EDITED BY
Jo Freeman
State University of New York
College at Purchase

WOMEN:
A FEMINIST PERSPECTIVE

Mayfield Publishing Company

Library of Congress Catalog Card Number: 74-84579
International Standard Book Numbers: 0-87484-289-1 (paper)
0-87484-290-5 (cloth)

Manufactured in the United States of America

Mayfield Publishing Company
285 Hamilton Avenue, Palo Alto, California 94301

This book was set in Journal Roman by Libra Cold Type and was printed and bound by the George Banta Company. Sponsoring editor was Alden C. Paine; copy editors were Ellen Hershey and Autumn Stanley, under the supervision of Carole H. Norton. Production supervisor was Michelle Hogan and the book and cover design were by Nancy Sears.

The photograph on the cover and part title pages is from "Say It with Buttons" by Jo Freeman in the August 1974 issue of *Ms.*, and is used in modified form with the permission of *Ms.* Photographer is Susan Wood.

Contents

The Contributors

JO FREEMAN is Assistant Professor of Political Science at the State University of New York, College at Purchase. She holds a Ph.D. from the University of Chicago, where she was an organizer and participant in the Women's Liberation Movement since its inception. A founder and editor of the first national new feminist newsletter, *Voice of the Women's Liberation Movement* (1968), she is currently a member of the National Organization for Women, and the Women's Caucus for Political Science (WCPS). Her published articles include: "The Social Construction of the Second Sex," (in *Roles Women Play*, Michele Garskof, Ed., 1971); "The Tyranny of Structurelessness" (*Ms.*, July 1973); "The Origins of the Women's Liberation Movement" (*American Journal of Sociology*, January 1973); "Women on the Movement: Roots of Revolt" (in *Academic Women on the Move*, Alice Rossi, ed., 1973). She is the author of *The Politics of Women's Liberation: A Case Study of an Emerging Social Movement and Its Relation to the Policy Process* (1975).

$$* * * * * * *$$

PAULINE B. BART is Associate Professor of Sociology in Psychiatry at the Abraham Lincoln Medical School of the University of Illinois, Chicago. She teaches behavioral science to medical students and conducts interdisciplinary seminars on sex roles and health issues to students in sociology and the health professions. She is the author of a major study of depression among middle-aged women, "Portnoy's Mother's Complaint"; and she is co-author (with Diana Scully) of "A Funny Thing

Happened on the Way to the Orifice: Women in Gynecology Textbooks" *(American Journal of Sociology,* January 1973). Ms. Bart taught the first course on women at the University of California, Berkeley, is one of the founders of Sociologists for Women in Society, and was first chairperson for the Sex Roles section of the American Sociological Association. Her current research is concerned chiefly with the interface between sex roles, sexism, and such health issues as abortion and rape, gynecological and obstetrical care, and psychotherapy.

ROSALYN BAXANDALL is an Assistant Professor of American Studies at State University of New York, College at Old Westbury. She is an editor of *Life and Labor, an Anthology of Women's Work in America from 1620 to 1970,* to be published by Random House and Viking in 1975, and has contributed articles on day care to scholarly journals and women's movement publications. In 1967-68 she was active in the first women's liberation group in New York City and helped start several day care centers in that city. Ms. Baxandall served on the Mayor's Task Force on Day Care in 1970 and is presently a member of the Committee for Community Controlled Day Care. She also helped set up and obtain funding for the two day care centers now in operation at Old Westbury.

INGE BELL is an Associate Professor of Sociology at Pitzer College, Claremont, California, where she specializes in innovative teaching with special emphasis on placing students in the social science fields and encouraging them to work toward societal change. She is the author of *Involvement in Society Today* (1971), a book of field-work projects for introductory social science courses; and *CORE and the Strategy of Nonviolence* (1968). Ms. Bell has prepared an illustrated lecture that expands on the material contained in her contribution to this volume; she is currently working on making this lecture available in synchronized tape-slide form. She is also investigating the paths of individual liberation proffered by Eastern religions.

SHIRLEY BERNARD is an Instructor in English and Women's Studies at Fullerton College, Fullerton, California. She served for four years on the National Board of the National Organization for Women (NOW), and for two years as NOW Western Regional Director. In addition, she was a founder and steering committee member for both the Southern California National Women's Political Caucus (NWPC) and Women in California Higher Education (WICHE). Her column, "The Glib-Lib; *Or* What to Say to a Cliché," appeared regularly in the national feminist newsletter *NOW Acts*; and her article "Aggression in Women" is included in *The Radical Therapist* (Jerome Agel, ed., 1971).

FRANCINE BLAU is a Research Associate at the Center for Human Resource Research, Ohio State University. Prior to her present appointment (September 1974), she was an Instructor in Economics at Trinity College, Hartford, Connecticut, and taught extensively in the area of women's studies. Ms. Blau is a member of the American Economic Association Committee on the Status of Women in the Economics Profession. She has published several articles on the economic status of women and is presently completing work on her doctoral dissertation, "Pay Differentials and Differences in the Distribution of Employment of Female and Male Office Workers" (Harvard University).

MERRY BOLT is one of a team of investigators engaged in biomedical research at the University of Chicago. During 1969-71 she was active in Zero Population Growth and Illinois Citizens for the Medical Control of Abortion. Ms. Bolt received her M.S. degree in Nutrition in 1964.

LYVIA MORGAN BROWN is a graduate student of Minoan Archaeology at the University of London. After attending Art School, she studied History of Art at Sussex University, Brighton, and thereafter worked for two years in the Archaeology Department of the British Columbia Provincial Museum, Victoria.

PHYLLIS CHESLER is an Assistant Professor of Psychology at Richmond College, City University of New York, where her teaching curriculum includes classes on the psychology of women, women and society, women in film, and women in literature. She is founder and Policy Council member of the Association for Women in Psychology, and serves on the advisory boards of the National Organization for Women (NOW) and Women's Action Alliance. Ms. Chesler is the author of *Women and Madness* (1972), and many of her articles have been published in professional and popular journals and anthologies. Her works in progress include one book on "Male Psychology in the Twentieth Century" and another entitled "Conversations: R. D. Laing and Phyllis Chesler."

MARY EASTWOOD is an attorney in the U. S. Department of Justice, Washington, D. C. She was formerly a technical secretary for the Civil and Political Rights Committee of the President's Commission on the Status of Women, and has served as technical legal assistant to the Citizens' Advisory Council on the Status of Women. She is the author of several articles on legal theory and women's rights, and a founding member of the National Organization for Women (NOW), Federally Employed Women (FEW), and Human Rights for Women, Inc. She is a member of the board of directors of Human Rights for Women and a member of the National Council of the National Women's Party.

GAIL FALK is a staff attorney in the Charleston, West Virginia, office of the United Mine Workers of America. She holds a J. D. degree from Yale University, and is co-author (with Ann Freedman and others) of "The Equal Rights Amendment: A Constitutional Basis for Equal Rights for Women" (*Yale Law Journal*, 871 [1971]). Ms. Falk was formerly a staff attorney at the Legal Aid Society of Charleston, West Virginia, and in 1971 she co-taught an undergraduate course on women and the law at Yale College.

DAIR L. GILLESPIE is a graduate student in Sociology at the University of California, Berkeley, a position she says she has "held for several years." In addition to contributing to scholarly journals, she has published articles in women's movement publications, the most recent being "Academic Feminists and the Women's Movement," which she co-authored with Ann Leffler and Elinor Lerner-Ratner. She received her M. A. in Sociology at the University of Houston.

KATHLEEN GOUGH is a Research Associate in Anthropology at the University of British Columbia, Vancouver. She is the co-editor (with David M. Schneider) of *Matrilineal Kinship* (1974), and (with Hari P. Sharma) of *Imperialism and Revolution in South Asia* (1973). She has contributed numerous articles on family roles and kinship in India to scholarly journals and anthologies.

SUSAN GRIFFIN is a poet and an Instructor in Women's Studies at the University of California Extension, Berkeley. Her first book of poetry, *Dear Sky*, and a collection of her short stories, *The Sink*, have been published by the Shameless Hussy Press; her second book of poetry, *Let Them Be Said*, was published by MaMa Press. Her play *Voices*, written with funds from the National Endowment for the Arts, went into production at station KPFA in San Francisco early in 1974.

HELEN MAYER HACKER is a Professor of Sociology at Adelphi University, Garden City, N.Y. She is the author of a number of widely reprinted articles concerning gender roles, including, in addition to the one contained in the present volume, "The New Burdens of Masculinity" (*Marriage and Family Living*, August 1957) and "Why Can't a Woman . . . ?" (*The Humanist*, January-February 1971). She contributed three chapters on societal, class, and ethnic differences in gender roles to *The Sociology of Gender Roles* (Lucile Duberman, ed., 1974), and recently completed a module entitled "A Sociological Approach to the Status of Women."

Ms. Hacker is currently working on a textbook for Harper and Row, as well as a manuscript entitled "Women in Cooperative Communities: A Study of Equality in Israel," for Praeger.

NANCY HENLEY has worked several years on the staff of the critical mental health journal *Rough Times* (formerly *Radical Therapist*). She has taught social psychology, psycholinguistics, and "Psychology and Women" at the University of Maryland, Baltimore County, and elsewhere. She is now writing one book on the politics of touch, and co-editing another on sex differences in language. Her numerous published works in scholarly journals include the widely reprinted "Politics of Touch," and "Power, Sex, and Nonverbal Communication" (*Berkeley Journal of Sociology*, 18, 1973). Ms. Henley has pursued postdoctoral research in nonverbal communication at Harvard University and is an active, long-standing member of the Association for Women in Psychology.

JUDITH HOLE is the Associate Archivist of CBS News. She is a member of the CBS Women's Advisory Council, a group elected by the women employees to advise CBS top management on programs and policies affecting women. Ms. Hole is the co-author (with Ellen Levine) of *Rebirth of Feminism* (1971). In 1970, as a CBS News Researcher, she compiled a backgrounder on the August 26 women's strike to be used by editors, reporters, and producers in their coverage of the event. She continues to write and lecture on the movement.

VIOLA KLEIN was a Reader (equivalent to Associate Professor) of Sociology at Reading University, Berkshire, Eng., until her sudden death in 1973. She is the author of *The Feminine Character: History of an Ideology* (1946 and 1973); *Women's Two Roles* (with Alva Myrdal, 1956); *Britain's Married Women Workers* (1965); *Women Workers* (1965); and a large number of articles and monographs on related subjects.

WENDY LARSEN, an attorney, is currently clerking for a Justice of the Illinois Supreme Court. She serves on the Women's Rights Committee of the American Civil Liberties Union, and is a former Editor-in-Chief of the *DePaul Law Review*. She received her B.D. degree from the University of Chicago and her J.D. from DePaul University, Chicago.

ELLEN LEVINE is a writer, cartoonist, and photographer, currently on the staff of the Consumers Union as an associate producer of films for television. She is the co-author (with Judith Hole) of *Rebirth of Feminism* (1971); co-editor (with Anne

Koedt and others) of *Radical Feminism* (1973); and an editor of the feminist journal *Notes*. Her most recently published work is a book of feminist cartoons, *All She Needs . . .* (1973).

NAOMI LYNN is an Assistant Professor of Political Science at Kansas State University, Manhattan. She is co-author (with Arthur F. McClure) of *The Fulbright Premise: Senator J. William Fulbright's Views on Presidential Power* (1973), and of *Undergraduate Research Guide to Women's Studies* (1974). She has done extensive research on the political participation of women and has contributed articles to a number of scholarly journals. She holds an M.A. degree from the University of Illinois, Urbana, and a Ph.D. from the University of Kansas, Lawrence.

PAULI MURRAY is an attorney, poet, legal scholar, teacher, and pioneer activist in the struggle against racial discrimination and sex discrimination. Since September 1973 she has been a full-time student at General Theological Seminary, New York City, in the hope of becoming a priest in the Episcopal Church. Her published works include *Dark Testament and Other Poems* (1970); *States' Laws on Race and Color* (1951; supplement 1955); and *Proud Shoes*, the biography of an American Negro family of multiple origins (1956 and 1973). Her poems and articles appear in numerous anthologies, and she has written extensively for law journals. She has also taught courses in law and political science at several universities, including Brandeis University; Boston University; and Ghana Law School, Accra. Ms. Murray has served on the National Board of the American Civil Liberties Union; the Board of Directors of NOW Legal Defense and Education Fund, Inc.; and as Vice-Chairman of the American Bar Association Committee on Women's Rights, Section on Individual Rights and Responsibilities.

MARY NELSON is a doctoral candidate in Social Psychology at the University of Chicago, and an Instructor in Witchcraft and Negotiation at the School for New Learning, an experimental college-level adult education program at DePaul University, Chicago. She is presently preparing a book manuscript entitled "The Art of Cohabitation," which is a negotiation-oriented guide to living outside conventional sex roles.

LINDA PHELPS is a Research Assistant at the Institute for Community Studies in Kansas City, Mo. She is active in the Kansas City Women's Liberation Union, and has published several articles in Women's Movement publications, including "What Is the Difference. Women's Rights and Women's Liberation."

KAY F. REINARTZ is an Assistant Professor of American Studies at State University of New York at Albany, where she is a member of the Faculty Women's Caucus. Her published works include "Domesticity," a poem, in *The New Feminism* (Lucy Komisar, ed., 1971), and "Walt Whitman and Feminism" (*Walt Whitman Review*, 19, 1973). Her dissertation, "American Women and Swedish Women: Changes Since World War II," is based in part on research conducted in Sweden in 1971-72 under a fellowship grant from the American-Scandinavian Foundation. Ms. Reinartz holds a Ph.D. from the University of New Mexico, and is a member of the National Organization for Women (NOW).

PAMELA ROBY is an Associate Professor of Sociology and Community Studies at the University of California, Santa Cruz. She is the editor of *Child Care—Who Cares? Foreign and Domestic Infant and Early Childhood Development Policies* (1973), and co-author (with S. M. Miller) of *The Future of Inequality* (1970). She is currently working on a preliminary study of the impact of social policies on women in working-class jobs.

KATHLEEN K. SHORTRIDGE is a Research Associate in the graduate school at the University of Michigan. She served as the equal employment analyst in a recent review of salary equity between men and women at the University of Michigan.

KIMBERLEY SNOW is currently engaged in research on feminism in nineteenth-century America. She helped organize the Women's Studies Program at the University of Kentucky, Lexington, where she has taught both introductory and advanced women's studies courses, and served as Women's Studies Bibliographer for the Margaret King Library. Ms. Snow has contributed several articles on women in literature to women's movement publications and originated the popular "Uppity Women Unite" button in 1968.

LENORE J. WEITZMAN is currently studying the effects of the California no-fault divorce law under a Ford Foundation fellowship. She is an Assistant Professor of Sociology at the University of California at Davis and has published articles on sex roles as portrayed in children's books (*American Journal of Sociology*, May 1972), on affirmative action (in *Academic Women on the Move*, Alice Rossi, ed., 1973), and on women's legal status (*Hastings Law Review*). She has also developed a multimedia show, *The Images of Males and Females in Elementary School Textbooks*, which will be distributed by the National Education Association. Her most recent article is an analysis of legal marriage (*California Law Review*, June 1974) in which she advocates contracts-in-lieu-of-marriage.

MARTHA STURM WHITE is a Research Psychologist at the University of California, San Francisco, where she teaches and is conducting a study of a new role in the medical profession, the nurse practitioner. She is also a member of the faculty of the California School of Professional Psychology, San Francisco. Her pioneering book on adult development, *The Next Step*, was published in 1964 while she was on the staff of the Radcliffe Institute; since then she has been active in developing guidance workshops for women, and in conducting further research in adult development, particularly that of educated and professional women. She has taught at Boston University, Cornell University, and San Francisco State University.

ANNE WILSON is a graduate student in Family and Community Development at the University of Maryland. She is currently studying the relationship between sex-role attitudes and adult preferences for male or female children.

Introduction

Jo Freeman

This book had its genesis in 1968 at the first, and so far only, national conference of what was to become the younger branch of the women's liberation movement. Many of us there had just begun voraciously reading everything we could find on women, and we were appalled by the scarcity of perceptive pieces and occasionally delighted by the few rare gems brilliantly raising new ideas in that traditional era. At that time there were no books or anthologies presenting a feminist perspective on women's status, and, ironically for members of a movement that has subsequently produced so much writing, most of us felt unable to express our newly rising consciousness in words. Why not, we thought, bring together those few pieces that were worthwhile, so that other women would not have to seek them out laboriously one by one among the many that were not?

That was a task I took on, unfortunately at the same time that I started working for my Ph.D. It has taken me much longer to finish the anthology than the degree. But this often nerve-racking snail's pace was not without its benefits. This book has been able to grow and change with the movement, and it is infinitely better than it would have been had I been able to finish it in one or two years. Of the original selections, only those by Hacker and Klein remain. All of the other articles reflect the new research, the new thinking, and the new interpretations of old research on women that have been inspired by the women's liberation movement.

Some of the pieces to follow are reprints, but most are being published for the first time. The former papers are among the best feminists have written to date. The original articles were solicited specifically for this book to cover topics that had not yet been adequately dealt with. In keeping with the egalitarian concepts of the women's liberation movement, this solicitation was not limited to the friends and acquaintances of the editor. Instead ads requesting manuscripts were placed in most of the feminist media, and some organizations, notably the Women's History Research Library of Berkeley and KNOW of Pittsburgh, sent out special notices with their regular mailings. The response was overwhelming, and well over a year was spent reading and editing the submissions.

From the beginning a high standard was set for comprehensiveness and substance. In the early years of the women's movement, new feminists responded emotionally and often rhetorically to the sexist institutions their new consciousness made them keenly aware of. Partly because adequate research on women was lacking and partly because what little there was had rarely been systematically brought together, systematic, substantiated analysis was difficult. During the last two or three years the problem of correcting these deficiencies has been attacked, and a new body of substantive research on women from a feminist perspective has begun to emerge. The papers in this volume are part of this development; they employ the traditional scholarly disciplines to assess the effects of sexism, to document the status of women, and to analyze the complex interaction of institutions and values that keep women in their place.

The uniform criterion applied in these analyses is what I have called a feminist perspective. That is, starting from the premise that women and men have the same potential for individual development, this view examines the way social institutions create differences. It is a social control perspective; it rejects the idea that there is any meaningful choice for members of either sex as long as there are socially prescribed sex roles and social penalties for those who deviate from them. This is a perspective that is largely alien to Americans. We have so thoroughly absorbed the national ideology about living in a "free society" that whatever else we may question, we are reluctant to admit the extent to which our society, as well as others, controls the lives of its members. We are even more reluctant to face the often subtle ways that our own attitudes and our own lives are being controlled by that same society.

It is no wonder, then, that materially well-off, educated Americans—women as well as men—find it so difficult to accept the idea that women are oppressed. The "freedom of choice" argument, which maintains that women are free to do what they want, fails to consider why women think they want what they say they want. But what people think they want is precisely what society must control if it is to maintain the status quo. As Sandra and Daryl Bem put it, "We overlook the fact that the society that has spent twenty years carefully marking the woman's ballot for her has nothing to lose in that twenty-first year by pretending to let her

The socialization process, the climate of opinion in which people live, the value structure, the legal system, and the distribution of economic opportunities are just some of the means society has at its disposal to channel people into the roles it finds necessary for its maintenance.

cast it for the alternative of her choice. Society has controlled not her alternatives but her motivation to choose any but one of those alternatives."*

There are many mechanisms of social control, some more subtle than others and some more sophisticated. The socialization process, the climate of opinion in which people live, the value structure, the legal system, and the distribution of economic opportunities are just some of the means society has at its disposal to channel people into the roles it finds necessary for its maintenance. These mechanisms and many more are incisively examined and challenged in this book, in the belief that only by first understanding how they operate will we gain the wisdom to dismantle them and create a more just society.

The book's organization allows the reader to begin by looking at herself, and then moves out in ever widening circles that bring in the social and historical context, concluding with a section on feminism as the historical and contemporary challenge to women's status. Nonetheless, the inclusive nature of many of the pieces, and their topics, means that the global and the personal are often combined.

In Section I, "The Body and Its Control," Wilson, Bolt, and Larsen first show how the most intimate of functions, reproduction, has been one of the most highly controlled aspects of human life, and how our historically pro-natalist attitude has logically led to the current population explosion. They argue that only when society ceases its emphasis on motherhood as the most socially acceptable and available "career" for women can voluntary population control become realistic. Turning to sex, Phelps shows how for many women the sexual liberation of the 1960's merely resulted in another form of sexual alienation, and Griffin examines the role of rape in physically intimidating and controlling women. So much has been written on abortion that a separate paper on the subject did not seem necessary here. Instead an analysis of the recent Supreme Court decisions governing the circumstances of legal abortion is included by Eastwood in her paper in Section VI.

The family has been the primary social institution to which women have been confined, and thus it is not surprising that new feminists have been quick to attack the patriarchal family. In Section II, Gough puts the family in an historical and

---

* "We're All Nonconscious Sexists," *Psychology Today*, 4, 6 (1970), 26.

anthropological context; Gillespie shows how power distribution within the family is biased in favor of the husband/father by social institutions and values; and Baxandall explores the continuing need for adequate day-care facilities to aid U.S. employed mothers, pointing out how the absence of day care operates as a disincentive to seeking employment out of the home.

It is via socialization and education that women are steered away from participating in the major social and economic institutions of our society. In Section III, Weitzman contributes a major tour de force of the socialization literature with her own interpretation of how and why women emerge from this process in the way they do. Bell and Bart examine the consequences for older women of accepting the social norms of the female life cycle, and Roby shows how higher education, the great equalizer of American society, is not so equal for women.

In Section IV the economic consequences of this channeling are clearly delineated by Blau, who points out that there are two distinct labor markets—one male and one female—and that the latter is economically depressed. Women's direct share in the material wealth of this country, by and large, is not proportionate to their productive contribution. Instead a woman's economic status is determined largely by her relationship to a man, whose economic status extends to her. This point is reemphasized by Bernard, who succinctly abolishes the myth that women have most of the wealth of this country. How cruel a hoax this has been is illustrated by Shortridge in her article on poor working women. The female labor market is so depressed that even working full-time, many women cannot earn enough to rise above the poverty line. Shortridge makes it clear that poverty is a woman's problem, caused in large part by discriminatory employment practices that restrict the access of women at all educational levels to higher-paying jobs. Comparatively few families that contain an able-bodied, employable male are living in poverty, but millions of families living only on the incomes of full-time employed women are unable to make ends meet. White shows how women's employment problems are not limited to poor women but extend even to the professions, where education and merit are supposed to be the primary determinants of success. Even in the highest professions a penis is a more valuable asset than a degree. Falk describes how women have been denied access to the working person's major vehicle for economic justice—the labor union. In fact, unions have been among the most persistent discriminators against women; yet they are still one of the best potential avenues for rectifying that discrimination. In conclusion, this section makes it abundantly clear that in order for women to have economic independence—the sine qua non of liberation—the male and female labor markets must be integrated.

Taking a different tack, Snow, Reinartz, and Brown explore images of women in three different media—literature, popular songs, and art. Despite their different foci, these authors have each discovered a similar pattern. Whatever the medium, women have basically two images—one of purity and one of evil. Neither corresponds well to the complex lives of real women and their artificiality suggests that women are not perceived—by men at least—as real people.

More overt institutions of social control are analyzed in Section VI. Eastwood shows the role of law in both suppressing women and rectifying discrimination. Nelson turns to history to analyze the original witchhunts, which she attributes to fear of a new economic independence among women. Murray kindly allowed us to reprint her excellent essay on what women's liberation has to offer black women and what black women have to offer women's liberation. Incisively cutting through the myth of the black matriarchy, she illuminates the particular problems black women must face to eliminate both race and sex discrimination, and asserts that their role is strategic for the success of both causes. Lynn comprehensively tackles the major problem of women's participation in political institutions. Her evidence shows that women's participation is not negligible, as many claim, but merely kept to the doorbell level. Chesler takes on two social institutions at once, concluding that marriage and psychotherapy serve the same social function of isolating women and making them dependent on an authority figure. A less obvious but very pernicious sphere is charted by Henley and Freeman, whose examination of interpersonal behavior reveals the pervasiveness of sexism as well as the constant reinforcement of appropriate sex role behavior in our society.

The last section is devoted to feminism past and present, a subject well worth a book in itself. Although Klein's historical treatment is primarily confined to England, the patterns of development were similar in the United States, and hers is the best succinct analysis done to date. Hole and Levine detail the accomplishments of the first feminist wave. And Freeman concludes with a brief description of the new feminist movement and its emerging ideas of equality and liberation.

The scholarly disciplines, like society at large, are dominated by those on the inside. They reflect a desire to explain, justify, and maintain the status quo of human and institutional relationships. The result is a consistency of approach that is almost stifling. It may be politically convenient to view the world through the most comfortable lenses, but the resulting distortion is scientifically unacceptable. Only when one changes position, views the world through another's eyes, and relaxes one's claims to a monopoly on truth can new knowledge be gained.

The papers in this book show how feminist thought can contribute to this process by providing a new perspective from which to reexamine basic concepts in many spheres of learning. They not only point out the sexist prejudices of old research but show how new human opportunities can be created by changing outworn institutions and values. A feminist perspective is practical as well as theoreti-

A feminist perspective is practical as well as theoretical; it illuminates possibilities for the future as well as criticizes the limitations of the present.

cal; it illuminates possibilities for the future as well as criticizes the limitations of the present.

Yet these new ideas can have real meaning only within the context of a political movement organized to put them into practice. They will not be adopted merely because they appear in print. For proof of this fact, we need only look at what happened during and after the last feminist movement. We are, after all, not the first scholars to challenge traditional attitudes toward women. Within the limits of the scholarly tools then available to them, our feminist forebears did this once before. One has only to visit the library of the National Women's Party in Washington or the Schlesinger Library in Cambridge, Mass. or the library of the Fawcett Society in London to realize the awesome proportions of their work. And one has only to think about how this work was relegated to dusty shelves and ignored after the last wave of feminism ended to feel a certain amount of despair: clearly new ideas are not espoused by society on the basis of merit alone.

Thus we are in the position of calling "new" what is in fact very old. The feminist ideas of today are "new" only in the sense that most people now alive have not been exposed to them until recently and in the sense that the more advanced methodology of the scholarly disciplines can "renew" their significance. But if we are not to repeat history—if we are not to see our volumes ultimately join those on the dusty shelves of yore—we cannot complacently assume that they will be readily embraced. Instead we must recognize the political context in which they thrive and work to maintain that context until they are thoroughly incorporated into the everyday frame of mind.

I The Body and Its Control

Woman's Biology–Mankind's Destiny: The Population Explosion and Women's Changing Roles

Anne Wilson, Merry Bolt, and Wendy Larsen

The family is not our world — the world is our family.

— Anonymous

The issues of population growth and women's liberation are both often featured topics in the media, yet the fundamental interdependency between them tends to be overlooked. As long as motherhood continues to be defined as a woman's essential role and major responsibility with any outside employment seen as simply an addition to that role, real "equal opportunity" is impossible; and as long as women's roles continue to be defined in expectation of universal motherhood, population stabilization will be difficult to achieve.

Woman's biology has been used to explain how traditional sex roles have developed and why they are similar in so many cultures. In this "biological" view, woman's lesser physical strength leads naturally to her lesser power and status, and her vulnerability during pregnancy and lactation sets limits to her achievement. Often an innately different psychology is ascribed to the female, based on the nurturant

3

qualities required by motherhood, or on a maternal instinct or drive. Sometimes these real and supposed differences have been eulogized;[1] simultaneously, and without conscious contradiction, however, they have served to justify and maintain women's inferior status, and to dictate a certain role (motherhood as the primary career) as peculiarly appropriate to women.

Historically, women have had little control over their reproductive function. Motherhood was almost inevitable for any sexually active, fertile woman. Such fecundity only slightly overbalanced the high death rate, however, and was necessary for survival of the species. Biology *was* destiny in that the idea of separating procreative functions from other female sex roles was scarcely even entertained.

As long as there was a high death rate, positive attitudes toward marriage and reproduction were desirable, and we should keep in mind when we analyze these attitudes that from time to time famine, disease, and war have taken heavy tolls in human populations even during fairly recent recorded history. The Black Death, for example, may have killed more than a quarter of the population of England and Europe within a two-year time span in the fourteenth century.[2] World War II claimed millions of lives only thirty years ago; and even today, thousands are dying in Subsaharan Africa owing to a combination of age-old scourges. Nevertheless, death rates in most parts of the world have now dropped dramatically. Moreover, most of this recent decline in the death rate has been in infant and child mortality,[3] which has a more serious effect on population growth than a drop in deaths among people aged 45–60. Population growth depends not just on fertility rates, but also on survival to reproductive age and status. Thus, despite the trend to smaller families in certain countries, we still face a problem of excess fertility both in the United States and in the world as a whole.

Much has been said about the nature and extent of the population problem. The world now has almost four billion people and will probably have two to three billion more by the turn of the century.[4] In the United States all this talk has caused less concern than one might expect, because it has been followed by talk of our having achieved zero population growth (ZPG) and of a "baby bust" instead of a "baby boom."[5]

Contrary to the impression some have gained from the news media, the United States is a long way from ZPG. Our natural growth rate has indeed slowed down 1 percent per year (doubling every 70 years) to .8 percent per year (doubling every 87 years). At the same time, however, projections based on present fertility trends seem to indicate that fertility may be about at replacement level, where one child survives to replace each adult. This would result in ZPG when the age structure of the population becomes stable approximately 70 years from now (the average lifespan),[6] if fertility remains at this low level.* While there is some evidence that this slower population growth is due in part to a shift in the ideal family size,[7] the decline has been paralleled by economic recession. Thus it is difficult to tell how much is a real decline and how much is merely delayed fertility that could lead to another baby boom if economic conditions improve.[8]

Still, Americans constitute only 5 percent of the world's population,[9] and many people find it hard to understand why it is important to limit growth in this country at all. The connection between affluent America and the rest of the world is not obvious. Most Americans do not realize how dependent we are on the resources of the world to support our standard of living, and how inequitable distribution of those resources supports our illusion of abundance. Yet even in our own country, hunger and malnutrition exist amidst plenty because substantial numbers of people do not have the money to buy nutritious food. Economic surpluses are not necessarily real surpluses. This situation can be seen more clearly when we look at trade between developed and underdeveloped nations. We tend to feel in this country that we are feeding the world singlehandedly with our shipments of excess wheat. But protein is the actual limiting nutritional factor, and we in the United States import more pounds of protein than we export.[10] Peru, which was once a major producer of protein-rich fish meal, exported most of it to Europe, the United States, and Japan to be used for livestock and poultry feed, while there was widespread protein malnutrition in Peru and the rest of Latin America.** Similarly, the energy crisis has exposed our dependence on other countries' selling us their resources (in this case, oil) cheaply.† At the same time that we are trying to maintain our lifestyle at the expense of the future development of the rest of the world, however, we tout the glories of technology and development, encouraging everyone to aspire to owning two cars, an air-conditioned four-bedroom house, a swimming pool, and a color TV.[11]

---

* Technical distinctions in demographic terms are not the issue here. Adroit choice of appropriate data can support almost any conclusion. Furthermore, demographic projections require estimates that are inherently unreliable. For a fuller discussion of the actual problems and distinctions see the original report by George Grier (see note 6) or the Population Reference Bureau publication, "Population Statistics: What do they Mean?" (see note 4).

** And when the Peruvian anchovy fishing collapsed, the price of chicken and other meat soared in the United States. See C. P. Idyll, "The Anchovy Crisis," *Scientific American*, 228(6): 22-29, 1973.

† According to U.S. Department of Transportation figures cited in the ZPG *National Reporter*, 5(7):9, 1973, about a fourth of our annual oil consumption is imported.

Ecologists have warned that there is no simple technological solution to our environmental problems.[12] Unfortunately, population experts have tended to ignore these warnings. The solutions they propose to the population problem range from increasing the availability of contraceptives, finding safer, more effective contraceptives, and giving free abortions, to licensing parenthood.[13] Although some of these proposals have merit (it makes no sense, for example, to force people to have babies they don't want at the same time one is encouraging people to forgo having babies they do want), people's lives and particularly women's lives are involved in these decisions. Typically the desires of the people involved are highhandedly dismissed as unimportant, or important only as an obstacle to the public welfare.

Meanwhile, people—including women—continue to want too many children. Although concern about overpopulation has removed some of the societal-duty aspect of parenthood, and expected family size is at an all-time low, people still expect families of a size somewhat above the replacement level of 2.1 children per couple.[14] Also, people continue to have planned children.[15] Research seems to indicate that couples are more likely to practice effective contraception when they have reached or exceeded their desired family size, and that desired family size is a fair, if conservative, predictor* of actual fertility.[16] We would argue, then, that as long as marriage and motherhood are regarded and promulgated as a woman's primary role, women will continue to want "too many" children.

The pronatalist attitudes of our society and government have a long history behind them that is not easily erased. The Biblical tradition, one primary source of Western views on sex and women, sees men and women as incomplete without each other; in relation to each other through marriage and parenthood they form the

---

* An exception to this is the poor, who tend to expect—and find—birth control to be ineffective, and who tend to be somewhat fatalistic about family planning. See Catherine S. Chilman, "Some Psychological Aspects of Fertility, Family Planning, and Population Policy in the United States," in J. T. Fawcett, ed., *Psychological Perspectives on Population* (New York: Basic Books, 1973), especially p. 177; and Lee Rainwater, *And the Poor Get Children* (Chicago: Quadrangle Books, 1960). It is just a myth, however, that the poor, black mothers receiving Aid to Dependent Children are largely responsible for population growth in this country, and that if they would just restrain themselves from having children they can't afford (through compulsory abortion or sterilization, for example), the problem would be solved. Most (68 percent) of the population growth in this country between 1960 and 1970 has been due to the third and fourth children of middle-class families. See "U. S. Population Facts" in the Population Reference Bureau's journal *People,* 1(1):1, 1970. Also, most poor families in this country are white (Ehrlich and Ehrlich, p. 322). If black and Spanish-speaking people in this country (rich or poor) had had *no* children at all during the 1960's, our population would be merely 4 percent smaller, compared to the 13 percent attributable to the white majority (Commission on Population Growth and the American Future, pp. 71-72).

image of divine life. The primary emphasis in this sexual relationship is on producing offspring, especially boys, as it is through posterity that a Jew participates in the Messianic age. After the Exile, every Jewish man had to marry and to produce at least one son and one daughter; sterility made the marriage void.

Christianity, developing under the influence of Greek asceticism and Eastern religions, gradually downgraded sex. The Roman Catholic tradition, as seen especially in Aquinas, saw sex as a hindrance to the spiritual life, therefore sinful and in need of justification. Reproduction—and only reproduction—can provide this justification because it brings souls into the world as candidates for salvation; thus the Catholic position on birth control.

In not banning either birth control or divorce, Protestantism sowed the seeds of a change in the status of women. However, that change was a long time coming; the Reformation envisioned no change in basic attitudes toward women and sex. Luther maintained that men and women had originally been created equal, but that since a woman had been largely responsible for the Fall, women must be subject to their husbands and bear the pain of labor and the responsibility of childrearing. With Protestantism's lesser emphasis on celibacy and virginity, marriage did become a more honorable estate, although the only justification for sex was still procreation.

Nineteenth-century science made it possible to question literal interpretations of the Bible. Simultaneously, nineteenth-century industrial development restricted the family to immediate relatives and narrowed the wife's role as men left the farms and home industries for the factories.[17] With advances in sanitation and public health, the death rate began to drop, followed by the birth rate,[18] and feminism developed. Ironically, the "biology is destiny" credo seemed to reach full flower even as people began to control their fertility and the birth rate fell in Great Britain and the United States. Pressures designating motherhood as the natural path to feminine fulfillment seem to have intensified into a sentimental mystique under the auspices of Freud and Queen Victoria just as women caught a glimpse of other options. There was fear of "race suicide" if feminism took hold.

The birth rate declined further during the Great Depression of the 1930's.[19] Although fertility never dropped even to the present level, and although our population continued to grow, people tended to attribute to the statistics a mind of their own, and to fear that the downward trend might be extrapolated out to zero and the end of mankind.

From associating economic depression and contraction with a declining birth rate, it seemed natural conversely to associate prosperity and industrial expansion with a rising birth rate, and to create the "growth is good" ethic that characterized the post-war years. Population growth was seen as beneficial to the economy and therefore desirable.[20] Having children might almost have been considered a civic duty. Lee Rainwater's study of attitudes toward childbearing, presumably reflecting the feelings prevalent during the late 1950's and early 1960's found agreement that it was selfish not to have children, that people should have all the children they can afford.[21] Economists reinforced this belief even to the end of the 1960's, predicting disaster if zero population growth should ever be attained.

The post-industrial decline in family size was somewhat balanced by a trend for more women to marry and to marry at younger ages.[22]. It is not unreasonable to assume that this in part reflects stronger societal pressure toward a norm of universal marriage (better dead than unwed)[23] and parenthood as well as a relaxation of obstacles to marriage as individual autonomy increased with industrialization. Of American women born in 1901–5, almost one in ten remained single despite few apparent alternatives to marriage at that time; and of those who did marry, about a third had only one child or no children at all.[24] Reliable estimates are of course difficult to obtain in a time of flux such as this, but as of 1972, projections for American women born in 1948–54 (now aged 20–26) are that only one in twenty will not marry. Of those marrying, only 3.6 percent expect to remain childless, and 9.8 percent expect to have one child.[25]

This sort of phenomenon has circular effects, for as marriage becomes nearly universal, the unmarried do not fit in. They find the world organized by and for couples. A few years later in the life cycle, when all their friends have had children, the childless feel out of place as discussions turn to *Sesame Street* and diaper service. It is not just women talking about domestic matters that leads to a feeling of exclusion, for men are prone to replay the latest Little League game, inning by inning. Those not experiencing similar joys and frustrations are not appreciated, particularly if they should respond by talking about how much they enjoy their own free lifestyle.

American industry has carefully fostered society's pronatalist prejudices while cashing in on them, selling the marriage ideal along with its deodorant, mouthwash, and orange-blossom-scented douches, honoring superbreeders as "Mothers of the Year" for producing more little consumers. It is interesting to speculate why ads for feminine deodorant sprays are acceptable for television and radio, while contraceptive devices are not. Contraceptives, in fact, are not extensively advertised anywhere, even where there are no laws forbidding such ads.

The American government, too, has traditionally given official sanction to the sex-role norms, reflecting both the dominant social values and the view that a large population is beneficial in maintaining military strength. Thus even with recent changes in the federal income tax structure, there are still tax advantages in being married, particularly if the wife does not work. Similarly, social security benefits

Those who fear themselves to be selfish and egocentric may have large families to prove to themselves and others that they are not selfish and self-centered.

are often greater for married women who have never worked than for women who have worked all their lives. At the local level, where the basic tax is the property tax, the family with twelve children pays no more for the expenses of schools, recreational facilities, transportation, police, and fire protection than the family with no children, except insofar as larger families may tend to own larger and thus possibly more valuable homes.

There has been talk of changing the official pronatalism, but little has actually been done.* The Population Stabilization Resolution initiated by Congress in 1972 was not passed. The President's Commission on Population and the American Future came out with an excellent report, but President Nixon refused to accept it, and it has largely been ignored. Family-planning funds have been cut, and President Nixon has impounded the funds that would have put the Population Education Act into effect.

Unofficially, pressure to marry and have children seems reinforced even today by holdovers of the puritan ethic. "Getting married and settling down" is still prescribed as an antidote to irresponsibility. Those who fear themselves to be selfish and egocentric may have large families to prove to themselves and others that they are not selfish and self-centered.[26] The norm that parents should be mature may be taken to mean that those who forego parenthood are immature, or that having children in and of itself makes one mature.

Childlessness has become more socially acceptable, perhaps, and there is at least one national organization[27] lobbying to end discrimination against the single and childless. Yet most mothers probably perceive this new attitude as a devaluation of their life's work, and hope that their daughters do not take such talk too seriously. And the evidence seems to be that generally their daughters do share their values. Sorensen reported in 1972 that 92 percent of the teenage girls interviewed in his survey expected ultimately to marry and have children.[28]

Even among some feminists who are challenging the old restrictive role, motherhood may become very important. It can be used to prove both to society

---

* This inaction is, in part, due to the problem of finding measures that will not adversely affect the children of large families who should not be made innocent victims in any attempt to discourage large families.

and to these women themselves that they are indeed "normal females" with the proper maternal instincts. It keeps them from being called man-hating, unloving, frustrated castrators.

In the face of all these pressures to marry and reproduce, perhaps the institutions of marriage and parenthood—and thus, inevitably, woman's traditional role—should be reexamined. For if they really are all glamour and romance, the one true path to personal happiness, maturity, and self-actualization, if they bring security, love, and a stable, lifelong source of companionship and emotional gratification, why are they sold so hard? We must begin to recognize that the traditional feminine role not only contributes to overpopulation, but also commonly fails to live up to its promises of fulfillment.

Sunday supplements make it hard to ignore that one in three or four American marriages ends in divorce.[29] Even for lasting marriages, the picture is often unattractive. J. R. Udry states after a review of the data: "The young person contemplating marriage might be advised that the *usual* experience is gradual devitalization, although none will accept this as representing his own future."[30]

Still, it requires strength not to conform and there are indications that those with lower ego strength and poorer social adjustment tend to be among the first to seek the social security of early marriage.[31] Society seldom questions the decision of a woman to "give up everything" and marry, but it often questions the motives of those who want more than marriage. In a study of the adjustment of unmarried women, Baker found that when a single woman took a positive view of her state, her chances of feeling fulfilled were as good as those of married women.[32] Unfortunately, our society does all it can to make it difficult for women past a certain age to take a positive view of being single.

Similarly, parenthood continues to be romanticized, perhaps even more than marriage. One may recognize that one's parents' marriage was less than ideal, but, by logical necessity, children grow up in, and are therefore best acquainted with, families with children. Alternative adult models are scarce, particularly in suburbia. It may be difficult to escape the idea that parenthood is the normal culmination of every adult's life.

Whether all people are universally suited to parenthood, deriving their major life satisfactions from it is open to question, however. Family research does not substantiate the myths that children patch up unhappy marriages and generally contribute to marital euphoria.

Practically speaking, moreover, children are expensive. Recent (1969-70) estimates are that an American family with two children and an annual income of $10,000 will spend about $20,000 per child between birth and age 18,[33] and another $10,000 to put each child through college. Under current economic conditions of recession and inflation, children are not merely a serious responsibility but a severe economic strain for struggling couples.

Worse, the togetherness and harmony that are supposed to compensate parents for their sacrifices are not always forthcoming. Several studies of marital satisfaction show wives' complaints increasing with the advent of children, reaching a peak when children begin school and then tapering off somewhat, particularly when the husband retires.[34] Although one should be cautious in attributing the wives' rising dissatisfaction directly to the influence of children, nonetheless it does conflict with the idealized pattern wherein children are supposed to revitalize and strengthen the relationship between their parents, and bring new love and happiness into the family. In a more carefully controlled longitudinal study, wives' complaints of lack of attention from their husbands increased following the birth of a first child.[35] Masters and Johnson, studying pregnancy, report that a substantial number of husbands begin affairs during their wives' pregnancies, and often continue them afterwards.[36]

If we seem unduly cynical, let us add that we are not suggesting that there are no happy marriages or that parenthood is always disappointing and lacking in gratification. Happy marriages do exist, and children can be a great source of joy and satisfaction in their appreciation of life.* We only wish to suggest that marriage is undesirable as a universal goal and ideal. No one should rush into it, be pushed into it, or drift into it for lack of other alternatives. Likewise, parenthood is something to be planned, to be undertaken seriously and realistically, with a full understanding of the problems, responsibilities, and restrictions attendant upon bringing another person into the world. Children are more than cute pets; they have identities all their own and may or may not fulfill their parents' expectations.

The obstacles in the way of a career for the well-socialized woman are still great today, and the escape hatch to instant identity through motherhood is always open. As a mother, a woman may receive all the praise and attention she felt lacking before. Unfortunately the discovery that motherhood is not always enough often comes too late for the situation to be easily rectified, for children require a long-term commitment and a large part of the family resources. Returning to a career after dropping out is often difficult. Certain kinds of training become obsolete rapidly, especially in the technical fields, and refresher courses do not always exist. Educational institutions are not geared to the needs of women who have

---

* For a description of some satisfying marriages and families, see John F. Cuber and Peggy G. Harroff, *Sex and the Significant Americans* (Baltimore: Penguin Books, 1965). These "vital" marriages are not suggested as ideal relationships, but simply as possible; the actual sex roles portrayed may appear somewhat dated.

children to care for, and neither are most jobs. These conditions need to be changed so that women will not be trapped in a cycle of housewifery where producing and rearing children is the only creative option readily available to them.

Once a woman begins having children, social forces seem to conspire to keep her at home. Unless they have no husbands or are otherwise forced to work, mothers are expected to stay home with preschool children, even though maternal employment apparently does the children no harm under normal conditions of adequate care and parental affection.[37] On the contrary, some evidence suggests that women who want to work are "better mothers" if they follow their inclination than if they stay home out of duty.[38] Maternal employment may sometimes positively benefit children by fostering greater independence.[39] But the image of even school-age children returning to an empty house and an empty cookie jar continues to pull at heartstrings as if there were no other choices.

One or two children are not a full-time, lifelong career. The three or four children our mothers had were not, either, but since our mothers were encouraged to ignore this problem, they were confronted with twenty or thirty empty years between the time their children left home and the time their husbands retired. Many of them have entered the labor market, yet such women often feel trapped— too old to start a new career and unable to find challenging work utilizing their potential.

We must finally accept careers outside the home as the rule rather than the exception. If marriage and childbearing are placed in this perspective, then women may be able to plan more realistically to achieve satisfaction through their own abilities and efforts rather than through the lives of their husbands and children, probably to the relief of both of those groups.

To achieve this end, however, women will have to come to terms both with their own sexuality and with heterosexual relations in general. Without birth control (including abortion), biology is still destiny. Both premarital sex and births out of wedlock are increasingly common among adolescents.[40] About half of unmarried nineteen-year-old females in the United States are estimated to be sexually active.[41] Unfortunately, casual sex is often characterized by casual contraception and inaccurate sexual knowledge.[42] Sexual freedom carries with it as great a potential for the exploitation of women as did the traditional role. Possibly, indeed, a greater potential, for it places on women the entire burden of child support as well as childrearing, if responsible paternity is not insisted upon.

Women seem intent upon pleasing men, inside or outside of marriage. Insofar as this is reciprocated by men's genuinely caring about the welfare of their sex partners, this is not necessarily bad. However, women need to recognize their vulnerability, and to be prepared to look after themselves.* Unintentional motherhood resulting from "sexual liberation" curtails a woman's options as severely as do culturally imposed social and psychological definitions of sex roles—and often at an earlier age.

Only when women are truly free, both culturally and biologically, to be producers of ideas, art, inventions, and leadership as well as of babies, will we have come very far toward a real solution to the population crisis in this country.

Notes

1. Ashley Montague, *The Natural Superiority of Women* (New York: Macmillan, 1968).
2. William L. Langer, "The Black Death," *Scientific American,* 210(2):114-21, 1964.
3. The American Assembly, Columbia Univ., *The Population Dilemma,* 2nd ed., ed. by Philip Hauser (Englewood Cliffs, N.J.: Prentice-Hall, 1969), p. 15.
4. Population Reference Bureau (PRB), *1973 World Population Data Sheet,* available at Bureau headquarters, 1755 Massachusetts Ave. NW, Washington, D.C.; Paul Ehrlich and Anne Ehrlich, *Population, Resources and Environment,* 2nd ed. (San Francisco: W. H. Freeman, 1972), p. 50.
5. George Grier, "Baby Bust Replaces Baby Boom," report released by Washington Center for Metropolitan Studies, 1717 Massachusetts Ave. NW, Washington, D.C., 1971.
6. PRB, *1973 World Population Data Sheet, op. cit.*
7. Bureau of the Census, "Birth Expectations of American Wives: June 1973," and "Birth Expectation and Fertility, June 1972." *Current Population Reports,* Series P-20 #254 and
8. Philip Hauser, "Population Outlook," testimony before the Special Sub-Committee on Human Resources, U. S. Senate Committee on Labor and Public Welfare, Washington, D.C., Oct. 14, 1971.
9. PRB, *1973 World Population Data Sheet, op. cit.*
10. Ehrlich and Ehrlich, pp. 112-13.
11. For further discussion of the interrelations between population and other problems, see Donella Meadows, Dennis Meadows, Jørgen Randers, and William Behrens, III, *The Limits to Growth* (New York: Universe Books, 1972); Commission on Population Growth and the American Future, *Population and the American Future,* G. P. O., Stock #5258-2002, Washington, D.C., 1972; Committee on Resources and Man, National Academy of Sciences - National Research Council, *Resources and Man* (San Francisco: W. H. Freeman & Co.), 1969; Paul Ehrlich, *The Population Bomb,* 2nd ed. (New York: Ballantine Books, Inc., 1971).
12. Barry Commoner, *The Closing Circle: Nature, Man and Technology* (New York: Knopf,

---

* Only 28 percent of Sorensen's nonvirgin males "often worried" about making a girl pregnant. Forty-six percent of the males who were sexually active at the time of the study had sometimes "just trusted to luck that the girl wouldn't become pregnant," during the preceding month. See Robert C. Sorensen, *Adolescent Sexuality in Contemporary America,* pp 305, 453.

1971); Garrett Hardin, *Exploring New Ethics for Survival: the Voyage of the Spaceship Beagle* (New York: Viking Press, 1972).

13. Lenni W. Kangas, "Integrated Incentives for Fertility Control," *Science* 169:1278-83, 1970; Edgar R. Chasteen, *The Case for Compulsory Birth Control* (Englewood Cliffs, N.J.: Prentice-Hall, 1971); Roger W. McIntire, "Parenthood Training or Mandatory Birth Control: Take Your Choice," *Psychology Today*, 7(5):34, 1973; Bernard Berelson, "Beyond Family Planning," *Science*, 163: 533-43, 1969.
14. Bureau of the Census, "Birth Expectations: 1973" and ". . . 1972." *op. cit.*
15. Commission on Population Growth and the American Future, *op. cit.*, p. 97.
16. Lee Rainwater, *Family Design: Marital Sexuality, Family Size and Contraception* (Chicago: Aldine, 1965), pp. 228-30; "Birth Expectations: 1972," p. 2.
17. W. A. O'Neil, *Everyone Was Brave: The Rise and Fall of Feminism in America* (Chicago: Quadrangle Books, 1969), p. 4.
18. Commission on Population Growth and the American Future, *op. cit.*, pp. 16-17.
19. R. E. Miles, "The Population Challenge of the '70's," *Population Bulletin* 16(1):7, 1970.
20. Commission on Population Growth and the American Future, *op. cit.*, p. 41.
21. Rainwater, 1965, *op. cit.*, pp. 280-81.
22. Bureau of the Census, "Marriage, Divorce, and Remarriage by Year of Birth: June 1971," *Current Population Reports*, Series P-20 #239, 1972, pp. 4-5.
23. Jessie Bernard, *Women and the Public Interest* (Chicago: Aldine-Atherton, 1971), p. 180.
24. N. B. Ryder, "The Emergence of a Modern Fertility Pattern: United States, 1917-66," in *Fertility and Family Planning*, ed. S. J. Behrman, L. Corsa, and R. Freedman (Ann Arbor: University of Michigan Press, 1970), pp. 102-4.
25. Bureau of the Census, "Birth Expectations: 1973," p. 1 and ". . . 1972," p. 19.
26. Rainwater, 1965, *op. cit.*, 194-95.
27. NON (National Organization for Non-Parents), 220 Miramonte Ave., Palo Alto, Calif. 94306.
28. Robert C. Sorensen, *Adolescent Sexuality in Contemporary America* (New York: World Publishing, 1973), p. 358.
29. Bureau of the Census, "Marriage: 1971," *op. cit.*, p. 5; Commission on Population Growth and the American Future, *op. cit.*, p. 67.
30. J. R. Udry, *The Social Context of Marriage*, (Philadelphia: Lippincott, 1966), p. 301.
31. K. W. Bartz and F. I. Nye, "Early Marriage: A Propositional Formulation," *Journal of Marriage and the Family*, 32:258, 1970; Floyd M. Martinson, "Ego Deficiency As a Factor in Marriage," *American Sociological Review*, 20:163, 1955.
32. Luther G. Baker, Jr., "The Personality and Social Adjustment of the Never-Married Woman," *Journal of Marriage and the Family*, 30:473, 1968.
33. Commission on Population Growth and the American Future, *op. cit.*, p. 81; "Cost of Rearing Child Held $5,000 Greater Than in '61," *N.Y. Times*, Feb. 22, 1970, p. 53.
34. Wesley Burr, "Satisfactions with Various Aspects of Marriage Over the Life Cycle: A Random Middle Class Sample," *Journal of Marriage and The Family*, 32:54, 1970; Boyd Rollins and Harold Feldman, "Marital Satisfaction over the Family Life Cycle," *Journal of Marriage and the Family*, 32: 20, 1970; Karen S. Renne, "Correlates of Dissatisfaction in Marriage," *Journal of Marriage and the Family*, 32: 54, 1970; J. R. Hurley and D. Palonen, "Marital Satisfaction and Child Density Among University Student Parents," *Journal of Marriage and the Family*, 29: 483, 1967.

35. Robert G. Ryder, "Longitudinal Data Relating Marriage Satisfaction and Having a Child," *Journal of Marriage and the Family,* 35: 604, 1973.
36. Ruth Brecher and Edward Brecher, "Sex During and After Pregnancy," in *An Analysis of Human Sexual Response* ed. by Brecher and Brecher (New York: New American Library, 1966), p. 93.
37. L. W. Hoffman and F. I. Nye, *The Employed Mother in America* (Chicago: Rand McNally, 1963).
38. Marion Yarrow, Phyllis Scott, Louise de Leeuw and Christine Heinig, "Child Rearing in Families of Working and Non-Working Mothers," *Sociometry,* 25(2): 102-40, 1962.
39. Faye H. Von Mering, "Professional and Non-Professional Women as Mothers," *The Journal of Social Psychology,* 42: 21-34, 1955.
40. Commission on Population Growth and the American Future, *op. cit.,* pp. 88-89.
41. *Ibid.,* p. 85; Sorensen, *op. cit.,* p. 189.
42. *Ibid.,* pp. 303-27; Commission on Population Growth and the American Future, *op. cit.,* p. 85.

Female Sexual Alienation

Linda Phelps

I n the last few years, the so-called sexual revolution has turned sour. The end of inhibition and the release of sexual energies so often thought of as initiating the revolutionary culture are now beginning to be seen as just another fraud. After the countless rapes at music festivals and anti-war gatherings, after the demands raised at People's Park (Berkeley, California, 1969) for "Free Land, Free Dope, Free Women," after the analyses of (male) rock culture, women are beginning to realize that nothing new has happened in male-female sexual relations. What we have is simply a more sophisticated (and thus more insidious) version of male sexual culture, a kind of sexual "freedom" that has meant more opportunity for men, not a new kind of experience for women. At first it was, perhaps, a new experience for women as traditional, puritanical notions of female sexuality were partly discarded. But underneath the guilt that we had learned were needs for self-protection that were much more real. Somehow the rules of the game were still male.

Many of us who only a few years before had felt sexually "liberated" now suddenly found ourselves more sympathetic with the problems of our

Another version of this article appeared in *Liberation* (May 1971) and in *The Ladder* (August-September 1971).

Not only are females confined to a small number of socially acceptable roles, but they are given conflicting messages about these roles.

mothers and grandmothers—feeling a loss of interest in sex, a hatred of sex, or a disgust with our own sexual fantasies. This turn-about happened very fast in many cases, and I think it happened because we opened ourselves up in consciousness-raising and a lot of bad feelings that we did not quite understand floated to the top. It has been good to get these feelings out and look at them. But can we explain them, can we understand what has happened to our sexuality?

I would like to suggest that we can understand the distortion of female sexuality if we conceptualize it as a special case of alienation.

Alienation is a much-used and little-explained term. Put simply, it refers to the progressive sense of separation between our selves or personalities and everything around us that occurs when we are powerless. As Ernest Becker put it in an important essay on alienation: "People break down when they aren't 'doing'—when the world around them does not reflect the active involvement of their own creative powers. . . . Alienated man [sic] is man separated from involvement with and responsibility for the effective use of his *self-powers*." The opposite of powerlessness is self-actualization; and the healthy, self-actualizing human being moves through the world as an autonomous source of action, in touch with her/his own experience.

Since self-actualization seems so obviously preferable, it is worth asking precisely how alienation comes about in our lives as individuals. Becker suggests several ways in his tri-dimensional analysis of alienation.

1) *Alienation occurs along the dimension of time.* As children we learn certain patterns of behavior that bring us approval and help us function in the world. But as we grow older, we face situations not covered by the old patterns, situations calling for new kinds of behavior. If our early childhood training has been too rigid, we cannot go beyond the old patterns, and we become increasingly unable to handle our own experiences. Withdrawal is a natural response in these circumstances.

2) *Alienation also occurs within the dimension of the roles we play.* We are called upon to play more than one role in life, and sometimes the behavior expected in one role conflicts with the behavior expected in another. These contradictions set us at odds with parts of our lives. Not only are females confined to a small number of socially acceptable roles, but they are given conflicting messages

about these roles. Motherhood, for example, is viewed as a sacred task, but mothers are not taken seriously when they act outside their kitchens and homes. Child-rearing is seen as a woman's job, but a woman must not use her intuition or experience in doing it; (largely male) psychologists, child psychiatrists, and educational researchers will tell her how. Girls are encouraged to become educated, but discouraged from doing anything meaningful with that education.

3) *The third dimension of alienation* is more complex. Put simply, it *is the stage at which* the conflicts just described become too severe, the gaps between thought and experience, mind and body become too great, and *an actual breakdown of self is likely to occur.* It is this kind of breakdown that makes people unable to function and lands them in mental hospitals. Becker calls this extreme form of alienation "schizophrenia" and I would like to adopt his usage, realizing that powerlessness can sometimes drive us literally "out of our minds." R. D. Laing is probably right in his contention that there is no such thing as "schizophrenia" as that term has usually been used in the mental health field,* yet for want of another term I would like to use it here in the specialized sense explained above: an extreme form of alienation in which people lose touch with their own experience of reality.

This tri-dimensional concept of alienation is complex, but I think it can help us understand some parts of our own experience of male-female sexual relationships, especially if we extend it to include a political dimension. Both Laing and Becker describe alienation as growing out of power relationships between people as well as out of the condition of being human. As human beings we come to understand and experience ourselves as we interact with other people. It is in grappling with the outside world, in trying out our powers of thought and emotion, that we become full, self-actualized people. In this self-directed behavior, we test ourselves and gain some understanding of ourselves and our environment. And the more positive and successful experiences we build up, the more secure we are as whole persons. This is the mechanism by which we become liberated; the reverse process is alienation.

As alienated people, we begin to deny our own reality; we lose important parts of ourselves. When alienation becomes extreme, we take refuge in a world of

---

* R. D. Laing and A. Esterson, *Sanity, Madness, and the Family: Families of Schizophrenics* (Baltimore, Md.: Penguin Books, 1970). As Laing sees it, behaviors that have often been called schizophrenic are understandable reactions to social situations in which people are powerless, their experiences and perceptions denied and mystified by others. A woman in Laing's study broke down when she lost "any sense of being the agent of her own thoughts and words" (p. 42). Another young woman who had been in a mental hospital for ten years felt that "she was forbidden to see for herself and think for herself. Any expression of her own was simply ignored, disparaged, ridiculed" (p. 60).

**I would argue that as females we become sex-
ually alienated, at points even schizophrenic,
because we relate ... to a false world of
symbol and fantasy ... the world of sex as
seen through male eyes.**

symbols; we become accustomed to relating to symbol-objects rather than person-objects and in doing so we lose contact with our own self-powers.

I would argue that as females we become sexually alienated, at points even schizophrenic, because we relate neither to ourselves as self-directed persons nor to our partners as the objects of our desire, but to a false world of symbol and fantasy. This fantasy world that veils our experience is the world of sex as seen through male eyes. It is a world where eroticism is defined in terms of female powerlessness, dependency, and submission. It is a world of sado-masochistic sex.

If this seems doubtful, think of the erotic themes of most of the novels, comic books, movies, jokes, cartoons, and songs ever published. The most frequent sexual theme is the drama of conquest and submission: the male takes the initiative and the female waits, waits in a thousand variations on a single theme—eagerly, coyly, shyly, angrily, and, at the outer edge of pornography and fantasy, against her will. Usually it is more subtle. The female stands in awe of the hero's abilities, his powers; she is willing when he takes the initiative, guides her by the elbow, puts his arm around her waist, maneuvers her into the bedroom. What is it that makes such descriptions arousing? Not a mere catalogue of anatomy, for this may not even be given, but the tension in the social situation as male advances on female, whether she is willing or not.

Such submission is acceptable in our culture if the man is superior, and this leads to the search for the man who is smarter, taller, more self-confident—someone to look up to and thus worthy of giving in to.

> In each of our lives, there was a first man for whom we were prepared like lambs for the slaughter. My fantasy of him was a composite of Prince Valiant, Gary Cooper, and my father. Trained in submission, in silence, I awaited him through a series of *adolescent boyfriends who were not masterful enough to fit the dream* ... because I would not really graduate to the estate of womanhood until I had been taken by a strong man.[2]

Our culture's eroticism mirrors the power dynamics between the sexes, but in a particularly cruel way. With the right man and the right circumstances, the picture of female powerlessness can be highly arousing. In this way, sexism gets built into our very biological impulses.

A rather narrow form of male-dominated heterosexuality has become the norm which shapes our sexual impulses. In a study of sexual behavior,[3] psychologist Abe Maslow confirmed this norm, reporting that women who find their male partners more dominant than they are usually make the best sexual "adjustment." For example, a very sexually active women in his study failed to reach orgasm with several male partners because she considered them weaker than herself and thus could not "give in to them." Thus, "normal" sexual happiness occurs in our society when the male plays the dominant role.

If we come to view male-dominated heterosexuality as the only healthy form of sex, it is because we are bombarded with that model for our sexual fantasies long before we experience sex itself. Sexual images of conquest and submission pervade our imagination from an early age and determine how we will later look upon and experience sex. Through the television set and the storybook, we live out in imagination society's definition of sex and love. Rapunzel waits in her tower for years in hopes of the young prince who will free her body from its imprisonment. Sleeping Beauty's desires slumber until they are awakened and fulfilled by the kiss of the young prince. The sexual fable in the stories of these fairy-tale princesses is quite clear, and very nearly as powerful today as it was a century ago. There are few women, no matter how intelligent, no matter how dedicated to the pursuit of a goal, who will not finally be conquered—and like it. And if they are not conquered, it is understood that no man desired them anyway.

By experiencing such sexual fantasies at an early age, women become alienated from their own later experiences (Becker's first dimension). Locked early into a set of fantasy images that define female sexual roles as passive, they must deny feelings that do not fit the definition. And so all-pervasive is the male bias of our culture that we seldom notice that the fantasies we take in, the images that describe to us how to act, are male fantasies about females. In a male world, female sexuality is from the beginning unable to get a clear picture of itself.

Moreover, also from the beginning, women experience Becker's second dimension of alienation: the role of woman as a sexual being is subject to contradictory evaluations by society. Young girls become attuned to society's ambivalent view of female sexuality. Women are considered synonomous with sex, yet female sexuality is seen as valid only under certain conditions, such as marriage. Even in more permissive ages like our own, there are still limits. One of these is the point where a female can be labeled promiscuous. Another is the point where she attempts to exercise any power: women who initiate and direct sexual activity with male partners find that they have gone too far and are feared and rejected as "castrators."

In all these ways, female sexuality becomes distorted, swallowed up in a fantasy world of symbol-objects rather than real people. Like the schizophrenic, we are alienated from our own experience and from our own powers of initiation. This form of alienation affects sex directly: it means that women do not often take the initiative in relation to men. As Becker describes it:

> Schizophrenic passivity is a direct reflex of the abrogation of one's powers in the face of the object. . . . If you relate to an object under your own initiatory powers, then it becomes an object which enriches your own nature. If you lack initiatory powers over the object, it takes on a different value, for it then becomes an individual which crowds your own nature. . . . A girl really comes to exist as a feminine sex object for the adolescent only as he learns to exercise active courtship powers in relation to her.[4]

If women become objects of sexual desire for men in the social process of male-initiated relationships, how does the male become an object of sexual desire for the female? In a sense, perhaps he does not. It is not clear, in fact, that the male body *per se* is arousing for women, certainly not in the same way that the female body is for men. Indeed, many women find the male body ugly. They respond narcissistically to the bombardment of images of the female body as sexual stimuli: and think of sex in terms of what is being done to them rather than projecting sexual desire onto the male. The female is taught to be the object of sexual desires rather than to be a self-directed sexual being oriented toward another; she is taught to be adored rather than adoring. As Shulamith Firestone points out in *The Dialectic of Sex,* "Cultural distortion of sexuality also explains how female sexuality gets twisted in narcissism: women make love to themselves vicariously through the man rather than directly making love to him."[5]

Two things would seem to happen to female sexuality. On the one hand, with little acceptable sexual imagery—either male or female—available in this culture for women, many do not allow themselves any sexual desires or fantasies at all. (Masters and Johnson, having found that many women who could not focus on sexual imagery had difficulty having orgasm, have tried to encourage sexual fantasy through the reading of arousing material.) Women who do have fantasies often have the same sado-masochistic ones as men do. In these fantasy episodes, the female does not always play the masochistic role. She may take the part of the male, the female, or an onlooker, but there is almost always a powerless female in the scene.

How do women tolerate a situation in which men control and define the experience of sex? Only, I believe, in the same way the schizophrenic tolerates her/his world—by separation from it. We experience our sexuality in symbolic terms at the expense of active physical involvement. Sex is reinterpreted to us by society in symbolic messages of passivity and conquest. Like the symbolic world of the schizophrenic, women's fantasy life—our desire to be taken, overpowered, mastered—allow us to play the passive role and perhaps even to enjoy it *if we fully accept the world as defined by men.* Caught between the demands of a male-dominated society and the demands of our own self-definition, we survive by fully accepting the masochistic symbol-world given to us by male society at the expense of our own experience. In fact, our physical experience has been denied and distorted for so long that most of us are not even aware of the sacrifice we have made. We are only uneasy that all is not well.

Yet ultimately in the lives of those women for whom fantasy and reality become too far apart, a crisis occurs. The crisis may arise in some cases merely because the male becomes demystified after years of marriage. It is hard to hold onto fantasies of male power when confronted with the reality of a pot-bellied, lethargic husband. In other cases, as more women become involved in the women's movement, the whole fragile structure of fantasy and power may fall along with the myth of male supremacy. Such a crisis most commonly results either in a transfer of fantasy to a new male or in a loss of interest in sex altogether.

Women, then, are alienated from their sexuality along several dimensions. From an early age, we are alienated from ourselves as sexual beings by a male society's ambivalent definition of our sexuality: we are sexy, but we are pure; we are insatiable, but we are frigid; we have beautiful bodies, but we must paint and shave and deodorize them. We are also alienated because we are separated from our own experience by the prevailing male cultural definition of sex—the male fantasy of active man and passive woman. From an early age, our sexual impulses are turned back upon ourselves in the narcissistic counterpart of the male fantasy world. In social relations with men, we are alienated from ourselves as initiating, self-directed persons. Only a few women are able to hold all these contradictory parts together. Far more are now beginning to question whether they should have to try.

Calling into question our traditional female role, however, has meant calling into question more and more layers of our experience. With this questioning has come the discovery that there is very little worth saving in male-female relations as we have known them. Kate Millett showed us in *Sexual Politics* that fascism—the relations of dominance and submission that begin with sex and extend throughout our society—is at the very core of our cultural experience. So it is with little joy and much sadness that we peel back the layers of our consciousness and see our sexual experience for what it really is. And it is also with much sadness that we admit that there is no easy answer. It does no good to say that we have been merely the victims of male power plays. For whatever reasons, the sado-masochistic content is in the heads of women too. As long as female powerlessness is the unspoken reality of much of our cultural imagination, then women will want to be conquered. As long as our cultural vision for the future is the projection of male desires, women will not be able to understand even their own alienation.

To say this is to suggest some ways out of our cultural and sexual alienation. Yet we should never assume, as we often do, that the pervasive sexual distortion will easily be corrected. We have pushed beyond the economic revolution and the cultural revolution to come face to face with the real sexual revolution, and we are not sure just what we have left in the way of hope and affirmation.

Perhaps the most courageous and in the long run the most positive thing we can do is to acknowledge the pain we feel now and the profound damage we have sustained—and in doing so avoid despair. Sometimes it is necessary to touch bottom in order to push up for air.

Notes

1. Ernest Becker, "Mills' Social Psychology and the Great Historical Convergence on the Problem of Alienation," in Irving Horowitz, ed., *The New Sociology, Essays in Social Science and Social Theory in Honor of C. Wright Mills* (New York: Oxford University Press, 1964), pp. 108-33.
2. *Motherlode*, vol. 1. no. 1, p. 1.
3. A. H. Maslow, "Self-Esteem (Dominance-feeling) and Sexuality in Women," in Hendrik M. Ruitenbeek, *Psychoanalysis and Female Sexuality* (New Haven, Conn.: College and University Press, 1966), pp. 161-97.
4. Becker, *op. cit.,* p. 125.
5. Shulamith Firestone, *The Dialectic of Sex* (New York: William Morrow, 1970), p. 78.

Rape:
The All-American Crime

Susan Griffin

I have never been free of the fear of rape. From a very early age I, like most women, have thought of rape as part of my natural environment—something to be feared and prayed against like fire or lightning. I never asked why men raped; I simply thought it one of the many mysteries of human nature.

I was, however, curious enough about the violent side of humanity to read every crime magazine I was able to ferret away from my grandfather. Each issue featured at least one "sex crime," with pictures of a victim, usually in a pearl necklace, and of the ditch or the orchard where her body was found. I was never certain why the victims were always women, nor what the motives of the murderer were, but I did guess that the world was not a safe place for women. I observed that my grandmother was meticulous about locks and quick to draw the shades before anyone removed so much as a shoe. I sensed that danger lurked outside.

At the age of eight, my suspicions were confirmed. My grandmother took me to the back of the house where the men wouldn't hear, and told me that strange men wanted to do harm to little girls. I learned not to walk on dark streets, not to talk to

But though rape and the fear of rape are a daily part of every woman's consciousness, the subject is so rarely discussed by that unofficial staff of male intellectuals . . . that one begins to suspect a conspiracy of silence.

strangers or get into strange cars, to lock doors, and to be modest. She never explained why a man would want to harm a little girl, and I never asked.

If I thought for a while that my grandmother's fears were imaginary, the illusion was brief. That year, on the way home from school, a schoolmate a few years older than I tried to rape me. Later, in an obscure aisle of the local library (while I was reading *Freddy the Pig*) I turned to discover a man exposing himself. Then, the friendly man around the corner was arrested for child molesting.

My initiation to sexuality was typical. Every woman has similar stories to tell—the first man who attacked her may have been a neighbor, a family friend, an uncle, her doctor, or perhaps her own father. And women who grow up in New York City always have tales about the subway.

But though rape and the fear of rape are a daily part of every woman's consciousness, the subject is so rarely discussed by that unofficial staff of male intellectuals (who write the books which study seemingly every other form of male activity) that one begins to suspect a conspiracy of silence. And indeed, the obscurity of rape in print exists in marked contrast to the frequency of rape in reality, for *forcible rape is the most frequently committed violent crime in America today.* The Federal Bureau of Investigation classes three crimes as violent: murder, aggravated assault and forcible rape. In 1968, 31,060 rapes were *reported.* According to the FBI and independent criminologists, however, to approach accuracy this figure must be multiplied by at least a factor of ten to compensate for the fact that most rapes are not reported; when these compensatory mathematics are used, there are more rapes committed than aggravated assaults and homicides.

When I asked Berkeley, California's Police Inspector in charge of rape investigation if he knew why men rape women, he replied that he had not spoken with "these people and delved into what really makes them tick, because that really isn't my job." However, when I asked him how a woman might prevent being raped, he was not so reticent. "I wouldn't advise any female to go walking around alone at night . . . and she should lock her car at all times." The Inspector illustrated his warning with a grisly story about a man who lay in wait for women in the back seats of their cars while they were shopping in a local supermarket. This man eventually murdered one of his rape victims. "Always lock your car," the Inspector repeated, and then added, without a hint of irony, "Of course, you don't have to be paranoid about this type of thing."

The Inspector wondered why I wanted to write about rape. Like most men he did not understand the urgency of the topic, for, after all, men are not raped. But like most women I had spent considerable time speculating on the true nature of the rapist. When I was very young, my image of the "sexual offender" was a nightmarish amalgamation of the bogey man and Captain Hook: he wore a black cape, and he cackled. As I matured, so did my image of the rapist. Born into the psychoanalytic age, I tried to "understand" the rapist. Rape, I came to believe, was only one of many unfortunate evils produced by sexual repression. Reasoning by tautology, I concluded that any man who would rape a woman must be out of his mind.

Yet, though the theory that rapists are insane is a popular one, this belief has no basis in fact. According to Professor Menachem Amir's study of 646 rape cases in Philadelphia, *Patterns in Forcible Rape,* men who rape are not abnormal. Amir writes, "Studies indicate that sex offenders do not constitute a unique or psychopathological type; nor are they as a group invariably more disturbed than the control groups to which they are compared." Alan Taylor, a parole officer who has worked with rapists in the prison facilities at San Luis Obispo, California, stated the question in plainer language: "Those men were the most normal men there. They had a lot of hang-ups, but they were the same hang-ups as men walking out on the street."

Another canon in the apologetics of rape is that, if it were not for learned social controls, all men would rape. Rape is held to be natural behavior, and not to rape must be learned. But in truth rape is not universal to the human species. Moreover, studies of rape in our culture reveal that, far from being impulsive behavior, most rape is planned. Professor Amir's study reveals that in cases of group rape (the "gangbang" of masculine slang) 90 percent . . . were planned; in pair rapes, 83 percent . . . were planned; and in single rapes, 58 percent were planned. These figures should significantly discredit the image of the rapist as a man who is suddenly overcome by sexual needs society does not allow him to fulfill.

Far from the social control of rape being learned, comparisons with other cultures lead one to suspect that, in our society, it is rape itself that is learned. (The fact that rape is against the law should not be considered proof that rape is not in fact encouraged as part of our culture.)

This culture's concept of rape as an illegal, but still understandable, form of behavior is not a universal one. In her study *Sex and Temperament,* Margaret Mead describes a society that does not share our views. The Arapesh do not ". . . have any conception of the male nature that might make rape understandable to them." Indeed our interpretation of rape is a product of our conception of the nature of male sexuality. A common retort to the question, why don't women rape men, is the myth that men have greater sexual needs, that their sexuality is more urgent than women's. And it is the nature of human beings to want to live up to what is expected of them.

And this same culture which expects aggression from the male expects passivity from the female. Conveniently, the companion myth about the nature of female sexuality is that all women secretly want to be raped. Lurking beneath her modest female exterior is a subconscious desire to be ravished. The following description of a stag movie, written by Brenda Starr in Los Angeles' underground paper, *Everywoman*, typifies this male fantasy. The movie "showed a woman in her underclothes reading on her bed. She is interrupted by a rapist with a knife. He immediately wins her over with his charm and they get busy sucking and fucking." An advertisement in the *Berkeley Barb* reads, "Now as all women know from their daydreams, rape has a lot of advantages. Best of all it's so simple. No preparation necessary, no planning ahead of time, no wondering if you should or shouldn't; just whang! bang!" Thanks to Masters and Johnson even the scientific canon recognizes that for the female, "whang! bang!" can scarcely be described as pleasurable.

Still the male psyche persists in believing that, protestations and struggles to the contrary, deep inside her mysterious feminine soul, the female victim has wished for her own fate. A young woman who was raped by the husband of a friend said that days after the incident the man returned to her home, pounded on the door and screamed to her, "Jane, Jane. You loved it. You know you loved it."

The theory that women like being raped extends itself by deduction into the proposition that most or much of rape is provoked by the victim. But this too is only myth. Though provocation, considered a mitigating factor in a court of law, may consist of only "a gesture," according to the Federal Commission on Crimes of Violence, only 4 percent of reported rapes involved any precipitative behavior by the woman.

The notion that rape is enjoyed by the victim is also convenient for the man who, though he would not commit forcible rape, enjoys the idea of its existence, as if rape confirms that enormous sexual potency which he secretly knows to be his own. It is for the pleasure of the armchair rapist that detailed accounts of violent rapes exist in the media. Indeed, many men appear to take sexual pleasure from nearly all forms of violence. Whatever the motivation, male sexuality and violence in our culture seem to be inseparable. James Bond alternately whips out his revolver and his cock, and though there is no known connection between the skills of gun-fighting and love-making, pacifism seems suspiciously effeminate.

In a recent fictional treatment of the Manson case, Frank Conroy writes of his vicarious titillation when describing the murders to his wife:

. . . in the spectrum of male behavior, rape, the perfect combination of sex and violence, is the penultimate act.

"Every single person there was killed." She didn't move.
"It sounds like there was torture," I said. As the words left my mouth I knew there was no need to say them to frighten her into believing that she needed me for protection.

The pleasure he feels as his wife's protector is inextricably mixed with pleasure in the violence itself. Conroy writes, "I was excited by the killings, as one is excited by catastrophe on a grand scale, as one is alert to pre-echoes of unknown changes, hints of unrevealed secrets, rumblings of chaos. . . ."

The attraction of the male in our culture to violence and death is a tradition Manson and his admirers are carrying on with tireless avidity (even presuming Manson's innocence, he dreams of the purification of fire and destruction). It was Malraux in his *Anti-Memoirs* who said that, for the male, facing death was *the* illuminating experience analogous to childbirth for the female. Certainly our culture does glorify war and shroud the agonies of the gun-fighter in veils of mystery.

And in the spectrum of male behavior, rape, the perfect combination of sex and violence, is the penultimate act. Erotic pleasure cannot be separated from culture, and in our culture male eroticism is wedded to power. Not only should a man be taller and stronger than a female in the perfect love-match, but he must also demonstrate his superior strength in gestures of dominance which are perceived as amorous. Though the law attempts to make a clear division between rape and sexual intercourse, in fact the courts find it difficult to distinguish between a case where the decision to copulate was mutual and one where a man forced himself upon his partner.

The scenario is even further complicated by the expectation that, not only does a woman mean "yes" when she says "no," but that a really decent woman ought to begin by saying "no," and then be led down the primrose path to acquiescence. Ovid, the author of Western Civilization's most celebrated sex manual, makes this expectation perfectly clear: "and when I beg you to say "yes," say "no." Then let me lie outside your bolted door. . . . So Love grows strong."

That the basic elements of rape are involved in all heterosexual relationships may explain why men often identify with the offender in this crime. But to regard the rapist as the victim, a man driven by his inherent sexual needs to take what will not be given him, reveals a basic ignorance of sexual politics. For in our culture heterosexual love finds an erotic expression through male dominance and female submission. A man who derives pleasure from raping a woman clearly must enjoy force and dominance as much as or more than the simple pleasures of the flesh. Coitus cannot be experienced in isolation. The weather, the state of the nation, the level of sugar in the blood—all will affect a man's ability to achieve orgasm. If a man can achieve sexual pleasure after terrorizing and humiliating the object of his passion, and in fact while inflicting pain upon her, one must assume he derives pleasure directly from terrorizing, humiliating and harming a woman. According to Amir's study of forcible rape, on a statistical average the man who has been convicted of rape was found to have a normal sexual personality, tending to be different from the normal, well-adjusted male only in having a greater tendency to express violence and rage.

And if the professional rapist is to be separated from the average dominant heterosexual, it may be mainly a quantitative difference. For the existence of rape as an index to masculinity is not entirely metaphorical. Though this measure of masculinity seems to be more publicly exhibited among "bad boys" or aging bikers who practice sexual initiation through group rape, in fact "good boys" engage in the same rites to prove their manhood. In Stockton, a small town in California which epitomizes silent-majority America, a bachelor party was given [in the early 1970's] for a young man about to be married. A woman was hired to dance "topless" for the amusement of the guests. At the high point of the evening the bridegroom-to-be dragged the woman into a bedroom. No move was made by any of his companions to stop what was clearly going to be an attempted rape. Far from it. As the woman described, "I tried to keep him away—told him of my Herpes Genitalis, et cetera, but he couldn't face the guys if he didn't screw me." After the bridegroom had finished raping the woman and returned with her to the party, far from chastising him, his friends heckled the woman and covered her with wine.

It was fortunate for the dancer that the bridegroom's friends did not follow him into the bedroom for, though one might suppose that in group rape, since the victim is outnumbered, less force would be inflicted on her, in fact, Amir's studies indicate, "the most excessive degrees of violence occurred in group rape." Far from discouraging violence, the presence of other men may in fact encourage sadism, and even cause the behavior. In an unpublished study of group rape by Gilbert Geis and Duncan Chappell, the authors refer to a study by W. H. Blanchard which relates, "The leader of the male group . . . apparently precipitated and maintained the activity, despite misgivings, because of a need to fulfill the role that the other two men had assigned to him. 'I was scared when it began to happen,' he says. 'I wanted to leave but I didn't want to say it to the other guys—you know—that I was scared.' "

Thus it becomes clear that not only does our culture teach men the rudiments of rape, but society, or more specifically other men, encourage the practice of it.

II

Every man I meet wants to protect me. Can't figure out what from.

— Mae West

If a male society rewards aggressive, domineering sexual behavior, it contains within itself a sexual schizophrenia. For the masculine man is also expected to prove his mettle as a protector of women. To the naive eye, this dichotomy implies that men fall into one of two categories: those who rape and those who protect. In fact, life does not prove so simple. In a study euphemistically entitled "Sex Aggression by College Men," it was discovered that men who believe in a double standard of morality for men and women, who in fact believe most fervently in the ultimate value of virginity, are more liable to commit "this aggressive variety of sexual exploitation."

(At this point in our narrative it should come as no surprise that Sir Thomas Malory, creator of that classic tale of chivalry [*La morte d'Artur*], was himself arrested and found guilty for repeated incidents of rape.)

In the system of chivalry, men protect women against men. This is not unlike the protection relationship which the Mafia established with small businesses in the early part of this century. Indeed, chivalry is an age-old protection racket which depends for its existence on rape.

According to the male mythology which defines and perpetuates rape, [the desire to rape] is an animal instinct inherent in the male. The story goes that sometime in our pre-historical past, the male, more hirsute and burly than today's counterpart, roamed about an uncivilized landscape until he found a desirable female. (Oddly enough, this female is *not* pictured as more muscular than the modern woman.) Her mate does not bother with courtship. He simply grabs her by the hair and drags her to the closest cave. Presumably, one of the major advantages of modern civilization for the female has been the civilizing of the male. We call it chivalry.

But women do not get chivalry for free. According to the logic of sexual politics, we too have to civilize our behavior. (Enter chastity. Enter virginity. Enter monogamy.) For the female, civilized behavior means chastity before marriage and faithfulness within it. Chivalrous behavior in the male is supposed to protect that chastity from involuntary defilement. The fly in the ointment of this otherwise peaceful system is the fallen woman. She does not behave. And therefore she does not deserve protection. Or, to use another argument, a major tenet of the same value system, what has once been defiled cannot again be violated. One begins to suspect that it is the behavior of the fallen woman and not that of the male, that civilization aims to control.

The assumption that a woman who does not respect this double standard deserves whatever she gets (or at the very least "asks for it") operates in the courts today. While in some states a man's previous rape convictions are not considered admissible evidence, the sexual reputation of the rape victim is considered a crucial element of the facts upon which the court must decide innocence or guilt.

The court's respect for the double standard manifested itself particularly clearly in the case of the People v. Jerry Plotkin. Mr. Plotkin, a 36-year-old jeweler, was tried for rape [in 1971] in a San Francisco Superior Court. According to the woman who brought the charges, Plotkin, along with three other men, forced her at gunpoint to enter a car one night in October 1970. She was taken to Mr. Plotkin's fashionable apartment where he and the three other men first raped her and then, in the delicate language of the *San Francisco Chronicle,* "subjected her to perverted sex acts." She was, she said, set free in the morning with the warning that she would be killed if she spoke to anyone about the event. She did report the incident to the police, who then searched Plotkin's apartment and discovered a long list of names of women. Her name was on the list and had been crossed out.

In addition to the woman's account of her abduction and rape, the prosecution submitted four of Plotkin's address books containing the names of hundreds of women. Plotkin claimed he did not know all of the women since some of the names had been given to him by friends and he had not yet called on them. Several women, however, did testify in court that Plotkin had, to cite the *Chronicle,* "lured them up to his apartment under one pretext or another, and forced his sexual attentions on them."

Plotkin's defense rested on two premises. First, through his own testimony Plotkin established a reputation for himself as a sexual libertine who frequently picked up girls in bars and took them to his house where sexual relations often took place. He was the Playboy. He claimed that the accusation of rape, therefore, was false—this incident had simply been one of many casual sexual relationships, the victim one of many playmates. The second premise of the defense was that his accuser was also a sexual libertine. However, the picture created of the young woman (fully thirteen years younger than Plotkin) was not akin to the light-hearted, gay-bachelor image projected by the defendant. On the contrary, the day after the defense cross-examined the woman, the *Chronicle* printed a story head-lined, "Grueling Day For Rape Case Victim." (A leaflet passed out by women in

According to the double standard a woman who has had sexual intercourse out of wedlock cannot be raped. Rape is not only a crime of aggression against the body; it is a transgression against chastity as defined by men.

front of the courtroom was more succinct, "rape was committed by four men in a private apartment in October; on Thursday, it was done by a judge and a lawyer in a public courtroom.")

Through skillful questioning fraught with innuendo, Plotkin's defense attorney James Martin MacInnis portrayed the young woman as a licentious opportunist and unfit mother. MacInnis began by asking the young woman (then employed as a secretary) whether or not it was true that she was "familiar with liquor" and had worked as a "cocktail waitress." The young woman replied (the *Chronicle* wrote "admitted") that she had worked once or twice as a cocktail waitress. The attorney then asked if she had worked as a secretary in the financial district but had "left that employment after it was discovered that you had sexual intercourse on a couch in the office." The woman replied, "That is a lie. I left because I didn't like working in a one-girl office. It was too lonely." Then the defense asked if, while working as an attendant at a health club, "you were accused of having a sexual affair with a man?" Again the woman denied the story: "I was never accused of that."

Plotkin's attorney then sought to establish that his client's accuser was living with a married man. She responded that the man was separated from his wife. Finally he told the court that she had "spent the night" with another man who lived in the same building.

At this point in the testimony the woman asked Plotkin's defense attorney, "Am I on trial? . . . It is embarrassing and personal to admit these things to all these people. . . . I did not commit a crime. I am a human being." The lawyer, true to the chivalry of his class, apologized and immediately resumed questioning her, turning his attention to her children. (She is divorced, and the children at the time of the trial were in a foster home.) "Isn't it true that your two children have a sex game in which one gets on top of another and they—" "That is a lie!" the young woman interrupted him. She ended her testimony by explaining "They are wonderful children. They are not perverted."

The jury, divided in favor of acquittal ten to two, asked the court stenographer to read the woman's testimony back to them. After this reading, the Superior Court acquitted the defendant of both the charges of rape and kidnapping.

According to the double standard a woman who has had sexual intercourse out of wedlock cannot be raped. Rape is not only a crime of aggression against the body; it is a transgression against chastity as defined by men. When a woman is forced into a sexual relationship, she has, according to the male ethos, been violated. But she is also defiled if she does not behave according to the double standard, by maintaining her chastity, or confining her sexual activities to a monogamous relationship.

One should not assume, however, that a woman can avoid the possibility of rape simply by behaving. Though myth would have it that mainly "bad girls" are raped, this theory has no basis in fact. Available statistics would lead one to believe that a safer course is promiscuity. In a study of rape done in the District of Columbia, it was found that 82 percent of the rape victims had a "good reputation." Even the Police Inspector's advice to stay off the streets is rather useless, for almost half of reported rapes occur in the home of the victim and are committed by a man she has never before seen. Like indiscriminate terrorism, rape can happen to any woman, and few women are ever without this knowledge.

But the courts and the police, both dominated by white males, continue to suspect the rape victim, *sui generis,* of provoking or asking for her own assault. According to Amir's study, the police tend to believe that a woman without a good reputation cannot be raped. The rape victim is usually submitted to countless questions about her own sexual mores and behavior by the police investigator. This preoccupation is partially justified by the legal requirements for prosecution in a rape case. The rape victim must have been penetrated, and she must have made it clear to her assailant that she did not want penetration (unless of course she is unconscious). A [woman's] refusal to accompany a man to some isolated place to allow him to touch her does not in the eyes of the court [make the subsequent act a] rape. She must have said "no" at the crucial genital moment. And the rape victim, to qualify as such, must also have put up a physical struggle—unless she can prove that to do so would have been to endanger her life.

But the zealous interest the police frequently exhibit in the physical details of a rape case is only partially explained by the requirements of the court. A woman who was raped in Berkeley was asked to tell the story of her rape four different times "right out in the street," while her assailant was escaping. She was then required to submit to a pelvic examination to prove that penetration had taken place. Later, she was taken to the police station where she was asked the same questions again: "Were you forced?" "Did he penetrate?" "Are you sure your life was in danger and you had no other choice?" This woman had been pulled off the street by a man who held a 10-inch knife at her throat and forcibly raped her. She was raped at midnight and was not able to return to her home until five in the morning. Police contacted her twice again in the next week, once by telephone at two in the morning and once at four in the morning. In her words, "The rape was probably the least traumatic incident of the whole evening. If I'm ever raped again . . . I wouldn't report it to the police because of all the degradation. . . ."

If white women are subjected to unnecessary and often hostile questioning after having been raped, third world women are often not believed at all. According to the white male ethos (which is not only sexist but racist), third world women are defined from birth as "impure." Thus the white male is provided with a pool of women who are fair game for sexual imperialism. Third world women frequently do not report rape and for good reason. When blues singer Billie Holliday was ten years old, she was taken off to a local house by a neighbor and raped. Her mother brought the police to rescue her, and she was taken to the local police station crying and bleeding:

> When we got there, instead of treating me and Mom like somebody who called the cops for help, they treated me like I'd killed somebody . . . I guess they had me figured for having enticed this old goat into the whorehouse. . . . All I know for sure is they threw me into a cell . . . a fat white matron . . . saw I was still bleeding, she felt sorry for me and gave me a couple glasses of milk. But nobody else did anything for me except give me filthy looks and snicker to themselves.
> After a couple of days in a cell they dragged me into a court. Mr. Dick got sentenced to five years. They sentenced me to a Catholic institution.

Clearly the white man's chivalry is aimed only to protect the chastity of "his" women.

As a final irony, that same system of sexual values from which chivalry is derived has also provided womankind with an unwritten code of behavior, called femininity, which makes a feminine woman the perfect victim of sexual aggression. If being chaste does not ward off the possibility of assault, being feminine certainly increases the chances that it will succeed. To be submissive is to defer to masculine strength; is to lack muscular development or any interest in defending oneself; is to let doors be opened, to have one's arm held when crossing the street. To be feminine is to wear shoes which make it difficult to run; skirts which inhibit one's stride; underclothes which inhibit the circulation. Is it not an intriguing observation that those very clothes which are thought to be flattering to the female and attractive to the male are those which make it impossible for a woman to defend herself against aggression?

Each girl as she grows into womanhood is taught fear. Fear is the form in which the female internalizes both chivalry and the double standard. Since, biologically speaking, women in fact have the same if not greater potential for sexual expression as do men, the woman who is taught that she must behave differently from a man must also learn to distrust her own carnality. She must deny her own feelings and learn not to act from them. She fears herself. This is the essence of passivity, and of course, a woman's passivity is not simply sexual but functions to cripple her from self-expression in every area of her life.

Passivity itself prevents a woman from ever considering her own potential for self-defense and forces her to look to men for protection. The woman is taught fear, but this time fear of the other; and yet her only relief from this fear is to seek out the other. Moreover, the passive woman is taught to regard herself as impotent, unable to act, unable even to perceive, in no way self-sufficient, and, finally, as the object and not the subject of human behavior. It is in this sense that a woman is deprived of the status of a human being. She is not free to be.

III

Since Ibsen's Nora slammed the door on her patriarchical husband, woman's attempt to be free has been more or less fashionable. In this nineteenth-century portrait of a woman leaving her marriage, Nora tells her husband, "Our home has been nothing but a playroom. I have been your doll-wife just as at home I was papa's doll-child." And, at least on the stage, "The Doll's House" crumbled, leaving audiences with hope for the fate of the modern woman. And today, as in the past, womankind has not lacked examples of liberated women to emulate: Emma Goldman, Greta Garbo and Isadora Duncan all denounced marriage and the double standard, and believed their right to freedom included sexual independence; but still their example has not affected the lives of millions of women who continue to marry, divorce and remarry, living out their lives dependent on the status and economic power of men. Patriarchy still holds the average woman prisoner not because she lacks the courage of an Isadora Duncan, but because the material conditions of her life prevent her from being anything but an object.

In the *Elementary Structures of Kinship,* Claude Levi-Strauss gives to marriage this universal description, "It is always a system of exchange that we find at the origin of the rules of marriage." In this system of exchange, a woman is the "most precious possession." Levi-Strauss continues that the custom of including women as booty in the marketplace is still so general that "a whole volume would not be sufficient to enumerate instances of it." Levi-Strauss makes it clear that he does not exclude Western Civilization from his definition of "universal" and cites examples from modern wedding ceremonies. (The marriage ceremony is still one in which the husband and wife become one, and "that one is the husband.")

The legal proscription against rape reflects this possessory view of women. An article in the 1952-53 *Yale Law Journal* describes the legal rationale behind laws against rape: "In our society sexual taboos, often enacted into law, buttress a

The laws against rape exist to protect rights of the male as possessor of the female body, and not the right of the female over her own body.

system of monogamy based upon the law of 'free bargaining' of the potential spouses. Within this process the woman's power to withhold or grant sexual access is an important bargaining weapon." Presumably then, laws against rape are intended to protect the right of a woman, not for physical self-determination, but for physical "bargaining." The article goes on to explain explicitly why the preservation of the bodies of women is important to men:

> The consent standard in our society does more than protect a significant item of social currency for women; it fosters, and is in turn bolstered by, a masculine pride in the exclusive possession of a sexual object. The consent of a woman to sexual intercourse awards the man a privilege of bodily access, a personal "prize" whose value is enhanced by sole ownership. An additional reason for the man's condemnation of rape may be found in the threat to his status from a decrease in the "value" of his sexual possession which would result from forcible violation.

The passage concludes by making clear whose interest the law is designed to protect. "The man responds to this undercutting of his status as *possessor* of the girl with hostility toward the rapist; no other restitution device is available. The law of rape provides an orderly outlet for his vengeance." Presumably the female victim in any case will have been sufficiently socialized so as not to consciously feel any strong need for vengeance. If she does feel this need, society does not speak to it.

The laws against rape exist to protect rights of the male as possessor of the female body, and not the right of the female over her own body. Even without this enlightening passage from the *Yale Law Review*, the laws themselves are clear: in no state can a man be accused of raping his wife. How can any man steal what already belongs to him? It is in the sense of rape as theft of another man's property that Kate Millett writes, "Traditionally rape has been viewed as an offense one male commits against another—a matter of abusing his woman." In raping another man's woman, a man may aggrandize his own manhood and concurrently reduce that of another man. Thus a man's honor is not subject directly to rape, but only indirectly, through "his" woman.

If the basic social unit is the family, in which the woman is a possession of her husband, the super-structure of society is a male hierarchy, in which men dominate other men (or patriarchal families dominate other patriarchal families). And it is no small irony that, while the very social fabric of our male-dominated culture denies women equal access to political, economic and legal power, the literature, myth and humor of our culture depict women not only as the power behind the throne, but the real source of the oppression of men. The religious version of this fairy tale blames Eve for both carnality and eating of the tree of knowledge, at the same time making her gullible to the obvious devices of a serpent. Adam, of course, is merely the trusting victim of love. Certainly this is a biased story. But no more biased than the one television audiences receive today from the latest slick comedians. Through a medium which is owned by men, censored by a State dominated by men, all the evils of this social system which make a man's life unpleasant are blamed upon "the wife." The theory is: were it not for the female who waits and plots to "trap" the male into marriage, modern man would be able to achieve Olympian freedom. She is made the scapegoat for a system which is in fact run by men.

Nowhere is this more clear than in the white racist use of the concept of white womanhood. The white male's open rape of black women, coupled with his overweening concern for the chastity and protection of his wife and daughters, represents an extreme of sexist and racist hypocrisy. While on the one hand she was held up as the standard for purity and virtue, on the other the Southern white woman was never asked if she wanted to be on a pedestal, and in fact any deviance from the male-defined standards for white womanhood was treated severely. (It is a powerful commentary on American racism that the historical role of Blacks as slaves, and thus possessions without power, has robbed black women of legal and economic protection through marriage. Thus black women in Southern society and in the ghettoes of the North have long been easy game for white rapists.) The fear that black men would rape white women was, and is, classic paranoia. Quoting from Ann Breen's unpublished study of racism and sexism in the South, "The New South: White Man's Country," Frederick Douglass legitimately points out that had the black man wished to rape white women, he had ample opportunity to do so during the Civil War when white women, the wives, sisters, daughters and mothers of the rebels, were left in the care of Blacks. But yet not a single act of rape was committed during this time. The Ku Klux Klan, who tarred and feathered black men and lynched them in the honor of the purity of white womanhood, also applied tar and feathers to a Southern white woman accused of bigamy, which leads one to suspect that Southern white men were not so much outraged at the violation of the woman as a person, in the few instances where rape was actually committed by black men, but at the violation of his property rights. In the situation where a black man was found to be having sexual relations with a white woman, the white woman could exercise skin-privilege, and claim that she had been raped, in which case the black man was lynched. But if she did not claim rape, she herself was subject to lynching.

In constructing the myth of white womanhood so as to justify the lynching and oppression of black men and women, the white male has created a convenient symbol of his own power which has resulted in black hostility toward the white "bitch," accompanied by an unreasonable fear on the part of many white women of the black rapist. Moreover, it is not surprising that after being told for two centuries that he wants to rape white women, occasionally a black man does actually commit that act. But it is crucial to note that the frequency of this practice is outrageously exaggerated in the white mythos. Ninety percent of reported rape is intra- not inter-racial.

In *Soul on Ice*, Eldridge Cleaver has described the mixing of a rage against white power with the internalized sexism of a black man raping a white woman. "Somehow I arrived at the conclusion that, as a matter of principle, it was of paramount importance for me to have an antagonistic, ruthless attitude toward white women. . . . Rape was an insurrectionary act. It delighted me that I was defying and trampling upon the white man's law, upon his system of values and that I was defiling his women—and this point, I believe, was the most satisfying to me because I was very resentful over the historical fact of how the white man had used the black woman." Thus a black man uses white women to take out his rage against white men. But in fact, whenever a rape of a white woman by a black man does take place, it is again the white man who benefits. First, the act itself terrorizes the white woman and makes her more dependent on the white male for protection. Then, if the woman prosecutes her attacker, the white man is afforded legal opportunity to exercise overt racism. Of course, the knowledge of the rape helps to perpetuate two myths which are beneficial to white male rule—the bestiality of the black man and the desirability of white women. Finally, the white man surely benefits because he himself is not the object of attack—he has been allowed to stay in power.

Indeed, the existence of rape in any form is beneficial to the ruling class of white males. For rape is a kind of terrorism which severely limits the freedom of women and makes women dependent on men. Moreover, in the act of rape, the rage that one man may harbor toward another higher in the male hierarchy can be deflected toward a female scapegoat. For every man there is always someone lower on the social scale on whom he can take out his aggressions. And that is any woman alive.

This oppressive attitude toward women finds its institutionalization in the traditional family. For it is assumed that a man "wears the pants" in his family—he exercises the option of rule whenever he so chooses. Not that he makes all the decisions—clearly women make most of the important day-to-day decisions in a family. But when a conflict of interest arises, it is the man's interest which will prevail. His word, in itself, is more powerful. He lords it over his wife in the same way his boss lords it over him, so that the very process of exercising his power becomes as important an act as obtaining whatever it is his power can get for him. This notion of power is key to the male ego in this culture, for the two acceptable measures of masculinity are a man's power over women and his power over other men. A man may boast to his friends that "I have 20 men working for me." It is also aggrandizement of his ego if he has the financial power to clothe his wife in furs and jewels. And, if a man lacks the wherewithal to acquire such power, he can always express his rage through equally masculine activities—rape and theft. Since male society defines the female as a possession, it is not surprising that the felony most often committed together with rape is theft. . . .

Rape is an act of aggression in which the victim is denied her self-determination. It is an act of violence which, if not actually followed by beatings or murder, nevertheless always carries with it the threat of death. And finally, rape is a form of mass terrorism, for the victims of rape are chosen indiscriminately, but the propagandists for male supremacy broadcast that it is women who cause rape by being unchaste or in the wrong place at the wrong time—in essence, by behaving as though they were free. . . .

But rape is not an isolated act that can be rooted out from patriarchy without ending patriarchy itself. The same men and power structure who victimize women are engaged in the act of raping Vietnam, raping Black people and the very earth we live upon. Rape is a classic act of domination where, in the words of Kate Millett, "the emotions of hatred, contempt, and the desire to break or violate personality" takes place. This breaking of the personality characterizes modern life itself. No simple reforms can eliminate rape. As the symbolic expression of the white male hierarchy, rape is the quintessential act of our civilization, one which, Valerie Solanis warns, is in danger of "humping itself to death."

The Origin of the Family

Kathleen Gough

The trouble with the origin of the family is that no one really knows. Since [Friedrich] Engels wrote *The Origin of the Family, Private Property and the State . . .* in 1884,* a great deal of new evidence has come in. Yet the gaps are still enormous. It is not known *when* the family originated, although it was probably between two million and 100,000 years ago. It is not known whether it developed once or in separate times and places. It is not known whether some kind of embryonic family came before, with, or after the origin of language. Since language is the accepted criterion of humanness, this means that we do not even know whether our ancestors acquired the basics of family life before or after they were human.

---

* EDITOR'S NOTE: The full original title of this volume is *Der Ursprung der Familie, des Privateigenthums und des Staats. Im Anschluss an Lewis H. Morgan's Forschungen* (Hottingen-Zurich, 1884). It is based on Lewis H. Morgan, *Ancient Society; Or, Researches in the Lines of Human Progress from Savagery, through Barbarism to Civilization* (New York, 1877). Ms. Gough has consulted the English translation of the Engels work: *The Origin of the Family, Private Property and the State in the Light of the Researches of Lewis H. Morgan,* 4th ed. (New York and London, 1942); this is the work referred to in her article as "Morgan and Engels."

Reprinted, with minor editorial changes, from *Journal of Marriage and the Family* (November 1971), pp. 760-71, with permission of the author and the publisher.

The chances are that language and the family developed together over a long period. But the evidence is sketchy.

Although the origin of the family is speculative, it is better to speculate with than without evidence. The evidence comes from three sources. One is the social and physical lives of non-human primates—especially the New and Old World monkeys and, still more, the great apes, humanity's closest relatives. The second source is the tools and home sites of prehistoric humans and proto-humans. The third is the family lives of hunters and gatherers of wild provender who have been studied in modern times.

Each of these sources is imperfect: monkeys and apes, because they are *not* pre-human ancestors, although they are our cousins; fossil hominids, because they left so little vestige of their social life; hunters and gatherers, because none of them has, in historic times, possessed a technology and society as primitive as those of early humans. All show the results of long endeavor in specialized, marginal environments. But together, these sources give valuable clues.

DEFINING THE FAMILY

To discuss the origin of something we must first decide what it is. I shall define the family as "a married couple or other group of adult kinsfolk who cooperate economically and in the upbringing of children, and all or most of whom share a common dwelling."

This includes all forms of kin-based household. Some are extended families containing three generations of married brothers or sisters. Some are "grand-families" descended from a single pair of grandparents. Some are matrilineage households, in which brothers and sisters share a house with the sisters' children, and men merely visit their wives in other homes. Some are compound families, in which one man has several wives, or one woman, several husbands. Others are nuclear families composed of a father, mother and children.

Some kind of family exists in all known human societies, although it is not found in every segment or class of all stratified, state societies. Greek and American slaves, for example, were prevented from forming legal families, and their social families were often disrupted by sale, forced labor, or sexual exploitation. Even so, the family was an ideal which all classes and most people attained when they could.

The family implies several other universals. (1) Rules forbid sexual relations and marriage between close relatives. Which relatives are forbidden varies, but all [known] societies forbid mother-son mating, and most, father-daughter and brother-sister. Some societies allow sex relations, but forbid marriage, between certain degrees of kin. (2) The men and women of a family cooperate through a division of labor based on gender. Again, the sexual division of labor varies in rigidity and in the tasks performed. But in no human society to date is it wholly absent. Child-care, household tasks and crafts closely connected with the household, tend to be done by women; war, hunting, and government, by men. (3) Marriage exists as a socially recognized, durable, although not necessarily lifelong relationship between individual men and women. From it springs social fatherhood, some kind of special bond between a man and the child of his wife, whether or not they are his own children physiologically. Even in polyandrous societies, where women have several husbands, or in matrilineal societies, where group membership and property pass through women, each child has one or more designated "fathers" with whom he has a special social, and often religious, relationship. This bond of *social* fatherhood is recognized among people who do not know about the male role in procreation, or where, for various reasons, it is not clear who the physiological father of a particular infant is. Social fatherhood seems to come from the division and interdependence of male and female tasks, especially in relation to children, rather than directly from physiological fatherhood, although in most societies, the social father of a child is usually presumed to be its physiological father as well. Contrary to the beliefs of some feminists, however, I think that in no human society do men, as a whole category, have *only* the role of insemination, and *no* other social or economic role, in relation to women and children. (4) Men in general have higher status and authority over the women of their families, although older women may have influence, even some authority, over junior men. The omnipresence of male authority, too, goes contrary to the belief of some feminists that in "matriarchal" societies, women were either completely equal to, or had paramount authority over, men, either in the home or in society at large.

It is true that in some matrilineal societies, such as the Hopi of Arizona or the Ashanti of Ghana, men exert little authority over their wives. In some, such as the Nayars of South India or the Minangkabau of Sumatra, men may even live separately from their wives and children, that is, in different families. In such societies, however, the fact is that women and children fall under greater or lesser authority from the women's kinsmen—their eldest brothers, mothers' brothers, or even their grown up sons.

In matrilineal societies, where property, rank, office and group membership are inherited through the female line, it is true that women tend to have greater independence than in patrilineal societies. This is especially so in matrilineal tribal societies where the state has not yet developed, and especially in those tribal societies where residence is matrilocal—that is, men come to live in the homes or villages of their wives. Even so, in all matrilineal societies for which adequate descriptions are available, the ultimate headship of household, lineages and local groups is usually with men.*

There is in fact no true "matriarchal" as distinct from "matrilineal," society in existence or known from literature, and the changes are that there never has been.† This does not mean that women and men have never had relations that were dignified and creative for both sexes, appropriate to the knowledge, skills and technology of their times. Nor does it mean that the sexes cannot be equal in the future, or that the sexual division of labor cannot be abolished. I believe that it can and must be. But it is not necessary to believe myths of a feminist Golden Age in order to plan for parity in the future.

PRIMATE SOCIETIES

Within the primate order, humans are most closely related to the anthropoid apes (the African chimpanzee and gorilla and the Southeast Asian orang-utan and gibbon), and of these, to the chimpanzee and the gorilla. More distantly related are the Old, and then the New World, monkeys, and finally, the lemurs, tarsiers and tree-shrews.

All primates share characteristics without which the family could not have developed. The young are born relatively helpless. They suckle for several months or years and need prolonged care afterwards. Childhood is longer, the closer the species is to humans. Most monkeys reach puberty at about four to five and mature socially between about five and ten. Chimpanzees, by contrast, suckle for up to three years. Females reach puberty at seven to ten; males enter mature social and sexual relations as late as thirteen. The long childhood and maternal care produce close relations between children of the same mother, who play together and help tend their juniors until they grow up.

---

* See David M. Schneider and Kathleen Gough, eds., *Matrilineal Kinship* (Berkeley, Calif., 1961), for common and variant features of matrilineal systems.

† The Iroquois are often quoted as a "matriarchal" society, but in fact Morgan himself refers to "the absence of equality between the sexes" and notes that women were subordinate to men, ate after men, and that women (not men) were publicly whipped as punishment for adultery. Warleaders, tribal chiefs, and *sachems* (heads of matrilineal lineages) were men. Women did, however, have a large say in the government of the long-house or home of the matrilocal extended family, and women figured as tribal counsellors and religious officials, as well as in arranging marriages. (Lewis H. Morgan: The League of the *Ho-de-ne Sau-nee* or *Iroquois*, Human Relations Area Files, 1954).

Monkeys and apes, like humans, mate in all months of the year instead of in a rutting season. Unlike humans, however, female apes experience unusually strong sexual desire for a few days shortly before and during ovulation (the oestrus period), and have intensive sexual relations at that time. The males are attracted to the females by their scent or by brightly colored swellings in the sexual region. Oestrus-mating appears to be especially pronounced in primate species more remote from humans. The apes and some monkeys carry on less intensive, month-round sexuality in addition to oestrus-mating, approaching human patterns more closely. In humans, sexual desires and relations are regulated less by hormonal changes and more by mental images, emotions, cultural rules and individual preferences.

Year-round (if not always month-round) sexuality means that males and females socialize more continuously among primates than among most other mammals. All primates form bands or troops composed of both sexes plus children. The numbers and proportions of the sexes vary, and in some species an individual, a mother with her young, or a subsidiary troop of male juveniles may temporarily travel alone. But in general, males and females socialize continually through mutual grooming* and playing as well as through frequent sex relations. Keeping close to the females, primate males play with their children and tend to protect both females and young from predators. A "division of labor" based on gender is thus already found in primate society between a female role of prolonged child care and a male role of defense. Males may also carry or take care of children briefly, and non-nursing females may fight. But a kind of generalized "fatherlinesss" appears in the protective role of adult males toward young, even in species where the sexes do not form long-term individual attachments.

SEXUAL BONDS AMONG PRIMATES

Some non-human primates do have enduring sexual bonds and restrictions, superficially similar to those in some human societies. Among gibbons a single male and female live together with their young. The male drives off other males and the female, other females. When a juvenile reaches puberty it is thought to leave or be expelled by the parent of the same sex, and eventually find a mate elsewhere. Similar *de facto*, rudimentary "incest prohibitions" may have been passed on to humans from their prehuman ancestors and later codified and elaborated through language, moral custom and law. Whether this is so may become clearer when we know more about the mating patterns of the other great apes, especially of our closest relatives,

---

* Combing the hair and removing parasites with hands or teeth.

the chimpanzees. Present evidence suggests that male chimpanzees do not mate with their mothers.

Orang-utans live in small, tree-dwelling groups like gibbons, but their forms are less regular. One or two mothers may wander alone with their young, mating at intervals with a male, or a male-female pair, or several juvenile males, may travel together.

Among mountain gorillas of Uganda, South Indian langurs, and hamadryas baboons of Ethiopia, a single, fully mature male mates with several females, especially in their oestrus periods. If younger adult males are present, the females may have occasional relations with them if the leader is tired or not looking.

Among East and South African baboons, rhesus macaques, and South American woolly monkeys, the troop is bigger, numbering up to two hundred. It contains a number of adult males and a much larger number of females. The males are strictly ranked in terms of dominance based on both physical strength and intelligence. The more dominant males copulate intensively with the females during the latter's oestrus periods. Toward the end of oestrus a female may briefly attach herself to a single dominant male. At other times she may have relations with any male of higher or lower rank provided that those of higher rank permit it.

Among some baboons and macaques the young males travel on the outskirts of the group and have little access to females. Some macaques expel from the troop a proportion of the young males, who then form "bachelor troops." Bachelors may later form new troops with young females.

Other primates are more thoroughly promiscuous, or rather indiscriminate, in mating. Chimpanzees, and also South American howler monkeys, live in loosely structured groups, again (as in most monkey and ape societies) with a preponderance of females. The mother-child unit is the only stable group. The sexes copulate almost at random, and most intensively and indiscriminately during oestrus.

A number of well-known anthropologists have argued that various attitudes and customs often found in human societies are instinctual rather than culturally learned, and come from our primate heritage. They include hierarchies of ranking among men, male political power over women, and the greater tendency of men to form friendships with one another, as opposed to women's tendencies to cling to a man.*

I cannot accept these conclusions and think that they stem from the male chauvinism of our own society. A "scientific" argument which states that all such

---

* See, for example, Desmond Morris, *The Naked Ape*, [Dell, 1969] ; Robin Fox, *Kinship and Marriage*, [Penguin, 1968] . [Editor's note: see also Lionel Tiger, *Men in Groups*, Random House, 1969.]

features of female inferiority are instinctive is obviously a powerful weapon in maintaining the traditional family with male dominance. But in fact, these features are *not* universal among non-human primates, including some of the most closely related to humans. Chimpanzees have a low degree of male dominance and male hierarchy and are sexually virtually indiscriminate. Gibbons have a kind of fidelity for both sexes and almost no male dominance or hierarchy. Howler monkeys are sexually indiscriminate and lack male hierarchies or dominance.

The fact is that among non-human primates male dominance and male hierarchies seem to be adaptations to particular environments, some of which did become genetically established through natural selection. Among humans, however, these features are present in variable degrees and are almost certainly learned, not inherited at all. Among non-human primates there are fairly general differences between those that live mainly in trees and those that live largely on the ground. The tree dwellers (for example gibbons, orang-utans, South American howler and woolly monkeys) tend to have to defend themselves less against predators than do the ground-dwellers (such as baboons, macaques or gorillas). Where defense is important, males are much larger and stronger than females, exert dominance over females, and are strictly hierarchized and organized in relation to one another. Where defense is less important there is much less sexual dimorphism (difference in size between male and female), less or no male dominance, a less pronounced male hierarchy, and greater sexual indiscriminancy.

Comparatively speaking, humans have a rather small degree of sexual dimorphism, similar to [that found in] chimpanzees. Chimpanzees live much in trees but also partly on the ground, in forest or semi-forest habitats. They build individual nests to sleep in, sometimes on the ground but usually in trees. They flee into trees from danger. Chimpanzees go mainly on all fours, but sometimes on two feet, and can use and make simple tools. Males are dominant, but not very dominant, over females. The rank hierarchy among males is unstable, and males often move between groups, which vary in size from two to fifty individuals. Food is vegetarian, supplemented with worms, grubs, or occasional small animals. A mother and her young form the only stable unit. Sexual relations are largely indiscriminate, but nearby males defend young animals from danger. The chances are that our pre-human ancestors had a similar social life. Morgan and Engels were probably right in concluding that we came from a state of "original promiscuity" before we were fully human.

HUMAN EVOLUTION

Judging from the fossil record, apes ancestral to humans, gorillas, and chimpanzees

Out of the sexual division of labor came, for the first time, home life as well as group cooperation.

roamed widely in Asia, Europe, and Africa some twelve to twenty-eight million years ago. Toward the end of that period (the Miocene) one appears in North India and East Africa, Ramapithecus, who may be ancestral both to later hominids and to modern humans. His species were small like gibbons, walked upright on two feet, had human rather than ape corner-teeth, and therefore probably used hands rather than teeth to tear their food. From that time evolution toward humanness must have proceeded through various phases until the emergence of modern *homo sapiens,* about 70,000 years ago.

In the Miocene period before Ramapithecus appeared, there were several time-spans in which, over large areas, the climate became drier and sub-tropical forests dwindled or disappeared. A standard reconstruction of events, which I accept, is that groups of apes, probably in Africa, had to come down from the trees and adapt to terrestrial life. Through natural selection, probably over millions of years, they developed specialized feet for walking. Thus freed, the hands came to be used not only (as among apes) for grasping and tearing, but for regular carrying of objects such as weapons (which had hitherto been sporadic) or of infants (which had hitherto clung to their mothers' body hair).

The spread of indigestible grasses on the open savannahs may have encouraged, if it did not compel, the early ground dwellers to become active hunters rather than to simply forage for small, sick, or dead animals that came their way. Collective hunting and tool use involved group cooperation and helped foster the growth of language out of the call-systems of apes. Language meant the use of symbols to refer to events not present. It allowed greatly increased foresight, memory, planning and division of tasks—in short, the capacity for human thought.

With the change to hunting, group territories became much larger. Apes range only a few thousand feet daily; hunters, several miles. But because their infants were helpless, nursing women could hunt only small game close to home. This then produced the sexual division of labor on which the human family has since been founded. Women elaborated upon ape methods of child care, and greatly expanded foraging, which in most areas remained the primary and most stable source of food. Men improved upon ape methods of fighting off other animals, and of group protection in general. They adapted these methods to hunting, using weapons which for millennia remained the same for the chase as for human warfare.

Out of the sexual division of labor came, for the first time, home life as well as group cooperation. Female apes nest with and provide foraged food for their infants. But adult apes do not cooperate in food getting or nest building. They build new nests each night wherever they may happen to be. With the development of a hunting-gathering complex, it became necessary to have a G.H.Q., or home. Men could bring meat to this place for several days' supply. Women and children could meet men there after the day's hunting, and could bring their vegetable produce for general consumption. Men, women, and children could build joint shelters, butcher meat, and treat skins for clothing.

Later, fire came into use for protection against wild animals, for lighting, and eventually for cooking. The hearth then provided the focus and symbol of home. With the development of cookery, some humans—chiefly women, and perhaps some children and old men—came to spend more time preparing nutrition so that all people need spend less time in chewing and tearing their food. Meals—already less frequent because of the change to a carnivorous diet—now became brief, periodic events instead of the long feeding sessions of apes.

The change to humanness brought two bodily changes that affected birth and child care. These were head-size and width of the pelvis. Walking upright produced a narrower pelvis to hold the guts in position. Yet as language developed, brains and hence heads grew much bigger relative to body size. To compensate, humans are born at an earlier stage of growth than apes. They are helpless longer and require longer and more total care. This in turn caused early women to concentrate more on child care and less on defense than do female apes.

Language made possible not only a division and cooperation in labor but also all forms of tradition, rules, morality and cultural learning. Rules banning sex relations among close kinfolk must have come very early. Precisely how or why they developed is unknown, but they had at least two useful functions. They helped to preserve order in the family as a cooperative unit, by outlawing competition for mates. They also created bonds *between* families, or even between separate bands, and so provided a basis for wider cooperation in the struggle for livelihood and the expansion of knowledge.

It is not clear when all these changes took place. Climatic change with increased drought began regionally up to 28 million years ago. The divergence between pre-human and gorilla-chimpanzee stems had occurred in both Africa and India at least 12 million years ago. The pre-human stem led to the Australopithecenes of East and South Africa, about 1,750,000 years ago. These were pygmy-like, two-footed, upright hominids with larger-than-ape brains, who made tools and probably hunted in savannah regions. It is unlikely that they knew the use of fire.

The first known use of fire is that of cave-dwelling hominids (Sinanthropus, a branch of the Pithecanthropines) at Choukoutien near Peking, some half a million years ago during the second ice age. Fire was used regularly in hearths, suggesting cookery, by the time of the Acheulean and Mousterian cultures of Neanderthal man in Europe, Africa, and Asia before, during, and after the third ice age, some 150,000 to 100,000 years ago. These people, too, were often cave dwellers, and buried their dead ceremonially in caves. Cave-dwelling by night as well as by day was probably, in fact, not safe for humans until fire came into use to drive away predators.

Most anthropologists conclude that home life, the family, and language had developed by the time of Neanderthal man, who was closely similar and may have been ancestral to modern *homo sapiens.* At least two anthropologists, however, believe that the Australopithecenes already had language nearly two million years ago, while another thinks that language and incest prohibitions did not evolve until the time of *homo sapiens* some 70,000 to 50,000 years ago.* I am myself inclined to think that family life built around tool use, the use of language, cookery, and a sexual division of labor, must have been established sometime between about 500,000 and 200,000 years ago.

HUNTERS AND GATHERERS

Most of the hunting and gathering societies studied in the eighteenth to twentieth centuries had technologies similar to those that were widespread in the Mesolithic period, which occurred about 15,000 to 10,000 years ago, after the ice ages ended but before cultivation was invented and animals domesticated.

Modern hunters live in marginal forest, mountain, arctic, or desert environments where cultivation is impracticable. Although by no means "primeval," the hunters of recent times do offer clues to the types of family found during that 99 percent of human history before the agricultural revolution. They include the Eskimo, many Canadian and South American Indian groups, the forest BaMbuti (pygmies) and the desert Bushmen of Southern Africa, the Kadar of South India, the Veddah of Ceylon, and the Andaman Islanders of the Indian Ocean. About 175 hunting and gathering cultures in Oceania, Asia, Africa, and America have been described in fair detail.

---

* For the former view, see Charles F. Hockett and Robert Ascher, "The Human Revolution," in Yehudi A. Cohen, ed., *Man in Adaptation: The Biosocial Background,* Aldine, 1968; for the latter, Frank B. Livingstone, "Genetics, Ecology and the Origin of Incest and Exogamy," *Current Anthropology,* February 1969.

In spite of their varied environments, hunters share certain features of social life. They live in bands of about 20 to 200 people, the majority of bands having fewer than 50. Bands are divided into families, which may forage alone in some seasons. Hunters have simple but ingenious technologies. Bows and arrows, spears, needles, skin clothing, and temporary leaf or wood shelters are common. Most hunters do some fishing. The band forages and hunts in a large territory and usually moves camp often.

Social life is egalitarian. There is of course no state, nor organized government. Apart from religious shamans or magicians, the division of labor is based only on sex and age. Resources are owned communally; tools and personal possessions are freely exchanged. Everyone works who can. Band leadership goes to whichever man has the intelligence, courage, and foresight to command the respect of his fellows. Intelligent older women are also looked up to.

The household is the main unit of economic cooperation, with the men, women, and children dividing the labor and pooling their produce. In 97 percent of the 175 societies classified by G. P. Murdock, hunting is confined to men; in the other three percent it is chiefly a male pursuit. Gathering of wild plants, fruits, and nuts is women's work. In 60 percent of societies, only women gather, while in another 32 percent gathering is mainly feminine. Fishing is solely or mainly men's work in 93 percent of the hunting societies where it occurs.

For the rest, men monopolize fighting, although interband warfare is rare. Women tend children and shelters and usually do most of the cooking, processing, and storage of food. Women tend also to be foremost in the early household crafts such as basketry, leather work, the making of skin or bark clothing, and in the more advanced hunting societies, pottery. (Considering that women probably *invented* all of these crafts, in addition to cookery, food storage and preservation, agriculture, spinning, weaving, and perhaps even house construction, it is clear that women played quite as important roles as men in early cultural development.) Building dwellings and making tools and ornaments are variously divided between the sexes, while boat-building is largely done by men. Girls help the women, and boys play at hunting or hunt small game until they reach puberty, when both take on the roles of adults. Where the environment makes it desirable, the men of a whole band or of some smaller cluster of households cooperate in hunting or fishing and divide their spoils. Women of nearby families often go gathering together.

Family composition varies among hunters as it does in other kinds of societies. About half or more of known hunting societies have nuclear families (father, mother and children), with polygynous households (a man, two or more wives, and children) as occasional variants. Clearly, nuclear families are the most common among hunters, although hunters have a slightly higher proportion of polygynous families than do non-hunting societies.

About a third of hunting societies contain some "stem-family" households—that is, older parents live together with one married child and grandchildren, while the other married children live in independent dwellings. A still smaller proportion live in large extended families containing several married brothers (or several married sisters), their spouses, and children.* Hunters have fewer extended and stem families than do non-hunting societies. These larger households become common with the rise of agriculture. They are especially found in large, pre-industrial agrarian states such as ancient Greece, Rome, India, the Islamic empires, China, etc.

Hunting societies also have few households composed of a widow or divorcee and her children. This is understandable, for neither men nor women can survive long without the work and produce of the other sex, and marriage is the way to obtain them. That is why so often young men must show proof of hunting prowess, and girls of cooking, before they are allowed to marry.

The family, together with territorial grouping, provides the framework of society among hunters. Indeed, as Morgan and Engels clearly saw, kinship and territory are the foundations of all societies before the rise of the state. Not only hunting and gathering bands, but the larger and more complex tribes and chiefdoms of primitive cultivators and herders organize people through descent from common ancestors or through marriage ties between groups. Among hunters, things are simple. There is only the family, and beyond it the band. With the domestication of plants and animals, the economy becomes more productive. More people can live together. Tribes form, containing several thousand people loosely organized into large kin-groups such as clans and lineages, each composed of a number of related families. With still further development of the productive forces the society throws up a central political leadership, together with craft specialization and trade, and so the chiefdom emerges. But this, too, is structured through ranked allegiances and marriage ties between kin groups.

Only with the rise of the state does class, independently of kinship, provide the basis for relations of production, distribution, and power. Even then, kin groups remain large in the agrarian state and kinship persists as the prime organizing principle within each class until the rise of capitalism. The reduction in significance of the family that we see today is the outgrowth of a decline in the importance of "famil-

---

* For exact figures, see G. P. Murdock, *World Ethnographic Sample,* American Anthropologist, 1957; Allan D. Coult, *Cross Tabulations of Murdock's World Ethnographic Sample,* University of Missouri, 1965; and G. P. Murdock, *Ethnographic Atlas,* University of Pittsburgh, 1967. In the last-named survey, out of 175 hunting societies, 47 percent had nuclear family households, 38 percent had stem families, and 14 percent had extended families.

ism" relative to other institutions, that began with the rise of the state but became speeded up with the development of capitalism and machine industry. In most modern socialist societies, the family is even less significant as an organizing principle. It is reasonable to suppose that in the future it will become minimal or may disappear at least as a legally constituted unit for exclusive forms of sexual and economic cooperation and of child-care.

Morgan and Engels (1942) thought that from a state of original promiscuity, early humans at first banned sex relations between the generations of parents and children, but continued to allow them indiscriminately between brothers, sisters and all kinds of cousins within the band. They called this the "consanguineal family." They thought that later, all mating within the family or some larger kin group became forbidden, but that there was a stage (the "punaluan") in which a group of sisters or other close kinswomen from one band were married jointly to a group of brothers or other close kinsmen from another. They thought that only later still, and especially with the domestication of plants and animals, did the "pairing family" develop in which each man was married to one or two women individually.

These writers drew their conclusions not from evidence of actual group-marriage among primitive peoples but from the kinship terms found today in certain tribal and chiefly societies. Some of these equate all kin of the same sex in the parents' generation, suggesting brother-sister marriage. Others equate the father's brothers with the father, and the mother's sisters with the mother, suggesting the marriage of a group of brothers with a group of sisters.

Modern evidence does not bear out these conclusions about early society. All known hunters and gatherers live in families, not in communal sexual arrangements. Most hunters even live in nuclear families rather than in large extended kin groups. Mating is individualized, although one man may occasionally have two wives, or (very rarely) a woman may have two husbands. Economic life is built primarily around the division of labor and partnership between individual men and women. The hearths, caves and other remains of Upper Palaeolithic hunters suggest that this was probably an early arrangement. We cannot say that Engels' sequences are completely ruled out for very early hominids—the evidence is simply not available. But it is hard to see what economic arrangements among hunters would give rise to group rather than individual or "pairing" marriage arrangements, and this Engels does not explain.

Soviet anthropologists continued to believe in Morgan and Engels' early "stages" longer than did anthropologists in the West. Today, most Russian anthropologists admit the lack of evidence for "consanguineal" and "punaluan" arrangements, but some still believe that a different kind of group marriage intervened between indiscriminate mating and the pairing family. Semyonov, for example, argues that in the stage of group marriage, mating was forbidden within the hunting band, but that the men of two neighboring bands had multiple, visiting sex relations with women of the opposite band.*

While such an arrangement cannot be ruled out, it seems unlikely because many of the customs which Semyonov regards as "survivals" of such group marriage (for example, visiting husbands, matrilineage dwelling groups, widespread clans, multiple spouses for both sexes, men's and women's communal houses, and prohibitions of sexual intercourse inside the huts of the village) are actually found not so much among hunters as among horticultural tribes, and even quite complex agricultural states. Whether or not such a stage of group marriage occurred in the earliest societies, there seems little doubt that pairing marriage (involving family households) came about with the development of elaborate methods of hunting, cooking, and the preparation of clothing and shelters—that is, with a fully-fledged division of labor.

Even so, there *are* some senses in which mating among hunters has more of a group character than in archaic agrarian states or in capitalist society. Murdock's sample shows that sex relations before marriage are strictly prohibited in only 26 percent of hunting societies. In the rest, marriage is either arranged so early that pre-marital sex is unlikely, or (more usually) sex relations are permitted more or less freely before marriage.

With marriage, monogamy is the normal *practice* at any given time for most hunters, but it is not the normal *rule.* Only 19 percent in Murdock's survey prohibit plural unions. Where polygyny is found (79 percent) the most common type is for a man to marry two sisters or other closely related women of the same kin group— for example, the daughters of two sisters or of two brothers. When a woman dies it is common for a sister to replace her in the marriage, and when a man dies, for a brother to replace him.

Similarly, many hunting societies hold that the wives of brothers or other close kinsmen are in some senses wives of the group. They can be called on in emergencies [times of illness]. Again, many hunting societies have special times for sexual license between men and women of a local group who are not married to each other, such as the "lights out" games of Eskimos sharing a communal snow-house. In other situations, an Eskimo wife will spend the night with a chance guest of her husband's. All parties expect this as normal hospitality. Finally, adultery,

---

* Y. I. Semyonov, "Group Marriage, its Nature and Role in the Evolution of Marriage and Family Relations," *Seventh International Congress of Anthropological and Ethnological Sciences,* vol. 4, Moscow, 1967.

although often punished, tends to be common in hunting societies, and few if any of them forbid divorce or the remarriage of divorcees and widows.

The reason for all this seems to be that marriage and sexual restrictions are practical arrangements among hunters designed mainly to serve economic and survival needs. In these societies, some kind of rather stable pairing best accomplishes the division of labor and cooperation of men and women and the care of children. Beyond the immediate family, either a larger family group or the whole band has other, less intensive but important, kinds of cooperative activities. Therefore, the husbands and wives of individuals within that group can be summoned to stand in for each other if need arises. In the case of Eskimo wife-lending, the extreme climate and the need for lone wandering in search of game dictate high standards of hospitality. This evidently becomes extended to sexual sharing.

In the case of sororal polygyny or marriage to the dead wife's sister, it is natural that when two women fill the same role—either together or in sequence— they should be sisters, for sisters are more alike than other women. They are likely to care more for each other's children. The replacement of a dead spouse by a sister or a brother also preserves existing intergroup relations. For the rest, where the economic and survival bonds of marriage are not at stake, people can afford to be freely companionate and tolerant. Hence pre-marital sexual freedom, seasonal group license, and a pragmatic approach to adultery.

Marriages among hunters are usually arranged by elders when a young couple are ready for adult responsibilities. But the couple know each other and usually have some choice. If the first marriage does not work, the second mate will almost certainly be self-selected. Both sexual and companionate love between individual men and women are known and are deeply experienced. With comparative freedom of mating, love is often less separated from or opposed to marriage than in archaic states or even in some modern nations.

THE POSITION OF WOMEN

Even in hunting societies it seems that women are always in some sense the "second sex," with greater or less subordination to men. This varies. Eskimo and Australian aboriginal women are far more subordinate than women among the Kadar, the Andamanese or the Congo Pygmies—all forest people.

I suggest that women have greater power and independence among hunters when they are important food-obtainers than when they are mainly processors of meat or other supplies provided by men. The former situation is likelier to exist in societies where hunting is small-scale and intensive than where it is extensive over a

**In general in hunting societies . . . women are
less subordinated in certain crucial respects
than they are in most, if not all, of the archaic
states, or even in some capitalist nations.**

large terrain, and in societies where gathering is important by comparison with
hunting.

In general in hunting societies, however, women are less subordinated in certain crucial respects than they are in most, if not all, of the archaic states, or even in
some capitalist nations. These respects include men's ability to deny women sexuality or to force it upon them; to command or exploit their labor or to control their
produce; to control or rob them of their children; to confine them physically and
prevent their movement; to use them as objects in male transactions; to cramp their
creativeness; or to withhold from them large areas of the society's knowledge and
cultural attainments.

Especially lacking in hunting societies is the kind of male possessiveness and
exclusiveness regarding women that leads to such institutions as savage punishments
or death for female adultery, the jealous guarding of female chastity and virginity,
the denial of divorce to women, or the ban on a woman's remarriage after her
husband's death.

For these reasons, I do not think we can speak, as some writers do, of a class-
division between men and women in hunting societies. True, men are more mobile
than women and they lead in public affairs. But class society requires that one class
control the means of production, dictate its use by the other classes, and expropri-
ate the surplus. These conditions do not exist among hunters. Land and other
resources are held communally, although women may monopolize certain gathering
areas, and men, their hunting grounds. There is rank difference, role difference, and
some difference respecting degrees of authority, between the sexes, but there is
reciprocity rather than domination or exploitation.

As Engels saw, the power of men to exploit women systematically springs
from the existence of surplus wealth, and more directly, from the state, social
stratification, and the control of property by men. With the rise of the state,
because of their monopoly over weapons, and because freedom from child-care
allows them to enter specialized economic and political roles, some men—especially
ruling-class men—acquire power over other men and over women. Almost all men
acquire it over women of their own or lower classes, especially within their own
kinship groups. These kinds of male power are shadowy among hunters.

To the extent that men *have* power over women in hunting societies, this seems to spring from the male monopoly of heavy weapons, from the particular division of labor between the sexes, or both. Although men seldom use weapons against women, they *possess* them (or possess superior weapons) in addition to their physical strength. This does give men an ultimate control of force. When old people or babies must be killed to ensure band or family survival, it is usually men who kill them. Infanticide—rather common among hunters, who must limit the mouths to feed—is more often female infanticide than male.

The hunting of men seems more often to require them to organize in groups than does the work of women. Perhaps because of this, about 60 percent of hunting societies have predominantly virilocal residence. That is, men choose which band to live in (often, their fathers'), and women move with their husbands. This gives a man advantages over his wife in terms of familiarity and loyalties, for the wife is often a stranger. Sixteen to 17 percent of hunting societies are, however, uxorilocal, with men moving to the households of their wives, while 15 to 17 percent are bilocal—that is, either sex may move in with the other on marriage.

Probably because of male cooperation in defense and hunting, men are more prominent in band councils and leadership, in medicine and magic, and in public rituals designed to increase game, to ward off sickness, or to initiate boys into manhood. Women do, however, often take part in band councils; they are not excluded from law and government as in many agrarian states. Some women are respected as wise leaders, story tellers, doctors, or magicians, or are feared as witches. Women have their own ceremonies of fertility, birth, and healing, from which men are often excluded.

In some societies, although men control the most sacred objects, women are believed to have discovered them. Among the Congo Pygmies, religion centers about a beneficent spirit, the Animal of the Forest. It is represented by wooden trumpets that are owned and played by men. Their possession and use are hidden from the women and they are played at night when hunting is bad, someone falls ill, or death occurs. During the playing men dance in the public campfire, which is sacred and is associated with the forest. Yet the men believe that women originally owned the trumpet and that it was a woman who stole fire from the chimpanzees or from the forest spirit. When a woman has failed to bear children for several years, a special ceremony is held. Women lead in the songs that usually accompany the trumpets, and an old woman kicks apart the campfire. Temporary female dominance seems to be thought necessary to restore fertility.

In some hunting societies women are exchanged between local groups, which are thus knit together through marriages. Sometimes, men of different bands directly exchange their sisters. More often there is a generalized exchange of women between two or more groups, or a one-way movement of women within a circle of groups. Sometimes the husband's family pays weapons, tools or ornaments to the wife's in return for the wife's services and later, her children.

In such societies, although they may be well treated and their consent sought, women are clearly the moveable partners in an arrangement controlled by men. Male anthropologists have seized on this as evidence of original male dominance and patrilocal residence. Fox and others, for example, have argued that until recently, *all* hunting societies formed out-marrying patrilocal bands, linked together politically by the exchange of women. The fact that fewer than two-thirds of hunting societies are patrilocal today, and only 41 percent have band-exogamy, is explained in terms of modern conquest, economic change and depopulation.

I cannot accept this formula. It is true that modern hunting societies have been severely changed, de-culturated, and often depopulated, by capitalist imperialism. I can see little evidence, however, that the ones that are patrilocal today have undergone less change than those that are not. It is hard to believe that in spite of enormous environmental diversity and the passage of thousands, perhaps millions, of years, hunting societies all had band exogamy with patrilocal residence until they were disturbed by western imperialism. It is more likely that early band societies, like later agricultural·tribes, developed variety in family life and the status of women as they spread over the earth.

There is also some likelihood that the earliest hunters had matrilocal rather than patrilocal families. Among apes and monkeys, it is almost always males who leave the troop or are driven out. Females stay closer to their mothers and their original site; males move about, attaching themselves to females where availability and competition permit. Removal of the wife to the husband's home or band may have been a relatively late development in societies where male cooperation in hunting assumed overwhelming importance.* Conversely, after the development of horticulture (which was probably invented and is mainly carried out by women), those tribes in which horticulture predominated over stock-raising were most likely to be or to remain matrilocal and to develop matrilineal descent groups with a relatively high status of women. But where extensive hunting of large animals, or later, the herding of large domesticates, predominated, patrilocal residence flour-

---

* Upper Palaeolithic hunters produced female figurines that were obvious emblems of fertility. The cult continued through the Mesolithic and into the Neolithic period. Goddesses and spirits of fertility are found in some patrilineal as well as matrilineal societies, but they tend to be more prominent in the latter. It is thus possible that in many areas even late Stone Age hunters had matrilocal residence and perhaps matrilineal descent, and that in some regions this pattern continued through the age of horticulture and even—as in the case of the Nayars of Kerola and the Minangkabau of Sumatra—into the age of plow agriculture, of writing, and of the small-scale state.

ished and women were used to form alliances between male-centered groups. With the invention of metallurgy and of agriculture as distinct from horticulture after 4000 B.C., men came to control agriculture and many crafts, and most of the great agrarian states had patrilocal residence with patriarchal, male-dominant families.

CONCLUSIONS

The family is a human institution, not found in its totality in any pre-human species. It required language, planning, cooperation, self-control, foresight, and cultural learning, and probably developed along with these.

The family was made desirable by the early human combination of prolonged child-care with the need for hunting with weapons over large terrains. The sexual division of labor on which it was based grew out of a rudimentary pre-human division between male defense and female child care. But among humans this sexual division of functions for the first time became crucial for food production and so laid the basis for future economic specialization and cooperation.

Morgan and Engels were probably right in thinking that the human family was preceded by sexual indiscriminacy. They were also right in seeing an egalitarian group-quality about early economic and marriage arrangements. They were without evidence, however, in believing that the earliest mating and economic patterns were entirely group relations.

Together with extensive tool use and language, the family was no doubt the most significant invention of the human revolution. All three required reflective thought, which above all accounts for the vast superiority in consciousness that separates humans from apes.

The family provided the framework for all pre-state society and the fount of its creativeness. In groping for survival and for knowledge, human beings learned to control their sexual desires and to suppress their individual selfishness, aggression, and competition. The other side of this self-control was an increased capacity for love—not only the love of a mother for her child, which is seen among apes, but of male for female in enduring relationships, and of each sex for ever-widening groups of humans. Civilization would have been impossible without this initial self-control, seen in incest prohibitions and in the generosity and moral orderliness of primitive family life.

From the start, women have been subordinate to men in certain key areas of status, mobility and public leadership. But before the agricultural revolution, and even for several thousands of years thereafter, the inequality was based chiefly on the unalterable fact of prolonged child-care combined with the exigencies of primi-

Knowledge of how the family arose is interesting to women because it tells us how we differ from pre-humans, what our past has been, and what have been the biological and cultural limitations from which we are emerging.

tive technology. The extent of inequality varied according to the ecology and the resulting sexual division of tasks. But in any case it was largely a matter of survival rather than of man-made cultural impositions. Hence the impressions we receive of dignity, freedom, and mutual respect between men and women in primitive hunting and horticultural societies. This is true whether these societies are patrilocal, bilocal, or matrilocal, although matrilocal societies, with matrilineal inheritance, offer greater freedom to women than do patrilocal and patrilineal societies of the same level of productivity and political development.

A distinct change occurred with the growth of individual and family property in herds, in durable craft objects and trade objects, and in stable, irrigated farm-sites or other forms of heritable wealth. This crystallized in the rise of the state, about 4000 B.C. With the growth of class society and of male dominance in the ruling class of the state, women's subordination increased, and eventually reached its depths in the patriarchal families of the great agrarian states.

Knowledge of how the family arose is interesting to women because it tells us how we differ from pre-humans, what our past has been, and what have been the biological and cultural limitations from which we are emerging. It shows us how generations of male scholars have distorted or over-interpreted the evidence to bolster beliefs in the inferiority of women's mental processes—for which there is no foundation in fact. Knowing about early families is also important to correct a reverse bias among some feminist writers, who hold that in "matriarchal" societies women were completely equal with or were even dominant over men. For this, too, there seems to be no basis in evidence.

The past of the family does not limit its future. Although the family probably emerged with humanity, neither the family itself nor particular family forms are genetically determined. The sexual division of labor—until recently, universal—need not, and in my opinion should not, survive in industrial society. Prolonged child-care ceases to be a basis for female subordination when artificial birth control, spaced births, small families, patent feeding and communal nurseries allow it to be shared by men. Automation and cybernation remove most of the heavy work for which women are less well equipped than men. The exploitation of women that came with the rise of the state and of class society will presumably disappear in post-state, classless society—for which the technological and scientific basis already exists.

The family was essential to the dawn of civilization, allowing a vast qualitative leap forward in cooperation, purposive knowledge, love, and creativeness. But today the confinement of women in homes and small families—like their subordination in work—artificially limits these human capacities [rather than enhancing them]. It may be that the human gift for personal love will make some form of voluntary, long-term mating and of individual devotion between parents and children continue indefinitely, side by side with public responsibility for domestic tasks and for the care and upbringing of children. There is no need to legislate personal relations out of existence. But neither need we fear a social life in which the family is no more.

Who Has the Power? The Marital Struggle

Dair L. Gillespie

> *Marriage is the destiny traditionally offered to women by
> society. It is still true that most women are married, or have
> been, or plan to be, or suffer from not being. The celibate
> [single] woman is to be explained and defined with reference
> to marriage whether she is frustrated, rebellious, or even
> indifferent in regard to that institution.*
>
> — *Simone de Beauvoir*

THE CHANGING POWER STRUCTURE

Modern theorists of the family agree that the
American family has evolved from a paternalistic to a much more democratic form. Before the
Civil War married women had many duties, few
rights. They were not permitted to control their property, even when it was theirs by inheritance or dower,
or to make a will. To all intents and purposes they
did not own property. The husband had the right to
collect and use the wife's wages, to decide upon the
education and religion of the children, and to punish
his wife if she displeased him. The right to will children, even unborn, to other guardians was retained by
the husband. In the case of divorce, when granted at

Reprinted from *Journal of
Marriage and the Family* (August 1971), pp. 445-58, with
permission of the author and
the publisher.

all, the husband had the right to determine the control of the children. To a married woman, her husband was her superior, her companion, her master. In every sector of the social arena, women were in a subordinate position. The church was one of the most potent forces for maintaining them in this position. Within the church, women were segregated from men, were not allowed to sing, preach or take public action. There were no high schools for girls, and no college in the world admitted women. Unpropertied males, slaves, and all women were not allowed into the political process at all.

Today, as the textbooks never tire of telling us, couples are more free to choose partners than formerly, they are able to separate more easily, the differences in age and culture between husband and wife are less marked than formerly, the husband recognizes more willingly the independence of his wife's demands, they may share housekeeping and diversions, and the wife may even work. In fact, sociologists claim that the modern husband and wife are so nearly equal in power that marriage today can be termed "democratic," "equalitarian," or "egalitarian."

These changes in the form of marriage are generally attributed to the entrance of women into the economic structure and to the extension of an equalitarian ideology to cover women. This type of explanation is careful to emphasize socioeconomic conditions of the past and the "rise of women" in the American economy. However, socioeconomic conditions of the present are no longer examined, for it is assumed that women have won their rights in all social arenas, and if they haven't—well, ideology takes a while to filter down to the masses. New egalitarian ideals, they tell us, will bring about further socioeconomic changes and a better position for women.

In a major research project on the modern American family, Blood and Wolfe state:

> Under former historical circumstances, the husband's economic and social role almost automatically gave him pre-eminence. Under modern conditions, the roles of men and women have changed so much that husbands and wives are potential equals—with the balance of power tipped sometimes one way, sometimes the other. It is no longer possible to assume that just because a man is a man, he is the boss. Once upon a time, the function of culture was to rationalize the predominance of the male sex. Today the function of culture is to develop a philosophy of equal rights under which the saying goes, "May the best man win!"—and the best man is sometimes a woman. The role of culture has shifted from sanctioning a competent sex over an incompetent sex to sanctioning the competent marriage partner over the incompetent one, regardless of sex.[1]

There is good evidence, however, that the balance of power is tipped the same

**There is good evidence . . . that the balance of
power is tipped the same way it always was,
and that the best man is very seldom a woman.**

way it always was, and that the best man is very seldom a woman. I am arguing,
then, against the *personal* resource theory and am positing that, in fact, this is still a
caste/class system rationalizing the preeminence of the male sex.

THE MEASUREMENT OF POWER

Before examining the causes of male dominance in marital power, I would like to
examine first how Blood and Wolfe* conceive of power and how they measure it.
Operationally, power is restricted to who makes the final decision in each of eight
areas, ranging from those traditionally held entirely by the husband to those held
entirely by the wife. These eight areas include:

1. What job the husband should take.
2. What car to get.
3. Whether or not to buy life insurance.
4. Where to go on a vacation.
5. What house or apartment to take.
6. Whether or not the wife should go to work or quit work.
7. What doctor to have when someone is sick.
8. How much money the family can afford to spend per week on food.

These questions were asked because (a) they are all relatively important, (b) they
are questions which nearly all couples have to face, and (c) they range from typically masculine to typically feminine decisions, but affect the family as a whole.[2]

This measurement of power leaves much to be desired. Safilios-Rothschild has
made probably the most telling criticisms of such studies. She points out that all
decisions are given equal weight even though not all decisions have "objectively"
the same degree of importance for the entire life of the family. Which job the husband would take (with important consequences in terms of time to be spent away
from home, location of job, salary level, amount of leisure available, etc.) and

---

* Blood and Wolfe's work plays a major part in this paper because it has been one of the most
influential studies of marriage in the last 10 years.

which doctor to call were considered decisions equally affecting the family and the balance of power within the family. Further, some decisions are made less frequently than others; thus, while a decision such as "what food to buy" requires a daily or weekly enactment, a decision such as "what car to buy" is only made every few years. In addition, some decisions are "important" and frequent, others frequent but not "important," others "important" and not frequent, and still others not important and not frequent. Thus, the familial power structure may not be solely determined on the number of areas of decisions that one can appropriate for himself/herself. She also mentioned the multidimensionality of some of the decision-making areas and suggested that it is possible that one spouse decides which make of car to buy and the other specifies color.[3]

It seems, then, that the conception and measurement of power is already biased in that it does not expose certain kinds of power which automatically accrue to the husband by virtue of his work; and second, that it takes no account of the differential importance of the eight decisions in the power structure of the marriage. Further, there is good evidence that even if we accepted Blood and Wolfe's measures as being true measures of power, the husband still controls most of the power decisions in the family (Figure 1). I must conclude, then, that the husband has much more power than he appears to have according to Blood and Wolfe's analysis.

FIGURE 1   **Husband's Mean Power in Family Decision Making Areas**

Percentage of decisions in which husband prevails

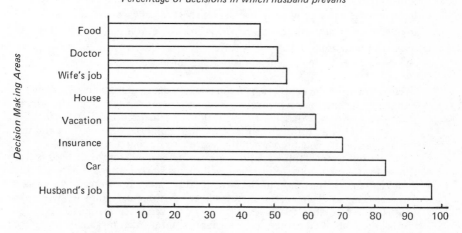

Source: Plotted from data contained in Robert O. Blood, Jr., and Donald M. Wolfe, Husbands and Wives: The Dynamics of Married Living (New York: Free Press, 1960).

Their discussion of "who decides" is even more convincing evidence that there are power differentials which are being overlooked. For example, they explain:

> That the husband should be more involved in his wife's job decisions than she with his is understandable. For one thing, her work is seldom her major preoccupation in life the way it is for a man. Even if she works just as many hours a week, she does not usually make the same lifelong commitment to the world of work. Nor is her pay-check indispensable to the family finances (if only because it is smaller). In such ways the choice of whether to work or not is less vital to a woman than to a man.
>
> In addition, the wife's decisions about working have repercussions on the husband. If his wife goes to work, he will have to help out more around the house. If he is a business executive, he may prefer to have her concentrate her energy on entertaining prospective clients at home. As a small business-man or independent professional, he may need her services in his own enter-prise. On the other hand, regardless of his own occupation, he may want her to work in order to help him buy a house or a business or pay for the chil-dren's education.
>
> It may be, then, that the work role is so much the responsibility of the husband in marriage that even the wife's work is but an adjunct of his instru-mental leadership, leaving this decision in his hands.[4]

In these *justifications* of the division of power, Blood and Wolfe use the device of examining why a husband would want more power in particular areas. The basic assumption is, of course, that he can have it if he wants it. I think a more pertinent question would be not who wants power, since there are always myriad reasons why anyone would want power, but why he is able to get it if he wants it. This question is not even broached.

William Goode . . . comments on this aspect of power and authority:

> After evaluating the conflicting comments and data published by Shaffner, Rodnick, Schelski and Wruzbacher, Baumert comes to the conclusion, which seems eminently reasonable, that claims of fundamental equalitarianism in the German family (or in any other European family) are not correct and that an unequivocally equalitarian family is rarely to be found. In the final analysis, only a few family relations are not determined by the male. It is not possible at present to state just how well such a statement could be applied to other countries. In reality, in all countries there are many women who man-age to dominate the man, but it seems likely that in most countries, when the husband tries to dominate he can still do this. Even when the husband per-forms the household chores, his participation means that he gains power—the household becoming a further domain for the exercise of prerogatives for making decisions.

Perhaps the crucial qualitative difference is to be found in the extent to which, in one country or another, the male can still dominate *without* a definite effort to do so.[5]

Goode calls this "negative authority—the right to prevent others from doing what they want."[6]

I must conclude, then, that the power structure is much more lopsided than Blood and Wolfe lead us to believe, and that it is the husband who holds this hidden power. Why does the husband have all this power? How does he obtain it? How does he maintain it?

It is assumed that most marriages begin with partners at a somewhat egalitarian level. All evidence points to homogamous marriage, i.e., that the woman's *husband* and *father* occupy similar positions in the socioeconomic structure. However, regardless of her background, "her future rank is mainly determined by the future job achievement of the man she marries, rather than by the class position of his family,"[7] or hers, needless to say. In discussing differentials in power which emerge in marriage, most social scientists use an individualistic perspective as do Blood and Wolfe in *Husbands and Wives*. They remark:

> The balance of power is, after all, an interpersonal affair, and the wife's own characteristics cannot long be disregarded if we are to understand who makes the decisions. Whenever possible it is desirable to compare the wife and the husband on the same characteristics, for then the comparative resourcefulness and competence of the two partners can be discovered. Once we know which partner has more education, more organizational experience, a higher status background, etc. we will know who tends to make the most decisions.[8]

The major error made by Blood and Wolfe (and others who use this perspective) is in assuming that this control of competence and resources occurs in individual couples by chance rather than being structurally predetermined (in a statistical sense) in favor of the male. To state it more clearly, I am arguing that it is still a caste/class system, rationalizing the preponderance of dominant males. The distribution of power is not an interpersonal affair, but a class affair. Blood and Wolfe continue:

> Some husbands today are just as powerful as their grandfathers were—but they can no longer take for granted the authority held by older generations of men. No longer is the husband able to exercise power just because he is the "man of the house." Rather, he must prove his right to power, or win power by virtue of his own skills and accomplishments *in competition with his wife*.[9]

If we assume that the marriage contract is a mutual mobility bet for gaining ascendancy in power, personal autonomy, and self-realization, we will find that the opportunity for winning the bet is very slim for the woman.

I am arguing that in the competition with his wife, the man has most of the advantages. If we assume that the marriage contract is a mutual mobility bet for gaining ascendancy in power, personal autonomy, and self-realization, we will find that the opportunity for winning the bet is very slim for the woman. She is already at a disadvantage when she signs the contract. For further self-realization, for further gains in status and experience as compared with her husband, the cards are already stacked against her, for women are *structurally* deprived of equal opportunities to develop their capacities, resources, and competence in competition with males.

Since theorists of marriage have a quite notable tendency to disregard the psychological, legal, and social blocks put in the way of women as a class when they are discussing power differentials and their sources, I would like to examine some of these differences.

SOURCES OF MARITAL POWER

Socialization

Men and women are differentially socialized. By the time women reach marriageable age, we have already been damaged by the socialization process. We have been systematically trained to accept second best, not to strive, and to accept the "fact" that we are unworthy of more. Naomi Weisstein's *Kinde, Küche, Kirche As Scientific Law* states this process clearly:

> How are women characterized in our culture, and in psychology? They are inconsistent, emotionally unstable, lacking in strong conscience or superego, weaker, "nurturant" rather than productive, "intuitive" rather than intelligent, and if they are at all "normal," suited to the home and family. In short, the list adds up to a typical minority group stereotype of inferiority: if they know their place, which is in the home, they are really quite loveable, happy, childlike, loving creatures. In a review of the intellectual differences between little boys and little girls, Eleanor Maccoby has shown that there are no intellectual differences until about high school, or if there are, girls are slightly ahead of boys. At high school, the achievement of women now measured in

terms of productivity and accomplishment, drops off even more rapidly. There are a number of other, non-intellectual tests which show sex differences; I chose the intellectual differences since it is seen clearly that women start becoming inferior. It is no use to talk about women being different but equal; all of the tests I can think of have a "good" outcome and a "bad" outcome. Women usually end up at the "bad" outcome. In light of social expectations about women, what is surprising is not that women end up where society expects they will; what is surprising is that little girls don't get the message that they are supposed to be stupid until high school, and what is even more remarkable is that some women resist this message even after high school, college, and graduate school.[10]

Thus, women begin at a psychological disadvantage when we sign the marriage contract, for we have differential training and expectations.

Marriage: A Free Contract Between Equals

Sociologists universally fail to discuss legal differences in power when the marriage contract is signed.* Marriage is ordinarily considered a contract freely entered into by both partners, and the partners are assumed to stand on common footing of equal rights and duties. Sheila Cronan[11] examined this "free" contract between equals and found a few unlisted terms.

Sex. She found that the husband can legally force his wife to have sexual intercourse with him against her will, an act which if committed against any other woman would constitute the crime of rape. By definition, a husband cannot be guilty of raping his own wife, for "the crime (of rape) is ordinarily that of forcing intercourse on someone other than the wife of the person accused."[12] Women are well aware of the "right" of the husband to "insist" and the "duty" of the wife to submit to sexual intercourse. The compulsory nature of sex in marriage operates to the advantage of the male, for though the husband theoretically has the duty to have intercourse with his wife, this normally cannot occur against his will. (Both partners are protected in that a marriage can be annulled by either party if the marriage has not been consummated.)

Other marital responsibilities. Women believe that we are voluntarily giving our household services, but the courts hold that the husband is legally entitled to

---

* It should be made clear that legality is not necessarily a basis for decision making. It merely reflects the position of society as to how the power is to be distributed when such distributions are contested in the courts. This normally occurs upon dissolution of marriage and not in an ongoing relationship.

. . . the courts hold that the husband is legally entitled to his wife's services, and further, that she cannot be paid for her work.

his wife's services, and further, that *she cannot be paid for her work.* In *Your Marriage and the Law,* Pilpel and Savin state:

> As part of the rights of consortium, the husband is entitled to the services of his wife. If the wife works outside the home for strangers, she is usually entitled to her own earnings. But domestic services or assistances which she gives her husband are generally considered part of her wifely duties. The wife's services and society are so essential a part of what the law considers the husband is entitled to as part of the marriage that it will not recognize any agreement between spouses which provides that the husband is to pay for such services or society.
>
> In a Texas case David promised his wife, Fannie, that he would give her $5000 if she would stay with him while he lived and continue taking care of the house and farm accounts, selling his butter and doing all the other tasks which she had done since their marriage. After David's death, Fannie sued his estate for the money which had been promised her. The court held that the contract was unenforceable since Fannie had agreed to do nothing which she was not already legally and morally bound to do as David's wife.[13]

The legal responsibilities of a wife are to live in the home established by her husband, to perform the domestic chores (cleaning, cooking, washing, etc.) necessary to help maintain that home, and to care for her husband and children (Gallen 1967:4). The husband, in return, is obligated to provide her with basic maintenance which includes "necessities" such as food, clothing, medical care, and a place to live, in accordance with his income. She has no legal right to any part of his cash income, nor any legal voice in spending it.[14] Were he to employ a live-in servant in place of a wife, he would have to pay the servant a salary, provide her with her own room (as opposed to "bed"), food, and the necessary equipment for doing her job. She would get at least one day a week off and probably would be required to do considerably less work than a wife and would not be required to provide sexual services.

Thus, being a wife is a full-time job for which one is not entitled to pay. (Chase Manhattan Bank estimates a woman's overall work week at 99.6 hours.) Furthermore, the wife is not entitled to freedom of movement. The husband has the right to decide where the family will live. If he decides to move, his wife is obliged to go with him. If she refuses, he can charge her with desertion. This has been upheld by the courts even in cases where the wife could be required to change her citizenship. In states where desertion is grounds for divorce (47 states plus the District of Columbia), the wife would be the "guilty party" and would therefore be entitled to no monetary settlement.[15]

A married woman's name. Leo Kanowitz . . . found that the change in a woman's name upon marriage is not only consistent with social custom, it also appears to be generally required by law.

> The probable effects of this unilateral name change upon the relations between the sexes, though subtle in character, are profound. In a very real sense, the loss of a woman's surname represents the destruction of an important part of her personality and its submersion in that of her husband. . . . This name change is consistent with the characterization of coverture as "the old common-law fiction that the husband and wife are one . . . [which] has worked out in reality to mean that the one is the husband."[16]

The law of support. The universal rule is that it is the primary obligation of the husband to provide financial support for the family. Kanowitz explored some of the legal ramifications of this general rule.

> The effects of the basic rule upon the marital relationship itself are complex. In common law marital property jurisdictions, the husband's legal obligation to support the family is not an unmixed blessing for the wife. That obligation has been cited, for example, as justifying his right to choose the family home. It has no doubt also played an important part in solidifying his legal role as head and master of the family. For in according the husband this position within the family, the law often seems to be applying on a grand scale the modest principle that "he who pays the piper calls the tune." However, even in the community property states, in which a wife's services in the home are theoretically viewed as being equal to or exceeding in monetary value the husband's earnings outside of the home, husbands have generally been given the rights to manage and control the community property, along with other superior rights and interests in it.[17]

Thus, it is clear that husbands have access to legal advantages which wives do not have. True the wife does gain legal protection against capricious action by the male, but in exchange, she becomes his vassal. He is the economic head of the joint household, and hence, represents it in view of society. She takes his name and belongs to his class. She follows where his work calls to determine their place of residence. Their lives are geared to the daily, weekly, annual rhythms of his life. She gives him her person and her private labor, but he wants more.

The "White Man's Burden." In today's "love match," the husband does not merely require an obedient and efficient worker, he wants something more. He wants his wife to love him, that is, to freely choose over and over again to be subjected to the control of the other, to make his welfare the center of her being.[18] [Yet this] very demand is the crux of what husbands term their "oppression" as Simone de Beauvoir has so clearly observed:

> Her very devotion seems annoying, importunate; it is transformed for the husband into a tyranny from which he tries to escape; and yet he it is who imposes it upon his wife as her supreme, her unique justification. In marrying her, he obliges her to give herself entirely to him; but he does not assume the corresponding obligation, which is to accept this gift and all its consequences.
>
> It is the duplicity of the husband that dooms his wife to a misfortune of which he complains that he is himself the victim. Just as he wants her to be at once warm and cool in bed, he requires her to be wholly his and yet no burden; he wishes her to establish him in a fixed place on earth and to leave him free; to assume the monotonous daily round and not to bore him; to be always at hand and never importunate; he wants to have her all to himself and not to belong to her, to live as one of a couple, and to remain alone. Thus she is betrayed from the day he marries her. Her life through, she measures the extent of that betrayal.[19]

Throughout their lives together, she attempts to wrest back from him some measure of her independence. Surely it is not entirely an accident that divorce rates are highest at this early phase of the marriage cycle and drop with the birth of children, when women are most dependent upon the husband economically and emotionally.

Economic Sources of Power

It is clear that an economic base of power is important in marriage, for the higher the husband on the social scale, the greater his decision-making [power] in the family. Using three indices of success in the community, Blood and Wolfe found that all three affected power differentials in the family.

1. The higher the husband's occupational prestige, the greater his voice in marital decisions.
2. Income was an even more sensitive indicator of power than occupation. The higher the husband's income, the greater his power.
3. The higher the husband's status (based on occupation, income, education, and ethnic background), the more power he had to make decisions.

The major break in power fell between white-collar and blue-collar husbands. High white-collar workers had the most power, then low white-collar workers. Within the blue-collar category, however, low blue-collar husbands had more power than high blue-collar husbands when compared on the basis of their relative occupational prestige and social status. I shall discuss some of the possible causes of this deviation in the section on education.

These material bases of power were operant despite the fact that middle-class husbands espouse a more egalitarian ideology than do working-class husbands. William Goode commented on this tension between the ideal and the real distributions of power.

> Since at present this philosophy [of equalitarianism in the family] is most strongly held among better educated segments of the population, and among women more than among men, two interesting tensions may be seen: Lower-class men concede fewer rights *ideologically* than their women in fact *obtain*, and the more educated men are more likely to concede *more* rights ideologically than they in fact grant.[20]

He then supplies us with an excellent example of how ideology may be modified to justify the current distribution of power:

> One partial resolution of the latter tension is to be found in the frequent assertion from families of professional men that they should not make demands which would interfere with his *work*: He takes preference as a *professional*, not as a family head or as a male; nevertheless, the precedence is his. By contrast, lower-class men demand deference as *men*, as heads of families.

As we can see, marital power is a function of income to a large extent, and egalitarian philosophies have very little impact on the actual distribution of power. It seems clear that the authority of the male is used as a justification of power where it is useful (working-class), and new justifications will arise as they are useful, as in the case of professional men who demand deference because of their work, thus enabling them to accept the doctrine of equality while at the same time undermining it for their own benefit as males. If this is the effect of that much touted egalitarian ideology which will bring about better conditions for women and racial and ethnic minorities as soon as it filters down to the masses, it seems we will have a long, long wait for cosmic justice.

Blood and Wolfe claim that this superior power of high-status husbands is not due to coercion, but to the recognition by both partners that the husband is the one eminently qualified to make the decisions in the family. This argument is reminiscent of arguments in labor relations. The labor contract is assumed to be freely entered into by both partners. The power conferred on the one party by the difference in class position—the real economic position of both—is not taken into account. That economic relations compel the worker to surrender even the last semblance of equal rights is of no concern. Coercion (however subtle) based on economic power is still coercion, whether it involves wife-beating or not.

Women who work have more power vis-a-vis their husbands than do non-working wives, regardless of race or class.

As further evidence that individual competence and resourcefulness (regardless of sex) are not the real issues, we must examine Blood and Wolfe's discussion of the *deviant* case—[the dominant wife]. In these cases, they claim that wives who have superior power acquire it, not because they have access to pragmatic sources of power or because they are more competent than their husbands (heaven forbid!), but by default.

> We will find throughout this study dissatisfaction associated with wife-dominance. This is not, however, simply a reflection of the breaking of social rules. Rather, the circumstances which lead to the wife's dominance involve corresponding inadequacies on the husband's part. An inadequate husband is by definition unable to make a satisfactory marriage partner. So the dominant wife is not exultant over her "victory" but exercises power regretfully by default of her "no good" or incapacitated husband.[21]

For Blood and Wolfe, wives can never gain dominance legitimately; it falls in our unhappy laps and is accepted only unwillingly and with much bitterness.

Despite the superior power gained by the husband because of his economic position, there are conditions under which wives do erode that power to some extent. Not surprisingly, the wife's participation in the work force is an important variable. Women who work have more power vis-a-vis their husbands than do non-working wives, regardless of race or class. The number of years the wife has worked also affects the balance of power—the longer she has worked, the more power she is able to obtain. This, to some extent, explains why blue-collar wives have more power than white-collar wives (in comparison to their husbands), since their participation in the work force is much higher than for the wives of high-status, high-income husbands.[22]

Organizational Participation

Organizational participation, too, is a factor which affects marital decision making as shown by Blood and Wolfe's data. Women with much more organizational participation than their husbands alter the balance of power in the wife's direction. In those cases where the participation is equal or in which the husband is superior (by far the most frequent), the balance of power increases in the husband's direction.[23]

Education

Education was also influential in the distribution of power. The more education the husband has, the greater his power. High white-collar husbands continue to gain power if they exceed their wives' education (and chances are good that they do, in fact, exceed), and they lose it if they fall short of the wife. The same trend holds within the low white-collar and high blue-collar groups, leaving a low blue-collar reversal, i.e., low blue-collar husbands have more power even when their wives have superior educations.[24]

Mirra Komarovski has drawn attention to the fact that education is a much more important variable when the husband's income and social status are relatively low. In working-class families, the less educated and unskilled husbands have more power than do those with higher incomes. She attempted to explain some of the causes of this power anomaly. First, patriarchal attitudes are more prevalent among the less educated and hence, a source of power in some families. High school graduates, because of a social milieu which does not sanction patriarchal authority (though it does sanction male privilege), tend to lose power. Second, among the less-educated, the husband is more likely to excel in personal resources for the exercise of influence, and this margin of male superiority narrows among the high school graduates. Among the less-educated, the husband has wider contacts in the community than his wife. He represents the world to his family, and he is the family's "secretary of state." In contrast, a few of the more educated wives enjoy wider contacts and higher status outside the home than their husbands. Third, the education of the spouses was found to affect their degrees of power because of mating patterns. The effect of educational inequality appears to explain the lower power of skilled workers in comparison with the semi-skilled. The skilled worker is more likely than the semi-skilled worker to marry a high school graduate. By virtue of their relatively high earnings, skilled workers may be able to marry better-educated women, but by marrying "upward" they lose the degree of power enjoyed by the semi-skilled over their less-educated wives. Fourth, male prestige or social rank was a source of power in low blue-collar families.[25]

Physical Coercion

Komarovski is one of the few sociologists who has mentioned physical coercion as a source of power in the family. In her discussion of the low blue-collar family, she found that the use of physical violence was a source of masculine power. However, not only the use of physical violence, but its *threat* can be an effective form of control. She reports that one woman said of her husband: "He is a big man and terribly strong. One time when he got sore at me, he pulled off the banister and ripped up three steps." With the evidence of this damage in view, this woman realized, as she put it, what her husband could do to her if he should decide to strike her.[26]

Lynn O'Connor has suggested that threats of violence (in gestures of dominance) are not limited to any particular class, but are a universal source of male power and control. After discussing dominance gestures in primates, she states:

> Although there have been no systematic studies of the gestures of dominance and submission in human groups, the most casual observation will show their crucial role in the day to day mechanics of oppression. An example should clarify.
>
> A husband and wife are at a party. The wife says something that the husband does not want her to say (perhaps it reveals something about him that might threaten his ranking with other men). He quickly tightens the muscles around his jaw and gives her a rapid but intense direct stare. Outsiders don't notice the interaction, though they may have a vaguely uncomfortable feeling that they are intruding on something private. The wife, who is acutely sensitive to the gestures of the man on whom she is dependent, immediately stops the conversation, lowers or turns her head slightly, averts her eyes, or gives off some other gestures of submission which communicate acquiescence to her husband and reduce his aggression. Peace is restored; the wife has been put in her place. If the wife does not respond with submission, she can expect to be punished. When gestures of dominance fail, the dominant animal usually resorts to violence. We all know stories about husbands beating up their wives after the party when they have reached the privacy of their home. Many of us have experienced at least a few blows from husbands or lovers when we refuse to submit to them. It is difficult to assess the frequency of physical attacks within so-called love relationships, because women rarely tell even one another when they have taken place. By developing a complicated ethic of loyalty (described above in terms of privacy), men have protected themselves from such reports leaking out and becoming public information. Having already been punished for stepping out of role, the woman is more than a little reluctant to tell anyone of the punishment because it would mean violating the loyalty code, which is an even worse infraction of the rules and most likely would result in further and perhaps more severe punishment.[27]

That violence or the threat of violence may be more widespread than is currently admitted is also suggested by complaints made by wives in divorce. Goode found that almost one-third (32 percent) of the wives reported "authority-cruelty" as the reason for divorce. Authority problems are defined as being disagreements concerning permissible degree of dominance over wife and include cruelty, beating, jealousy, and "wanted to have own way."[28] Since Goode did not code cruelty or beating separately, we have no definite evidence as to the frequency of such behavior, but there is evidence that problems with male dominance are widespread in the population. Goode comments:

> . . . In different strata and groups, the husband may be permitted different control techniques. For example, the middle-class male will very likely be censured more if he uses force to control his wife than if he uses techniques of nagging, jealousy, or sulking. On the other hand, there is a strong reservoir of attitude on the part of the American male generally, that he has a *right* to tell his wife what to do. This attitude is given more overt expression, and is more frequently backed by force, in the lower strata. It is not so much that beating and cruelty are viewed as an obvious male right in marriage, but only that this is one of the techniques used from time to time, and with little or no subsequent guilt, for keeping control of the wife. . . . In our society, the husband who successfully asserts his dominance does enjoy some approval and even a modicum of envy from other males. Male dominance is to some extent actually approved.[29]

Suburbanization

Blood and Wolfe also found that families living in the suburbs were more husband-dominant than those which live in the central city. This directly contradicts the popular image of suburban life as being dominated by women and therefore, oriented toward the satisfaction of women's needs. The data showed that suburban families were more husband-dominant at every status level than their urban peers. They then speculated that suburban husbands were more powerful "because suburban wives feel more indebted to their husbands for providing them with a place to live which is more attractive than the industrial city of Detroit. If so, this fits the theory that power accrues to those husbands who are able to provide for their wives especially well."[30]

In a recent study on the working class in suburbia, Tallman has suggested that other factors than the wife's gratitude might be working to build up the husband's power. He constructed a profile of the working-class marriage which indicated consistently that wives tend to maintain close ties with relatives and old girl friends while husbands continue their premarital peer group associations. Social and psychological support emanates, then, not from marriage partners, but from same-sex friends, and kin from long standing and tight-knit social networks. As a consequence, there is a relatively high degree of conjugal role segmentation which is characterized in part by a lack of communication between the spouses. In general the experiences of working class women are more localized and circumscribed than their male counterparts. Since their security and identity depend upon their position vis-a-vis a small group of intimates, their opinions and beliefs are both dependent upon and in accord with this group. Blue-collar women have minimal experience in the external world and tend to view it fearfully. Men, on the other hand, have more frequent social contacts, in part for occupational reasons, but also because they have been socialized into male roles which define them as family representatives to the outside world.

Tallman concluded that suburban women are more isolated because of disruptions in the primary group relations. The disruption of friendship and kinship ties are not only personally disintegrating for the wife but also demand fundamental changes in the role allocations in the family. Suburban wives are more dependent upon their husbands for a variety of services previously provided by members of tight-knit networks. In brief, he found that moving to the suburbs was experienced as a disintegrative force in the lives of many working-class women, leading to a greater isolation and dependence upon the husbands.[31] This partial explanation of the husband's increased power in the suburbs as being due to the wife's increased isolation and dependence seems eminently more reasonable than Blood and Wolfe's explanation that it is due to gratitude on the part of the wife. Tallman's data also indicates that the wife frequently regrets the move to the suburbs, despite more pleasant living conditions, because of its disruption of the kinship and friendship network.

Race

Blood and Wolfe report very little on black families, except to say that Negro husbands have unusually low power. Their data show that white husbands are always more powerful than their Negro status equals and that this is true within each occupational stratum, each income bracket, and each social level.* They concede that "the label 'black' is almost a synonym for low status in our society—and

---

* Blood and Wolfe's report of the data is so skimpy that it makes interpretation difficult. For example, they say the 35 high income husbands (over $4,000) have lower mean power (4.09) than their 68 less affluent colleagues (4.56). This is possibly analogous to the distribution in the white blue-collar class, where low blue-collar husbands have more power than the high blue-collar husbands. Comparisons are difficult because, for the general population, income was broken into five groups, while for black families they used only two—over $4000 and below $4000. They reported that "the generalization that the husband's power is correlated with occupational status also holds within the Negro race" (4.31, 4.60, no cases, and 5.00 respectively). The only mention of Negro husbands and social status was that the few white husbands in the lowest status groups differ sharply from their powerless negro counterparts (no figures reported).

Detroit Negroes are no exception in having less education, lower incomes, inferior jobs, and lower prestige generally than whites. Since low status white husbands make relatively few decisions, we would expect Negro husbands to exercise little power, too."[32]

What they fail to take into account (among other things) is that black women, too, are discriminated against in this society. They, too, have less education, lower incomes, inferior jobs, and lower prestige generally than whites. The fact that blacks are discriminated against does not explain power differentials within black families. To explain power differentials in black families, just as for white families, the sources of power for black men and black women must be examined and compared. Blood and Wolfe fail to do this.

Their primary purpose seems to be to demonstrate gross differences between black and white families, without bothering to report differences within black families. Andrew and Amy Tate Billingsley have criticized just this approach used in sociological studies, [drawing] attention to the fact that class variables are as important in black families as in white families. "Negro families are not only Negroes to be compared and contrasted with white families, they may also be upper-class (10 percent), middle-class (40 percent), or lower-class (50 percent), with urban or rural moorings, with southern or northern residence, and most importantly, they may be meaningfully compared and contrasted with each other."[33]

The Billingsleys account to some extent for what may be part of the white/black differentials in overall power. [They note] that Negro samples are dominated by low-income families and point out that even where income levels between whites and blacks are similar, the groups are not truly comparable, for the Negro group reflects not only its income level but its experience with prejudice and subjugation as well.

Because both black husbands and black wives are discriminated against in this society, it is absurd to explain power differentials between them as being due to race (as Blood and Wolfe do), unless there are mitigating factors brought about by racial discrimination which operate in favor of one sex's access to sources of marital power. Since data on the black family are so sadly inadequate, I can at this point only examine some demographic data which have possible implications for power distributions in black families.

Black women comprised 40 percent of all black workers in 1960. They earned considerably less than black men. The median earnings of full-time year round black women in 1959 was two-fifths that of black men. (In 1964, it was 64.2 percent.) The unemployment rate for black women is higher than for black men. In 1967, for Negro men aged 20–64, the unemployment rate was 3.7. For Negro women it was 6.0. The unemployment rates for black women under 20 were also higher than for Negro men. Clearly, then, black women are not superior to black men in income.[34]

In occupational status, we find that Negro women are most frequently in service jobs while Negro men are predominantly blue-collar workers. However, relatively more Negro women than men had professional or technical jobs, this being due primarily to their extensive employment as teachers and nurses. Of all full-time year-round Negro workers in 1960, Negro women constituted nearly all the private household workers. They were more than half the number of Negroes employed as professional workers (61 percent) and other service workers (51 percent). Except for the clerical group in which the numbers were about equal, the remaining occupational groups (sales, managers, operatives, crafts, laborers, and farmers) had fewer Negro women than men.[35]

Negro women in general had a higher median education than Negro men. (This is also true in the white population.) The median educational level of non-white women was 8.5 years in 1960, but for men it was 7.9. However, at the top of the educational ladder, just as for the white population, men are more numerous.[36]

Though there are differences, we find that the relations *between the sexes* for both Negroes and whites are similar. Obviously, black men have suffered from discrimination in this society. This is evident in the figures of income, occupation, and education. However, it is also evident that Negro women have suffered discrimination, not only because of race, but also because of their sex. Thus, they are doubly oppressed. This, too, is evident in figures of income, occupation, and education.

Jessie Bernard . . . has suggested still another variable which must be taken into account in Negro family patterns. She reports that there is an extraordinarily low sex ratio (number of males per 100 females) among urban Negroes as compared to whites. The ratio is especially low (88.4) in the critical years of marriageability. Bernard conjectures that the low sex ratio means that Negro women are competing for a relatively scarce "good" when they look forward to marriage, being buyers in a sellers' market.[37] While this is certainly not the cause of power distributions in the black family, it does suggest a source of male power.* Delores Mack, in a study of black and white families, supports this contention:

What these findings suggest is that researchers have not carefully evaluated

---

* This has also been suggested in several articles in *The Black Woman*, edited by Toni Cade (New York: New American Library, 1970), particularly "Dear Black Man," Fran Sanders; "Who Will Revere the Black Woman?", Abbey Lincoln; "The Black Woman as Woman," Kay Lindsey; "Double Jeopardy: To Be Black and Female," Frances Beale; "On the Issue of Roles," Toni Cade; "Black Man, My Man, Listen!," Gail Stokes; "Is the Black Man Castrated?," Jean Carey Bond and Pat Peery.

> **There is more than a little truth in the old saw that the best way to control a woman is to "keep her barefoot and pregnant," for there is evidence that the power of the wife declines as the number of children grows.**

the logic of the assumptions of their hypotheses. They have looked at the white community; there they have observed that education, occupation, and income are important sources of power. . . . They have ignored the possibility that the sources of power in the Black community may be different from that in the white community. In fact, they have ignored one of the most potent forms of power in any marriage, but particularly sex power in Black marriages. Certainly researchers have noted the preoccupation of the Black male with sex. Some have viewed this preoccupation with sex as a form of escapism, failing to realize that this concentration on sexual activities may be a main source of power. The Black male is well aware, as Eldridge Cleaver notes, that he is the desired sex object for both the white and the Black female. He may use this power in his marriage, much as the white male uses his education and earning power as a lever in his marriage.[38]

The threat or use of physical violence (as discussed above) is another factor which must be taken into account to explain power distributions in black as well as in white families. Obviously, a great deal of research on the differences within black families is needed, as Billingsley has suggested.

Life Cycle

The stages of the family life cycle also affect the marital power distribution. In the early (childless) stage of marriage, the wife is frequently working, but the pressure of social discrimination against women is already beginning to be exerted. Women are unable to procure anything but low paying, low status jobs as compared with their husbands. Already status background and autonomous experiences are being eroded. Though the married childless woman maintains some sort of independent social and economic status if she works, it is below that of her husband. During this period, the power of the husband is moderate.

With the birth of children, there is a substantial jump in power differentials, the husband universally gaining.[39] There is more than a little truth in the old saw that the best way to control a woman is to "keep her barefoot and pregnant," for there is evidence that the power of the wife declines as the number of children grows.[40] At this period after the first child is born, but before the oldest child is in school, the power of the husband reaches its maximum. Many women stop working during this stage and in doing so, become isolated and almost totally dependent socially, economically, and emotionally upon their husbands, further eroding any strength they may have gained due to earning power or participation in organizations. [A woman who stops working] loses her position, cannot keep up with developments in her field, does not build up seniority. Further, she loses that precious "organizational" experience, the growth of competence and resources in the outside world, the community positions which contribute to power in the marriage. The boundaries of her world contract, the possibilities of growth diminish. If she returns to work, and most women do, she must begin again at a low-status job and she stays there—underemployed and underpaid. As her children grow up, she gradually regains some power in the family.

These data again call into question the theory of individual resources as the source of power in marriage. As David Heer pointed out, there is no reason, according to Blood and Wolfe's theory, for the power of the wife to be greater before she has borne children than when her children are pre-school age. Surely the wife with pre-school children is contributing more resources to the marriage than she did before their children were born.[41] Power, then, is clearly not the result of individual contributions and resources in the marriage, but is related to questions of social worth; and the value of women and women's work, as viewed by society, is obviously very low. The contributions of women in the home are of little concern and are consequently little valued, as Margaret Benston explained: "The Political Economy of Women's Liberation."[42]

> In sheer quantity, household labor, including child care, constitutes a huge amount of socially necessary production. Nevertheless, in a society based on commodity production, it is not usually considered "real work" since it is outside of trade and market place. It is pre-capitalist in a very real sense. The assignment of household work as the function of a special category "women" meant that this group *does* stand in a different relation to the production than the group "men." We will tentatively define women, then, as that group of people who are responsible for the production of simple use-values in those activities associated with the home and the family.
> Since men carry no responsibility for such production, the difference between the two groups lies here. Notice that women are not excluded from commodity production. Their participation in wage labor occurs, but as a group, they have no structural responsibility in this area and such participation is ordinarily regarded as transient. Men, on the other hand, are responsible for commodity production; they are not, in principle, given any role in household labor. . . . The material basis for the inferior status of women is to be found in just this definition of women. In a society in which money determines value, women are a group who work outside the money economy. Their work is not worth money, is therefore valueless, is therefore not even

real work. And women themselves, who do this valueless work, can hardly be expected to be worth as much as men, who work for money. In structural terms, the closest thing to the condition of women is the condition of others who are or were outside of commodity production, i.e., peasants or serfs.

THE HUSBAND: MOST LIKELY TO SUCCEED

Thus, it is clear that for a wife to gain even a modicum of power in the marital relationship, she must obtain it from external sources, i.e., she must participate in the work force, her education must be superior to that of her husband, and her participation in organizations must excel his. Equality of resources leaves the power in the hands of the husband. Access to these sources of power are structurally blocked for women, however.

In the general population, women are unable to procure anything but low-status, low-paying, dead-end jobs as compared with their husbands, be it [in the] factory or [in the] university.[43] Partly as a result of unequal pay for the same work, partly as a consequence of channeling women into low-paying jobs, the median income of women is far less than that of men workers. Black women tend to fare slightly better in relation to black men, but make only two-thirds as much as white women.

Median Income of Year-Round Full-Time Workers by Sex and Color, 1964.[44]

	Men	Women	Women as % of Men
White	$6,497	$3,859	59.4
Nonwhite	4,285	2,674	62.2

In higher socioeconomic classes, the husband is more likely to excel his wife in formal education than he is among blue-collar workers. Men predominate among college graduates, regardless of race, but adult women have a higher median of education (12.1 for women, 12.0 for men in 1964.)[45] (We have already seen that the educational attainment of the non-white population is lower (8.5 for women, 7.9 for men), reflecting discrimination on the basis of race.)

All of these areas are sources of power in the marital relationship, and in all of these areas women are structurally blocked from realizing our capacities. It is not because of individual resources or personal competence, then, that husbands obtain power in marriage, but because of the discrimination against women in the larger

> **Men gain resources as a class, not as individuals, and women are blocked as a class, not as individuals.**

society. Men gain resources as a class, not as individuals, and women are blocked as a class, not as individuals.

In our mutual mobility bet the woman (as a class) always loses in the fight for power within the marital relationship. We live in a system of institutionalized male supremacy, and the cards are systematically stacked against women in all areas—occupational, political, educational, legal, [and familial]. As long as the structure of society remains the same, as long as categorical discrimination against women is carried out, there is relatively little chance for the woman to gain autonomy, *regardless* of how much good will there is on the part of her husband.

The equalitarian marriage as a norm is a myth. Under some conditions, women can gain power vis-a-vis their husbands; i.e., working women [and] women with higher educations than their husbands have more power than housewives or women with lesser or identical education . . . but more power is not equal power. Equal power we do not have. Equal power we will never get so long as the present socioeconomic system remains.

Notes

1. Robert O. Blood, Jr. and Donald M. Wolfe, *Husbands and Wives: The Dynamics of Married Living* (New York: Free Press, 1960), pp. 29-30.
2. *Ibid.*, pp. 19-20.
3. Constantia Safilios-Rothschild, "Family Sociology or Wives' Family Sociology? A Cross-Cultural Examination of Decision Making," *Journal of Marriage and the Family,* 31 (May 1969): 297-98.
4. Blood and Wolfe, p. 22.
5. William Goode, *World Revolution and Family Patterns* (New York: Free Press, 1963), p. 70.
6. *The Family* (Englewood Cliffs, N.J.: Prentice-Hall, 1964), p. 75.
7. *Ibid.*, p. 87.
8. Blood and Wolfe, p. 37.
9. *Ibid.*, p. 29; emphasis mine.
10. *Kinde, Kuche, Kirche As Scientific Law: Psychology Constructs the Female* (pamphlet; New York: New England Free Press, 1969), p. 7.
11. "Marriage," *The Feminist* (New York, 1969), pp. 2-4.
12. Richard T. Gallen, *Wives' Legal Rights* (New York: Dell, 1967), p. 6.

13. Harriet F. Pilpel and Theodora Zavin, *Your Marriage and the Law* (New York: Collier Books, 1964), p. 65.
14. *Know Your Rights: What a Working Wife Should Know About Her Legal Rights* (U. S. Department of Labor, Women's Bureau, 1965), p. 1.
15. Gallen, p. 6.
16. *Women and the Law: The Unfinished Revolution* (Albuquerque: University of New Mexico Press, 1969), p. 41.
17. *Ibid.*, p. 69.
18. Conversation with Ann Leffler, U. C. Berkeley, 1969.
19. *The Second Sex* (New York: Bantam Books, 1968), p. 451.
20. *World Revolution and Family Patterns*, p. 21.
21. Blood and Wolfe, p. 45.
22. *Ibid.*, pp. 40-41.
23. *Ibid.*, p. 39.
24. *Ibid.*, pp. 28, 38.
25. *Blue Collar Marriage* (New York: Vintage Books, 1967), pp. 226-29.
26. *Ibid.*, p. 227.
27. Lynn O'Connor, "Male Dominance, the Nitty-Gritty of Oppression," *It Ain't Me, Babe,* 1 (June 11–July 1, 1970): 9–11.
28. *Women in Divorce* (New York: Free Press, 1956), pp. 120, 123.
29. *Ibid.*, p. 122.
30. Blood and Wolfe, p. 36.
31. Irving Tallman, "Working Class Wives in Suburbia: Fulfillment or Crisis?" *Journal of Marriage and the Family*, 31 (Feb. 1969): 66-69.
32. Blood and Wolfe, p. 34.
33. Andrew Billingsley and Amy Tate Billingsley, *Black Families in White America* (Englewood Cliffs, N.J.: Prentice-Hall, 1968), p. 8.
34. *Negro Women Workers in 1960*, U.S. Department of Labor, Women's Bureau, 1964, pp. 23-25; *Fact Sheet on the Relative Position of Women and Men Workers in the Economy*, U.S. Department of Labor, Women's Bureau, 1965, p. 3; U.S. Department of Labor, Bureau of Labor Statistics, *Employment and Earnings*, vol. 16, no. 7, Jan. 1970, Table A-1 (data under "Negro" heading are for "Negro and Other Races").
35. *Negro Women Workers*, pp. 23-25.
36. *Ibid.*, pp. 13-14.
37. *Marriage and Family Among Negroes* (Englewood Cliffs, N.J.: Prentice-Hall, 1966), p. 69.
38. "The Husband-Wife Power Relationship in Black Families and White Families," Ph.D. Dissertation, Stanford University.
39. Blood and Wolfe, pp. 41-44.
40. David M. Heer, "Dominance and the Working Wife," *Social Forces*, 36 (May 1958): 341-47.
41. Heer, "The Measurement and Bases of Family Power: An Overview," *Marriage and Family Living*, 25 (May 1963): 138.
42. "The Political Economy of Women's Liberation," *Monthly Review*, Sept. 1969, pp. 3-4.
43. *Handbook on Women Workers*, U. S. Department of Labor, Women's Bureau, 1965, pp. 34-35.
44. *Fact Sheet on the Relative Position . . .*, p. 3.
45. *Handbook on Women Workers*, p. 172.

Who Shall Care for Our Children? The History and Development of Day Care in the United States

Rosalyn F. Baxandall

Given America's expressed concern for the well-being of children and the shocking extent of childhood poverty, it is all the more ironical that of all groups among the poor it is children who have been most neglected and most shabbily treated by current social policies.[1] Recently, however, there has been a growing concern for the welfare of children. Many child-care programs are under debate or in the early stages of development. Thus it is important that we should analyze various policies and programs to determine if possible which will be most beneficial over the long haul. Such an analysis, limited to the problem of day care, will be undertaken here with an eye to proposals for an effective and meaningful day-care policy.[2]

In planning a child-care policy for today it is extremely important to examine the programs of yesterday. Much of present day-care policy stems from the idea that the nuclear family ought to be a self-sufficient unit, performing according to its structure a series of economic, educative, protective, recreational, sexual, and biological functions.[3] Moreover, it is considered that a natural division of labor occurs within this family unit, with nurturance allotted to the mother and breadwinning to the father. Provision for early child-care is seen then as a private matter—to be carried out by the nuclear family, and specifically the mother. Yet not so long ago, and not only in rural areas, child-rearing was shared among members of two or more generations, by mothers-in-law and grandmothers, often living under the same roof or nearby, and was not the sole province of the young children's mothers. The situation today is of course much different. Most families live in single-generational units, and usually at some distance from relatives.

At the same time that child-rearing has become chiefly the responsibility of the single-family unit, a tendency toward family breakups has developed. According to 1969 figures, one marriage in three results in divorce.[4] Of public resources allocated to child-welfare services, 70 percent now goes to foster care.[5] Moreover, more than 11.6 million mothers work; and of these more than 4 million have children under six years of age.[6] Even among those whose children are old enough to be in school, few can be home as early as their children. Where the single-family unit no longer exists as a unit, or is overburdened in one way or another, some other solution must be found. Communal living, a return to extended families, and various forms of day care are among the most frequently mentioned solutions, but only the last will concern us here.

HISTORICAL PERSPECTIVES

The first infant school in the United States seems to have been organized by Robert Owen in New Lanark, Pennsylvania, in the 1830's, after Owen had visited Pestalozzi's infant nursery (modelled on Rousseau's) in Switzerland.[7] Owen's school was, however, a utopian experiment that did not inspire many imitators. The next nursery was opened in 1854 in New York City: the Nursery for Children of the Poor. It was followed by the Virginia Nursery (1872) and the Bethany Day (1887), also in New York.[8] These nurseries provided philanthropic assistance, at first to children of Civil War widows, and later to children who were left during the day by their mothers of immigrant origin while they worked in factories or in domestic service. The care was custodial; wealthy women performed it. The purpose was described as being to "feed the starving, clothe the naked, enlighten the soul."[9]

Parallel with the growth of the day nurseries was the rise of the kindergarten movement that took its inspiration from Friedrich Froebel. German liberals brought Froebel's thought to the United States after 1848. Froebel stressed the freeing of little children from harsh discipline and fear, and he sought to encourage children's natural development through creative play, nature study, art, and music.[10] Many settlements adopted kindergarten programs. Elizabeth Peabody House in Boston began as a combination settlement and kindergarten. At Hull House in Chicago, the settlement activist Mary McDowell taught kindergarten. Many neighborhood kindergartens established in Boston in the 1840's and 1880's became settlements in the 1890's.

On the whole, the kindergarten tradition with its stress on education for the normal child led to the establishment of private nursery schools for the well-to-do. In marked contrast, the day nurseries originated in a welfare tradition that emphasized care and protection for the neglected child and family. Of course, the separation of emphasis was by no means rigid. Day care benefitted greatly from improvements in medicine, hygiene, nutrition, and knowledge of child development. Nevertheless, two distinct traditions developed in the field of child care outside the home in this country. This distinction survives today.

In 1896 a National Federation of Day Nurseries was organized to work for higher standards. In 1905 physicians began to inspect day-care facilities and examine the children who used the centers. A new concern for research and experimentation in the area of educational aids for the underprivileged followed from the establishment of special teacher-training schools at Bank Street in New York, Merrill Palmer in Detroit, and elsewhere. These schools, with their emphasis on teacher training, marked the entrance of professionals into the field. Most of these professionals, however, have gone to nurseries and kindergartens rather than into day-care centers. The teachers in day care belong to a *welfare* union, and they are not nearly so well paid as regular teachers who belong to a *teachers'* union.

In 1919 the day nursery was first included in the National Conference of Social Work. By the 1930's, social-work concepts, emphasizing the value of the day nursery in uplifting family life, were particularly being stressed in the day nurseries sponsored by social agencies. For example, Sophie Van S. Theis found "all child caring agencies, irrespective of the particular type of service which they give . . . have come to think in recent years of casework as an essential part of a good child care program."[11] She goes on to say that traditionally, by charter and by history, the day nursery is a social agency. This social-work legacy—not, of course, a part of nursery-school education—led to further emphasis on day care as a welfare service for the unfortunate, deprived, and maladjusted and to further separation between the two traditions.

The major impetus for day-care development in the United States has been furnished by depression and war. Federally financed nursery schools were established in the 1930's—the greatest era of growth for day care—under the Federal Emergency Relief Administration (FERA), later known as the Works Progress Administration (WPA). The primary purpose of federal action in 1933 was to create employment for needy teachers, nutritionists, clerical workers, cooks, and janitors, all part of a larger program to counteract massive unemployment.[12] The WPA spent large sums of public funds on group programs for children aged two to five from welfare-recipient families, and on staff training and parent education. Outstanding people from the child-development field were enlisted for the extensive training programs, which included brief, intensive teacher-training courses to supply immediate staff needs.[13]

WPA day care was conceived primarily as a residual welfare service. The WPA nursery school, by contrast, was identified as an educational service. Nutrition and health services were likewise stressed. Most of the nurseries (except those in New York City) were located in Board of Education facilities and were staffed by jobless school teachers. (In New York City in 1938, of fourteen WPA nurseries only one was located in a public school; the rest were set up in settlements and other social agencies and even in vacant lots, churches, cellars, stores. These were staffed by recreation directors, nurses, and teachers.) By and large the WPA nurseries were kept open ten to twelve hours a day six days a week. By 1937, 40,000 American children were being provided with what most professionals today still consider high standards of care and education.

In October of 1942 the Federal government notified WPA nurseries that they were no longer needed as a source of employment. Therefore, relief-status children need not be served, although children of working mothers might be cared for, so that these mothers could supply the war industries with much-needed womanpower. Also, there were fewer and fewer unemployed teachers to staff the centers; on the contrary, teacher-shortages were beginning to appear.

In 1941 when World War II began, thousands of women entered industrial production to replace the men who had to leave for the armed forces. The demand for women workers was so great that single and childless women alone could not fill it.[14] Women with young children could not work without child care. Consequently in 1941 Congress passed, in a record two weeks, the Community Facilities Act, usually referred to as the Lanham Act. This Act made federal funds available to states on a fifty-fifty matching basis for the expansion of day-care centers and nursery schools in defense areas. These funds could also be used to convert WPA facilities into wartime nurseries. The Children's Bureau was responsible for the development and extension of day-care centers, whereas the United States Office of Education under the aegis of local school boards handled nursery-school operations. Again the separation of approaches, with the more well-to-do children getting education and the poorer children receiving therapeutic services. The Children's Bureau proved quite ambivalent about the idea of women at work; it felt that in the long run a mother's absence would be destructive to the family and to basic American values. Most social-work leaders joined the Children's Bureau in the concern that publicly funded nurseries might sanction the employment of women.[15] However, widespread popular acceptance of these day-care centers is indicated by the fact that by July of 1945 the Children's Bureau was responsible for 3,100 day-care centers serving 130,000 children,[16] and about 1,600,000 children were receiving care financed largely by federal funds.[17] Every state except New Mexico had some day-care centers. California supported the most: 392 nurseries.

The purpose of these nurseries was first to relieve unemployment and later to encourage the employment of mothers. When the Second World War ended, and women were no longer wanted in the factories, Congress withdrew the Lanham Act funds for day care. Without funds, most of the nurseries had to close. In Chicago there were 23 wartime centers; in 1968 there were none in the entire state of Illinois. In Detroit during the war there were 80 centers, but by 1957, just three remained. In California, where there was a continued demand for women workers in the electronic and aircraft industries, the Lanham Act funds were not withdrawn, and in fact continue to this day on a "temporary" basis, administered through the State Department of Labor.

New York City has a special history. The Lanham Act did not apply to this city because it was not designated a "war-impact" area. However with the threat of withdrawal of funds to the WPA nurseries, active groups of parents and professionals and labor union representatives sent hundreds of petitions, and publicly pressured Mayor LaGuardia not only to keep open existing city-supported nurseries but also to expand the program. The campaign was successful, and day care survived in New York City.

The 1962 Public Welfare amendments to the Social Security Act mark the first time that day care was included in a federal program that was not part of an emergency or wartime measure. However, the major thrust of these amendments was to be in the direction of rehabilitative social services. Day care was provided to protect children whose parents were unable to provide adequate parental supervision for their children. More money ($800,000) was made available for day-care services under the 1962 amendments, but the sum was still far from adequate. The funds were allotted on a matching basis to the states, and it was up to each state to decide whether, and if so how, to launch or extend a day-care program for children.[18] Unfortunately, the poorest, most conservative states with the greatest need generally make the least provision for child care.

The passage of the Economic Opportunity Act in 1964 was another major step in the history of day care. Project Headstart, as an arm of the Office of Economic Opportunity (OEO), directed specific attention to programs for children. Here again, the program was made available only through the states, and the emphasis was on giving poor, deprived children a "head start" rather than on developing day care as a fundamental development service for all. At least 90 percent of the children in Headstart programs must be from families whose income falls below the poverty line, defined as $4,000 for a family of four.[19]

THE NEED

More mothers are working outside the home now than ever before. In the 1940's only 9 percent of all mothers with children under eighteen worked for wages. In 1968, 38 percent of mothers with minor children worked, including 29 percent with children under six and 21 percent with children under three. The labor-participation rate of mothers has increased two times faster than the participation rate of all women, and the labor-participation rate has increased even more rapidly for mothers of pre-school-age children than it has for mothers of school-age children. More women (60 percent) work when the husband has absented himself from the family household, than when the husband is present (30 percent). Among mothers of children under six, a greater proportion of non-white women (42 percent) than white women (25 percent) work for wages.[20]

Day-care facilities have not increased commensurately with the increase in employment of mothers. Licensed public and voluntary day-care centers now care for only one-sixth the number of children cared for at the end of World War II.[21] The gap between availability and need has widened over a period of thirty years. Only in the last few years has the trend been reversed and that, only to a slight degree.[22]

What are the child-care arrangements for these children of working mothers? Forty-six percent of them were cared for in their own homes; 15 percent were cared for by the father; 21 percent by a relative; and 9 percent by a non-relative. Nearly 8 percent looked after themselves; and 4 percent of these were under six, undoubtedly an underestimate, as most women would hesitate to admit that they have no other alternative. Only 2 percent of the children were cared for in group care, whether day-care nurseries or after-school programs.[23]

How many parents would use day care if it were available? The figures are of course impossible to provide. An indication of need is that in New York City in 1970 there were 8,000 children on the waiting list for day-care centers operated by the Department of Social Services. No official waiting lists exist or are available from Central Head Start, but many Head Start centers in 1970 recorded waiting lists as long as the lists of those currently enrolled.[24] Many women are known to be unable to take jobs because there is no day care for their children. The Labor

Studies show that there are no detrimental effects on the child [of a working mother] if the mother makes an effort to spend an hour or two a day with the child when she is home.

Department made a study of underemployment and unemployment in ten high-poverty areas. They found that one out of every five residents who was not in the labor force but who desired a regular job, gave as the principal reason for not looking for work an inability to arrange child care.[25]

Families who can afford to pay for day care do not have enough nursery facilities, either. For one thing, the suburban areas where many of them live have health and zoning laws precluding establishment of nursery schools in many residential areas.[26] At private nurseries in 1970, competition for admission was record-high, with applications outnumbering vacancies by as much as 150 to one.[27]

ATTITUDES TOWARD DAY CARE

Since there seems clearly to be a desperate need for day care, why is the need unmet? Part of the reason is that day care has been stigmatized by its welfare origins. It is thought of as something needed by the problem family. The *Ladies' Home Journal* carried a series on day care from June through November of 1967. One conclusion of this series was that "the concept of day care has not been more widely accepted because it was being presented as something solely for the poor and not for every mother."[28] Day care is often equated with maternal deprivation and emotional problems. Mr. Charles Tobin, secretary of the New York State Welfare Conference, said, "The child who needs day care has a family problem which makes it impossible for his parents to fulfill their parental responsibilities without supplementary help"[29]

Psychiatrists and social workers with their stress on the early mother-child relationship have certainly contributed to the negative attitude toward day care. No one has ever bothered to explore the importance of the *paternal relationship,* or other alternatives to the maternal nexus. As Barbara Wooten, a British sociologist, wrote: "But so long as the study of the role of the father continues to be so much neglected as compared with that of the mother, no opinion on the subject [the emphasis on the young child's need for its mother] can be regarded as more than purely speculative."[30] In the Soviet Union, where group child care from infancy onward is provided for all children as a right, Bronfenbrenner found that not only were the children better socialized, but there was greater companionship between parents and children, and Soviet parents spent even more time with their children than did American parents.[31]

Studies show that there are no detrimental effects on the child if the mother makes an effort to spend an hour or two a day with the child when she is home. Another study illustrates that if a mother enjoys her job, a child benefits from the mother's working. There seems no reason, then, to equate day care with maternal deprivation.[32]

A general prejudice against women's working has also prevented the development of adequate child care facilities outside the home in the United States. A recent study that originated in the Child Welfare League found that the average opinionmaker in the community, including the educator and the social worker, does not believe women should work. If they do work, they are working for frivolous reasons and therefore might better take care of their own children.[33] Another kind of negative attitude toward working women is exemplified by Samuel Nocella, International Vice President of the Amalgamated Clothing Workers, who says: "We have looked upon the presence of women in industry a little cynically because years ago we felt that the only way we could solve the problem of unemployment was for women to stay home so that men could have jobs."[34]

The attitude toward women's employment has often been tied in with the general mythology, or conventional wisdom, regarding a nurturing role for women. Part of this myth holds that only the biological mother can effectively "mother," and that a child will obviously therefore be harmed by the mother's absence in a work situation. The welfare mother has been the brunt, then, of contradictory attitudes: on the one hand she is urged to get off the tax rolls and into the job market; on the other hand she is mindful of the approval to be had from staying home to care for her children. Studies show that there is, on the whole, no higher rate of delinquency among the children of working mothers, nor is there evidence that either the husband-wife or the child-parent relationship is impaired.[35] Maternal employment has not been shown to have other harmful consequences for children, either.[36] In general, the impact of a mother's employment upon her child or children varies with the adequacy of the substitute arrangement, or the mother-child relationship prior to the separation for work, and with the mother's motivation to work and the gratification she receives from her employment.[37] In fact, "group care . . . has positive features. Often those in charge of children's groups are better trained, more patient, and objective in dealing with children than the mothers. A child can be allowed greater freedom to run, climb, and throw in a nursery school than in a home full of breakable objects."[38] "There has been some speculation that greater variety of stimulation provided by several close mother figures may be intellectually stimulating and promote flexibility."[39] Day care in various experiments and full-scale programs in the Soviet Union, East Germany, Czechoslovakia, Hungary, Israel, Greece, and France seems to have benefitted children.[40]

Since day care has never been studied from a feminist perspective, there have been few studies on the importance of day care *for the mother.* However, anyone who has been a mother knows that mothers need some kind of break from routine, some breathing spell, and some time for recreation, socializing, and creative pursuits—impossible on any meaningful scale without day care of some kind. In fact, most mothers are better mothers when they have some satisfying independent life of their own.[41] Mothers should not be forced to place their children in day care centers, but the option should always be present.

Part of the reason why professionals in the child-care field oppose women's working and group care for children of working mothers is that these professionals equate maternal separation, even for a few hours a day, with maternal deprivation. They seem to think that maternal separation for any reason and in any manner has to have traumatic, deleterious effects on young children.[42] This misunderstanding comes out of the Bowlby, Spitz, Roudinesco, and Goldfarb studies showing that children who lived in impersonal institutions and were totally bereft, not only of maternal care but also of adequate maternal substitution, developed irreversible psychopathic or autistic characteristics. But these studies have little bearing on the situation of the child of a working mother generally considered; and they probably have little relevance even to questions of maternal deprivation. Barbara Wooten has questioned the scientific validity of these maternal-deprivation studies, inasmuch as they tended to use only disturbed children in institutions as a sample, never following the subjects into later experiences, whereas their clinical observations and statistics altered with time.[43] Regrettably, these studies are still respected in professional psychological and educational circles. It is true generally that scientific evaluations of the effects of day care on mothers and children are colored by cultural norms. And in a society where one must be considered abnormal in order to qualify for the day-care center, how is the evaluation of such services to be contemplated along guidelines that might with accuracy be termed scientific?

PERSPECTIVES AND PROBLEMS

Day care can be viewed as a benefit in kind, as opposed to a cash benefit. Benefits in kind are preferred when a quality service is too expensive to be purchased on an individual basis.[44] In 1970 it was estimated that decent day care cost $1,600 per year per child.[45] Together with large sums of money, complex administrative and technological and educational skills are required if the demand for adequate day care is to be met. Individual families cannot be expected to meet these expensive, complex demands themselves. Even if they could, there is a view of society whereby the wellbeing of children is too important a priority to be left to individual family discretion; childhood and education are societal rather than individual functions, since they ensure the continuity and survival of the society as a whole.

Day care, then, should be seen as a universal entitlement, like public education, rather than as it is now perceived, as a means-tested provision on the order of welfare. Means tests are not efficient as a way of concentrating help on those in need.[46] Means tests usually degrade and stigmatize and therefore only reinforce the conditions they are intended to alleviate and widen the inequity gap they purport to diminish.[47] In a society such as ours, which sets great emphasis on monetary reward and success, an admission of poverty and failure can prove so detrimental that it outweighs the reward it brings.[48] Many liberal-minded people believe that those who could pay for day care should do so on a sliding scale. However, because of the lingering welfare associations of day care, I feel the only way to make day care available without stigma must be to treat it as an unconditionally free public utility.

One of the problems with benefits in kind, however, is that they are often employed as mechanisms for social control.[49] Day care has in the past been used in this way. At present, day care is made available only on condition that women on welfare become enrolled in Special Work Incentive Programs (WIN) and Concentrated Employment Programs (CEPS). The proposed Nixon Family Assistance Plan (FAP) would likewise combine day care with work.

In FAP plans, the welfare recipients would be provided vouchers enabling them to purchase day care from government or private profit-making centers. This would constitute a windfall for private, franchised centers that would exist for profit rather than owing to any special evinced vocation for child care. Such centers would naturally seek to cut corners to increase their profits. The existing ones generally are overcrowded, with inadequate equipment and untrained part-time personnel. They are geared not toward child development but rather toward the readiest means to give parents the impression that their children are happy. They also seek to inveigle the parents into purchasing the products made by the day-care franchisers.[50]

The only way to prevent this balance-sheet-dominated kind of day care is to be insistent about having genuine parental control. With this, certain criteria and health and education standards should be maintained in day care. Unlike the present Code enforcement, such standards and criteria should not militate against experiment and innovation. Different communities should be able to develop vary-ing centers to meet their needs. For example: in an area where many parents are employed at night, the day-care center should be open 24 hours a day. In contrast, where parents sought care for half-days only, this too should be made possible, and with due budgetary benefit.

Day care has begun to be a factor in labor-market planning. Recently the AVCO Corporation of Dorchester, Massachusetts, Bell Telephone, Whirlpool, and the Rochester Clothing Company have commenced to use day care as a fringe benefit to attract and attach women workers to relatively poorly paid jobs.[51] This is a genuine benefit and may take the place of another $100 or more a month in salary. Moreover, insofar as it succeeds in reducing turnover, it may be taken up by other industries. However, since many of the women in most need of the pro-gram would find it difficult to get another job, clearly the plan can also be used to control workers. Women are also less apt to engage in action that threatens the firm: organizing strikes, picketing, etc., when the threat is not only loss of a job, but loss of day care.

Day care should be financed by the federal government. This should be done from general tax revenue, rather than from any wage-related tax. Wage-related taxes are often employed to psychologically reinforce a relationship between par-ticipation in the labor force and receipt of a benefit.[52] And taxes applied from the general tax revenues are on the whole considered to be of universal benefit. It is true the cost of universal day care stands to be enormous—perhaps as much as 6 to 10 billion dollars annually. The issue, however, is not in fact one of economic feasibility. In the world's wealthiest country the issue is rather one of priorities and readiness. Day-care services might best be administered under a special Early Childhood Agency rather than be distributed among the existing (bureaucratic, outmoded, but entrenched) education or welfare systems. It would probably prove simpler to innovate, and to go directly to the task with a new agency structured for it. Early childhood education is a special field, with educational, health, nutri-tional, developmental, and behavioral components.

Another question often raised when universal day care is proposed is that of work incentive. Will the widespread availability of day care encourage women to engage in economically productive labor? And if so, with what consequences? Al-ready we have explored the social and psychological consequences, and found no necessarily detrimental results, but rather the possibility of beneficial results both for the mother and for the child. As to economic consequences, these might in-clude an even stronger influx of women into the labor market, adding to the unem-ployment problem. Yet with a growing unemployment among men to match the institutionalized unemployment (housewifery) among women, there might be more incentive for a rethinking of the entire question of the duration and constitution of the work week. Part-time work for all might prove to be a partial solution to unemployment and to family needs alike, especially if men are encouraged to share in housekeeping. Also, it might be argued that day care could in the short run reduce the public assistance rolls, as it would leave welfare mothers free to work. It is estimated that in New York City alone, 250,000 women on welfare would be employable if day-care centers and job training were provided.[53]

At present, the absence of day care operates as a work disincentive. The cost of babysitters and nurseries, transportation, work clothing, and lunches often makes it financially unfeasible for women to work, especially those with low pay. Work-related expenses plus taxes are estimated to take 50 percent of a mother's paycheck.[54]

In the past a combination of voluntary and publicly sponsored day care has been controlled by boards of directors, the welfare apparatus, or the tendencies of the labor market, and shaped to respond to the welfare and therapeutic needs of special families and the labor-productive sector. Yet day care is a unique and invaluable service. It is not interchangeable with other institutions for the structuring of human resources. Obstacles to universal day care seem to consist of its origin in welfare arrangements; negative attitudes on the subject of working women; the psychiatric social-work emphasis on the mother's role in early childhood; the tradition of a single dominant maternal role; the confusion between separation and deprivation; the association of day care with communism;[55] and a general emphasis in our modern psychological and educational theory on individual as opposed to group or contextual development and achievement.[56]

It is time for Americans to face the present realities—the breakdown of the nuclear family, the transformation of women's roles, the new awareness of human (child and parental) needs. It is accordingly time to reorient day-care policy to correspond to this changed reality. This in turn must call forth federally funded, community-controlled, universal day care, under a distinct administration for early childhood purposes.

Notes

1. Eveline Burns, "Childhood Poverty and the Children's Allowance," in Eveline Burns, ed., *Children's Allowances and the Economic Welfare of Children* (New York: Citizens' Committee for Children, 1968), p. 3.
2. *New York Times*, Dec. 19 and 29, 1970; Jan. 11, 1971.
3. Alva Myrdal, *Nation and Family* (Cambridge, Mass.: M.I.T. Press, 1941), pp. 3-5.
4. *Statistical Abstracts of the United States*, 1970, Department of Commerce, Bureau of the Census, 91st edition, p. 47.

5. Eveline Burns, "The Government's Role in Child and Family Welfare," in *The Nation's Children*, vol. 3, *Problems and Prospects*, ed., Eli Ginzberg (New York: Columbia University Press, 1960), p. 161.
6. *New York Times*, Nov. 30, 1970, p. 1.
7. Ethel Beer, *The Day Nursery* (New York: E. P. Dutton & Co., 1930).
8. Bernice Fleiss, "The Relationship of the Mayor's Committee on Wartime Care of Children to Day Care in New York City," doctoral thesis (Education), New York University, 1962; and Mary Bogue and Mary Moran, "Day Nurseries" in *Social Work Yearbook*, vol. 1 (1929), pp. 118-19.
9. Child Welfare League of America, "A Historical Sketch of the Day Nursery Movement," New York, 1940 (typescript in Child Welfare League of America Library).
10. Allen F. Davis, *Spearheads for Reform: The Social Settlements and The Progressive Movement, 1890-1914* (New York: Oxford University Press, 1967), pp. 43-46.
11. Fleiss, *op. cit.,* who quotes from Sophie Van S. Theis, *The Importance of Casework in the Day Nursery* (New York: National Federation of Day Nurseries, 1935), p. 1.
12. Anna Mayer, *Day Care as a Social Instrument, A Policy Paper,* Columbia University School of Social Work, Jan. 1965, p. 24.
13. Fleiss, *op. cit.* Most of my material on the 1930's comes from the Fleiss thesis, and from Gussack Anne LeWine and R. Alice McCabe, *The Public Voluntary Agency-Sponsored Day-Care Program for Children in New York City,* an Administrative Study prepared for the Subcommittee on Day Care of the Committee on Family and Child Welfare, Community Service Society, Dept. of Public Affairs, July 1965.
14. Valerie Oppenheimer, *The Female Labor Force in The United States: Demographic and Economic Factors Governing Its Growth and Changing Composition* (Berkeley: University of California Press, 1970).
15. Mayer, *op. cit.,* p. 27.
16. Fleiss, *op. cit.,* p. 82, who quotes Alice Dashiell, "Trends in Day Care," *The Child,* 2 (Sept. 1946): 56.
17. Mayer, *op. cit.,* p. 27.
18. Katherine Oettinger, "Day Care Today: A Foundation for Progress," in *Report of a Consultation on Working Women and Day-Care Needs* (Wash., D.C.: United States Department of Labor), June 1, 1967 (hereafter, *Report*); Title I, Section 102B, of the Social Security Act as amended in 1962.
19. *Children Are Waiting* (Washington, D.C.: Human Resources Administration, Task Force on Early Childhood Development, July 1970; pamphlet), Appendix A, p. 2.
20. *1969 Handbook of Women Workers,* Women's Bureau Bulletin 294, pp. 40-43.
21. Florence Ruderman, *Child Care and Working Mothers: A Study of Arrangements Made for Daytime Care of Children,* Child Welfare League of America, 1968, p. 10.
22. Mary Keyserling, "Working Mothers and Their Children: The Urgent Need for Day-Care Services," in *Report,* see footnote 20, p. 3.
23. Seth Low and Pearl Spindler, *Child-Care Arrangements of Working Mothers in the United States,* Children's Bureau and Women's Bureau, 1968, pp. 15-16 (based on a study done in 1965).
24. *Children Are Waiting,* p. 8.
25. Keyserling, *op. cit.,* pp. 5-6.
26. *Ibid,* p. 6.

27. Martin Tolchin, "Nursery Schools Arouse Rivalry," *New York Times*, Feb. 17, 1964.

28. Keyserling, *op. cit.*, p. 8.

29. *Guides to State Welfare Agencies for the Development of Day-Care Services*, (Washington, D.C.: United States Dept. of Health, Education and Welfare, Children's Bureau, Welfare Administration, 1963).

30. Barbara Wooton, *Social Science and Social Pathology* (New York: Macmillan, 1959), p. 144.

31. Urie Bronfenbrenner, *Two Worlds of Childhood: U.S. and U.S.S.R.* (New York: Russell Sage Foundation, 1970).

32. F. Ivan Nye and Lois Wladis Hoffman, eds., *The Employed Mother in America* (Chicago: Rand McNally, 1963).

33. Joseph Reid, "Legislation for Day Care," in *Report*, p. 35.

34. "Innovative Approaches — a Panel," *Ibid.*, p. 55.

35. Rose A. John, "Child Development and the Part-Time Mother," *Children* (Nov.-Dec. 1959): 213-18; and Leon Yarrow, "Conceptualizing the Early Environment," in Laura L. Dittman, ed., *Early Child Care: The New Perspectives* (New York: Atherton, 1968), pp. 15-27.

36. Bettye Caldwell and Julius Richmond, "Programmed Day Care for the Very Young Child — A Preliminary Report," *Child Welfare*, 44 (Mar. 1965): 134-42; and Stig Sjolin, "Care of Well Children in Day-Care Centers," *Care of Children in Day Care Centers* (Geneva: World Health Organization, 1964), p. 22.

37. Milton Willner, "Day Care, a Reassessment," *Child Welfare*, 44 (Mar. 1967): 126-27.

38. Eleanor Maccoby, "Children and Working Mothers," *Children*, 5-6 (1958-59): 86.

39. Yarrow, *op. cit.*, pp. 22-23.

40. Dale Meers and Allen Marans, "Group Care of Infants in Other Countries," in Dittman, *op. cit.*, pp. 234-82.

41. Willner, *op. cit.*, p. 129.

42. Julius Richmond, "Twenty Percent of the Nation," *Spotlight on Day Care: Proceedings of the National Conference on Day-Care Services, May 13-15, 1965* (Washington, D.C.: United States Department of Health, Education, and Welfare), p. 45.

43. Wooton, *op. cit.*, pp. 146, 151, 153.

44. Gerald Holden, "A Consideration of Benefits in Kind for Children," *Children's Allowances and the Economic Welfare of Children* (New York: Citizens' Committee for Children, 1968), pp. 150-52.

45. *New York Times*, Nov. 30, 1970, p. 51.

46. David Bull, "Action for Welfare Rights," in *The Fifth Social Service: Nine Fabian Essays* (London: Fabian Society, May 1970; pamphlet), p. 148.

47. Peter Townsend, Introduction, "Does Selectivity Mean a Nation Divided," *Social Services for All: Eleven Fabian Essays* (London: Fabian Society, Sept. 1968), pp. 1-6.

48. Brian Abel Smith, Conclusion, "The Need for Social Planning," *Ibid.*, p. 114.

49. Holden, *op. cit.*, p. 151 and Myrdal, *op. cit.*, p. 150.

50. Joseph Featherstone, "The Day-Care Problem: Kentucky Fried Chicken," *The New Republic*, Sept. 12, 1970, pp. 12-16; and Ann Cook and Herbert Mack, "Business Education, the Discovery Center Hustle," *Social Policy*, Sept.-Oct. 1970, pp. 3-11; *New York Times*, Dec. 27, 1969. For example, if Creative Playthings (a toy corporation) runs a day-care center, they will try to convince the parents of the children that certain Creative Playthings toys are needed for the children's educational development.

51. *New York Times,* Jan. 21, 1970, pp. 59 and 65, and Oct. 29, 1970.
52. Shlakman, *op. cit.,* p. 28.
53. *New York Times,* Dec. 15 and 29, 1970.
54. Nadine Brozan, "To Many Working Mothers, a Job Is Almost a Losing Proposition," *New York Times,* Jan. 5, 1971, p. 30.
55. Mayer, *op. cit.,* p. 129, who is quoting Raymond J. Gallagher, Secretary of the National Conference of Catholic Charities, in testimony on Public Welfare Amendments of 1962, Bill No. 10032, *Congressional Record,* 87th Congress, 2d Sess., pp. 578-80.
56. Rochelle Paul Wortis, "Child-Rearing and Women's Liberation," paper delivered at Women's Weekend, Ruskin College, Oxford University, February 28, 1970; pamphlet, p. 1.

Sex-Role Socialization

Lenore J. Weitzman *

In our society women are characterized as passive, dependent and emotional in contrast to men, who are considered aggressive, active and instrumental. How can these differences be explained? Are women "naturally" more passive, or are they taught to be more passive? Are men inherently more aggressive, or does our society socialize men into more aggressive roles?

To shed some light on the continued controversy over whether (or to what degree) these observed differences are learned or inherent, this paper will focus on the socialization process. I want to examine how the socialization process shapes the sex roles that women and men come to accept as entirely natural and self-evident.

First, however, let us consider a wider range of data suggesting that studying socialization will be fruitful in helping us to understand sex roles as we

---

* This paper was originally written in 1970 and 1971. I wish to thank Ruth Dixon, Ann Freedman, and Jo Freeman for their comments on the earlier drafts, and Sheryl Ruzeck for her research assistance. I am especially indebted to William J. Goode for his extensive suggestions and provocative comments.

The varied sex-role assignments given to men and women in different cultures suggest that the characteristics of maleness and femaleness are not biologically determined; rather they are based on cultural definitions of sex-appropriate behavior.

know them today: data from studies of cross-cultural variation in sex roles and data from studies of sex roles acquired by persons with biologically ambiguous sexual identities.

Anthropologists who have examined sex roles cross-culturally have found great diversity in the roles assumed "natural" for men and women, and in the extent of differentiation between the sexes. Margaret Mead's classic study of three New Guinea tribes provides impressive evidence of this cross-cultural variation in assigned sex roles.[2] She found that the Arapesh regarded both men and women as cooperative, unaggressive, and responsive to the needs of others—characteristics we would normally label as feminine or maternal. Among the Mundugumor, she found both men and women to be aggressive, unresponsive, and individualistic—traits we would normally call masculine. Neither the Arapesh nor the Mundugumor ascribed contrasting personality characteristics to men and women: the Arapesh ideal man—like the ideal woman—was mild and responsive; the Mundugumor ideal for both man and woman was violent and aggressive. In the third society Mead studied, the Tchambuli, there was a reversal of the typical sex roles found in Western cultures. The Tchambuli women were dominant, impersonal and managing; the men were emotionally dependent and less responsible than women.

Cross-cultural data such as those collected by Mead are illuminating because they make us realize that some of our most basic assumptions about what is "natural" are based on cultural beliefs rather than biological necessity. For example, although we have long assumed that women were not fit for war (because they were "naturally" weaker and less aggressive than men) women in other societies, such as Dahomey, were great warriors. * Similarly, we have traditionally regarded women as "naturally" more nurturant, and therefore uniquely qualified to rear children: but other societies have assumed males were more nurturant, while still others regard child care as the exclusive domain of trained experts.[3]

The varied sex-role assignments given to men and women in different cultures suggest that the characteristics of maleness and femaleness are not biologically

---

* It should be noted that physical strength is almost irrelevant in modern society. Certainly an industrial society does not give its highest rewards of money, power, or prestige on the basis of physical strength.

determined; rather they are based on cultural definitions of sex-appropriate behavior. Since there is no reason to assume that the biological makeup of men and women in Mead's tribes or in other societies differs from that of men and women in the United States in any basic way, the observed differences between the sexes in these cultures and our own would seem to be culturally determined. The compelling logic of this conclusion becomes more obvious when we consider the alternative: if we hypothetically assume a biological basis for these differences we would then have to conclude that Tchambuli men were dependent because they had more female hormones. This would be akin to concluding that Latin American men are more *macho* than American men because of higher levels of male hormones, or that Oriental women are less aggressive than American women because they have more female hormones.* Since we know that there is no such cross-cultural variation in biological or hormonal sex, we must recognize the great influence of cultural learning in order to explain these differences.

The power of cultural factors is also suggested by a very different line of research: the work of Money, Hampson, and Eckhardt on hermaphrodites.[4] The complete hermaphrodite—a person who possesses complete sets of both male and female genitalia and reproductive organs—is extremely rare, but a fair number of babies are born each year whose sex is difficult to determine with certainty. Some of these infants appear to be female, but are biologically male. Others may appear to be male but are biologically female. Dr. John Money and his associates at Johns Hopkins University have spent almost twenty years following the life histories of some of these babies. Of most interest to us here are those who were assigned one sex at birth and were later found to belong biologically (genetically, gonadally, hormonally) to the opposite sex. In virtually all cases, the sex of assignment (and thus of rearing) proved dominant. Thus, babies assigned as males at birth and brought up as boys by their parents (who were unaware of their child's female genetic and hormonal makeup) thereafter thought of themselves as boys, played with boys' toys, enjoyed boys' sports, preferred boy's clothing, developed male sex fantasies, and in due course fell in love with girls. And the reverse was true for babies who were biologically male but reared as girls: they followed the typical feminine pattern of development—they preferred marriage over a career, enjoyed domestic and homemaking duties, and saw their future fulfillment in the traditional woman's role.

---

* As the Bems have observed, "If female hormones are responsible for keeping women from high level jobs, we would have to assume that women in the Soviet Union have different hormones, because they comprise 33 percent of the engineers and 75 percent of the doctors." Sandra Bem and Daryl Bem, "Training Woman to Know Her Place: The Power of a Nonconscious Ideology," *Psychology Today*, November, 1970.

This research dramatically illustrates the impact of socialization—even when it contradicts biological sex—and thus further supports the importance of learned differences as powerful determinants of current sex roles. Having shown the great influence of socialization, let us now examine the dynamics of the sex-role socialization process.

EARLY CHILDHOOD SOCIALIZATION

Socialization begins at birth. From the minute a newborn baby girl is wrapped in a pink blanket and her brother in a blue one, the two children are treated differently. The difference starts with the subtle tone of voice of the adults cooing over the two cradles, and continues with the father's mock wrestling with his baby boy and gentler play with his fragile daughter.[5] Researchers have observed sex differences in behavior of male and female babies at amazingly young ages, most of it directly traceable to parents' differential treatment of infant boys and girls.

Moss's observations of mothers with infants at three weeks and three months show that even the newborn baby is consistently being given reinforcement for appropriate behavior.[6] Moss, in fact, has tentatively suggested that patterns leading to verbal ability in girls and aggression in boys were being selectively encouraged in the infants he observed.[7]

Infant Socialization

In observing thirteen-month-old babies, Goldberg and Lewis found that the little girls clung to, looked at, and talked to their mothers more often than the little boys.[8] Each of these behavioral differences, however, was linked to differential treatment by the mother when the babies were younger. The researchers had observed the same mothers with their babies when the babies were six months old. At that stage they observed that mothers of girl babies touched their infant girls more often than did mothers of infant boys. They also talked to and handled their daughters more often.[9] By the time these same children were thirteen months old, the researchers observed that the girl babies had learned to respond to the more frequent stimuli they received from their mothers: they reciprocated their mothers' attention with the result that by thirteen months they talked to and touched their mothers more often than the boys did. In order to establish the causal relationship, i.e., that high frequency of touching at six months causes babies to seek more touching at thirteen months, Goldberg and Lewis reclassified the mothers they had observed at six months into groups with high and low rates of touching. They found that the children (both boys and girls) of mothers with high touching rates at six months sought the most maternal contact at thirteen months.[10]

This research vividly illustrates socialization at its earliest stages. It indicates that sex-role socialization begins before the child is even aware of a sexual identity: before he or she can have an internal motive for conforming to sex-role standards. It also indicates that cultural assumptions about what is "natural" for a boy or for a girl are so deeply ingrained that parents may treat their children differently without even being aware of it. Presumably, if we interviewed mothers of six-month-old babies, they would not tell us that they expected their young sons to be independent and assertive while still in the cradle. Yet, it appears that at some level mothers do have such expectations, and these expectations are successfully communicated to very young babies. Thus, wittingly or unwittingly, parents encourage and reinforce sex-appropriate behavior, and little boys and little girls respond to parental encouragement and rewards. So little boys learn to be independent, active, and aggressive; their sisters learn to be dependent and passive.

Early Cognitive Socialization

We have been discussing the first type of socialization an infant experiences: simple behavioral reinforcement. A second type of socialization begins with cognitive learning—when the child is able to sort out and make conceptual distinctions about the social world and herself or himself. Around the age of three or four, the child begins to make sex-role distinctions and express sex-role preferences. Rabban found that at the age of three both boys and girls still showed incomplete recognition of sex differences and were unaware of the appropriateness of sex-typed toy objects.[11] Each year, however, children's cognitive abilities increase: by age six they are able to clearly distinguish the male and female role, and to identify themselves appropriately. Sex-role learning in these preschool years may be divided into three analytic processes. The child learns:

1. to *distinguish* between men and women and between boys and girls, and to know what kinds of behavior are characteristic of each;
2. to express appropriate sex-role *preferences* for himself or herself;
3. and to *behave* in accordance with sex-role standards.

In labeling these processes I have avoided the term *identification* because of the distinct meaning of this word in the socialization literature. Identification, a frequently used concept in Freudian theory, assumes that sex-role learning is limited to the same-sex parent. This theory will be discussed (and criticized) in the final section of this paper. In the following pages each of the three processes listed above will be discussed separately because each presents a different set of contingencies for the growing boy or girl.

Distinguishing Between Male and Female Roles

Both boys and girls learn to distinguish the male from the female role by observing the men and women around them: their parents, brothers and sisters, neighbors, and friends. In addition to serving as models for the young child, these adults and older boys and girls often provide explicit instructions on proper behavior. Little girls are told what is considered nice and ladylike, and little boys are told what is expected of big strong men.

As already noted, parents are especially influential in defining the male or female role for the young child. They do this both consciously and unconsciously, by example and proscription, by reward and punishment. There is some evidence that fathers are more concerned than mothers with sex-typing in young children. Goodenough's interviews with the parents of two- to four-year-old children indicated that fathers more strictly differentiated sex roles and encouraged stronger sex typing in children than did mothers.[12]

Picture books are another important source of sex-role learning for young children. Through books, children learn about the world outside their immediate environment: they learn what other boys and girls do, say, and feel, and they learn what is expected of children of their age. In a recent study of prize-winning preschool picture books, Weitzman, Eifler, Hokada, and Ross found girls portrayed as passive, doll-like creatures, while the boys were active and adventuresome.[13] Most of the little girls engaged in service activities directed toward pleasing and helping their brothers and fathers. In contrast, the boys were engaged in a variety of tasks requiring independence and self-confidence.

Picture books also provide children with role models—images of what they will be like when they grow up. Weitzman *et al.* found the adult women portrayed in these award-winning books were consistently stereotyped and limited. Most were identified only as wives or mothers. The men were shown in a wide variety of occupations and professions, whereas not one of the adult women had an outside job or profession. The authors conclude that in the world of picture books:

> Little girls receive attention and praise for their attractiveness, while boys are admired for their achievements and cleverness. For girls, achievement is marriage and becoming a mother. Most of the women in picture books have status by virtue of their relationships to specific men—they are the wives of the kings, judges, adventurers and explorers, but they themselves are not the rulers, judges, adventurers and explorers.

**The world of picture books never tells little
girls that as women they might find fulfillment outside of their homes or through
intellectual pursuits . . . .**

Through picture books, girls are taught to have low aspirations because
there are so few opportunities portrayed as available to them. The world of
picture books never tells little girls that as women they might find fulfillment
outside of their homes or through intellectual pursuits. . . .

In a country with close to 40 percent of the women in the labor force it
is absurd to find that women in picture books remain only mothers and
wives. . . .

Their future occupational world is presented as consisting primarily of
glamour and service. Women are excluded from the world of sports, politics
and science. They can achieve only by being attractive, congenial and serving
others.[14]

Another influential source of sex-role socialization for young children is television. Gardner's study of the program *Sesame Street* (another supposed ideal)
indicated that television contributes equally to severe sex-role stereotypes:

On one program, Big Bird (having said that he would like to be a member of a
family and having been told that Gordon and Susan would be his family) is
told that he will have to help with the work and that since he is a boy bird, he
will have to do men's work—the heavy work, the *"important"* work and also
that he should get a girl (bird) to help Susan with *her* work arranging flowers,
redecorating, etc. There was more and virtually all of it emphasized that there
is men's work and then there is women's work—that men's work is outside
the home and women's work is in the home. (This in spite of the fact that 17
million children under eighteen have mothers who are employed outside the
home; of these 4.5 million are under six.)[15]

Although the images in children's books and TV programs appear to be more
stereotyped and rigid than reality, interviews with young children indicate the
extent to which these clearly differentiated sex roles are internalized by the child.
Hartley asked a sample of young boys what they thought was expected of boys and
girls. Her respondents described boys as follows:

They have to be able to fight in case a bully comes along; they have to be
athletic; . . . they must be able to play rough games . . . they need to be
smart; they need to be able to take care of themselves; they should know
what girls don't know . . . they should have more ability than girls . . . they
are expected to get dirty; to mess up the house; to be naughty; to be outside
more than girls are; not to be cry babies, not to be softies; and to get into
trouble more than girls do.[16]

Girls, according to the boy respondents,

> have to stay close to home; they are expected to play quietly and more gently than boys; they are often afraid; they must not be rough; they have to keep clean; they cry when scared or hurt; their activities consist of "fopperies" like playing with dolls, fussing over babies, and sitting and talking about dresses; they need to know how to cook, sew and take care of children, but spelling and arithmetic are not as important for them as for boys.[17]

When Hartley asked her young respondents about adults, she found their images of the two sexes even more disparate. In the children's eyes men are active and intelligent,

> strong, ready to make decisions, protect women and children in emergencies. . . . They must be able to fix things, they must get money to support their families, and have a good business head. Men are the boss in the family and have the authority to dispose of money and they get first choice in the use of the most comfortable chair in the house and the daily paper. . . . They laugh and make more jokes than women do. Compared with mothers, fathers are more fun to be with: they are exciting to have around and they have the best ideas.[18]

In contrast, women are seen as a rather tired and unintelligent group.

> They are indecisive and they are afraid of many things; they make a fuss over things; they get tired a lot . . . they don't know what to do in an emergency, they cannot do dangerous things, they are scared of getting wet or getting an electric shock, they are not very intelligent. . . . Women do things like cooking and washing and sewing because that's all they can do.[19]

Expressing Sex-role Preferences

Once the child has learned to distinguish males from females and has determined the types of behavior that are appropriate for each, he or she may begin to express sex-role preferences. At age three, Rabban found that both boys and girls decidedly prefer the mother role when asked to choose which parent they would prefer to be like.[20] Other studies have corroborated this preference of young children for the mother.* According to the reasons the children themselves give for their preference, they like best the parent who caters to their material wants, who expresses affection for them, who plays with them most, and who punishes them least.[21]

But the sex-role preferences of children soon change. By age five most boys, and a significant minority of girls, say they prefer the masculine role. Brown, inter-

---

* These preferences of the young children challenge Freud's theory of penis envy. They suggest, rather, that the young boys may experience something akin to breast envy.

viewing five- and six-year-old children, found more cross-sex preferences among girls (indicating a desire to be boys) than among boys.[22] In addition, the boys show a significantly stronger preference for the masculine role than girls reveal for the feminine role.[23] The research of Hartup and Zook corroborates the finding about strength of preference[24] and indicates, further, that with each year more girls prefer to identify with the masculine role than boys with the feminine role.[25] Sex-role preference is strongly influenced, however, by social class. Upper- and middle-class boys say they prefer the male role strikingly more often than do lower-class boys.[26]

One explanation for why both girls and boys in middle-class families prefer the male role is that they have learned that it is more prestigious in our society. Thus, it is preferable. Hartley's study, cited above, clearly indicates that children perceive the superior status and privileges of the masculine role. They know which sex gets the best chair in the house, and which sex is expected to do the cleaning.[27] Brown, using the values children give to sex-typed toys, also concluded that the children saw the masculine role as having greater prestige and value.[28] Smith has found evidence to suggest that as children grow older, they increasingly learn to give males more prestige.[29] He asked children from eight to fifteen to vote on whether boys or girls have desirable or undesirable traits. With increasing age both boys and girls increasingly ascribed the desirable traits to boys. In addition, boys expressed a progressively better opinion of themselves while self-conceptions of girls' progressively weakened.[30]

Thus children learn that it is better to be a male than a female because it is men who exhibit the highly valued traits and are accorded the privilege and prestige in our society.* No wonder, then, that girls are reluctant to express "appropriate" sex-role preferences, and instead continue wishing they were boys. Boys, by contrast, find it easy to express "appropriate" sex role preferences.

Learning Sex-Role Behavior

The third component of the socialization process consists in learning to act like a girl or a boy. Boys are described as having more difficulty learning appropriate sex-role behavior. Their difficulty stems from three sources: the lack of continuous

---

* Alice Rossi has suggested that girls get a more subtle message with regard to the relative prestige of men and women. They learn that outside the home men are the bosses of women; however, in the home, father does not know best. The message thus communicated to little girls is that women can be important only in the family. Alice Rossi, "Equality Between the Sexes," in *The Woman in America* (Boston: Houghton Mifflin, 1964), p. 105.

male role models, the rigidity and harshness of masculine sex-role demands, and the negative nature of male sex-role proscriptions.

Several theorists have suggested that boys know less about the masculine role because of the relative lack of salience of the father as a model. Lynn notes that the father is in the home much less than the mother, and even when he is there, he usually participates in fewer intimate activities with the child than the mother does.[31] Both the amount of time spent with the child, and the intimacy and intensity of parental contact are thought to be important for the child's learning. Since the girl is able to observe her mother throughout the day and has continuous and intimate contact with her, she supposedly finds it easier to use her mother as a model, and to imitate appropriate sex-role behavior.

Lynn has further theorized that because boys have less direct exposure to male models they tend to develop stereotypical images of masculinity.[32] This view has been supported by studies which have shown that fatherless boys have more exaggerated notions of masculinity than boys who have a father in the home.[33] The tendency of boys to pattern themselves after a male stereotype may help account for the exaggerated forms of masculinity encouraged by male peer groups. In the absence of fuller role models to emulate, boys may view exaggerated "toughness" and aggression as appropriate male behavior.

Hartley has suggested that boys have the additional problem of a more rigorous sex-role definition: "Demands that boys conform to social notions of what is manly come much earlier and are enforced with much more vigor than similar attitudes with respect to girls. These demands are frequently enforced harshly, impressing the small boy with the danger of deviating from them, while he does not quite understand what they are."[34] By contrast, very young girls are allowed a wider range of behavior and are punished less severely for deviation, especially in the middle class. (At young ages it is easier for a girl to be a tomboy than for a boy to be a sissy.) Upon reaching adolescence, however, the behavior of girls is more sharply constricted than is boys'.

In addition to the relative absence of male role models and the rigidity of the male sex role, the socialization of boys is said to be characterized by negative proscriptions.[35] Boys are constantly warned *not* to be sissies, and *not* to engage in other feminine behavior. The literature on learning suggests that it is harder to learn from punishment than from rewards, because the desired behavior is not enunciated in the sanction and therefore remains obscure.[36] Thus some theorists have asserted that the socialization of boys is particularly conducive to anxiety. In Hartley's words,

the child is asked to do something which is not clearly defined for him, based

The little girl is . . . aware of the fact that she is being pushed, albeit gently, into a set of behaviors that are neither considered desirable nor rewarded by the society at large.

on reasons he cannot possibly appreciate, and enforced with threats, punishments, and anger by those who are close to him. . . . Anxiety frequently expresses itself in over-straining to be masculine, in virtual panic at being caught doing anything traditionally defined as feminine, and in hostility toward anything even hinting at "femininity," including females themselves.[37]

In contrast to the anxiety-producing sex-role learning of the boy, the socialization literature characterizes the young girl's experiences as easy. She is supposedly provided with more positive opportunities to learn appropriate role behavior through her frequent interaction with her mother* as well as the chance to try out her feminine role in her doll play.[38] This idyllic view of the learning process for girls appears naive to any woman who has been socialized in a middle-class family. It is clear that the sex-role socialization process is equally anxiety-producing for girls, although for somewhat different reasons. The girl is provided with a female model, and is afforded more opportunity to "play out" the "appropriate" behavior, but the role she is asked to play is clearly not a desirable one. As already noted, children understand the relative worth of the two sexes at quite young ages. The little girl is therefore aware of the fact that she is being pushed, albeit gently, into a set of behaviors that are neither considered desirable nor rewarded by the society at large. For example, she is told that it is feminine to play house: to wash dishes, set the table, dress her doll, vacuum the floor, and cook the dinner. In many middle-class homes these activities are delegated to paid domestics, or performed with obvious distaste. Why, then, should the little girl want to imitate these behaviors? I would hypothesize that the little girl becomes quite anxious about being encouraged to perform a series of behaviors that are held in low esteem. I would hypothesize further that she experiences considerable internal conflict when she realizes that her mother, a loved model, receives neither recognition nor satisfaction for such activities, and yet encourages them in her.

---

* This statement presumes a family in which the mother stays at home. It ignores the reality in most lower-class families and in an increasingly significant number of middle-class families, which is that the mothers of preschool children work and may thus have no more frequent contact with their children than working fathers do.

In addition to perceiving the low evaluation of feminine activities, many young girls find boys' activities intrinsically more enjoyable. For example, boys' toys allow a much broader range of activity as well as more active and adventure-some involvement. One study found that the average price of boys' toys was much greater than that of girls' toys for each age group.[39] More girls in Ward's sample preferred boys' toys than preferred girls' toys.[40] Respondents in Komarovsky's study expressed a similar interest in boys' toys—in chemistry sets, baseball gloves, and electric trains. "One of my biggest disappointments as a child," wrote a girl in Komarovsky's study, "happened one Christmas. I asked for a set of tools . . . only to find a sewing set."[41]

Since most growing children enjoy being active, running and playing outside, getting dirty if necessary, and being allowed to explore their own interests, it is not surprising that many girls prefer "boys' " activities, and resent being restricted to being "a sweet little girl." Komarovsky's students reported that they envied the freedom their brothers and other boys were allowed, and resented being con-strained to play with "girls' toys," to be sedentary, quiet, and neat in their play.[42]

In reviewing the socialization literature I was struck by the fact that the harsh restrictions placed on boys are often discussed, but those placed on girls are ignored. In fact, there is considerable support for the view that it is the socialization of girls that involves the greater restrictiveness, control, and protectiveness.[43] Boys may be punished more often, but girls' activities are likely to be so severely con-strained to begin with that they never have a chance to engage in punishable behav-ior. It is also possible that the kinds of sanctions used to socialize women may be more subtle—but no less severe: boys are spanked, but girls may be made to feel unworthy, deviant, guilty, or queer.[44] The following quotes from Komarovsky's study indicate the powerful sanctions and the resulting anguish experienced by girls whose desires conflict with the sex-role preferences of their parents:

> I started life as a little tomboy but as I grew older, Mother got worried about my unladylike ways. She removed my tops, marbles, football, and skates and tried to replace these with dolls, tea sets and sewing games. To interest me in dolls she collected dolls of different nations, dressed exquisitely in their native costumes. . . . When despite her efforts she caught me one day trying to climb a tree in the park she became thoroughly exasperated and called me a little "freak."
>
> Once I got very dirty playing and Mother told me that if I didn't learn to play quietly and keep myself neat no man would ever want to marry me.
>
> I was a member of a Brownie Troop when I was seven and we were to have a party one day to which each child was to bring her favorite toy. My favorite toy at that time was a set of tin soldiers. Grandmother was shocked and insisted that I would disgrace her by bringing such an unladylike toy. But

I refused to take a doll, with the result that I was forced to miss the party. But Grandmother succeeded in making me feel quite "queer" because I didn't like dolls.[45]

These quotes suggest the very real pressures that are brought to bear on the girl whose temperamental preferences do not conform to the feminine stereotype.

In summary, the socialization of boys and of girls may present different sets of difficulties, but difficulties and anxiety in the socialization process are common to both girls and boys. Typically, girls have more readily available role models, but they probably have less motivation to imitate those models because they (correctly) view the role as more confining and less rewarding than the masculine role. Boys may have less salient role models, and experience more frequent physical punishment, but they have more motivation to learn the masculine role because they (correctly) view it as more highly valued than the feminine role, allowing more exciting and interesting activities.

Consequently, socialization must be understood as an anxiety-producing process for both boys and girls because it requires them both to conform to rigid sex-role standards that are often in conflict with their individual temperaments or preferences. To the extent that we continue to define appropriate sex-role behavior for men and women as polar opposites, we will continue to push many individuals into unnatural molds.

The Learning Process: Reactions, Rewards and Punishment

Let us now briefly consider how specific characteristics are encouraged in children of each sex. According to Kagan, the typical child seeks the acceptance of parents and peers and wants to avoid their rejection. These motives predispose her or him to shun inappropriate activities, and to choose responses that are congruent with sex-role standards.[46]

Parents say that they want their daughters to be passive, nurturing, and dependent and their sons to be aggressive and independent. Therefore, most parents punish aggression in their daughters, and passivity and dependency in their sons.[47] For example, the little girl is allowed to cling to her mother's apron, but her brother is told that he can't be a "sissy" and must go off on his own. The dependency and affection-seeking responses seen as normal for both boys and girls in early childhood become defined as feminine in older children.[48] The result, as Bardwick has noted, is that girls are not separated from their parents as sources of support and nurturance, and they are therefore not forced to develop internal controls and an independent sense of self.[49] Instead, the self that they value is one that emanates from the appraisals of others. Consequently girls develop a greater need for the approval of others and a greater fear of rejection[50] than do boys.

Kagan has observed that our definition of femininity *requires* reactions from other people. The young girl cannot assess whether she is attractive, nurturing, or passive without continual interaction and feedback from others.[51] She is thus forced to be dependent upon people and to court their acceptance in order to obtain those experiences that help to establish sex-typed behaviors.[52]

In contrast, the boy is encouraged to be self-reliant. Many masculine sex-typed behaviors, especially those involving physical skills, can be developed alone. A boy is taught to stand up for himself and engage in certain behavior because he, as a person, feels that it is appropriate. In fact, men who stand by their individual principles despite opposition and the scorn of others often become cultural heroes.

According to Bronfenbrenner, different methods of child training are used for boys than for girls. Boys are subjected to more physical punishment, whereas psychological punishments, such as the threat of withdrawal of love, are more frequently used for girls.[53] Children trained with physical punishment have been shown typically to be more self-reliant and independent.[54] The other method of child training—the love-oriented or psychological method—usually produces children who are more obedient and dependent.[55] As girls are most often trained with psychological methods they are exposed to more affection and less punishment than boys. But they are also made more anxious about the withdrawal of love.

Thus, specific methods of child training and the cultural definition of femininity (which necessitates reliance on the approval of others) both encourage dependency in women. Kagan links the crucial significance of others—and their acceptance or rejection—to the finding that girls are often more conforming and more concerned about socially desirable behavior than boys.[56] Another interpretation of female conformity links it to doll-play training. David Matza has hypothesized that girls are taught to be more conforming and concerned with socially acceptable behavior because they are trained to act as socializing agents with their dolls. By talking to, and "training" their dolls to do the right thing, the girls themselves gain a vast amount of experience in articulating and sanctioning the cultural norms.[57]

Class, Racial and Other Variations in Sex-roles

Thus far we have suggested that girls are socialized to be dependent and conforming whereas boys learn to be independent and aggressive. It should be kept in mind, however, that the specific content of sex-role standards varies among social classes and racial and ethnic groups.[58] And even within these large subgroupings, various aspects of family composition affect both the content and the potency of sex-role socialization. It has been impossible in a paper of this length to consider all of these factors in each section, and we have instead focused on the most prevalent section of the population: the broadly defined white middle class. It is important, however, to consider briefly some of the variation in sex-role standards.

Differentiation between the sexes appears to be sharpest in lower-class families.[59] According to Kohn, lower-class mothers are more concerned with sex typing and encourage it more consistently than middle-class mothers.[60] Rabban found that children from working-class families differentiate sex roles at earlier ages and have more traditional sex-role standards than middle-class children.[61] He showed that working-class boys were aware of the appropriate sex-typed toy choices by age four or five; but middle-class boys were not aware of them until age six.[62] The class differences are even greater for girls than for boys. Middle-class girls not only showed later awareness of sex typing than working-class girls, but were less traditional in their sex-role concepts.[63]

Further specification of sex-role standards occurs along ethnic and racial lines. We all have the impression that Italians, Jews, Asian Americans, Chicanos, Irish, Polish, blacks, and Puerto Ricans have distinctive conceptions of appropriate behavior for men and women. With few exceptions, however,[64] ethnic and racial variation in sex-role standards has been ignored in the socialization literature.[65] Ladner's recent work on sex roles in the black community indicates the fruitfulness of further exploration of this area.[66] Ladner's research suggests that black girls are encouraged to be more independent than white girls—irrespective of social class. She notes that the realities of life in the ghetto, where aggressiveness and toughness are requisites for survival, make the ideal of a dependent passive middle-class housewife almost unimaginable.

Ladner found that young black girls most frequently identify with and aspire to the image of the "strong black woman"—the resourceful, hardworking, economically independent female.[67] The teenage girls she interviewed saw this woman as the one who kept the home intact—by caring for children, carrying out household tasks, and often supporting the family financially. Ladner's subjects described this role as a strong role, for they perceived a personal struggle for life's bare necessities and the possibility of never achieving a secure life. A variant of this model is the image of the educated and upwardly mobile middle-class woman, with an emphasis on acquiring skills that would allow the girl to escape the ghetto.[68]

Black girls' ambivalence about the role of the hard-working woman who lacks glamour and appeal gives rise to another image of womanhood, the image of the "carefree" woman. This woman enjoys life, is carefree, a bit loose, and unfaithful to husband or lovers. Ladner argues that girls have problems justifying this role as a legitimate one; nonetheless it is a popular image.[69]

But whichever role a black girl chooses, she expects to have a considerable degree of autonomy, strength, and independence. And these general characteristics are outgrowths of the kind of socialization the black girl undergoes. This socialization begins in the home, but the home is quite different from that in which the white girl is socialized. The black girl is more likely to live with a single parent or in a three-generational household than is the white girl. Her parents may be in the home less frequently, and from an early age she may be cared for by older siblings, other relatives, or neighbors. Consequently, socializing agents other than the parents are likely to influence her development. As Ladner points out, peer groups and various adult female relatives and acquaintances take on great significance as role models and reinforcers of appropriate sex-role behavior.[70]

Nevertheless, Ladner and others acknowledge the strong influence that the mother has on the adult role expectations of black girls. Kandel has reported that among the working-class high school girls she studied, black girls had a consistently closer and more intense relationships with their mothers in many aspects of family life than the white girls had.[71] And, not surprisingly, a greater proportion of black than white girls wanted to be like their mothers in most ways.[72]

In addition to class and race, another important variable in sex-role behavior is the family constellation—the number, spacing, and sex ratio of the children in the family. Brim, reanalyzing Helen Koch's data on two-child families, found that children with cross-sex siblings exhibited more traits of the opposite sex than did those with same-sex siblings.[73] This effect was particularly strong when opposite-sex siblings were older. Thus, boys with older sisters and girls with older brothers are more likely to exhibit the traits of the opposite sex. Brim's study points out the importance of siblings (and peers) in sex-role definitions.

CONTINUING SOCIALIZATION

Although boys and girls learn sex roles at an early age, the definition of appropriate sex-role behavior changes with age. The female sex role at age five is specific to the attributes of a five-year-old, and different from the female sex role at age twenty-five.[74] Sex-role socialization continues throughout the child's life as she or he learns age-specific sex-role behavior.

Thus far we have focused largely on socialization within the family. As the child matures and begins to participate in social relations outside the family, teachers, peers, and other socializing agents become more significant in defining and sanctioning appropriate sex-role behavior.

The Influence of the School

Once the child enters school, her or his experiences there assume great importance. The educational system has generally reinforced sex-role stereotypes. For girls, this implies a series of pressures to conform to traditional women's roles. One of the first messages communicated to girls at school is that they are less important than boys. For example, in a study of all third-grade readers published since 1930, Child, Potter and Levine found 73 percent of the stories were about male characters, while only 27 percent were about females.[75] Girls' impressions that they are not very important are reinforced by the portrait of the few women who do appear in the texts. Child *et al.* found girls and women shown as timid, inactive, unambitious, and uncreative. Females were not only the moral inferiors of males in these books (they are shown lazy twice as often as males), but their intellectual inferiors as well:

> The persons who supply information are predominantly male. . . . Males, in short, are being portrayed as the bearers of knowledge and wisdom, and as the persons through whom knowledge can come to the child.[76]

Although Child's work was published in 1960, more recent examinations of elementary school readers indicate that even the newest textbooks retain the same stereotypes.[77] Nor are these stereotypes restricted to readers. Weitzman and Rizzo have found that spelling, mathematics, science, and social studies textbooks purvey an equally limited image of women.[78] Rarely are women mentioned in important roles in history, as government leaders, or as great scientists. This study found the stereotyping to be most extreme in the science textbooks, where only 6 percent of the pictures included adult women. Weitzman and Rizzo hypothesize that the presentation of science as a prototypical masculine endeavor may help to explain how young girls are "cooled out" of science—and channeled into more traditional "feminine" fields.[79]

Guidance counselors and teachers also help to reinforce conformity to the traditional female role. They encourage the girl to take home economics and not to "bother" with physics or advanced algebra. They let her know that she doesn't have to worry about developing her mind. (After all, girls will be wives and mothers, not scientists and politicians.) The tracking system often ensures that she doesn't have to develop her body, either. Girls are excluded from the more rigorous sports activities and from school teams and athletic competition. The sex-stereotyped tracking system has traditionally served to keep girls from learning many skills that would be useful in the home (skills that boys learn in shop) and to keep boys blissfully ignorant of cooking and other domestic skills. Women who have achieved, who could be presented as exciting role models to the growing girls, are ignored. Instead of

> Although we have every reason to believe that
> girls' intellectual achievements do decline
> during high school, it should be noted that the
> typical measures of intelligence and scholastic
> achievement at this age have a strong male bias.

opening doors to new possibilities for both girls and boys, the educational system pushes them both through the same old ones.

Intellectual and Analytic Ability

Despite the discouragement they receive, girls consistently do better than boys in reading, mathematics, and speaking until they reach high school.[80] During high school, girls' performance in school and on ability tests begins to drop. Although we have every reason to believe that girls' intellectual achievements do decline during high school, it should be noted that the typical measures of intelligence and scholastic achievement at this age have a strong male bias. Milton's research illustrates this clearly.[81] He found that when adolescent or adult subjects were presented with problems involving primarily mathematical or geometric reasoning, the males consistently obtained higher scores than females. However, if the problem—involving identical logical steps and computations—dealt with feminine content such as cooking and gardening materials, the women scored much better than if the problem dealt with guns, money, or geometric designs.[82] Apparently the typical female believes that the ability to solve problems involving geometry, physics, logic, or arithmetic is a uniquely masculine skill, and her motivation even to attack such problems is low—for unusual excellence in solving them may be equated with loss of femininity.[83]

Since the erroneous finding that women are less analytic than men is often quoted, it deserves some attention here. It has been postulated that analytic thinking is developed by early independence training: how soon a child is encouraged to assume initiative, to take responsibility for herself or himself, and to solve problems alone rather than to rely on others for help or direction.[84] Each of these characteristics, as already reviewed, is encouraged in boys and discouraged in girls. When women are socialized to be dependent and passive, they are supposedly being trained to be more "field-dependent" or "contextual" and less analytic in their thinking.

In a devastating review of the scientific literature on what is usually called analytic ability, Sherman has pointed out that the term analytic ability is misleading.[85] It implies a general intellectual skill, whereas what is apparently being

measured in most of the studies is the much more limited ability of spatial perception—the ability to visualize objects out of their context.[86] Boys are generally
"field independent" in their spatial perception, whereas girls are more "contextual." Girls score lower on tests of spatial relationships, but in verbal perception—
certainly an area that is equally, if not more, important in analytic thinking—they
score higher than boys.[87]

It seems ironic that researchers have labeled spatial perception "analytic ability." One might speculate that if women had higher scores on spatial perception
and men had higher scores on verbal perception, the latter would have been called
analytic ability—for what the researchers have done is to seize upon one of the few
traits in which males score higher and label it analytic ability.

Actually, spatial ability has little to do with analytic thinking in any of the
usual meanings of that term.[88] Strictly analytic ability has to do with the structure
of arguments, the logical closure of propositions and syllogisms, and patterns of
logic. Since World War I (in the work of Whitehead and Russell), and certainly by
the 1930's with Wittgenstein's work in modern logic, we generally understand that
the underlying structure of logic (and thus of mathematics as well) is ultimately a
language pattern, resting on our understanding of linguistic connections. One might
therefore argue that people who are best in language and show the most facility in
language analysis and construction would potentially have the greatest ability in
analytic thinking—in the perception of logical connections and in the understanding of the strength or weakness of arguments.[89] However, this would lead us
to conclude that women have superior analytic ability, and the strong anti-female
bias pervading the literature on intelligence and analytic thinking precludes this
logical conclusion.

It is interesting to note that spatial ability appears to be learned, and is especially strong in individuals who have hobbies or jobs of a mechanical or technical
nature. Since the sex disparity in skills related to this ability widens greatly at age
seventeen, it is tempting to connect the superior performance of males with the
training they receive in high school classes in mechanical drawing, analytic geometry, and shop (as well as their spare-time activities with cars).

If both spatial and verbal ability can be learned, findings of sex differences in
these areas should direct us once again to the socialization process. As Professor
William Goode has noted, "Although we encourage the verbal fluency of girls and
their ease in writing and speaking, we are more likely to criticize boys for their
weakness in logic (we forgive girls that fault; it is an endearing weakness, it is cute).
In short, although males have a lower potential we strengthen their (boys') ability
in logic. We do not, in contrast, strengthen girls' ability in spatial connections or
facilitate girls' growth in the areas in which they appear most talented, i.e., the

grasp of language construction, logical progressions, syllogisms, and all the apparatus of clear analytic thinking."[90]

The Influence of Parents

It is not the school alone that channels girls and boys in different directions and emphasizes certain skills over others. Parents have different sex-related expectations for their male and female children as well. Aberle and Naegele have reported that middle-class fathers show concern over their sons' lack of aggressiveness, good school performance, responsibility, and initiative. In contrast, their concerns for their daughters focus on attractiveness and popularity. As the authors report:

> In all of these categories boys were the object of concern . . . ; satisfaction with girls seemed to focus strongly on their daughters being nice, sweet, pretty, affectionate, and well liked.[91]

With respect to future careers for their daughters, half of the fathers rejected the possibility out of hand. The other half said they would accept the possibility, but preferred and expected their daughters to marry—a career was unnecessary. Only two of the twenty fathers said they wanted their daughters to know how to earn a living.[92]

The Aberle and Naegele study was done in 1952 and might be out of date. However, more recent studies of parental influence on their children's educational aspirations indicate that girls are still less likely to receive parental support than boys. Sewell and Shah indicate that parents continue to encourage their sons more than their daughters.[93] Similarly, most of Bordua's male adolescents reported that their parents "stress college a lot," whereas most of the girls reported that their parents "don't care one way or the other."[94] Elder suggests that sex differences in parental stress on college have a more important effect than the intentions of the adolescents. He notes that lack of parental backing, especially financial support, may explain why fewer qualified girls than qualified boys enroll in college each year.[95]

Parental pressures on the working-class girl to follow a traditional female role are probably even greater than those on the middle-class girl.[96] The working-class girl who aspires to a career is seen as especially threatening because her occupational aspirations (if achieved) would result in her being more successful than her father and brothers, in addition to being "unfeminine." Her middle-class counterpart usually faces only the problem of being regarded as unfeminine.

In contrast to both lower-class and middle-class white girls, black girls do not fear being considered unfeminine because of educational or occupational aspira-

> . . . instead of being discouraged from aspiring
> to college or a career, the black girl may have
> her aspirations actively supported by her family.
> For her, it is reliance on men and marriage for
> future security that may be discouraged.

tions. Ladner reports no such conflict among her subjects. In fact, she suggests that within the black community so many women head households and must support their families that working is regarded as a perfectly appropriate female role. Thus high educational and occupational aspirations are viewed positively as means of bettering one's life situation.[97]

Kandel's recent study revealed that black mothers in female-headed families had higher educational aspirations for their daughters than for their sons. But what is really remarkable is that in intact black families, there was no difference in aspirations for boys and girls as there was in white families.[98] Thus, instead of being discouraged from aspiring to college or a career, the black girl may have her aspirations actively supported by her family. For her, it is reliance on men and marriage for future security that may be discouraged. Ladner has indicated that young black girls want to marry a man who fits the model of protector, supporter, and companion. But with increasing age they come to believe that very few men can fulfill these roles, and they become more ambivalent toward men. (Some girls had firmly established the view that men are "no good" by the time they were eight years old.)[99] Thus, black girls come to rely on their own achievements. As a student of mine wrote in an autobiographical socialization paper, "Black girls don't dream of being rescued by "Prince Charming." They know that "Snow White" is White, and that if they want to get something or somewhere, they are going to have to get it themselves."[100]

White parents not only discourage intellectual interests and careers for their daughters, but also restrict their daughters' opportunities for independent action more than their sons'. Boys are allowed more freedom to play away from home, to return home later, and to choose their own activities.[101] As one of Komarovsky's students complained:

> My brother is 15, three years younger than I am. When he goes out after supper, mother calls out, "Where are you going, Jimmy?" "Oh, out." Could I get away with that? Not on your life. I would have to tell them in detail where to, with whom, and if I am half an hour late, mother sits on the edge of the living room sofa watching the door.[102]

Komarovsky concludes that the "risk of this kind of traditional upbringing resides in the failure to develop in the girl independence, inner resources, and that degree of self-assertion which life will demand of her."[103] Thus, both the school and her parents impede the growing girl's social and intellectual independence.

The Influence of Peers

This equation of intellectual success with a loss of femininity appears to be common among high school peer groups. According to the Kennistons, high school girls feel they must hide their intelligence if they are to be popular with boys.

> Girls soon learn that "popularity"—that peculiar American ecstasy from which all other goods flow—accrues to her who hides any intelligence she may have, flatters the often precarious maleness of adolescent boys, and devotes herself to activities that can in no way challenge their sex. The popular girls in high schools are seldom the brilliant girls; or if they are, it is only because they are so brilliant they can hide their brilliance from less brilliant boys. . . . Most American public schools (like many private schools) make a girl with passionate intellectual interests feel a strong sense of her own inadequacy as a woman, feel guilty about these "masculine" outlooks, perhaps even wonder about her own normality.[104]

In light of these cultural pressures on a girl not to appear too smart, and certainly not to surpass boys in anything, Freeman finds it unsurprising that girls believe the development of their minds will have only negative results.[105]

Thus, school, parents, and peers make it clear to girls that the only criterion for feminine success is attractiveness to men. Pierce found high achievement motivation for women related to success in marriage, not, as for males, to academic success.[106] In Pierce's view, girls see that to achieve in life they need to excel in non-academic ways, i.e., in attaining beauty in person and dress, in finding a desirable social status, and in marrying the right man.[107]

The mass media reinforce this perception and provide explicit instruction on attaining these goals. *Seventeen, Glamour,* and *Mademoiselle* provide endless pages of fashion, make-up, and dating advice. The girl learns that she must know how to attract, talk to, kiss, keep (or get rid of) a boy, depending on the circumstances. The magazines suggest which eye shadow, hair spray, lipstick, and blusher to use to accomplish these all-important ends. While fashion magazines tell her how to dress and use cosmetics, movies instruct on how to undress—and on the explicit use of sexuality. "On the whole, mass media and popular fiction continue to portray career women as mannish, loose, or both; and the happy ending for working girls still involves abandoning work, marrying, and having many children—and there the story ends."[108]

In sum, the well-socialized American girl learns three clear lessons: one concerning her personality, a second concerning her capability, and a third concerning her future role. With regard to her personality, she "knows" that to be truly feminine she will be sweet, expressive, not too intelligent, nurturing, cooperative, pretty, and fairly passive. With regard to her capability, she "knows" she will always be less capable and less important than most men. With regard to her future, she "knows" she will be a wife and mother. If she is a successful woman, she will acquire this status soon. Although Ladner reports a similar emphasis on attractiveness, sexuality, and "managing" men among black girls, the well-socialized black girls learns somewhat different lessons about her personality, capacity, and future role.[109] She is likely to view herself as strong and independent, at least as capable as black men, and to see her future as a mother with major responsibility for her family's support.

Socialization Pressures on the College Girl

For the college-oriented girl the process just described is probably delayed four years—it occurs during the last two years of college, rather than during high school. Middle-class college-oriented girls may be allowed considerable latitude during adolescence—by the educational system, their parents, and their peers. However, many of the same pressures are exerted on them in college. For example, 40 percent of the women in Komarovsky's 1946 research at Barnard College admitted they played dumb on dates.[110] Many of the students in her sample felt they were caught between the traditional feminine role and the more modern role—with inconsistent expectations pressuring them simultaneously. For example:

> Uncle John telephones every Sunday morning. His first question is: "Did you go out last night?" He would think me a grind if I were to stay home Saturday night to finish a term paper. My father expects me to get an "A" in every subject and is disappointed by a "B". He says I have plenty of time for social life. Mother says, "That 'A' in Philosophy is very nice, dear, but please don't become so deep that no man will be good enough for you."[111]

Komarovsky's study was done a quarter of a century ago, and one might speculate that women in college today are not being subjected to the same severe pressures. Although their parents may still encourage them to see marriage as the ultimate goal, it is possible that peer definitions of feminine roles are more liberal. The ideology of the current women's liberation movement certainly supports independent achievement for women.

Since I know of no study that has dealt with this possibility in a systematic fashion, I will cite some personal data from an experiment on changing roles to indicate both the continued pressure and some changes among college students in the United States today.[112] After a discussion of the ideology and goals of the women's liberation movement in my 1972 undergraduate course on the family, I asked the students to try out the feminist ideals we had discussed in a heterosexual situation of at least one hour's duration.

The most common response encountered by those who completed the assignment, reported by 27 percent of the female students, was a rejection of the feminist behavior by their male companion. In some cases the women were asked to change their behavior: "So after I told him why I was doing it, he said, 'Stop it, please, I don't want you to be a member of women's liberation.' " In other cases, the man treated the woman's ideas or actions as nonserious, tossing them off as a joke or "putting her down as crazy":

> Then I bought two pretzels and gave my boyfriend one. By this time he's had enough. "What's wrong with you?" he said. "Are you crazy?"
> I told him I thought being a housewife and a mother was a bore and a lot of shitwork. Well, this really got to him and he said I was crazy. . . . Just then his roommate came in and he related my "weird" ideas to him and they both had a good laugh.
> He said it wasn't a man's job to do the housework . . . and that any woman who had decided that she didn't want children was crazy.

In several instances, the friends and boyfriends were so angered or upset by the women's behavior that they refused to deal with it. They tried to terminate the interaction by telling the women they would never attract a man if they continued to act in such an unfeminine manner:

> Bill said I'd have to put an ad in the paper to find a man who'd put up with that.
> He told me that if I wanted a man I should start acting like a woman because any man would ball me but if I wanted a husband I'd better do the right things.

In contrast to these emotional reactions, some of the men were more intellectual about their rejection, trying to answer the feminist arguments "rationally" by arguing that motherhood was fulfilling, or that a woman's career was too disruptive to a marriage:

> He said that if I went to law school I'd be challenging him at his own career and would be sacrificing our home life for a materialistic job. . . . He felt women with careers neglected their husbands and children and that they were basically selfish. . . . When I confessed that I was doing a class assignment he

seemed relieved but later continued to discuss the disadvantages of a career for a woman.

He thought a woman should have a career or a family and that most housewives were fulfilled by their role.

The second most common reaction (17 percent) was that boyfriends or dates were merely surprised and uncomfortable:

(After the girl stopped over at the apartment of a man she had just met): He sat and talked to me, but it was clear that he was uncomfortable and just couldn't figure out what was happening.

All of this made him feel uncomfortable, especially when I said this other guy had a good ass.

The third most common response, reported by 12 percent of the students, was subtle resistance by dates and male friends. Although not explicitly challenging the women, the men attempted to regain control of the situation:

He asked how much the dinner cost and told me how much to leave for the tip.

He asked if he could drive instead because he didn't like it to look as if he was being chauffeured around.

Each time I did something out of the ordinary, he countered it with a comment to try to make me fit into a more ladylike role (by telling me that my voice was soft and pure, or that I could model for *Vogue*).

I was sitting on the chair so he came over and handed me the broom, asking me to hold it, but really trying to put me into my proper role.

Most of these men denied trying to regain the dominant position in the relationship, contending that they were "just trying to be helpful."

Some of the women (8 percent) reported that their dates or boyfriends did not seem to resent their behavior, but other friends and observers did:

The waiter seemed to feel sympathy for my boyfriend for being with such an assertive, pushy woman, while the cashier sided with me, assuming that by paying my share, I was being taken advantage of. She said sympathetically, "I've got one at home just like him."

They couldn't understand how Jerry could let me act so aggressively.

These quotes indicate the extent to which third parties observe and try to reinforce conventional behavior, even when the couple is content with new roles.

In contrast to the reactions just described, some 10 percent reported that the males they chose reacted positively to their behavior:

He said he dug me in that particular role and that I should come across like that more often.

. . . although it appears that a majority of . . . women university students are still being constrained by their male peers to conform to more traditional standards of feminine behavior, change is also evident.

> He said he admired intelligent women who he could really talk to . . . he didn't enjoy sissies and he appreciated treating me as an equal.
> He confessed that he looked for more companionship from women, rather than pure femininity. He said, "I'd rather have someone who would dig building a cabinet with me instead of worrying about ironing my shirts."

It is interesting to note than 27 percent of the women in the class found they could not carry out the assignment because acting liberated was so normal for them that none of their friends noticed any difference in their conversation or actions.

> Since this is the way I always act, no one reacted to anything I did.
> I rarely come into contact with people (especially men) who aren't in a liberated circle of people, and when I do, they don't have much to say.

If we combine this 27 percent of the students with the 10 percent who received positive reactions and the 8 percent who were hassled only by outsiders, we find that for almost half of the women in the group, there is positive peer support for rejecting the traditional feminine role. Thus, although it appears that a majority of these women university students are still being constrained by their male peers to conform to more traditional standards of feminine behavior, change is also evident. Those women who said they typically act in accordance with the ideals of the women's movement report strong support from their network of close friends.

The class assignment did have an interesting side effect: one-third of the men in the class who did the assignment reported that the experience of articulating the arguments for women's liberation had a positive effect on them:

> I think the most significant reaction was within myself. After discussing all the points that were made in class, I became more of a feminist. I think I convinced her about the movement, but I also convinced myself.

When I read the results of this study to my class, several students who had reported they received support for their actions said that this support had definite limits. Many had chosen "low-risk" situations for the class assignment—situations in which neither the man nor the woman had a great stake in the relationship and the woman's behavior was not of critical importance. Both these women and those who had characterized themselves as "already liberated" felt that when they were seriously involved with a man there were more pressures on them to play a more "feminine" role.

Another reaction among the liberated women in the class was that the degree of peer support for their new role had been exaggerated. They reported that although they themselves felt comfortable in the role, there were still considerable problems involved in establishing relationships with men. Several felt they were no longer so attractive to men, or that most men did not know how to handle the new women—or preferred not to. As one woman reported, "I get a lot of support from both men and women, but most men say something like 'even though I'm really supportive of what you are, I just can't handle it . . . I'm still hung up on having a more feminine woman who will support me.' " Thus, although peers may appreciate the independence and intellectual companionship of the liberated woman, they may let her know they do not consider her a real woman.

It would seem, then, that peer support for the new feminist role may derive primarily from other women, and may be weaker among male peers than the original results suggested. This final quotation seems to express the situation of a majority of those who reported that they already embodied the ideals of the women's liberation movement:

> It's wonderful to have a group of women who really care about you and who are always supporting your independence. On the other hand, many of my relationships with men remain frustrating. They are more open and real than they ever were before—but they are also so much more complicated. I'm committed to "the new me" but I know it's going to involve a struggle all the way. I guess I still want a man somewhere in my life.

Other recent research on college women suggests that the pressures for more traditional roles may grow especially severe during their junior and senior years in college. Horner's interviews with Radcliffe students indicate that parents and boyfriends exert great pressure on them to "return" to traditional feminine roles during their last two years in college, and generally at this time their intellectual performance drops.[113] Because of such continued pressures on college women, Rossi contends they are not seriously oriented toward careers—even when they are being trained for future occupations.[114] She reports that college women study and prepare for a job "only in case I have to work."* Thus the middle-class girl, unlike her future-oriented brother, often fails to prepare herself for the future. But even if

---

* Of course this lack of preparation for a future career does not prevent women from working. Most women will both have families and work. It does, however, prevent planning and training for a career instead of a job. And it is likely they will believe their future job status is due to inherent inferiority rather than this socialized failure to plan.

she does prepare for a relatively high-status occupation (in relation to "women's work") such as social work, teaching, librarianship, or nursing, she may be hampered by her "job" rather than "career" orientation. Some sociologists have suggested that this "job orientation" results from women's valuing devotion to their families above commitment to work. And they argue that this ordering of priorities seriously hampers women's advancement within professions.[115]

Perhaps part of the reason for the lack of future or career orientation on the part of college women is their own sense of inferiority. After being told that women are less intelligent and less worthy than men for so many years, many believe it and do not take themselves seriously. This is illustrated in the following quotation from Howe about the internalized inferiority among the women in her writing seminar:

> What I learned from listening to my women students was that they consistently considered women writers (and hence themselves) inferior to men. . . . Why should naturally inferior writers attempt anything ambitious? . . . Their comments ranged from "I don't have any ideas" to "I can't write anything really interesting" to "I used to have ideas and imagination but I don't any more."[116]

Goldberg finds this sense of female inferiority generalized to all women. His research involved giving college women a set of six articles, three purportedly by men and three purportedly by women, and asking them to rate the scholarship and professional competence of the authors.[117] Although each girl received an identical set of articles, the names of the authors were varied. The article bearing the author's name "*John* T. McKay" in half the sets was attributed to "*Joan* T. McKay" in the other half.

> The girls consistently found an article more valuable—and its author more competent—when the article bore a male name. Though the articles were exactly the same, the girls felt that those written by John McKay were more impressive, and reflected more glory on their authors, than did the mediocre offerings of the Joan McKays.[118]

The Goldberg study indicates that women are not taken seriously even by women. It implies that women's achievements, even when equal to men's will not be equally recognized.

Another reason for the lack of career orientation among college women may be the images they have of the career woman. Horner has shown that among women, a successful career is associated with strong fears of social rejection, doubts about femininity or normality, and guilt or despair over success.[119] She concludes that most women, consciously or unconsciously, equate intellectual achievement with loss of femininity:

> A bright woman is caught in a double bind. In testing and other achievement-oriented situations she worries not only about failure, but also about success. If she fails, she is not living up to her own standards of performance; if she succeeds, she is not living up to societal expectations about the female role. Men in our society do not experience this kind of ambivalence, because they are not only permitted but actively encouraged to do well. For women, then, the desire to achieve is often contaminated by what I call the *motive to avoid success.* I define it as the fear that success in competitive situations will lead to negative consequences, such as unpopularity and loss of femininity.[120]

Horner's findings are discouraging[121] because they indicate the extent to which even the brightest women seem to have internalized the cultural definition of femininity as incompatible with career success.*

In sum, the rewards for women seem to be "stacked" on the side of internalizing the culturally defined feminine role. It hardly seems realistic to speak of the "choice" between marriage and a career. The word "choice" implies that there are alternatives, but most American women have little contact with women who have chosen careers, or have knowledge of the career option. As Professors Sandra and Daryl Bem of Stanford University have noted, "We overlook the fact that the society has spent twenty years carefully marking the woman's ballot for her, and has nothing to lose in that twenty-first year by pretending to let her cast it for the alternative of her choice. Society has controlled not her alternatives but her motivation to choose any but one of those alternatives."[122]

WOMEN'S ACHIEVEMENT

Although this discussion has emphasized formal academic and occupational achievement throughout, it should be clear that there are other areas in which both men and women are motivated to achieve.** For example, some people make lifetime careers of philanthropy or unpaid volunteer work. Some devote their energies to

---

* The other side of this coin is the identification of career success with masculinity. There is no doubt that many men suffer from the pressure exerted on them to "prove" their masculinity by occupational success. Those men who deviate from the culturally defined appropriate sex-role behavior (and fail at work) are stigmatized in the same way as women who succeed.

** I am indebted to Sheryl Ruzeck for suggesting this to me.

civic affairs. Others aspire to positions of responsibility in religious or recreational organizations. Still others undertake technical or creative pursuits such as photography, rock collecting, or wine-making. And all of these unpaid endeavors may give participants a sense of achievement and success.

Nonetheless, there are limits to the status rewards these activities can bring. For in American society, status is closely related to monetary rewards, which generally come from occupational achievements. And it is clear that men, not women, are socialized to adopt the personality characteristics that are related to success in the more prestigious and financially lucrative occupations.

With the relentless conditioning we have just reviewed, it seems remarkable that some girls do not get the message that they are supposed to be less intelligent and less successful until high school,* and that some escape through their college years. Further, in spite of the overwhelming pressures to conform to the traditional feminine role, many women do aspire to intellectual and professional success, and a significant number of them attain it. How can we account for these women? Are they deviants, or have we presented an oversocialized portrait of women in this essay?

Women Achievers As Deviant

In the statistical sense, women who have attained professional success are deviants; but it is important to realize what a significant minority they are. In an effort to summarize a large body of literature I have focused on the average woman. This average woman has been portrayed as more dependent and less achievement-oriented than the average man. However, this does not mean that all women are dependent, or that all women accept the traditional feminine role. It is clear that there is a great deal of variation among individuals of both sexes with regard to personality characteristics, intelligence, and achievement motivation. In fact, the range of differences within each sex is much greater than the differences between the average members of opposite sexes.[123]

After a review of the literature on sex differences, Jo Freeman observes that what is deemed typical of one sex or the other is based on the average performance of two-thirds of the subjects.[124] But this takes no account of the behavior of the remaining one-third of each sex. Thus, when we speak of averages we obscure the great range of variation within each sex—and leave one-third of the relevant population unaccounted for.

---

* This question was raised by Naomi Weisstein in "Kinder, Kuche, Kirche as Scientific Law," *Motive,* April 1969.

In this section we shall focus on this "deviant" group, composed of female doctors, lawyers, engineers, architects, professors, scientists, corporation executives, writers, etc., and ask what has been different about the socialization of these women. The following discussion will, of necessity, be speculative, because there has not yet been a systematic study of the socialization of high-achieving women. It is meant to be suggestive.

Family Background

One might speculate on various family situations that would encourage a girl's occupational aspirations: being the only child of a successful businessman who has been encouraged to take over her family's business; being the daughter of a female doctor who is encouraged to assist in her mother's office; or being the oldest sibling in a large family for whom leadership and authority are natural. Achievement motivation and occupational aspirations may arise from a great variety of sources that are beyond the limited scope of this paper to explore.

Several studies have indicated that the role of the mother is especially important. If the mother works, or has worked, the girl is more likely to see a career as "natural" for a woman. In Hartley's study of girls between the ages of eight and eleven, the girls' future plans were significantly related to their mothers' work roles. When asked what they expected to do when they grew up, significantly more daughters of nonworking mothers gave "housewife" as their primary choice and more daughters of working mothers mentioned nontraditional professional areas (such as medicine, law, creative work) as their vocational choices. Also, daughters of working mothers were more likely to plan to continue working after marrying and having children.[125]

Traditional identification theory assumed that the same-sex parent was the more crucial in determining the sex-role identity of the child. This theory, which grew out of Freudian theory, asserted that the child must, in order to identify properly as a member of his or her sex, have a same-sex model to imitate.[126] Thus by imitating the father the boy would learn and internalize masculine behavior. Similarly, it was assumed, the girl would learn how to be feminine by imitating the behavior of her mother. According to this theory, the child internalizes not only the particular behavior observed, but a complex integrated pattern of sex-related behavior.[127] I would suggest, instead, that a large amount of sex-role behavior can be learned only through interaction with the opposite sex. This is especially true of the "feminine role," which is often defined in terms of relationships with others. It is thus possible that the father teaches the girl how to be feminine as much as the mother does.

Identification theory may be challenged on another ground as well. Identification theorists have assumed that it is necessary for adult rőle-models to have clearly differentiated sex roles, so that the child can clearly distinguish what is masculine and what is feminine behavior.[128] However, Slater has indicated that adult role-models who exhibit stereotyped sex-role identification may impede, rather than facilitate, the child's sex-role identification. Children may find it easier to identify with less differentiated and less stereotyped parental role models.[129] It is more likely that they will internalize parental values when nurturance (the typically feminine role) and discipline (the typically masculine role) come from the same source.

Both of these challenges to traditional identification theory indicate that the father may play as important a role as the mother in a daughter's socialization. In fact, Heilbrun has shown that highly successful girls tend to have an especially close relationship with, and identify with, a masculine father.[130]

Although there are no direct data, we might speculate that an especially strong stimulus to achievement motivation in women would be a strong father-daughter relationship in which the father encourages his daughter and makes his love and approval dependent on her performance. Most fathers show unconditional support for their daughters, whether or not they achieve, because most fathers do not consider a woman's achievements crucial to her success in life.

The importance of this father-daughter tie has been noted by Goode, who has observed that a large number of successful women were their fathers' "favorite" child.[131] This can be a great spur to "masculine" achievement, especially when there are no sons in the family and the father supports and assists his daughter's aspirations.

This hypothesis has its parallel in research on male achievement motivation. McClelland's work has shown that a strong mother-son relationship (in which the mother bases conditional love on her son's success) is most conducive to masculine achievement motivation.[132] And Strodbeck has shown that the typical Italian mother does not stimulate high achievement motivation in her son because she makes it clear that she will love him irrespective of his performance.[133] In contrast, the typical Jewish mother is concerned about her child's performance and continually prods him on by threatening to withdraw love if he doesn't succeed.[134]

The Oversocialized Portrait of Women

Thus far, we have considered high occupational achievement and achievement motivation in women as if it were deviant, and therefore required a special explanation. However, an alternative view would suggest that, in fact, most women *are* motivated to achieve. This would lead one to conclude that the socialization literature presents an oversocialized view of women. It is clear that the socialization literature reviewed in this paper exaggerates in two ways:

a. Women are assumed to internalize the feminine role *completely*.
b. The pressures on women are presented as *unidimensional*.

Let us examine each of these.

The socialization literature has probably overestimated the effectiveness of the socialization process. It is assumed that women have been successfully socialized and have internalized the feminine role. However, if this were so, women would feel fulfilled within that role, whereas in fact almost every study of women's fulfillment has shown that those who conform most closely to the feminine role are least fulfilled.[135] Both Dr. Jessie Bernard[136] and Betty Friedan,[137] after reviewing the literature on feminine happiness and fulfillment, conclude that most women are not content with their traditional role.

In addition to exaggerating the effectiveness of the socialization process for women, the literature incorrectly treats the pressures on women as unidimensional. Women are viewed as being consistently rewarded for feminine behavior and consistently punished for or discouraged from unfeminine behavior. Social learning theory, which is the basis for the bulk of the material presented in this paper, holds that sex-appropriate responses are consistently rewarded and reinforced—and sex-inappropriate behavior consistently discouraged or punished—in the young girl until she comes to learn and internalize the feminine role.[138]

Without denying the pressures on women to conform to the feminine role, one can see that women are socialized in an ambivalent fashion. At the same time that girls are rewarded for typical feminine behavior, they are also rewarded for some types of "masculine" behavior. This is because what is labeled masculine behavior is generally highly regarded and rewarded in our society. The girl who excels in school, wins the tennis championship, or fixes a broken car receives approval for each of these activities. Although she may be regarded as too aggressive or masculine, she is also admired for her accomplishments.

Thus, the feminine role is not consistently reinforced. Women are rewarded for *both* masculine and feminine behavior. Heilbrun's study of successful adolescent women indicates that they are both instrumental and expressive; that is, they exhibit the goal-directedness of typically successful males as well as the interpersonal sensitivity of typically successful females.[139]

It is reasonable to assume that ambivalent socialization results in a very different kind of learning than consistent rewards or punishment. Skinner and his associates have called this pattern intermittent, or random, reinforcement. They argue that behavior patterns learned in this manner are the most difficult to unlearn.[140] Skinnerian learning theory would thus lead us to predict that the socialization of women to succeed in areas that are typically designated as masculine may be even stronger than that of men. To assert that women have been socialized to achieve is not to deny that considerable anxiety may accompany this motive when women attempt to achieve outside of traditional female roles. As already noted, Horner's research indicates that although women want to succeed, they are afraid of the implications of success for a woman.[141]

If we are correct in asserting that the socialization of women into the traditional female roles is neither totally effective nor totally consistent, then one might legitimately ask why there are not more visible examples of high-achieving women. If, as we have asserted, many women are actually motivated to high achievement, why has the proportion of women in the professions and in other high-status occupations remained so low?

There are two possible answers to this question. The first is that women's achievement is channeled in a different direction. As noted above, Pierce has shown that women with high achievement motivation are oriented toward finding high-status husbands.[142] Press and Whitney and Lipman-Blumen have also suggested that women see success in terms of heterosexual relationships, and that they attain vicarious gratification from the achievements of their husbands and sons.[143] Press and Whitney suggest that women with high achievement motivation pick males who will succeed, so that they may experience success vicariously.[144]

But even though women have been socialized to regard personal occupational success as difficult or undesirable, it seems unlikely that many women with high achievement motivation would be content with vicarious achievement alone. Unless they are allowed to play a significant role in their husbands' or sons' careers, they are likely to channel their energies elsewhere. It is obvious that the energies of many capable women are channeled into volunteer work or into other nonremunerative pursuits. Other high-achievement-oriented women may be found in frustrating jobs that are much below their capability, or in positions that involve power and capabilities that are neither recognized nor rewarded (with either money or position) by their employers.

A second answer to the question of why there are not more visible examples of high-achieving women lies in the structural opportunities available to women in this society. When women are denied real opportunities for advancement and are discriminated against at every stage of the process leading to a professional position, it is not surprising that they have not "made it." Thus, the answer to this question probably lies not so much in the socialization of women as in the structural opportunities available to them in our society.

As long as women are denied real career options, it is a realistic decision not to aim for a career. As long as they lack role models of successful career women, are denied structural supports to aid a career, are told they are neurotic or unfeminine if they are dedicated to an occupation, we cannot expect young women to take the career option seriously. The only way to change their (accurate) perceptions about future options is to create *real options* for them.

NOTES

1. The work on this paper was partially supported by the Institute of Governmental Affairs, University of California at Davis.
2. Margaret Mead, *Sex and Temperament in Three Primitive Societies* (New York: Morrow, 1939; Mentor Books, 1950).
3. Milton Spiro, *Children of the Kibbutz* (New York: Schoken Books, 1960).
4. John Money, *Sex Research: New Developments* (New York: Holt, Rinehart, 1965); and "Sex Hormones and Other Variables in Human Eroticism," in William C. Young (ed.), *Sex and Internal Secretions,* 3rd ed., vol. 2 (Baltimore: Williams and Wilkins, 1961), pp. 1383-1400; John L. Hampson and Joan Hampson, "The Ontogenesis of Sexual Behavior in Man," in *ibid.,* pp. 1401-32.
5. Mirra Komarovsky, *Women in the Modern World* (Boston: Little, Brown, 1953).
6. Howard A. Moss, "Sex, Age, and State as Determinants of Mother-Infant Interaction," *Merrill-Palmer Quarterly,* 13, 1 (1967): 19-36, 28, 30.
7. *Ibid.*
8. Susan Goldberg and Michael Lewis, "Play Behavior in the Year-Old Infant; Early Sex Differences," *Child Development,* 40 (1969): 21-30.
9. Jerome Kagan and Michael Lewis, "Studies of Attention in the Human Infant," *Merrill-Palmer Quarterly,* 2 (1965): 95–127.
10. Goldberg and Lewis, p. 29.
11. Meyer L. Rabban, "Sex Role Identification in Young Children in Two Diverse Social Groups," *Genetic Psychological Monographs,* vol. 42 (1950), pp. 81-158.
12. Evelyn Wiltshire Goodenough, "Interests in Persons as an Aspect of Sex Differences in the Early Years," *Genetic Psychological Monographs,* vol. 55 (1957), p. 312.
13. Lenore J. Weitzman, Deborah Eifler, Elizabeth Hokada, and Catherine Ross, "Sex Role Socialization in Picture Books for Pre-School Children," *American Journal of Sociology,* May, 1972.
14. *Ibid.* Parts of this quote were paraphrased from the original.
15. Jo Ann Gardner, "*Sesame Street* and Sex Role Stereotypes," in *Women,* 1, 3 (Spring 1970).
16. Ruth E. Hartley, "Sex-Role Pressures and the Socialization of the Male Child," *Psychological Reports,* 5 (1959): 457-68, 461.
17. *Ibid.*
18. *Ibid.*
19. *Ibid.*
20. Rabban, p. 145.
21. M. S. Simpson, "Parent Preferences of Young Children," *Contributing Education,* No. 682 (New York: Teachers College, Columbia Univ., 1935).

22. Daniel G. Brown, "Sex-Role Preference in Young Children," *Psychological Monographs,* 70, 14 (1956): 1-19.
23. *Ibid.*
24. Willard W. Hartup and Elsie A. Zook, "Sex-Role Preferences in Three- and Four-Year-Old Children," *Journal of Consulting Psychology,* 24 (Dec. 1960): 420-26.
25. Willard W. Hartup, "Some Correlates of Parental Imitation in Young Children," *Child Development,* 33 (1962): 85-96.
26. Alex Inkeles, "Society, Social Structure, and Child Socialization," in John Clausen, ed., *Socialization and Society* (Boston: Little, Brown, 1968): 122-23.
27. Hartley, *op. cit.*
28. Brown, *op. cit.*
29. S. Smith, "Age and Sex Differences in Children's Opinion Concerning Sex Differences," *Journal of Genetic Psychology,* 54 (1939): 17-25.
30. *Ibid.*
31. David B. Lynn, *Parental and Sex Role Identification: A Theoretical Formulation* (Berkeley, Calif.: McCrutchan Publishing Corp., 1969), p. 24.
32. *Ibid.*
33. David B. Lynn, "A Note on Sex Differences in the Development of Masculine and Feminine Identification," *Psychological Review,* 66, 2 (1959): 126-35.
34. Hartley, p. 458.
35. *Ibid.*
36. For an excellent review of the learning literatures and the effects of punishment versus rewards, see William J. Goode, "The Uses of Dispraise," in *The Celebration of Heroes* (forthcoming 1974).
37. Hartley, *op. cit.*
38. Ruth E. Hartley, "A Developmental View of Female Sex-Role Definition and Identification," *Merrill-Palmer Quarterly,* 10, 1 (Jan. 1964): 3-17, 4.
39. Janet Lever, "Christmas Toys for Girls and Boys," report to Sociology 62a, Sociological Perspectives on Women, Sociology Department, Fall 1970, Yale University, Professor L. Weitzman.
40. William D. Ward, "Variance of Sex-Role Preference Among Boys and Girls," *Psychological Reports,* 23, 2 (1968): 467-70.
41. Komarovsky, *op. cit.*
42. *Ibid.*
43. Pauline R. Sears, Eleanor Maccoby, and Harry Levin, *Patterns of Child Rearing* (Evanston, Ill.: Row, Peterson, 1957).
44. Urie Bronfenbrenner, "Some Familial Antecedents of Responsibility and Leadership in Adolescents," in Luigi Petrullo, and Bernard M. Bass, eds., *Leadership and Interpersonal Behavior* (New York: Holt, Rinehart, 1961).
45. Komarovsky, p. 55.
46. Jerome Kagan, "Acquisition and Significance of Sex Typing and Sex-Role Identity," in Martin Leon Hoffman and Lois Wladis Hoffman, eds., *Review of Child Development Research* (New York: Russell Sage Foundation, 1964), pp. 137-67, 151.
47. David Aberle and Kasper Naegele, "Middle Class Father's Occupational Role and Attitudes Toward Children," in Norman W. Bell and Ezra F. Vogel, eds., *The Family,* rev. ed. (New York: Free Press, 1968): Melvin L. Kohn, "Social Class and Parental Values," *American*

Journal of Sociology, 64 (Jan. 1959): pp. 337-51; Sears, Maccoby, and Levin, *op. cit.*; Paul H. Mussen, John U. Conger, and Jerome Kagan, *Child Development and Personality,* 2nd ed., (New York: Harper and Row, 1963).

48. Judith M. Bardwick, Elizabeth Douvan, Matina S. Horner, and David Gutmann, *Feminine Personality and Conflict,* (Belmont, Calif.: Brooks/Cole Publishing Co., 1970), p. 4.
49. *Ibid.*
50. *Ibid.*
51. Kagan 1964, p. 151.
52. *Ibid.*
53. Urie Bronfenbrenner, "The Changing American Child: A Speculative Analysis," *Merrill-Palmer Quarterly,* 7 (Apr. 1961): 73-83, 9.
54. Stanley Schachter, *The Psychology of Affiliation* (Stanford, Calif.: Stanford University Press, 1959; Bronfenbrenner 1961).
55. Bronfenbrenner, 1961.
56. Kagan,1964, p. 151.
57. Personal conversation, Dec. 1971.
58. For a more extensive review of the literature, see William J. Goode, Elizabeth Hopkins, and Helen M. McClure, *Social Systems and Family Structures* (Indianapolis: Bobbs-Merrill, 1971).
59. *Ibid.*
60. Melvin L. Kohn, "Social Class and Parental Values," *American Journal of Sociology,* 64 (Jan. 1959): 337-51.
61. Rabban 1950.
62. *Ibid.*
63. *Ibid.*
64. See, for example, Herbert Gans, "The Urban Villagers" (New York: Free Press, 1962).
65. Although there has been no systematic study of racial differences in parental treatment of young children, we do know that black mothers, irrespective of class, have much less exposure to child-rearing experts. See, for example, Zena Smith Blau, "Exposure to Child-Rearing Experts: A Structural Interpretation of Class-Color Differences," *American Journal of Sociology,* 69 (May 1964): 596-608.
66. Joyce A. Ladner, *Tomorrow's Tomorrow: The Black Woman* (Garden City, N.Y.: Doubleday, 1971), especially pp. 120-76.
67. *Ibid.*
68. *Ibid.*
69. *Ibid.*
70. *Ibid.*
71. Denis B. Kandel, "Race, Maternal Authority, and Adolescent Aspirations," *American Journal of Sociology,* 76, 6 (May 1971): 999-1020, 1009. We should note that there were no significant differences between intact and non-intact black families.
72. *Ibid.*
73. Orville G. Brim, "Family Structure and Sex Role Learning by Children," *Sociometry,* 21 (1958): 1-16; Helen L. Koch, "The Relation of Certain Family Constellation Characteristics and the Attitudes of Children Toward Adults," *Child Development,* 26 (Mar. 1955): 13-40.
74. Hartley 1964.

75. Irwin Child, Elmer Potter, and Estelle Levine, "Children's Textbooks and Personality Development: An Exploration in the Social Psychology of Education," in Morris L. Haimowitz and Natalie Reader Haimowitz, eds., *Human Development: Selected Readings* (New York: Thomas Y. Crowell Co., 1960), pp. 292-305.

76. *Ibid.,* p. 302.

77. Women on Words and Images, *Dick and Jane as Victims* (Princeton, N.J., 1972); Marcia Federbush, *"Let Them Aspire,"* (Ann Arbor, Michigan, 1972); and Terry Sario, Carol Nagy Jacklin, and Carol Kehr Tittle, "Sex Role Stereotyping in the Public Schools," *Harvard Educational Review*, vol. 43, no. 3 (Aug. 1973).

78. Lenore J. Weitzman and Diane Rizzo, "Images of Males and Females in Elementary School Textbooks," New York, National Organization for Women's Legal Defense and Education Fund, 1974.

79. *Ibid.*

80. Eleanor E. Maccoby, "Sex Differences in Intellectual Functioning," in Maccoby, ed., *The Development of Sex Differences* (Stanford, Calif.: Stanford University Press, 1966).

81. G. A. Milton, *Five Studies of the Relation Between Sex Role Identification and Achievement in Problem Solving,* Technical Report No. 3, Dept. of Industrial Admin., Department of Psychology, Yale University, Dec. 1958.

82. *Ibid.*

83. Kagan 1964, p. 157.

84. Eleanor E. Maccoby, "Woman's Intellect," in *The Potential of Women,* Seymour L. Farber and Roger H. L. Wilson, eds. (New York: McGraw-Hill, 1963), p. 31.

85. Julia A. Sherman, "Problems of Sex Differences in Space Perception and Aspects of Intellectual Functioning," *Psychological Review*, 74, 4 (1967): 290-99.

86. *Ibid.*

87. *Ibid.*

88. The following is paraphrased from comments of Professor William Goode, Jo Freeman, and myself in personal communications, 1971-74.

89. Similar assumptions about the linkage of male abilities and the traits most useful in managerial positions have been challenged in William J. Goode, "Family Life of the Successful Woman" in Eli Ginzberg and Alice Yohalem, eds. *Corporate Lib* (Baltimore: Johns Hopkins University Press, 1973), p. 97-117.

90. Personal communication, Jan. 1974.

91. Aberle and Naegele, 1952.

92. *Ibid.*

93. This finding is taken from Table 4, p. 569, in William H. Sewell and Vimal P. Shah, "Social Class, Parental Encouragement, and Educational Aspirations," *American Journal of Sociology,* 73, 5 (Mar. 1968): 559-72.

94. David Bordua, "Educational Aspirations and Parental Stress on College," *Social Forces,* 38 (1960): p. 267.

95. Glen H. Elder, Jr., *Adolescent Achievement and Mobility Aspirations* (Chapel Hill, N.C.: Institute for Research in Social Science, 1962), pp. 159-60.

96. Sex differences in parental encouragement persist even when social class and intelligence are held constant; Sewell and Shah, p. 570.

97. Ladner, *op. cit.*

98. Kandel, p. 1009.

99. Ladner, pp. 187-88.
100. Tansey Thomas, "Growing Up in the Ghetto," Student Report, Sociology 131, University of California, Davis, Fall, 1971.
101. Mirra Komarovsky, "Functional Analysis of Sex Roles," *American Sociological Review*, 15 (Aug. 1950): 508-16.
102. *Ibid.*
103. *Ibid.*
104. "An American Anachronism: the Image of Women and Work," *Daedalus*, Summer 1964.
105. Jo Freeman, "The Social Construction of the Second Sex," in Michele Barskof, ed., *Roles Women Play* (Belmont, Calif.: Brooks/Cole, 1971).
106. James V. Pierce, "Sex Differences in Achievement Motivation of Able High School Students," Cooperative Research Project No. 1097, University of Chicago, Dec. 1961.
107. *Ibid.*
108. Keniston, 1964.
109. Ladner, *op. cit.*
110. Mirra Komarovsky, "Cultural Contradictions and Sex Roles," *American Journal of Sociology*, 52 (1946); 184-89.
111. *Ibid.*
112. I am indebted to Robert Ross for his assistance in analyzing these data.
113. Personal conversation, Jan. 1971.
114. Rossi, "Equality Between the Sexes."
115. A. Etzioni, ed., *The Semi-Professions and Their Organization* (New York: Free Press, 1969).
116. Florence Howe, "Identity and Expression: A Writing Course for Women," unpublished paper.
117. Philip Goldberg, "Are Women Prejudiced Against Women?" *Trans-Action*, Apr. 1968.
118. *Ibid.*
119. Matina S. Horner, "Women's Need to Fail," *Psychology Today*, Nov. 1969.
120. *Ibid.*
121. See also Horner's more recent article, "Toward an Understanding of Achievement-Related Conflicts in Women," *Journal of Social Issues*, 28, 2 (1972): 157-75.
122. Bem and Bem, 1970.
123. Leona E. Tyler, "Sex Differences" under "Individual Differences" in the *International Encyclopedia of the Social Sciences*, vol. 7 (New York: Macmillan, 1968), pp. 207-13.
124. Jo Freeman, "The Social Construction of the Second Sex."
125. Ruth E. Hartley, "Children's Concept of Male and Female Roles," *Merrill-Palmer Quarterly*, 6 (1960): 83-91.
126. Paul H. Mussen, "Early Sex-Role Development," in David A. Goslin, ed., *Handbook of Socialization Theory and Research* (Chicago: Rand McNally, 1969).
127. *Ibid.*
128. Talcott Parsons, "Family Structure and the Socialization of the Child," in Talcott Parsons and Robert F. Bales, eds., *Family, Socialization, and Interaction Process* (New York: Free Press, 1955), p. 80.
129. Philip Slater, "Parental Role Differentiation," *The American Journal of Sociology*, 47, 3 (Nov. 1961): pp. 296-331.
130. Alfred B. Heilbrun, Jr., "Sex Role, Instrumental-Expressive Behavior, and Psychopathology in Females," *Journal of Abnormal Psychology*, 73, 2 (1958): 131-36.

131. William J. Goode, personal conversation, Dec. 1970.
132. David McClelland, *The Achieving Society* (New York: Free Press, 1964).
133. Fred Strodbeck, "Family Interaction, Values, and Achievement," in David McClelland, Alfred Baldwin, Urie Bronfenbrenner, and Fred Strodbeck, eds., *Talent and Society* (Princeton, N.J.: Van Nostrand, 1968), pp. 135-94.
134. *Ibid.*
135. Abraham H. Maslow, "Dominance, Personality and Social Behavior in Women," *Journal of Social Psychology*, 10 (1942): 259-94.
136. Jessie Bernard, "The Myth of the Happy Marriage" in V. Gornick and R. Morgan, eds., *Women in a Sexist Society* (New York: Basic Books, 1971) and *The Future of Marriage* (New York: World Books, 1972).
137. Betty Friedan, *The Feminine Mystique* (New York: W. W. Norton, 1963).
138. Mussen, *op. cit.*; Walter Mischel, "A Social-Learning View of Sex Differences" in Eleanor E. Maccoby, ed. *The Development of Sex Differences* (Stanford, Calif.: Stanford University Press, 1966).
139. Heilbrun, p. 134.
140. See Goode, "The Uses of Dispraise," for a review of the learning literature and effects of rewards and punishments.
141. Horner, *op. cit.*
142. J. Pierce, *op. cit.*
143. Jean M. Press and Fraine E. Whitney, "Achievement Syndromes in Women: Vicarious or Conflict-Ridden," paper presented at the Forty-First Annual Meeting of the Eastern Sociological Society, April 1971; and Jean Lippman-Blumen, "How Ideology Shapes Women's Lives," *Scientific American*, 226, 1 (Jan. 1972).
144. *Ibid.*

The Double Standard: Age

Inge Powell Bell

T here is a reason why women are coy about their age. For most purposes, society pictures them as "old" ten or 15 years sooner than men. Nobody in this culture, man or woman, wants to grow old; age is not honored among us. Yet women must endure the specter of aging much sooner than men, and this cultural definition of aging gives men a decided psychological, sexual and economic advantage over women.

It is surely a truism of our culture that, except for a few kinky souls, the inevitable physical symptoms of aging make women sexually unattractive much earlier than men. The multimillion dollar cosmetics advertising industry is dedicated to creating a fear of aging in women, so that it may sell them its emollients of sheep's fat, turtle sweat and synthetic chemicals which claim, falsely, to stem the terrible tide. "Did you panic when you looked into the mirror this morning and noticed that those laugh lines are turning into crow's-feet?" "Don't let your eyes speak your age!" "What a face-lift can do for your morale!"

A man's wrinkles will not define him as sexually undesirable until he reaches his late fifties. For

Reprinted from *Trans-Action* (November-December 1970), pp. 75-80, by permission of Transaction Inc.

him, sexual value is defined much more in terms of personality, intelligence and earning power than physical appearance. Women, however, must rest their case largely on their bodies. Their ability to attain status in other than physical ways and to translate that status into sexual attractiveness is severely limited by the culture. Indeed, what status women have is based almost entirely on their sexuality. The young girl of 18 or 25 may well believe that her position in society is equal to, or even higher than that of men. As she approaches middle age, however, she begins to notice a change in the way people treat her. Reflected in the growing indifference of others toward her looks, toward her sexuality, she can see and measure the decline of her worth, her status in the world. In Simone de Beauvoir's words:

> she has gambled much more heavily than man on the sexual values she possesses; to hold her husband and to assure herself of his protection, and to keep most of her jobs, it is necessary for her to be attractive, to please; she is allowed no hold on the world save through the mediation of some man. What is to become of her when she no longer has any hold on him: This is what she anxiously asks herself while she helplessly looks on the degeneration of this fleshly object which she identifies with herself.

The middle-aged woman who thickly masks her face with makeup, who submits to surgical face and breast lifting, who dyes her hair and corsets her body is as much a victim of socially instilled self-hatred as the black person who straightens his hair and applies bleaching creams to his skin.

The most dramatic institutionalization of different age definitions for men and women is the cultural rules governing the age at which one can marry. It is perfectly acceptable for men to marry women as much as 15 or 20 years younger than they are, but it is generally unacceptable for them to marry women more than four or five years older. These cultural rules show up very plainly in the marriage statistics gathered by the Department of Health, Education and Welfare. At the time of first marriage the age differential is relatively small; the groom is on the average 2.2 years older than his bride. When widowers remarry, however, the gap is 8.3 years; and when divorced men do, the gap is 4.5 years.

These age differentials put the woman at a disadvantage in several ways. First, whatever may be the truth about age and sexual performance, our culture defines the young as sexually more vigorous and desirable. Thus, the customary age differential means that the man gets the more desirable partner; the woman must settle for the less desirable.

More important, the divorced or widowed woman is severely handicapped when it comes to finding another marital partner. Let us take, for example, a couple who divorce when both are in their thirties. What is the difference in the supply of future marriage partners for the man and for the woman? The man can choose among all women his own age or younger. This includes all those women below 25, many more of whom are as yet unmarried. The woman, by contrast, is limited by custom to men her own age or older. She has access only to age brackets in which most people are married. She is thus reduced to the supply of men who come back on the marriage market as a result of divorce or widowerhood or to those few who have not yet married. It is easy to see which of the two will have an easier time finding companionship or a marriage partner. It is also easy to surmise that the awareness of this difference makes divorce a much more painful option for women than for men and thus puts many women at a continuous disadvantage within a strained marriage.

Statistics bear out our supposition that women have a harder time remarrying than men (see table). It has been estimated that, while three-quarters of divorced men remarry, only two-thirds of divorced women ever do. In a study of widows and widowers done in 1948, Paul Glick found that half the men who had been widowed during the five years preceding the study had remarried, but three-quarters of the women were still alone. Among those who had been widowed from five to 14 years, two-thirds of the men had remarried, but only one-third of the women had.

How Many Men and Women in Different Age Groups Remarry? (Number of marriages per 1000)

Widowed	Women	Men
45–64	16.2	70.1
65 and over	2.0	17.4
Divorced		
25–44	179.0	306.6
45–64	45.2	89.5
65 and over	9.7	26.5

Only a small proportion of these discrepancies is due to the shorter life expectancy of men and thus their relative scarcity in the upper-age brackets. For example, in the age brackets 45–64, there are a little over three times as many widowed and divorced women without mates as there are single widowed and divorced men. Yet in the total population the ratio of women to men in that age bracket is only 1.05 to 1. In the over-65 age bracket there are over three and a half times as many divorced and widowed women still alone; yet in the population as a whole, the ratio of women to men in this age bracket is only 1.2 to 1.

Still, the difference in life expectancy between the two sexes does work to a woman's disadvantage in another way. The gentleman in the ad below is making explicit an expectation which is made implicitly by most men:

> Occupation is man's major role . . . . The question "What do you do?" is seldom answered, "Well, I'm married and a father . . . ."

RECENTLY DIVORCED, 53, affectionate, virile, tall, good-looking, yearns for the one utterly feminine, attractive, loving woman in her 30s, 40s with whom he can share a beautiful new life.

At age 50, this gentleman had a life expectancy of 23 years. (It is a little less now.) If he finds a woman of 35, her life expectancy will be 41.27. In other words, he is affectionately offering her a statistical chance of 18 years of widowhood. And she will be widowed at an age when men of her own age will be looking for women in their thirties and forties. At best, he may live to a ripe old age. When he is 75 she will be 57.

Now let us consider the case of a much larger group: women who have husbands. As middle age approaches, many of these married women find that they, too, are vulnerable to the difficulties posed by the different definitions of age in men and women. For them, however devoutly they may wish it as they tidy their homes, take care of their teen-aged children or play bridge, sexual adventure is usually out of the question. This is not just because of the more restrictive mores that bind them to fidelity; their age has already disqualified them for anything else. Not so for the husband. If he is a successful man, his virility will be seen as still intact, if not actually enhanced, and the affair becomes very much the question. Indeed, if he is engaged in a middle-class occupation, he is almost inevitably surrounded by attractive, young females, many of whom—the receptionist, the cocktail waitress at the downtown bar, the airplane hostess—have been deliberately selected to flatter his ego and arouse his fancy. In addition, many of the women hired to fulfill more ordinary functions—the secretaries, typists and the like—find the older man desirable by virtue of his success and wealth. Thus, the middle-aged wife, unless she is one of the statistically few whose husband is truly happy and faithful, is put into competition with the cards stacked against her. And even if her husband doesn't leave her for a younger woman or begin having affairs, she will probably experience anxiety and a sense of diminished self-esteem.

The mass media glamorize and legitimate the older man-younger woman relationship. Successful actors continue to play romantic leads well into their fifties and sometimes sixties (vide Cary Grant). Frequently they are cast opposite actresses at least half their age, and the story line rarely even acknowledges the difference.

They are simply an "average" romantic couple. The question of whether the 20-year-old heroine is out of her mind to marry the greying 55-year-old hero isn't even raised.

THE PRESTIGE LOSS

Occupation is man's major role, unemployment or failure in his occupational life the worst disaster that can befall him. The question "What do you do?" is seldom answered, "Well, I'm married and a father. . . ." But because men draw their self-esteem and establish their connections to others very largely through their jobs, retirement is a time of psychic difficulty and discomfort for most men. The woman faces a similar role loss much earlier. Her primary role in life is that of mother: her secondary role is that of homemaker, and her tertiary that of sexual partner. We have already seen that the role of sexual partner, and sexually desirable object, is impaired for many women as middle age approaches. Now we must contemplate the additional fact that the woman's primary role—that of mother—also disappears during middle age.

Indeed, with decreasing family size and increasingly common patterns of early marriage, women are losing their mother role much earlier than formerly. In 1890 the average woman took care of children until her mid-fifties. Today most women see their children leave home when they are in their late forties. Whereas in 1890 the average woman lived 30 years after her last child had entered school and 12 years after her last child married, today, with longer life expectancy, the average woman lives 40 years after her last child enters school and 25 years after her last child marries. Thus, women lose their major role long before the retirement age arrives for men.

Loss of sexual attractiveness and the maternal role comes at a time when the husband is likely to be at the peak of his career and deeply involved in satisfying job activities. Bernice Neugarten, in describing how people become aware of middle age, says:

> Women, but not men, tend to define their age status in terms of timing of events within the family world, and even unmarried career women often discuss middle age in terms of the family they might have had . . .
>
> Men, on the other hand, perceive the onset of middle age by cues presented outside the family context, often from the deferential behavior accorded them in the work setting. One man described the first time a younger associate helped open a door for him; another, being called by his official title by a newcomer in the company; another, the first time he was ceremoniously asked for advice by a younger man.

The Double Standard: Age   **149**

Little research has been done on the prestige accorded men and women in different age brackets. The few studies available point to older women as the lowest prestige group in society. In a projective test asking middle-aged persons to make up a story about a picture which showed a young couple and a middle-aged couple in conversation, Neugarten found that the older woman was seen as more uncomfortable in her role than any of the others and was the only figure who was as often described in negative as in positive terms. Mary Laurence found that respondents tended to rate women as having more undesirable personality traits than men through all age ranges, but the age group rated most severely was women over 40.

A study of characters in American magazine fiction from 1890 to 1955 found a decline in the number of older women appearing as characters. By 1955 there were none at all. The middle-aged woman almost never sees herself and her problems depicted in print or on the screen. When they are, she sees mostly negative stereotypes. Her dilemma is very similar to that of the black ghetto child who finds in the "Dick and Jane" first reader a world that is irrelevant at best, invidious at worst. To have oneself and one's experiences verified in the mythology and art of one's culture is a fundamental psychological need at every stage of the life cycle.

Women's own attitudes toward aging are shown in the interesting finding that, in the listings of the Directory of the American Psychological Association, women are ten times as likely to omit their age as men. Thus, even professional women, who presumably have roles which extend undamaged into middle age, are much more likely than men to feel that their advancing age is a serious impairment.

On the question of whether middle-aged women are actually unhappier or more maladjusted than middle-aged men, the evidence is conflicting and inconclusive. A few studies by various researchers found little or no difference between middle-aged and old men and women on such factors as personality change, engagement with life and reported satisfaction with life. One study found older women more satisfied than older men.

One problem with these efforts, though, is that some of them lump together the middle-aged group with persons past retirement age. Some of the findings may therefore be due to the fact that the retirement age is far more stressful and acute for men than for women. Women have never invested much in careers and have been adjusting to role loss for many years. In old age an additional factor works in favor of women. Women are closer to relatives and thus more sheltered from complete isolation.

The studies present another problem in that the respondents themselves judged how happy or satisfied they were. The trouble with this is that subordinated groups learn to expect less and therefore to be satisfied with less. A middle-aged woman whose husband has had several affairs may report that her marriage has been satisfying because society has taught her to expect infidelity from her husband. A man whose wife had behaved in similar fashion would be less likely to regard his marriage as satisfying. Indeed, social conditioning would probably dictate a more painful crisis for the cuckolded husband. Moreover, measuring the satisfaction levels of people who are already so thoroughly "socialized" doesn't take into account the wife's feelings the first time she saw her own mother experience such treatment from her father and realized that a similar fate was in store for herself. It does not measure the emotional cost of adjusting to the expectation of abuse. In fact, if we were to confine our evidence to degrees of self-reported satisfaction, we might conclude that a great variety of social inequities create no emotional hardships for the subjugated. Elsewhere, however, Pauline Bart shows that middle age is much more stressful for women than for men and this finding corroborates the work of Judd Marmor who has reported that middle-aged women manifest psychiatric disorders three to four times as frequently as middle-aged men.

THE ECONOMIC LOSS

Discrimination against older women in employment is important because of the large number of people affected. The number of older women in the labor force has been growing rapidly in recent decades. In 1965, 50.3 percent of women in the age range of 45 to 54 and 41.4 percent of those 55 to 64 were employed. These percentages had risen sharply from 1940, when they were 24.5 percent and 18 percent respectively. In 1960, 40 percent of the total female work force was over 45 years old.

Discrimination against older workers of both sexes in industry is well documented. A 1965 Department of Labor survey concluded that half the job openings in the private economy are closed to applicants over 55 years of age, and one-fourth are closed to applicants over 45. Women are particularly disadvantaged by this discrimination because, as a result of their typical work and child-rearing cycle, many women come back on the labor market after a long period of absence (and are perhaps entering the market for the first time) during precisely these years. There is very little evidence on the question of whether older women are relatively more disadvantaged than older men. Edwin Lewis states that age is a greater detriment to women than to men but cites no evidence. A Department of Labor publication on age discrimination in employment claims that men are slightly favored, but the evidence is very incomplete. The study found that, compared to the percentage of unemployed older men and women, women were hired in somewhat greater numbers. But unemployment rates are based on self-reporting and are notoriously influenced by the optimism of a given group about the prospects of finding employment. Older women, many of whom are married, are less likely to report themselves as seeking work if they are pessimistic about the possibilities of getting any. The study also surveyed the employment practices of 540 firms and found that, although differences were slight, men were disadvantaged in a larger number of occupational categories. But in clerical work, in which 24 percent of women over 45 are engaged, discrimination against women was decidedly greater.

The problem of discrimination against older men and women is complicated by the fact that a study would have to take into account whether discrimination was practiced because of expected lack of physical strength, long training or internship programs or physical attractiveness. The former two considerations figure much more frequently in the case of men and certainly have more legitimacy as grounds for discriminating than the factor of physical attractiveness, which usually arises solely because the woman is seen as a sex object before she is seen as a productive worker. As long as this is the employer's orientation, it will probably do little good to cite him the studies proving that middle-aged women office workers are superior to young women in work attendance, performance and ability to get along agreeably with others. It would also be necessary to see how much relative discrimination there is within occupational categories. There is little discrimination in certain low-paid, undesirable jobs because the supply of workers in these categories is short. Women tend to be predominantly clustered in precisely these job categories.

A check of one Sunday's *Los Angeles Times* want ads yielded a count of 1,067 jobs advertised for women and 2,272 advertised for men. For both sexes specific upper-age limits or the term "young" were attached to less than 1 percent of the job listings, and there was almost no difference between men and women. However, 97 (or 9 percent) of the female ads used the term "girl" or "gal," while only two of the 2,272 male ads used the term "boy."

To check out my hunch that "girl" is an indirect way of communicating an age limitation, in a state where discrimination by age is supposedly illegal, I called five employment agencies in southern California and asked an interviewer who handles secretarial and clerical placement what he or she thought the term "girl" meant from the employer's side and how it would be interpreted by the average job seeker. Four of the five employment interviewers stated that the term definitely carries an age connotation for employer and job seeker alike. They defined the age implied variously as: "under 30"; "under 35—if we were looking in the 35–45 category we would use the term 'mature'; over 45 we don't say anything"; "It means a youngster. I certainly don't think a 45-year-old would go in if she saw that

> **The use of the term "girl" . . . [in want ads]
> underscores the extent to which women's jobs
> are still considered young girls' jobs, that is,
> the relatively unimportant work that a girl
> does before she gets married.**

ad"; "It does mean age, which is why we always use the term 'women' in our company's ads (although we may use the term 'girl' on a specific listing)." The last person would not state a specific age because she was obviously worried about being caught in violation of the law, to which she frequently alluded. Only one of the five replied in the negative, saying "to me 'girl' is just another word for 'woman.' You can hardly use the term 'woman' in the wording of an ad." Everyone I questioned agreed that the term "girl Friday" (a tiny proportion of our cases) carries no age connotation. Several, however, mentioned that the terms "trainee," "recent high school grad" and "high school grad" were used to communicate an age limitation.

Along with the term "girl," a number of ads use physical descriptions—almost entirely lacking in men's ads. "Attractive gal for receptionist job" is typical. More specific are the following excerpts from the columns in the *Los Angeles Times*: "Exciting young atty seeks a sharp gal who wants a challenge"; "Young, dynamic contractor who is brilliant but disorganized needs girl he can depend on completely"; and one headlined "Lawyer's Pet" which goes on to say "Looking for a future: want challenge, 'variety,' $$$? Young attorney who handles all phases of 'law' will train you to become his 'right hand.'" Few women over 30 would consider themselves qualified to apply for these jobs.

The use of the term "girl" and the reaction of one employment agency interviewer who considered this as the only proper way to connote "woman" in a want ad underscores the extent to which women's jobs are still considered young girls' jobs, that is, the relatively unimportant work that a girl does before she gets married. One employment agency interviewer stated that his agency frequently had requests for a certain age level because companies want to keep the age range in a certain department homogeneous for the sake of congeniality. It is significant that he mentioned only the "twenties" or "thirties" as examples of such desirable age ranges.

One is tempted to make a comparison between the term "girl" and the insulting racist use of "boy" for all blacks, regardless of age. In both cases, the term indicates that the species under discussion is not considered capable of full adulthood. In both cases, blacks and women are acceptable and even likable when very old, as "uncle" and "grandmother," but somehow both are anachronistic as mature adults.

Given the scarcity and conflicting nature of the data, it is impossible to say with certainty that older women suffer more from discrimination than older men. The question certainly merits further and more systematic exploration.

CASTE AND CLASS

The division of this article into sexual, prestige and economic loss was taken from John Dollard's analysis of the sexual, prestige and economic gains of whites at the expense of blacks in his classic study, *Caste and Class in a Southern Town.* The choice was not an accident; spokesmen of women's liberation have often drawn heavily on the analogy between the problems of blacks and of women. Yet equally often one hears objections to the analogy. Blacks are, as a group, isolated in the lowest economic strata and physically ghettoed into the worst parts of town, while women, being inextricably connected to men through familial ties, do not share a drastic, common disability. It has also been suggested that to compare the plight of women with that of blacks is to belittle the importance of the need for black liberation. Most of these critics care as little for black liberation as for the liberation of women and need not be taken seriously.

Yet the intellectual objections to the analogy should be discussed. The argument actually rests on the assumption that middle-class status cushions all of life's shocks and that middle-class women are always comfortably imbedded in middle-class primary groups. It assumes further that the woes of lower-class women are all essentially class-connected rather than specifically sex-connected. The loneliness of widowhood, the anguish of a woman losing her husband to a younger woman, the perplexity of the woman whose children have left home and who finds herself unwanted on the labor market—these are real hurts, and they go deep, even in the middle class. Further, the notion of the individual as being deeply rooted in his primary groups certainly reflects a partial and outmoded view in a highly individualistic society where the nuclear family, usually the only long-lasting primary group, has become extremely unstable. In our society, men and women are expected to get through life essentially alone. This is true even of the woman who is able to maintain good family ties throughout her life. It is even truer for those who suffer the more common fate of having these ties weakened by discord or severed by death or separation. For the lower-class woman, of course, these difficulties are harsher and more unrelieved, but in every class the woman must bear them alone.

The differential definition of age in men and women represents a palpable advantage to men at the expense of women. It multiplies the options for emotional satisfaction on his side while it diminishes them on hers. It raises his prestige and self-esteem at the expense of hers. All men in our society benefit to some degree from this custom, while not a single woman who lives into middle age escapes bearing some of the cost. If we are ever to restructure this society into one of true equality for both sexes, this is one of the crucial points at which we must begin.

The Loneliness of the Long-Distance Mother

Pauline Bart

> *I don't want to be alone, and I'm going to be alone, and my children will go their way and get married . . . of which I'm wishing for it . . . and then I'll still be alone, and I got more and more alone, and more and more alone.*
>
> *—Sara*

This article draws on data used in Pauline Bart, "Mother Portnoy's Complaint," *Trans-Action* (November-December 1970).

Middle age, like adolescence, is a time of physiological as well as sociological changes. At one time the stress often characterizing both these ages was considered physiological in origin and therefore universal. In order to test the so-called "Sturm und Drang" hypothesis concerning adolescents, Margaret Mead went to Samoa, where she found adolescence not stressful at all. As there seemed little reason to assume significant physiological differences between Americans and Samoans, she reasoned that adolescent stress in Western nations had cultural origins. I went to other cultures—unfortunately only through their anthropological records—to learn whether the changes of mid-life were psychologically stressful for women, thus becoming, as it were, the Margaret Mead of the menopause. I studied the roles available to women who were past childbearing and whether women typically had problems with menopause.* I was particularly looking for an absence of depression appearing for the first time in middle age.

Unfortunately, data on the menopause were scarce—available for only five out of the thirty societies I studied. Clearly, anthropologists are generally male and thus not interested in pursuing such information—or unable to, for when the anthropologists were female or when teams included females, information about menopause was reported. Psychiatric data were also scarce, but there was enough information on post-maternal roles and on the relative status of women to allow me to determine whether that status rose or fell in middle age.

It appears that in each culture there is a favored stage in the life cycle of women. For instance, if a woman has high status when she is young, her power and prestige can be expected to decline as she matures, and vice versa. Rather than the usual image of society as a pyramid or ladder, one can think of society as a social ferris wheel.[1] I attempted to correlate these age-related changes in status with cultural and structural factors in the society, paying special attention to roles for post-menopausal women.

Most cultures had definite roles that women were expected to fill after they were through with childbearing and -rearing, but these roles varied from society to society. They included, in addition to the wife role, the roles of grandmother, economic producer, mother and mother-in-law, participant in government, performer of magic and ritual, and daughter of aged parents. The higher-status roles on the list were those of grandmother, mother-in-law and participator in government, since the available economic role for women was generally limited to performing hard work of little prestige.

Using the following indices for higher status—more freedom (especially from taboos), more respect, special privileges and more power and influence—I found that in seventeen out of the thirty cultures, women registered *higher* status during middle age by at least one index.** In twelve out of the thirty they had more

---

* The cultures and peoples studied were all pre-literate, peasant or traditional: the Andaman Islanders, Serbs, Toda, Twi, Nupe, Tiv, Yoruba, Azande, Bushmen, Lovedu, Bedouin, Wolof, Aleuts, Comanche, Yurok, Navajo, Zuni, Ifugao, Aranda, Trobrianders, Samoans, Marquesans, Pukapukans, Jivaro; and peasant or traditional cultures in Burma, China, rural Ireland, Poland, India, the Soviet Union, and the Philippines. The following aspects of all these cultures were studied: ontogeny, social personality, personality traits, and personality disorders, division of labor by sex, age stratification, sex status, celibacy, family relationships, grandparents and grandchildren, dependency, old-age dependency, adulthood, senescence, and the activities, status, and treatment of the aged.

** Middle age will be defined here as the years from 40 to 65.

respect, in eight they had more power and influence, in seven they had special privileges, and in four they had more freedom. In eleven cultures middle-aged women registered neither an increase nor a decrease in social status on any of these indices. In only two cultures, those of the Marquesans and the Trobrianders—cultures in a number of ways similar to our own—did women have less power and influence in middle age than when they were younger.

The cross-cultural study therefore indicated that middle age was not usually considered an especially stressful period for women. Consequently, purely biological explanations of the stress felt at this time by Western woman can be rejected. Middle age need not be fraught with difficulty.

It needs to be noted, however, that a major buffer against problems facing women in mid-life has been the kinship group. The literature I surveyed showed that a strong tie to family and kin rather than a strong marital tie, an extended-family system rather than a nuclear-family system, an institutionalized grandmother role, a mother-in-law role rather than no role for a woman in relationship to her son- or daughter-in-law, plus residence patterns keeping one close to one's parents and siblings—all these factors strengthen kinship ties and tend to improve the woman's position in middle age. Thus, very clearly, a woman's status after she stops bearing children can be associated with the structural arrangements and cultural values of her society. Specifically, the associations charted below seem to hold true:

Raised Status in Middle Age	Lowered Status in Middle Age
Strong tie to parents, siblings, cousins and other kin	Marital tie stronger than tie to nuclear family
Extended-family system	Nuclear-family system
Reproduction important	Sex an end in itself
Strong mother-child relationship reciprocal in later life	Weak maternal bond, adult-oriented culture
Institutionalized grandmother role	Noninstitutionalized grandmother role, grandmother role not important
Institutionalized mother-in-law role	Noninstitutionalized mother-in-law role, mother-in-law does not train daughter-in-law
Extensive menstrual taboos	Minimal menstrual taboos
Matrilocal, patrilocal or duolocal residence pattern	Residence pattern that isolates women from kin and grown children, e.g. neolocal, avuncular
Age valued over youth	Youth valued over age

Turning to our own society with this chart in mind, we can begin to see why middle-aged women so often feel stress. In each instance, except for the mother-child bond, which in our society is strong but nonreciprocal, we fall on the right side, where the status of women drops in middle age. For women whose lives have not been child-centered and whose strong marital ties continue, or for those whose children set up residence near them, the transition to middle age may be buffered. But child-centered women note that the relationship with their children is non-reciprocal—that all they are entitled to is "respect." A child once reaching maturity in our culture need honor and look after her/his mother only on Mother's Day, unless she is widowed. And both for these women, and for those who have empha-sized the maternal role or the glamour role, middle age may be a difficult stage in the life cycle. Our emphasis on youth and our stipulation that mothers-in-law should not interfere and grandmothers not meddle makes the middle years a time of stress for many thousands, if not millions, of American women.* But let one such woman, one of twenty I interviewed and tested in mental hospitals, speak for herself.

SARA: THE MARTYR MOTHER

This is Sara's second admission to a mental hospital. The first time, the diagnosis was "psychophysiological gastro-intestinal reaction," but this time, knowing more about her, doctors have diagnosed "involutional depression."

Sara is Jewish. In her early sixties, she is divorced and in what has been called the "empty nest" stage. She represents an almost ideal type of all of the problems that beset an aging woman in our society, in addition to some that began in child-hood. Not only did her mother reject her, not only did her husband reject her, but now her children and grandchildren are rejecting her, and she is unable to partici-pate in work or voluntary activities that could give her life meaning because she is physically ill, and transportation is inaccessible. She needs to keep busy, and her activities are severely restricted. She must live alone, and she is phobic about being alone.

Sara has had many physical problems—arthritis, kidney trouble, and, at the time I saw, her, severely swollen feet. She has had a hysterectomy and gall bladder surgery. According to her record, her frightened, depressed state was "induced by

---

* See, however, Neugarten's work on healthy middle-aged women: Bernice Neugarten, ed., *Middle-Aged and Aging: A Reader in Social Psychology* (University of Chicago Press, 1968).

fear of living in an apartment in Las Vegas where she felt abandoned and unprotected." This feeling has been present "ever since she was asked to move out of her son's home in order to placate the anger of her daughter-in-law who felt she caused trouble by trying to absorb all of her son's time and sympathy." Her (male) psychiatrist characterizes Sara as hypochondriachal and self-pitying.

I asked Sara one question and she immediately launched into a long description of her troubles: her fears of being alone, the failure of medication to alleviate these fears, her physical illnesses, and more:

> I first of all have a lot of fears, and it isn't very easy I guess . . . to do something about it. And . . . these fears just follow me, and just push me in the wrong direction. I'm not really doing what I want to do. I want to go one way, but it just seems to take me the other way and I — can't control them . . . . The minute nobody's here, and those fears start working with me. Everything seems closed up, and everything looks dark.

Sara told me that as a child she felt she was "really nothing." Her Russian-born father died when she was about six, but she always felt close to him. Even now she believes that if he had lived,

> He would have always made me feel that I'm not alone, and that someone loves me. I am very strong for love. . . . This is a very big thing to me, and I wasn't very fortunate because Mother didn't give it to me, and I was hungry for it, and when I married I also thought it was going to be a wonderful thing because somebody is going to care, but my marriage never turned out good.

While Sara's first child, a son, was a baby, her husband started a produce store. Sara would go to the store four miles from their home at four o'clock in the morning in a horse and wagon holding the baby in her arms, feeding him.

> I worked hard my whole life and I thought that if I worked for him he would—he would be good to me, but he took all that good [I gave him]. . . . He didn't feel that I was human, too.

A daughter was born, but the marriage continued no better. Her husband was repeatedly unfaithful, and apparently contracted venereal disease. Since he needed to work during the night, he refused to let her have company during the day or evening so that he could rest and sleep. He was rude to her friends. And "even with sex he was very, very rude about it."

> Me: How was he rude with sex?
> Sara: Very much so. He was concerned . . . about himself. nothing about me. . . . He had another woman that he took out, and I found out about it, but I didn't let on. I thought, well, if that's a weakness, maybe he'll overcome it. Let me try and, uh, cope with it enough to see if I couldn't get

. . . nine years after the divorce, a hysterectomy was necessary . . . . "To me it feels like Sara died."

him to reason . . . maybe later I could. But I couldn't. He would always run away when I wanted to reason with him. He would slam the door and go away for a few days, come back and throw the dirty clothes into the bathroom hamper, and everything was coming to him, but nothing was coming to me.

Me: Were you ever able to have sex satisfactory for you?

Sara: I say no. He—he always felt that he was tired and it was "necessary" and it "wasn't necessary" when he thought it was. [What she apparently means is that he had sexual relations with her only when he wanted to.]

Years later, with her son in the army and her daughter still at home, Sara decided she could not "take" her marriage anymore. She divorced her husband. But after the divorce she became very frightened about having to be on her own. Although she had a job at the time, this did little to lessen her insecurity. In addition, she was "very hurt" at having had to get a divorce. This feeling was heightened whenever she sublet her apartment; her tenants made her feel it wasn't "nice" to divorce. It never occurred to her to consult a psychiatrist, either during her marriage or immediately after her divorce because "At those times if you went to a psychiatrist people thought you were insane."

She became physically ill immediately after the divorce. She had to have gall bladder surgery. Then she became anemic and had to be under a doctor's care. Then, nine years after the divorce, a hysterectomy was necessary. Ever since this operation she believes she has been "entirely different." "To me it feels like Sara died."

Sara has four grandchildren. When they were very small she took care of them, but now that they are older she is expected to leave them alone. Their lack of concern and respect hurts her, although she loves them "very dearly." Some years ago on the advice of her doctor and at the invitation of her daughter-in-law she left her home in New Jersey and went to Las Vegas to reap the benefits of the Nevada climate and to live with and help take care of her son's family. But when the grandchildren matured, Sara was no longer needed. Rather than tell her this, the daughter-in-law tried to drive Sara out with unkind treatment: "She just treated me so that—it just made me go. You know what I mean? You can treat a person enough to make them feel they want to go."

At that time her daughter in New Jersey was expecting a baby and so Sara seized the chance to go and help her. Before she left, her son told her that if she wanted to return to Las Vegas she would have to find another place to live. He pointed out that perhaps she hadn't realized that living with them was a "temporary thing." Sara believes her daughter-in-law pressured him to do this. In New Jersey, she contacted friends to see whether she could remain in the East, but no one was willing to help her.

She returned to Las Vegas and tried to find work as a saleslady, but this was possible only during the Christmas rush.

> It's very difficult in that town to get a job at my age, because it's considered as attraction and they—hire the young girls. . . . I couldn't get no work and I was pretty disappointed because I felt that there was nothing else in this Vegas that I could do.

She had belonged to the Sisterhood of the local temple and enjoyed attending services, being present at meetings and doing volunteer work. Now, living alone, she needed transportation so that she could participate in these activities. When her son did take her to services, he would rush her home as soon as possible after they were over, saying, "I'm not going to stay here all night, you know."

She asked her daughter-in-law, who was active in the Sisterhood, to inform the temple that she would be willing to help with any work that needed to be done. Her daughter-in-law said,

> "They don't want people like you. Our organization wants young people . . . they want young blood that can do things. . . . What can you do?"

Not only was Sara unable to do volunteer work, she was no longer permitted to sing in the choir. When the synagogue had been small the cantor had asked her to sing. Then the Jewish community had built a larger temple and hired a new cantor who limited participation to people who could read music. Sara asked for a chance to learn how, but the cantor never offered to teach her or have anyone else teach her.

I asked Sara if she had been happier before her children left home, and she said, "Yes and no. Because my husband never let any of us enjoy it." When I asked specifically what changes in her own feelings of self-worth she had noticed since her children left, she replied: "I don't . . . I don't feel like . . . I don't feel at all that I'm wanted. I just feel like nothing."

Then I asked Sara what was the worst thing that had ever happened to her.

> When I had to break up and be by myself, and be alone, and I'm just—I really feel that I'm not—not only not loved but not even liked sometimes by my own children. . . . They could respect me. If—they can't say good why should

they . . . hurt my feelings and make my cry, and then call me a crybaby, or tell me that I ought to know better or something like that. My worst thing is that I'm alone, I'm not wanted, nobody interested themselves in me. Nobody cares.

Sara couldn't think of the best thing that had ever happened to her, but the best times of her life, she said, were when she was pregnant and when her children were babies.

I was glad that God gave me . . . the privilege of being a mother and—and I loved them. In fact, I wrapped my love so much around them.

She felt grateful to her husband, since "if it weren't for him it wouldn't be the children. *They were my whole life, that was it.*"

ROLE LOSS, RELIGION, AND DEPRESSION; OR WHY NOT TO BE A JEWISH MOTHER

Sara was typical in many ways of the twenty middle-aged women I interviewed in mental hospitals,* all but one of whom were or had been married and had children. All but two of these women were depressed, and eleven were Jewish. I had predicted that the Jewish mother, especially if she had limited herself to being a housewife, would be the one to find the departure of children most stressful, since this departure, according to my hypothesis, is most difficult for women whose primary role is that of mother. The devotion of the Jewish woman to her children is legendary, eulogized in songs and stories and more recently satirized by comedians and writers. From the widely selling books of such prominent Jewish sons as Phillip Roth (*Portnoy's Complaint*, 1967), Bruce J. Friedman (*A Mother's Kisses*, 1964), and Dan Greenburg (*How to Be A Jewish Mother*, 1965) we have been led to see that the other side of the coin of extreme devotion to children is overprotection, controlling behavior, and the development of a "martyr complex" by the mother.

When some crucial items in the interview protocols were analyzed, certain

---

* Of the women interviewed eleven were married, one separated, six divorced, one widowed and one single. Of the eight women whose children had all departed (the empty-nest women), four were married, and four divorced, widowed, or separated. Of those who had at least one child out of the home but at least one child still at home (partially empty-nest) three were married and none were divorced, widowed, or separated. Four women had marital but not maternal role loss, one had partial marital role loss but not maternal role loss, and four had no role loss. Eighteen of the twenty were diagnosed depressed. Eleven women were Jewish and nine women were housewives.

factors reminiscent of the cross-cultural survey, began to emerge. These women did not have a kinship network to whom they could turn in times of trouble (here it should be noted that my data were gathered in Los Angeles, where this lack is probably more prevalent than in many other areas of the country). Though they did not believe that their children "owed" them anything, it was clear from the interviews that the Jewish women in particular had expectations of their children that were not being met. None of the women were spending time caring for their grandchildren, but several had done so when the grandchildren were younger, and these women had had to cope with the loss of both mother and grandmother roles. When asked what they were most proud of, the women said their children. In general, they were least proud of their failure to have happy homes. Most of the women felt they were expected to keep busy and not "interfere" once their children were raised. They considered their lives lonelier now than when they were younger, and mentioned that they were less busy. This decline in activity, however, was not an asset, since it gave them more time to ruminate on their problems.

Perhaps the interview item most relevant for this essay was the one asking the women to rank in order of importance seven possible roles. These were: being a homemaker; taking part in church, club, and community activities; being a companion to my husband; helping my parents; being a sexual partner to my husband; my paying job; and helping my children.

Significantly, the mother role—"helping my children"—was most frequently ranked first or second. The role of homemaker was also ranked high. Roles such as "my paying job" and "taking part in church, club, and community activities" were considered unimportant. Thus, precisely those roles that become constricted with age were viewed as important, whereas the roles that could be expanded—the occupational and the organizational roles—were dismissed as unimportant.

All the Jewish women interviewed (but see below for epidemiological data), as expected, had had overprotective or overinvolved relationships with their children, and had experienced feelings of depression when the children left. My analysis of the interviews also showed that many of the women had severe physical illnesses before their hospitalization for depression and that in some cases the physical illness was associated with the failure of their marriages, since when ill they could not meet the expectations of their husbands. A strikingly high proportion of the women had lost their fathers at an early age. This loss deprived them of the opportunity to learn role relationships in an intact family, and therefore may have led to an over-involvement in the maternal role and to depression when the role was lost.

The departure of their children seemed related to the depression of all of the empty-nest mothers, Jewish and non-Jewish alike. The major difference appeared to be that the non-Jewish mothers "keep a stiff upper lip"—they do not complain about their children, they do not express a desire to see them more often or state that they want to live with them—whereas two of the Jewish "empty-nest" mothers I interviewed said openly that they wanted to live with their children. They also talked about wanting a grandmother role.

The interview material lent support to the epidemiological data I had gathered earlier from the records of 533 women between the ages of 40 and 59, hospitalized for the first time for mental illness. The five hospitals varied from an upper-class private hospital to two state hospitals. Among these women, maternal role-loss seemed important only for those in the empty-nest stage. For women with some children still at home, depression seemed associated with other factors. On the basis of the epidemiological data the women with more than one role-loss—for example, both marital and maternal—did not have a higher rate of depression than the women with only one role-loss. However, these data showed only the presence or absence of depression, and nothing about the severity or intensity of the depression where present.* When the intensity of depression could be observed, as in the interviews, those women with a multiple role-loss did appear to be in a worse situation than those with a single loss.

The epidemiological data did not support the hypothesis that maternal role loss would be especially stressful for Jewish women, primarily because the Jewish women in this group were found to be more likely to be depressed whatever their role state. Indeed, one of the most striking relationships to come to light is the high degree of association between being Jewish and being depressed. When ethnicity was cross-tabulated with depression, Jews had a higher rate than any other group— 84 percent; Wasps had 47 percent and blacks 22 percent. In other words, whereas more than four out of every five of the Jewish women patients studied were diagnosed as depressed, less than half the non-Jewish sample had this diagnosis. If this high incidence of depression originates in the traditional Jewish socialization process, which makes aggression taboo and uses guilt as a means of social control, then depression should be less common among Jews from less traditional homes. Indeed, evidence to support this hypothesis was found, in the higher rate of depression among Jewish women with foreign-born mothers—only 67 percent of those with native-born mothers were depressed, as compared with 92 percent of those with foreign-born mothers (but the numbers were small).

All in all, however, the Jewish women were more depressed than the non-Jewish women for whatever category they were compared, although significantly, the difference in depression between Jews and non-Jews was markedly reduced

---

* I did not find that women diagnosed as psychotic had more severe symptoms than those with "neurotic" depression. Diagnosis depended primarily on hospital.

. . . my findings indicate that it is the women . . . who are housewives, are not aggressive, are centered on their children, who in short, have "bought" the cultural proscriptions— who are most prone to depression when their children leave.

when *only housewives with overprotective relationships with their children were studied.** Non-Jews in this category also had an extremely high rate of depression. So you don't have to be Jewish to be a Jewish mother. The pathological effect of an overprotective mother on her children has been discussed by clinicians for many years. This investigation demonstrated that overprotection can be pathological for the mother. And Jews are more likely to have overinvolved relationships with their children than are non-Jews.

Contrary to my original hypothesis that women in high-status occupations would be relatively mildly affected by the loss of the maternal role, the epidemiological data showed that women with professional or managerial occupations had a high rate of depression. (The interview material bore less directly on this question, for the one woman among the twenty with role-loss who had had a job considered professional—she was a nurse—was not greatly involved in her profession. Far from considering it a "calling," she had become a nurse only after her first divorce and had stopped working outside the home during her first marriage.) The norms of our society are such that a woman is not expected to "fulfill" herself through an occupational role, but rather through the traditional feminine roles of housewife and mother. In addition, many women in high-status occupations suffer because of double messages about achievement, nonegalitarian marriages in which the wife's job is considered less important than the husband's and she is responsible for the housework, and the discrimination they experience at work. The fourteen women in the epidemiological sample with high-status occupations and maternal role-loss were also found to be either unhappily married or divorced. In view of a woman's cultural expectations and the considerable stresses and role contradictions she may face in a high-status occupation in a sexist society, it is not surprising that the occupational role could not be expanded to compensate for a lost maternal or marital role.

Nevertheless, my study did not support the theory advanced by a number of psychiatrists, most notably Helene Deutsch and Theresa Benedek,[2] that it is the so-called feminine and mothering woman who has the easiest time during the meno-

---

* But in this comparison 80 percent of the Jewish women had such a relationship while only 48 percent of the non-Jewish women did.

pause and that it is the—in Deutsch's phrase—"masculine protester" who has the most difficulty. On the contrary, my findings indicate that it is the women who play the traditional feminine role—who are housewives, are not aggressive, are centered on their children, who in short, have "bought" the cultural proscriptions —who are most prone to depression when their children leave. The depressed women I studied, far from being masculine protesters, were half a standard deviation more "feminine" on the MMPI test than the mean for the criterion group.

This is not to say that all housewives who are overinvolved or overprotective with their children are hospitalized when their children leave home, or that all housewives become depressed in middle age. Under the following conditions the women would continue to receive vicarious gratification:

1. Their husbands are financially successful
2. Their husbands do not become interested in other women, nor want a divorce, nor die
3. Their children fulfill their expectations, i.e.,
   a. The son obtains a good job
   b. The daughter makes a "good" marriage
   c. The mother-child relationship can continue through frequent phone calls and visits

If these conditions are met, then women of the type we have been discussing need not become depressed. But if any one of these conditions is not fulfilled, then such a woman may be in a dangerous situation. All of these cases depend on the actions of other people rather than the woman herself.

INTEGRATION OF PSYCHIATRIC AND SOCIOLOGICAL THEORY

Both the psychodynamic and the existential theories of depression state that depression is a result of loss. Psychodynamically oriented psychiatrists consider the loss that of an ambivalently loved object, whereas existentialists, such as Ernest Becker, consider the loss to be a loss of meaning. In Freudian terms, depressives are understood as individuals who, instead of expressing anger toward the ambivalently loved lost object, turn the anger inward, against themselves. One possible way of combining the Freudian and existentialist views is as follows:

People who are intrapunitive, who do not express their anger, especially if they are women, are conforming to the cultural norms. Since they are "good," they expect to be rewarded. Should their husbands or children leave them, their life may seem meaningless; their world may no longer "make sense." Their introjected anger has led to "proper" behavior, which in turn has led to expectations of reward. If the reward does not materialize, but in fact tragedy strikes, they will suffer from a loss of meaning and become depressed.

The loss that was the independent variable for this study was role-loss, especially the loss of the maternal role for middle-aged women who had overinvolved or overprotective relationships with their children. There is no direct evidence that the "lost" children were ambivalently loved, although some of the interviews I held might suggest that ambivalence was present. It was, however, quite clear that both the interviewees and the epidemiological sample were made up of "norm-following" women.

In *The Revolution in Psychiatry*, Ernest Becker says that it is the women who have been too closely integrated into the social structure who become depressed when they find that their "sacrifice," their exemplary behavior, has been in vain. They discover that it is the exploiters rather than the martyrs who are rewarded, contrary to what they have always believed. They were told that as women they should live for their children. They did so. Their husbands became interested in other women or preoccupied with their jobs, or they died. Their children left home. Since their feeling of being useful stemmed primarily from husband and children, these losses left them with no sense of worth.[3]

Durkheim's work is also relevant to the stresses a mother may feel when her children leave, particularly his concepts of *egoistic* and *anomic* suicide. According to Durkheim it is not marriage that protects a woman from egoistic suicide, as it is for men. Rather it is the birth of children that reduces the suicide rate for women, and immunity to suicide increases with the "density" of the family. This density diminishes, needless to say, when the children mature and leave.

Durkheim focused on problems stemming from normlessness, from anomie. There are indeed few norms governing the relationship between an American woman and her adult children. When the children leave, the woman's situation is consequently normless. There would be, for example, no folkway, no pattern, no mores that could indicate to Sara just what she should expect from her children, just what their relationship should be with her.[4]

All the women I interviewed said their children "owed" them nothing. But there was an additional element of normative confusion faced by the Jewish women. The norms considered appropriate in parent-child relationships in traditional Jewish culture—and therefore adhered to by the women—may not have been completely internalized by their children. The children were also exposed to Anglo-Saxon parent-child relationships, which are more restrained and place more emphasis, at least on the verbal level, on the parent's desire for independence, both for her child and for herself.

WHAT NEEDS TO BE DONE

The cross-cultural study, showing the multiplicity of possible roles for middle-aged women, made it clear that not only need status not drop in mid-life, but in most cultures it actually rises. That fact, however, would be cold comfort to the American women we have studied who are already depressed. It is unreasonable to expect them to change their value systems or personality structures or characteristic patterns of interaction at this stage of the game. These women are not psychotic, if by psychotic we mean the patient does not know what reality is. They know exactly what their reality is: that is why they are depressed. We must change society so that these tragedies will not be repeated. More basic changes are required than the "band-aid" reforms making it easier for older women to re-enter the labor force. The entire system of sex roles should be changed so that women could, if they chose, remain in the labor force after childbearing. (This is particularly important for professional women and those whose occupations have changing skills.) Not only should there be adequate 24-hour-a-day, parent-controlled day-care centers, but men should share the child-care and housekeeping responsibilities. The value system should change so that a man's "masculinity" will not be measured by his occupational achievement, freeing him then to devote more time and energy to his family; and a woman's sense of adequacy should not be dependent on her fulfilling the traditional female roles of wife and mother in the traditional manner. She should have other options, such as not being considered a failure if she does not marry, and deciding not to have children even if she does marry. There are many industrialized societies—such as the Soviet Union, Poland, Sweden, and Finland—where women play a vital part in the economy. Our record on the participation of women in the professions is shameful when we look at that of these other countries. It is interesting to note, however, that even there, when professions (e.g., medicine or pharmacy) have changed from primarily masculine to primarily feminine, they are redefined so as to require "naturally feminine" qualities and skills.

Age discrimination as well as sex discrimination and sexism should be overcome. Although both older men and older women are discriminated against, such discrimination hurts women earlier because of the double standard in aging. A woman's physical attractiveness is one of her assets and a requirement for certain jobs, such as receptionist, hostess, waitress.

The increasing participation of women in the labor force (if not prevented by a decreased demand for workers in the 1970's), declining desired and actual fecundity, the power of the women's movement in fighting sex discrimination and loosening sex role stereotypes, and the increasing self-esteem and self-confidence of women in general should improve the situation of middle-aged women.

Most imperative of all, we must nurture a new sense of worth in the girls of our society, to ensure that as women they will not feel useless when their children or their husbands leave them. If one's satisfaction, one's sense of value, comes from other people rather than from one's own accomplishments, it follows that when these people depart, one is left with an empty shell in place of self. On the other hand, if one's sense of self comes from her own accomplishments, one is not so vulnerable to breakdown when significant others leave.

The woman's liberation movement, by pointing out alternative life styles, by providing the emotional support necessary for deviating from the conventional sex roles, and by emphasizing the importance of women actualizing their own selves, fulfilling their own potentials, can aid in the development of personhood for both men and women.

Notes

1. Pauline Bart, "Why Women's Status Changes in Middle Age: The Turns of the Social Ferris Wheel," *Sociological Symposium,* Fall 1969, p. 1.
2. Helene Deutsch, *The Psychology of Women: A Psychoanalytic Interpretation* (New York: Grune and Stratton, 1945), vol. 2; Theresa Benedek and Boris Rubenstein, *Psychosexual Functions in Women* (New York: Ronald Press, 1952), pp. 1-11.
3. Ernest Becker, *The Revolution in Psychiatry* (Glencoe, Ill.: Free Press, 1964).
4. Emile Durkheim, *Suicide,* tr. John A. Spaulding and George Simpson (Glencoe, Ill.: Free Press, 1951).

Structural and Internalized Barriers to Women in Higher Education

Pamela Roby *

L ooking at educational statistics in a national perspective, we find

- 50.6 percent of the nation's high school diplomas are granted to women
- 75.0 percent of all intellectually qualified youngsters who do not enter college are girls
- 40.4 percent of bachelor's or first professional degrees are awarded to women
- 33.8 percent of master's degrees go to women
- 11.6 percent of the nation's doctoral degrees are awarded to females[1]
- 8.3 percent of the medical students in the United States are women
- 5.9 percent of the nation's law students are women.[2]

When these statistics are viewed in a historical perspective, we find that the picture for women has worsened rather than improved. In 1930, women were granted 40 rather than 34 percent of the mas-

Reprinted from *Toward a Sociology of Women,* Constantina Safilios-Rothschild, ed. (Lexington, Mass.: Xerox College Publishing, 1972), by permission.

---

* I wish to thank Jo-Ann Gardner, Kay Cassell, Daphne Joslin, and Ruth Oltman for assisting me in gathering material for this article.

171

> Regardless of intelligence or past academic
> performance, female applicants frequently
> find themselves confronted by barriers never
> experienced by men during the admission
> process.

ter's degrees and 15 rather than 12 percent of the doctorates.[3]

Turning to the nonacademic side of undergraduate life, Ruth Oltman, in a survey based on a random sample of 200 coeducational colleges and universities, found that in

85 percent of the institutions, *men* held the position of student-body president *all three academic years* from 1967–68 through 1969–70

81 percent of the schools, men were class presidents all three years

70 percent of the schools, men were chairmen of the campus judicial board all three years

61 percent of the institutions, men were chairmen of the union, senate, or board of governors all three years

75 percent of the (sixty-six reporting) institutions, men held the top SDS post all three years.[4]

The above illustrative figures give a good idea of the nature of barriers women are confronted with in higher education today. In this article we will first analyze the structural or institutional barriers which confront women in higher education. Secondly, we will examine the social attitudes and norms which, once internalized by women, further bar women from obtaining education and from utilizing the education they have obtained. In the last section, we will suggest steps which must be taken to provide women with equal educational opportunities.

STRUCTURAL BARRIERS TO WOMEN IN HIGHER EDUCATION

Structural barriers refers to those organizational patterns and practices in higher education which hinder or halt female students in their efforts to obtain college or university educations. These organizational barriers include practices pertaining to student admission and the granting of financial aid, to rules governing life on campus, to residency and full-time-study requirements, to the sexist character of much subject matter taught within universities today, to the composition of faculties, and to maternity and paternity leaves and married students' domestic responsibilities.

Admission

The first hurdle which confronts all students seeking higher education is that of admission. Regardless of intelligence or past academic performance, female applicants frequently find themselves confronted by barriers never experienced by men during the admission process. Discriminatory admission policies are disguised in various garb. One is the concern that men enjoy parity with women in those departments or colleges where, on the basis of their qualifications for admission, women "threaten" to outnumber men. The concern leads to a policy in which admission is refused to women who have higher qualifications than men who are granted admission. Such a practice at first appears equitable: "We don't after all, want to discriminate *against* men," it is said. Then one notices that in other colleges or departments of the same university where men far outnumber women (the medical and engineering schools are always good examples), the concern with sexual parity is strikingly absent.[5]

A second type of discriminatory admissions policy simply gives special attention to women's applications. In the *American Bar Association Journal* Beatrice Dinerman notes, for example:

> Although no law school uses either a formal or informal quota system to limit the number of females enrolled, they do admit to scrutinizing female applicants more closely for ability and motivation. Some schools give close consideration to the marital status of women before granting admission, and other schools take into account the possibility that a female student might not graduate and continue to practice. It follows that a male applicant is often chosen over an equally qualified female.[6]

Other traditional admissions policies, the entrance examination and the requirement that entering students provide recent recommendations from teachers and professors, discriminate against older college applicants. Because women are more likely than men to delay their college education, they are disproportionately affected by the policy. College Entrance Examinations, Graduate Record Examinations, and the SATs are all based on knowledge taught in high school or lower-division college courses. These exams, which are relatively easy for students who have recently completed their high school or college course work, are extremely difficult for even the brightest students who have been away from the classroom for ten or twenty years.

Another prevalent discriminatory admissions policy is that which restricts the student population to men or sets a lower quota for female than male students.[7] Quotas and selective admissions policies are often supported on the ground that men are more likely than women to complete their course of study. Time and again, however, in the very universities where this argument is given, a visit to the recorder's office reveals that not only do women students have higher grade averages than men, but a higher portion of the entering women than the entering men have obtained their degrees.[8]

Financial Aid

Following admission, students must face the question of how they are to pay for their education. The height of this hurdle varies both by economic class and by sex. Upper-middle-income parents generally consider the undergraduate education of both sons and daughters to be part of their parental responsibilities. These parents generally feel that their responsibility in the case of sons extends through law or medical school, but that in the case of daughters, it has been fulfilled after four or five years of college. Many also believe that they would be doing their daughters a disservice by helping them obtain education beyond the B.A. or M.A. level, for doing so might make catching the right man difficult.

While the financing of undergraduate education is virtually guaranteed for upper-middle-class men and women, such is not the case for working-class students. At this income level, parents, who cannot afford to send all of their children to college, generally make considerable sacrifices in order to put their sons through four years of college but do not offer to finance their daughters' college educations. The daughters may take two-year nursing courses, three-month courses to qualify as beauticians, or one-year secretarial courses. Others, immediately following high school, apply for jobs typing, waitressing, selling, or working in factories. Some help their parents pay for their brothers' educations.

Within the university, women are frequently discriminated against in the distribution of fellowship aid. As in the case of admission, many departments subtly discriminate against women, who on the average have higher mean grades than men, by ruling that fellowship aid be distributed to men and women students in proportion to the ratio of men and women students in the department. The general consequence of such a rule is that men who have lower qualifications than women are given aid.[9] Many of the best scholarships, as Bernice Sandler has pointed out before the Senate Judiciary Committee, are limited to men only.[10] Only under considerable pressure from Women's Liberation did New York University Law School agree to consider women, who make up one-third of its student body, for some of the highly coveted $10,000 law scholarships. Married women who must combine schooling with [other] responsibilities are excluded from competing for practically all federal scholarship and loan aid as well as many university scholarships by the limitation of these prizes to students engaging in full-time study, an impossibility for a woman who is managing a household. Unmarried female students, unlike their male counterparts, are also discouraged from borrowing heavily to pay for their education because doing so may overly burden their future husbands.

Married females not only face difficulties in obtaining financial resources for themselves but are expected, no matter what their own educational desires, to help their husbands through college and the first years of their careers. "Putting hubby through" usually means the assumption of a full-time job as well as household chores. The advent of better means of birth control has not lightened the burdens of young wives: now their graduate-student husbands can pursue their studies, often taking the time to switch from one area to another, without the pressure of knowing that they may soon have to assume the family's financial responsibilities. Meanwhile, the child-bearing and -rearing stage of the wives' lives is postponed, delaying the time when they may eventually return to school. Many universities' hardened view and actual support of these women's plight is illustrated by an account from Yale University. The *Yale-Break* reported: "The wives of graduating medical students at Yale were 'dishonored' this spring by a 'PHT' degree. In fancy lettering, on creamy parchment, signed by Dean Redlich's wife, the diploma read 'Congratulations for PUTTING HUBBY THROUGH.' " One of the "PHT" recipients, angered that Yale obviously defined herself and others only in terms of the men they were attached to, sent her "degree" back.[11]

Campus Rules and Counseling

After they have surmounted the hurdles of admission and financial aid and have arrived on the university campus, women face not only the "normal" trials of university life which constitute the common complaints of all students, but a whole new set of obstacles to their education which are peculiar to their sex.

Both freshmen and graduate students are also greeted by a "college counselor." This advisor, whom they will meet with intermittently throughout their college careers, frequently counsels women students away from rigorous, traditionally masculine courses of study or away from the university altogether. At the University of Maryland, Bernice Sandler reports, a male member of her own department "feels strongly that women should not be professionals and tells this to his women students."[12] At New York University women students in the School of Education report that one of their professors teaches that "the fact that women have produced less than men professionally and artistically is an indicator of women's lesser ability."[13] At Princeton, in a proposed memo to the university's first female undergraduate students, a well-meaning career services officer suggested that "although it sounded old-fashioned, it really was a good idea for women to have secretarial skills to fall back on."[14] My first-day experience at Columbia University's graduate school included a meeting with a professor who, rather than counseling me as to which courses I might take, proceeded for a quarter of an hour to tell me that "*since I was a woman* [my emphasis], I had better be very serious about the business of pursuing a graduate career." Friends from nearly every school and department outside of education and social work in major universities throughout the nation have told of similar or worse experiences they have had.

The serious effects which such experiences can have on women's academic and career decisions are shown by the findings of a four-year longitudinal study involving interviews and psychological tests of female undergraduate students at Stanford. The data reported from the study show that "women students need special encouragement to develop intellectual, artistic and professional ambitions." Repeatedly, their college histories "indicated the effect of encouragement or lack of such encouragement as a catalytic agent." The study revealed further that "an interested male has the power to communicate to the maturing young woman that she is not damaging her femininity by developing her mind and skills. Sometimes even a subtle form of consent or disapproval from a male served as a stimulus for a young woman to advance or retreat."[15]

Degree Requirements

Those women who have the fortune to be encouraged by counselors and professors and those who persevere in spite of discouraging counselors next face the multiple obstacles of university residency, full-time study, and course-credit requirements. Because wives traditionally follow their husbands, female students must move from campus to campus more often than men. Undergraduate and graduate degree course-credit requirements, which vary from college to college, as well as residency requirements obviously deter mobile students. These barriers should be among the easiest to remove from the paths of women, for, as Cless has observed, most students attend colleges and universities which are members of one of the six regional accreditation commissions of higher education. Since all these institutions belong to the National Federation of Accreditation Commissions, "it would be expected that credit for similar courses at different institutions would be automatically interchangeable among accredited colleges or universities; that requirements for the field of concentration would be similar; and that residency requirements would be nonexistent."[16]

Many colleges and universities are now loosening some of their degree requirements by granting credit for Peace Corps, VISTA, teacher-aid, and ghetto tutoring

> Introductory sociology texts, which are required reading for over a hundred thousand students a year, mention women only in chapters on the family.

experience. Equity suggests that institutions of higher education should grant female students who have returned to college after raising a family similar credit for the experiences they have had managing families, raising and tutoring their children, budgeting expenses, and serving the community. Demonstration programs in women's continuing education suggest that schools might be well rewarded for assisting the older student. They have shown that no matter how well women had performed in college when eighteen to twenty-one years of age, they did better when they returned to formal study after the age of thirty.[17]

The final obstacle which peers out of many college catalogs at women is the full-time study requirement. Not only does the requirement that students enroll for a full-time course of study prevent the woman who must devote part of her time to familial responsibilities from studying, but it coercively shapes the marital patterns of all couples in which one partner is a student. An increasing number of young husbands and wives are attempting to share family and household responsibilities equally.[18] The requirement that one partner must study or work full time makes the achievement of an equal division of familial responsibilities more difficult, if not impossible.

Subject Matter: Or, Where Have All Our Women Gone?

Once in the classroom, women soon discover that instructors and textbook writers in every field have, consciously or unconsciously, joined hands to keep "women in their place." Introductory sociology texts, which are required reading for over a hundred thousand students a year, mention women only in chapters on the family. In these chapters women are described in their "traditional" roles as full-time homemakers and mothers unlinked to the economic and political world—roles which in fact only the upper, or in some societies also the upper-middle, classes can afford.[19] Most "Marriage and the Family" courses leave problems of the modern family as an institution unexamined and reinforce the rapidly disappearing social belief that brides must be virgins for a marriage to be "happy."[20] In sociological theory courses, Betty Friedan has noted, structural-functionalists, "by giving an absolute meaning and a sanctimonious value to the generic term 'woman's role' . . . put American women into a kind of deep freeze."[21] As in the case of Talcott

Parsons's widely read essay on social stratification, these theorists' discussions of "what is" quickly become interpreted as "what should be." Perhaps a million college women have been instructed to read the following passage by Parsons:

> Absolute equality of opportunity is clearly incompatible with any positive solidarity of the family. . . . Where married women are employed outside the home, it is, for the great majority, in occupations which are not in direct competition for status with those of men of their own class. Women's interests, and the standard of judgment applied to them, run, in our society, far more in the direction of personal adornment. . . . It is suggested that this difference is functionally related to maintaining family solidarity in our class structure.[22]

Neither Parsons himself nor most professors who discuss his article go on to question the desirability of the class structure he describes or the need for such family solidarity.

Female aggression, initiative, and creativity are not ignored solely by sociologists. History courses skip over feminist movements and overlook the contributions (except for that of Betsy Ross), achievements, and oppression of women. Literature students are fed a constant diet of male writers—Ernest Hemingway, James Joyce, Norman Mailer, etc.—while the notable accomplishments of female writers go unanalyzed. In schools of medicine, engineering, and architecture, where the subject matter itself cannot be used to reinforce male and depress female egos, women students are continuously, informally pressed into "feminine" areas such as pediatrics, gynecology, or interior design. In the engineering school of a midwestern university, a female student found that all the lockers assigned to students for their laboratory equipment and clothes were in the men's lavatory.[23] Women who persevere in such areas as surgery despite the negative sanctions of male students and male professors find themselves eventually blocked when no hospital will allow them to fulfill their surgical internship requirements.

The continual emphasis which college and university professors have placed on the culture and achievements of white males has naturally served to motivate white male students, who feel comfortable with the culture and with the models who are like themselves. For blacks and women it has done the opposite. It has clearly carried the message, "You do not belong among those who make important decisions for or significant contributions to society." And for women, additionally, "If you try to become something other than housewives or low-income workers, you will be unsuccessful." Rather than degrade themselves by memorizing and regurgitating such "facts" as "women's place is in the home," many able women have dropped out of college or have discontinued their education after completing their B.A.; others have capitulated to their male colleagues and professors by

> **The absence of women in faculty and administrative positions serves as a silent but potent message to female students that "aiming high" would be foolish indeed.**

becoming interior designers rather than architects or contractors, pediatricians rather than surgeons, kindergarten teachers rather than university professors.

Today, women, like blacks a half decade ago, are discovering that they have a history and that there are alternatives to a male-dominated sexist society. Around the nation new courses are being developed and offered on the sociology and history of women. Textbooks (like this one) are beginning to be written and published on the subject of women. At least one literature instructor, Elaine Showalter of Douglass College, has switched to teaching about Mary McCarthy and other female writers. She reports, "The whole quality of the classroom and quality of term papers has changed since we switched to McCarthy!" Now she knows why her all-female class had difficulty identifying with the adolescent times of Hemingway and Joyce![24] The new developments are exciting, but to date, a female student is lucky if she gets one course out of ten which is not characterized by male chauvinism and sexist bias. In January 1971, fifty-five out of 2600 colleges and universities offered one or more courses in women's studies.[25] All should offer them. Large numbers of additional female faculty are needed to teach courses on women, to help male faculty recognize and overcome their sexist practices, and to serve as role models and confidantes for female students.

Role Models: Faculty Women

The statistics cited at the beginning of this article show that although half the students in America's prestigious institutions of higher education are women, less than one-tenth of their faculty is female and that most of these female faculty members are to be found on the lower rungs of the professorial ladder.[26] Even seventy out of seventy-four directors of the largest college and university libraries are men.[27] The absence of women in faculty and administrative positions serves as a silent but potent message to female students that "aiming high" would be foolish indeed. Outright sexist discrimination in hiring and promotion, nepotism rules, full-time work requirements, lack of child-care facilities, and maternity-paternity leaves, as well as barriers to women's attaining higher education account for females' low representation in high-ranking university positions.

Outright discrimination in university hiring and promotion of women has been frequently revealed. The Women's Equity Action League and the National Organization for Women in the spring of 1970 charged forty-three colleges and universities with discriminatory employment practices against women under Executive Orders 11246 and 11375, which forbid discrimination by federal contractors on the basis of race, color, religion, national origin, or sex. The colleges charged with discrimination were from every part of the nation, and their number included large and small, rich and poor institutions.[28]

The depth of sexist discrimination in university hiring practices was discovered by Lawrence Simpson in 1968. For his Ph.D. dissertation, Simpson distributed mock resumes of "men" and "women" to 234 representative deans, departmental chairmen, and faculty members who were involved in faculty hiring. The responses to the resumes showed that "where qualifications of men and women were equal, substantially more men were chosen, although the selection should have been almost equal, based on the previously determined choices of the faculty panel when no sex identification was given. In a choice between a superior woman and a less qualified man, the employers selected a significant number of women."[29] The nature of these hiring agents' sexist attitudes is illustrated by a conversation Jo Freeman had with Professor Arthur Mann of Chicago University's history department:

> [Mann] said his department would be happy to hire more women, but that there were only three good women historians in the country and none of them were available. He may be right in his assessment of the top historians, but he is wrong if he meant that only the best people in any field ever teach at the University of Chicago. . . . Judging the status of women by that of the most successful is not only a sham, but a dangerous one because it perpetuates tokenism and clothes it in a self-righteous mythology. It cannot be said that women are judged equally with men until ordinary men are judged by the same standards.[30]

The common arguments given by institutions for discrimination against academic women have been explained and refuted by Martha Griffiths on the floor of the United States Congress:

> For years there has been a shortage of college teachers, yet there has been little serious effort to recruit women for college faculties. The excuse often given that there is a shortage of qualified women is ridiculous. For example, at Columbia University women receive about 25 percent of its doctoral degrees, but comprise only 2 percent of the tenured faculty in its graduate schools. Furthermore, contrary to academic mythology, a higher percentage of women with doctorates go into college teaching than do men with doctorates. The argument that women are lost to the academic world when they

marry is also a myth, since over 90 percent of the women with doctorates are in the labor force.[31]

Universities' closest sources of women qualified to fill faculty positions and to serve as role models for female students are faculty wives, the very women against whom colleges have erected the highest barriers. Antinepotism rules which hold that husbands and wives cannot teach within either the same department or the same university are the most obvious form of discrimination against faculty wives. Supporters of the rules, who maintain that granting positions to both husbands and wives would constitute a form of departmental patronage, overlook the facts that universities and colleges annually lure scholars to their campuses by guaranteeing their proteges positions as assistant or associate professors, and that since persons with similar educational backgrounds frequently marry, both husbands and wives are likely to be qualified for university positions. Other supporters of the nepotism rules argue that the task of faculty selection would be more difficult if the nepotism rules were dropped. They maintain that in the cases of couples where the husband and wife do all their writing together (and, therefore, the acceptance of the second spouse, that is, the wife could not bring "new" ideas into the department) and where one has considerably higher qualifications than the other, the department would have to face the prospect of accepting one and rejecting the other. Women, on the other hand, are responding that although no one likes the job of having to reject students or prospective faculty, such rejections are obviously made every day. Therefore why should a selection committee's task be made easier solely in the case of married couples? Specifically, why should it be made easier by a policy which deprives universities of much talent and leads to blanket discrimination against women? These women point out that underlying these questions is a basic issue of power: Are the lives of selection committees or the lives of women to be made difficult?

Women are beginning to refuse to carry such burdens continually. In Arizona, faculty wives have begun, successfully, to contest the state university system's antinepotism rule.[32] Meanwhile, most other universities, rather than use qualified and talented faculty wives as a resource, isolate them and thereby create an entire community of negative role models for female students—role models which daily say: No matter how much education you have, you may expect to forget your career if you marry.

One Yale faculty wife has described her position as follows:

Today was a rather typical day. The morning and afternoon were spent at home alone with the baby. I'm not free to study or pursue a career and I haven't even the satisfaction of developing close friendships with other faculty wives. We are isolated from one another and, by the nature of our husbands' careers, we are transient, in fact, maddeningly so. This evening I wanted to go to a political meeting; my husband felt he should go back to the lab. And so, of course, I'm still at home babysitting. . . .

I am not so naive as to think that I could have an interesting and challenging job in my field if only I had more time and more freedom. Three years ago I took a job at Yale which required a B.A. in English and some knowledge of Latin. I was optimistic that I would be doing work which utilized my knowledge and would allow me to follow through with my interest in English. I soon learned that a knowledge of Latin was deemed necessary for proofreading Latin texts and a degree in English considered essential for writing routine business letters.[33]

Once women are hired for faculty positions, they face discrimination in regard to promotion, salaries, and day-to-day matters of university life. At the University of Michigan when a world-renowned scientist retired as the director of the Gerontology Institute, it was learned that her salary was equivalent to that of many assistant professors. Men with markedly lesser reputations who were considered to replace her were all offered well over twice her retiring salary.[34] At that university, the University of Chicago, and numerous other prestigious institutions most female Ph.D.'s are placed in neither directorships nor faculty positions and are given instead temporary positions as research associates.[35] As such, they are "allowed" to teach at low salaries and without a faculty vote; the years of teaching they accumulate do not lead to associate and full professorships, for these higher positions require that one begin her career with the title "assistant professor." Since many assistant professors primarily do research and teach a course or two on the side, the distinction between "assistant professor" and "research associate" is a matter of title only, but it is a matter of important consequence for one's later career.

Maternity and Paternity Leaves, Child Care, Meal Service, Part-Time Work and Study

Working women spend an average of twenty-eight hours a week on household tasks and child care.[36] The burden of household tasks and child care must be shared equally between men and women if women are to be considered to have an "equal opportunity" to study or work in institutions of higher education. If colleges and universities are to provide young married women with equal educational opportunities and attract sizable numbers of women to serve as faculty role models for all female students, they must not only destroy discriminatory rules and practices but also provide married students and faculty with maternity and paternity leaves, twenty-four-hour child-care facilities, meal service, and part-time work and study arrangements. Present university regulations which exclude maternity and paternity leaves and forbid part-time work or study for men and women not only force women to withdraw from academic life for longer than they would like but also prevent men from assuming parental responsibilities during their children's early years.[37]

The availability of excellent child-care facilities is, as shown by a longitudinal study of students graduating from college in 1961, the most important condition affecting women's decisions to attend graduate school.[38] Despite this critical finding, universities have continued to ignore female students' and faculty members' cries for nurseries and child care. After months of confrontation with university officials, Princeton's chapter of the National Organization for Women in the autumn of 1970 was able to get the university to provide space and funds for a nursery which is expected to meet the child-care needs of one-third of its faculty and students. At least Princeton has made a start. Hundreds of colleges and universities have yet to follow its lead. Until they do, the necessity of child care will continue to bar many women from pursuing or using their higher education.

Not only child care, but household tasks and meal preparation hamper wives who wish to develop or utilize their talents. Unless other women are to be enslaved as domestics, husbands are academic women's only source of household help. University policies must be reshaped to encourage rather than discourage faculty and student men from sharing domestic responsibilities. Universities might also construct communal dining rooms for families such as those in American dormitories or Swedish "service apartment houses" which would relieve faculty and student *couples* of the task of preparing meals.

INTERNALIZED BARRIERS TO WOMEN IN HIGHER EDUCATION

> ... prejudices and outmoded customs act as barriers to the full realization of women's basic rights which should be respected and fostered as part of our Nation's commitment to human dignity, freedom, and democracy.... (John F. Kennedy, in establishing the President's Commission on the Status of Women in 1961)

The structural barriers to women in higher education which we have reviewed above are buttressed by the social attitudes and norms taught both men and women concerning "feminine" behavior.[39] Today's American college women received their first bit of socialization concerning sex roles when, as newborn infants, they were carefully wrapped in pretty pink blankets. Later as young children, they were encouraged by their families to play house, take care of their baby dolls, and act like "ladies." "Masculine" traits such as physical and intellectual aggression, problem-solving ability, and overt hostility, while encouraged in their brothers, were severely discouraged in them. Their grade-school teachers continued to socialize them to "their roles." Despite the increasing proportion of mothers in the national labor force, their grade-school readers seldom, if ever, portrayed mothers at work. Their own mothers were expected to be available to assist teachers on field trips and to bake cookies for class parties.

In high school their activities and career plans were viewed in relationship to traditional "women's roles." Teachers and guidance counselors gently persuaded them that it was not proper to run for class president, that they would be better off not pursuing physics and third-year algebra, and that despite the nation's desperate need for physicians and innovative leaders, they would be happier as nurses than as doctors, as secretaries than as politicians. They were taught that while women can only be truly fulfilled as mothers and wives, it is compatible with the "feminine nature" and perhaps necessary that they also seek to bring "peace and comfort into the world" as social workers, nurses, sympathetic assistants, and primary-school teachers.[40] This form of socialization is perhaps best described by the following reflection of an MIT student:

> For years I have had to fight to retain my interest in aeronautics. My high school teacher thought I was crazy to even think of going into aeronautical engineering. My mother said I'd never find a man willing to marry a woman who likes to "tinker with motors," as she put it. My professors say I won't get a job in industry and should switch to another engineering specialty.[41]

In addition to being socialized away from "unfeminine" careers and from positions which might challenge the status of their future mates, young women were taught to compete with other women for the admiration and attention of men and ultimately for a husband.[42] Other women were to be distrusted; women were to place their faith in men. They saw that, in the minds of their parents and teachers, having a date (however dull) for the junior prom took precedence over writing a creative essay, tutoring a poor child, and myriad other things. Life was defined for them in terms of being the "other half" of some man, a subordinate, submissive, dependent, unequal position.

Such wisdom imparted by parents and teachers was reinforced by the mass media. Whenever they flicked on the television they either saw themselves portrayed by liquor, cigarette, and auto advertisements as sexual objects whose goal was to give men pleasure, or were induced by the doting-wife-mother image portrayed in household ads to feel that indeed their only desire was to please a husband and his children.[43] Many came to feel that they had little of worth to say, that what they had to say could probably be said better by someone else (most likely a boy), and that they really were silly, emotional creatures. Those who, despite this consistent socialization to "feminine roles," continued to question their own roles in life usually found themselves talking with psychiatrists who treated their "problems" as requiring personal rather than societal change and urged them to find self-fulfillment through devotion to marriage and parenthood.[44]

Philip Goldberg's study of women's prejudice against women[45] proved quite clearly the tremendous effects of current sex-role socialization upon the self-images of women. In the same vein, in a study of students at six California high schools, Don McNeily III found that girls as young as thirteen or fourteen years old had already been socialized to believe that powerful social roles are not for them. When asked whether they "could be" President, only 13 percent of them, as compared with 31 percent of the boys, said yes, and when asked about the possibility of becoming governor, 17 percent of the girls and 44 percent of the boys replied that they could see themselves as someday holding that office.[46]

During the early fifties David McClelland and his colleagues isolated a psychological characteristic which they termed the "need to achieve." Subsequently, McClelland's students studied many aspects of this internalized motivation to excel. In each of the studies, however, women were conspicuously absent, for early in the studies the female subjects had produced inconsistent, confusing results and the investigators had decided to leave them out. Ten years later, Matina Horner decided to investigate the success needs of women. Her first consistent finding on women was that they had much higher test-anxiety scores than men. With the use of the TAT (Thematic Apperception Test) and a story-completion test concerning a successful male and a successful female medical student, Horner went on to isolate in women a fear of success. Horner concluded that the motive to avoid success was born in her female subjects when they learned the truth of Samuel Johnson's comment, "A man is in general better pleased when he has a good dinner upon his table, than when his wife talks Greek."[47]

What about the women who do "succeed" in academia? Jessie Bernard reports that a study of 706 college teachers in Minnesota, 27 percent of whom were women, found that the women had been much more tentative, much more modest, and much more influenced by others in their career choices than the men. On the basis of the study's findings, Bernard noted that an academic career appeared to be something almost thrust upon these women, something which they would not of themselves have aspired to.[48] Thus, these "successful women" had also learned not to seek success aggressively, as this would not have been considered "ladylike," but to deny their aspirations and to allow their career paths to be shaped by whether or

> **. . . for generations women have been advised to seek change by working harder individually or by being "twice as good as men." Women have tried this strategy and have found that it doesn't work.**

not someone happened to offer them a college teaching position.

Women's lack of confidence in other women, their "need to fail," their fear of acting aggressively are societally taught norms which, once internalized, become formidable psychological barriers buttressing the structural barriers to the higher education of women. These norms as well as organizational features of universities which deter women must be transformed if women are to enjoy the basic rights which Kennedy declared "should be respected and fostered as part of our Nation's commitment to human dignity, freedom, and democracy. . . ."

WOMEN UNITE! EDUCATION'S A RIGHT!

How can persons who seek educational opportunities for women abolish the structural and psychological barriers which confront women in higher education today? Glancing backward, we see that for generations women have been advised to seek change by working harder individually or by being "twice as good as men." Women have tried this strategy and have found that it doesn't work. The individual woman who struggles and finally becomes an outstanding scholar may be hired by a top-notch university, but her appointment guarantees neither that ordinary women, like ordinary men, will be hired by that university nor that she will not at some future time be discriminated against purely on the basis of her sex.

Feminists must work together and become politically organized if they are to destroy the barriers which confront women in higher education and other areas of life. Ours is a politically organized society which, as Richard Quinney notes, is based on an interest structure characterized by an unequal distribution of power and by conflict. Various segments of any society have different interests. The distribution of power, which is determined by conflict, determines the laws, policies, and practices of societies.[49] The conflict may involve violence or social conditioning.[50] When members of an interest group are split by geographical barriers or political conditioning, they are more vulnerable to socialization which supports norms and ideologies counter to their own interests. Marx, for example, noted that in his day Irish and English workers were separated by political conditioning to ideologies which misrepresented their interests, and that in feudal times peasants had been geographically separated.[51] Now in the 1970s, women are coming to realize, as blacks did some ten years ago, that through their socialization to individual and class competition, they too have been politically separated from one another. This separation has made them vulnerable to discrimination and sexist socialization in all spheres of life.[52] The effects of this separation may be countered only if women analyze the means by which they have been separated and exploited, resocialize themselves to their own interests, and act politically on the basis of these interests.

The discussion in the first two sections of this paper suggests many steps which feminists, as a politically organized segment of society, must take to provide women with equal educational opportunities. As a first step, overt and covert sexist discrimination in university admissions and financial aid practices must be halted. The addition of women to admissions and financial aid staffs will not guarantee fair practices but would be a step in the right direction. Admissions and financial aid staffs must work toward evaluating applications without regard to or information concerning sex, as they have done in the case of race. The practice whereby one sector of a university discriminates against women so as to maintain an even ratio of men to women while other sectors with a high ratio of men do nothing to obtain an even sexual balance must be stopped. Entrance examinations which discriminate against older applicants, most of whom are women, should be abolished. The limitation of many scholarships and fellowships to men must be contested. Until such time as sexist discrimination is abolished in elementary and high schools, admissions and financial aid policies should be designed, as they have been in the case of blacks, to favor women, particularly women from families which cannot afford to send all their children to college. Institutions of higher education which are found to have sexist admissions and financial aid practices must be sanctioned. Toward this end, the Civil Rights Act of 1964 should be amended to authorize the Attorney General of the United States both to aid women and, in the case of girls under twenty-one, parents in suits seeking equal access to public education (Title V), and to make a survey concerning the lack of equal educational opportunities for individuals by reason of sex (Title IX).

Second, college counseling should be made to broaden rather than restrict women's views of career possibilities. College counseling is one point at which women may be helped to reexamine their attitudes, taught by the media and other socializing agents, concerning their roles and status. College counselors should discuss with female students the significant changes which have occurred in the life-patterns of American women since 1900 and their grandmothers' day. These changes include the twenty-five-year extension of the average American woman's life; a continually decreasing housework load; birth control, which has resulted in smaller families and, in the last nine years, in an increasing proportion of twenty- to twenty-four-year-old wives who have no children and therefore have greater freedom to work or continue their schooling; and changing attitudes concerning the wisdom of mothers' full-time presence with their young children.[53] Counselors should next help women evaluate their educational and career choices in the context of these changes.

Women's Liberation groups on college campuses might help counselors reexamine their attitudes concerning women and might work with the counselors in advising groups of female students. Many women have already found that small "Women's Lib" group discussions provide a valuable basis for reexamining their personal goals and values.

Not only must counselors stop discouraging and begin encouraging women to develop their full potential, but universities must remove the degree requirements which bar many women from completing their education. In 1963 the President's Commission on the Status of Women stated that changes in degree requirements were among the basic essentials for the provision of adequate education for women. The commission recommended the provision of ready transfer of credits from college to college, increased use of testing for credit, the substitution of life experience for course work, the facilitation of part-time study, the lifting of age limits, and the reassessment of time requirements.[54]

Women now realize that, in addition to the "essentials" outlined by the 1963 commission, courses on women should be added to college curricula, large numbers of female faculty should be added to college staffs at all levels of the professorial and administrative hierarchies, and child-care facilities plus maternity and paternity leaves must be provided. Recently the American Federation of Teachers has begun to construct lesson plans on women's history and to conduct a major investigation of how high school history books portray the struggle for women's rights.[55] Similar efforts need to be made at the college level. In addition, the works of women writers plus texts analyzing them and examining the images of women in literature should be introduced in English classes. Social science instructors across the nation might follow the lead of Leni Weitzman, who at Yale University uses a collection of advertisements as a teaching aid to alert both men and women to the oppressive, manipulative nature of advertising and the role that it plays in shaping the population's image of women. Excellent courses specifically on the role of women in society have been instituted in some colleges and high schools, and similar courses should be made available at all American colleges and universities.

Large numbers of female faculty should be added to college staffs at all levels of the professorial and administrative hierarchies so that female like male students may have faculty role models and representatives of their own sex. In order to hire adequate numbers of female faculty, universities will have to recruit women active-

> **... sexism is an integral part of the present social structure and ... those in power benefit from it ....**

ly and abolish written and *de facto* nepotism rules and sexist hiring practices. Executive Orders 11246 and 11375, which, as mentioned earlier, forbid discrimination by federal contractors, including universities, on the basis of race, color, religion, national origin, or sex, must be enforced. The United States Office of Education's Higher Education General Information Surveys should include questions on the sex of teaching personnel.

So that male members of the academic community will not be forced to lead lopsided lives with little or no domestic activity and their wives will not be forced into unending isolation within the home, more flexible part-time employment arrangements should be made available to all university personnel, and part-time study arrangements should be offered to students. All institutions of higher education should also provide maternity and paternity leaves and child-development centers to all members of their communities. Until good preschool child-care centers and after-school centers are available for all children in the society and until husbands come to share domestic responsibilities equitably with their wives—or until the family institution is totally transformed—all should recognize that *in the United States women do not enjoy equal rights.*

As feminists strive to destroy the structural and attitudinal barriers confronting women in higher education and other spheres of life, they see more clearly the political and exploitative base which underlies the barriers. Destroying institutional barriers to women and changing traditional patterns of socialization will be difficult. The present barriers and forms of sexist socialization are not accidental: the inculcation of values and goals through the socialization process is universally the strongest means where dominators can exert social control over those they dominate. That sexism is an integral part of the present social structure and that those in power benefit from it is illustrated by the quick appearance of vengeful hostility when women seek freedom, power, or status greater than that given to or defined for them in their "feminine role." Like the label of "black racist" pinned on blacks struggling for freedom, the labels "man-hater," "castrating bitch," "lesbian," and "tough" are hurled at women who wish to define their destinies and goals for themselves. To have the strength to ignore such labels and to eradicate sexism in society, feminists must unite and treat the question of sex politically, as those who discriminate against women have done.

Notes

1. Elizabeth Cless, "A Modest Proposal for the Educating of Women," *American Scholar,* 38 (Autumn 1969): 620; U.S. Department of Labor, Women's Bureau, *Handbook on Women Workers* (Washington, D.C.: Government Printing Office, 1969).
2. *Report of the Presidential Task Force on Women's Rights and Responsibilities* (Washington, D.C.: Government Printing Office, 1969), sec. 3C.
3. "Discrimination," *Parade* (Sunday Magazine of the *Washington Post*), June 15, 1969.
4. Ruth M. Oltman, "Status of Women on Campus," stenciled (Washington, D.C.: American Association of University Women, Apr. 9, 1970), p. 1; cf. Marge Piercy, "The Movement: For Men Only?" *Guardian,* Jan. 31, Feb. 7, 14, 1970.
5. Cf. Kathleen Shortridge, "Women as University Nigger: How the 'U' Keeps Females in Their Place," *The Daily Magazine,* Apr. 12, 1970; Jean D. Grambs, "Editorial," *Women's Education,* 7 (Mar. 1968); Eric Wentworth, "Women Seek College Equality," *Washington Post,* June 22, 1970.
6. "Sex Discrimination in the Legal Profession," *American Bar Association Journal,* 55 (Oct. 1969), p. 951.
7. Only recently, legal action forced the state of Virginia to admit women to the University College of Arts and Sciences at Charlottesville (*Kirstein et al. v. University of Virginia,* F.C. Va. Civil Action No. 220–69R). The suit, which charged the university with the violation of women's rights under the First and Fourteenth amendments, was dropped because the university changed its policy to admit women (*Washington Post,* June 26, 1969).
8. Jo Freeman, "Women on the Social Science Faculties of the University of Chicago Since 1892," stenciled (Chicago: University of Chicago, Department of Political Science, Winter 1969).
9. Cf. Anne Row, "Women in Science," *Personnel and Guidance Journal,* 44 (Apr. 1966).
10. Bernice Sandler, "Statement Regarding the Equal Rights for Women," in U.S. Congress, Senate, Judiciary Committee, Subcommittee on Constitutional Amendments [Re S.J. Res. 61], May 6, 1970.
11. Editors, "Atrocity of the Month," *Yale-Break,* 1 (June 1, 1970).
12. Sandler, *op. cit.*
13. Personal communications with women students at the School of Education of New York University.
14. Elaine Showalter, "Women and the University," *Princeton Alumni Weekly* (Feb. 24, 1970), p. 8. Harold I. Kaplan, M.D., who conducted a seven-year study under a National Institute of Mental Health grant of medical schools' attitudes toward women students, recently said that "some replies to [my] questions were so 'scandalous' that [I] did not include them in [my] final report," which concluded that "widespread prejudice is depriving the nation of urgently needed physicians." See "Women Seek Bigger Medical Role," *American Medical News,* Nov. 23, 1970, p. 1.
15. Marjorie M. Lozoff, "Abstract of *College Influences on the Role Development of Female Undergraduates,*" stenciled (Palo Alto, Calif.: Stanford Institute for the Study of Human Problems, 1969), p. 3.
16. Cless, *op. cit.*, p. 624.
17. *Ibid.*, p. 623.
18. "Women's Lib Movement Inspires More Couples to Strive for Equality," *The Wall Street Journal,* Aug. 4, 1970; Pat Mainardi, "The Politics of Housework," in Robin Morgan, ed.,

Sisterhood Is Powerful (New York: Random House, 1970), pp. 447-455; Alix Shulman, "A Marriage Agreement," in Sookie Stambler, ed., *Women's Liberation: Blueprint for the Future* (New York: Ace Books, 1970), pp. 211-216.

19. Marlene Dixon has noted that "in Mexico, with its modified purdah and machismo . . . it is the middle-class women who are inferior, irrelevant, held in contempt—peasant women contribute too much to the support of the household, farm, and industry to be placed in the totally subservient position of middle-class Mexican women. Women have it bad everywhere, but with the loss of necessary economic functions, the position seems less psychologically bearable, not to mention the loss of all power except manipulation" (Marlene D. Dixon, "A Position Paper on Radical Women in the Professions," stenciled (Chicago: University of Chicago, Department of Sociology, 1967). Cf. Thorstein Bevlen, *The Theory of the Leisure Class: An Economic Study of Institutions* (New York: Macmillan, 1899).

20. Among the most blatantly sexist texts is Henry A. Bowman, *Marriage for Moderns* (New York: McGraw-Hill, 1942). In recent years a small number of articles and texts have appeared which have questioned the traditional writings of American family sociologists. Most of these have been by non-Americans or by sociologists who do not consider themselves "family sociologists." Cf. Barrington Moore, "Thoughts on the Future of the Family," in Frank Lindenfield, ed., *Radical Perspectives on Social Problems* (New York: Macmillan, 1968); Constantina Safilios-Rothschild, "Toward a Cross-Cultural Conceptualization of Family Modernity," *Journal of Comparative Family Studies*, 1 (Fall 1970): 17-25; Safilios-Rothschild, "A Cross-Cultural Examination of Women's Familial Educational and Occupational Options," *Acta Sociologica* 14 (Winter 1971); Safilios-Rothschild, "Marital Expectations: Discrepancies Between Ideals and Realities," in C. Presvellou and Pierre de Bie, eds., *Images and Counter-Images of Young Families* (Louvain: International Scientific Commission on the Family, 1970), pp. 169-74; and Safilios-Rothschild, "The Influence of Wives' Work Commitment upon Some Aspects of Family Organization and Dynamics," *Journal of Marriage and the Family*, 32, (Nov. 1970): 681-91.

21. *The Feminine Mystique* (New York: Dell Publishing Co., 1963), p. 118.

22. "An Analytical Approach to the Theory of Social Stratification," *Essays in Sociological Theory*, rev. ed. (New York: Free Press, 1965), pp. 79-80.

23. Esther Westervelt (Paper delivered at the Midwest Regional Pilot Conference, co-sponsored by the Women's Bureau of the U.S. Department of Labor and the U.S. Office of Education on "New Approaches to Counseling Girls in the 1960's," University of Chicago, Feb. 26-27, 1965).

24. S. Dianne Dublier, "What Makes A Feminist?" *Trenton* (May 1970), p. 18.

25. Women at San Diego (Calif.) State College organized the first complete women's studies program, with courses including women in comparative cultures, the socialization process of women, contemporary issues in the liberation of women, women in history, women in literature, the status of women under various economic systems, and women and education, among other subjects. According to the *Guardian*, the women have encountered considerable faculty and administrative resistance. Visiting Professor Roberta Salper reported that many faculty members "make comments like, 'This is absurd. Women come to college to get husbands and we all know that' " (see "Women Win Courses at 55 Schools," *Guardian* [Jan. 2, 1971], p. 7).

26. Caroline Bynum and Janet Martin, "The Sad Status of Women Teaching at Harvard or 'From what you said I would never have known you were a woman,' " *The Radcliffe*

Quarterly (June 1970), pp. 12-14; Women's Caucus, The Western Political Science Association, "Report on Women on the UCLA and Stanford Faculties," *The Spokeswoman,* 1, (July 30, 1970): 2,; Jo Freeman, *op. cit.*; Kathleen Shortridge, *op. cit.*

27. Women's Liberation meeting announcement (American Library Association Conference, Detroit, June 29, 1970).

28. Nancy Gruchow, "Discrimination: Women Charge Universities, Colleges with Bias," *Science,* 168 (May 1, 1970): 559.

29. Lawrence A. Simpson, "A Study of Employing Agents' Attitudes Toward Academic Women in Higher Education" (Ph.D. dissertation, Pennsylvania State University, 1968).

30. Freeman, *op. cit.*

31. U.S. Congress, House of Representatives, *Congressional Record,* 91st Cong. 2d sess., 1970, vol. 116; cf. Helen S. Astin, *The Woman Doctorate in America* (New York: Russell Sage Foundation, 1969); Patricia Graham, "Women in Academe," *Science,* 169 (Sept. 26, 1970): 1284-89.

32. The *Spokeswoman* reported, "An anti-nepotism rule that operated to exclude faculty wives from faculty positions in the Arizona state university system has been rescinded. The Board of Regents abolished its long-standing policy while a class declaratory judgment action attacking the rule was pending in the state courts. Brought by five faculty wives who had been affected by the rule, the complaint asked the court to declare it invalid under state law and the federal constitution. The case remains before the court, as of July 1970, while the plaintiffs watch what action the administration takes to implement the policy change" (vol. 1, no. 3 [July 30, 1970], p. 4).

33. Anonymous, "Status Woe," *Yale-Break,* 1 (June 1, 1970): 3.

34. Discussion between the author and Louis A. Ferman, Professor, The Institute of Labor and Industrial Relations, University of Michigan, Sept. 1969.

35. *Ibid.*

36. Astin, *op. cit.*, p. 95.

37. Cf. Lynda Lytle Holmstrom, "Career Patterns of Married Couples" (Paper delivered at the Seventh World Congress of the International Sociological Association, Varna, Bulgaria, Sept. 19, 1970). In Sweden, Prime Minister Olof Palme has noted, the large trade unions "have prepared their own programmes which will make it possible for men to share the child care with the women" ("The Emancipation of Man" [Address to the Women's National Democratic Club, Washington, D.C., June 8, 1970], p. 9).

38. U.S. Department of Health, Education, and Welfare, National Institutes of Health, *Women and Graduate Study* (Washington, D.C.: Government Printing Office, 1968), p. 9.

39. See Sandra L. Bem and Daryl J. Bem, "Training the Woman to Know Her Place," Kathleen Barry, "A View from the Doll Corner," Leah Heyn, "Children's Books," Jamie K. Frisof, "Textbooks and Conditioning," and Donna Keek, "The Art of Maiming Women" (an analysis of television commercials), all in *Women,* 1 (Fall 1969); and Jennifer Gardner, "Woman as Child: Notes from a Meeting," stenciled (The Radical Women of New York, 1968), p. 2; Elizabeth Fisher, "Children's Books: The Second Sex, Junior Division," *New York Times Book Review* (1970) pp. 89-94, rpt. in Sookie Stambler, ed., *Women's Liberation: Blueprint for the Future;* Cynthis Fuchs Epstein, *Woman's Place Options and Limits in Professional Careers* (Berkeley: University of California Press, 1970), pp. 50-86; Ruth Hartley and A. Klein, "Sex-Role Concepts among Elementary School-Age Girls," *Marriage and Family Living,* vol. 21 (Feb. 1959), pp. 59-64; and Ann Eliasberg, "Are You Hurting

Your Daughter Without Knowing It?" *Family Circle* (Feb. 1971).

40. An extreme example of sexist attitudes and of a belief in the "feminine nature" became a national controversy during the summer of 1970, when in response to Congresswoman Patsy Mink's request that the Democratic party's Committee on National Priorities "give the cause of women's rights the highest priority it deserves," Dr. Edgar F. Berman, a retired surgeon and a member of the committee, declared that physical factors, particularly the menstrual cycle and menopause, disqualified women for key executive positions. Subsequently, psychiatrists and endocrinologists noted that menopause is "usually most upsetting to women who stay home and think about it rather than do a good day's work" and that, even when women have menstrual dysfunctions, they don't "usually stay off the job or go off at noon and drink too much liquor as so many men do" (Christopher Lydon, "Role of Women Sparks Debate by Congresswoman and Doctor," *New York Times,* July 26, 1970; Marilyn Bender, "Doctors Deny Woman's Hormones Affect Her as an Executive," *New York Times,* July 31, 1970, p. 33).

41. Alice Rossi, "Job Discrimination and What Women Can Do About It," *Atlantic,* 225 (Mar. 1970): 99.

42. Redstockings Collective, "How Women Are Kept Apart," in Stambler, ed., *Women's Liberation: Blueprint for the Future,* pp. 23-39.

43. Cf. Sue Munaker, Evelyn Goldfield, and Naomi Weisstein, "A Woman Is a Sometime Thing," in Priscilla Long, ed. *The New Left: A Collection of Essays* (Boston: Porter Sargent, 1969), pp. 236-71; Alice Embree, "Media Images: Madison Avenue Brainwashing" and Florika, "Media Images 2: Body Odor and Social Order," in Morgan, ed., *Sisterhood Is Powerful* pp. 175-97.

44. Cf. Alice Rossi, "Equality Between the Sexes: An Immodest Proposal," *Daedalus,* 93 (Spring 1964): 607-52; and Rossi, "Sex Equality: The Beginnings of Ideology," *The Humanist,* 28-29 (Sept.-Oct. 1969): 3-6.

45. Philip Goldberg's article is contained in Chapter 1 of this volume.

46. Editors, "Research Round-Up," *Trans-Action,* 8 (Feb. 1971): 4, 6, 10.

47. Matina Horner, "A Bright Woman Is Caught in a Double Bind," *Psychology Today,* 3 (Nov. 1969): pp. 36-38, 62.

48. Jesse Bernard, *Academic Women* (University Park, Pa.: The Pennsylvania State University Press, 1964), p. 65.

49. Richard Quinney, ed., *Crime and Justice in Society* (Boston: Little, Brown, 1969), pp. 25-29.

50. Cf. Kate Millett, *Sexual Politics* (Garden City, N.Y.: Doubleday & Co., 1970), pp. 23-58; and Hannah Arendt, "Speculations on Violence," *New York Review of Books,* 12 (Feb. 27, 1969), p. 24.

51. Karl Marx, *The Eighteenth Brumaire of Louis Bonaparte* (New York: International Publishers, 1926).

52. Cf. Bem and Bem, *op. cit.*

53. U.S. Department of Labor, Bureau of Labor Statistics, "Marital and Family Characteristics of Workers, March 1969," Advance Summary: *Special Labor Force Report* (Washington, D.C.: Government Printing Office, 1970), pp. 2-7.

54. The President's Commission on the Status of Women, *American Women* (Washington, D.C.: Government Printing Office, 1963).

55. *Spokeswoman,* 1 (Sept. 30, 1970): 7.

to Discriminate
...st Women
Without Really Trying

Jo Freeman

"Any girl who gets this far has got to be a kook"
  one distinguished (male) member of the
University of Chicago faculty told a female graduate
student who had come to see him about being on
her dissertation committee.

This was just one of many such statements collected by women students at the University in the
spring of 1969 to illustrate their contention that
"some of our professors have different expectations
about our performance than about the performance
of male graduate students—expectations based not
on our ability as individuals but on the fact that we
are women." There were many others. They included:

"The admissions committee didn't do their job.
There is not one goodlooking girl in the entering class."

"They've been sending me too many women
advisees. I've got to do something about that."

"You have no business looking for work with
a child that age."

"I'm sorry you lost your fellowship. You're
getting married, aren't you?"

"We expect women who come here to be competent, good students; but we don't expect them to
be brilliant or original."

"I see the number of women entering this year has increased. I hope the quality has increased as well."

And most telling of all: "I know you're competent and your thesis advisor knows you're competent. The question in our minds is are you *really serious* about what you're doing." This was said to a young woman who had already spent five years and over $10,000 getting to that point in her Ph.D. program.

These comments hardly contribute to a student's self-image as a scholar. Often made in jest, they are typical of those used by professors on the University of Chicago campus and other campuses to express the only socially acceptable prejudice left—that against women. But if you were to ask these same professors whether they discriminate against women students and colleagues, most would answer that they do not.

Until a few years ago, most women would have agreed with them. Since then, many of the women students and faculty toward whom these comments were aimed have looked at the actions behind the words and concluded that most professors discriminate against women whether they are conscious of it or not.

Women in one social science department openly declared that their professors frequently discouraged them from going to or staying in graduate school. They said the attitude of their professors indicated "that we are expected to be decorative objects in the classroom, that we're not likely to finish a Ph.D. and if we do, there must be something wrong with us." They pointed out that no woman had held a faculty position in their department since the University was founded in 1892 and that this lack of role models was hardly encouraging to women students.

At the time the University community was recovering from a massive sit-in the previous quarter (winter 1969) caused by the firing of Marlene Dixon, the first woman to teach in the Sociology Department in nineteen years. Though women's issues were not the primary concern of the protest, they had been raised publicly for the first time during the course of it, (thanks largely to the efforts of Dixon herself and of the campus women's liberation group), and had generated the greatest response from the University community.

One such response was from the students, who began to organize into departmental caucuses, put out position papers, and confront the faculty with their new feminist consciousness. The other response was from the faculty and the administration. The Committee of the Council of the Academic Senate appointed a Committee on University Women (COUW) to study "the situation and opportunities presently enjoyed by women in the University community." The COUW created a student subcommittee (SCOUW) of six students and three faculty members, of which I was chairperson.

THE STUDY

As part of its duties SCOUW developed a detailed, self-administered questionnaire. The design of the study* involved distributing the questionnaire to a sample of approximately 50 male and 50 female respondents from each of the seventeen graduate and undergraduate divisions and professional schools at the University of Chicago at the beginning of the following fall quarter (1969–70). These numbers were chosen to provide adequate samples for comparison. In the final tally each 100-person unit was weighted to represent the actual relative strength of its school or division in the University. The sampling intervals were determined individually for each unit and sex, and the sample was drawn by selecting every n^{th} name from alphabetical lists of students registered that spring.

Although the expected 30 percent loss rate was compensated for, the inevitable elimination of the drop-outs in itself involves a bias: our study excluded the University's casualties, who may well have been those most fruitful to examine. This is analogous to studying the effects of a disease by looking only at its survivors. Although the study no doubt included many who would later drop out, the possibility of bias still exists. One could maintain that those women who perceive discrimination most sharply or get the least support from the University environment are the ones to leave. To a certain extent we are dealing with a group of self-selected women who have at least partially adapted to the system.

The questionnaire took about twenty minutes to complete as most of the questions had precoded answers from which the respondent picked one or more. Students maintained their anonymity by turning in their completed questionnaires separately from a card with their name on it. When a name card was received, the respondent's name was removed from the sample list. Thus at any given moment we had a list of those who had not returned their questionnaires and who could be followed up by phone calls.

The overall response rate was 77 percent. The loss was due partially to nonreturning students and partially to failure to turn in the questionnaires. Unfortunately, the rather low response rate was not the only problem the study ran into. Other problems that could bias its results were encountered in three spheres:

1. *The Administration.* The staff had received assurances from intermediate-level administrators that if the questionnaire was not offensive, it would

---

* The study was directed by Ellen Fried, formerly of the National Opinion Research Center, assisted by Nancy Hartsock, then a graduate student in political science at the University of Chicago and now teaching at the Johns Hopkins University. The responses to the questionnaire have been published in *Women in the University of Chicago* (May 1970), available from the Office of Public Information, University of Chicago.

be distributed at registration. Unfortunately, the Provost later decided to avoid any possible complications of the registration procedure and rejected the questionnaire without even looking at it. It might be noted that it is not uncommon for material to be distributed and studies undertaken at registration time. Only four years previously, permission had been given for a study requiring every registering student to fill out a questionnaire on teeth-gnashing. Other studies using the registration handout procedure had been done in the interim. Our low response rate can be attributed largely to this administrative reversal, for the officials of some of the professional schools gave us full cooperation and those units had response rates near 90 percent.

2. *The Faculty.* The study was originally intended to be a far-ranging one that would probe the causes of the problems women students faced in general. Unfortunately, a majority of the faculty members of COUW and SCOUW felt the survey should be used primarily to determine the extent to which women perceived overt discrimination in the classroom and in university services. It was felt that only items leading to explicit recommendations to the University should be included. For example, questions on the amount of time spent in child care were opposed on the grounds that there was nothing the University could do about any sex differential that might exist here. The Null Environment Hypothesis which will be discussed in detail below, was one of the few nonspecific concerns to survive this weeding out.

3. *The Students.* Members of the campus women's liberation group decided to boycott the questionnaire for political reasons on which they did not elaborate. Most of them were undergraduate women in the social sciences, and this is where we found our lowest return rate—62 percent. Some differences in return rates were certainly due to the different distribution and follow-up methods we had to use. However, the procedures used in this unit were identical for men and women, and the men had a response rate of 81 percent. There is good reason to believe, therefore, that the boycott was effective and that the responses from this unit do not adequately represent the militant feminist viewpoint. Nonetheless, the results were quite striking.

THE NULL ENVIRONMENT HYPOTHESIS

The Null Environment Hypothesis was a response to the contention of one of the

. . . an academic situation that neither encourages nor discourages students of either sex is inherently discriminatory against women because it fails to take into account the differentiating external environments from which women and men students come.

faculty members of SCOUW that the faculty did not discriminate between women and men students—they treated them all poorly. Succinctly put, the hypothesis states that an academic situation that neither encourages nor discourages students of either sex is inherently discriminatory against women because it fails to take into account the differentiating external environments from which women and men students come. As Horner has pointed out, many women enter school with a "motive to avoid success" because they fear social rejection or find academic success in conflict with a feminine identity.[1] Even those who have not internalized this notion often find little or no support for intellectual aspirations—particularly at the postgraduate level—because their endeavors are not taken seriously. Thus women enter with a handicap which a "null" academic environment does nothing to decrease and may well reinforce. In other words, professors don't have to make it a specific point to discourage their female students. Society will do that job for them. All they have to do is to fail to encourage them. Professors can discriminate against women without really trying.

Obviously, we first had to find out whether the hypothesized null environment existed at the University. Did the faculty provide a supportive environment for the students or did they not? Did they strongly encourage them to develop their potential or did they not?

We asked students how they thought the faculty felt about their going to or being in graduate or professional school and about their having a career. We interpreted a response of "very favorable" to mean that a student felt he or she received positive support. As can be seen in Tables I and II, only 47 percent of the male students and 32 percent of the female students felt they got positive support or encouragement for postgraduate education, either from the male 94 percent or the female 6 percent of the faculty.* Even fewer felt the faculty were very favorable to their having a career. Thus if we define a null academic environment as one with a significant lack of positive support, we can say that such an environment did indeed

---

* Female faculty members scored identically to males, for instance (see Table IV), in the percentage rated "very favorable" to women graduate students' having a career, and only 2.6 percent higher in "very favorable" attitudes toward women's being in graduate or professional school.

exist at the University of Chicago. The lack of positive support for women was especially evident. Only a little over two-thirds as many female as male students thought the male faculty were "very favorable" to their having advanced education and a lesser proportion thought they were favorable to their having a career.

If students do not receive support from faculties for going on with their education and careers, where do they get it? Much of it comes from personal commitment. The presence of this internal support mechanism is always assumed in men. Women are supposed to be less deeply committed, and this supposition is often used both as an explanation of their lesser success and as a justification for preferential treatment for men. Ignoring for the moment the self-fulfilling prophecy inherent in such an assumption, we wanted to know exactly how deeply committed our women students were.

TABLE I Response to: "How do you think these people feel about your going to (being in) graduate or professional school?" by Sex

(Percent Saying Person is "Very Favorable")

| | Sex of respondent | |
Person	Male	Female
Male faculty	47%	32%
Female faculty	37%	35%

TABLE II Response to: "How do the following people feel about your having a career?" by Sex

(Percent Saying Person is "Very Favorable")

| | Sex of respondent | |
Person	Male	Female
Male faculty	46%	27%
Female faculty	35%	27%

We found that they were more deeply committed than the men students. When asked how they themselves felt about having a career, 75 percent of the women as against 60 percent of the men were very favorable. When asked "If you could have a choice, would you choose to have a career at all?" 92 percent of the women compared to 81 percent of the men said yes. So much for the "women have no career commitment" myth.

There is another myth which says that women will drop out before completing their degree. We had no way to test what our subjects would do in the future, but we could test how strongly they felt about the possibility of dropping out. We discovered that 62 percent of the women said they would be very disappointed if they left school before completing their education, whereas only 53 percent of the men said this; 31.6 percent of the men said they were in school primarily to stay out of the draft.

Further support comes from the external environment, the general atmosphere and mores of the society. We are all aware that our society is more favorable to men's getting advanced education and having a career than to women's doing these things. We also know that we are influenced by these values. But we had no real way of measuring the amount or importance of this influence. This variable had to remain undetermined.

We could, however, measure the perception by our students of positive sup-

TABLE III Response to: "How do you think these people feel about your going to (being in) graduate or professional school?"

		Very favorable	Somewhat favorable	Not too favorable	Don't know
Yourself	M	66.9%	24.1%	6.1%	2.9%
	W	67.6%	23.1%	4.1%	5.2%
Father	M	74.6%	18.7%	4.6%	2.0%
	W	66.8%	19.4%	7.4%	6.4%
Mother	M	77.7%	19.1%	2.4%	0.9%
	W	62.0%	27.4%	5.8%	4.8%
Siblings	M	58.3%	26.7%	1.9%	13.1%
	W	44.7%	26.2%	4.0%	25.1%
Other relatives	M	55.2%	23.5%	3.4%	17.9%
	W	37.5%	24.6%	7.9%	30.0%
Most friends of opposite sex	M	51.4%	28.5%	1.4%	18.7%
	W	40.0%	33.1%	6.3%	20.6%
Most same-sex friends	M	51.1%	29.8%	2.8%	16.3%
	W	46.9%	33.3%	4.5%	15.3%
Spouse, boy- or girlfriend	M	64.5%	26.4%	2.7%	6.5%
	W	62.8%	23.4%	6.0%	7.8%
Male faculty member	M	46.7%	20.0%	2.1%	31.3%
	W	32.2%	22.8%	5.2%	39.8%
Female faculty member	M	37.1%	15.8%	0.9%	46.2%
	W	34.8%	12.7%	1.0%	51.4%
Any significant older people	M	56.2%	19.1%	1.4%	23.3%
	W	44.9%	21.1%	3.3%	30.8%

port by specific people. We could determine whether they felt their relatives, friends, and spouses were very favorable to their education and their career. This was not adequate to measure the total influence of the nonacademic environment in which our students lived, but it did give us some indicators. Therefore we asked the same questions about the attitudes of these other people as we had about the attitudes of the faculty.

Here, too, the difference was quite apparent. As seen in Tables III and IV, men in all cases perceived more support than women—in most cases considerably more. The difference is greatest of all on the question about careers. This should not be surprising: it is much more socially acceptable for a woman to be well educated than for her to earn money with that education.

Much more surprising was a comparison of the attitudes of faculty, nonfac-

TABLE IV Response to: "How do the following people feel about your having a career?" by sex

		Very favorable	Somewhat favorable	Not too favorable	Don't know
Yourself	M	60.3%	24.1%	11.1%	4.4%
	W	75.3%	15.1%	6.1%	3.5%
Father	M	77.0%	19.0%	0.8%	3.1%
	W	47.5%	37.0%	6.1%	9.4%
Mother	M	79.1%	17.3%	1.0%	2.6%
	W	49.3%	33.4%	10.9%	6.4%
Siblings	M	52.7%	31.3%	1.5%	14.5%
	W	33.8%	27.4%	5.2%	33.6%
Other relatives	M	61.1%	25.2%	1.1%	12.6%
	W	20.8%	30.6%	13.7%	34.9%
Most friends of opposite sex	M	43.4%	37.6%	1.7%	17.3%
	W	22.9%	45.8%	10.8%	20.5%
Most same-sex friends	M	42.9%	39.9%	2.5%	14.8%
	W	30.7%	45.1%	7.5%	16.7%
Spouse, boy- or girlfriend	M	62.0%	29.4%	2.1%	6.5%
	W	51.1%	32.2%	7.8%	8.9%
Male faculty member	M	46.3%	26.6%	1.1%	26.0%
	W	26.6%	30.6%	1.9%	41.0%
Female faculty member	M	35.3%	22.3%	0.7%	41.6%
	W	26.6%	19.5%	0.6%	53.3%
Any significant older people	M	53.8%	25.0%	0.3%	21.0%
	W	35.5%	28.1%	1.8%	34.6%

ulty, and the students themselves toward their graduate education and career. First, for the most part the weakest support of all came from the faculty—the very people from whom students should have reason to expect the strongest support. Not only is this further confirmation of a tendency toward a null environment at the University of Chicago, but it implies that it is well within the faculty's power to significantly increase the total support students receive for going on with their education.

Second, the men frequently reported more favorable attitudes from others than from themselves. This could imply that the encouragement (or pressure) they receive from parents, spouses, and friends makes up for what they do not receive from the faculty. The women, by contrast, always report a more favorable attitude from themselves, with the difference most noticeable in the case of attitudes toward a career. Obviously women need their higher levels of internal commitment. The cognitive dissonance between their attitudes toward their own potential and the attitudes of others toward it must create a stress endurable only with the help of a strong personal determination to pursue both education and careers.

To test our hypothesis further, we had to know whether the faculty were openly discouraging the students, male and female, or whether their attitude was, in fact, null. The tendency toward the latter was confirmed by the very low percentage of students who felt that the faculty were noticeably unfavorable to their pursuing graduate education or careers and by the very high percentage who answered "Don't know." Among women in particular, this was the most frequent response to the two questions. Among men, however, "favorable," though low, had the highest response rate.

The University of Chicago is essentially a graduate and professional school that prides itself on its low student-faculty ratio. Even undergraduates, less than a third of the student body, are expected to attend mostly small lectures and seminars and do a good deal of guided independent study. Therefore we wanted to check the extent of student-faculty interaction and the effect this interaction had on students. One way we did this was by asking students whether a faculty member had ever revealed to them his/her opinion about the students' seriousness, academic progress, suitability for the field of work, intellectual ability, and the other concerns students have about faculty estimations. From 43 to 93 percent of both women and men students answered that not a single faculty member had expressed an opinion, or implied one, on any of these matters. The intellectual environment was indeed very parched.

Yet the overall picture appeared more sterile for women than for men. The number of "don't know" responses given by women indicates that not only do they experience low levels of support, but they do not get enough feedback from the

TABLE V Response to: "Since you have been at the University of Chicago, has any faculty member in your department (or collegiate division) ever told you or given you the impression that he thought . . . . . ?"

		No one	Yes, one faculty member	Yes, more than one faculty member
That you should apply for a	M	55.8%	18.8%	25.4%
scholarship or fellowship	W	56.4%	22.2%	21.4%
That the rate at which you are mov-	M	84.6%	9.2%	6.2%
ing through the program is too slow	W	88.4%	9.7%	2.7%
That you are not working up to the	M	87.0%	9.7%	3.3%
University's standards	W	88.4%	8.9%	2.7%
That you should switch	M	93.5%	5.4%	1.1%
to another field	W	87.3%	11.1%	1.6%
That you are well-suited for	M	47.9%	19.4%	32.6%
the field you are in	W	43.6%	23.8%	32.7%
That you are not a	M	89.8%	7.5%	2.7%
serious student	W	89.3%	8.5%	2.1%
You are one of the best students in	M	57.5%	26.1%	16.4%
one of his classes or department	W	59.8%	27.6%	12.6%
That you write well	M	52.9%	24.4%	22.7%
	W	49.4%	23.5%	27.1%

faculty to know where they stand. The University does not care enough about the women within it even to respond negatively. Its discouragement is much more insidious: it fails to respond at all.

This discouragement by default manifests itself in many ways besides lack of faculty encouragement for women students. The very structure of the University is geared to meet the needs of men and those women whose lives most closely resemble men's. Since the life-styles of the population of intellectually qualified women are more heterogeneous and the demands made upon them more diverse than those of an intellectually similar population of men, fewer can comfortably fit into the University environment.

The two most obvious examples of this are lack of child-care facilities and lack of female role models among the professors. The University will deliberately keep a balance between younger and older faculty because some students relate better to the former and some to the latter. It will also try to have representatives from various fields within a discipline. But it sees no need to provide a sexual representation. The result is that few women have examples before them of how to be a female professional.

The idea of meeting the different needs of different students with different backgrounds is nothing new or radical. Traditionally the University has provided, within limits, fellowships, loans, and jobs for those who need money; housing for those who are married or are undergraduates and can stand dormitories; jobs for student wives (though seldom for student husbands); remedial courses for those whose academic background is scanty; special programs for those who find the traditional ones too confining; sports programs (primarily for men), recreational facilities; health services (usually without gynecological care); and a host of other opportunities.

What the University fails to acknowledge is that all of these needs are met within the confines of male standards. Because most of academia is male it has never stopped to consider that what is good and necessary for most men is not always good and necessary for most women. Thus the University proved very understanding and flexible in its readiness to accommodate men with draft problems. It gave them draft-exempt jobs, letters of recommendation and standing, showed them as enrolled in courses they were not taking to preserve their deferments, and, if worst came to worst, held their fellowships for them until they came back. But a pregnant woman will often have to drop out—or be forced to leave by losing her fellowship—because the university feels no responsibility to provide child-care centers. Even when she does not leave school, or has her children before she enters, she usually has the major responsibility for their care and this can be quite detrimental to full academic involvement.

This sex-related difference was clearly evident among our students when they were asked how children affected their academic work. Of all those who were parents, 15 percent of the women and only 1 percent of the men said children had a very unfavorable effect. Conversely, 16 percent of the men and a predictable zero percent of the women felt children had a very favorable effect. This is just one example of how the specific needs of women students are not met because the needs of men students provide the standards the university feels obligated to meet.

THE EXTERNAL ENVIRONMENT

Most important for our study, however, is the fact that students are presumed to come from and exist in a supportive external environment. In reality, that presumption is far more valid for most men than for most women. In many different ways men have been expected and encouraged to go on with their advanced education and need little mental effort to picture themselves in a professional role. Their parents, their undergraduate professors, their friends, their other role models, their spouses, all contribute to this environment. Even if they have neither positive stimulus nor positive goal, their draft boards (at the time of this study) and the gnawing realization that they will, after all, have to do something with their lives, provides a negative spur that is only slightly less effective than a positive one.

For women this is not the case. Instead, the general social atmosphere in which they function tends to work against them. They learn to see women who achieve in the traditional sense of financial success and professional advancement as deviants and correctly perceive that such success often costs more than it gains in personal terms. Several research projects (in addition to the Horner research cited earlier) have documented what most women have always known. Beatrice Lipinski showed that women students think of success as something that is achieved by men but not by women.[2] Others have shown that women are reluctant to violate this social standard. As Kagan and Moss have noted, "The universe of appropriate behaviors for males and females is delineated early in development and it is difficult for the child to cross these culturally given frontiers without considerable conflict and tension."[3] These barriers account for Pierce's finding that high achievement-motivation among high-school women correlates much more closely with early marriage than with success in school.[4] Those women who do cross the frontiers must, according to Maccoby, pay a high price in anxiety and "it is this anxiety which helps to account for the lack of productivity among those women who do make intellectual careers." She feels that "this tells something of a horror story. It would appear that even when a woman is suitably endowed intellectually and develops the right temperament and habits of thought to make use of her endowment, she must be fleet of foot indeed to scale the hurdles society has erected for her and to remain a whole and happy person while continuing to follow her intellectual bent."

Thus it should not be surprising that women tend to aspire at a lower level than men and to require even greater stimulus from the academic environment. As Gropper and Fitzpatrick have pointed out, "Women appear to be less influenced than men by their high grades in deciding *in favor* of advanced education. But they are more influenced than men by their low grades in deciding *against* advanced education."[6] As a group, women are deprived of the rich external environment of high expectations and high encouragement that research indicates is best for personal growth and creative production. Unless they have exceptional backgrounds, they have little to go on but their own internal commitment.

The attrition rates alone testify that this is rarely enough. During the sixties women have earned roughly 53 percent of all high school diplomas, 36 percent of all bachelor's degrees, 31 percent of all master's degrees and 10 percent of all doctorates. The greatest drop-off is after the master's degree. Women seem to lack the stimulus to go on to the doctorate. In retrospect, this is a very logical response to the environment. It is socially expected for women to graduate from high school, generally expected and always acceptable for women to get a B.A. or a B.S., somewhat acceptable and occasionally necessary for a woman to get a master's degree (since many of the professions in which women predominate require it). But Ph.D.'s and some professional degrees are considered unnecessary and often undesirable for a woman to obtain if she is to remain within the purview of social acceptability. And, given the job and salary inequities for holders of such degrees, they are not always economically useful.

The University does little to remedy this situation and much to exacerbate it. It offers virtually no courses on women and there is little material on women in the regular courses. This lack contributes to the feeling that women are not worth studying. There are few women on the faculty—less than half the percentage that prevails in the Ph.D. pool from which the University draws. These are concentrated at the bottom of the academic ladder or are off it entirely, despite the fact that the percentage of women in the older Ph.D. pool is considerably larger than that in the younger and that women Ph.D.'s as a group have higher I.Q.'s, higher grade-point averages, and higher class ranks than their male counterparts. This situation gives many students the idea that high-quality academic women are rare. Some 40 percent of the women students in the SCOUW survey felt that the faculty were less receptive to female students than to male students.

One has only to look at the Rosenthal-Jacobson experiments to see what a depressing effect this environment can have on the aspirations of women students. Although they did not use sex as a salient variable, these experimentors showed that when teachers were told that certain students (actually selected at random) would perform exceptionally well or poorly, those students altered their normal performance in the predicted direction to a significant degree. The teachers stated that they were treating all students exactly alike, yet investigation showed that they were subtly, unconsciously, encouraging or discouraging the chosen ones.[7]

In many ways this environment of subtle discouragement by neglect is more pernicious than a strongly negative one would be. As Eric Berne has theorized, everyone needs "strokes"; and although good strokes are better than bad strokes, bad strokes are better than none. In academic terms, this translates that women will do better when they are pointedly told that their sex makes their abilities and their commitment suspect. At least overt negative response provides women with some interaction and some standards by which they can judge their behavior. It also creates a challenge—something to be overcome. If women are conscious of the roadblocks they face as women at the University and in society they are in a better position to muster the energy to struggle against them. They not only know exactly what they have to face, but by sharing their struggle with other women they can create the context of emotional support that every student needs for high achievement.

Historically it is also evident that overt opposition is preferable to motivational malnutrition. Women did better when things were worse. From the time they first pounded on the doors of higher education their progress was steadily upward until thirty or forty years ago. By then they no longer had to overcome the obstacle of disbelief, but at the same time they no longer had the internal stimulus of knowing they were pioneers. Once women had made it, no one cared—one way or the other. Their place was still seen to be in the home, and the graduate schools did little more than provide a few loopholes for the hardy. The percentage of women earning Ph.D.'s began to go down in the 1920's and has risen only slightly since its nadir in 1950.

In summation, one can say that if the University and the behavior of its faculty do not directly discriminate against women, they indirectly and insidiously discriminate against them. The University is less of an intellectual seedbed than a psychological gauntlet—and it is one that the male students run in full armor, while the women students trip through in their bare skins.

Perhaps the best analogy for understanding the differentiating effect on men and women of the null environment is to be drawn from agriculture. If a farmer transplants into a field two groups of seedlings—one having been nourished thus far in rich, fertilized loam and the other malnourished for having struggled in desert sand—and that farmer then tends all the seedlings with virtually equal lack of care, fertilizer, and water (perhaps favoring the loam-grown seedlings slightly because they look more promising), no one should be surprised if the lesser harvest is reaped from the desert-bred plants. Nor should we, with all the modern farm apparatus and information available, shrug complacently and lament that there is no way to make the desert bloom.

Notes

1. Matina Horner, "Why Bright Women Fail" *Psychology Today,* Nov. 1970.
2. Beatrice Lipinski, *Sex-Role Conflict and Achievement Motivation in College Women,* unpublished Ph.D. dissertation, University of Cincinnati, 1965.
3. Jerome Kagan and Howard A. Moss, *Birth to Maturity: A Study in Psychological Development* (New York and London: Wiley 1962), p. 270.

4. James V. Pierce, *Sex Differences in Achievement Motivation of Able High School Students*, Cooperative Research Project No. 1097, University of Chicago, Dec. 1961.
5. Eleanor Maccoby, "Women's Intellect," in Farber and Wilson, eds., *The Potential of Women* (New York: McGraw-Hill, 1963).
6. G. L. Gropper and Robert Fitzpatrick, *Who Goes to Graduate School?* (Pittsburgh: American Institute for Research, 1959).
7. R. Rosenthal and L. Jacobson, *Pygmalion in the Classroom: Teacher Expectations and Pupils' Intellectual Development* (New York: Holt, Rinehart, 1968).

IV The Working Woman

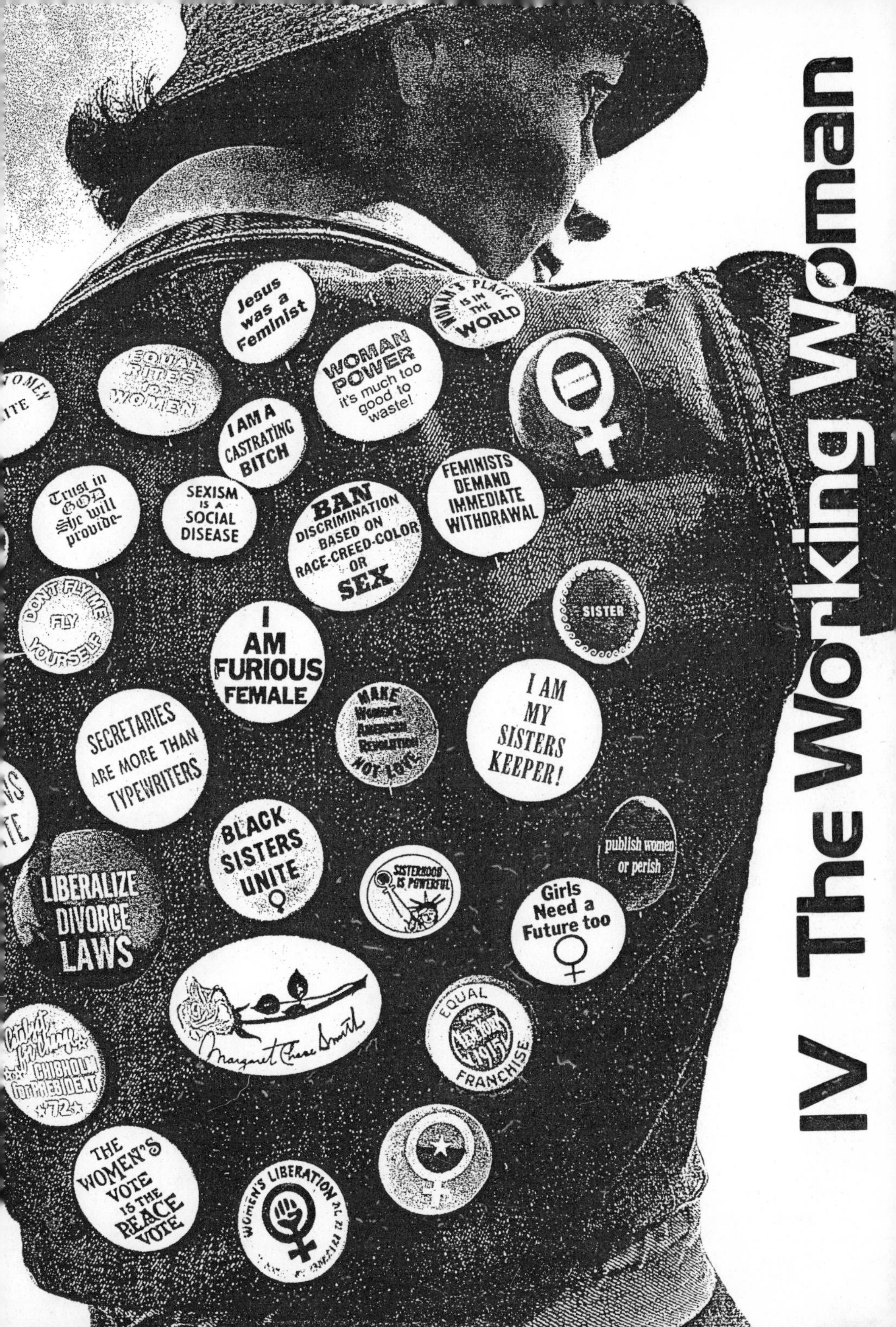

Women in the Labor Force: An Overview

Francine D. Blau

Women have traditionally engaged in three types of economically productive work. First, they have produced goods and services for their family's own consumption; second, they have engaged in household production for sale or exchange on the market; third, they have worked for pay outside the home. The process of industrialization has brought about a reallocation in the relative importance of these three types of economic activities, greatly increasing the absolute and relative number of women who seek and obtain paid employment. In this paper we shall briefly trace this evolution in the working woman's role and summarize the trends in women's involvement in work outside the home. We shall then examine the status of women in the labor market in terms of their employment and earnings. Finally, we shall attempt to draw some conclusions regarding the changes that must be made in employment patterns if women are to gain equality in the labor market.

HISTORICAL PERSPECTIVES

In the preindustrial economy of the American Colonial period, work was frequently allocated on the basis of sex, but there could be little question that the work of women was as essential to the survival of the community as that of men. Unlike England and the Continental countries, where women were routinely employed as reapers, mowers, and haymakers, the Colonies left their agricultural work mostly to the men, at least among the nonslave population.[1] This departure from the customs of the mother country may have been due to the economic importance of the household industries carried on primarily by women and children, who produced most of the manufactured goods for the Colonies. In addition to cleaning, cooking, and caring for their children, Colonial women considered spinning, weaving, and making lace, soap, shoes, and candles part of their ordinary housekeeping duties, for the Colonial economy at first provided no other source for these goods and services.[2]

Moreover, the pressures of a struggling frontier society, faced with a continual labor shortage and imbued with a puritanical abhorrence of idleness, opened up a wide range of business activities to women. They could be found working as tavern keepers, store managers, traders, speculators, printers and publishers, as well as in the more traditional women's occupations of domestic servant, seamstress, and tailor.[3] But many of the Colonial businesswomen were widows, frequently with small children to provide for, who carried on their husband's enterprise after his death.[4] In some cases opportunities for women to remain single and self-supporting were curtailed, perhaps because of women's economic value in the home. For example, in early New England female family heads were given their proportion of planting land, and in Salem even unmarried women at first also received a small allotment. "The custom of granting 'maid's lotts,' however, was soon discontinued in order to avoid 'all presedents and evil events of graunting lotts unto single maidens not disposed of.' "[5]

Although conditions peculiar to the Colonies may have contributed to the relatively high status of American women, the more general point has been made that before the Industrial Revolution separated the home from the place of work, women were able to take a more active role in the economic life of the community.[6] The broad thrust of industrialization may indeed have diminished the participation of women in certain kinds of economically productive work. Particularly in America, however, women played a crucial role in the development of the first important manufacturing industry, the textile industry.

During the seventeenth century, when spinning and weaving were household industries done primarily by women and children, each household provided its own raw materials and produced chiefly to meet its own needs. But it was not uncommon for women to market part of their output, selling it directly to their own customers or to shopkeepers for credit against their account.[7] With the expansion of the industry in the latter half of the eighteenth century, it became more common for women to be employed by merchants to spin yarn in their own home. Under this commission system the merchants would sell the yarn or put it out again to be woven into cloth. The first factories in America embodied no new technology. They were "merely rooms where several looms were gathered and where a place of business could be maintained." Women delivered yarn they had spun at home to these establishments and were paid for it there.[8]

The first textile factory to incorporate power machinery was established in Pawtucket, Rhode Island, in 1789 by Samuel Slater, a British immigrant. Slater's factory used a water-powered spinning frame. By 1800 fifteen mills had been established in New England for the carding and spinning of yarn. When the power loom was introduced in 1814, the whole process of cloth manufacture could be carried on in the new factories.[9] But if cloth was no longer made solely in the home, it was still made primarily by women and children, who constituted the bulk of the new industrial work force.

> The earliest factories did not open any new occupations to women. So long as they were only "spinning mills" there was merely a transferring of women's work from the home to the factory, and by the time that the establishment of the power loom had made weaving also a profitable factory operation, women had become so largely employed as weavers that they were only following this occupation, too, as it left the home. It may, in brief, be said that the result of the introduction of the factory system in the textile industries was that the work which women had been doing in the home could be done more efficiently outside of the home, but women were carrying on the same processes in the making of yarn or cloth.[10]

Perhaps even more interesting than the pioneering role of women in the industry is the reaction of illustrious contemporaries to the employment of women outside the home. Alexander Hamilton, for example, claimed that one of the great advantages of the establishment of manufacturing was "the employment of persons who would otherwise be idle (and in many cases a burthen on the community) . . . . It is worthy of particular remark, that, in general, women and children are rendered more useful, and the latter more early useful, by the manufacturing establishments, than they would otherwise be."[11] The notion that a farmer's masculinity might be threatened by the entry of his wife and children into paid employment apparently did not trouble American men of the time. Hamilton noted, on the contrary, that men would benefit from having a new source of income in the family.[12] Others claimed that the new factories not only opened up a new source of income but also built character in their employees:

> The rise of manufactures was said to have "elevated the females belonging to the families of the cultivators of the soil from a state of penury and idleness to competence and industry" . . . . In the same spirit of unreasoning exaggeration the women in villages remote from manufacturing centers were described as "doomed to idleness and its inseparable attendants, vice and guilt."[13]

Since the economy of the United States during this period, was predominantly agricultural, with an extremely favorable land-to-labor ratio, women and children were virtually the only readily available source of labor for the infant manufacturing industry. This would seem to be an important factor in the approval with which the entry of women into the wage-labor force was greeted. The existence of a factor of production, women, which was more productive in the new industrial pursuits than in the home, was cited as an argument for the passage of protective tariffs to encourage the development of the textile industry in a country that appeared to have a clear comparative advantage in agriculture.*

Of course, present day attitudes toward women working outside the home are not nearly so encouraging. While a careful investigation of the causes for the change remains to be undertaken, it seems reasonable to suggest that the gradual diminution of the supply of unsettled land coupled with the waves of immigrants that provided a more abundant source of labor shifted public concern to the problem of providing sufficient employment for men. In any case, by the turn of the century sentiment against the "intrusion" of women into the industrial work force was strong enough to compel Edith Abbott to answer this charge specifically in her classic study, *Women in Industry.* Her words add a valuable perspective to contemporary discussions of the issue as well:

> Women have been from the beginning of our history an important factor in American industry. In the early days of the factory system they were an indispensable factor. Any theory, therefore, that women are a new element in our industrial life, or that they are doing "men's work," or that they have "driven out the men," is a theory unsupported by the facts.[14]

---

* "To the 'Friends of Industry,' as the early protectionists loved to call themselves, it was . . . a useful argument to be able to say that of all the employees in our manufacturing establishments not one fourth were able-bodied men fit for farming." Edith Abbott, *Women in Industry* (New York: Appleton, 1910), p. 51. The same author noted (p. 52, n. 1) that "manufactures are lauded because of their 'subserviency to the public defense; their employment of women and children, machinery, cattle, fire, fuel, steam, water, and even wind—instead of our ploughmen and male laborers.'"

A careful investigation of the facts also leads us to further qualify the statement that the separation of the home from the place of work during the Industrial Revolution tended to reduce the participation of American women, particularly married women, in many kinds of economically productive work. For one thing, though it is estimated that in 1890 only 5 percent of married women had jobs outside the home,[15] this pattern did not prevail among all groups in the female population. For another, various types of work done in the home continued to be important in the economy throughout the nineteenth century.

The two major groups of married women for whom work outside the home was fairly common were black women, the majority of whom still lived in the South, and immigrant women in the textile-manufacturing towns of New England. In 1890 one quarter of black wives and two-thirds of the large number of black widows were gainfully employed. Most of these women worked either as field hands or as domestic servants, the same kinds of jobs black women had always done under slavery.[16] Undoubtedly the tendency of black wives to engage in market activity can be explained in large part by the low incomes of black men.

The women who worked in the New England textile mills were carrying on the long tradition of the participation of women in this industry. In two Massachusetts towns, Fall River and Lowell, for example, nearly one-fifth of all married women worked outside the home in 1890. Most were first- or second-generation immigrants of French-Canadian or Irish ancestry. The low wages of men working in the textile mills frequently made it necessary for other family members, including children, to work in the mills too. Thus it was often for family reasons as well as financial reasons that married women went to work: "Since many of the older children worked in the mills, their mothers were not needed at home to care for them. Indeed, a mother whose children worked could look after them better if she went to work in the same mill."[17]

In addition to women from these two groups, married women from many sectors of the population were forced to seek market work when they suffered certain kinds of misfortunes against which there was little social protection in the nineteenth and early twentieth centuries. Some indication of the kinds of problems these women faced can be gained from the results of a study conducted by the United States Bureau of Labor Statistics in 1908:

> Among one group of 140 wives and widows who were employed in the glass industry, 94 were widows, or had been deserted, or were married to men who were permanently disabled. Thirteen were married to drunkards or loafers who would not work. The husbands of ten were temporarily unable to work because of sickness or injury. Seventeen were married to unskilled laborers who received minimum wages for uncertain employment. Only six were

married to regularly employed workers above the grade of unskilled labor.[18]

The types of employment and working conditions of urban women who earned money for work done in the home varied widely. Some women took in boarders or did laundry or sewing. Others, in New York, Chicago, and other major cities, eked out a meager existence doing home work in the garment industry, while Bohemian and German women in New York's upper East Side tenements provided a cheap source of labor for the cigar industry.[19]

Another element of home work, the production of goods and services for the family's own use, remained extremely important throughout the nineteenth century, even in urban areas. Women frequently kept livestock and poultry and raised fruits and vegetables in small home gardens. Even foodstuffs bought at the market were usually in their natural, unprocessed form. Preserving, pickling, canning, and jelly making, as well as baking the family bread, were normal household duties. Much of the family's clothing, curtains, and linens were sewn or knitted in the home. And, of course, the housekeeping tasks of cleaning, washing, and cooking were all undertaken without the benefit of modern appliances.[20]

THE FEMALE LABOR FORCE SINCE 1890

If the process of industrialization has meant that many of the goods and services women have traditionally produced in the home have increasingly been provided by the market economy, it has also brought about the incorporation of ever-increasing numbers of women into the paid labor force. Since fairly reliable data on the female labor force did not become available until 1890, we shall confine our discussion of the trends in female labor force participation to the period 1890–1970. The figures in Table 1 indicate a relatively slow rate of increase in the proportion of women of working age that were in the labor force in the early decades of this period.* Be-

---

* There is some question whether there was any increase at all in female labor force participation during the 1890–1930 period. The 1910 census, in which enumerators were given special instructions *not* to overlook women workers, especially unpaid family workers, yielded a participation rate of 25 percent. Robert W. Smuts has argued that women workers were undercounted in the 1900, the 1920, and perhaps the 1930 census as well, but that over the period, gradual improvements in technique, broader definitions of labor force status, and a redistribution of the female work force from unpaid farm work to paid employment resulted in an apparent rather than a true increase in the female participation rate. Smuts, "The Female Labor Force," *Journal of the American Statistical Association*, March 1960, pp. 71–79. For a discussion of this issue see Valerie Kincade Oppenheimer, *The Female Labor Force in the United States* (Berkeley: Univ. of Calif., Institute of International Studies, 1970), pp. 3–5.

tween 1940 and 1970, however, more dramatic changes in women's labor force status occurred. In 1940 less than 29 percent of the female population 16 years of age and over was in the labor force. By 1970 the figure had risen to 43 percent, and nearly half of all women between the ages of 16 and 64 were working or seeking work. Women workers increased from one quarter to nearly two-fifths of the civilian labor force.

TABLE I   Women in the Civilian Labor Force, Selected Years, 1890–1970

Year	No. (in thousands)	As percentage of all workers	As percentage of female population
1890	3,704	17.0	18.2
1900	4,999	18.1	20.0
1920	8,229	20.4	22.7
1930	10,396	21.9	23.6
1940	13,783	25.4	28.6
1945	19,290	36.1	38.1
1947	16,664	27.9	30.8
1950	18,389	29.6	33.9
1955	20,548	31.6	35.7
1960	23,240	33.4	37.7
1965	26,200	35.2	39.2
1970	31,520	38.1	43.3

Sources: U. S. Dept. of Labor, Women's Bureau, 1969 Handbook on Women Workers, p. 10; U. S. Dept. of Labor, Manpower Administration, Manpower Report of the President, April 1971, pp. 203, 205.
Note: Pre-1940 figures include women 14 years of age and over; figures for 1940 and after include women 16 years of age and over.

When we take into account the World War II experience, however, these changes look less impressive. Between 1940 and 1945 the female labor force expanded by 5.5 million, and 38 percent of all women 16 years of age and over were working. As the 1947 figures indicate, considerable ground was lost in the immediate postwar period. In fact, it was not until 1953 that the absolute number of women workers surpassed its wartime peak. Participation rates did not regain their 1945 levels until 1961.[21]

The long-term growth in the female labor force that has occurred since 1940 was accomplished primarily by the entry of new groups of women into the labor market. Before 1940 the typical female worker was young and single. The peak age-specific participation rate occurred among women 20 to 24 years of age, as Figure 1 shows. In the next twenty years older married women entered or re-entered the labor force in increasing numbers, while the labor force participation rates of women between 20 and 34 years of age remained relatively constant. Since 1960 there has been a sizable increase in the participation rates of all women under 65. The fastest increase, however, has occurred among young married women, many with preschool-age children.

FIGURE 1   Labor Force Participation Rates of Women by Age, 1940-1970

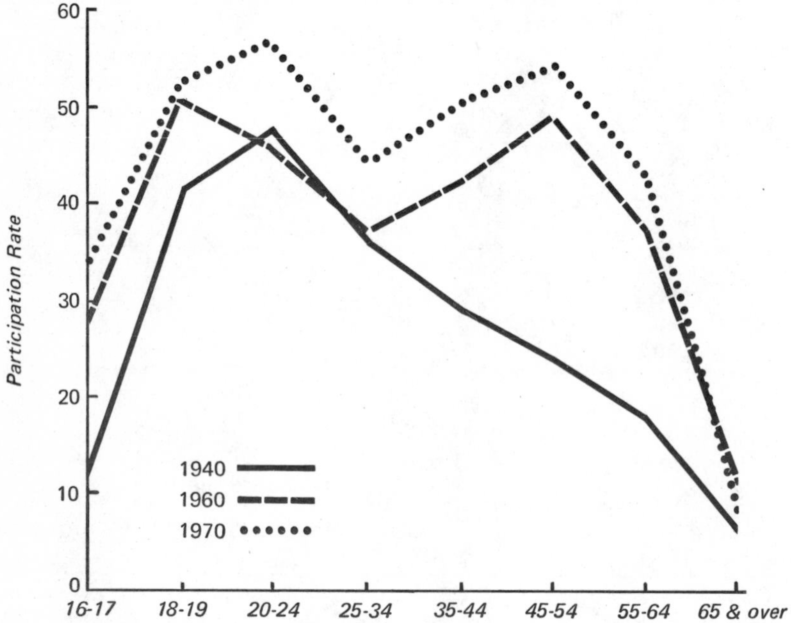

Sources: U. S. Dept. of Labor, Women's Bureau, 1969 Handbook on Women Workers, p. 18; U. S. Dept. of Labor, Manpower Administration, Manpower Report of the President, March 1972, pp. 160–62.

The result of the sequential entry into the labor force of black and immigrant women, young single women from all ethnic groups, and older married women, and most recently the increased labor force participation of the younger group of married women, is that the female labor force has come to resemble much more closely the total female population. That is, women who engage in market work have been drawing closer to the total female population in terms of their racial composition, age, educational attainment, marital and family status and other characteristics.[22] Thus it is rapidly becoming more difficult to consider working women as in some sense an unrepresentative or atypical group.

Valerie Oppenheimer has identified the growth in the sex-specific demand for women workers as an important factor in the increase in the female labor force and in its changing composition. As we shall see in greater detail in the next section, the employment of women is restricted chiefly to a limited number of industries and occupational categories. The growing importance of service industries and white-collar work has provided greatly expanded employment opportunities for women, within the framework of the sexually segregated labor market. Moreover, the increase in these jobs, coupled with the appearance of new female occupations between 1940 and 1960, created a demand that greatly exceeded the supply of young single women workers, once the backbone of the female labor force. Thus, as Oppenheimer concludes,

> "The combination of the rising demand for female labor and the declining supply of the typical worker opened up job opportunities for married women and older women that had not previously existed. . . . The great influx of older married women into the labor force, was, in good part a *response* to increased job opportunities—not the creator of such opportunities."[23]

Oppenheimer also points out that under the pressures of labor shortages, employers were forced to abandon their prejudices against employing older married women.[24] Further research may show that a similar process has operated to the benefit of young married women in the period since 1960. There is some evidence that employers have been reluctant to hire married women with young children, either because they feared such women would have high rates of absenteeism or because they made a moralistic judgment that mothers of preschool-age children should remain at home.[25] Some employers may have been forced to discard these concerns in order to meet their demand for female labor, thus making possible the rapid increase in the labor force participation of women in this group that has occurred in recent years.

If, as Oppenheimer contends, the growing demand for women workers was a crucial factor in the expansion of the female labor force, the question arises whether large numbers of women are outside the labor force simply because sufficient opportunities for work have not been present. The extreme responsiveness of women to the demands created by the emergency conditions of World War II and the evidence that the female labor force tends to grow more quickly during upswings in the business cycle than during recessions would support this view.[26] If we further take into account the extremely limited availability of child care centers and the narrow range of jobs open to women, it becomes difficult to regard the decision whether or not to seek paid employment solely as a matter of free choice or personal preference for many women.

Occupational Distribution

Table 2 shows the distribution of female and male workers by occupation in 1971.

TABLE 2   Occupational Distribution of the Labor Force, by Sex, 1971

Occupation Group	Distribution (%)	
	Males	Females
Total employed	100.0	100.0
White-collar workers	40.9	60.6
Professional and technical	13.7	14.5
Managers, officials and proprietors	14.6	5.0
Clerical workers	6.7	33.9
Sales workers	5.9	7.2
Blue-collar workers	45.9	15.4
Craftsmen and foremen	19.9	1.3
Operatives	18.3	13.3
Nonfarm laborers	7.7	0.8
Service workers	8.2	22.3
Private household workers	0.1	4.9
Other service workers	8.1	17.4
Farmworkers	5.1	1.7
Farmers and farm managers	3.2	0.3
Farm laborers and foremen	1.9	1.4

Source: U. S. Dept. of Labor, Manpower Administration, Manpower Report of the President, March 1972, p. 173.

The patterns of employment displayed by the two groups diverged widely: almost 70 percent of male white-collar workers, or 28 percent of all working men, were in the professional and technical or managerial category, whereas only about 32 percent of female white-collar workers, or 20 percent of all working women, were in one of these categories. Furthermore, while a slightly greater proportion of women than men were employed as professional or technical workers, the majority of the women in this category were concentrated in the two traditionally female professions of elementary or secondary school teacher and nurse.[27] Nearly 56 percent of female white-collar workers, or over one-third of all employed women, were working in clerical jobs.

Men also had a larger share of the higher-paying, higher-status blue-collar jobs. Only 8 percent of female blue-collar workers, or 1.3 percent of all working women, were employed as craftsmen or foremen. By contrast, over 40 percent of male blue-collar workers, or 20 percent of all working men, were employed as craftsmen or foremen. The percentage of women workers in the generally low-paying service-worker category was much greater than the percentage of men. In 1971 some 22 percent of all working women held service jobs, as compared to 8 percent of working men.

The occupational distribution of nonwhite women was even more skewed toward the bottom of the occupational ladder. Fifty percent held service jobs in 1968, and fully half of this group were private household workers, the lowest-paying occupation. Only 30 percent of nonwhite women were white-collar workers, as compared to 60 percent of the total female labor force.[28]

A more specific examination of the occupational distribution of female employees highlights two aspects of the position of women in the labor market. First, women workers are heavily concentrated in an extremely small number of occupations. Half of all working women were employed in just 21 of the 250 detailed occupations listed by the Bureau of the Census in 1969. Just five occupations—secretary-stenographer, household worker, bookkeeper, elementary school teacher, and waitress—accounted for one quarter of all employed women. Men workers were much more widely distributed throughout the occupational structure, with half of them employed in 65 occupations.[29] Second, most women work in predominantly female jobs. A list of the occupations in which 70 percent or more of the workers were women was compiled by Oppenheimer from 1900 and 1960 census figures. She found that in both years well over half of all working women were in these "women's jobs."[30] The only major change over the period was an increase in the number of occupations on the list.

A study by Edward Gross further supports the conclusion that occupational segregation is as severe now as it was in 1900. Gross constructed an "index of segregation" for each census year between 1900 and 1960. The index for any given year can be construed as the percentage of women (or men) who would have to change jobs in order for the occupational distribution of women workers to match that of men. Despite two world wars and a major depression, the index shows a remarkable stability over the years, ranging from a low point of 65.6 percent for 1950 to a high point of 69.0 percent for 1910 and 1940—a difference of less than 4 percent. The absolute magnitude of the indices is also striking, for it indicates that about two-thirds of the female labor force would have had to change jobs in any given census year for the occupational distribution of women to correspond to that of men. According to this measure, indeed, the segregation of occupations by sex has been even more severe than segregation by race. In 1960 the index of racial segregation was 46.8 percent, as compared to 68.4 percent for sexual segregation. Gross concludes:

> Those concerned with sexual segregation as a social problem can take small comfort from these figures. They suggest that the movement of women into the labor market has not meant the disappearance of sexual typing in occupation. Rather, the great expansion in female employment has been accomplished through the expansion of occupations that were already heavily female, through the emergence of wholly new occupations (such as that of key punch operator) which were defined as female from the start, and through females taking over previously male occupations. This last may be compared to the process of racial invasion in American cities. From the group's point of view, such invasion provides new opportunities but still in a segregated context.[31]

Earnings

In 1971 the annual median earnings of working women were $2,986, only 40 percent of the annual median earnings of working men. Part of this difference is due to the greater prevalence of part-time work among women. Even women who worked full-time, year-round, however, had a median income of only $5,593, or 60 percent of that of working men.[32] Nonwhite women were even more disadvantaged. The median income of those who were full-time, year-round workers was only $3,677 in 1968, or 46 percent of the median income of white men.[33] Furthermore, the gap between the earnings of women and men increased between 1956 and 1969, and has narrowed only slightly since.[34]

A further measure of the problem can be gained by comparing the earnings distribution of female and male workers. In 1970, 45 percent of the women working full-time, year-round, earned less than $5,000, and 12 percent earned less than $3,000. Only 14 percent of the men earned less than $5,000, and only 5 percent earned less than $3,000. At the upper end of the income scale, 1 percent of the women working full-time, year-round, earned over $15,000, as compared to 14 percent of the men.[35] These earnings differentials persist even when we control for major occupation group. In 1971 full-time women sales workers earned only 42 percent as much, based on median income, as men sales workers; women in a managerial capacity earned 53 percent as much as men; women craftsmen and foremen, 56 percent; women service workers (except private household workers), 58 percent; women operatives, 60 percent; women clerical workers, 62 percent; and women professional or technical workers, 66 percent.[36]

Since earnings are directly tied to both work experience and job tenure, the intermittent labor force participation of women workers and their shorter average length of time on a particular job would lead us to expect some differences in median earnings between women and men workers.[37] The observed earnings differentials, however, exceed what could be expected to result from these factors. These extremely high differentials can best be understood in terms of the sexual segregation of the labor market discussed in the preceding section. Women are heavily concentrated in predominantly female occupational categories. Even when women and men are in the same occupation, they are likely to be employed in different industries or establishments.[38] At the risk of some oversimplification, the effect of the resulting "dual labor market" on women's earnings can be explained in terms of supply and demand.

The demand for women workers is mainly restricted to a small number of sexually segregated occupations. At the same time, the supply of women available for work is highly responsive to small changes in the wages offered as well as to employment opportunities in general. Moreover, employers can attract more women into a job simply by increasing the flexibility of work schedules. In all likelihood, the same situation exists even in the traditional women's jobs that require a high level of general education. The reserve pool of qualified women outside the labor market who would be willing to enter it if the price or the job were right certainly exerts a downward pressure on earnings.

In the framework of Marxist analysis, the women outside of the labor force may be viewed as a kind of "reserve army of the unemployed" that is guaranteed its subsistence through the institutions of marriage and the family. Since the labor market is sexually segregated, however, this reserve acts most directly to hold down the earnings of women workers and only indirectly affects the more protected group of men workers. Thus it is not surprising that the rapid expansion of the female work force in recent years has corresponded to an increasing gap between the earnings of women and men. Of course, this does not suggest that women and men never work together on the same job in the same establishment, or that even in that case wage differentials do not exist. Rather it suggests that the practice of unequal pay for equal work is made possible by the limited job opportunities open to women, who have little choice but to accept the disparity. Moreover, nominal differences in job definitions sometimes provide a further excuse for unequal pay even in the case of comparable work.

There are some who argue that women do not need to earn as much as men, and hence that the low earning power of working women is not a significant social problem. Single women who work are only biding their time before marriage, so the argument goes, and married women are only supplementing their husbands' already ample incomes. The assumptions underlying this view—that single women do not need to make a living wage or to be able to save for the future, and that all husbands earn enough to provide adequately for their wives and children—are left un-examined.

We shall cite evidence showing that work is a financial necessity for significant numbers of women, but two additional points should be made at the outset. First, in a society in which value often means monetary value, it is extremely unlikely that women can attain "equality," however that may be defined, without equal earning opportunities. Second, a significant change in women's social status would seem to require the real possibility of economic independence for women, and not simply limited earning opportunities at low income levels.

Returning to the initial point, some indication of the financial importance of paid employment for women can be gained from data on the female labor force. Of the women in the labor force in March 1971, 23 percent were single and an additional 19 percent were widowed, divorced, or separated from their husbands. Of the married women, who constituted the remaining 58 percent, 23 percent had husbands who incomes were below $5,000. Undoubtedly most of these women, and many whose husbands earned more than $5,000, were also working for compelling economic reasons.[39]

The plight of female-headed families is particularly serious. Although these families constituted only about 11 percent of all American families in 1969, they accounted for 47 percent of all poor families with children in that year. Nearly one-third of all black families were headed by women in March 1970, and 60 percent of these had incomes below the poverty line.[40] Thus any discussion of the issue of poverty that does not concern itself with the disadvantaged position of women in the labor market can hardly be regarded as a serious attempt to deal with the problem.

CONCLUSION

The data presented so far amply demonstrate that women are not at the present time equal participants in the labor market. The question that remains, of course, is what policies are necessary to enable women to attain economic equality? A wide variety of changes in prevailing occupational structures and institutional arrangements must be made if this goal is to be achieved. Clearly, however, the elimination of occupational segregation is one of the most important steps. As we have seen, occupational segregation restricts the employment opportunities open to women; it results in lower earnings for women, owing to the oversupply of labor available for "women's jobs"; and it permits the low status accorded women by society at large to be carried over to predominantly female occupations, which are generally regarded as less prestigious or important than other occupations.

Of course, the finding that occupational segregation is an obstacle to the attainment of economic equality for women is hardly surprising, since there is no reason to assume that the doctrine of "separate but equal" should be any more valid for women than it has proved to be for other groups in our society. Yet, to define the problem in these terms is extremely useful because it points to policies that would affect all working women, not just those at the upper levels. It means, for example, that we must have more women sales workers in wholesale trade, more women electricians, more women chefs, as well as more women doctors, lawyers, and business executives. It also means that more men must move into predominantly female jobs.

Since women presently constitute nearly two-fifths of the civilian labor force and since they are so heavily concentrated in predominantly female jobs, complete integration is a task of enormous proportions. Once a substantial movement of women into the male sector of the labor market took place, however, we could expect the incomes of women in predominantly female occupations to increase, since the supply of labor for these jobs would no longer be so abundant. This in turn should attract men into presently female occupations. Thus the long-range benefits of a sizable movement toward increased integration could be very great.

Notes

1. Edith Abbott, *Women in Industry* (New York: Appleton, 1910), pp. 11–12.
2. Eleanor Flexner, *Century of Struggle: The Women's Rights Movement in the United States* (New York: Atheneum 1968), p. 9.
3. Abbott, pp. 13–18. "It should be noted that the domestic servant in the seventeenth and eighteenth centuries was employed for a considerable part of her time in processes of manufacture and that, without going far wrong, one might classify this as an industrial occupation." *Ibid.*, p. 16.
4. Flexner, p. 9.
5. Abbott, pp. 11–12.
6. Viola Klein and Alva Myrdal, *Women's Two Roles* (London: Routledge and Kegan Paul, 1956), p. 1.
7. Abbott, pp. 18–19.
8. *Ibid.*, p. 19, and for quote, p. 37.
9. Elizabeth Faulkner Baker, *Technology and Women's Work* (New York: Columbia Univ. Press, 1964), p. 5.
10. Abbott, p. 14.
11. Alexander Hamilton, *Report on Manufactures*, vol. 1, cited in Baker, p. 6.
12. Hamilton, *Report on Manufactures*, cited in Abbott, p. 50.
13. Abbott, p. 57.
14. *Ibid.*, p. 317.

15. Robert W. Smuts, *Women and Work in America* (New York: Columbia Univ. Press, 1959), p. 23.
16. *Ibid.*, pp. 10, 56.
17. *Ibid.*, p. 57.
18. *Ibid.*, p. 51.
19. *Ibid.*, pp. 14–17.
20. *Ibid.*, pp. 11–13.
21. U.S. Dept. of Labor, Manpower Administration, *Manpower Report of the President,* March 1970, p. 217.
22. Janice Neipert Hedges, "Women Workers and Manpower Demands in the 1970's," *Monthly Labor Review,* June 1970, p. 21.
23. Oppenheimer, *Female Labor Force,* p. 187.
24. *Ibid.*, p. 188.
25. See for example, Georgina M. Smith, *Help Wanted—Female: A Study of Demand and Supply in a Local Job Market for Women* (Rutgers, N.J.: Rutgers Univ., Institute of Management and Labor Relations, 1964), pp. 18–19.
26. See Gertrude Bancroft McNally, "Patterns of Female Labor Force Activity," *Industrial Relations,* May 1968, pp. 204–18.
27. Hedges, pp. 22–23.
28. U.S. Dept. of Labor, Women's Bureau, *1969 Handbook on Women Workers,* Bulletin 294 (Washington, D.C.: GPO, 1969), pp. 105–6.
29. Hedges, p. 19.
30. Valerie Kincade Oppenheimer, "The Sex-Labeling of Jobs," *Industrial Relations,* May 1968, Table 6, p. 220.
31. Edward Gross, "Plus Ca Change . . . ? The Sexual Structure of Occupations Over Time," *Social Problems,* Fall 1968, p. 202.
32. *Economic Report of the President,* Jan. 1973, p. 103.
33. U.S. Dept. of Commerce, Bureau of the Census, *Current Population Reports,* p. 60.
34. *Economic Report of the President,* Jan. 1973, p. 103.
35. *Current Population Reports,* P-60, No. 80.
36. *Economic Report of the President,* Jan. 1973, table 28, p. 104.
37. In addition, full-time hours for women tend to be less than those of men on the average. For the effect of adjustment for this factor on the earnings differential, see *ibid.*
38. See, for example, Donald McNulty, "Differences in Pay Between Men and Women Workers," *Monthly Labor Review,* Dec. 1967.
39. Elizabeth Waldman and Kathryn R. Gover, "Marital and Family Characteristics of the Labor Force," *Monthly Labor Review,* April 1972, p. 5; Janice Neipert Hedges and Jeanne K. Barnett, "Working Women and the Division of Household Tasks," *ibid.*, p. 10.
40. Robert L. Stein, "The Economic Status of Families Headed by Women," *Monthly Labor Review,* Dec. 1970, pp. 4–5.

Women in the Professions: Psychological and Social Barriers to Women in Science

Martha S. White

T alented and educated women with family responsibilities often face special problems of
identity and self-esteem when they attempt to continue their professional activity. Although many do
so successfully and encounter few problems, others
find it more difficult. I first became aware of some
special aspects of these problems when I interviewed
women scholars at the Radcliffe Institute—women
with outstanding intellectual and creative ability who
had been awarded fellowships so that they might
continue their professional interests on a part-time
basis.[1]

The Institute members were particularly questioned about their feelings of identity as a professional. Did they feel any more professional as a result
of their fellowship at the Institute? What made a
person feel professional? Had their commitment to
their work changed as a result of their Institute experience? At the time, I hypothesized that one outcome
of the fellowship, of the opportunity to work deeply
and seriously on a project, would be a greater sense
of competence. The greater the sense of inner competence, my reasoning went, the greater would be the
sense of commitment to future productive work. This
proved to be only partially true.

Reprinted from *Science* 170
(23 October 1970): 413-16.
Copyright 1970 by the American Association for the Advancement of Science. Published originally under the
title "Psychological and Social
Barriers to Women in Science."

. . . one of the main barriers to women's achievement of excellence and commitment is the expectation that women's career patterns and motivation will be the same as men's.

Many indicated that the fellowship program had resulted in a genuine change in the conceptions of themselves as professionals, but their responses suggested that this change was rarely due solely to the opportunity to work on their projects. Although this was important, equally significant was the access to stimulating colleagues, both within and outside the Institute, which the special status conferred by the fellowship made possible. Appraisals of their work by others, coupled with acceptance and recognition by people whose professional opinions were relevant and appropriate, made a significant difference in determining whether a woman felt like a professional, and whether she in turn had a strong sense of commitment to future work.

Challenging interaction with other professionals is frequently as necessary to creative work as is the opportunity for solitude and thought.[2] Yet comments from many women indicate that it is particularly difficult for them to attain, especially for the woman who seeks reentry. As one woman astutely noted:

> Those of us who have interrupted our careers because of children or moving with our husbands across the country have special difficulties. Our departments maintain no ties with us. Often no one knows us, and the articles and books on which we are working may not be published for another three to five years. Meanwhile, if we are to be productive, we need to be professionally involved again.

Although women offer unique qualities to intellectual and creative endeavors, one of the main barriers to women's achievement of excellence and commitment is the expectation that women's career patterns and motivation will be the same as men's. When they are not, there are many phrases ("lost to marriage," "didn't pan out," "dropped out") which indicate the disappointing nature of their acts, the hopelessness of their making choices which are uniquely theirs as women. Many, possessing energy and talent, will choose the same career paths and find great personal satisfaction in meeting the same demands as many men. But others who live life differently, and who may choose differently from the traditional career pattern, also have much to offer, and our gain is greater if we can include their talents among those which society and science utilize. Attracted to scholarship and scientific research, they continue on to graduate school or professional school after college because of their deep interest in a field. Many have clear and well-defined plans for a career, while others wish to combine "worthwhile work" with homemaking. Because of their serious intellectual interest and involvement, such women usually do well academically and are excellent students. Yet they find that their interest in learning and in excellence does not receive the same recognition after college or graduate school as it did before unless they determinedly indicate that they plan a full-time uninterrupted career. But clearly the dominant (and in many cases preferred) life pattern for many a highly trained woman still includes multiple roles, dual commitments, and occasional interruptions. If she wishes to continue her professional activity on a flexible or modified schedule, or faces temporal or geographic discontinuities, she is frequently excluded from important aspects of what the sociologists call "socialization into a profession."

PROFESSIONAL SOCIALIZATION

In the normal course of men's and women's professional careers, only a part of their professional training takes place in college, in graduate or professional schools, or in a training program. Many professions and occupations have periods analogous to that of the medical intern or resident (though these stages are frequently informal and rarely explicitly recognized) during which the individual learns to behave in ways which other people in the field regard as "professional." Such "socialization" usually occurs during graduate school as well as during the first decade of employment after one is launched on a career, and consists of learning the roles, the informal values and attitudes, and the expectations which are an important part of real professional life. During this stage of a career, the person not only learns occupational roles and skills, but gains a firmer image of himself as competent and adequate. Appraisals of his work by others permit self-criticism to grow and standards of judgment to develop. Such a sense of competence may come quickly and early for some, but develop slowly and gradually for others. Once a person has this sense of competence and regards himself as a professional, it is probable that he has less need to learn from colleagues and indeed may have greater freedom to diverge from the accepted way of doing things, seeking his own pathway instead. It is this firm sense of professional identity and capability which women, regardless of their ability, may find difficult to achieve, or achieve only at a high personal price.

Many people are unaware of this period of role learning in scholarly, scientific or academic professions and fail to realize how important such a stage is and how lengthy it has become because of the increased complexity of professional life. Everett Hughes, the sociologist, has noted that many still think of professions as they were in the nineteenth century, although they have vastly changed since then.[3] Many professions are practiced in complicated organizations, with consequent nuances of status and levels of organization to contend with. There are elaborate social systems in all parts of academic and business life, and purely techical training is rarely enough. The aspiring young scientist must be knowledgeable about many aspects of institutions, journals, professional meetings, methods of obtaining source materials, and funding grant applications. Knowing how to command these technical and institutional facilities requires numerous skills, many unanticipated by the young student. But once gained, such skills often seem very simple in retrospect and even thoughtful professionals forget that they were once not second nature. This is the kind of learning we speak of as "caught," not "taught," and it is a valued by-product of acceptance and challenging association with other professionals.

SPONSORSHIP

Studies of professions and professional identity have also stressed the importance of sponsorship as a device for influencing commitment and affecting the self-image. Referred to by some writers[4] as the "protégé system," sponsorship is common to the upper echelons of almost all professions, including the scientific fields. One must be "in" both to learn crucial trade secrets and to advance within the field. Unfortunately a man may be hesitant about encouraging a woman as a protégé. He may be delighted to have her as an assistant, but he may not see her as his successor, or as one who will carry on his ideas, or as a colleague. He may believe that she is less likely to be a good gamble, a risk for him to exert himself for, or that she is financially less dependent upon a job. Because of subtle pressures from his wife, he may temper his publicly expressed enthusiasm or interest. He may fail to introduce her to colleagues or sponsor her for jobs. And as one of Anne Roe's studies of eminent scientists indicated,[5] the advancement and success of protégés are important to the sponsor's own feelings of satisfaction in his professional efforts; nonachieving protégés reflect on the sponsor's public and private image.

In addition, sponsorship affects the recognition an individual receives. One might assume (or hope) that excellence and productivity in scientific work is all that is needed for recognition, but in reality ideas are more likely to be accepted if they are promoted or mentioned by eminent sponsors, or if they are the products of joint authorship with a well-known professional or derive from a well-known laboratory or university. Whether a woman is "sponsored" in these ways will partially determine who reads her work, listens to her reports, or even offers friendly comments on the draft of a paper. Such informal signs of recognition increase motivation and affect one's subjective feelings of commitment to a field, as well as feelings of professional identity.

ARE WOMEN IN THE CLUB?

A recent study of women Ph.D.'s[6] showed that the full-time employed woman Ph.D. published as much as her male colleagues and was more likely than the average male scientist to be in research. She was involved in the activities of her professional organization, was sought out as a consultant, and was more likely to be awarded fellowships and be accepted in honorary societies. Despite all this evidence of productivity and commitment, the authors of the study noted that the women often felt left out, and suggested that

> the problem which bothers the woman Ph.D. who is a full-time contributor to her profession is that she is denied many of the informal signs of belonging and recognition. These women report that even on such daily activities as finding someone to have lunch or take a coffee break with, or finding someone with whom she can chew over an idea, or on larger issues such as finding a partner with whom she can share a research interest, the woman Ph.D. has a special and lower status.

This exclusion from the informal channels of communication is of particular importance in fast-moving science, where, as Sir Alfred Egerton has noted, "of the total information extant, only part is in the literature. Much of it is sorted in the many brains of scientists and technologists. We are as dependent on biological storage as on mechanical or library storage." Jessie Bernard astutely comments: "It is this access—[to] the brains of fellow scientists—that may be more limited for women than for men."[7]

The need for stimulating colleagues was also attested to in a study by Perrucci of women engineers and scientists.[8] She found that women were more apt than men to endorse as important the opportunity "to work with colleagues who are interested in the latest developments in their field" and "to associate with other engineers and scientists of recognized ability." Interestingly enough, no differences appeared between men and women of comparable education as to whether they desired challenging work or work involving "people versus things."

The evidence also seems to indicate, however, that in many cases women are reluctant to put themselves forward or to protest their being left out. It is a vicious circle: men indifferent or unaware of excluding women; women insecure and hesitant of intruding. The remedy is not necessarily more individual boldness, but must include new institutional arrangements and programs which do not depend on individual initiative.[9] However, as the Radcliffe data indicated, such arrangements and programs are not too difficult to achieve.

There have been lone individuals who have flourished on society's neglect and produced great ideas or masterpieces, but this is not characteristic of those in the professions or the majority of people. For most people, acceptance by others and interaction with challenging groups or organizations are a source of deep personal significance and of creative energy as well. Yet it is this acceptance and this interaction which are often denied, both purposefully and inadvertently, to women, whether they participate full time or on a flexible schedule, whether they remain continuously in the field or seek reentry.

A NEW CAREER CONCEPT

Because of their life patterns, many women with scientific training have nonprofessional roles and identifications to which they are deeply committed. They seek an occupational or professional identity which recognizes and takes into account this dual commitment. For women with these values, a new concept of professional "career" may be necessary.

Numerous women, either because of their own inclination or their personal situations, enjoy and competently manage full-time work and a full-time career. Others, however, seem to be seeking to invent for themselves a new and more varied conception of career, one which has not existed before and for which there are few models or patterns available. They have a full-time commitment, but do not always plan to work on a full-time basis; their lives and where they work are governed to a greater degree by nonoccupational factors. As a result of the smaller size of families, and the shorter span of child-rearing, few of these women see their maternal role as bringing their professional life to an end. They think of themselves as a permanent part of the working force, and regard flexible schedules and part-time work as a necessary part of the solution. Some seem to be seeking an alternative career model which is neither upward-moving nor "success-oriented," but which recognizes their commitment to family responsibilities as an important part of their choice. To accommodate this lateral career, or "career of limited ambition,"[10] they seek to improvise a new professional role which is more differentiated and diversified than the accepted pattern. (I should note parenthetically that this interest in new career patterns is by no means limited to women.) Such an alternative mode might be represented schematically by an ascending spiral movement, indicating career choices which are upward in direction but slowly paced, with long horizontal stopovers. Deeper knowledge or more varied experience would be the goals of such a career: not greater status, but greater esteem; not primarily extrinsic rewards, but intrinsic satisfactions.[11]

Such new models are long overdue. Almost a century of experimentation has been spent in attempting to fit women's career patterns into those followed by most men, and the result has not been phenomenally successful. If such alternative career patterns can gain general recognition, the result may be more productive, creative work. As Epstein[12] has so succinctly noted, the barriers to women's advancement and achievement are not merely a function of prejudice or incapacity. The structures of professions, narrow and inflexible as they often are, may create limits which are largely unintended. But groups and colleagues are powerful forces in shaping attitudes and behavior; the institutional settings and social mechanisms which inhibit commitment and identity can also be used to promote change and to encourage different consequences.

SUGGESTIONS

What can women do to cope with these barriers and discriminatory practices which intensify the effects of discontinuity in their lives? How can they fully utilize their talents, yet make choices that are suitable to their goals and life styles? What constructive action can be taken to remedy the inadequate socialization which the current structure of the professions makes inevitable for many women?

In overcoming the barriers, the importance of sponsorship and the maintenance of communication with stimulating colleagues should not be underestimated. When a woman has to interrupt her training, graduate study, or employment, she should talk over future alternatives or avenues of return with an adviser and ask for letters of recommendation which may be used when a return is contemplated. She can seek ways to keep in touch with her department or work group. As one successful woman observed, "She should leave no gap unfilled."

Women with similar fields of interest can often profit by forming or joining other women in associations which provide professional stimulation and motivation, as well as information and access to new opportunities. Such groups can be particularly effective in assisting women who have temporarily retired to return to or keep up with their field. Several studies[13] suggest the possibility that women who are more ambitious in the traditional male-career sense may be more stimulated to achieve by the presence of men who are achieving, while women who regard intellectual achievement as part of the feminine role may react more favorably to the presence of capable women colleagues. This at least suggests that many talented younger women might be more encouraged by knowing and observing in the professional role other women who value the feminine family role. Such models are still too often a rarity.

Part-time work has only begun to be utilized effectively. Many men have long known that they are most productive when they engage in a variety of functions, carrying out activities which complement but may have very little immediate relation to each other. Although the initial stages of learning how to accomplish this are not easy, many women are discovering that such juggling can work even in complex and demanding scientific and engineering fields. Pilot projects using women scientists in the federal government have found both a shorter week and a shorter day successful.[14] Enthusiastic women report that they get almost as much done, while employers note that they get more than their money's worth, since there is little wasted time and important thinking time often comes free. In fields with hard-to-find skills such as data processing, part-time job opportunities may make it easier to recruit employees. An innovation which has been used with great success in education, social work, library work and medical residencies is to have two women share one job. Thoughtfully and carefully planned, the partnership job has proved not only eminently suitable to the needs of women, but of benefit to employers as well.[15] Partnership teaching has proved so useful in education that one wonders why it was not thought of before.

Sometimes women create their own part-time opportunities. In the San Francisco area, a group of women biologists found they lacked opportunities for part-time work and for keeping up with their fields while their children were small. They organized a talent pool, incorporating as an educational group, Natural Science Education Resources. They have since offered a unique series of classes on plants and animals to mothers and their preschool children, served as consultants to teachers and schools, developed new ecology programs, presented adult education courses, and obtained a pilot National Science Foundation grant. Several women have now moved on to other jobs, leaving a vacant place which is eagerly taken by someone else seeking such a part-time opportunity.

Although all of these part-time approaches serve to prevent technical obsolescence, retraining programs and reentry techniques are also needed. Although some writers counsel noninterruption as the only answer, it seems more realistic to assume that discontinuity will continue to be a fact of life for many women. A

. . . our attempts to foster a social climate which meets the complex needs of women today may well be pointing the way toward meeting the diverse needs of both the men and the women of tomorrow.

woman's interests change between the time she is in college and the point at which she decides to involve herself more deeply again. Fortunately mid-career retraining is becoming mandatory for many scientific fields; if reentry opportunities for women can only be included by companies, universities, and professional societies along with the continuing education programs for full-time professionals, these transitions can be more easily accomplished.

Some women have planned their own transitional reentry programs. One woman chemist talked to a local college professor and offered to assist him in his laboratory courses during the year in order to bring her knowledge up to date. She proved so capable that he admitted her to advanced seminars, supervised her in tutorial reading, and is now working to retain her in a permanent capacity in the department.

Master's degree programs aimed at updating skills are particularly promising. Rutgers University has had one for mathematicians, and Wellesley College has had a two-year program for chemists.

Some may raise the question: Aren't women now insisting on the same opportunities as men? Do women want the same opportunities or do they want special opportunities? The answer is simply that they need both. Career commitment takes a variety of forms for women and may increasingly do so for men. Longevity, population pressures, and the explosion of knowledge have created new needs and life stages for us all. If we become obsessed with simply giving women the same opportunities as men (important though this may be), we not only obstruct effective recognition of the differences in women's lives, but may fail to note what is already a trend—more complex educational and occupational patterns for both men and women. Many of the programs and innovations developed to suit women's needs are needed for men as well. They too are feeling the impact of new knowledge, the expectation of intellectual retooling every decade, and the need for part-time refresher courses to update proficiency. They too have discovered that interests change after twenty years in a field, that challenge can outweigh security, and that mid-life may bring a desire to shift the focus of a career. And surely we are all learning the lesson that education is most useful when one is most ready for it. Many young students are no longer so eager to cram all their education and professional training into the beginning of their adult years.

While the patterns of women's lives may be more varied, the interruptions more pronounced and profound, and possibly the needs for guidance greater, our attempts to foster a social climate which meets the complex needs of women today may well be pointing the way toward meeting the diverse needs of both the men and the women of tomorrow.

SUMMARY

Commitment and creativity in science are not merely a function of an individual's competence or excellence, but are a product of the social environment as well. Acceptance and recognition from significant other people (one's peers and other professionals) and opportunities for stimulating and challenging interaction are essential for developing a strong occupational or professional identity, and for creating the inner sense of role competence which can lead to greater commitment and productivity in professional work. Unfortunately women, especially those who have experienced interrupted or discontinuous careers, find such opportunities and acceptance difficult to obtain.

The scientific community can foster the professional development and effectiveness of women in science by permitting women more flexible opportunities for professional participation, by being more aware of practices which exclude women on the basis of gender rather than ability, and by separating standards of excellence from time schedules.

Women can help themselves by keeping up contacts with others in their fields, participating in professional groups, becoming familiar with new part-time approaches and reentry skills, creating their own retraining and employment opportunities, and instituting new programs appropriate to their needs.

"Restriction of opportunity not only blights hope; it excludes the person from the chance to acquire the knowledge and skill that would in turn enable him to surmount the barriers to effectiveness."[16]

Notes

1. M. S. White, "Conversations with the Scholars" (report submitted to the Radcliffe Institute, 1966). The Radcliffe Institute supports part-time scholars, provides funds for domestic and child care help, a place to work and access to the library and intellectual resources of Radcliffe and Harvard. The scholars neither work for a degree nor take courses, but engage in creative or scholarly work within their fields. Many already have their doctorate, or its equivalent in achievement. In addition, the Institute sponsors other fellow-

ship programs for part-time graduate study and medical residency training, and conducts a research program.

2. D. C. Pelz, "Creative Tensions in the Research and Development Climate," *Science* 157 (1967), 160; H. S. Becker and J. W. Carper, *American Journal of Sociology,* 41 (1956) 289; J. J. Sherwood, "Self-Identity and Referent Others," *Sociometry,* 28 (1965), 66.
3. E. C. Hughes, "Professions," *Daedalus, 92* (1963), 655.
4. C. F. Epstein, *Woman's Place* (Berkeley: Univ. of California Press, 1970).
5. A. Roe, "Women in Science," *Personnel and Guidance Journal,* 54 (1966), 784.
6. R. J. Simon, S. M. Clark, and K. Galway, "The Woman Ph.D.: A Recent Profile," *Social Problems,* 15 (1967), 221.
7. J. Bernard, *Academic Women* (University Park, Pa.: State College, The Pennsylvania Press, 1964), p. 303.
8. C. C. Perrucci, "The Female Engineer and Scientist: Factors Associated with the Pursuit of a Professional Career" (unpub. report, 1968).
9. See U.S. Civil Service Commission, *Changing Patterns: A Report on the Federal Women's Program Review Seminar* (Washington, D.C.: Government Printing Office, 1969); A. L. Dement, "The College Woman as a Science Major," *Journal of Higher Education,* 33 (1962), 487.
10. M. K. Sanders, "The New American Female: Demi-Feminism Takes Over," *Harper's,* 231 (1965), 37.
11. R. H. Turner, "Some Aspects of Women's Ambition," *American Journal of Sociology,* 70 (1964), 271.
12. Epstein.
13. E. G. French and G. S. Lesser, "Some Characteristics of the Achievement Motive in Women," *Journal of Abnormal Social Psychology,* 68 (1964), 119; C. A. Leland and M. M. Lozoff, *College Influences on the Role Development of Undergraduates* (Stanford, Calif.: Institute for the Study of Human Problems, Stanford Univ. 1969), pp. 46–90.
14. U.S. Civil Service Commission, *Changing Patterns;* Dement.
15. I. Zwerling, "Part-Time Insured Staff," *Hospital and Community Psychiatry,* 21 (1970), 59; W. A. Thompson et al., "An Answer to the Computer Programmer Shortage." *Adult Leadership,* vol. 18, no. 7 (Jan. 1970), p. 213.
16. M. B. Smith, in *Socialization and Society,* ed. J. A. Clausen (Boston: Little, Brown, 1968), p. 313.

Women's Economic Status: Some Clichés and Some Facts

Shirley Bernard

Women are poor. Compared with men, they are very poor. They get about half as much as men in wages, and less than half as much in other income. And this disparity is found at every level of society, from the working poor, who are most often women, to the wealthy, who are most often men.

Yet the notion persists that women own most of the wealth of the nation. In fact, this notion is so prevalent that it has become a cliché. It's a cruel cliché. It perpetuates the belief that women work for fun, or to get out of the house, or to pass the time until marriage, or to meet men, or for almost any reason except to earn money. Everyone repeats the cliché—even women themselves.

As a consequence, employed women are unpaid and underpaid; untitled and unpromoted; unorganized and unappreciated; and until now—uncomplaining. But no more. When the President's Task Force on Women's Rights and Responsibilities reports that "almost two-thirds of the adult poor are women," when the Department of Labor Women's Bureau reports that 40 percent of working women are single, divorced, or separated, and dependent upon their earnings to support themselves and their families, when two out of ten American households are headed by women, when it takes the combined earnings of both parents to lift thousands of families out of poverty, when a cliché demoralizes and impoverishes, then the nation cannot afford its comfort. Especially when it affords but cold comfort for so many.

In order to assess the damage done to women and their families by these false notions, one must have the facts. The following statistics provide a more accurate picture of the economic position of women in the United States.

In a society where money means power, most of the money must come to the dominant group if it is to maintain the status quo. In our society white males are dominant; as Table 1 shows, they earn substantially more than nonwhites and females. Among full-time workers, nonwhite males, who share "maleness" with the dominant group, earn about 70 percent as much as white males. White females, who share "whiteness" with the dominant group, earn about 58 percent as much as white males. Nonwhite females, who share no characteristic of the dominant group, earn about 50 percent as much as white males.

TABLE I   Average Salaries Earned by Working Men and Women, 1970

Workers	Average salary
Full-time, year-round	
White men	$9,375
Nonwhite men	6,598
White women	5,490
Nonwhite women	4,674
Full-time and part-time	
Men	$7,939
Women	3,785

Source: U. S. Dept. of Commerce, Census Bureau, Current Population Report (1970), Bulletin P-60, no. 80, p. 129.

The plight of part-time women workers is especially severe. Their relative income is sharply lower, while their relative number is substantially greater. Many more women than men suffer the particular privations of the part-time worker, which often include not only lower salaries, but also lack of job security and loss of fringe benefits.

Discrimination against women has an immediate impact upon their families. Of the families headed by women, 38.3 percent live in poverty, according to the *Statistical Abstracts of the United States, 1971.* By contrast, only 8.3 percent of the families headed by men fall into that category. Their dire straits frequently force women heads of families to seek public assistance. Approximately 3,982,000 females survive on some form of public assistance or welfare, as compared with only 1,498,000 males.[1] One reason for this discrepancy may be the relatively few sources of income for females as compared with males. For example, unemployment and workman's compensation, government employee pensions, and veterans' payments are sources of income for 8,532,000 males as compared with 3,401,000 females.[2] These factors, plus the generally depressed salaries for women, plus many other factors, such as the lack of child care as well as educational and employment opportunities, all contribute to the poverty of women. But one fact is abundantly clear. A substantial number of women—30 percent more than men—cannot make enough money either from wages or from other sources to bring their standard of living above the poverty level. And they are not alone in their misery. Their children suffer, too.

In the upper income brackets the disparity in earnings between men and women continues. Males hold around 90 percent of the jobs that pay $10,000 a year or more, leaving only 10 percent for females. The disparity in income from sources other than wages is not as sharp, but it still exists. A comparison between nonwhite men and women cannot be made in the highest brackets since the Census Bureau does not consider their numbers statistically significant enough to be recorded. But in the $10,000 to $25,000 brackets, as Table 2 shows, it is clear that nonwhite males do somewhat better than nonwhite females. In the highest brackets the factor of inherited wealth becomes evident. American fortunes have been amassed primarily by white families; therefore, white females share in that kind of

TABLE 2 Percentages of White and Nonwhite Men and Women with Incomes over $10,000, 1972

Income	Men		Women	
	White	Nonwhite	White	Nonwhite
From wages				
$10,000 – 14,999	24.4	13.3	4.4	4.2
$15,000 – 24,999	11.3	2.8	0.6	0.5
$25,000 and over	2.8	0.4	0.1	0.2
From sources other than wages				
$10,000 – 14,999	1.4	0.1	0.8	0.1
$15,000 – 24,999	0.5	0.1	0.3	—
$25,000 and over	0.3	—	0.2	—

Source: U. S. Dept. of Commerce, Bureau of the Census, Current Population Report (Dec. 1973), Bulletin P-60, no. 90, pp. 151, 152.

income. However, even at these levels the income of white women is considerably lower than that of white men.

Another common illusion is that women control most of the assets of this country. In fact, about 61 percent of the persons holding assets of $60,000 or more composed of real estate, bonds, corporate stock, cash, notes and mortgages, insurance equity, and other are men, whereas only about 39 percent are women.[3] Some 24 percent of the country's stock is owned by individual men and only 18 percent by individual women.* And even these figures overstate the assets held by women. A 1964 survey of leading brokerage houses revealed that "many accounts are held in the names of wives, girl friends and other women for tax and other purposes."[4] There is no reason to believe that the situation has changed since then. As for controlling the money exchanges, the story is the same. A woman on Wall Street is a rarity. Women hold only 5 percent of all sales jobs in brokerage firms and 6.5 percent of management jobs—usually on the lower levels of management—according to Equal Employment Opportunity Commission statistics.

Finally—according to the cliché—women inherit most of the wealth of the country, since they live longer than men. The older women are, the richer they become, so the theory goes. But a comparison of the estates left by men and women refutes such a notion. In fact, the chances of being a rich dead man are a lot better than the chances of being a rich dead woman: estates of $60,000 or more are left 61.4 percent of the time by men, and only 38.6 percent of the time by women.[5]

A study of the facts thoroughly discredits the clichés about women and their wealth. Not only are poor women poorer than poor men, but rich men are richer than rich women. At no time in life, (yea, even unto death) do women have more money than men. In fact, the contrary is true. Men, not women, earn, own, and control most of the wealth of this country.

Notes

1. U.S. Dept. of Commerce, Bureau of the Census, *Current Population Report* (Dec. 1973), Bulletin P-60, no. 90, p. 153.
2. *Ibid.*
3. *Statistical Abstracts of the United States, 1971,* p. 327.
4. Survey quoted in the *Los Angeles Times,* Aug. 9, 1964.
5. *Statistical Abstracts of the United States, 1971,* p. 327.

---

* U.S. Dept. of Labor, Women's Bureau, Bulletin no. 294, p. 146. The rest is held by institutions.

Working Poor Women

Kathleen Shortridge

" Pity the poor working girl," they said in the
bad old days before industrial democracy
brought prosperity to the workers. Today there are
more "poor working girls," more utterly impoverished
working women, than there were women working in
the factories and sweatshops and mills during the
depths of the nineteenth century Industrial Revolution.[1] Six million American women work full-time,
year-round, and earn less than $4,000 per year.[2]
Their jobs are hard and unpleasant. Most work in
private households, in agriculture, or in small retail
and service establishments. Their jobs bring no
respect, and little remuneration.

 The working poor form a class of workers who
have been bypassed by the great gains in economic
and social power made by most American workers.
Men outnumber women in the more prosperous segments of the work force, but among the working
poor, women are in the majority. Women constitute
21 percent of the full-time, year-round force, but 55
percent of the full-time, year-round workers who earn
less than $4,000 per year.[3] Some 39 percent of white
women and 61 percent of black women, working
full-time, year-round, earned less than $4,000 in

1968. Only 11 percent of white men and 31 percent of black men did as badly.[4] While the worker's cause has advanced through organization and legislation, millions of working women have remained untouched and impoverished.

Who are these working poor women? Some 1.6 million of them are private household workers—often called domestics, maids, or servants. They try to earn a living doing the classic women's work, cleaning, cooking, and caring for children. Theirs is the least valued job in our economy and the third most common occupation of women. According to the National Committee on Household Employment,[5] about two-thirds of the private household workers in 1968 were black. Most of them—54 percent—worked in the South. Most of them had little education, though 20 percent had finished high school and 4.2 percent had some college education. There are more women with college education than there are men of any description doing private household work. Two-thirds of the women in private household employment are single, widowed, divorced, or separated, and 200,000 are single heads of families.

The snide bumper sticker "I fight poverty—I work" is not too amusing to the household worker, waiting to catch a bus home* after her eight-hour day of cleaning up other people's dirt, looking after other people's children, and cooking other people's food. The federal minimum wage, $2.00 per hour, which is set by the Fair Labor Standards Act, does not apply to private household workers. The median annual income of full-time household workers in 1968 was $1,523; 82 percent had total cash incomes from all sources, including Social Security and public assistance, of less than $2,000.

Furthermore, private household workers are denied the fringe benefits that have become such an important part of the American worker's wage. Overtime pay, sick leave, unemployment compensation, paid vacations, medical plans, pensions, and so on have come to constitute 23 percent of the average worker's effective pay.[6] The private household worker gets none of these. Some are eligible for Social Security, but many of their employers are unwilling to pay for it, and some of the workers themselves cannot afford to have anything deducted from their already hopelessly inadequate checks. Thus the private household worker's wage is even lower, compared to most workers, than her miserable take-home pay would suggest.

Of course, insult is added to poverty. Employers often treat household workers disrespectfully. To the National Committee on Household Employment (NCHE), the use of such terms as maid, servant, and girl, and the common habit of calling grown women by their first names, are only the most obvious of demeaning

---

* The great majority of household workers do go home after work. Only 11 percent live in with their employers.

working conditions. To compensate for a sense of personal inadequacy, some housewives tyrannize their household workers. Racial prejudice often aggravates the problem, since the traditionally exploited and abused black woman often works in a white household. As Edith B. Sloan of NCHE says, "Many household workers find themselves today, in 1970, confronted with employers who consciously or subconsciously pattern their behavior after the stereotype of Scarlett O'Hara."

The undervaluation of "women's work" has resulted in the exploitation and degradation of private household workers, and now women are beginning to refuse to do this work. The need for private household employees is great and growing; more women than ever before want or need to join the work force outside the home, and they in turn need help with housework and child care. The growing population of elderly people desperately needs household help. If the trend toward remaining single continues, as the last census suggests, many working single people may want help with their housework and be able to afford it. Yet today there are fewer household workers than there were a decade ago. Private household workers are an older group—six years older than the average working woman—and as they become incapacitated or die (few can ever afford to retire), young women are not replacing them. Unless the conditions of private household employees change radically, an acute shortage of these important workers will certainly develop.

Another substantial group of impoverished working women works in agriculture. About 665,000 women work on farms, and many are not covered by the federal minimum wage—$1.30 in agriculture in 1973.[7] Eleanor A. Eaton of the American Friends Service Committee writes that women farm workers "operate under the same conditions as men do . . . and have family responsibilities in addition."[8] The women share the often appalling working conditions with the men— long hours, hard work, hot sun, poor food, dreadful housing, and sometimes migrancy. On top of this they must cook, clean, and care for their families. The average annual income of agricultural workers, including both farm and nonfarm earnings, is $1,886.[9] Those excluded from federal minimum wage coverage certainly fall below the average. Women generally earn less than men, and between family and field, they work even harder.

Some 4.3 million women in the impoverished working class are service workers. Women are far more likely than men to be doing service work—cooking, cleaning offices and hospitals and hotels, taking tickets, waiting tables, emptying bedpans. One out of five working women but only one out of fourteen working men does service work. The average woman service worker makes $2,815 if she works full-time, year-round—55 percent of what the average man service worker makes.[10] Service workers employed by small establishments with under $250,000 in receipts annually are not covered by the $1.60-per-hour federal minimum wage.

TABLE 1 Proportion of Saleswomen and Salesmen Employed in Various Retail Trades, by Salary Level, 1970

Occupations with average weekly salary	Saleswomen Number (in thousands)	%	Salesmen Number (in thousands)	%
Over $120 (e.g. motor vehicle dealers)	104.0	1.9	762.6	9.7
$110 – 119.99 (e.g. building materials and farm equipment)	122.3	2.2	652.0	8.3
$100 – 109.99 (e.g. furniture and home furnishings)	928.5	17.0	2756.4	35.2
$90 – 99.99 (e.g. mail order houses)	81.3	1.5	51.2	.7
$80 – 89.99 (e.g. grocery, meat and vegetable stores)	593.8	10.9	1168.0	14.9
$70 – 79.99 (e.g. department stores)	1667.5	30.6	1235.5	15.8
$60 – 69.99 (e.g. women's ready-to-wear stores)	313.7	5.8	65.0	.8
$50 – 59.99 (e.g. eating and drinking places)	1644.5	30.1	1151.1	14.7
Total	5455.6	100.0	7841.8	100.1[a]

Note: Trades included in this table met the following criteria: 1) they provided information on the total number of men employed, the total number of women employed, and the 1970 average weekly salary; and 2) they did not subsume another more specific category that could be used.

Source: U. S. Dept. of Labor, Bureau of Labor Statistics, Employment and Earnings Statistics for the U. S., 1909-1971, Bulletin No. 1312-8 (Washington, D. C., 1971).

[a]Does not sum to 100% because of rounding.

Like private household workers and farm workers, women service workers are doing some of the hardest, most unpleasant work our society requires; they reap the reward of living the hardest, most unpleasant lives that poverty can buy.

The 1.9 million women who work full-time, year-round in retail sales make a median wage of $1.49 per hour, or $3,103 per year. Almost half of these women work in small stores not covered by the federal minimum wage. Saleswomen earn

**Saleswomen earn on the average 40 percent
of what salesmen earn, because salesmen and
saleswomen sell different things.**

on the average 40 percent of what salesmen earn, because salesmen and saleswomen sell different things.[11] The retail trades are segregated sharply by sex, with women clustered thickly in those sales occupations that earn the least. Table 1 demonstrates that most salesmen are in the relatively higher-paying trades, and most saleswomen in the relatively lower-paying trades. But perhaps the most striking illustration is a simple comparison of the men's and women's clothing trades. In 1970, 42 percent of the sales force were women, and the average weekly salary was $88.56. In women's ready-to-wear, 88 percent of the sales force were women, and the average weekly salary was $64.16.[12]

With one-third of its female labor force employed in the least valued, lowest-paying jobs in the economy—retail sales, services, agricultural labor, and household labor—the United States has an enormous population of poor women. Sixty-two percent of the adults who live in poverty are women. One-fourth of the full-time, year-round women workers had annual incomes from all sources of less than $3,000. Sixty percent of the children who live in poverty depend solely on the earnings of women. Nineteen percent of the families headed by white working women and 50 percent of the families headed by nonwhite working women fall below the poverty level.[13] The problem of poverty in the United States is disproportionately a problem for women, and to an alarming extent, a problem for working women.

What are some of the disabilities that keep so many women in the class of the working poor? Of course, all the problems plaguing the poor generally also plague the working poor woman: ill health, low education,* unfamiliarity with bureau-

---

* But contrary to the stay-in-school advertising campaign, more education is not in itself the answer for working women. At each educational level, there is a substantial gap between the earnings of men and those of women. Indeed, at the lowest educational level—less than eight years of schooling—women do relatively better than at higher levels. In 1970, women elementary school dropouts earned 62.8 percent as much as men with the same education, while women elementary school graduates earned only 55.5 percent as much, and women high school graduates, 58.3 percent as much. Women who had completed high school and worked full-time, year-round, earned less on the average than male elementary school dropouts—$5580 as compared to $6043. See U.S. Dept. of Labor, Women's Bureau, "Fact Sheet on the Earnings Gap."

cratic structures, poor nutrition, racial prejudice, a tight economy. But on top of these general problems, working poor women have the added burden of sex-related low earning power. It is well known that women are frequently paid less than men for doing precisely the same work.[14] Sometimes men are given different job titles to disguise the discrimination: thus a man doing a charwoman's work may be called a janitor, a caretaker, or an industrial cleaner. Sometimes the only discernible difference between a man's job and a woman's is in their paychecks. At the bottom of the economic spectrum this kind of discrimination is not even illegal, for the provision of the Fair Labor Standards Act requiring equal pay for equal work applies only to jobs that are covered by the minimum wage.

It is also well known—and we have already presented evidence for this point—that employers reserve the lowest-paying, least valued work, like private household and service work, for women. Of the 33 occupations listed in *Employment and Earnings Statistics for the United States* which paid on the average less than $75 per week in 1967 and for which information on the proportion of women employed was available, only five had less than 50 percent women employees; none had less than 30 percent women; and twelve had over 80 percent women. The manufacture of certain leather goods, certain household furnishings, and cigars turn out to be highly feminine occupations. Dorothy Haener of the Women's Committee of the United Auto Workers has said, perhaps bitterly but with clear justification, "If a job will command a living wage, it's a man's job."

There are many rationales and excuses for excluding women from high-paying jobs. To begin with, myths like the supposedly high absentee and turnover rates of women make employers reluctant to hire, train, and promote women. The Department of Labor has analyzed surveys that demonstrate the inaccuracy of these myths: "Women workers have favorable records of attendance and labor turnover when compared with men employed at similar job levels and under similar circumstances."[15] But male employers remain unconvinced.

Economic mechanisms also operate to devalue women's work. A significant factor in the passage of the Fair Labor Standards Act of 1938, which provided for the establishment of a federal minimum wage, was the lobbying by many employers who paid adequate wages themselves and resented competitors who cut costs by paying low wages.[16] Employers of household workers do not have to contend with competitors, however, but only with laborers. Thus their interest lies not in establishing a floor under wages but in reducing wages as much as possible. Clearly the competition factor will never persuade employers of household workers to favor a minimum wage.

Legal factors, especially state "protective" laws, often operate to the detriment of women workers. Legal opinion on the effect of these laws in the face of the 1964 Civil Rights Act is in flux. Traditionally, however, employers have refused to hire women for certain jobs because the work would require them to lift weights or work hours in excess of those permitted women by state law, or to do work considered too dangerous for women by state law. Thus women have been legislated out of better-paying unskilled work in industry and pushed into low-paying service jobs.

The prejudices of lawmakers and public administrators help perpetuate the low earning power of women. For example, the Job Corps, an effort to train poor people for good jobs, clearly aimed to train men. The Johnson Administration's original Job Corps bill specified "male individuals," and no one had seriously considered including young women in the program until Congresswoman Edith Green insisted. Despite this, two years after the passage of the Equal Opportunity Act of 1964, Congress had to pass an amendment ensuring that women would compose at least 23 percent of the Job Corps. Congresswoman Green recalled, "I have fought for an amendment allowing 50 percent enrollment for girls. We have never even achieved that. Girls have never constituted even 30 percent of Job Corps enrollment. Our Education and Labor Committee of the House has legislated to discriminate."[17] This imbalance exists despite the fact that a clear majority of the nation's poor are women, and the unemployment rate for women is consistently higher than that of men. In 1967, for example, the unemployment rate for non-white girls aged 16–19 reached a staggering 29.5 percent.[18]

Social roles and social myths also detract from women's earning power. Girls who grow up expecting to take care of a family while a male breadwinner takes care of them are not motivated to acquire the marketable skills necessary to obtain a well-paying job. Yet over 12 million single, widowed, divorced, and separated women are in the labor force. Social roles prescribe a particularly heavy burden for women family heads, and one in ten American families is headed by a woman.[19] Women as heads of single-parent families outnumber men by more than four to one; given social expectations about the responsibilities of motherhood, this could hardly be otherwise. Responsibility for child care falls on the mother; it is not shared by society or by the employer, and all too often, it is not shared by the father. Thus many women who grow up expecting to be housewives end up in the labor market, often solely responsible for their families, with the devastating combination of great financial need and poor employment opportunity.

Do the women of the impoverished working class have any alternative to lives of drudgery and poverty? Several possibilities come to mind: welfare, marriage, government regulation, and organization.

Why don't women who are working full-time, year-round for poverty-level wages go on welfare? In the first place, many are not eligible. Residency and domi-

**It would be impossible . . . for every woman
in the United States to marry, unless our
society were willing to tolerate polygamy.**

cile requirements have excluded hundreds of thousands of migrant workers and newcomers from welfare rolls over the years. Furthermore, many impoverished working women, including half the private household workers, reside in the South, where the requirements tend to be the stiffest and the payments the smallest. Inadequacy of payments is a serious problem all over the nation, however. Mitchell Goodman, head of New York City's Welfare Department, told the National Advisory Commission on Civil Disorders that "the welfare system is designed to save money instead of people, and tragically ends up doing neither."

Far from trying to save people, some welfare administrators deliberately exploit welfare recipients. Nick Kotz described the actual operation of federal food aid programs in parts of the South and Southwest. Surplus commodities were distributed in the winter, when there were no jobs on the plantations and farms. In the spring, when the $3-a-day planting jobs opened up, food aid stopped. "The federal government eased the planter's responsibility by keeping his workers alive during the winter, then permitted counties to withdraw that meager support during the planting season—forcing workers to accept the near-starvation wages in order to survive," Kotz wrote. "Thus the United States government worked hand in hand with the most feudal system of agricultural peonage."[20]

Even for those who meet eligibility requirements for welfare programs, the system operates to make being on welfare so unpleasant that no one who has any alternative—even the most miserable and low-paying job—would choose welfare. This may effectively serve the function of keeping those who can work off the rolls, but at a certain cost. It compounds the misery of those who have no choice, and it forces many whose low earning power would justify their being on welfare to toil hopelessly at starvation wages instead.[21] What of marriage, the traditional alternative for the "career girl"? The social myth persists that the adult American woman's destiny is to be married and dependent on the earnings of her husband. The reality is otherwise. One-third of the women of marriageable age are not married,[22] and 40 percent of those who are married are in the labor force. However, society simply does not view women workers as permanent members of the labor force. Few opportunities are provided for them, for to offer them good jobs, good pay, and child care facilities would be to acknowledge their financial independence from men.

It would be impossible, in fact, for every woman in the United States to marry, unless our society were willing to tolerate polygamy. There are five million more women than men in the United States, according to the 1970 census. The discrepancy is especially pronounced among the elderly and the black populations, both of which have high percentages of impoverished women. Furthermore, since people tend to marry people like themselves, poor people tend to marry poor people. Two poverty-level checks instead of one do not permit much real improvement in a family's standard of living. Thus the marriage alternative turns out to be a cruel hoax. It penalizes those who do not conform to the expectation that all women will marry, and it often fails to deliver on its promise of lifetime maintenance for those who do.

Another possible source of assistance for the working poor is the extension of the Fair Employment Practices Act and particularly the minimum wage. This is not an especially generous alternative, for the minimum wage, at $3,326 per year, falls below poverty level. Still, many of those concerned with poverty in America—the United Automobile Workers, the AFL–CIO, the Department of Labor, the the NCHE, for example—view the extension of the minimum wage as an important step for the impoverished working class. If an absolute minimum wage of $2 per hour were established, one-third of the poor in America—those who live in families with a full-time wage earner—would be pulled above the poverty level for a family of four.[23] *

A negative income tax could be a supplement or an alternative to an extended minimum wage. Under such a plan people work for whatever wage they can command, and the government makes up any difference between their wage and some established minimum income. Clearly, strict audits and tight controls would have to be maintained over employers whose employees drew negative income tax payments to ensure that the government was not in effect subsidizing employers who offered unconscionably low wages.

This plan has advantages if some essential jobs are insufficiently productive to bear the federal minimum wage. Paying a woman service worker in a nursing home a negative income tax instead of a salary increase would in effect subsidize the hospital, and perhaps ultimately lower hospitalization costs. Paying a farm worker a negative income tax instead of higher wages would help keep the cost of vegetables within the buying power of most consumers. The current economic structure keeps

---

* [Editor's Note: The $2.00 per hour minimum wage became effective for many on May 1, 1974 with provisions for further increases to $2.30 per hour until January, 1977. However, at the time of this writing inflation had effectively raised the poverty level well above the income provided by the new minimum wage.]

costs down at the expense of the worker. But if low costs and economic competition in certain sectors of the economy are desirable national goals, the costs should certainly be borne by the nation—in the form of a negative income tax—and not by the poorest among us.

Perhaps the most hopeful alternative for working poor women is organization. Historically, organization has brought economic and social power to American workers; the working poor, who do not share this power, are overwhelmingly unorganized. Of course, even working women who are organized must still struggle all too often against discrimination with their unions. Nonetheless, union members consistently earn more than nonmembers in comparable situations. Lucretia M. Dewey has reported that in occupations within which the comparison could be made, the difference in median yearly earnings between union and nonunion women was $1,540 in 1966. Thus organization seems to be a vital step in pulling women out of poverty.[24]

Poor women work in the hard-to-organize sections of the economy where the employees have the least power. Private household workers are totally atomized. Service workers have few specialized skills, and at the first rumblings of organization, some employers fire a batch of employees and hire a new staff willing to settle for things as they are. Tiny retail establishments are dispersed all over the cities and small towns of the nation, and often they are staffed by people who do not think of themselves as union types. Both the service occupations and the wholesale-retail trades are estimated to be less than 25 percent organized. They are ranked 31 and 32 out of 34 industries in terms of degree of organization.[25] In agricultural sections of the nation, legal, economic, and social power looms overwhelmingly on the side of the employers. Since so many women work in these nonunionized occupations, women workers are underorganized. While 30 percent of the male work force is organized, only 14 percent of the female work force is.[26]

Yet there are some hopeful signs. Two of the fastest growing unions in the nation, both in terms of overall membership and in terms of women members, are the Retail Clerks International Association and the Service Workers International Union. These organizations serve sections of the work force that have great importance to women in the impoverished working class. Perhaps the most dramatic story in current labor history is that of the National Farm Workers Organization, which has been unionizing the grape and lettuce workers in California. This movement will in all likelihood spread to the rest of the nation.

Private household employment has certain characteristics that make it uniquely difficult to organize; yet there are groups sprouting up with the aim to accomplish the task. The Professional Household Workers Union, Local 1, has recently been chartered by the New York Division of the Brotherhood of Sleeping

Car Porters. Many of those involved in efforts to organize private household workers believe that a restructuring of the field is essential. The National Household Employment Committee, for example, proposes that household workers band together in management cooperatives that will send out teams of workers to employers who contract with the agency. They believe that such a system, combined with specialized training for the workers, would increase the efficiency of the workers, make their work more valuable, and improve their relationship with their employers. Several model projects of this sort have been set up in various parts of the nation.

President Nixon told the Republican Governors' Conference that "scrubbing floors or emptying bedpans—my mother used to do that—is not enjoyable work, but a lot of people do it and there is as much dignity in that as there is in any other work to be done in this country." He is wrong. Work that does not pay enough for a woman to live on decently has no dignity. A woman doing this kind of work begins to feel that it is worthless, or that she is a fool to do so much for so little. But clearly she is not a fool; she is only desperate, and cruelly exploited by the society and the economy. Her poverty is not a personal indignity or an individual aberration. She belongs to the impoverished working class, and sex-related low earning power places her in that class. The "poor working girl" of today does not need pity; she needs money. She will get it when she and her six million sisters in the impoverished working class can organize to demand their shares.

Notes

1. The 1890 census enumerated about four million working girls and women, but this count is probably low. See Robert W. Smuts, *Women and Work in America* (New York: Columbia Univ. Press, 1959).
2. From studies done by the U.S. Census Bureau, cited by George Meany, president of the AFL–CIO, in testimony before the General Subcommittee on Labor, House Committee on Education and Labor, Hearings on a Bill to Amend the Fair Labor Standards Act, July 29, 1970. For perspective on this $4,000 figure, bear in mind that the federal government set the poverty line for a family of four at $3,743.
3. Calculations based on figures in the *1969 Handbook on Women Workers*, U.S. Dept. of Labor, Women's Bureau, Bulletin 294.
4. Meany's testimony, July 29, 1970.
5. My figures on private household employment all come from the National Committee on Household Employment. For more information write to them at 1346 Connecticut Ave. N.W., Washington, D.C. 20036.
6. Meany's testimony, July 29, 1970.
7. U.S. Dept. of Agriculture, "Agricultural Statistics, 1970."
8. Letter from Eleanor A. Eaton to the author, May 17, 1971.

9. "Agricultural Statistics, 1970."
10. See U.S. Dept. of Labor, Women's Bureau publications "Women in Poverty," April 1968, and "Women Workers Today," June 1970.
11. *Ibid.; 1969 Handbook on Women Workers.*
12. U.S. Dept. of Labor, Bureau of Labor Statistics, "Employment and Earnings Statistics for the U.S., 1909–1971."
13. See Census Bureau figures appended to Wilma Scott Heide's testimony before the House Committee on Education and Labor, Hearings to Amend the Fair Labor Standards Act Aug. 12, 1970; see also the U.S. Labor Dept. publications "Women in Poverty" and "The American Family in Poverty," April 1968.
14. The National Management Association found that one-third of the firms they surveyed paid women $5–15 per week less than men for precisely the same job and experience. Cited in Joy Osofsky and Harold Feldman, "Fact Sheet on Women," Cornell Univ., Fall 1969.
15. U.S. Dept. of Labor, Women's Bureau publication, "Facts About Women's Absenteeism and Labor Turnover," by Joan A. Wells.
16. U.S. Dept. of Labor, Women's Bureau publication, "Minimum Wage and the Woman Worker," by Regina Neitzer, pamphlet no. 8, 1960.
17. Hearings before the Special Subcommittee on Education of the House Committee on Education and Labor, on Section 805 of HE 16098 June 19, 1970.
18. "Women in Poverty."
19. *Ibid.;* "The American Family in Poverty."
20. Nick Kotz, *Let Them Eat Promises: The Politics of Hunger in America* (Englewood Cliffs, N.J.: Prentice-Hall, 1968), p. 25.
21. For a thought-provoking history of welfare reform, see Francis Fox Piven and Richard A. Cloward, "The Relief of Welfare," *Transaction,* May 1971.
22. *1969 Handbook on Women Workers.*
23. Meany's testimony, July 29, 1970.
24. Lucretia M. Dewey, "Women in Labor Unions," *Monthly Labor Review,* Feb. 1971, published by the U.S. Dept. of Labor, Bureau of Labor Statistics.
25. "Directory of National and International Labor Unions in the U.S., 1969," U.S. Dept. of Labor, Bureau of Labor Statistics, Bulletin 1665.
26. *Ibid.*

Sex Discrimination in the Trade Unions: Legal Resources for Change

Gail Falk

BACKGROUND

Nondiscriminatory representation of working women by labor unions and full participation by women in existing unions is an important goal in the broader attack on discrimination against women in employment. While some may argue that sex discrimination in the labor unions is so great that women are better off forming independent women's unions, this has not been the trend. The creation of separate unions excluding men would be in violation of Title VII of the 1964 Civil Rights Act.

The labor movement itself has, over the past century, consistently stressed the importance of unity and equality among workers. Federal legislation accepts the principle, at least on an abstract level, that workers in similar situations should be treated similarly. But in many cases the rhetoric fails to affect the practice of discrimination. The courts, the enforcement agencies, and the unions themselves do not yet behave as though women workers come within the category of workers.

Some of the patterns of discrimination in the unions are clear: women are underrepresented in the

From preliminary materials prepared by the Twentieth Century Fund's Task Force on Women and Employment. Printed by permission of The Twentieth Century Fund, 41 East 70th Street, New York 10021.

leadership of trade unions, even in the unions of which they constitute a large majority; the jobs, occupations, and industries in which women form a large portion of the work force are generally underorganized; most unions have been at best silent partners in sexist employment practices, and some have affirmatively encouraged employers to discriminate against women.

The tradition of sex discrimination in the unions has a long history. The earliest trade unions in America derived from working men's social clubs. Their language was male, and their meeting place was the neighborhood saloon.[1] The first unions to be established, in the 1820's, were among the printers, cordwainers, and carpenters, occupations in which there were no women. At this same time about 66,000 women were employed in New England cotton mills.[2] The fact that these women had serious grievances and an ability to act together was demonstrated as early as 1828, when the cotton mill workers of Dover, New Hampshire, marched out of work to protest a reduction of wages and eventually won their strike. But women's labor union activity during the next three decades remained separate from men's, though it developed along parallel lines. Separate women's unions were started among the collar workers, tailoresses, seamstresses, umbrella sewers, capmakers, textile workers, printers, laundresses, and furnishers.[3]

None of the nineteenth-century women's unions was able to sustain itself very long. Working women then, as now, frequently carried a double burden— responsibility for a home and family as well as responsibility for a job. Women lacked money for organization costs—for dues, for strike funds, for the expenses of spreading the word to other women—since they were generally paid only a fraction of what men were paid for the same work, and were employed almost entirely in unskilled jobs.[4] Women had traditionally been isolated from one another in the home; they were inexperienced as organizers and were unused to thinking of themselves as workers.*

Thus began a vicious circle that continues to be the pattern today: men excluded women workers from full participation in their unions, and women were unable to organize strong unions of their own; women, lacking bargaining power, were forced to work at lower wages under inferior working conditions; and employers could use women workers to undercut the wages and organizational efforts of men.

As the twentieth century began, the labor movement was dominated by the

---

* S. C. Hewitt, an organizer of the Fall River Mechanics Association, was far ahead of his time in 1844 in believing that women should be members of every labor movement. He discovered that he had to mention women explicitly in his writing and speaking because when he put out a call for "workingmen," women did not understand themselves to be included.

skilled craft unions of the American Federation of Labor, many of which openly excluded women. Although the practice gradually died, it died mainly because men's unions felt serious competition from nonunion working women rather than because the unions recognized morally or philosophically that women should have equal rights. In 1924 seven AF of L internationals still officially opposed the admission of women members, though women were working in all of the industries covered by these unions. The International Moulder's Union Constitution went so far as to say that "any member, honorary or active, who devotes his time in whole or in part to the instruction of female help in the foundry or in any branch of the trade shall be expelled from the union."[5]

There were also ways of excluding women without explicitly barring them from the union. High dues could be and were exclusionary in a period when many women's wages were below subsistence levels—and averaged about half of those earned by male coworkers. More important, lack of job skills kept women from entering unions of skilled craftsmen. The common way to become a skilled craft worker was through apprenticeship, but rigid apprenticeship regulations prevented women from becoming apprentices.[6]

Exclusionary policies were only the most clear cut of antiwomen policies. Once women were admitted to trade unions, they were generally treated as unwanted poor relations, or at best as second class citizens. In the 1920's a number of international unions set lower dues and lower initiation fees for women.[7] Then many unions made the amount of benefits received contingent upon the amount of dues paid, so that women members as a class ended up receiving lower strike benefits, sickness benefits, and death benefits than men. The United Leather Workers, for instance, set monthly dues for women and apprentices at $.60; the rate for men was $1.15. The strike benefits for women and apprentices were $3 a week, whereas for men they were $5 to $7.[8]

Although it was generally recognized that women organizers were more effective with women workers, only eight national unions had women organizers in 1924.[9] Even unions like the International Ladies Garment Workers, the Amalgamated Clothing Workers, and the Cap Makers, which put a certain amount of emphasis on female leadership and had a heavily female jurisdiction, hired only about one woman organizer in the 1920's for every three men organizers.[10] Similarly, women officers were rare, particularly at the higher levels of the union hierarchy, even in unions with large female memberships.

As justification for their discriminatory policies, union leaders frequently observed that women workers did not have time to be active union members because they had, in effect, two jobs: a job at work and a job at home. But if this burden was the main thing standing between women and active union membership, and if the unions were interested in having women members, they showed a singular lack of interest in demands such as day care, that might have eased that burden, and even less interest in encouraging their male members to share their wives's work at home.

The result of all these sexists policies was that women were broadly discouraged from joining unions. In 1929 Teresa Wolfson estimated that one in nine wage earners was organized, but only one in 34 women wage earners.[11] If anything, this was an overestimate.[12] In 1933 Elizabeth Christman estimated that about twice as many working women were members of the Young Women's Christian Association as were members of the AF of L.[13]

The unions' antiwomen practices were not the only reason why the number of women in labor unions was so small. Large numbers of women worked in occupations traditionally thought of as hard to organize, such as housekeeping and clerical and agricultural work.* Most women workers were unskilled or semiskilled, and the labor movement generally underrepresented low-skilled workers, regardless of sex. Most women workers accepted the social myths about women who work; they failed to think of themselves as permanent workers; they considered working a cause for shame; and they feared that identifying with a union was or would be considered unfeminine.[14]

Coupled with these barriers to organizing women, the unions' antiwomen attitudes had the effect of a self-fulfilling prophecy. Unions did not on the whole want women, and women did not on the whole join unions. And so the myth that women cannot be organized became established through its own momentum.

Two major factors encouraged union membership of women in the 1930's. The growth of industrial unionism brought more unskilled, semiskilled, and white-collar workers into unions. In addition, federal legislation began to recognize and protect the rights of union members, giving greater respectability to unions and making them more attractive to women. Balanced against this was the huge unemployment rate of the Depression years, which put a premium on jobs and generated pressures to shrink the size of the labor force. Women as a class were pictured as secondary workers and were a primary target of the struggle to limit the number of persons in the labor market. Many unions adopted policies against the hiring of women workers, particularly married women workers.

World War II reversed the labor situation. Women flowed into the work force to meet the labor shortages, and by 1944, 21.9 percent of the members of American trade unions were women. The war experience stimulated greater sensitivity to

---

* One cannot help wondering whether these occupations would be thought of as hard to organize if priority had been given to developing methods for organizing them.

the problems and interests of women on the part of many unions. A Women's Bureau survey of 80 midwestern union contracts revealed that half had clauses establishing equal pay for equal work.[15] Some unions had maternity-leave clauses written into contracts. The Amalgamated Clothing Workers included maternity benefits in its insurance plan and worked for decent day care. The United Auto Workers (UAW), whose membership was 28 percent women by 1945, brought a case against General Motors before the War Labor Board that established the principle that wage rates for women should be equal to rates for men.[16] The UAW's Women's Committee dates from World War II.

Women continued to be underrepresented in administrative and leadership positions in unions, however.[17] Some unions still excluded women; in 1943, at the height of the war effort, the American Civil Liberties Union counted 25 national unions that excluded women. While supporting equal pay for equal work, unions generally accepted sex segregation of jobs and separate seniority lists for men and women.[18]

The improved status of working women brought by the war faded as the war ended and the need for working women diminished. Returning veterans received their old jobs back and preference for any new openings. Large numbers of women were fired or demoted. Many left the working world entirely; others accepted part-time and/or lower-level jobs and less pay. The proportion of women labor union members declined, and union concern for the interests of women fell almost to the vanishing point during the following two decades.

PRESENT PRACTICES

The ranks of women trade unionists have grown in the past two decades, but not as fast as the number of employed women. Between 1954 and 1968 the number of union women went from 2.8 million to 3.7 million; yet only 14.1 percent of all working women were unionized in 1954, and only 12.5 percent in 1968.[19] This decline does not appear to have stopped, since the major influx of new women workers is into occupations that are heavily female and sparsely unionized, such as clerical work. There has also been a decline of male union membership in proportion to the male working population, but it has been less substantial; more than 30 percent of male workers are union members.

In addition to the lack of unionization in occupations dominated by women, a wide variety of other barriers has served to keep women out of existing unions. Present discriminatory practices have their roots in the traditions of the past; most of them would have seemed familiar to women trade unionists of fifty years ago.

Especially in the skilled trades, discrimination begins in the apprenticeship programs. Apprenticeship programs do not account for a huge number of jobs—there are fewer than 300,000 apprentices per year—but they control access to the skilled trade unions and the highest-paying jobs. Thus the competition for positions in many apprenticeship programs is fierce.

Women are kept out of apprenticeship programs by a number of devices. Craft unions tend to give preference to the sons of union members, or even restrict admission to them. Other unions require new members to be sponsored by old members. These exclusionary techniques are well known as methods of discriminating against blacks and, they have been even more effective in discriminating against women. While a little more than 3 percent of all apprentices were blacks in 1968, fewer than 1 percent were women.[20] This figure includes apprenticeships in jobs traditionally held by women, such as cosmetologist, dressmaker, fabric cutter, tailor, fur finisher, bookbinder, and dental technician.

A large proportion of apprenticeship programs are sponsored by a joint labor-management committee. In these, as well as the programs sponsored by unions alone, union choice—whether tacit or explicit—is a major factor in deciding which applicants are accepted. So far little attention has been paid to discrimination against women in selection for apprenticeships. Court suits challenging discrimination have focused instead on racial discrimination.[21] Similarly, affirmative recruiting programs have been designed to encourage minority group men, rather than women, to apply to apprenticeship programs.

More discrimination takes place at the hiring gate and in the hiring halls of the highly organized industries. If employers prefer not to hire women for certain jobs, then clearly there will not be many women in the unions. For example, unions point to the fact that General Motors hired women as clerical workers in its Norwood, Ohio, plant, but would not hire them in the production lines. Production workers at the plant were organized, but clerical workers were not. In Michigan, Ford explicitly told women they could not be hired for the production line in one of its major plants. The unions blame the employers for the dearth of women on the job, but the employers blame the unions. Of course, both the unions and the employers are generally dominated by men.

Bargaining units are frequently defined in a way that separates men and women workers employed at the same job or excludes women altogether. For most purposes, the definition of the bargaining unit comes under the jurisdiction of the National Labor Relations Board, but labor unions exercise practical control over the unit by deciding which workers to organize and which to ignore. Documenting the extent to which sexism shapes these decisions is difficult, however, because the factors involved in organizing workers are subtle and complicated. Nonetheless, enough cases exist illustrating union discrimination in defining the bargaining unit to suggest that segregation of women workers is a common pattern. In the case of *Cuneo Eastern Press,* [22] for example, the union petitioned for a bargaining unit composed of all women workers on the first and second shifts at the press; the men workers were organized into a separate unit. In a more recent case involving the United States Baking Company,[23] the Bakery Workers had organized men and women workers in the plant into two separate units, even though they all worked under the same conditions on an integrated straight-line operation.

Defining women out of bargaining units or into predominantly female units is encouraged by the pervasive sex segregation of jobs in most places of work. Sex segregation of jobs is not merely an invention of management; frequently unions turn out to have played a major role in establishing it. In the landmark Equal Pay Act case *Wirtz v. Wheaton Glass Co.,*[24] the judge's opinion describes how the Glass Bottle Blowers Association insisted on separate job categories for women after the company began to hire women in 1956. The union and the company agreed that the women would be paid 10 percent less than the men. At the bargaining table unions continue to represent their women members badly. During the 1968 General Electric strike, the demand that women's wages be raised to the base level for men's wages was dropped in the course of negotiations. Separate seniority lines for women continue to be common, and frequently the highest wage rate for women is below the lowest rate for men. There are exceptions. The United Auto Workers negotiated for maternity leave without pay and the Amalgamated Clothing Workers have included day care benefits in some of their collective agreements. But in general, unions take the position that matters of primary concern to women, such as day care and cash maternity benefits, should be provided by government rather than industry.

In internal union affairs women have not made much progress either. According to Alice Cook, "Women remain more the exception than the rule" on national organizing staffs, "rarely rising above the level of assistant to the department chief, although there have been a very few notable exceptions."[25] The largest proportion of women officers is found at the local level. Women are rarely found as officers of the intermediate bodies, the joint boards and district councils, and almost never appear on major negotiating teams, on national executive boards, on national staffs, or among the national officers.[26] Unions with a large proportion of women members have had a standard practice of "tokenism" whereby one or at the most two are placed on the national executive boards. Some unions have begun to make efforts to remedy this situation. The American Federation of State, County and Municipal Employees now employs the same proportion of women on the professional staff as there are women in the union's membership—40 percent.[27]

**Both men and women have been taught to
underrate the competence of women and may
vote for a male candidate because they think
he will be tougher at the bargaining table . . . .**

No one can deny that women are underrepresented in union leadership positions, but there is much disagreement about the causes of this situation. The fairest explanation is that women are squeezed out of leadership positions by the interaction of a number of factors. One is that domestic duty leaves women with families no time after work to engage in union activities that are steppingstones to union leadership. Another factor is that women commonly take ten to fifteen years away from the labor force when their children are small. This means that women are often out of the union during their twenties and early thirties, the ages when young men frequently take their first leadership positions.

These domestic barriers interact with psychological barriers. Both men and women have been taught to underrate the competence of women and may vote for a male candidate because they think he will be tougher at the bargaining table or simply because they think it is more appropriate for a man to hold a position of authority. Many women workers do not vote regularly in union elections or seek leadership positions in the union because they prefer to think of themselves as temporary workers who have no real stake in union efforts.

These psychological blocks could be overcome if unions were more welcoming, but they have shown little inclination in this direction. Writing in 1968, Alice Cook concluded,

> The hard fact in the late 1960's is that less attention is being paid by the unions today to the special needs and problems of their women members than was the case earlier in the century . . . Even when they are a majority, women play the role and are assigned the status, of a minority—moreover, a minority still in that state of political self-consciousness where "tokenism" suffices to meet its demands.[28]

A few unions, such as the United Auto Workers and the International Brotherhood of Electrical, Radio and Machine Workers, have provided significant if not groundbreaking support for their women members. However, the real evidence of progress by labor women since Cook wrote her critique has been in the changing policies of unions that previously showed no great concern for the interests of women. Among the most prominent have been the Communications Workers of America, The American Newspaper Guild, the American Federation of State, County, and Municipal

Employees, the American Federation of Teachers, and the Amalgamated Clothing Workers—all of which have a significant proportion of women members.

Even the giant AFL–CIO, which has been traditionally dominated by male bias despite the sizable female membership of many of its affiliates, shows signs of changing its official stance vis-à-vis women's rights. Since 1970 various state labor councils have sponsored women's conferences in which the issues of child care, seniority rights, abortion, and unequal pay have been addressed and the conventional sexists clichés about women workers denounced.[29] In October 1973 the AFL–CIO national convention reversed the organization's historic opposition to the Equal Rights Amendment and began slowly to mobilize its forces behind ratification.*

In addition to these progressive developments within the unions, trade union women have begun to see the need to organize themselves outside their occupational affiliates. The women who were pressing within their unions have formed a network to sponsor regional conferences on the problems of trade union women. These conferences culminated in a national gathering in Chicago in March 1974 to form the Coalition of Labor Union Women and elect a National Coordinating Committee.**

LEGAL REMEDIES

The current statutory and regulatory arsenal seems to present an impressive array of weapons for attacking the discriminatory practices of unions. Federal fair employment laws and regulations, including the Equal Pay Act of 1963, Title VII of the 1964 Civil Rights Act, and 1967 Age Discrimination Act, Executive Order 11246 as amended by Executive Order 11375, and Labor Department regulations for registered apprenticeship programs are all enforcible against labor unions. The federal relations laws have been interpreted to forbid many forms of discrimination by

---

* AUTHOR'S NOTE: Much of the material in this paper concerning the efforts of unions to eradicate sexism from their internal organization, was supplied by Erica Grubb, A Harvard Law School graduate.

** EDITOR'S NOTE: The Chicago meeting was attended by 3,200 women. The delegates were drawn from a total of 60 unions, and represented all age groups and all major racial minorities employed in the U. S. labor market. Olga Madar, a vice-president of United Auto Workers international, was named to chair the National Coordinating Committee, and Addie Wyatt of the Amalgamated Meat Cutters and Butchers International Union was named vice-chairperson. *The Spokeswoman* (Chicago), 4, 10 (April 15, 1974): 1–2.

labor unions. In addition, state fair employment laws in some states bar sex discrimination by unions.

But for the most part these remedies are little more than possibilities. Most have scarcely ever been applied to protect women in unions; some, never. Some are too unwieldy to provide effective means of broad-scale relief. Others provide such unsatisfactory relief that most aggrieved persons will not bother to make complaints, let alone follow through on them. Aspects of three of the major laws will be discussed in this section: the 1935 National Labor Relations Act, with its companion, the Railway Labor Act; Title VII of the 1964 Civil Rights Act; and the Equal Pay Act of 1963.

The National Labor Relations Act and the Railway Labor Act

The National Labor Relations Act (NLRA) and its major amendments, the Labor-Management Relations Act of 1947 (Taft-Hartley Act) and the Labor-Management Reporting and Disclosure Act of 1959 (Landrum-Griffin Act), define the structure and principles by which the federal government regulates labor relations. The Railway Labor Act (RLA) supplements the NLRA by regulating labor-management relations in the railroad and airline industries. Federal labor law has preempted the regulation of labor relations in all the areas it touches, so that state labor regulation has relatively little vitality now.

Major responsibility for administering the NLRA lies with the National Labor Relations Board (NLRB). The Board's many responsibilities include determining bargaining units, holding elections, and adjudicating disputes. Policing labor union discrimination against individual workers or classes of workers takes up only a small part of the Board's attention, and for the most part the authority to do so is not even explicitly delegated to the Board by Congress. However, as the government agency most responsible for shaping the development of labor union practices, as well as the agency with the largest staff and resources for regulating labor unions, the NLRB is in a special position to regulate sex discrimination by labor unions if it chooses.[30]

COVERAGE   The NLRA does not cover all job categories, and most of the ones it excludes have a high percentage of women workers. Workers in agricultural labor and domestic service are explicitly excepted from the NLRA's definition of employee.[31] Relatively few farm workers are women. However, 7.2 percent of all women workers are paid private household workers (domestic service), and 97.6 percent of all paid private household workers are women.[32] Excluded from the NLRA's definition of employers, moreover, are the federal government, state and municipal governments, and nonprofit hospitals. The exclusion of government agencies is particularly significant, since government is the fastest growing area of employment for women. In 1968 there were 5.3 million women on government payrolls, and women constituted 43.5 percent of all government workers.[33] In addition to the huge number of women filling clerical and receptionist jobs in government, this figure includes schoolteachers (elementary school teaching is the fourth highest occupational category for women) and federal, state, and municipal hospital workers.

Combined with the exclusion of nonprofit hospital workers, the exclusion of federal, state, and municipal hospital workers means that most hospital workers are not covered by the NLRA, since there are relatively few private proprietary hospitals. This, too, is very significant, since more than 1.3 million workers—81.3 percent of all hospital workers—were women in 1968.[34]

Altogether, the few categories of workers that are excluded from the NLRA and the RLA contain more than one-fourth of all women workers. Since the NLRA and the RLA provide important protections for workers attempting to organize, these exceptions are discriminatory in and of themselves.

Under the NLRA and the RLA there is extensive case law attempting to clarify the duty of a union to represent its members. A union that has been certified as the recognized agent of a bargaining unit has the power to represent and define the terms and conditions of employment of all employees in the unit, whether or not they are members of the union. Because all employees are bound by the collective agreement the union negotiates, and they may not contract independently for other terms with the employer, the courts have determined that unions have a duty to represent all employees fairly.

The duty of fair representation, not explicitly required by statute, was first enunciated in 1944 by the Supreme Court in a case under the RLA, *Steele v. Louisville & N.R. Co.*[35] Steele, a black man, was a locomotive fireman; he sued for an injunction and damages against the all-white Brotherhood of Locomotive Firemen and Enginemen, which was trying to replace black firemen with whites, thus forcing blacks out of their jobs. The Supreme Court held that federal courts had jurisdiction to entertain such a suit, explaining in the majority opinion by Chief Justice Stone,

> So long as a labor union assumes to act as the statutory representative of a craft, it cannot rightly refuse to perform the duty which is inseparable from the power of representation conferred upon it, to represent the entire membership of the craft . . . . [The statute requires the union] to represent non-union or minority members of the craft without hostile discrimination, fairly, impartially, and in good faith.

In the *Miranda Fuel Co.* case of 1962,[36] the NLRB carried the logic of *Steele* farther and found that violation of the duty of fair representation was an unfair labor practice. Since *Miranda* the NLRB has found that unfair representation violates the NLRA in a number of cases.[37]

No particular limits have been set on what activities the duty of fair representation covers. *Steele* required fair representation in negotiation of the collective agreement. *Conley v. Gibson*[38] extended the duty to fair administration of the contract, which includes fair processing of grievances arising under the collective agreement. In *Local Union No. 12, United Rubber, Cork, Linoleum and Plastic Workers of America*,[39] the Fifth Circuit Court held that the union was required to process grievances that were not specifically subjects of the collective agreement; in this case the grievances in question concerned segregated restrooms, showers, and dining rooms, and a whites-only golf course.

The extent to which the duty of fair representation obliges a union to refuse to accept or to strike to avoid a discriminatory contract is still uncertain. At least in cases of racial discrimination, the NLRB would probably go as far as to hold that a union may not accept a contract that confers its benefits on a discriminatory basis.[40] Breach of the duty of fair representation has been found and prohibited in nonracial cases where the discrimination has been hostile or arbitrary—for instance, in cases of unfair allocation of seniority when two companies merge.

One might think that union discrimination against women would be considered hostile or arbitrary, and therefore a violation of the duty of fair representation. However, the duty of fair representation has not yet been applied in any case to protect women, and in at least one case a court has found that discrimination against women comes within the "wide range of reasonableness" that the Supreme Court said it would allow to unions in deciding how best to represent their members.[41] In *Cortez v. Ford Motor Co.*[42] three women brought a class action on behalf of themselves and 105 other women employees of Ford's Dearborn stamping plant; joined as defendants were Ford, the United Auto Workers international, the UAW local, and the president of the UAW local. The women had all been laid off in 1950 and 1951, even though men with less seniority were kept on the job and new men were hired. The union refused to process the women's grievances, and the women filed suit for $3 million damages, claiming the layoffs violated the seniority provisions of the Ford-UAW collective agreement. In an unsatisfactory opinion the Michigan Supreme Court rejected the women's claim, explaining that union refusal to process grievances could be attacked only if bad faith, arbitrary action, or fraud could be shown. The union had "discretion to effect compromises and settlements in the interests of all members," said the court, and was not obligated to take the women's side. In other words, the court refused to characterize

> **The union explained its action by saying that keeping married women on the job at a time when work was scarce was seriously impairing personnel relations. The court accepted this explanation . . . .**

discrimination on the basis of sex as "arbitrary."

Cortez relied in part on an earlier Michigan case, *Hartley v. the Brotherhood of Railway and Steamship Clerks,*[43] which made more explicit the court's determination that discrimination against women was perfectly reasonable. In *Hartley* the union had sought and obtained a modification of the collective agreement. Originally the agreement had provided for promotion and layoff on the basis of seniority; the modified agreement provided that all married women were to be relieved of service unless there were extenuating circumstances. The union explained its action by saying that keeping married women on the job at a time when work was scarce was seriously impairing personnel relations. The court accepted this explanation and said the union had power to make the modification it believed was in the best interests of all the members. The court told the complainant that she had had all the relief she was entitled to when she appealed through the grievance procedure of the discriminating union.

Both *Cortez* and *Hartley* are Michigan state cases. No federal court has ever said that sex discrimination does not violate the duty of fair representation. But no federal court has ever said it does violate the duty either.*

There is no particular reason to think that sex discrimination should not constitute a violation of the duty of fair representation. Writing in 1957, Archibald Cox concluded that "the right of fair representation protects individuals and minorities against all forms of hostile discrimination or oppression at the hands of the

---

* And note the maddening case of *Union News v. Hildreth,* 395 F.2d 658 (6th Cir. 1961); ele F.2d 548; *cert. den.* 375 U.S. 326. In this case a lunch counter operator found that money was sometimes missing from his cash register at the end of the day, and the Hotel and Restaurant Employees and Bartenders International Unions permitted him to lay off five employees to see if the losses would stop. After the layoffs the losses did stop, and the five employees, all women, were fired by agreement between the union and the employer, even though none of them was shown to be personally guilty of stealing. The court found nothing improper in the union's refusal to process the women's grievances and said the women were entitled to no relief. There is no obvious evidence that the women were discriminated against as women, since they were replaced with other women. The union involved, however, was dominated by men, and it would be interesting to know whether they considered the job security of these low-status women employees insignificant.

bargaining representative."[44] The Equal Pay Act, Title VII of the 1964 Civil Rights Act, and Executive Orders 11246 and 11375 are all evidence of a federal policy that discrimination on the basis of sex is hostile and unacceptable. Moreover, the NLRB has refused in a few cases to approve bargaining units established along sex lines. The Board refused a request for bargaining units made up entirely of women on the first and second shifts in *Cuneo Eastern Press*,[45] explaining that bargaining units based on sex alone were inappropriate unless significant differences in skills were shown between the men and the women.[46]

The only real legal argument against considering sex discrimination a violation of the duty of fair representation goes back to the original *Steele* decision. In announcing its conclusion that the RLA obliges unions to represent fairly all workers in their jurisdiction, the Supreme Court suggested that such a conclusion might be Constitutionally required. For Congress to invest a union with quasilegislative power, said the Court, without imposing a commensurate duty to exercise the power without discrimination would raise the possibility that the Act violated the Fourteenth Amendment. If the duty of fair representation rested on Fourteenth Amendment grounds, it would arguably protect only against racial discrimination, since the Fourteenth Amendment has not been held clearly to bar sex discrimination.

However, the Supreme Court rested *Steele* on a statutory basis, and later decisions have found a duty of fair representation to be implied in the NLRA. In the *Miranda* case in 1962, as we have seen the NLRB held that violation of the duty of fair representation was an unfair labor practice under the Act. The Second Circuit Court denied enforcement in *Miranda,* but the decision did not constitute a review of the NLRB's interpretation of Section 8(b)(1). In 1966 the Fifth Circuit Court accepted the reasoning that the duty of fair representation is imposed by the statute.[47]

The crucial question is not so much whether sex discrimination violates the duty of fair representation, but how blatant the discrimination must be and how far the NLRB and the courts will be willing to go in enforcing remedies against it. The answer will lie in the development of the case law and in the generally inscrutable politics of the NLRB and labor relations law.

Title VII

Of all the legislation barring discrimination by unions, Title VII of the Civil Rights Act is the broadest and clearest in its delineation of the numbers of workers and types of practices covered. Under Title VII unions cannot exclude or expel any individual because of his or her race, color, religion, sex, or national origin. Nor can a

Sex-discriminatory seniority systems are a mainstay of the overall structure of employment discrimination against women.

union limit, segregate, or classify its membership on these bases. The language of Title VII is broad enough to cover virtually all areas in which unions might practice discrimination, including access to apprenticeship programs, employment opportunities, and membership. The most pertinent are discussed here.

Sex-discriminatory seniority systems are a mainstay of the overall structure of employment discrimination against women. A worker's employment security, rate of advancement, wages, benefits, and position within the union may all hinge on the provisions of a seniority system. Of course, since women are frequently the last hired and the first fired, their opportunities to gain seniority are limited. But in addition, unions frequently discriminate overtly against women by negotiating sex- segregated promotion and transfer ladders and separate lines of layoff and rehiring priority.

The use of seniority systems to institutionalize discrimination was aptly illustrated in *Bowe v. Colgate-Palmolive.* Women first entered the Colgate work force at the Albany, Indiana, plant during World War II. After the men returned, the company and union agreed that certain jobs should be reserved exclusively for each sex. Separate seniority lines for men's jobs and women's jobs were established under the collective agreement, with the highest pay rate for women equal to the lowest pay rate for men. The passage of Title VII clearly made it illegal to distinguish between "men's jobs" and "women's jobs," so the contract was modified to change the names of the jobs. The erstwhile women's jobs were defined as those not requiring the employee to lift more than 35 pounds and were opened up to men as well as women employees, while those jobs that might require lifting more than 35 pounds were restricted to men. This arrangement allowed the men to compete for the women's jobs in times when work was scarce, but it did not allow the women to compete for the men's jobs.

Several women at the plant brought a class action suit under Title VII against Colgate and their union, International Chemical Workers Local No. 15. The federal district court upheld the segregated job structure on the grounds that its purpose was really protection, not discrimination. However, on appeal, the Seventh Circuit Court gave a landmark decision to the contrary. It ordered Colgate to allow all workers to bid on jobs their respective seniority rights entitled them to, regardless of sex, and to give the women back pay from the time that Title VII had become law.[48]

Another case taken before the Equal Employment Opportunity Commission (EEOC), involved the seniority rights of a woman who became pregnant. The collective agreement provided for all women who became pregnant to be terminated permanently after their fourth month of pregnancy. The complainant wanted to continue working after her baby was born. The commission decided that an employer could be required to preserve the "recall rights" of a woman who takes a maternity leave.[49] The opinion contains this interesting reasoning:

> Though a woman who has just had a child is unlikely to return immediately to work, this is not sufficient reason for depriving those women who should wish to so return from enjoying the same rights that a man would enjoy should he wish to return to the labor force after a period of sustained illness or convalescence. Most of the women who will want to return to their jobs will do so because they must do so to provide for themselves and their children. It is in the national interest that children be born. But there is little benefit to anyone to make mother and baby public charges or to force her to seek other work. An arbitrary rule that severs her rights of tenure and seniority is neither desirable nor fair.

Such a decision represents real progress, in view of the discrimination women employees had suffered previously. As the commissioner noted, before World War II women employees had been discharged as soon as they married, and in the 1950's the collective agreement had provided that married women could stay on the job but would not be eligible for promotion.

Issues of seniority are difficult and complex, because more than any other term or condition of employment, seniority raises the question of what is to be done about the present effects of past discrimination. During Congressional debate over the 1964 Civil Rights Act, much was made of the fact that Title VII was not intended to allow "reverse discrimination"—that is, preferential hiring of minority groups or women. However, in the first seniority case under Title VII, *Quarles v. Philip Morris, Inc.* (and *Local 203 Tobacco Workers International Union*),[50] the court said, in answer to the argument that Congress did not intend to require reverse discrimination: "It is also apparent that Congress did not intend to freeze an entire generation of Negro employees into discriminatory patterns that existed before the Act." The Civil Rights Act, said the court, does not condone present differences that are the result of a past intent to discriminate. In the Philip Morris plant seniority lines followed departmental lines, and departments had been segregated before the Act on racial lines. The court ordered that black workers who qualified for the better-paying jobs in the white departments and had more seniority than the whites in line for the jobs must be invited to bid for the jobs. And it enjoined both the company and the union from doing anything that might interfere with the plan it had ordered. Subsequent decisions have broadened this interpretation.[51]

Sex segregation of seniority systems is a very common phenomenon, and where it appears it is just as invidious as racial discrimination because it links low pay with low status and menial or unpleasant work. Yet so far no cases have established for women what *Quarles* and other cases have established for blacks—that present disadvantages stemming from past discrimination are no more acceptable than present discrimination.

The practice of segregating union locals has a long history, but only recently has it been the subject of a suit under Title VII. In *Evans v. Sheraton Park Hotel*[52] a district court ruled against both a hotel and a union for discriminating against waitresses, who were organized into one local, and in favor of waiters, who were organized into another local of the same international union, in assigning them jobs. The discrimination had the effect of giving the waiters longer hours, greater total hourly compensation, larger gratuities, and fewer menial tasks. The court observed:

> The discrimination in reception assignments is a classic example of the abuse inherent in maintaining and recognizing separate female and male locals for co-workers performing the same duties. It is inevitable in such a situation that not only will controversy and suspicion arise between males and females, but that the more dominant group, in this case the male, will gain privileges of various kinds. The failure of Local 507 [the all-woman local] to support plaintiff's justifiable official complaints concerning uneven and unfair assignments demonstrates the inability of a Janus-headed union to safeguard sex-equality.

The court went on to rule that the maintenance of sex-segregated locals was a violation of Title VII, and awarded damages to the waitress who had filed the suit.

AFFIRMATIVE ACTION AGAINST DISCRIMINATION   Title VII makes it illegal for a union to fail to process grievances because of a member's sex or race. In addition, recent decisions under the NLRA have held that a union has a duty to press members' complaints about discrimination under the law.

In 1969 two blacks filed complaints about job discrimination because their company operated a whites only swimming pool and racially segregated teen clubs. The union gave them no help. It claimed that it was unaware of racial discrimination, that it had no machinery to process racial grievances, that it was ignorant of Title VII, that it had never discussed the questions with management, and that it had no instructions from the international union to process racial grievances. However, the EEOC held that "the union not only has the power, it has the obligation to process racial discrimination matters. By its refusal to do so, it violates Title

VII.["](53) The Fifth Circuit Court reached a similar result under the NLRA in the *Rubber Workers* case discussed above. There the court held that the unions had a duty to process grievances about facilities that were segregated in violation of Title VII.

Unions may now file complaints with the EEOC as aggrieved parties.[54] They may also sponsor suits under Title VII in the form of class actions.[55] This duty to press grievances about discrimination could be of great significance to women. Unions have the money to press individual complaints; they have the potential to develop sensitivity to and expertise in issues of employment discrimination; they are in touch with workers at the point of discrimination; they are in a position to follow through the lengthy complaint process and to bring a class action. Moreover, without backing by a union or some equivalent organization, few women's cases will be pressed. Women have nothing analogous to the NAACP Legal Defense Fund, which presses the job discrimination complaints of blacks, and few women workers have the money, stamina, and knowledge required to press a complaint on their own. The National Organization of Women (NOW) brought the original appeal in some Title VII cases because the working women involved could not afford to appeal on their own and their unions would not help them.[56]

ENFORCEMENT   Two factors have minimized the actual enforcement of Title VII against unions that discriminate against women. The first is the relatively small number of complaints women have made against unions. In fiscal 1967 the EEOC received a total of 208 complaints against union practices, as compared with 1,674 complaints against employers. Figures from fiscal 1972 indicate that even this low proportion had declined. That year there were 419 complaints against unions and 335 joint complaints against unions, employers, and employment agencies, as compared to 9,056 complaints against employers.[57] Similarly, a 1965 study revealed that only 5 percent of all complaints received by the California Fair Employment Practices Commission were against unions.[58] It may be that unions no longer discriminate against women, but this seems doubtful. More likely women do not think of filing complaints against unions for a number of reasons such as the prevailing social belief that unions are the worker's friend and that to make a complaint against a union is a form of scabbing; failure to see the union's role in the perpetuation of discrimination at the place of work; and lack of information about Title VII's applicability to unions. Frequently, too, the lack of a direct economic grievance against the union makes it impractical to file a complaint. A clear case of payroll discrimination, such as failing to grant a deserved promotion, would justify suit more readily than some of the more prevalent aspects of union discrimination against women, such as exclusion from leadership positions, which would involve a protracted and possibly expensive enforcement process.

For its part, the EEOC has increased its efforts to obtain enforcement against labor unions, and as a result unions are often later joined to an initial complaint against an employer. However, the EEOC can still improve its record. In any case where the EEOC receives a complaint about a practice that comes under the collective agreement it could and should join the union. Yet it has frequently failed to do so or has done so only halfheartedly. In *Rosenfeld v. Southern Pacific,*[59] for instance, it failed to notify the Transportation and Communication Employees Union of the complaint and to include the union in conciliation; when it sought to join the union in the federal court suit, it was too late. Even when the union has been included, the EEOC has not generally pushed for enforcement against the union but only against the employer; in the brief for the *Rosenfeld* case, the EEOC included only general and unsubstantiated allegations against the union.

Title VII and the NLRA

While virtually any instance of sex discrimination that would violate the duty of fair representation under the NLRA or the RLA would also violate Title VII of the Civil Rights Act, there are definite advantages to pursuing remedies under both acts. In the past the NLRA procedures were cheaper and simpler for the complainant and provided prompter remedies than those under Title VII.[60] Although the 1972 expansion of the EEOC's powers has somewhat changed this situation, the NLRB still has powerful tools for enforcing a union's duty of fair representation; women should take advantage of them.[61] The procedures are simpler, and as no deference period to a state agency is required, the overall time lapse between complaint and enforcement is generally shorter.[62]

Of particular importance, the NLRB can refuse to help a discriminating union that wants to be certified as a bargaining representative. For a weak union this is a serious sanction because an employer is not required to bargain with a union that is not certified and competing unions are not prohibited from trying to take over under the usual "contract bar" rule. The NLRB can bring unfair labor practice proceedings against the union. If a union is found to have committed an unfair labor practice, the Board may issue a cease-and-desist order or an order for another appropriate remedy, enforcible by contempt proceedings in federal court.

NLRB procedures are not a model of efficiency and effectiveness; political considerations strongly color the actions and opinions of the Board. However, since the *Bowe* decision an aggrieved individual may pursue parallel remedies under both Title VII and the NLRA, and plaintiffs have nothing to lose by filing charges simultaneously.

The Equal Pay Act

One provision of the Equal Pay Act makes it unlawful for any labor organization to cause or attempt to cause an employer to violate the Act.[63] A labor organization is defined as any organization of any kind, or any agency or employee representation committee or plan, in which employees participate and which exists for the purpose, in whole or in part, of dealing with employers concerning grievances, labor disputes, wages, rates of pay, hours of work, and conditions of employment.[64] This is the same definition of labor organization that is given in the Taft-Hartley Act.

Just how actively a union must "cause or attempt to cause" an employer to discriminate to be liable under the Act remains uncertain. Affirmative acts such as picketing to force an employer to establish a wage differential or demanding discriminatory terms at the collective bargaining table are certainly prohibited.[65] However, the current regulations suggest that passively to accept discriminatory terms may also be illegal. According to the regulations, Congress intended that unions should share with the employer responsibility for ensuring that the collective agreement is in compliance with the Equal Pay Act, and it will be no defense to say that any failure to comply is the product of negotiations.

But the courts will apparently not go so far as to require that a union strike to avoid a discriminatory condition. In *Wirtz v. Hayes Industry*, a suit under the Equal Pay Act, the defendant company moved to have the union held jointly liable as coauthor of the contract in question. The union president testified that he had attempted to have the discriminatory provisions changed at the contract negotiations and that he had filed a complaint of discrimination with the Wages and Hours Division of the Department of Labor after the employer refused to change his position. The court held that the union had done all it was legally required to do, and refused to hold the union jointly liable.[66] The limits of a union's duty to see that women receive equal pay have not been set, since virtually no Equal Pay Act suits have been brought against labor unions. To some extent, unequal pay for the same work in jobs covered by union contracts is more of historic than of current importance. Far more prevalent now is sex segregation in the labor force, which keeps women in different and generally inferior job categories from men.

Notes

1. Teresa Wolfson, *The Woman Worker and the Trade Unions* (New York: International Publishers, 1926), p. 56.
2. *Ibid.*, p. 58.
3. Philip S. Foner, *History of the Labor Movement in the United States* (New York: International Publishers, 1947), vol. 1, p. 383.

4. Eleanor Flexner, *Century of Struggle: The Woman's Rights Movement in the United States* (Cambridge, Mass.: Harvard University Press, 1959), pp. 57–60.

5. Alice Henry, *Women and the Labor Movement* (New York: George H. Duran, 1923), p. 100.

6. Sarah Simpson to Samuel Gompers, quoted in Foner, *History of the Labor Movement,* vol. 3, p. 227.

7. Wolfson, *Woman Worker,* p. 80. Wolfson lists 12 international unions with such policies.

8. *Ibid.,* p. 87.

9. *Ibid.,* p. 104.

10. *Ibid.,* p. 140.

11. Teresa Wolfson, "Trade Union Activities of Women," *Annals of the American Academy of Political and Social Science,* 143 (May 1929), 120. She estimated that 8,500,000 women were gainfully employed in 1927 and that 260,095 of these women were union members.

12. Gladys Dickason ("Women in Labor Unions," *Annals of the American Academy of Political and Social Science,* 251 [May 1947] , 70) estimated that there were 10,679,000 women in the labor force and 260,000 women trade union members in 1930. This comes to about one woman worker in 40.

13. Quoted in Grace Hutchins, *Women Who Work* (New York: International Publishers, 1952), p. 260.

14. For an excellent discussion of the ways social myths about women interacted with working women's experiences, see S. Eisenstein, "Bread and Roses: Working Women's Consciousness, 1905–1920," *The Human Factor: Journal of the Graduate Sociology Student Union of Columbia University,* 10 (Fall 1970), 33.

15. Dickason, "Women in Labor Unions," p. 78.

16. *Ibid.,* p. 73.

17. *Ibid.* In 1949 Dickason was able to count only 20 women officers of state labor organizations and 20 women directors of education and research, which was the traditional woman's job. At the time Dickason wrote her article, the Women's Department of the United Auto Workers was developing a questionnaire about women union officers.

18. *Ibid.,* p. 109.

19. Abbott L. Ferriss, *Indicators of Trends in the Status of American Women* (New York: Russell Sage Foundation, 1971), p. 177.

20. Women's Bureau, U.S. Dept. of Labor, *Handbook of Women Workers* (Washington, D.C.: GPO, 1969), p. 83.

21. For example, *Local 153, International Assoc. of Heat and Frost Insulators,* 407 F.2d 1047 (5th Cir. 1969); *Dobbins v. Local 212, International Brotherhood of Electrical Workers,* 292 F.Supp. 413 (S.D. Ohio 1968).

22. 106 NLRB 343, 32 LRRM 1446 (1953).

23. 165 NLRB 951 (1967).

24. 284 F.Supp. 23 (1968).

25. Alice Cook, "Women and American Trade Unions," *Annals of the American Academy of Political and Social Science,* 375 (Jan. 1968), 129.

26. *Ibid.,* pp. 130–32.

27. Telephone interview with Linda Tar-Whelan, Deputy Director, Program Development, American Federation of State, County, and Municipal Employees, Feb. 1, 1974.

28. Cook, "Women and American Trade Unions," p. 130.

29. Minutes of Women's Conference, Labor Temple, Wisconsin Rapids, Wis., March 7, 1970.

30. Although the subject is beyond the scope of this paper, the NLRB also has authority to regulate discrimination by employers. See, e.g., *Farmers Cooperative Congress*, 59 LCCR Lab. Cas. para. 13,234 (D.C. Cir. 1969).

31. 49 Stat. 449 sec. 101(2)(3)(1935).

32. *Handbook of Women Workers*, p. 38.

33. *Ibid.*, p. 113.

34. *Ibid.*, p. 116.

35. 323 U.S. 198 (1944).

36. 140 NLRB 181 (1962).

37. See, e.g., *Independent Metal Workers Union, Local No. 1 (Hughes Tool Co.)*, 147 NLRB 1573 (1964); theory approved in *Local Union No. 12, United Rubber, Cork, Linoleum and Plastic Workers of America*, 150 NLRB 312; *enforcement granted*, 368 F.2d 12 (5th Cir. 1966); *cert. den.*, 380 U.S. 837 (1967).

38. 355 U.S. 41 (1957).

39. *Rubber Workers, supra* note 37.

40. See, e.g., *Local 1367, International Longshoremen's Assoc.*, 148 NLRB 44 (1967): "Collective bargaining agreements which discriminate invidiously are not lawful under the Act . . . and both unions and employers are enjoined by the Act from entering into them."

41. *Ford Motor Co. v. Huffman*, 345 U.S. 330 (1953).

42. 349 Mich. 108, 84 N.W. 523 (Sup. Ct. Mich. 1957).

43. 283 Mich. 201, 277 N.W. 885 (Sup. Ct. Mich. 1938).

44. Archibald Cox, "The Duty of Fair Representation," *Villanova Law Review*, 2 (1957), 151, 160–61, citing *Mount v. Grand International Brotherhood of Locomotive Engineers*, 226 F.2d 604 (6th Cir. 1955).

45. 106 NLRB 343 (1953).

46. See also *Underwriters Salvage Co. of New York*. 99 NLRB 337 (1952); *Tom Thumb Stores*, 123 NLRB 99 (1959); *U.S. Baking Co.*, 165 NLRB 931 (1961).

47. *Rubber Workers, supra* note 37. See Michael I. Sovern's *Legal Restraints on Racial Discrimination in Employment* (New York: Twentieth Century Fund, 1966) for an outline of the arguments that unfair representation violates sections 8(b)(2) and 8(b)(3) as well as 8(b)(1).

48. 272 F.Supp. 332; *modified* at 416 F.2d 711; order entered 2 FEP Cases 463 (S.D. Ind. 2/25/70). See also the *Job Discrimination Handbook* (Washington, D.C.: Human Rights for Women, 1971), p. 10.

49. Bureau of National Affairs (BNA), Fair Employment Practices Reporter, 401:2001.

50. 279 F.Supp. 505, 516 (E.D. Va. 1968). See also *Robinson v. Lorillard*, 444 F.2d 91 (4th Cir. 1971).

51. See *U.S. v. Paper-makers Local 189*, 282 F.Supp. 39 (E.D. La.); *aff'd.*, 416 F.2d 980 (5th Cir. 1969). This case dealt with discrimination at Crown Zellerbach's Bogalusa, Louisiana, plant, where the highest pay for any of the black jobs was lower than the lowest pay for any of the white jobs. After the 1964 Civil Rights Act went into effect, the progression lines were merged on the basis of pay, with the result that blacks, no matter what their seniority in terms of length of service, were still at the bottom of all the progression ladders. The court ordered that a seniority system should be instituted based solely on length of service in the mill.

And in *Dobbins* (*supra* note 21) the court held that a referral system based on work experience in the union, which had excluded blacks from membership in the past, was discriminatory and illegal.

52. 5 FEP Cases 395 (D.D.C. 1973).
53. EEOC Decis. No. 70134, 2 FEP Cases 237 (9/5/69).
54. *Auto Workers v. H—— Corp.* and *Chemical Workers v. P—— Corp.*, BNA, Fair Employment Practices Reporter, 401:3001; adopted by federal court in *Chemical Workers v. Planters Mfg. Co.*, 1 FEP Cases 39, 63 LRRM 2213 (N.D. Miss. 1966).
55. *Quarles* (*supra* note 50) and *Dobbins* (*supra* note 21) were class actions. So was *Hall v. Werthen Bag*, 251 F.Supp. 184, 400 F.2d 28 (1968). The fifth Circuit Court reversed a lower court ruling that had refused to allow a class action by blacks working in different parts of the plant.
56. Betty Friedan, newsletter to members of NOW, Nov. 1969, p. 1, quoted in S. Ross, "Sex Discrimination and Title VII" (unpub. paper written for course at New York University Law School, 1969). Note, however, that NOW filed a brief as *amicus curiae*.
57. EEOC, 2d Annual Report (1968), 6th Annual Report (1972).
58. M. Tobriner, "California FEPC," *Hastings Law Review*, 16 (1965), 333.
59. 293 F.Supp. 1219 (C.D. Cal. 1968).
60. Jacques M. Dulin, "Comment on Recent Decisions," *George Washington Law Review*, vol. 34, pp. 155ff.
61. "Note: Union Liability for Sex Discrimination," *Hastings Law Review*, 23 (1971), 295.
62. For the steps of the NLRB enforcement procedure, see 29 C.F.R., pt. 101.
63. 29 U.S.C. no. 206 (d)(1), 1964.
64. 29 C.F.R., no. 800,109.
65. 29 C.F.R., no. 800,106.
66. *Wirtz v. Rainbo Baking Co.*, 58 Labor Cases, para. 32,085 (Sept. 1968); see also *Murphy v. Miller Brewing Co.*, 307 F.Supp. 829 (E.D. Wis. 1969).

V The Double Image

Women in the American Novel

Kimberley Snow

In 1852 Melville described Lucy Tartan in *Pierre*:

> . . . her cheeks were tinted with the most delicate white and red, the white predominating. Her eyes some god brought down from heaven; her hair was Danae's, spangled with Jove's shower; her teeth were dived for in the Persian Sea.

In 1930 Faulkner described Temple Drake in *Sanctuary*:

> Her face was quite pale, the two spots of rouge like paper discs pasted on her cheek bones, her mouth painted into a savage and perfect bow, also like something both symbolical and cryptic cut carefully from purple paper and pasted there. . . . her eyes blank right and left looking, cool, predatory and discreet.

This change from flower to Venus's flytrap took place neither suddenly nor completely. The earlier image of woman as the hand-wrought creation of the gods permeated our culture to such an extent that remnants and distortions of it may still be found. Despite its persistence on the periphery, however, it was gradually obscured and replaced by a more dominant image. In turn, that image was eclipsed by a newer one, until an evolving pattern emerged in

First published under the title "Images of Women in the American Novel" in *Aphra* (Winter 1970). Copyrighted by, and reprinted with the permission of, Kimberley Snow.

which a series of images grew out of, or in opposition to, one another. The contemporary image of woman as a mechanical yet threatening creature is but the current one in this succession. It is not difficult to trace the broad outlines of the evolutionary process that turned the darling of the gods into the witch of the Industrial Revolution.

There are, of course, individual characterizations of women that transcend the usual pattern and works that do not correspond to the dominant trend.* In spite of these exceptions, if one reviews a cross section of American literature for a certain time span, one finds that in general a common attitude toward women prevails and a particular image dominates. In works of literary merit, this portrait is presented in depth, while in popular literature, it tends to be more one-dimensional or stereotyped. But whether the characterization is deep or shallow, within a given time period the underlying attitude toward woman is often depressingly consistent.

In early American literature a number of different types of female characters are found. Several are transplants from European soil, although one, at least, reflects a more specifically American treatment. By the nineteenth century, these types of women and the attitudes behind them had jelled into an idealized portrait of woman. A change occurred around the end of the nineteenth century, and by the middle of the twentieth, the earlier image of woman was almost reversed. In order to trace the change in our literature from the idealized heroine of the nineteenth century to the current demonic one, it is necessary first to review a few of the conventional female types that were carried over into our literature from the European tradition.

The earliest American novels feature the sentimental heroine inherited from Samuel Richardson's *Clarissa Harlow*, published in 1748. The formula for these novels is simple: a heroine is (reluctantly or through chicanery) seduced, impregnated, and abandoned. In the end the parent/guardian/friend who initially drove her into the arms of the seducer arrives (miraculously) in time for a deathbed scene. Amid copious tears, recriminations, and forgiveness all around, the heroine presents them with her spotless baby (usually a girl) to bring up before she "raised her eyes to Heaven—and then closed them forever."[1] William Hill Brown's *The Power of Sympathy* (1789), Susanna Rowson's *Charlotte Temple* (1794), and Hannah Foster's *The Coquette* (1797) are all popular examples of this type.

Another popular heroine in the early literature is the one-dimensional female who flits through the historical romances of James Fenimore Cooper and William Gilmore Simms and their imitators. This woman exists essentially as a prop to be

---

* Such individual portraits as Isabel Archer and Hester Prynne immediately spring to mind.

brought on stage to swoon, scream, or sigh at the appropriate moment. Her chief function, apparently, is to be rescued by the hero.

Of all the early American novelists, Charles Brockden Brown was the most innovative in his treatment of women. Many of his contemporaries dealt with the idea of the "American Adam"—a second Adam who is given another chance in the second Eden of the New World. Brown, however, was the only one to deal with the New Woman* in the New World. In 1798 Brown, who had been influenced by Mary Wollstonecraft and the French feminists, wrote a dialogue called *Alcuin* that deals with the education and emancipation of women. In his novels he explored these ideas further by creating rational, self-directed heroines who embody many feminist ideals. Although Brown was not always successful in developing his heroines, his treatment of women, especially in *Wieland* (1798) and *Ormond* (1799), is extremely interesting.[2] His efforts in this area were truly pioneering, for it was not until nearly the end of the nineteenth century that the New Woman emerged as a dominant type in American letters.

In American literature of the late eighteenth and early nineteenth centuries, the sentimental and historical heroines are dominant. These two did not remain pure types, but became inextricably mixed. Leslie Fiedler, however, has pointed out that there is a curious lack of women of any type in many of the American classics throughout the nineteenth century. He points to *Moby Dick, Huckleberry Finn, The Last of the Mohicans,* and *The Red Badge of Courage* as examples. It is his thesis that excessive sentimentality has prevented American authors from portraying either woman or sex in a natural manner. The American novel, he writes, "is different from its European prototypes, and one of its essential differences arises from its chary treatment of woman and of sex."[3]

But Fiedler has oversimplified and exaggerated his case. The English novelists of the same period were no more realistic about sex than the Americans. Dickens, who had a tremendous influence on American novelists, was excessively sentimental about women and never failed to idealize them. Still, Fiedler is right in observing that sex and women do not play a dominant part in our nineteenth-century literature. The reason for this is simple: American novelists—in their novels—were simply concerned with other things. Since early American writers were strongly influenced by the Puritan meditative tradition, in which the soul is constantly being examined, American literature tends to deal more with the state of the soul than

---

* The New Woman is a term applied to the independent, self-motivated heroine of the Restoration drama. Her immediate origins lie in the Renaissance, although the liberated heroine appears throughout epic literature and mythology.

Theoretically, souls have no sex, but in a sexist society, they are perceived as male and represented as such.

with the individual in society. Theoretically, souls have no sex, but in a sexist society, they are perceived as male and represented as such.* Since women are thus seen in social, not metaphysical terms, it is not surprising that they play a large part in English novels, which deal with society and social relationships, but have a paler role in American literature, which deals with the isolated soul of man, his relationship with himself, or his relationship to God. Up to the novels of Henry James, social relationships, especially between men and women, are not as important in American literature as they are in English or Continental literature.

The Romantic movement in the United States, for example, has a peculiarly desexed quality about it when compared to the Romantic movement in Britain. None of the major American writers of this period show the combined interest in women and sex displayed by Blake and Shelley. Whitman was interested in sex, but except for "Children of Adam," not necessarily in connection with women. The high-minded Mr. Emerson and Mr. Thoreau were concerned neither with women nor with sex, but with philosophy. Poe has many women characters, but they all seem to be dead—or dying.

In spite of Fiedler's claims, the great American fiction writers of this period— Poe, Melville, and Hawthorne—created many women characters. Frequently, however, as would be expected in the type of novel involved, women are treated not as individuals but as symbols of some aspect of man's soul. Of course, to see women in symbolic terms was nothing new. In the Western tradition, with its persistent ideas of a Manichean universe, the dual aspects of man's nature have frequently found symbolic form. In Plato's parable of a chariot pulled by a black horse and a white horse, the dual aspects of man's nature are symbolized by the black horse, which pulls the chariot downward, and the white horse, which pulls it upward, while the charioteer struggles to keep a steady course.** Women are substituted for the horses in much of Western literature, but the basic struggle and the underlying symbolism remain the same. In this traditional, even archetypal pattern, the Dark Woman as Fiedler calls her, who symbolizes the evil side of man's nature, is placed

---

* One is reminded of the husband's comment: "My wife and I are one and I am he."

** Freud, using the same paradigm, calls them the id, ego, and superego.

in opposition to what he calls the Fair Maiden, who represents the good side. The hero is symbolically caught between the two. This symbolic representation, of course, prevents a realistic portrayal of the woman herself, as an individual in her own right.*

In the earlier versions of this symbolism, such as the one set forth in the sixteenth century by Spenser in *The Faerie Queene,* The Fair Maiden is closely identified with God and with the powers of the Establishment. Conversely, the Dark Woman is a temptress who is the agent of the underworld and the darker powers. By the Romantic era, however, the Dark Woman is no longer truly evil but has become increasingly idealized. At the same time she has also become more autonomous and self-motivated, for she is no longer the agent of the devil. In Scott's *Ivanhoe,* for example, Rebecca's Jewish ancestry connects her with the archetypal Dark Woman, although she is not evil herself. In the novels of Scott and his American followers, the Dark Woman becomes depressingly vapid and virtuous, only a pale carbon of the dangerous creature she once was. Even in Oliver Wendell Holmes's *Elsie Venner,* where the heroine has deep affinities with the dark powers, her viciousness is sympathetically attributed to a snake bite received by her mother. In the end Elsie repents in a tearful deathbed scene and dies like a good sentimental heroine.

This symbolic representation of the Dark Woman and the Fair Maiden is seen in Poe's "Ligeia," Melville's *Pierre,* and Hawthorne's *The Marble Faun,* as well as in numerous other American works. Usually the Dark Woman is pictured as being in love with the hero, and it is only some unfortunate circumstance (she is his sister, she is married, etc.) that prevents her from marrying him. Unlike her progenitors, she exists only for the hero; certainly she has no outside interests such as witchcraft or pacts with the devil. Frequently she has a past, but it remains shrouded in mystery and she gives up all connections with it for the hero. In fact, the Dark Woman's darkness lies mainly in the color of her hair and the obscurity of her origins. Likely as not, she loves the hero as purely and virtuously as the Fair Maiden. Usually, the hero is fascinated or even obsessed with the Dark Woman, but because she is outside the accepted structures of society, he marries the Fair Maiden.**

---

* Also, the fact that women are always connected with sex and are seen only in their relationships to men gives them a lopsided appearance in literature and prevents realistic characterization. The nonsexual aspects of a woman's life are almost never explored by male authors, and women characters do not think about anything except men. No doubt the fact that women exist in fiction as symbols of man's inner conflicts or as necessary props to his fantasy life indicates their true position in society.

** In Melville's *Pierre* the hero chooses the Dark Woman and all three members of the triangle are destroyed.

By the end of the century, when the image of woman was generally undergoing a change, novelists shifted their emphasis from the hero's struggle between the Dark Woman and the Fair Maiden to the point of view of one of the women. As the psychology of the Dark Woman was explored, she was portrayed in increasingly sympathetic terms. Ellen Olenska in Edith Wharton's *The Age of Innocence,* for example, is much more appealing than the fair, cold May Welland. In William Dean Howells's *The Rise of Silas Lapham,* a major portion of the plot hinges on the fact that the hero is in love with the Dark Woman, while everyone (including the women themselves) assumes that he is in love with the Fair Maiden. To today's reader the Dark Woman of the earlier novels is infinitely more interesting than her pale, pious sister, but this was not always the case.* Contemporary reviews of these novels reveal that the nineteenth-century sympathies were with the Fair Maiden, who stayed well inside the traditional woman's role.

The early women novelists, too, tended to keep women within the usual boundaries, but a study of the domestic novel reveals an unsuspected twist. These novels—written by, about, and for women—have long been dismissed with a sniff by academicians as being unworthy of study. It is true that their literary quality is usually very poor, and their portrayal of the ordinary woman's daily trials and sacrifices in the home, ludicrously heroic. But it was not because of literary quality that the work of such women as Mrs. E. D. E. N. Southworth and Augusta Jane Evans Wilson outsold that of better writers each year by a wide margin.

In one domestic novel after another, the heroine, who embodies all of the idealized traits of womanhood, glories in her role as wife and mother. She is worshipped because she is that mystical thing known as Woman, and she rules her father, husband, and children through "love." She is the mawkish product of the fireside poets, the epitome of the Victorian ideal of motherhood. The men in the novel, alas for their brute natures, do not always have the higher sensibilities necessary to appreciate these paragons. Thus in the domestic novel the roles of long-suffering martyr, forgiving wife, and indispensable helpmeet reach their apotheosis. No doubt these novels, with their glorification of women, served to keep women satisfied with their roles as wives and mothers, but they also helped to work out unconscious feelings of aggression and hostility by means of fantasy.

On the surface the domestic novel is merely a sentimentalization of woman, but this is only on the surface. When Helen Waite Papashvily analyzed a number of the books, she found that by the end, the husband's or father's great powers had

---

* Even as late as 1957, when the girls in a high school class were asked if they identified with Scarlett O'Hara or Melanie Wilkes, only one chose Scarlett. In 1970, however, three-fourths of the girls in a similar class said they identified with Scarlett.

been diminished or destroyed. Frequently the hero died and the novel ended in an orgy of tears at his bedside. (Did someone say wish-fulfillment?) Other times the hero was somehow mutilated, emasculated, bedridden, blinded, or otherwise incapacitated in the course of the novel, and was put under the complete control of the heroine by the end. Sometimes the hero reformed his evil ways (frequently he gave up drinking), but his burden of guilt rendered him as manageable to the heroine as the physical injuries sustained by the heroes of other novels did.

Papashvily writes that although their women characters retained the traditional women's roles, the domestic novels were "a witches' broth, a lethal draught brewed by women and used by women to destroy their common enemy, man": "No man, fortunately for his peace of mind, ever discovered that the domestic novels were handbooks of another kind of feminine revolt—that these pretty tales reflected and encouraged a pattern of feminine behavior so quietly ruthless, so subtly vicious that by comparison the ladies at Seneca appear angels of innocence."[4] Perhaps the true viciousness of these novels lies in their absolute lack of self-knowledge and honesty. While the self-righteous heroines exploit the roles that are sanctioned by society, their hate and hostility are completely unconscious and completely buried under sentimentality. Thus these women are able to devour their families by "love" and crush them with guilt—while God and society look on approvingly.

In the nineteenth-century popular literature written by men, the heroine shows many of the same characteristics found in the domestic novel, without her proclivities toward castration. A combination of the sentimental and Fair Maiden heroines, she emerges as an idealized, desexed creature, brimming over with piety, purity, and innocence. She has an innate moral sense vastly superior to that of the men around her. She is ethereally beautiful, sensitive, loving, kind, and generous, and if she is occasionally willful, she is just headstrong enough to add spice. She is all heart, and she acts on feminine instinct rather than on the basis of rationality. She is spoken of in diminutives and is invariably described with flower imagery. In fact, she could be called the Dew Drop heroine. Naturally, Dew Drop has no goal in life except marriage and few concerns outside of the domestic.

Dew Drop enjoyed a widespread revival in the popular culture of the 1950's. She was modernized to the extent that she was no longer pious and became inordinately fond of baseball, but she remained incorrigibly virginal and kittenish. Dew Drop reached her apotheosis in Doris Day, and while today the type may still easily be found in popular literature, girls' books, women's magazines and innumerable television series and commercials, her popularity is somewhat diminished.

Even in the nineteenth century, there was a reaction against the saccharine Dew Drop, and by the late 1900's, two different reactions were easily discernible.

In many of the popular novels written by men around the turn of the century, the New Woman is shown declaring her independence, making a mess of things, and then confessing that her way of thinking was mistaken and gratefully reverting to her role of Dew Drop.

One reaction sprang from the intellectual currents set in motion by realism and naturalism, and eventually led to a more realistic treatment of women. The other stemmed from the feminist movement and led to the reintroduction of the New Woman into American literature. In the case of the former, it is obvious that at first American novelists could be realistic and naturalistic about almost everything except their heroines. Generally, their women characters continue in the tradition of Dew Drop or they are lightly varnished over with a thin coating of realism or naturalism.

Such a novelist as Frank Norris, for example, who is hailed as a pioneer in naturalism, has given us the following description of a young woman: "She sat thus, as on a throne, raised about the rest, the radiance of the unseen crown of motherhood glowing from her forehead, the beauty of the perfect woman surrounding her like a glory."[5] Even in the most frequently cited example of American naturalism, *Maggie: A Girl of the Streets,* Stephen Crane is able to evoke sympathy for Maggie because she initially embodies so many of Dew Drop's characteristics: blushing shyness, innate delicacy and daintiness, love of beauty and flowers, and so on. Similarly, Theodore Dreiser's *Sister Carrie* is said to be naturalistic because it shows a woman controlled by external circumstances and animal instincts. However, much of the novel's naturalism is undercut by the sentimental overtones in Dreiser's description of Carrie. In time, of course, the heroine was treated with brutal realism, but the early attempts at realism and naturalism reveal how deeply the stereotype of the ideal heroine was imbedded at the turn of the century.

That the tide against Dew Drop was turning, however slowly, becomes clear when we consider the emergence of a new type of heroine—the New Woman. She has been described by Beatrice K. Hofstadter:

> At the turn of the century a new heroine appeared, epitomized in the drawings of Charles Dana Gibson and hailed everywhere as the "New Woman." She was tall and active, she held her body straight and her head high. Her free and easy manners shocked her genteel mother, and her determination to live her own life appalled her father and his world of domineering men.[6]

The New Woman, however, was not as universally admired as Hofstadter would lead one to believe. In many of the popular novels written by men around the turn of the century, the New Woman is shown declaring her independence, making a mess of things, and then confessing that her way of thinking was mistaken and gratefully reverting to her role of Dew Drop. In other novels she is simply satirized and her principles are deliberately misrepresented for a humorous effect. But despite these distortions and jibes, the New Woman had entered our literature for good. She was a product of the feminist movement and frequently, like Mary Johnston's Hagar, a fervent advocate of women's rights. At other times, as in the novels of Hamlin Garland, she simply embodied the feminist ideals—independence and control over her destiny—without actually advocating the franchise for women.

The New Woman is guided by her rational mind rather than intuitive emotion. This heroine is interested in specific reform instead of being invested with a vague spirituality and goodness. She is portrayed as having a sharp mind and an indomitable will, a combination that makes her successful in her attempts to control her destiny. The New Woman is more physical than spiritual; thus for the first time sex begins to enter into the portrait of the American heroine.

The New Woman is still with us today, but unfortunately she is no longer the dominant stereotype. She is most clearly seen in the figure of the popular girl detective, Nancy Drew. In the Nancy Drew stories Nancy is flanked by the dark and fair standbys of American literature. The blond is overly feminine, formless, and afraid of things, while the brunette lacks true feminity and womanly grace. With archetypal simplicity, Nancy is titian-haired, and she combines the best qualities of the blond and the brunette. In addition, she is a marvel of efficiency, independence, and self-reliance, rivaled only perhaps by Batman. When a homing pigeon falls at her feet, she immediately exclaims, "I'll wire the International Federation of American Homing Pigeon Fanciers and give them the number stamped on the bird's leg ring. All homing pigeons are registered by number so the owners can be traced."

Nancy would never be guilty of fluttering over the pigeon wondering what was to be done or looking to her football-hero friend, Ned Nikerson, for advice. In fact, when examined closely, Ned exists solely as a prop to Nancy—much as the Ken doll is a useful accessory for Barbie. Nancy's father, too, is only a shadowy figure in the background who supplies her with legal advice and new cars from time to time. Judging from the Nancy Drew cult that exists among young girls today, one can conclude that these books serve much the same function as the domestic novels did in the nineteenth century.*

---

* In a recent conversation about various heroines, a nine-year-old girl dismissed Beth of *Little Women* as one of those things in literature that are "not real—like houses that fly and animals that talk." She considered Nancy Drew to be quite real because "after all, girls do get kidnapped and things and they are a lot smarter than their boyfriends and fathers and policemen and everybody."

Various critics have pointed out that the heroine created by a male author is frequently a projection of his own hopes, fears, and frustrations.

In addition to supplying little girls with a model of feminism, the emergence of the New Woman in American letters had an adverse effect. Male authors, as Virginia Woolf pointed out, were so unsettled by this display of feminism that they came to write with what she called "the male side of their minds." The excessive maleness of Hemingway's novels are classic examples of this preoccupation with the masculine.*

From out of all this maleness, a new female stereotype emerged in American literature—the American Bitch. Prime examples are Temple Drake in Faulkner's *Sanctuary,* Daisy Buchanan in Fitzgerald's *The Great Gatsby,* and the heroines in Hemingway's "The Snows of Kilimanjaro" and "The Short Happy Life of Francis Macomber." No longer the innocent, suffering woman or the pliable Dew Drop, the American Bitch is utterly shallow and inhumane. She is the spoiled product of luxury and freedom, the self-centered child whose favorite pastime is destruction— especially the destruction of men. In many cases she is not only a bitch but a hypocrite, retreating behind the code that traditionally protects the ladies when she is challenged. Far from being pure, she is portrayed as being sexually insatiable, devouring the hapless men who attempt to satisfy her lust. Just as Dew Drop grew out of the Fair Maiden stereotype, the American Bitch is an updated version of the Dark Woman.

Even while the novelists of the 1920's and 1930's were creating these destructive monsters, many were also presenting an alternative image of woman: that of the mother-savior. This character is a strong, primitive matriarch, usually nonwhite, who symbolizes the traditional enduring qualities of love, sacrifice, maternal strength, and devotion. If the rest of the characters in the novel survive at all, it is because of her. Dilsey in Faulkner's *The Sound and the Fury,* Pilar in Hemingway's *For Whom the Bell Tolls* and Ma Joad in Steinbeck's *The Grapes of Wrath* are typical examples of the mother-savior figure.

Various critics have pointed out that the heroine created by a male author is frequently a projection of his own hopes, fears, and frustrations.[7] William Wasserstrom feels that in American literature the heroine reflects the national spirit as frequently as she does the personal aspirations of her creator. It is his thesis that

---

* It is difficult, however, to really hate Hemingway now that we have Norman Mailer.

Dew Drop embodies the optimism of nineteenth-century America and that Henry James's fledgling heroines in Europe reflect the emergence of our young country into the world arena. In these terms it could be argued that the novelists of the 1920's and 1930's used the American Bitch and mother-savior stereotypes to symbolize the conflicting value systems in American society—specifically the modern versus the traditional.

Certainly, the American Bitch is sometimes so closely identified with industrialization as to be indistinguishable from it. She is described in mechanical imagery, and her emasculating, threatening qualities seem to reflect the depersonalizing influences of an industrial society. In contrast, the mother-savior is a primitive or peasant woman closely connected with the simple agrarian life and the traditional values associated with it.

By the 1960's, however, the two characters, savior and destroyer, had merged, and only the negative side remained. The strong matriarch was replaced by Ken Kesey's Big Nurse in *One Flew Over the Cuckoo's Nest.* Thus the destroyer absorbed the savior, and symbolically, all hope that the agrarian ethic would save modern man was lost. Big Nurse became the objective correlative for the Super State, a monster with complete legal control over man, but inhuman and rotten to the core.

Also by the 1960's, the American Bitch had reached hysterical proportions in the novels of such writers as Norman Mailer, Bernard Malamud, Gore Vidal, and John Updike. Not since the days of Saint Augustine has woman been so reviled as she is by these novelists. As one would expect when woman is viewed as an evil force, man-woman relationships in these novels are reduced to a vicious battle. The struggles range from the relatively mild ones in Updike's *Couples,* where the relationships are based on a tedious expediency, to the more violent ones in Mailer's *An American Dream,* which are filled with pain and hate. Kate Millett points out that much of Mailer's degradation of women lies in his specifically lower-class attitude toward them.[8] No doubt it is machismo—an excessive concern with maleness—that makes his novels read like extended castration fantasies.

In addition to serving as a sort of inkblot into which the author projects his personal fears, the Ultramodern American Bitch is identified with her society, as was the traditional American Bitch before her:

> Woman becomes something far more insidious than a mere scold; she becomes that force in life which not only has its own unconquerable and even indefinable power but also operates to rob man of his last shred of purpose and dignity. Sexually, she is all hunger and depredation. In terms other than those of sexual desire she is an empty shell, as empty and meaningless as the society in which we find her and with which she has come to be so disastrously identified.[9]

Thus, as our society has disintegrated, so has our heroine—both to the point that one wonders whether either can be redeemed.

In order to rebalance and humanize the image of woman in American literature—to show that she, too, is the victim and not just the product of our society—women novelists must present the female point of view. Moreover, they must write as well as men novelists and receive equal consideration from readers and reviewers. Within our culture, however, the difficulties involved in doing this are almost overwhelming. In order to write well, as Virginia Woolf points out, a woman must have a substantial income and a room of her own with a lock on the door.[10] Even then, just writing well is not enough, as the fate of Kate Chopin and of her novel, *The Awakening,* painfully shows.

This novel, published in 1899, is the story of the awakening of Edna Pontellier, the wife of a wealthy but stuffy New Orleans businessman. Through a lover she awakens first to physical passion and then to herself as a human being. In her quest for self-discovery and personal growth, she gradually awakens to the true nature of the position of woman in society and to the restrictions imposed on her because she is a woman. Edna begins to realize that her lover, like her husband, is insensible to her need for autonomy. As she awakens from her illusions about romantic love, she realizes that a series of lovers will probably follow her present one and that such socially unacceptable behavior on her part will destroy her children. In the end she decides not to sacrifice her essential being by resuming her empty role as wife and mother, and chooses death instead.

Naturally, Kate Chopin had trouble getting her novel published. Not only is its theme outrageous for 1899, but the novel is written with a detached simplicity that never argues for or against the heroine's actions. When it was finally published, it created a scandal. Even in her home town, Saint Louis, the citizens—including T. S. Eliot's mother—demanded that it be removed from the library shelves. A newspaper proclaimed that it was "too strong drink for moral babes and should be labeled poison." Chopin, stunned by these vicious attacks, withdrew from society, never to write again. She died a few years later.

Although *The Awakening* is beautifully written and contains many themes that were later to become major ones in American fiction, it has been forgotten. Since it not only contains a deeply unsettling image of woman that totally contradicted the prevailing stereotype at the time of its publication but also projects a most unflattering portrait of a successful businessman, one suspects that it was too disconcerting to win the attention it deserved. Even today, when Kate Chopin is mentioned at all, her name is usually mispronounced* and she is relegated to that

---

* It should be pronounced like the composer's name.

innocuous pigeonhole of "local colorists." She is noted for her Creole stories, but *The Awakening* is rarely mentioned. The novel itself remained virtually unknown until it was reprinted in 1964. Even the cover of the 1964 edition hails it as "an American *Madame Bovary.*" This comparison not only somehow gives Flaubert the credit for the book's excellence but also undercuts its meaning, for if anything, *The Awakening* is a woman's answer to *Madame Bovary.*

The fate of Kate Chopin's *The Awakening* is but one example of how the feminine world view is banished from literature. Women are just beginning to be aware of—and to rebel against —the process that keeps the male mythology intact.[11] In the field of criticism, the male critic is able to destroy a book that threatens to present a dissenting view by ignoring it, by damning it with faint, paternalistic praise, or by distorting its meaning, whether as a result of simple blindness to feminine nuance or of a more conscious attempt to denigrate the feminine viewpoint. A subtle form of distortion is to relegate all feminine works to either the mediocrity of "popular" literature or the quaintness of "local color."

Another perennial tactic in criticism is to see women characters and authors only in biological terms.* One critic, for example, divides Faulkner's women into cows and bitches, while another relates the poems of Emily Dickinson to her menstrual cycles. Male characters and authors, however, are not reduced to their biological functions. No one divides Faulkner's men into studs and geldings or relates Carlyle's work to his indigestion, although the evidence is certainly there in both cases.

Women authors and characters are also frequently distorted in classroom discussions. It is not uncommon for a literature teacher to agonize over the trials that beset modern man as they are reflected in Quentin Compson's character, but to dismiss Caddy as a slut. Often women authors are completely ignored. It is perfectly possible today to received a bachelor's degree in literature without studying any female author other than Emily Dickinson; a master's degree by adding only Edith Wharton, Ellen Glasgow, and Willa Cather; and a doctorate by adding only another handful, usually the "local colorists."

While it is true that writers such as Sylvia Plath, Doris Lessing, and Joan Didion have begun to create new images of women, their work is usually not dealt with except in the few courses that deal specifically with women in literature. These specialized courses are a valuable first step, but until their insights and perspectives are incorporated into the larger literary framework, the image of women in literature, as in life, will continue to be created and perpetuated by the

---

* This is known among critics as "innovative criticism" and among feminists as "the biological put-down."

patriarchy. Since what is known as literature is almost entirely dictated by the taste of the male critic/publisher/professor, the image of woman is defined in *his* terms. Naturally this image tends to reinforce the traditional ideas of women with which the male is most comfortable. Thus, a woman striving to create a mature, well-integrated image for herself certainly cannot find a model for it in our well-known literature. Nor will she find her special problems honestly confronted, explored, or transcended there. Instead she will find stereotyped heroines—monstrous extremes of virtue and bitchery—acting out stereotyped responses.

In order to rebalance this image of woman in literature, it is not enough merely to increase the number of honest women authors or to rediscover perceptive female writers of the past. Only when women can make their influence felt in the fields of criticism, publishing, and education will literature serve to liberate rather than enslave the woman. Only then will the image of woman in American literature change and begin to reflect woman as a human being rather than a stereotype, symbol, or scapegoat.

Notes

1. This line from Susanna Rowson's *Charlotte Temple* is typical of the rhetorical tone of most sentimental novels.
2. For a complete discussion of Brown's treatment of women, see my article "The Continuity of Charles Brockden Brown: Feminism in *Alcuin, Weiland,* and *Ormond,*" *Women's Studies,* Fall 1973.
3. Leslie Fiedler, *Love and Death in the American Novel* (New York, 1960), p. 11.
4. Helen Waite Papashvily, *All the Happy Endings* (New York, 1956), p. xvii.
5. Frank Norris, *The Octopus* (New York, 1956), p. 504.
6. Beatrice K. Hofstadter, "Popular Culture and the Romantic Heroine," *American Scholar,* XXX (Winter, 1960–61), 98-116.
7. See Simone de Beauvoir, *The Second Sex* (New York, 1968); William Wasserstrom, *The Heiress of All the Ages* (Minneapolis, 1959); and H. R. Hays, *The Dangerous Sex: The Myth of Feminine Evil* (New York, 1964).
8. Kate Millett, *Sexual Politics* (New York, 1970).
9. Diana Trilling, "The Image of Women in Contemporary Literature," in *The Woman in America,* ed. R. J. Lifton (Boston, 1965), p. 63.
10. Virginia Woolf, *A Room of One's Own* (New York, 1957).
11. See Mary Ellman, *Thinking About Women* (New York, 1968).

The Paper Doll: Images of American Woman in Popular Songs

Kay F. Reinartz

'm goin' to buy a Paper Doll I can call my own
A doll that other fellows cannot steal
. . .
When I come home at night she will be waiting
She'll be the truest doll in all this world.
. . .
I'd rather have a Paper Doll I can call my own,
Than to have a fickle-minded real live girl.[1]

"Paper Doll" originally appeared in 1915 and was an immediate top hit. In 1942 it was revived and enjoyed even more popularity than it had two decades earlier. In 1957 Arthur Miller used it as the theme song symbolizing the central female figure in *A View from the Bridge.* Why has this particular song, which appears to be little more than a very ordinary melody coupled with a lyrical variation of the romantic dream-girl quest, enjoyed such popularity? Semanticist S. I. Hayakawa suggests that its repeated popularity is indicative of men's rejection of women as real human beings who have personal differences and needs of their own beyond catering to the egos of men. He remarks that "when the world of reality proves unmanageable, a common practice is to retreat into a symbolic world, since symbols are more manageable and predictable than the extensional realities for which they stand."[2] Although women were not commonly referred to as "dolls" in songs until the twentieth century ("Oh, You Beautiful Doll," 1911), the use of this term is simply a modern expression of an attitude toward woman that has existed in various forms throughout Western culture since ancient times.

Songs are cultural symbols that help us organize and classify our environment and experiences, thus helping us establish order, meaning, and a sense of security in our lives. Sigmund Spaeth, America's foremost authority on popular music, has commented that "the popular song has become a most revealing index to American life in general. It sums up the ethics, habits, slang, and intimate character of a generation and will tell as much to future students of current civilization as any histories, biographies or newspapers of the times."[3] In a recent study Arnold Shaw describes popular music as "spontaneous and unashamed in embodying the romantic dreams, the anxieties, the fulfillment, and frustrations of the American people."[4] In this article the images and values that have been associated with American woman over the past ninety years as revealed by the lyrics of popular songs of the period are examined.

After studying all forms of popular American music of the past one hundred years, Shaw finds that there has been a gradual movement away from cliches toward a more realistic and artistic expression of human values.[5] I find that cliches have remained intact significantly more often in songs dealing with women than in songs dealing with blacks, youth, or marriage. A comparison of these stereotypes with their historical precedents reveals how dominant and pervasive the stereotype of woman has been. Clearly it has much to tell us about American cultural values.

Since ancient times the songs of a people have been the traditional means of transmitting the mythology of their culture. This phenomenon is observable in a significant percentage of American popular songs. While not all hit songs are socially significant, within the mass of songs there regularly appear songs that do carry serious implications of society's beliefs. It is this group of songs that have been culled from the mass to be studied here. This study begins with 1880, since this date marks the beginning of the popular song as we know it today.

Some observers have charged that popular songs cannot be taken seriously as indicators of cultural values. They point out that in addition to being artificially promoted in the mass media, these songs are frequently formula-made. In fact, the fabled Tin Pan Alley song industry was originally based on the idea of the formula hit. But far from regarding this fact as an argument against the real-life basis of the song content, Isaac Goldberg finds it to be the best recommendation possible. The repeated appeal of the formula ingredients, he reasons, implies that they reflect the desires and ideas of a large number of people.[6] Another objection is that the public has no control over which songs become popular because popular tastes are dictated by the artists and entrepreneurs of the music industry. According to Irwin Stambler, however, careful study has shown that to be successful, a piece of popular music must strike a responsive chord in the mass audience and must "reflect culture at that point in history."[7] Actually, it is hard to believe that several million people would listen to and sing a song over and over unless the song meant something to them. Indeed, such casual sources as roving reporter interviews have revealed that teenagers prefer certain songs because "they are so true."[8]

The cultural significance of popular song content cannot be understood without a general awareness of the dominance of male values in American society and culture. A favorite despairing cry of American men in the thirty years since Philip Wylie's invective unveiling of the American "mom" in his popular book *Generation of Vipers,* has been that the United States is becoming a matriarchy in which the men are controlled by the women. The noted historian Charles W. Ferguson makes it clear that this claim of feminine dominance is pure fabrication. He finds that at every point of American history, cultural as well as political, men have been clearly, absolutely, and cleverly in charge; hence the notion of dominance of women can only be regarded as a myth created by men to attract unwarranted sympathy and to assuage their own guilt. History proves beyond question that both the primitive and the civilized world have been a man's world, dominated by male values, ideas, and symbols. When women have been allowed on the stage of society, they have appeared in the image that men have molded for them, doing and saying the things that men have wanted or allowed.[9]

Men have dominated the music entertainment world, just as they have dominated other aspects of our society. Thus, on the legitimate stage as well as in Tin Pan Alley, men have always done and still do most of the writing, directing, producing, reviewing, and advertising of what reaches the public. Those few women who do get into the entertainment business, usually in the role of vocalist, actress, "girl Friday," or clerk, "behave as men want, direct, and imagine them to be."[10] In short, men rule the world of popular music, through which their impressions, attitudes, and prejudices can be magnified and passed to the rest of society. This study is based on an examination of approximately 2,000 songs, the vast majority of them—roughly 90 percent—written by men. The viewpoint expressed in almost all of those that deal with love, sex, marriage, and women is explicitly male. In the past decade the percentage of female song writers has increased over the percentage in the fifty years preceding; however, it is still very small. Not surprisingly, female vocalists almost always sing songs composed by males; thus the mythology expressed in their songs, which occasionally even claim to express a woman's viewpoint, is still a fairly pure expression of the male mind and spirit. Throughout the following analysis the goal has been to present typical examples of themes commonly expressed in song lyrics. Of course, such factors as a song's purely musical attributes and the style in which it is sung are also highly significant indicators of cultural values.[11] But it would be impractical to try to discuss them in a paper this size.

Ferguson, in his ten-year study of the male attitude in the United States, concludes that woman is perceived in two major ways in this country. Sometimes she is seen as an angel—a creature on a pedestal elevated to an absurdly unreal and hypocritical ideal. Other times she is seen as an embodiment of evil—a Pandora creature of corruption and deceit bringing sorrow to man; man's inevitable appendage (not always happily accepted); and a problem that should be avoided as much as possible except for superficial contacts.[12] Many psychologists and anthropologists refer to this polarity as the male's virgin-prostitute complex. In the mythology of popular song, these views of woman are expressed with metronomic monotony in the theme of the sadness of the man's lot as the result of some woman's mistreatment or in expressions of vague, giddy, frivolous feelings of love, which are frequently merely euphemisms for sexual desire. The three things men value women for—service, sex, and love—are the main topics discussed in the vast majority of popular songs. The values of love and sex receive the most reinforcement in song mythology, with service appearing regularly, but not as often. Many of the songs of the past ninety years have been dedicated in one way or another to the task of clarifying the roles, attitudes, and behavior patterns deemed appropriate for the female. The images and values associated with the Victorian woman will be considered first and then those associated with woman in the twentieth century.

To the Victorian mentality, life was divided into two parts: the province of the home, where women and children dwelled; and the adventurous outside world, reserved strictly for men—and women of "questionable reputation." Since woman was the appointed guardian of virtue, man was effectively released to act amorally in the outside world.[13] Thus he could consort with "loose" women—actresses, dancers, and ordinary prostitutes—and not actually be contradicting his sanctimonious attitudes at home and the high value he placed on chastity and family life. The man was the undisputed king of his domain and made all of the rules for his womenfolk to obey. In short, the average woman was expected to live in a separate, unreal world of her own, where she made a fetish of respectability.[14] The only defense available in the limited world to which she was relegated became self-righteousness and frequently "sour-grapes" piety. Songs glorifying the home, motherhood, and domestic life constitute at least 50 percent of the popular songs of the period 1880–1910. They go by such telling titles as "Home Sweet Home" (1825), "My Old New Hampshire Home" (1898), "The Dearest Spot Is Home" (1891), "I'll Take You Home Again Kathleen" (1880), "There's Another Picture in

My Mama's Frame" (1880's), "For Sale a Baby" (1903), "Mud-Pie Days" (1880's), "Baby Hands" (1880's), "My Mama Lives Up in the Sky" (1890's), "My Mother's Kiss" (1890's), "Always Take Mother's Advice" (1884).

It was in the Victorian period that the double standard, as we have known it in the twentieth century, became rigidly set. This standard compels the male to be the active, aggressive member at all times, while the woman plays a dumb, passive role that effectively denies her any opportunity to express her own preferences.[15] The promotion of chastity as a feminine quality is obvious support for the double standard, and the reinforcement of chastity and general inexperience as values for women is much in evidence in Victorian songs. For example, in a song called "Sweet Marie" (1893), the woman is favored by her lover

> Not because your face is fair, love, to see
> But your soul so pure and sweet
> Makes my happiness complete
> Makes me falter at your feet, Sweet Marie.[16]

Another lover is smitten with love at first sight:

> Ah! So pure. Ah! So bright burst her beauty on my sight!
> So mild, so divine, She beguiled this heart of mine.
> 'Reft of aim, ere she came
> Dark the future seemed to loom.
> 'Til her clear brilliant sphere
> New with light, dispelled the gloom.[17]

Through the mythology of song, domestic values and roles were reinforced for Victorian woman, not so much by glorification of household drudgery as through lyrical reminders of the awful fate that lay in store for the woman who considered venturing into the outside world. "And Her Hair Hung Down Her Back" (1894) tells the story of a simple, pure, shy maiden who goes alone to New York City on a trip, "but, alas, alack—she's gone back, with a naughty little twinkle in her eye."[18] A more serious statement of the punishment in store for the woman who longs for a worldly life is revealed in "We Never Speak As We Pass By" (1882):

> The spell is past, the dream is o'er,
> And though we meet, we love no more.
> One heart is crushed to droop and die,
> And for relief must heav'nward fly.

> No life on earth more pure than ours
> In that dear home midst field and flow'rs
> Until the tempter came to Nell—
> It dazzled her, alas she fell.

We never speak as we pass by,
Although a tear bedims her eye;
I know she thinks of her past life
When we were loving man and wife.[19]

The very popular song "The Picture That Is Turned to the Wall" (1891) furnished a good warning to the young woman who might dally with the idea of taking a lover or seeking adventures of her own in the world outside the hallowed, safe, and confining walls of her home. The song describes the domestic sorrow wreaked by a runaway daughter.

There's a name that's never spoken
And a mother's heart's half broken,
There is just another missing from the dear old home,
    that is all;
There is still a memory living,
There's a father unforgiving,
And a picture that is turned toward the wall.[20]

It has been suggested by H. R. Hays that the double standard these songs obviously reinforce springs from the man's desire to control, through custom, the woman's sexual fulfillment, since its customary accompanying pattern of feminine sexual passivity creates the illusion that the woman has less sexual need. Hays further suggests that the jealous and emotional "never darken my door again" reaction of the Victorian father to his daughter's running away from home with her lover springs from the father's unacknowledged incestuous desires, which cause him to feel that his daughter has betrayed him for her lover.[21]

The image of woman as a grown-up child, introduced long before the Victorian period, is much in evidence in the popular songs of that era as well as the twentieth century. Lord Chesterfield's description of women, recorded in a letter to his son in the late eighteenth century, summarizes the characteristic stereotyped thinking about woman's qualities that lie behind this belittling image: "Women then are only children of larger growth; they have an entertaining rattle, and sometimes wit; but not solid reasoning, or good sense. I never knew in my life one that had it or one who reasoned or acted consequently for four and twenty hours together." Chesterfield advises his son that a man of sense merely trifles and plays with women by humoring and flattering them, much as one would treat a bright child. He neither consults them nor trusts them with anything of consequence, though it is tactful to make them think that a man trusts them, for this is "the thing in the world that they are most proud of."[22]

Paternalism is a manner frequently adopted by one who prejudicially considers himself superior to another. The long-standing pattern of paternalism in the behavior of the white toward the black in the South is well known. Evidence of it is easily observed in the customs of referring to the black man as "a child with the body of a man," and to an individual black as a "boy" or a "girl," regardless of age. In Victorian America a paternalistic attitude toward woman is evident in the very titles of such hits as "She Is More To Be Pitied Than Censured" and "She Might Have Seen Better Days." In the twentieth century, references to a woman as a "girl," "little girl," 'baby," or the like are stock cliches. The following lines are a typical contemporary example of this stereotype of woman: "Somewhere in this big, big world there's gotta be a little-bitty girl for me. I've got a big, big love for this little-bitty girl."* Man's "dream girl" notion and his view of woman as a love/ sex object (the sexual implications of giving his big, big love are readily apparent) are also reflected in this song. The traditional depiction of women as grown-up children is further evidence of man's long-standing rejection of them as equal human beings.

Throughout the first four decades of the twentieth century, very few songs specifically dwelled on the more down-to-earth qualities to be desired in a woman. Rather, this period is characterized by the angel image, in which idealized qualities are projected onto woman, almost invariably in association with romantic love. Typical examples are "You Are Love" (1928) and "All the Things You Are" (1939). In the latter song, by Jerome Kern, the woman is described in such metaphores as "the promised kiss of spring," the "breathless hush of evening," and the "angel glow that lights a star."[23] In "You Were Meant for Me," by Arthur Freed and Nacio Brown, a top hit of 1929, woman is characteristically referred to as "all the sweet things rolled up in one which must have been sent by the angels."[24]

Since World War II, however, the percentage of songs that have taken this approach has diminished. "I Enjoy Being a Girl," a top Rodgers and Hammerstein hit of 1958, is an example of the songs that have more concretely clarified the stereotyped qualities and values associated with femininity and the feminine role in America since mid-century. In this song a girl happily sees herself as a delicate sex-object. Moreover, she is unabashedly vain, frivolous, childlike, sentimental, talkative, and giddy. She regards herself as "strictly a female female" who looks forward to a future in the "home of a brave and free male."[25] Chris Gantry's "The Dreams of the Everyday Housewife" (1969) similarly reinforces the popular image of women as basically childish, sentimental, vain, foolish creatures whose egos are tied up with their appearance, their lost youth, and male opinion. These alleged

---

*Fred Tobias and Clint Ballard Jr., "Little Bitty Girl." Copyright © 1960 Post Music, Inc., New York. Used by permission.

feminine characteristics, as well as the things that supposedly preoccupy women—men, flowers, clothes, flattery, and warding off wrinkles—are carefully detailed. Thus the housewife stands before her mirror staring at the wrinkles "that weren't there yesterday" and thinking of the young man she almost married. " 'What would he think if he saw her this way?' " she wonders.[26] In both of these songs the "good life" for a woman is defined as a frivolous round of dates and parties. There is not even a hint that it could revolve around something other than men, such as rewarding work, travel, or commitment to a career. A revealing point in "Everyday Housewife" is the idea that the woman gives up the good life for her man. The overall reasoning is that a woman must sacrifice everything she enjoyed while single for the privilege of being "an everyday housewife."

The value system women are depicted as having in these two songs is precisely the same as that remarked upon by Lord Chesterfield nearly two hundred years ago: "Women are much more like each other than men; they have in truth, but two passions: vanity and love. These are their universal characteristics."[27] Gordon Allport points out that this judgment, which our twentieth-century song mythology reinforces, contains the two elementary components of prejudice: denigration and gross overgeneralization.[28] Lord Chesterfield, like the modern male songwriter, neither allows for individual differences among women nor inquires whether women's alleged attributes are actually more common among women than among men. Furthermore, Chesterfield's condescending description of women, like that of the songwriters, reminds one of the unreal stereotypes die-hard segregationists still apply to blacks.

Although the image of woman as provider of services is less commonly the theme of popular songs than are love and sex, enough songs do deal with this theme to suggest that Freud's conclusion that women's main role in society is to be "ministering angels to the needs and comforts of men" is still the predominant attitude.[29] The explicitness with which this role for woman is discussed in songs has steadily increased in the past twenty years. Rodgers and Hammerstein's "A Fellow Needs a Girl" (1947) discusses the joys of being the modern wife of an ambitious man and the psychological services a wife must provide, including sitting by her husband's side at the end of a weary day to "listen to him talk and agree with the things he'll say."[30] This song makes it clear that one of a wife's primary functions is to support her man's sagging ego without making any personal demands of her own. Her greatest privilege is to console him in his failures and reassure him that he is indeed brilliant and capable.

In his satirical song on the same theme, "Happy to Keep His Dinner Warm" (1961), Frank Loesser emphasized the basic neglect of the wife's own interests that the American wifely role requires.

I'll be so happy to keep his dinner warm,
While he goes onward and upward
Happy to keep his dinner warm 'til he comes wearily home
      from downtown.
I'll be there waiting until his mind is clear
While he looks through me right through me
Waiting to say "Good evening, dear—I'm pregnant,
      what's new from downtown."

Oh! To be loved by a man I respect,
To bask in the glow of his perfectly understandable neglect.
Oh! To be in the aura of his frown, darling busy frown.
Such heaven wearing the wifely uniform while he goes
      onward and upward.
Happy to keep his dinner warm 'til he comes wearily home.*

The score notes for this song indicate that the song is to be sung "happily." The fact that this song is intended as satire only further enhances its value as an indicator of contemporary role prescription for woman.

Among all of the songs surveyed not a single one was found in which a man offers a woman much more than the abstractions of "love," "paradise," "eternal bliss," or perhaps a more mundane rose-covered cottage or a baby or two. There are no offers of human consolation and certainly no promises to support her career or boost her ego.

Burt Bacharach and Hal David's "Wives and Lovers" (1963), reminds the modern wife, "don't you think because there is a ring on your finger you needn't try anymore."** Indeed, woman is instructed that she must constantly strive to keep the interest of her man by catering to him and working hard at retaining the youth, beauty, and romantic qualities that he supposedly married her for. Moreover, since her husband is exposed to attractive women at the office, she must never let him see her in curlers and she should dress up for him daily and serve him candlelight dinners so he will not be tempted to look elsewhere for romance. Actually, the song reads like a paraphrase of Margaret Mead's description of modern American marriage in *Male and Female*: "A marriage is something that has to be worked at each day. . . . The wife has to face the possibility of losing her [job], of finding herself companionless. . . . The wife in curl-papers is replaced by a wife who puts on

---

*From "Happy to Keep His Dinner Warm," by Frank Loesser, © 1961, Frank Music Corp., New York. Used by permission.

**Copyright © 1963 by Famous Music Corporation, New York. Used by permission.

A favorite cliche about woman is that she is by nature masochistic.

lip-stick before she wakes her husband. . . . It is her obligation to make herself continuingly desirable."[31]

Mead's description, written in 1949, stressed that in contemporary society the wife is expected to accept her homemaking role as her most important and main occupation. A survey of the hit songs of the late 1960's shows that this is still the predominant attitude toward woman's role. "Wedding Cake Blues" (1968) and "Queen of the House" (1969) are two cheery little musical sermons that take it upon themselves to list the housewife's duties, such as changing dirty diapers, washing floors, wiping snotty noses, cleaning, preparing endless meals, and "fixing up" for her husband each evening before he gets home from work. These tasks, according to the first song, all come with the wedding cake, or according to the second, make a woman happy to be queen of the house.

One aspect of society's stereotype of woman, reinforced by song mythology, is that she has an absolute need for a man's love. Supposedly this need is so overwhelming and undeniable that no woman can have a meaningful life without its being fulfilled. Women are incessantly reminded that "You've Got to Be Loved" (1968) and "It's a Woman's World When She's in Love" (1955) but only because she has him. Men are admonished, "If You Love Her Tell Her So" (1965), for a woman is born to hear those words; indeed, a woman lives only to hear those words.[32] Women are told over and over in song of the joys that are to be found in "just living for a man." As one happy woman sings,

Everything I do is just for you. . . .
Take me in your arms and make me realize
That all I ever need is just in your eyes
Knowing nothing else will do. . . .*

Practically speaking, cultivating in women the notion that securing and retaining the love of a man should be the focal point of their lives keeps their energies focused on pleasing men rather than on cultivating their own interests and talents, and perhaps ultimately competing with men.

A favorite cliche about woman is that she is by nature masochistic. This idea

---

*"Love Eyes." Copyright © 1967, Granite Music Corp., Hollywood. Used by permission.

is usually expressed in songs that characteristically link this quality with woman's obsessive need for a man's love. The resulting songs typically depict a woman more or less happily accepting her man's incredibly mediocre qualities or even his abuse in exchange for his love and kisses. "Bill" (1927), "The Man I Love" (1924), "Can't Help Lovin' Dat Man of Mine" (1927), and "What's the Use of Wonderin' " (1945) are examples of such songs that have enjoyed popularity over the past forty years. "Bill" is the prototype of the male who has practically nothing to recommend him. Indeed, he is described by his sweetheart as having a somewhat less than ideal face, brain, and body. Yet he is loved for just being himself.[33] Rodgers and Hammerstein's "What's the Use of Wonderin' " is a typical expression of a woman's simple, unconditional acceptance of her man as he is—"whether he's false or true"— because he is her sweetheart.[34] Many less well-known songs, such as "He Hasn't a Thing Except Me" (1936), include long lists of specific abuses or hardships brought upon the woman by her man, all of which she more or less happily accepts for the sake of love. A 1969 version of this basic theme, "I Like What You're Doing," has the modern feature of the woman accepting her man in spite of all because, as she says, "Baby I like what you're doing to me."[35] Perhaps the implication that the woman is accepting mistreatment because her man is good in bed is the contribution of the female songwriter who collaborated on this song. These songs would not be remarkable if there existed a comparable number of songs expressing man's unqualified and unconditional acceptance of woman. The fact that only an occasional song reflects this attitude in a man (and these few examples usually convey a feeling of self-pity that the typical woman's song does not) is further evidence of society's double standard of behavior for the sexes. Furthermore, these songs could be viewed as projections by their male authors of an idealized situation in which the man has the guaranteed love of a woman and yet retains his full freedom to pursue romantic or sexual adventures as well as to abuse the faithful woman if he is so inclined.

Just as domestic values and the man-centered life are clearly promoted for women in songs, independence and the pursuit of a career are emphatically not encouraged. On the contrary, they are associated with sorrow and unhappiness for both man and woman. Although direct criticism of feminine independence is occasionally found in songs from the early 1880's, the theme does not regularly appear until the 1940's, the decade when wartime conditions brought about the first mass exodus of women from the home to outside work. Thus in 1949 "Ballerina" made the top hit list for over half a year. This song tells the story of a dancer who lost her lover because she gave her art priority over her man. "So on with your career," it laments, "you can't afford a backward glance."[36] "You Can't Get a Man with a Gun" (1957) tells us by both word and symbol that it is unacceptable for a woman to "act like a man"—that is, excel at things in which she might be competing with men.[37] "One Hundred Easy Ways (to Lose a Man)," by Betty Comden and Adolf Green (1958), presents a number of hypothetical situations in which a woman is faced with the choice of two alternative modes of behavior: a) consistently helpless, dumb, and impressed by whatever her man does; or b) intelligent and capable herself. The song makes it clear that if she acts intelligent and capable, she is likely to lose her man.[38] Many of the songs of the late 1960's link career involvement with women who mistreat men. For example, "Later Than Night" (1969) is all about a career woman who literally kicks her man out onto the street.[39]

"The Girl That I Marry," a top hit in both 1947 and 1957, explicitly outlines the basically weak, accommodating, and outlandish qualities that were projected, at least throughout the 1950's, as ideal for a woman.

> The girl that I marry will have to be as soft and as
>   pink as a nursery
> The girl I call my own will wear satins and laces
>   and smell of cologne. . . .
> A doll I can carry the girl that I marry must be.*

In his comprehensive study of the myth of feminine evil, H. R. Hays concludes that the historical and contemporary definitions and images of woman are rooted in man's long-standing rejection of her as an equal human being. He finds that this rejection is also the motivation behind the continuing insistence in the present day that women "should be kept in their place, or fulfill some unreal role which neutralizes them and removes them from the sphere of competition."[40] After examining literally hundreds of songs that in one form or another project a highly decorative, accommodating, and passively unreal woman as the feminine ideal, it can only be concluded that the average American male is not interested in a real woman who is just a human being more or less like himself, but is eternally looking for the incredible dream girl: the Paper Doll. While the search for the Paper Doll continues unabated, modern woman's increasing reluctance to limit and deny her humanity has apparently aroused anxiety and hostility in men—at least, that is what popular song lyrics of the 1960's and 1970's seem to indicate.

In the past decade an increasingly common theme in songs is that man feels woman is trying to dominate him. The feeling is very evident in songs going by such telling titles as "You'll Never Tame Me" (1962) and "Lose Her" (1966). The latter song frankly recommends that a man get rid of his woman if she tries to make the decisions. "American Woman" (1970) openly accuses American women of being

---

*"The Girl That I Marry," by Irving Berlin. Copyright © 1946 by Irving Berlin. Reprinted by permission of Irving Berlin Music Corporation.

responsible for a wide range of American men's current problems. Many of these songs express strong feelings of aggressive hostility toward woman and threaten to "get her" in a manner that goes far beyond the sexual toying of the 1950's. For example, "Wild One" (1963) the man warns the woman:

Wild One—I'm gonna tame you down
Wild One—I'll get you yet you bet
    You little doll, all you do is play
    You got a new baby every day
        But someday it's gonna be me, me and only me!
Wild One—I'll make you settle down
Wild One—I'll clip your wings and things
    You got the lips that I'm mad about
    I got the lips that will knock you out.*

"Stop Foolin' Around" (1968) expressed the same male desire to tie the woman down. In this case the man, who is obviously upset by the woman's free behavior, threatens to cut her down to size and "fix" her. Indeed, he is determined that "You ain't going to put me down."[41]

Charles Ferguson suggests that "vituperation and charges of [female] dominance might be symbolic pyrotechnic signals of distress within the male ego."[42] Perhaps it is the status of men that has changed. Beginning in the early 1960's, psychiatrists, psychologists, and family counselors (mostly male) have reported treating ever increasing numbers of passive, dependent males. Experts agree that this mass decline of the dominant, assertive, aggressive, hell-for-leather male personality has been paralleled by an increase in male paranoia.[43]

In 1969 Phil Ochs wrote a number of songs with the specific goal of expressing the insecurity, paranoia, and hostility felt by the contemporary American male. In "Pretty Smart on My Part," essentially a catalog of the greatest fears and threats that men suffer from today, a man sees a pretty woman approaching, with "bold" breasts and a large mouth. "She wants to get me, she wants to hurt me, she wants to bring me down," he sings. Perhaps Ochs began the song with the appearance of a woman because he believes that modern man views her as his greatest threat—a feeling that men at other times in history have certainly shared. Like "Wild One" and "Stop Foolin' Around," Ochs's song then focuses on the man's desire to curtail the woman's personal freedom. It openly states that he will subdue her by leading her to the altar, after which "I'll tie her all in leather, and then I'm going to whip her." In the final verse Ochs exposes the American male's castration complex. The

---

*Bernie Lowe, Dave Appell, and Kal Mann, "Wild One." Copyright © 1963, Lowe Music Corp. and Kalmann Music, Inc. Used by permission.

Although political, education, and social equality for the sexes is a modern ideal, the ageless prejudices against women . . . continue to exist on a level that is only slightly less obvious today than before.

essence of man's ancient and continuing ambivalent attitude toward woman is summarized here. General fear of woman's sexuality is the underlying theme of the song, and the man's reaction combines the conventional way of controlling women —the institution of marriage—with an image of brutal sexual sadism. The male's fear of castration, rightly shown to be at the hands of another male (contrary to the misogynistic Freudian view, it is men who have always castrated men, not women) is portrayed as his second specific sexual fear.[44]

This survey of popular music has attempted to verify that over the years the American male has lyrically drawn the female in images that have changed little from the past and are thus revered as true and eternal. Although political, education, and social equality for the sexes is a modern ideal, the ageless prejudices against woman, which are expressed through a jungle of unreal and frequently negative or derogatory images and stereotypes, continue to exist on a level that is only slightly less obvious today than before. Many of the stereotypes—women are deceitful, excessively emotional, sentimental, illogical, frivolous—embody the very rationalizations which men still use everyday to explain why women cannot function in politics, vital research, scientific professions and other non-domestic spheres—spheres of competition with males. Many Americans believe that discrimination against women in this country can be eliminated through the passage and enforcement of laws that prevent social, occupation, and wage inequities. But a genuine understanding of how deeply sexism is embedded in our culture will dissolve this belief. The stereotyped image of woman as generally inferior to man is strengthened and perpetuated daily by such cultural tools as the popular song.

The sociologist David Riesman has suggested that a significant role of popular music is to create a standardized picture of a woman's place in society, and man-woman relationships, so that people can avoid coping with the problems that acknowledging woman's individualities would involve. Riesman further points out that adolescent girls are more likely than boys to adopt the self-image dictated by popular song. "As the subordinate group, with fewer outlets, girls can less afford even a conventionalized resistance" to the stereotypes projected.[45] Riesman's findings are supported by those of S. I. Hayakawa, who after studying the social significance of song lyrics, concluded that the popular song, "often memorized and sung most in adolescence—when awareness of the opposite sex is awakening—contributes to the false image and helps prevent a realistic, mature view of [woman] from being attainable in adulthood."[46]

The depth and degree of the prejudice against woman in the United States will only be discovered as each aspect of the culture and its accompanying institutions is individually examined and analyzed. The resulting understanding of our culture will serve as a foundation for the new attitudes and institutions necessary if our society is to offer each member a genuine opportunity to develop to her or his fullest potential regardless of sex.

Notes

1. Johnny S. Black, "Paper Doll" (New York: Marks Music, 1915, 1942, 1943).
2. S. I. Hayakawa, "Popular Songs vs. the Facts of Life," *ETC.: Review of General Semantics,* vol. 12, no. 1 (Winter 1955), pp. 88-89.
3. Sigmund Spaeth, *Fifty Years of American Music* (New York: Random House, 1953), 185.
4. Arnold Shaw, "Popular Music from Minstrel Songs to Rock 'n' Roll," in Paul Henry Lang, *One Hundred Years of Music in America* (New York: Schirmer, 1961), 140.
5. *Ibid.*
6. Isaac Goldberg, *Tin Pan Alley* (New York: John Day, 1930), 100.
7. Irwin Stambler, *Encyclopedia of Popular Music* (New York: St. Martin's Press, 1965), xii.
8. Warren G. French, "Pop Songs vs. the Blues: Comments on Hayakawa's Article," *ETC.: A Review of General Semantics,* vol. 12, no. 2 (Winter 1955), p. 128.
9. Charles W. Ferguson, *The Male Attitude* (Boston: Little, Brown, 1966), 4.
10. *Ibid.,* 266.
11. The best study of the cultural significance of musical style is Allan Lomax's *Folk Song Style and Culture* (Washington, D.C.: American Association for the Advancement of Science, 1968).
12. Ferguson, 4.
13. John William Ward, *Andrew Jackson: Symbol for an Age* (New York: Oxford University Press, 1953), 193.
14. David Ewen, *The Life and Death of Tin Pan Alley: The Golden Age of American Popular Music* (New York: Funk and Wagnalls, 1964), 37-38.
15. H. R. Hays, *The Dangerous Sex: The Myth of Feminine Evil* (New York: Putnam's Sons, 1964), 281.
16. Raymond Moore and C. Warre, "Sweet Marie" (1893). Throughout the article each song quoted is accompanied by a textual or footnote citation of as much reference documentation as was available to the writer. In a number of cases the documentation is incomplete, since often printed lyric sheets and discs do not provide the specifics of author, date, place of publication, or publishing company.
17. Von Flotow, "Ah! So Pure! So Bright!" (ca. 1890).
18. Mark Rosenfeld and F. McGlennon, "And Her Hair Hung Down Her Back" (New York: Leo Feist Music, 1894).
19. Frank Egerton, "We Never Speak As We Pass By" (1882).

20. Charles Graham, "The Picture That Is Turned to the Wall" (New York: M. Witmark and Sons Music, 1891).

21. Hays, 290.

22. C. Strachey, ed., *The Letters of the Earl of Chesterfield to His Son* (New York: Putnam's Sons, 1925), I, 261.

23. Jerome Kern, "All the Things You Are" (New York: T. B. Harms Music, 1939).

24. Arthur Freed and Nacio Herb Brown, "You Were Meant For Me" (New York: Robbins Music, 1929).

25. Richard Rodgers and Oscar Hammerstein II, "I Enjoy Being a Girl" (New York: Williamson Music, 1958).

26. Chris Gantry, "Dreams of the Everyday Housewife" (New York: Combine Music, 1969).

27. Strachey, ed., *Letters of Chesterfield*, II, 5.

28. Gordon Allport, *The Nature of Prejudice* (Garden City, N.Y.: Doubleday, 1954), 33.

29. Ernest Jones, *The Life and Times of Sigmund Freud*, III (New York, 1955), 414, 421.

30. Richard Rodgers and Oscar Hammerstein II, "A Fellow Needs a Girl" (New York: Williamson Music, 1947).

31. Margaret Mead, *Male and Female* (New York: Dell, 1949), 336-37.

32. Screiber, "If You Love Her Tell Her So" (1965).

33. Jerome Kern, P. G. Wodehouse, and Oscar Hammerstein II, "Bill" (New York: T. B. Harms, 1927, 1955).

34. Richard Rodgers and Oscar Hammerstein II, "What's the Use of Wonderin' " (New York: Williamson Music, 1945).

35. Betty Crutcher, Homer Banks, and Raymond Jackson, "I Like What You're Doing" (Memphis, Tenn.: East-Memphis Music, 1969).

36. Bob Russell and Carl Sigman, "Ballerina" (New York: Jefferson Music, 1949).

37. Irving Berlin, "You Can't Get a Man With a Gun" (New York: Irving Berlin Music, 1946).

38. Betty Comden and Adolph Green, "One Hundred Easy Ways (To Lose a Man)" (New York: Chappell, 1953).

39. Frank Zappa, "Later Than Night" (New York: Zappa Music, 1969).

40. Hays, 281.

41. Kal Mann and Bernie Lowe, "Stop Foolin' Around" (Philadelphia: Lowe Music and Kalmann Music, 1963).

42. Ferguson, 14.

43. *Ibid.*

44. Phil Ochs, "Pretty Smart on My Part" (Hollywood, Calif.: Barricade Music, 1971).

45. David Riesman, "Listening to Popular Music," in Bernard Rosenberg and David M. White, eds., *Mass Culture: The Popular Arts in America* (New York: Free Press, 1957), 410-12.

46. Hayakawa, 94.

Sexism in Western Art

Lyvia Morgan Brown

In the history of Western art, the paintings that depict women as independent individuals can virtually be counted on one's fingers. The rest depict them most often in one of two familiar roles: either as the pure and humble servant of man (or God) who bear his children, or as the sex-pot, the sinful temptress who, in this obsessive fantasy, lives for nothing but to give man pleasure. Somewhere between these stereotypes lies a third role: the unapproachable ideal of the cult of beauty. These three objects of male wish fulfillment—the Madonna, Eve, and Venus—turn up in almost infinite disguises in Western Art.

It is perhaps too obvious to recall that art has been the domain of men. So strongly does a patriarchal culture define its stereotypes that even on the rare occasions when women were patrons (as in the Rococo period), the fluffy female exhibiting her body as an end in itself was still the ultimate theme of art. There are no weak males being set upon and raped by women in armor; no coy, baby-hugging men look at themselves in mirrors; and with the startling exception of "Young Spartans" by Degas, there are no Amazon equals of men.* No one ever questioned the rightness of the images, nor saw the damaging effect that visual stereotypes could have on the individuals in a society. Let us, then, take a closer look at the man's eye view of women in art, in order to further our understanding of how certain expectations of men have forced women into passive acceptance of their roles. It is important to emphasize that we will not be discussing the esthetic values of paintings but certain images depicted in them. For this reason, great and inferior painters alike will be subject to scrutiny.

Post-Renaissance depictions of women developed out of the Christian prototypes: Eve and the Madonna, the Virgin Mother. The importance of the Madonna in art lies in her contradictory condition: she is a virgin but she has mothered a god. The humble, submissive, chaste woman became a cult figure. In the middle of the fifth century numerous pictures of the Madonna found their way onto church walls, into homes, onto garments and even onto furniture. In early Christian art, the depiction of Madonna and Child was a symbol of the doctrine of the Incarnation. Gradually the Madonna became a queen. In the Middle Ages the mystical side of the Madonna's motherhood gained in importance, and at about this time the cult of virginity found popular appeal and the ideal of feminine perfection was established. The next stage was inevitable: in the fourteenth and fifteenth centuries, the gold background characteristic of the medieval icon was replaced by an enclosed garden ("Hortus Conclusus"),** and finally in the Renaissance the domestic and sentimental aspects of the Holy Family group came to the fore. As religious painting declined, in the seventeenth and eighteenth centuries, the Virgin lost her importance as a subject; yet we find remnants of the sentimental state in the modern popular theme of mother and child. The idea of miraculous conception is not restricted to Christianity; it is found in many primitive and oriental religions as well. But the stress laid on both chastity (with its connotations of submissiveness and

---

* Other rare depictions of Amazon or Spartan women, such as those by Rubens and Delacroix, deprecate the myth by portraying their subjects as buxom, feeble, and usually defeated.

** The garden in art was originally a symbol of the perfect age before sin: the Greek Golden Age, and Eden before the fall. It became a symbol of the Madonna's virginity and fruitfulness (this symbolism derived from the Song of Solomon, which refers to the bride as the secret enclosed garden, but it is also closely connected to the fertility aspect of Venus in her walled garden). Botticelli's "Primavera" is a good example of how in the Renaissance, Venus became fused with the Virgin Mother in the Hortus Conclusus precinct. Eventually, with for example Cranach's "The Golden Age," this ideal setting became linked with sensual love—a pleasure garden. Bosch's triptych "A Garden of Earthly Delights" depicts the garden in its three stages: Eden, or bliss; earthly sexual delight; and finally hell, the punishment for sexual sin. See Robert Hughes, *Heaven and Hell in Western Art* (London: Weidenfeld and Nicolson, 1968), pp. 47-68.

obedience) and motherhood served an important purpose in counteracting man's other view of feminine nature.

Just as the Virgin was shown in her specifically "female" role, so Eve became the prototype for all that was sinful, woman being the cause of sin in man as well as in herself.* In Medieval art her position was ambiguous. With the perfection of the Virgin as an ideal, artists depicted Eve as a naive, weak vessel unable to withstand temptation, rather than as a wicked, knowledgeable temptress. But perhaps in an effort to avoid any association of the sinful serpent with masculine power (the phallus), the serpent was frequently depicted with female breasts and head, in accordance with a theological tradition. Since the Christian tradition emphasized the association between female sin and sexual knowledge—as the convention of hiding the pudendum with a fig leaf, a hand, or a well placed leg or flower shows— the naked body became the symbol of shame and sin instead of the image of divine perfection that it had been for the Greeks. Only in the fourteenth century did sexuality in the female body emerge in art.

The degree to which Eve is blamed for the original sin varies enormously among Renaissance artists. In Masaccio's magnificent fresco "Adam and Eve Expelled from Paradise," the shame and guilt is shared equally by the two distraught figures. And in Bosch's version of the temptation in a detail of "The Haywain," the serpent's expression betrays doubt about whether his offering will be accepted, while Adam and Eve stand by discussing the situation. But by the end of the Renaissance an enormous change had taken place, exemplified by Titian's "Adam and Eve," in which Eve eagerly takes the apple while Adam tries to stop her with his hand. Rubens, the ultimate male chauvinist of Western art, made a direct copy of this composition.

With the change of convention, there was no longer any need to portray the serpent as female: it could remain neuter, for Eve herself had come to represent sin. The innocent naked figure had turned into a contemporary temptress bereft of her clothes, but with her jewels and her coiffured hair intact. In place of the conventional fig leaf, she now held a piece of transparent drapery seductively wafting over her pudendum. Her face had grown older, her mouth and eyes had become more pronounced, and she had begun to smile knowingly at us—the spectators of the scene. The fact that the nude had been associated with sin now emphasized its eroticism. This new Eve, whose forebears were the Northern Gothic ladies of the fifteenth century, with their pale, slender beauty, was well established in art by the

---

* We do well to remember that bearing children in sorrow and serving our husbands, who rule over us, was no more than the punishment imposed on us by a wrathful masculine god (Genesis 3:16). The concept of original female sin is not restricted to the Christian tradition.

late Renaissance in Venice. Eve at this time was changing into Venus, a secular goddess the Greeks would never have recognized.

This was the age when considerable time and energy were spent on elaborate hair styles embedded with tiny jewels. Their use for erotic purposes in art associated the woman with the material world of wealth and ownership. Art was being used as a vehicle for sexual wish fulfillment—a way of making woman an object for man's contemplation and erotic desire. Cranach's girls are the first important example of the use of jewels and seductive drapery; yet they retain their independence and delicacy. In the work of Rubens, by contrast, the woman is seen as fluffy object. The portrait Rubens painted of his wife, "Helene Fourment in a Fur Coat," has her standing in her fat and earrings, with an ingeniously arranged fur coat covering her back and pudendum, and held so that her breasts are pushed up into two enormous bulbs.

It is in the numerous representations of "Vanity" or "Vanity and Death" that the erotic association of woman with her finery is most clearly connected with the image of the sinfulness of her sex. "Vanity" is recognizable in many images of the reclining Venus with her mirror (for example, in works by Bellini, Titian, and Rubens). Similarly, in Cranach's "Venus and Cupid," Venus's elaborately curled ringlets, and above all, the jewelry around her neck and waist, represent wealth and vanity. Being so tight, the jewelry also suggests slavery. More directly, numerous pictures of "Vanity" show the naked maiden with long streaming hair smiling into her mirror. The gruesome sequel to this is the theme "Vanity and Death." In works by the early sixteenth-century painters Hans Baldung Grien and Niklaus Manuel-Deutsch, for example, the naked woman is being grasped from behind by a leering or lecherous skeleton. In more recent times Munch brilliantly switched this image by making the voluptuous young woman embrace and kiss the skeleton, whose bone-leg slides between her legs.

The new Venus originally expressed the dual nature of sensuousness and chastity, as in Botticelli's "Birth of Venus." But soon sin became more important than purity, and the new themes of provocation and coyness were contrasted with the idea of masculine power. Two comparisons will illustrate the change that was taking place.

The classical theme of "Mars and Venus" shows the traditional form of female power. Mars has infinite power, but in the presence of the beautiful Venus he is overcome by her mystical love force. Botticelli, in his painting of this theme, portrayed Mars naked and reclining, calm, his eyes closed; Venus is clothed and looks on peacefully, smiling at Mars; she has no need to exert her power forcefully. In a painting of the same subject Veronese, who was born in 1528, eighteen years after Botticelli's death, showed Mars dressed in armor, complete with a horse;

**Rubens was preoccupied above all with the
female body, which he depicted as a bundle
of self-satisfied flesh.**

Venus, a blond, buxom, bejewelled nude, is about to be lifted up by the powerful
Mars. She is defenseless, and her drapery is slung to one side. We recognize all the
modern trappings of the striptease and the romantic male-power symbols of armor
and horse. It seems that Veronese was unable to accept the idea that Venus could
have mystical power over Mars and thought only that Mars must have sexual power
over Venus.

The second comparison is between Giorgione's "Sleeping Venus" and Titian's
"Venus of Urbino," two pictures that became the prototypes for reclining nudes
for the next four centuries. Giorgione's Venus lies, improbably, in the middle of a
landscape. She covers her hairless pudendum with her hand, and she is asleep, an
untouchable ideal. Titian's Venus is reclining on a couch indoors. Although she is in
almost the same pose as Giorgione's Venus, she is aware of her sexuality: her hair
flows over her shoulder, her lips are darkly accentuated, and her smouldering eyes
gaze on the spectator. She has become approachable. Woman had become an object
of the fantasies of masculine desire, and as such she had to be young, beautiful,
naked, and empty-headed. The sensitivity of Botticelli's Venus was gone and a new
era had begun. With the reclining nude, the artist was often so eager to show all the
erotic aspects—breasts, belly, buttocks, thigh—that the figure was twisted into
excruciating positions, while still retaining an ecstatic expression.

The French School of Fontainebleau of the sixteenth century developed a
peculiar form of frigid, naked eroticism deriving from Bronzino's "Venus, Cupid,
Folly and Time." This picture, with the wax-white skin, the elongated, contrived
poses, the excessively long kissing Cupid who fingers Venus's breast, lends an
uneasy sense of perversion to the theme. The School of Fontainebleau nudes, with
their elegant, stylized bodies and contrived smiles, their jewels, neck ruffs and
pinched nipples, were important as decorative elements extolling luxury and the
glory of the king.

It is with Correggio that the nude's role of arousing men's desire becomes
evident. He chose his subjects with this purpose in mind: thus Jupiter in disguise
seduces Io, Antiope, Danae, Leda, with hazy light (chiaroscuro) caressing the forms.
But it was in the Baroque period, with Rubens, that the emphasis on sexual innuendo became most obvious. At last Venus was attainable. Rubens was preoccupied
above all with the female body, which he depicted as a bundle of self-satisfied flesh.

Color, chiaroscuro, facial expression, the handling of flesh, and above all the flaunting poses of the naked bodies—all were used to stress the woman's new role as a sex object. In "Madonna with Saints" Rubens reveals his feeling for the dichotomy between male and female: a male saint wears armor, while a female saint has bare breasts. So preoccupied was Rubens with female flesh that in "Marie Arrives at Marseilles," in which Queen Marie naturally had to be a clothed, regal creature, he relegated the main scene onto a small mid-picture plane, and in the center foreground placed huge, pink sea-women rising naked from the quay; they show us alternately front, side, and back views as though, like the Three Graces, they were the subject of the painting.

At about this time, women in art were often presented as sex objects (the theme of rape) or as figures for male contemplation (the theme of the indolent nude). Rubens was master of both. It is enlightening to compare the biblical theme of "Bathsheba" as painted by Rubens and by Rembrandt. Both paintings show her at the moment when, busy at her toilette, she receives from her servant a letter from her lover, David, which brings the news that her husband has died as a result of David's order that he should fight in the front line of battle. But Rubens's Bathsheba has no thought beyond the triviality of having her hair combed and holding her necklace. Her clothes are consciously arranged so that her leg and breasts are bare, and her interest in the servant who brings the message from David amounts to no more than a questioning look. Rembrandt portrayed Bathsheba as a young woman of beauty, but her body, compared to artistic ideals, is not generalized, and she does not sit in a lounging, sensuous position; she holds the letter in her hand and her face expresses deep thought, intelligence, and understanding that go far beyond her nakedness. This is a rare picture.

Woman as contemplated object or cuddly toy was the chief theme of the Rococo period. The Rococo female is a soft plump body, a pretty, doll-like creature replacing the mature, languid figure of the Baroque. She is a coquette, veiling her sexual areas with coy enticement. Pale colors and the use of pastels as a medium emphasize the softness of the new pleasure-seeking life. This was the age of mistresses, boudoirs, mirrors, and frivolity. Everything in art, from furniture and interior design down to the smallest knick-knack, was designed for the leisured taste of aristocratic mistresses. The most typical painters of the era are Boucher and Fragonard. Boucher painted a new ideal—the petite. He designed the sentimental flurry of petals, precocious cupid babes, doves, and above all ripe, naked ladies. Miss Morphise O'Murphy lies on her front on a couch, sensually aware of the cushions beneath her, her legs apart and buttocks prominent. Venus has become a Rococo doll. Fragonard's clothed women are as flirtatious and trivial as his nudes; they delicately flee their pursuers in a garden scene filled with flowers and sculptures. Chubby naked boys (putti) emphasize the sentimentality. In "The Useless Resistance" the contented flesh-pot pretends to resist her surprise visitor. "The Bathers" shows bodies of pink fluff like generalized balls of coton wool that float weightlessly on water, grass, or air.

In a painting by Fragonard called "The New Model," there is no longer any effort to disguise the relationship between the artist as male-master and the model as female-object. A well dressed man stands nonchalantly lifting the skirts of a young girl with the end of his cane. She sits on a bed looking coyly away. A clothed woman who stands behind her is looking at the man as though for approval or directions and removing the girl's clothes so that her breasts are bare. The man smiles. But such blatant sexism was not possible until toward the end of the eighteenth century; up until then, and sometimes after, the woman-object had to be presented in mythological guise for the sake of propriety.

"The Judgment of Paris" as an artistic subject dates from classical Greece. But in Greek art the figures are clothed and stand firmly, not flaunting their bodies; they are still goddesses with other than sexual gifts to offer. In early Renaissance art, too, the figures are clothed and demure, and hardly distinguishable from religious figures. It was, once again, with the close of the Renaissance that body worship took over. In Cranach's version of the subject, the figures' eroticism is linked with a heightened awareness that they are objects of art. Each figure shows individually side, front, and back view to the spectators of the scene rather than to Paris, even though it is Paris who judges their beauty in the myth. Paris is in armor, and the scene takes place in the middle of a landscape. The women, however, are inevitably naked except for their large chain necklaces, a bit of drapery, and one enormous feathered hat. Niklaus Manuel Deutsch, in painting the same subject, added a sash and a feathered headdress to one of the naked beauties. The result is reminiscent of more modern beauty contests. Rubens, Boucher, and Renoir all used this theme to exhibit female flesh. And even though the bribes the goddesses individually offer to Paris in the myth are power (offered by Juno), wisdom (offered by Minerva), and the love of the fairest mortal woman, Helen (offered by Venus), it soon became a convention that the goddesses should all appear to be offering themselves.

Perhaps it was the theme of rape that depended most on the license of mythology. Certainly the Greek myths provided more than adequate material on the subject. Yet on close inspection it becomes clear that artists have concentrated on the power of the man or masculine god and the defenselessness of the woman rather than on the wealth of different situations described in the myths.

With the exception of the rape of the Sabine women, most mythical rapes are committed by gods or by beast-men (satyrs, centaurs, or wild men). The woman in a rape scene is at times identified with the evil temptress* and always appears as a defenseless object. The rape is usually associated with a chase, surprise, or capture, unless, as in the case of divine rape, the woman is unaware of what is happening. Jupiter was particularly fond of transforming himself into guises for seduction: a swan for Leda, a cloudy shadow for Io (who in Correggio's portrayal swoons like a prey to his embrace), a golden ray for Danae, a faun for Antiope, a bull for Europa. All these find their place in post-Rènaissance art, and in particular in works by Correggio, Titian, and Rubens. These myths offer at least as many pictorial possibilities as the story of the Virgin Mary, but it goes without saying that the Virgin is never depicted as a naked, swooning woman being carried off by a divine spirit, while such a scene is invariably selected from any suitable Greek myth. The rape scenes do not, of course, show actual penetration (with the rare exception of an occasional "Leda and the Swan"), but rather show the moment of abduction immediately prior to the rape. The female is seen struggling, though her helplessness is obvious, and the male is seen exerting his power and strength; the consequences are left to the spectator's imagination.

The distortion of a myth for the purpose of emphasizing this theme of power versus helplessness was not uncommon among artists. A picture like "The Rape of Dejanira" by Pollaiuolo (late fifteenth century) is a good example. The story goes that Dejanira was given to Hercules for marriage. He was bringing her to his own country when he was stopped by a river in flood. He agreed that the centaur Nessus should take Dejanira on his back across the water. When Nessus was halfway across, he prepared to abduct the woman. Hercules shot him with an arrow, and Nessus, dying, tricked Dejanira by giving her his bloodstained tunic with instructions that her husband must wear it in order that he might love her forever. She persuaded Hercules to wear the tunic, not realizing its deadly nature. He, mortally stricken, built his own funeral pyre and begged his friend Philoctetes to set it on fire. From this long, rich myth, Pollaiuolo painted only the abduction by Nessus, calling it a "rape" even though Nessus was unsuccessful, and omitting the vital tunic and Hercules altogether.

In "The Rape of Lucretia" Titian showed Lucretia naked (except for her jewelry) on a bed, being attacked by a man with a dagger. Actually the dagger only comes into the myth after the rape, when Lucretia, in shame, kills herself. Numerous other artists twisted their themes to achieve pictorial effects, but there is not enough space here to discuss them.

---

* The legend of Saint John Chrysostom tells how he met a woman in a forest, seduced her, and was then so overcome with remorse that to atone for his sin he promptly threw her off a cliff. Hughes, *Heaven and Hell in Western Art,* p. 254.

Another favorite scene shows a naked woman or goddess surprised in the forest by a lecherous creature (sometimes by several). (Why a woman is out naked in the forest, resting languorously on a luxurious piece of cloth, nobody knows.) "Angelica and the Hermit" is one such theme: a voluptuous sleeping woman is surprised by a wizened old man (one of Rubens's subjects). Otherwise the male figure is a satyr, a centaur, or a man in armor. Rubens even managed to fit beast-men, attacking and raping women, into his painting of "The Last Judgment." The theme also infiltrated nineteenth-century painting. Delacroix's women are frequently about to be crushed, whether by men or by horses' hooves.* Vulgar adaptations were popular later in the century.

Closely connected with the idea of woman as a sinful but usable object is the correlation between exotica and erotica. It began toward the end of the eighteenth century but found its true vocation in nineteenth-century art. But Ingres and Delacroix developed a love of the exotic, using it for the purpose of displaying servile, slothful women. "Thetis," by Ingres, shows a naked woman crouching obseqiously at the feet of a vast, muscle-bound god who sits solidly on his throne ignoring her. "Le Bain Turc" exhibits dozens of naked bodies that with another title would have been more appropriate as a harem.

The "Odalisque" was a popular theme among French painters of the nineteenth century, during the height of French colonialism in North Africa. The word itself is a French derivative of the Turkish word for a female slave or concubine, and paintings on this theme usually show a reclining, lavishly dressed woman in a Turkish setting. "The Sphinx," an evil, exotic creature, was another nineteenth-century favorite. In England the exotic slave was a popular subject among Victorian painters. Alma Tadema specialized in Roman settings of indolence, while the little-known painter Ernest Normand created an extraordinary picture, "In Bondage," that tries to show a Near Eastern slave trade of proud foreign women and timid white maidens. The result is an erotic fiasco that defies description.

A further development was the orgy of generalized bodies. The habit of putting into a composition unnecessary nude females, often emphasizing the power of a man with their adulation, began in the seventeenth century and reached its peak in the nineteenth. In England a spate of painters of frisking fairies was the result; but the ultimate painting of this type came from France—Bouguereau's "Les Oreades." Exhibited in the 1890's, this picture was a great success: three horny, muscular satyrs watch as thirty to forty naked, identical women float up into the

---

* The notable exception is "Liberty Guiding the People," in which, for once, the woman is depicted as "Liberty," strong and important; here her bare breasts are a sign of liberation and not of her use as a sex object.

sky in an entangled confusion of arms, legs, breasts, and passive faces.

Erotic fantasies were rife amid Victorian prudery. Eve and the Virgin emerged with new names. Morality pictures showed the downfall of respectable women through their sexuality. "Sin" emerged as a naked femme fatale wrapping around her body a giant snake. Theatrical eroticism lived in the world of art nouveau; swirling nymphs decorated not only paintings and illustrations but furniture, jugs, and lamps.

The modern forms of the old images have dropped their mythological trappings. The theme of rape is found in large scale only in Picasso's later works. It is woman as contemplated object that has found most appeal, as in the themes of "Toilette," "The Picnic," "Bathers," and "Artist and Model." In the nineteenth century eroticism in art was viewed by a double standard that had little to do with how much of the body was revealed. As an example we might look at "The Picnic" as a theme. The first painting to portray clothed men and a naked girl or girls nonchalantly picnicking in a landscape was Giorgione's "Fête Champêtre." In this theme the naked wood nymph has been transformed into a contemporary lady out for a jaunt with contemporary men; there is no sign of an orgy. The eighteenth-century French were fond of the picnic scene, for to them it represented society in nature, the dressed and the undressed. Yet in the nineteenth-century Manet's "Dejeuner sur l'Herbe," with its strong naked woman staring defiantly at us from the middle of a woodland picnic scene, caused an uproar. His "Olympia" created an even greater scandal. This picture is conventional at least in type—a reclining woman stares at the spectator-artist, a black servant behind her—but it is totally new inasmuch as the woman's body is unidealized, in fact squat, and her face has the look of independence rather than voluptuousness.* That these pictures were considered outrageous seems incongruous when we consider the typical academic painting that was so admired at the time, such as Cabanel's "Venus Anadyomene," with its swooning, outstretched nude, hairless pudendum uncovered, breasts sticking out, resting on the sea while five cherubs float above her.† This generalized pornographic work was easily accepted, while Manet's particular woman was a threat to the old stereotypes. Nineteenth-century viewers had one standard for the baby-faced, rosebud lady of Victorian keepsakes or the slick nude representing "Nonchalance" or "Leisure," and another for the nude depicted as an individual.

---

* Compare this with Cezanne's early exercise in orgiastic paint, "The New Olympia," in which the woman is a frenzy of pink fat sprawling before an aristocratic gentleman.

---

† The comparison between Cabanel's "Venus Anadyomene" and Manet's "Olympia" is made by Jean-Louis Vaudoyer in *The Female Nude* (London: Longmans, Green, 1957).

The themes of "Toilette" and "Bathers" are closely related. Renoir is quoted as saying, "The female nude rises from the sea or from her bed; she is called Venus or Nini. One can imagine nothing beyond that."* Certainly Renoir could imagine nothing beyond that, and so his fleshy pink masses rise either from the river or from the bed. "Bathers" is an old theme, going back at least to the fifteenth century, and popular with Boucher and Fragonard. It gives the painter an opportunity to show an orgy of flesh in that popular landscape background. Woman is seen as a luxurious, slothful creature who spends her entire time washing her body, braiding or combing her hair, and sitting in sunlight. There is always a sense of infinite time in these pictures. Renoir's women peer at themselves in mirrors, breasts bared, fingering jewels or a rose; or they hold their chubby babies to their chubby faces. Compare the nudes of Degas. His women actually wash, showing no concern for the spectator; Renoir's nudes simply stand, fat and sensuous, posing with water. Degas's figures have muscles and use them; Renoir's have none and would not know what to do with them even if they had. At least in the work of Degas, Toulouse-Lautrec, and Rodin, the female body became more individual.

The twentieth-century master of sexuality is Picasso, though it is really not until the works of the 1930's that his themes (particularly in his etchings) reach erotic obsession. Distortions are frequently used with erotic expression in mind, and always at the female's expense: her breasts become balloons; her thighs, belly, buttock line, vaginal slit, all swell outward to the spectator, while her head disappears into a tiny indistinguishable speck. One critic claimed that Picasso was showing how a woman experiences sex; another, more accurately perhaps, said he was showing the way a man (the artist) experiences a woman during sex. In a pastiche of Cranach's "Venus and Amor," Picasso put in all the Cranach elements except for the head, which he reduced to a formulaic blob—it is the body that obsesses him. Picasso's output is so enormous and complex that one could not hope to do him justice in a paper this size. It can be said, however, that this idea of women is undoubtedly from the masculine-power viewpoint. A recurrent theme is "Young Girl with Minotaur." Often violent, the beast-man mounts the defenseless girl; at other times he is merely lecherous or even quiet and defeated by a young, potent man. He represents instinctual lust, masculine power, and physical strength. "Artist and Model" is another favorite theme. In it Picasso at last makes explicit the relationship that remained veiled in works by earlier painters. He has created a brilliant visual pun in which a palette surrounds the artist's penis, which rises up amid emanating lines (i.e., the brushes) as he peers at the model. In works of the 1960's the theme becomes recognizably personalized: the model is young and

---

* Quoted by Vaudoyer, p. 6. Nini is the artist's model.

Above all, contemporary artists portray woman as a hated object.

beautiful; the artist (or sometimes clown or little king) is dwarfed, fat, and old, and he leers at the model. Or, more directly, the artist peers myopically at his painting while the model, far more sensuous than the artist's drawing, stands neglected near-by. In this and other similar themes, Picasso is showing that the painter should seduce the model instead of playing at sex with art (the palette-penis).

In contemporary art sexism is more explicitly expressed. In assessing art today we always have the problem of whether a work presents its own viewpoint or a satire on other viewpoints, but for the moment we shall ignore any subtleties of intention and look only at the content. In Pop Art we find the brazen world of the all-American girl, somewhere between Marilyn Monroe's image and Barbarella: legs, stockings, high-heeled shoes, half-cup bras, lipstick, nipples—these are the obsessive images. Tom Wesselman shows us Great American Nudes: all grin and boobs and sprawl. It is a world closely connected with language labels: "baby," "little doll," "honey-bun," "sugar-puss." The jewelry and transparent drapery have been re-placed by stockings, bras, and make-up. Pubic hair and nipples have emerged, but with a generalized eroticism instead of individual sexuality.

Above all, contemporary artists portray woman as a hated object. De Kooning gave us his caricatures—pink, bulbous, grinning, middle-aged. Hans Bellmer's "Peppermint Tower in Honor of Greedy Little Girls" is an obscenely violent depiction of a distorted, flabby female torso with numerous arms (no head or legs), stretching and shoving to push an enormous "tower" into her body. Richard Lindner creates a world of gangsters and cops—cardboard, power-ridden men—and women (molls) in elaborate corsets with holes for breasts that pop out, lipstick grins, and targets or "Hit" signs in the groin. Allen Jones makes sculptures of generalized female bodies, naked except for accessories—black stockings and G-string, black leather boots, long gloves. These creatures exist to hold up furniture; one kneels on all fours with a mirror in her hand and a transparent table top resting on her back; another is a chair; and so on. All these figures are without identity. Do they represent attacks on female sexuality itself or on conventional images of it? Either way, we look in vain for their male counterparts.

When women are no longer erotic objects, they become cuddly toys. This tradition goes back a long way. Think of the fluffy dog on the bed, tail dangling over its mistress's naked pudendum, in Fragonard's "Girl Making Her Dog Dance on

Her Bed;" or the convention of placing infants next to women, pink cheek by pink cheek. Sentimental portraits of girls with the emphasis on innocence are part of this tradition—a tradition kept alive in the comments of art historians when they use phrases like "sweet fruits" and "soft peach" in describing the women in such paintings. Eve or the Virgin, Venus or toy, erotic, raped, or naively coy—women are everything in art but themselves.

Selected Bibliography

When I wrote this paper there was, to my knowledge, no book dealing with sexism in Western art. Since then *Woman as Sex Object: Studies in Erotic Art, 1730–1970,* ed. Thomas B. Hess and Linda Nochlin (London: Allen Lane, 1973) has been published. Edward Lucie Smith's *Eroticism in Western Art* (London: Thames and Hudson, 1972) is also relevant. The following list does not include the numerous monographs on individual artists.

Bazin, Germain. *Baroque and Rococo.* London: Thames and Hudson, 1964.

Bell, Quentin. *Victorian Artists.* London: Routledge and Kegan Paul, 1967.

Berger, John. *Success and Failure of Picasso.* Harmonsworth, Eng.: Penguin, 1965.

Clark, Kenneth. *The Nude.* London: J. Murray, 1956.

Claviere, R. de Maulde la. *The Women of the Renaissance,* trans. George Herbert Ely. London: Swan Sonnerscheim, 1901. Chap. 3: "The Mission of Beauty."

Daniel, Howard. *Encyclopaedia of Themes and Subjects in Painting.* Introduction by John Berger. London: Thames and Hudson, 1971.

Fletcher, Jefferson Butler. *The Religion of Beauty in Woman.* New York: Haskell House, 1966.

Garland, Madge. *The Changing Face of Beauty.* London: Weidenfeld and Nicolson, 1957.

Gilot, Francoise. *Life with Picasso.* New York: McGraw-Hill, 1964.

Gombrich, E. H. "Botticelli's Mythologies." *Journal of the Warburg and Courtauld Institutes,* VIII (1945), 7-60.

Greer, Germaine. *The Female Eunuch.* London: Paladin, 1971.

Hale, Philip L. *Great Portraits: Women.* Boston: Bates and Guild, 1909.

Hess, Thomas B., and Baker, Elizabeth C. *Art and Sexual Politics.* New York: Macmillan, 1973.

Hirn, Yryo. *The Sacred Shrine: A Study of the Poetry and Art of the Catholic Church.* Boston: Beacon Press, 1957. First published in Sweden, 1909.

Hooten, Bruce, and Kaiden, Nina N., eds. *Mother and Child in Modern Art.* New York: Duell, Sloan, and Pearce, 1964.

Hughes, Robert. *Heaven and Hell in Western Art.* London: Weidenfeld and Nicolson, 1968.

Maas, Jeremy. *Victorian Painters.* London: Barrie and Rockliff, The Cresset Press, 1969.

Michaels, Sheila. *The Archetypal Woman.* New York: The Feminists.

Osborne, Harold. *Oxford Companion to Art.* Oxford, Eng.: The Clarendon Press, 1970.

Ovid. *Metamorphoses,* trans. Rolfe Humphries. Bloomington: Indiana University Press, 1958.

Putnam, Emily James. *The Lady.* Chicago: University of Chicago Press, 1970. First published, 1910.

Relouge, I. E., ed. *The Nude in Art,* trans. Mervyn Savill. Introduction by Bodo Cichy. London: B. T. Batsford, 1959.

Roe, Frederic Gordon. *The Nude from Cranach to Etty and Beyond.* Essex, Eng.: F. Lewis, 1944.

Vaudoyer, Jean-Louis. *The Female Nude in European Painting from Pre-history to the Present Day.* London: Longmans, Green, 1957.

Zucker, Paul. *Styles in Painting.* New York: Dover, 1963.

VI Institutions of Social Control

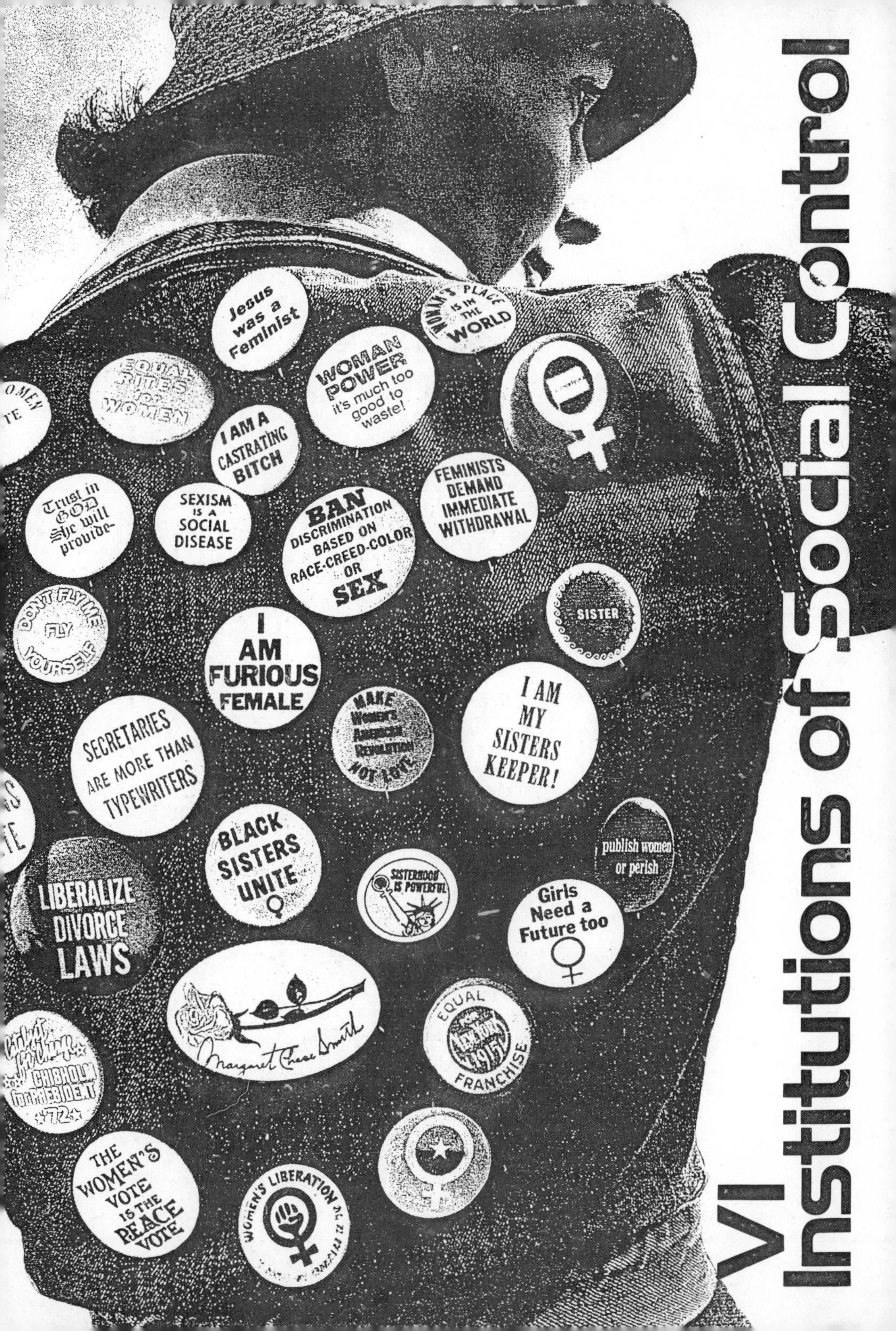

Feminism and the Law

Mary Eastwood

The women's movement is seeking (1) equal
treatment under the law; (2) protection from
discrimination on the basis of sex; (3) physical self-
determination; and (4) political and economic power
for women as a class. The tactics for achieving the
first three goals are, respectively: (1) litigation under
the Constitution and ratification of the proposed
Equal Rights Amendment; (2) the enactment and
enforcement of laws and regulations prohibiting
discrimination because of sex; and (3) abortion
litigation and abortion law repeal, and more recently, efforts to reform laws pertaining to rape and
other sexual assaults. With the achievement of the
first three goals, and the concomitant lifting of the
limitations imposed on women because of their sex,
the fourth goal should automatically follow.

This article outlines some of the cases and laws
relevant to the first three goals. The vehicle of the
law can be used to advance women's political and
economic power as well, but until the first three
goals are achieved both in the law and in women's
daily lives, there would be little practical value in
trying to achieve the fourth.

> ... The paramount destiny and mission of
> woman are to fulfill the noble and benign
> offices of wife and mother. This is the law
> of the Creator. (Bradwell v. Illinois, 1872)

EQUAL TREATMENT UNDER THE CONSTITUTION

The Fourteenth Amendment to the United States Constitution prohibits the states
from depriving any person of life, liberty, or property by any means that denies
her/him due process of law or equal protection of the law. The same basic prohibitions apply to the federal government under the due process clause of the Fifth
Amendment. Despite the protective purpose of these amendments, in the past
courts frequently refused to consider women as fully human "persons" under them,
and found laws that treated women as an inferior class to be constitutional nonetheless.

A century ago three Supreme Court justices, in a concurring opinion uphold-
ing the refusal of the State of Illinois to allow women to practice law, offered this
reasoning:

> The natural and proper timidity and delicacy which belongs to the female
> sex evidently unfits it for many of the occupations of civil life. The constitu-
> tion of the family organization, which is founded in the divine ordinance, as
> well as in the nature of things, indicates the domestic sphere as that which
> properly belongs to the domain and functions of womanhood . . . . The para-
> mount destiny and mission of woman are to fulfill the noble and benign
> offices of wife and mother. This is the law of the Creator.[1]

In other words, "the woman's place is in the home" because that is where God intended her to be.

In 1908, in the famous case of *Muller v. Oregon,*[2] the Supreme Court held
that an Oregon law establishing maximum hours of work only for women did not
violate the Fourteenth Amendment due process clause. At the time, the decision
was regarded as a major victory for those seeking decent standards of labor, but it
later became the bane of advocates of equal rights for women under the law. The
Court sustained special laws for women in the belief that women were an inferior
class of persons needing special protection: "[Woman] is properly placed in a
class by herself, and legislation designed for her protection may be sustained. It is
impossible to close one's eyes to the fact that she still looks to her brother and depends upon him."[3] Moreover, the Court reasoned, women are reproductive instru-
ments of the state, which therefore has an interest in controlling their activity and
protecting their health:

That woman's physical structure and the performance of maternal functions place her at a disadvantage in the struggle for subsistence is obvious. This is especially true when the burdens of motherhood are upon her. . . . As healthy mothers are essential to vigorous offspring, the physical well-being of woman becomes an object of public interest and care in order to preserve the strength and vigor of the race.[4]

As recently as 1961 the Supreme Court upheld a Florida law providing that no female be selected to serve on a jury unless she registers her willingness to serve with the circuit court clerk (whereas the law presumed men should serve). The Court said that "woman is still regarded as the center of home and family life."[5]

Lower courts likewise saw women in a special service capacity. In a 1968 case claiming that the exemption of women from the draft constituted discrimination on the basis of sex in violation of the Fifth Amendment, a federal district court stated: "In providing for involuntary service for men and voluntary service for women, Congress followed the teachings of history that if a nation is to survive, men must provide the first line of defense while women keep the home fires burning."[6] The recognition of women's function in the home as a basis for treating men and women differently under the law in reality has relegated women to a service class. Regardless of a woman's economic position, her status under the Constitution has been that of a servant—to man and to the state.

Recently, however, the Supreme Court has taken a more enlightened view of the position of women under the Constitution. In 1971 the Court held unconstitutional an Idaho statute giving preference to males in the appointment of administrators of estates.[7] In a landmark 1973 decision, *Frontiero v. Richardson*,[8] the Court held that federal statutes that permitted a male member of the uniformed services to claim his wife as a dependent without a showing that she was in fact dependent upon him for her support, but denied a female member dependency benefits for her husband unless he was in fact dependent upon her for over one-half of his support, violated the rights of female members under the due process clause of the Fifth Amendment. The following excerpts from the opinion of four of the justices in *Frontiero* represent a more enlightened and current view of the status of women under the Constitution:

> It is true, of course, that the position of women in America has improved markedly in recent decades. Nevertheless, it can hardly be doubted that, in part because of the high visibility of the sex characteristic, women still face pervasive, although at times more subtle, discrimination in our educational institutions, on the job market and perhaps most conspicuously, in the political arena . . . .

Moreover, since sex, like race and national origin, is an immutable characteristic determined solely by the accident of birth, the imposition of special disabilities upon the members of a particular sex because of their sex would seem to violate "the basic concept of our system that legal burdens should bear some relationship to individual responsibility . . . " [citation omitted] . And what differentiates sex from such nonsuspect statutes as intelligence or physical disability, and aligns it with the recognized suspect criteria, is that the sex characteristic frequently bears no relation to ability to perform or contribute to society. As a result, statutory distinctions between the sexes often have the effect of invidiously relegating the entire class of females to inferior legal status without regard to the actual capabilities of its individual members . . . .

With these considerations in mind, we can only conclude that classifications based upon sex, like classifications based upon race, alienage, or national origin, are inherently suspect, and must therefore be subjected to strict judicial scrutiny.

THE EQUAL RIGHTS AMENDMENT

The proposed Equal Rights Amendment to the Constitution provides that "equality of rights under the law shall not be denied or abridged by the United States or by any State on account of sex." The ERA was passed by the Congress on March 22, 1972, and at this writing has been ratified by 33 of the requisite 38 states. If it came into effect, such a constitutional requirement of absolute equality of the sexes would result in various changes in the application of laws that distinguish on the basis of sex.

Laws that benefit only one sex, such as minimum wage laws, certain preferential treatment of men or women in social security or other social benefits laws, and alimony, would be extended to both sexes, much as the voting laws were made applicable to blacks and women with the passage of the Fifteenth and Nineteenth amendments, respectively. The same is true of jury service and would be true of compulsory military service whenever the latter was in effect. These are responsibilities of citizenship, and to exclude women from their requirements relegates women to an inferior, unneeded class.

Laws that restrict or deny freedom to one sex, such as laws prohibiting women from working in certain types of jobs (e.g., as miners or bartenders), laws restricting the work hours of women only, and laws prohibiting night work by women in certain occupations, deny women equal employment opportunities and have kept them in the low-paid jobs traditionally relegated to them. These restrictions on women, once supported by organized labor as a basis for securing better

Segregation of the sexes in public restrooms or in sleeping facilities in state colleges and universities could continue under the ERA, provided the facilities were equal . . .

labor standards for all workers, including men, are now supported only by those advocating a sex-segregated work force.

Age distinctions based on sex, as in laws setting a lower minimum age for marriage for women, a lower age for boys under child labor laws, a higher age at which the right to parental support is cut off for boys, and a higher age for juvenile court jurisdiction for girls, would be eliminated by making the same age apply to males and females. The Citizens' Advisory Council on the Status of Women has suggested the following test to determine whether the higher or the lower age should apply: "If the age limitation restricts individual liberty and freedom the lower age applies; if the age limitation confers a right, benefit or privilege to the individuals concerned and does not limit individual freedom, the higher age applies."[9]

Segregation of the sexes in public restrooms or in sleeping facilities in state colleges and universities could continue under the ERA, provided the facilities were equal, the segregation did not operate to deny any individual of rights, and the segregation was necessary in order to protect the right to privacy.

LEGAL PROTECTION AGAINST SEX DISCRIMINATION

During the past decade a number of federal laws have been enacted that affirmatively prohibit discrimination against women (and in some instances minorities):

1. The Equal Pay Act[10] prohibits paying a woman at a lower rate than a man who is doing substantially the same work if the jobs require equal skill, effort, and responsibility. Different pay rates are allowed if they are based on a nondiscriminatory seniority or merit system, or a system that measures earnings by quality or quantity of production. The Equal Pay Act is administered by the Department of Labor.
2. Title VII of the Civil Rights Act of 1964, as amended,[11] prohibits discrimination on the basis of race, color, religion, sex, or national origin in all aspects of employment by employers covered by the Act. This law is enforced by the Equal Employment Opportunity Commission and the Department of Justice.

3. Executive Order 11246 of September 24, 1965, as amended, prohibits discrimination in employment under federal contracts and is administered by the Department of Labor.
4. Executive Order 11478 of August 8, 1969, prohibits discrimination in employment by the federal government itself and by the District of Columbia government. It is administered by the Civil Service Commission and the various government departments and agencies.
5. Title IX of the Education Amendments of 1972[12] prohibits discrimination on the basis of sex under education programs or activities receiving federal financial assistance, with certain exceptions. It is administered by the federal agencies extending the financial assistance, primarily the Department of Health, Education, and Welfare.

The sex discrimination provisions of Title VII of the Civil Rights Act of 1964 have been the subject of considerable litigation. An important effect of the law was to invalidate restrictive state labor laws and employer practices that preserved the better-paying and otherwise more desirable jobs for men. In a 1971 case, *Mengelkoch v. Industrial Welfare Commission*,[13] women employees challenged the consistency with Title VII (and the constitutionality) of California's restrictions on hours of work, which applied to women only. The effect of the restrictions was to deprive women of access to the higher-paid jobs, which might occasionally require some overtime work, and of the opportunity to earn overtime pay. A restraining order was entered against the company and the state, prohibiting discrimination against women on the basis of the state hours laws.

In *Bowe v. Colgate-Palmolive Co.*,[14] a 1969 decision, the United States Court of Appeals for the Seventh Circuit held that an employer-imposed practice of allowing only men to work on jobs requiring the lifting of 35 pounds or more at Colgate's Jeffersonville, Indiana, plant, was unlawful under Title VII. The court stated that Colgate must give all of its workers the opportunity to demonstrate their ability to perform more strenuous jobs, and then permit those who could to apply for any position to which their seniority entitled them.[15] Interestingly enough, the rule that purported to protect women at the Colgate plant from lifting more than 35 pounds had resulted in keeping all of them neatly at the bottom of the pay scale. The top rate for women employees equaled the bottom rate for men. The 35-pound rule also meant that some of the more tiring and difficult jobs were women's jobs; one such job required the worker to lift filled bottles of liquid Ajax repetitively, so that by the end of the day she had lifted over 17 tons.

In another 1969 case *Weeks v. Southern Bell Telephone & Telegraph Co.*,[16] the United States Court of Appeals for the Fifth Circuit similarly held that a 30-

pound weight-lifting limitation on women workers was unlawful under Title VII, as was the exclusion of women from jobs in order to protect them from having to work at night. The court pointed out:

> Title VII rejects just this type of romantic paternalism as unduly Victorian and instead vests individual women with the power to decide whether or not to take on unromantic tasks. Men have always had the right to determine whether the incremental increase in remuneration for strenuous, dangerous, obnoxious, boring or unromantic tasks is worth the candle. The promise of Title VII is that women are now to be on an equal footing.[17]

The first sex discrimination case under Title VII to be heard by the Supreme Court was *Phillips v. Martin Marietta Corporation* in 1971.[18] It involved the question whether an employer's policy of not hiring women with pre-school age children constituted illegal sex discrimination. The Court of Appeals for the Fifth Circuit had held that the policy did not, because the "discrimination was based on a two-pronged qualification, *i.e.* a woman with pre-school age children," rather than on sex alone.[19] The Supreme Court reversed the decision, stating in part: "The Civil Rights Act of 1964 requires that persons of like qualifications be given employment opportunities irrespective of their sex. The Court of Appeals therefore erred in reading this section as permitting one hiring policy for women and another for men —each having pre-school age children."[20]

THE RIGHT TO PHYSICAL SELF—DETERMINATION

Until recently, most states prohibited a woman from having an abortion unless it was necessary to save her life. A few permitted abortions in certain other cases such as when they were necessary to preserve the health of a pregnant woman or when the pregnancy had resulted from rape.

In January 1973 the Supreme Court ruled that the abortion statutes in effect in most states were unconstitutional. In two cases, involving the constitutionality of the Texas and Georgia abortion statutes, the Court held that the Fourteenth Amendment's protection against deprivation of life, liberty, or property without due process of law includes the protection of the right of privacy. The Court concluded that a woman's right of personal privacy includes her decision on whether or not to have an abortion.[21] Although the right of privacy is not absolute, it may be restricted by state regulation only if the regulation is necessitated by an overriding compelling governmental interest. The Court further held that "the word 'person,' as used in the Fourteenth Amendment, does not include the unborn."

That amendment, it said, has no "pre-natal application," and "the fetus, at most, represents only the potentiality of life."[22]

In applying these principles, the Court stated that after approximately the first trimester of pregnancy the state, "in promoting its interest in the health of the mother, may, if it chooses, regulate the abortion procedure in ways that are reasonably related to maternal health." With regard to the fetus, it said, "For the stage subsequent to viability the State, in promoting its interest in the potentiality of human life, may, if it chooses, regulate, and even proscribe, abortion except where it is necessary, in appropriate medical judgment, for the preservation of the life or health of the mother."[23]

The state may not require that an abortion be performed in a hospital during the first trimester. The state may not require that an abortion be approved by a hospital committee at any stage, since no other medical or surgical procedure requires committee approval. Nor can the concurrence of two other licensed physicians be required. Finally, the state may not impose a residency requirement for securing abortions.[24]

CONCLUSION

In the past ten years we have seen dramatic improvement in the law affecting women as a class, most notably the Supreme Court's decisions in *Frontiero* and the abortion cases, and the enactment of federal laws prohibiting discrimination on the basis of sex. However, it may take women several generations to fully exercise their legal rights, so that these rights will have a real effect on their lives. For example, a 55-year-old woman who has been denied educational or employment opportunities because of sex discrimination cannot make up for it now. It is too late for a 30-year-old welfare mother with eight children to benefit much from the Supreme Court's abortion rulings.

It should also be noted that although the courts that ruled on the cases and the Congress that enacted the laws were heavily dominated by men, their actions were not the result of benevolent paternalism. Women litigants with women lawyers brought many of the key cases, feminist organizations lobbied for the legislation and women in Congress helped push it through, and the activities of the women's movement generally have helped educate the lawmakers.

Finally, there are other legal issues that the women's movement is, or should be, addressing itself to. Is it possible to reform marriage and divorce laws so as to be consistent with feminist philosophy? Is the concept of adult dependency, imbedded in our income tax, social security, retirement, and other laws providing social benefits, consistent with feminist goals? Can reform of the rape laws protect women from violent sexual assaults? Are the legal issues respecting homosexuality, and particularly lesbianism, relevant to feminism? How should the law deal with prostitution, if at all? Perhaps in the next ten years these and other issues of concern to women will be resolved.

Notes

1. *Bradwell v. Illinois,* 83 U.S. (16 Wall.) 130 (1872).
2. 208 U.S. 412 (1908).
3. *Id.* at 422.
4. *Id.* at 421.
5. *Hoyt v. Florida,* 368 U.S. 57, 62.
6. *United States v. St. Clair,* 291 F.Supp. 122, 125 (S.D.N.Y. 1968).
7. *Reed v. Reed,* 404 U.S. 71.
8. 93 Sup. Ct. 1764.
9. Citizens' Advisory Council on the Status of Women, Memorandum on the Proposed Equal Rights Amendment, March 1970.
10. 29 U.S.C. 206(d).
11. 42 U.S.C. 2000e.
12. 20 U.S.C. 1681.
13. 442 F.2d 1119 (9th Cir. 1971).
14. 416 F.2d 711 (1969).
15. *Id.* at 718.
16. 408 F.2d 228 (1969).
17. *Id.* at 236.
18. 400 U.S. 542 (1971).
19. 411 F.2d 1, *rehearing denied,* 416 F.2d 1257 (1969).
20. 400 U.S. at 544.
21. *Roe v. Wade,* 410 U.S. 113; *Doe v. Bolton,* 410 U.S. 179.
22. *Roe v. Wade,* 410 U.S. at 157, 158.
23. *Id.* at 164, 165.
24. *Doe v. Bolton,* 410 U.S. 179.

Suggested Reading

Brown, Emerson, Falk and Freedman, "The Equal Rights Amendment: A Constitutional Basis for Equal Rights for Women," *Yale Law Journal,* 80 (1971), 871.

Chotiner, Renée, "Marriage and the Supreme Court: A Study of Judicial Attitudes and Woman's Legal Status," *Law and Women Series,* no. 2 (1973).

Crozier, Blanche, "Constitutionality of Discrimination Based on Sex," *Boston University Law Review,* 15 (1935), 723.

Crozier, Blanche, "Marital Support," *Boston University Law Review,* 15 (1935), 28.

Davidson, Kenneth M., *et. al., Sex-Based Discrimination: Text, Cases and Materials.* St. Paul: West Publishing Co., 1974.

De Crow, Karen, *Sexist Justice.* New York: McGraw-Hill, 1974.

Eastwood, Mary, "Fighting Job Discrimination—Three Federal Approaches," *Law and Women Series,* no. 1 (1971).

A Guide to Federal Laws Prohibiting Sex Discrimination, U.S. Commission on Civil Rights, 1974.

Handbook on Women Workers, Women's Bureau, U.S. Department of Labor, 1969.

Job Discrimination Handbook, Human Rights for Women, Inc., 1971.

Job-Related Maternity Benefits, Citizens' Advisory Council on Status of Women, position paper, Nov. 1970.

Kanowitz, Leo, *Sex Roles in Law and Society: Cases and Materials.* Albuquerque: University of New Mexico Press, 1973.

Kanowitz, Leo, *Women and the Law* (1969).

Lucas, Roy, "Federal Constitutional Limitations on the Enforcement and Administration of Abortion Statutes," *North Carolina Law Review,* 46 (1968), 730.

A Matter of Simple Justice, Report of the President's Task Force on Women's Rights and Responsibilities, 1970.

Murray, Pauli, and Mary Eastwood, "Jane Crow and the Law: Sex Discrimination and Title VII," *George Washington Law Review,* 34 (1965), 232.

The Proposed Equal Rights Amendment to the United States Constitution. Memorandum, Citizens' Advisory Council on the Status of Women, March 1970.

Report of the Task Force on Family Law and Policy. Citizens' Advisory Council on the Status of Women, 1968.

Report of the Committee on Civil and Political Rights. President's Commission on the Status of Women 1963.

Ross, Susan, *The Rights of Women.* New York: Avon, 1973.

Symposium, Equal Rights Amendment. *Harvard Civil Rights–Civil Liberties Law Review,* 6 (March 1971).

Symposium, Women and the Law, *Valparaiso University Law Review,* 5 (Spring 1971).

Symposium, Women and the Law. *Rutgers Law Review,* 25 (1970), 1.

Symposium, Women and the Criminal Law, 11 *American Criminal Law Review,* 11 (1973), 291.

Symposium, Women's Rights. *Hastings Law Journal,* 23 (1971), 1.

Symposium, Legal Rights of Women. *New York Law Forum,* 17 (1971), 335.

Why Witches Were W

Mary Nelson

Misplacement of one social order by another
leads inevitably to a set of issues and conflicts.
These arise like sparks at each point where the new
and the old make contact, where they treat the same
phenomenon differently. The crime of witchcraft in
Renaissance Europe arose at the points in time and
space where the new industrial order was displacing
the old feudal order.

One issue that arose was whether the Church or
the State is the final judge of human behavior. This
materialized as a jurisdictional dispute between ecclesiastical courts (the Inquisition) and secular courts. A
second issue was whether the feudal family or the
industrial job should have first claim on human
energies. This materialized as a dispute over the proper place of women. In the language of the time, it
became the question of who is a witch.

The practice of sorcery by the various European
tribes was probably a relic of the Stone Age, but the
crime of witchcraft was invented by the Inquisition
in the late fifteenth century. The Inquisitors' notions
of witchcraft, such as their belief that witches ride
broomsticks at night to orgiastic black masses in the
forest where they fornicate with the Devil and feast

Between the years 1400 and 1700 approximately half a million people, most of them women, were burned as witches.

on roasted children, was a mixture of archaic beliefs about sorcerers and contemporary fears of evil in women.* It was no harmless fantasy. Between the years 1400 and 1700 approximately half a million people, most of them women, were burned as witches.[1] The interest of the Inquisition and its successors in spreading a mortal fear of witches throughout western Europe and in developing a science for finding and punishing them is the first concern of this paper. The second is to explain why witches were women.

During the early Middle Ages, when western Europe was a disorganized backwash of the thriving Middle Eastern kingdoms, the magical arts were treated with leniency by Church and State. Sorcery was punished only by the State, and only when it had resulted in loss of life or the destruction of property.[2] In these cases the sorcerer was punished for the fruits of his craft, not for sorcery itself. The Church, for its part, maintained that witchcraft was an illusion.[3] Missionaries to the northern tribes hoped that as their charges became fully Christianized, the pagan lore would fall into disuse and be forgotten.[4] But it was not. Persons skilled in casting spells and concocting herbal medicines continued to be feared and employed at all levels of medieval society.[5]

Early in the thirteenth century a train of events began that eventually resulted in the creation of the crime of witchcraft and the burning of thousands of witches. It began in Toulouse, in southern France. The revival of trade on the Mediterranean had fostered there the growth of a tolerant and cosmopolitan society, in which painting and chivalrous poetry flourished.[6] Within this society an ascetic, dualistic

---

* In the Teutonic tradition there was a belief that witches were cannibals and that once a year, on the first of May or Saint Walpurgis's night, there was a nocturnal gathering of witches called the *trolla-thing*, where they ate and sang. What the Dominican Inquisitors added was the belief that witches made a pact with the Devil, that they ate specifically children at their nocturnal gathering, and that the primary activity at the gathering was fornication with the Devil. Whereas the traditional witch was something of a power unto herself because of her knowledge of herbs and potions, the witch of the Dominicans was merely a tool of the Devil, who possessed and controlled her. For a fuller description of the traditional beliefs, see H. C. Lea, *A History of the Inquisition of the Middle Ages,* 3 vols. (New York: Russell, 2d printing, 1956), III, 401–8. For a crosscultural and historical discussion of fertility cults, see J. L. Henderson and M. Oakes, *The Wisdom of the Serpent: The Myths of Death, Rebirth, and Resurrection* (New York: Collier, 1963).

sect from Bulgaria, known as the Cathars, made converts not only among the towns-folk but also among the nobility and the clergy.[7] Even the bishop was known to be interested in their views. Pope Innocent III was displeased by these developments, as one might expect. Fearing that the heretics would create a breach in the other-wise solid monarchy—Christendom—over which he ruled,[8] he sought first to lure them back into the fold with the gentle preaching of ascetic preachers who differed from the heretics only in that they remained loyal to the Church. The Dominican Order was created for this purpose; their emblem shows two dogs shepherding an unruly flock.[9] When their preaching failed to have the desired effect, Innocent called for a military crusade against the heretical province, much like the Crusades he and others before him had sent against the infidels in the Holy Land. The knights of northern France, who long had coveted the lands to the south, responded to Innocent's call.[10] Their victory was swift and bloody, but the heretics remained heretical and the local populace became still more united against the invaders from the north.

Innocent made one last effort to bring the heretics back to the Church and ensure the loyalty of the southerners to their new seignior, the King of France. He created the Inquisition, an ecclesastical court answerable only to himself. The in-quisitorial procedure was modeled after the Roman trial procedures for treason.[11] Inquisitors, most of whom were recruited from the Dominican Order, were em-powered to search out offenders, use torture to obtain confessions, deny legal advisers to the accused, and confiscate the property of the convicted. Their goal was to persuade heretics to repent. If, however, they decided that a heretic was irretrievably lost to God, he was handed over to the State to be executed.*

The new court proved to be an effective tool for handling the problems of disloyalty and heresy. In 1245 the last stronghold of the Cathars fell and two hundred were executed in a single day.[12] Survivors fled to Normandy or went underground to be periodically discovered by the Inquisition throughout the next century.[13] By 1250, however, the Inquisitors found themselves without heretics and began searching for new unruly flocks to shepherd. In 1257 they petitioned Pope Alexander IV to extend their jurisdiction to sorcery, but he refused.[14] He reaffirmed the official Church policy of treating witchcraft and sorcery as an illu-sion and urged the Inquisitors not to be distracted from their true work, that of recalling heretics to the Church. Subsequent popes were similarly petitioned, and they responded in the same way. During this time the Inquisitor Bernard Gui pub-

---

* J. Madaule, *The Albigensian Crusade: An Historical Essay,* trans. B. Wall (New York: Ford-ham Univ. Press, 1967). The Church dealt only with spiritual matters. The dispostion of the heretic's body thus fell to the State.

lished a handbook for interrogating sorcerers and a guide for recognizing magical practices.[15] Similar inquisitorial handbooks had previously appeared as guides to the prosecution of earlier heresies, such as Catharism and Waldensianism..Gui's guidelines make no mention of night-flying, which later became the inspiration for the Inquisitors' belief in the Sabat, as the black mass was called; nor do they mention the pact with the Devil and the sexual practices that later provided the basis for most of the accusations against witches. From this we may surmise that the Inquisitors did not yet hold these beliefs.

Despite official discouragement, the Inquisition conducted a small number of witch trials in the Pyrenees during this period.[16] Finally, in 1326, Pope John XXII provided the sanction the Inquisitors had sought for nearly seventy years. He had a personal stake in the issue because he feared that there were conspirators in his own palace who plotted to poison him using witchcraft. He issued a bull, the *Super illius specula,* which declared that although witchcraft is an illusion all who *used the services* of sorcerers were to be punished as heretics and all books on the subject were to be burned.[17] Armed with this authority, the Inquisition launched a witch craze in Toulouse and Normandy that continued for a full century, until the 1430's, and resulted in the execution of several hundred persons, mostly peasant women.[18] At the close of this period, more inquisitorial handbooks for witch hunting appeared, written by Inquisitors who participated in the craze in Toulouse.

The most important document to appear at this time was a paper issued in 1458 by the Inquisitor Nicholas Jaquerius,[19] who argued that the existing sect of witches was *different* from the traditional variety. Thus traditional Church policy, which held that witchcraft was an illusion, was no longer applicable. According to Jaquerius the new breed of witches all attended the Sabat, where they copulated with demons, desecrated Christian symbols, and feasted on unbaptized infants. Moreover, they were certainly heretics, for even if the Sabat were an illusion, the witches' belief in it indicated that they were followers of the Devil and pagan goddesses even in their waking hours.

The final victory of the Inquisition followed shortly. In 1451 the pope had appointed Hugh le Noir Inquisitor General in France, and he had already prosecuted a number of peasant women in the northern town of Arras.[20] In 1484 two Inquisitors, Jakob Sprenger and Henry Krämer, petitioned Pope Innocent VIII for a similar appointment to the Rhineland. He replied with the bull *Summis desiderantes,* which not only granted their petition but also affirmed the Church's belief in the heresy of witchcraft and in its responsibility, through the Inquisition, to remove that foul cancer from Christendom. The bull was published at the front of a handbook for witch hunters called the *Malleus Maleficarum (The Witches' Hammer).* Sprenger and Krämer wrote the *Malleus* a few years after they obtained the bull,

> **. . . since the Devil's ace in the hole was free
> sex, women were expected to be more prone
> to go over to his side because they were
> simply more lustful.**

but by placing the bull in the front they gave the appearance that the handbook
had been commissioned by Innocent.[21]

Of all the witch hunters' handbooks written, the *Malleus* was the most widely
used. It appeared to be authoritative, and since it was printed on the newly invented printing press, it was more widely distributed than any of the earlier handbooks could have been.[22] Even so, the *Malleus* contained little that was new. It
reiterated exhaustively the arguments of previous handbooks and restated Jaquerius's observations about the practices of the "new" witch cult. But an important
section was added to explain why witches were women, or rather, why women were
witches. The *Malleus* was thereby transformed into a classic statement of misogyny.
How did a woman become a witch? Through demonic possession. How did the
Devil come to possess a woman? According to the authors of the *Malleus*, her soul
was persuaded to shift its allegiance from God to the Devil. A strong spirit could
not be conned into such a bad bargain, but women were thought to have weak,
frivolous, even malicious natures. Any woman was an easy mark for the Devil,
while demonic possession remained rare, they believed, among men. Furthermore,
since the Devil's ace in the hole was free sex, women were expected to be more
prone to go over to his side because they were simply more lustful. As our authors
explained:

> All witchcraft comes from carnal lust, which is in women insatiable. See
> Proverbs xxx: There are three things that are never satisfied, yea, a fourth
> thing which say not, It is enough; that is, the mouth of the womb. Wherefore
> for the sake of fulfilling their lusts they consort even with devils. More such
> reasons could be brought forward, but to the understanding it is sufficiently
> clear that it is no matter for wonder that there are more women than men
> found infected with the heresy of witchcraft. And in consequence of this, it is
> better called the heresy of witches than of wizards, since the name is taken
> from the more powerful party. And blessed be the Highest Who has so far
> preserved the male sex from so great a crime: for since He was willing to be
> born and to suffer for us, therefore He has granted to men this privilege.[23]

No doubt the Inquisitors rejoiced at Innocent's bull, for it condoned and
even encouraged the witch hunting they had furtively engaged in already and promised to keep them in business a while longer. Ironically, however, it brought their

demise, for the secular authorities would not tolerate the use of such a powerful political tool as witch trials by anyone but themselves. The Inquisition was expelled from the Tyrol in 1485 and from France in 1491.[24] In both cases, Inquisitors had inadvisedly interfered with important persons of state by bringing them to trial for witchcraft. The Italian cities also refused to give the Inquisitors free rein. Most of the papal bulls dealing with witchcraft following the *Summis desiderantes* consisted of appointments of Inquisitors to uncooperative Italian cities.[25] Spain had succeeded in making the Inquisition a state institution just a few years before Innocent issued his bull. The Spanish Inquisitors were more interested in *conversos* than witches, but the principle was the same.* Isabel and Ferdinand allowed the Inquisition to function in their realm only while it remained under royal control.[26] In Germany the Inquisition had never been very active, and by 1517 it was unable to silence Martin Luther.†

In short, just at the time the Inquisition was in a position to hunt witches in the grand style, it was dismantled by the secular authorities, who took the task upon themselves. The witch craze the Inquisition had initiated continued for two more centuries and became far more brutal than it had ever been before.

During the 1500's the persecution of witches was conducted in connection with the Reformation and the Counter Reformation.[27] The Protestants found scriptural support for their witch hunting in Exodus 22: "Thou shalt not suffer a witch to live." They also relied on most of the Dominican demonology, even though they rejected the rest of Catholic doctrine.[28] Luther himself believed in witches and thought that his mother had been bewitched. He attributed the fact that he often felt sick when he visited Wartburg to spells cast by his adversaries there.[29] Like his Dominican predecessors, he believed that all witches attended the Sabat, that they made pacts with the Devil, and that they were lustful and prone to sexual misbehavior. Many of the persons who were actually executed as witches in Luther's Saxony were members of a rival Protestant sect, the Anabaptists, and particularly Anabaptist women preachers.[30] The Anabaptist men were generally accused of heresy instead. This practice was consistent with Luther's view that women should remain at home caring for their husbands and raising their children to

---

* The Inquisition concerned itself only with wayward Christians. Nonchristians were not under its jurisdiction. In Spain large numbers of Jews and Moors were registered with the State as converts to Christianity (*conversos*), and then accused of irregularities in the practice of their religion. In this way they became subject to the Inquisition.

† Lea, *History of the Inquisition*, II, 420–26. The Inquisition was finally discredited in Germany because of its participation in feuds among the theologians at the University of Cologne.

be proper members of the Elect.[31] Marriage, he felt, was a holy vocation. He closed convents and brothels alike and sent the inmates out to marry. Witchcraft became a crime in Saxony in 1572.[32]

Calvin was more skeptical of the Dominican witch beliefs than Luther. He believed that the Devil could do nothing without the permission of God and that he could never conquer the faithful. Nevertheless, Calvin regarded the Devil as an alert and energetic enemy.[33] In 1545 he led a campaign against witchcraft in Geneva that resulted in the execution of 31 witches. Calvinist missionaries succeeded in spreading the craze to Scotland in 1563. When James VI of Scotland, a Calvinist, became King of England, he revised the lenient statutes dealing with witchcraft and wrote his own handbook for witch hunters, the *Demonologie.* Under Queen Elizabeth the English witch craze became specifically anti-Catholic. Bishop Jewel of Switzerland demanded that Elizabeth take action against the witches lest they take over her kingdom. The witch craze that followed was worst in the Catholic counties of Essex and Lancashire. Calvinist missionaries from England also spread the craze to Bavaria, Baden, Württemberg, and Mecklenberg. Bishop Palladius, the Reformer of Denmark, declared that all who used Catholic prayers were witches and must be burned. [34]

During the Catholic reconquests beginning in the 1580's, the Jesuits were highly active at ferreting out witches. Many of the accused were obstinate Protestants. In France witches were found primarily in Huguenot areas, such as Orleans, Languedoc, Normandy, and Navarre. Up to that time France had remained relatively free of witch trials, in part because the monarchy wished to protect the good name of Joan of Arc,[35] who was burned by the Inquisition as a witch. But in the 1590's whole villages accused of witchcraft were burned in the Rhineland, and the Spanish bishops of Flanders launched an anti-Protestant witch craze there.[36]

Throughout both the Protestant and Catholic witch crazes, a large number of peasant women who were not particularly involved in the political conflicts at the root of the accusations found themselves accused nonetheless, for it was common practice to first accuse a few women and then, through the use of torture, elicit the names of suspected (male) political enemies or rivals from them.[37] The enemies were thus indicted and brought to trial not as Catholics or Protestants but as witches, making it nearly impossible for them to defend themselves. The continued execution of women along with political enemies served to reaffirm the validity of the fundamental witch beliefs. If all witchcraft accusations had been brought against political rivals, the political motivation of the trials would soon have become too transparent for the populace to tolerate, which in fact happened in the Tyrol in the 1520's.[38] As it was, the major critics of the witch hunts confined their remarks to the injustices in the trial procedures, particularly the use of torture, and never attacked the fundamental beliefs that supported the demonology. The critics sought to prevent the use of witch trials to harass the innocent, but they left intact the belief in the reality of demons and the possibility of demonic possession.[39] They did not question the misogyny of those beliefs. So long as witchcraft was seen as a preeminently female crime, it remained credible, since to their way of thinking it was in the nature of women to commit such atrocities. Thus, despite the fact that women were not the actual target of the Reformation and Counter Reformation witch hunts, they remained the inspiration for the underlying beliefs and continued to be the victims as well.

The final chapter in the witch craze was the worst of all. During the closing years of the Thirty Years' War there appeared a number of "burning judges" who grew rich from the property confiscated from the witches they had burned. A fairly large proportion of the persons accused of witchcraft during this period were men, especially wealthy men.[40] As many as fifty to one hundred were burned each year in villages in Bavaria and along the Rhine between 1620 and 1630,[41] and the judges who had condemned them subsequently appeared in fine carriages with their wives dressed in the most expensive gowns.[42] During these years the local princes and their small bureaucracies were hard-pressed for funds to maintain the machinery of government.[43] The Thirty Years' War had depleted their cash reserves, and often the surrounding land was ruined as well. Witch trials constituted a convenient and lucrative source of income.

The witch craze ended when it was suppressed. In Mecklenberg the trials were halted by the Swedes, who invaded in the 1630's. Frederick II halted the trials in Germany following the Thirty Years' War in order to establish some semblance of order and peace in his empire. The Anglican nobility of England had never been convinced of the need for witch trials and simply revoked the witch statutes of the Calvinist James VI after there had been no accusations of witchcraft for several decades.[44] Some students of the witch craze have argued that by the seventeenth century the witch trials had to end because the new spirit of science and progress made believing in witchcraft ludicrous.[45] It is possible that a growing habit of skepticism contributed to the final end of the craze, but the critics who wrote at the end of the period added virtually nothing to what the earliest critics of witch trials had written.[46] It appears more likely that the witch craze ended because the institutions that had found it advantageous to persecute witches no longer had the power to do so. The Inquisition was dismantled by the monarchs. The local judges, who once were the most active in burning witches in the Holy Roman Empire, were not able to continue after the Thirty Years' War because the legal system was centralized and kept under the control of the Emperor.

We have seen that there were three fairly distinct periods in the European

The theme of the witch hunts from the beginning was the culpability of women.

witch craze. The first, the ecclesiastical period, began approximately in the 1320's and continued intermittently until the 1490's, when the Inquisition was expelled from France and captured in Spain. The second was the period of the Reformation and Counter Reformation, during the 1560's through the 1590's, in which the craze was an extension of the religio-political conflicts of the time. This was followed by a short but essentially secular period in which the officers of the courts sought to profit personally from the conviction of witches. These "burning judges" appeared at the close of the Thirty Years' War. Throughout the witch craze the vast majority of the accused were women, particularly peasant women. The theme of the witch hunts from the beginning was the culpability of women. Some other equally disliked and defenseless group, such as Jews, lepers, or children, could have played the role just as well. The questions that remains, then is why witches were women.

The Dominican Inquisitors who wrote the *Malleus* and other related demonologies saw witches—and women, the two being inseparable—as a true threat to the survival of Christendom. Witches not only destroyed crops and sent storms to sailing expeditions, but threatened to destroy the whole population by killing infants in the womb and taking away men's generative powers. These fears were not entirely fantasy. At the time the Inquisitors were formulating their witch beliefs, enormous changes were taking place in the relationship of women to the social order. The development of an industrial system of producing goods and urban living patterns made the medieval family structure obsolete and required changes in the make-up of the labor force. Both of these new conditions made it necessary for women to step outside their traditional social roles. The medieval family was primarily a property-holding institution,[47] in which the wife's main duty was to provide male heirs for the family holdings, if any, and to add to her husband's fortunes through her dowry.[48] A woman who did not marry commonly entered a convent,[49] if her family was rich; otherwise she stayed home to help work the family land. When a family moved to the city, however, it became a buying unit dependent on a cash income. Members of the family accordingly sought employment in the guilds or with the large industrial manufacturers. Daughters who did not marry and could not afford to enter convents were either apprenticed to a trade or sent out to fend for themselves,[50] since very few urban-industrial families could afford to support unemployed members.

These new conditions raised the basic issues of women's participation in the industrial-urban labor force and the desirability of using various methods of birth control to limit family size. These may be reduced to a single issue: what is the proper relationship of a woman to the institution of the family? Medieval society gave two cultural responses. The first was to glorify woman's traditional role. In the fourteenth century (but beginning earlier in Languedoc, before the Crusade against the Cathars) woman became an object of respect, even of worship.[51] The Troubadors developed a poetry that consisted almost entirely of praise for the chaste lady locked in her castle tower.[52] At the same time there arose the cult of the Virgin Mary, in which the Virgin was worshipped as the ideal woman. She was viewed as entirely sexless (clerics argued about whether even her conception was immaculate, just as Christ's was)[53] and devoted to helping others. Numerous legends appeared at the time in which the Virgin intervened to protect mortals from assailants, Satan, and even the judgment of God.[54]

The second response to changes in women's role was the development of the witch beliefs, in which women were protrayed as the polar opposite of the Virgin. To understand this response fully, we must take a closer look at the economic and social conditions that faced women at the time.

The pressure on women to enter the labor force resulted not only from their dependence on cash income, mentioned earlier, but from the considerable hurdles to marriage in the new industrial society. To put it simply, marriageable men were in short supply.[55] Guild rules forbade members who had not yet reached the status of master to marry, and as the population increased in the late 1200's and again in the 1400's, a journeyman's prospects of becoming a master became poorer and poorer. At the same time, and this was perhaps more important than the problem of guild restrictions, men who were employed by the large manufacturers (usually in the textile and mining industries) lived too close to starvation to be able to marry. The new urban proletariat was drawn mainly from peasant families who could no longer support their children on the family land holdings. The rural emigrants to the cities were so plentiful that urban wages remained extremely low, and business fluctuations created chronic insecurity among the hordes of urban laborers.[56]

What was to become of women in the cities who could not find husbands? Very few had parents who were able to continue supporting them, in the traditional pattern. There are numerous records of the daughters of tradesmen being apprenticed to the family trade. Many were also apprenticed to enter the traditional female trades of spinning and weaving. However, if the family was unable to provide for an unmarried daughter in this way, she either became a prostitute or found employment with one of the large manufacturers, or both.[57] There are records of contemporary laborers complaining that employers used rural workers, women, and the foreign-born to break strikes and keep wages low.[58] There is some evidence, though records are understandably poor, that the number of prostitutes increased rapidly during the period of early industrial development.[59] In the late 1200's, in some towns, new laws were passed imposing stiff fines or public punishment for slandering a chaste woman by calling her a prostitute.[60] During the early 1300's the towns along the Rhine and in Alsace-Lorraine, where new industries were rapidly developing, passed laws aimed at confining prostitution to certain streets and houses.

There were some efforts to develop more acceptable alternatives for unmarried women than prostitution or entering the labor force. In the 1200's and 1300's a number of daughters of rich bourgeois families used their personal wealth to establish secular convents. If their families had been more wealthy, they would have bought their daughters' entrance into convents, as the aristocracy did. The secular convents they established, called Beguine houses, were open to all women who wished to remain chaste and earn their living by manual labor, usually spinning and weaving. The Beguines encountered enormous difficulties because the Church accused them of heresy and sought to place them under the supervision of the male clerical orders, the Dominicans and Franciscans. This proved unsatisfactory to the Beguines because they were harassed by monks seeking sexual favors from them. When they complained to the pope about these abuses, he responded by requiring all new members of the organization to be over forty years old. The Beguines were also harassed by the guilds, which considered them a source of economic competition and invoked city ordinances forbidding nonguild craft work to close the Beguine houses.[61] Most of the Beguines eventually became absorbed into the ecclesiastical structure as tertiaries (clerics who live in the world rather than the monastery and have no office in the Church). The few houses that survived became hospitals or poorhouses, primarily because the need for such institutions was very great.[62]

The economic expansion of the 1200's, as we have seen, created new work patterns and living arrangements for the peasantry and especially for women. It also led to the growth of numerous new cities along the Rhine, in Flanders, and in England, a substantial increase in population, the perfection of the money system, and even the settling of new lands.[63] It was interrupted in the 1300's by two serious natural disasters. The first was a terrible famine from 1315 to 1317, which appears to have taken a greater toll on the population than any previous European famine on record. Much more devastating was the second disaster, an epidemic of the Plague that killed about a third of the European population between 1347 and 1350. The disease reappeared in localized outbreaks until the end of the century. The death toll was especially high in the cities, though city dwellers escaping to the countryside succeeded in bringing the Plague there too.[64]

In the aftermath of the Plague, surviving peasants and wage laborers found themselves in an advantageous position. The labor shortage produced by the drop in population created a substantial increase both in real wages and in the prices peasants could command for the food they brought into the cities. For the first time they were able to include meat regularly in their own diets, and the economic insecurity they had experienced for nearly two centuries was alleviated. Under such favorable conditions, we might expect the population to increase rapidly to its former size. But it did not. In fact, the population of Europe did not begin its next growth spurt—one that extends to our own time—until the 1700's. This lag can be partly accounted for by the periodic return of the Plague and by the continuation of the Hundred Years' War in France and England. These factors were insufficient, however, to maintain the depressed level of the population. There is evidence that a third and more important factor was at work. During the second half of the fourteenth century, the reduction of the birth rate was considerably greater than the loss of population (i.e., potential parents). This indicates that some form of contraception or infanticide or both was being practiced.[65]

It is not difficult to account for the use of birth control at that time. A large part of the population had suddenly been introduced to a higher standard of living as a result of high wages. They did not wish to jeopardize their new prosperity by raising large families and were no longer on the land where they needed them. Many did not marry, and those who did limited the number of children they had. The Church complained of the widespread use of *coitus interruptus* by married and unmarried persons to prevent pregnancy,[66] which suggests that this was the most commonly used method of contraception. There is also evidence that infanticide was being practiced.[67] In England during the 1300's and 1400's, there was an "unmistakeable deficiency in the number of female children born, both among the more prosperous landholding groups and in servile families."[68]

Thus, during the century preceding the witch craze, when the demonology and witch beliefs of the Dominican Inquisitors were being formulated, women were responding to the demands of urban-industrial life by stepping outside the traditional female role. Owing to the shortage of available men, many were entering the labor market or turning to prostitution instead of marrying. Moreover, many were apparently using contraception and infanticide during the late 1300's and into the 1400's to limit the size of their families, against the teachings of the Churches. Seen in this context, the Dominicans' charge that witches took away men's generative powers, killed infants, and publicly indulged their sexual lust with with no eye to childbearing do not appear so bizarre. It is also reasonable that the Dominicans should have been especially suspicious of midwives, since they were

The Protestants killed Catholics as witches, the Catholics burned the Protestants, and certain enterprising judges burned whole villages . . . .

expert in methods of birth control, and most likely cooperated in abortions and infanticides. The demonologists were mistaken in their belief that these acts were committed for the purposes of demonic ritual; but it should not surprise us that the Dominicans responded to social innovations in religious terms.

The witch is the medieval stereotype of the "bad woman." She personally is sexually unproductive, and she destroys the fruit of other women's wombs. In addition, she is an adultress in the most fundamental way. Unlike the Virgin and the nun, who give themselves to God, the witch has turned from God to take another lover, the Devil. Some males were also accused of witchcraft, but the witch was preeminently female because of her special association with birth and the cycle of nature. From this perspective, we may see the witch beliefs as a backlash that occurred within a highly conventional and invested part of the feudal order in response to changes in the social function and behavior of a problematic but relatively powerless group—women. The *Malleus Maleficarum* and similar works on witchcraft were highly scholarly manifestations of a general fear of the changes taking place in the medieval social order, particularly in the medieval family. The witch was an excellent symbolic vehicle for expressing those fears. The Dominicans shared these fears even with the Humanists of the day, who showed great concern for the proper education of children and the need for women to remain good wives and mothers. Luther, as we saw earlier, was particularly eager that women should marry and find their true vocation in caring for their husbands and children.

In the fifteenth century the Dominicans needed new kinds of heresy to give their organization a purpose for continuing. They found that witchcraft was just the heresy they needed. In Spain, where industrialization had not begun, the Jews, an indigenous minority group that a large part of the Spanish population was eager to persecute, were selected as the target rather than women. Eventually the trials came to be used by other organizations to persecute their own demons. The Protestants killed Catholics as witches, the Catholics burned the Protestants, and certain enterprising judges burned whole villages, male and female, in order to confiscate their victims' wealth. In the end, the witch trials became a secular political tool.

The disjunctions in the female role that inspired the witch craze are still with us. We have yet to resolve the issues of birth control and the participation of women in the labor market. Clearly, the displacement of the feudal social order by the industrial order remains unfinished. Meanwhile, the industrial and urban system that precipitated the events we have discussed is itself being replaced by a highly centralized, cosmopolitan, bureaucratic, communications-oriented system that makes the familiar form of the debate on the viability of the family and the proper place of women in society obsolete. As the new order becomes stronger and displaces more and more of the old industrial order, new issues built into this new displacement process will replace the old ones.

Notes

1. G. L. Kittredge, *Notes on Witchcraft* (1907), as cited by E. P. Currie in "Crimes Without Criminals: Witchcraft and Its Controls in Renaissance Europe," *Law and Society Review,* III (1968), 10.
2. H. C. Lea, *A History of the Inquisition of the Middle Ages,* 3 vols. (New York: Russell, 2d printing, 1956), III, 408.
3. *Ibid.,* p. 494. Church policy was contained in the *capitulum Episcopi,* which is attributed to an obscure church council called the Council of Anquira.
4. *Ibid.,* pp. 485-96.
5. J. Michelet, *Satanism and Witchcraft: A Study in Medieval Superstition,* trans. A. R. Allison (New York: Citadel Press, 1939), pp. 86-87.
6. J. Madaule, *The Albigensian Crusade: An Historical Essay,* trans. B. Wall (New York: Fordham Univ. Press, 1967).
7. W. Wakefield and A. Evans, eds., *Heresies of the High Middle Ages* (New York: Columbia Univ. Press, 1969), p. 36.
8. Madaule, *Albigensian Crusade.*
9. .P. Mandonnet, *St. Dominic and His Work,* trans. M. B. Larkin (St. Louis, Mo.: Herder Book Co., 1944).
10. Madaule, *Albigensian Crusade.*
11. Lea, *History of the Inquisition,* I, 151.
12. T. Szasz, *The Manufacture of Madness: A Comparative Study of the Inquisition and the Mental Health Movement* (New York: Harper and Row, 1970), p. 294.
13. H. Trevor-Roper, *The European Witch-Craze of the Sixteenth and Seventeenth Centuries* (New York: Harper and Row, 1969), p. 175. Note discussion of G. L. Burr.
14. *Ibid.,* p. 103.
15. Lea, *History of the Inquisition,* III, 449.
16. Trevor-Roper, *European Witch-Craze,* p. 102.
17. Lea, *History of the Inquisition,* III, 452-53.
18. Trevor-Roper, *European Witch-Craze,* p. 103.
19. Lea, *History of the Inquisition,* III, 497.
20. *Ibid.,* pp. 519-30.
21. Trevor-Roper, *European Witch-Craze,* p. 101.
22. *Ibid.,* p. 102.
23. J. Sprenger and H. Krämer, *Malleus Maleficarum,* trans. M. Summers (Suffolk, Eng.: John Rodker, 1928), p. 47.

24. Lea, *History of the Inquisition,* III, 530, 541.
25. H. C. Lea, *Materials Toward a History of Witchcraft,* ed. A. C. Howland, 3 vols. (New York: Thomas Yoseloff, 1957), pp. 220–29.
26. H. C. Lea, *A History of the Inquisition of Spain* (London: Macmillan, 1906).
27. See G. Länglin, as cited in Lea, *Materials,* III, 1079.
28. Trevor-Roper, *European Witch-Craze,* p. 137.
29. Lea, *Materials,* III, 417.
30. R. Clifford, Univ. of Chicago School of Divinity, personal communication, March 1969.
31. R. Bainton, *Women of the Reformation in Germany and Italy* (Minneapolis: Augsburg Pub. House, 1971), p. 10.
32. Lea, *Materials,* I, 417.
33. *Ibid.,* p. 428.
34. Trevor-Roper, *European Witch-Craze,* p. 143.
35. Lea, *History of the Inquisition,* III, 530.
36. Trevor-Roper, *European Witch-Craze,* p. 139.
37. Lea, *History of the Inquisition,* III; see the discussion of the treatment of the witches of Arras, beginning p. 519, and for a discussion of the use of torture, see pp. 513–14.
38. Trevor-Roper, *European Witch-Craze,* p. 135.
39. *Ibid.,* p. 148.
40. E. P. Currie, "Crimes Without Criminals: Witchcraft and Its Controls in Renaissance Europe," *Law and Society Review,* III (1968), 25.
41. Trevor-Roper, *European Witch-Craze,* p. 156.
42. Currie, "Crimes Without Criminals," p. 22.
43. Trevor-Roper, *European Witch-Craze,* pp. 67–77.
44. Currie, "Crimes Without Criminals," p. 32.
45. For example, H. C. Lea, in the works cited above; Andrew Dickson White, *A History of the Warfare Between Science and Theology in Christendom* (New York: Appleton, 1896); and Joseph Hansen, *Quellen und Untersuchungen zur geschichte des hexenwahns* (Bonn, Germany: C. Georgi, 1901).
46. Trevor-Roper, *European Witch-Craze,* p. 161.
47. P. G. Aries, *Centuries of Childhood: A Social History of Family Life* (New York: Knopf, 1962). See also W. Goodsell, *History of the Family as a Social and Educational Institution* (New York: MacMillan, 1915).
48. B. Jarrett, *Social Theories of the Middle Ages,* 1200–1500 (London: Ernest Benn, 1926), p. 57.
49. E. W. McDonnell, *The Beguines and Beghards in Medieval Culture* (New Brunswick, N.J.: Rutgers Univ. Press, 1954), p. 83.
50. *Ibid.,* p. 87.
51. Editors of *Life, Epic of Man* (New York: Time, 1961). See also Michelet, *Satanism and Witchcraft,* p. 102.
52. Denis de Rougement, *Love in the Western World,* trans. M. Belgion (New York: Pantheon, 1956).
53. Lea, *History of the Inquisition,* III, 597–610.
54. Editors of *Life, Epic of Man.*
55. McDonnell, *Beguines and Beghards,* p. 84.
56. N. Cohn, *The Pursuit of the Millennium* (New York: Oxford Univ. Press, 1970). See also

R. F. Heilleiner, "The Population of Europe from the Black Death to the Eve of the Vital Revolution," in E. E. Rich and C. H. Wilson, eds., *The Cambridge Economic History of Europe* (Cambridge, Eng.: Cambridge Univ. Press, 1967), IV, 84.

57. McDonnell, *Beguines and Beghards,* p. 86.
58. P. Boissonnade, *Life and Work in Medieval Europe,* trans. E. Power (London: Routledge and Kegan Paul, 1927), p. 205.
59. Heilleiner, "Population of Europe," p. 72.
60. P. La Crois, *History of Prostitution,* trans. S. Putnam (Chicago: Pascal Covici, 1926), II, 113.
61. McDonnell, *Beguines and Beghards,* pp. 270–77.
62. *Ibid.,* p. 82.
63. H. Pirenne, *Economic and Social History of Medieval Europe* (New York: Harcourt, Brace, and World, 1937).
64. Heilleiner, "Population of Europe," p. 6.
65. *Ibid.,* p. 71.
66. *Ibid.,* p. 70.
67. W. Goodsell, *A History of the Family as a Social and Educational Institution* (New York: Macmillan, 1915), p. 212.
68. Heilleiner, "Population of Europe," p. 71.

The Liberation of Black Women

Pauli Murray

Black women, historically, have been doubly
victimized by the twin immoralities of Jim
Crow and Jane Crow. Jane Crow refers to the entire
range of assumptions, attitudes, stereotypes, customs,
and arrangements which have robbed women of a
positive self-concept and prevented them from participating fully in society as equals with men. Traditionally, racism and sexism in the United States have
shared some common origins, displayed similar manifestations, reinforced one another, and are so deeply
intertwined in the country's institutions that the
successful outcome of the struggle against racism will
depend in large part upon the simultaneous elimination of all discrimination based upon sex. Black
women, faced with these dual barriers, have often
found that sex bias is more formidable than racial
bias. If anyone should ask a Negro woman in America
what has been her greatest achievement, her honest
answer would be, "I survived!"

Negro women have endured their double
burden with remarkable strength and fortitude. With
dignity they have shared with black men a partnership as members of an embattled group excluded
from the normal protections of the society and en-

Reprinted from *Voices of the New Feminism,* Mary L. Thompson, ed. (Boston: Beacon, 1970), by permission of the author. Copyright © 1970 by Pauli Murray.

351

gaged in a struggle for survival during nearly four centuries of a barbarous slave trade, two centuries of chattel slavery, and a century or more of illusive citizenship. Throughout this struggle, into which has been poured most of the resources and much of the genius of successive generations of American Negroes, these women have often carried a disproportionate share of responsibility for the black family, as they strove to keep its integrity intact against a host of indignities to which it has been subjected. Black women have not only stood shoulder to shoulder with black men in every phase of the struggle, but they have often continued to stand firmly when their men were destroyed by it. Few blacks are unfamiliar with that heroic, if formidable, figure exhorting her children and grandchildren to overcome every obstacle and humiliation and to "Be somebody!"

In the battle for survival, Negro women developed a tradition of independence and self-reliance, characteristics which according to the late Dr. F. Franklin Frazier, Negro sociologist, have "provided generally a pattern of equalitarian relationship between men and women in America." The historical factors which have fostered the black women's feeling of independence have been the economic necessity to earn a living to help support their families—if indeed they were not the sole breadwinners—and the need for the black community to draw heavily upon the resources of all of its members in order to survive.

Yet these survival values have often been distorted, and the qualities of strength and independence observable in many Negro women have been stereotyped as "female dominance" attributed to the "matriarchal" character of the Negro family developed during slavery and its aftermath. The popular conception is that because society has emasculated the black male, he has been unable to assume his economic role as head of the household and the black woman's earning power has placed her in a dominant position. The black militant's cry for the retrieval of black manhood suggests an acceptance of this stereotype, an association of masculinity with male dominance and a tendency to treat the values of self-reliance and independence as purely masculine traits. Thus, while blacks generally have recognized the fusion of white supremacy and male dominance (note the popular expressions "The Man" and "Mr. Charlie"), male spokesmen for Negro rights have sometimes pandered to sexism in their fight against racism. When the nationally known civil rights leader James Farmer ran for Congress against Mrs. Shirley Chisholm in 1968, his campaign literature stressed the need for a "strong male image" and a "man's voice" in Washington.

If idealized values of masculinity and femininity are used as criteria, it would be hard to say whether the experience of slavery subjected the black male to any greater loss of his manhood than the black female of her womanhood. The chasm between the slave woman and her white counterpart (whose own enslavement was

If black males suffered from real and psychological castration, black females bore the burden of real or psychological rape.

masked by her position as a symbol of high virtue and an object of chivalry) was as impassable as the gulf between the male slave and his arrogant white master. If black males suffered from real and psychological castration, black females bore the burden of real or psychological rape. Both situations involved the negation of the individual's personal integrity and attacked the foundations of one's sense of personal worth.

The history of slavery suggests that black men and women shared a rough equality of hardship and degradation. While the black woman's position as sex object and breeder may have given her temporarily greater leverage in dealing with her white master than the black male enjoyed, in the long run it denied her a positive image of herself. On the other hand, the very nature of slavery foreclosed certain conditions experienced by white women. The black woman had few expectations of economic dependence upon the male or of derivative status through marriage. She emerged from slavery without the illusions of a specially protected position as a woman or the possibilities of a parasitic existence as a woman. As Dr. Frazier observed, "Neither economic necessity nor tradition has instilled in her the spirit of subordination to masculine authority. Emancipation only tended to confirm in many cases the spirit of self-sufficiency which slavery had taught."

Throughout the history of Black America, its women have been in the forefront of the struggle for human rights. A century ago Harriet Tubman and Sojourner Truth were titans of the Abolitionist movement. In the 1890's Ida B. Wells-Barnett carried on a one-woman crusade against lynching. Mary McLeod Bethune and Mary Church Terrell symbolize the stalwart woman leaders of the first half of the twentieth century. At the age of ninety, Mrs. Terrell successfully challenged segregation in public places in the nation's capital through a Supreme Court decision in 1953.

In contemporary times we have Rosa Parks setting off the mass struggle for civil rights in the South by refusing to move to the back of the bus in Montgomery in 1955; Daisy Bates guiding the Little Rock Nine through a series of school desegregation crises in 1957–59; Gloria Richardson facing down the National Guard in Cambridge, Maryland, in the early sixties; or Coretta Scott King picking up the fallen standard of her slain husband to continue the fight. Not only have these and many other women whose names are well known given this great human effort its peculiar vitality, but women in many communities whose names will never be known have revealed the courage and strength of the black woman in America. They are the mothers who stood in schoolyards of the South with their children, many times alone. One cannot help asking: "Would the black struggle have come this far without the indomitable determination of its women?"

Now that some attention is finally being given to the place of the Negro in American history, how much do we hear of the role of the Negro woman? Of the many books published on the Negro experience and the Black Revolution in recent times, to date not one has concerned itself with the struggles of black women and their contributions to history. Of approximately 800 full-length articles published in the *Journal of Negro History* since its inception in 1916, only six have dealt directly with the Negro woman. Only two have considered Negro women as a group: Carter G. Woodson's "The Negro Washerwoman: A Vanishing Figure" (14 *JNH,* 1930) and Jessie W. Pankhurst's "The Role of the Black Mammy in the Plantation Household" (28 *JNH,* 1938).

This historical neglect continues into the present. A significant feature of the civil rights revolution of the 1950's and 1960's was its inclusiveness, born of the broad participation of men, women, and children without regard to age and sex. As indicated, school children, often led by their mothers, in the 1950's won worldwide acclaim for their courage in desegregating the schools. A black child can have no finer heritage to give a sense of "somebodiness" than the knowledge of having personally been part of the great sweep of history. (An older generation, for example, takes pride in the use of the term "Negro," having been part of a 75-year effort to dignify the term by capitalizing it. Now some black militants with a woeful lack of historical perspective have allied themselves symbolically with white racists by downgrading the term to lower case again.) Yet, despite the crucial role which Negro women have played in the struggle, in the great mass of magazine and newspaper print expended on the racial crisis, the aspirations of the black community have been articulated almost exclusively by black males. There has been very little public discussion of the problems, objectives, or concerns of black women.

Reading through much of the current literature on the Black Revolution, one is left with the impression that for all the rhetoric about self-determination, the main thrust of black militancy is a bid of black males to share power with white males in a continuing patriarchal society in which both black and white females are relegated to a secondary status. For example, *Ebony* magazine published a special issue on the Negro woman in 1966. Some of the articles attempted to delineate the contributions of Negro women as heroines in the civil rights battle in Dixie, in the building of the New South, in the arts and professions, and as intellectuals. The editors, however, felt it necessary to include a full-page editorial to counter the possible effect of the articles by women contributors. After paying tribute to the Negro woman's contributions in the past, the editorial reminded *Ebony*'s readers that "the past is behind us," that "the immediate goal of the Negro woman today should be the establishment of a strong family unit in which the father is the dominant person," and that the Negro woman would do well to follow the example of the Jewish mother, "who pushed her husband to success, educated her male children first and engineered good marriages for her daughters." The editors also declared that the career woman "should be willing to postpone her aspirations until her children, too, are old enough to be on their own," and, as if the point had not been made clear enough, suggested that if "the woman should, by any chance, make more money than her husband, the marriage could be in real trouble."

While not as blatantly Victorian as *Ebony*, other writers on black militancy have shown only slightly less myopia. In *Black Power and Urban Crisis*, Dr. Nathan Wright, Chairman of the 1967 National Black Power Conference, made only three brief references to women: "the employment of female skills," "the beauty of black women," and housewives. His constant reference to Black Power was in terms of black males and black manhood. He appeared to be wholly unaware of the parallel struggles of women and youth for inclusion in decision making, for when he dealt with the reallocation of power, he noted that "the churches and housewives of America" are the most readily influential groups which can aid in this process.

In *Black Rage*, psychiatrists Greer and Cobbs devote a chapter to achieving womanhood. While they sympathetically describe the traumatic experience of self-depreciation which a black woman undergoes in a society in which the dominant standard of beauty is "the blond, blue-eyed, white-skinned girl with regular features," and make a telling point about the burden of the stereotype that Negro women are available to white men, they do not get beyond a framework in which the Negro woman is seen as a sex object. Emphasizing her concern with "feminine narcissism" and the need to be "lovable" and "attractive," they conclude: "Under the sign of discouragement and rejection which governs so much of her physical operation, she is inclined to organize her personal ambitions in terms of her achievements serving to compensate for other losses and hurts." Nowhere do the authors suggest that Negro women, like women generally, might be motivated to achieve as *persons*. Implied throughout the discussion is the sexuality of Negro females.

The ultimate expression of this bias is the statement attributed to a black militant male leader: "The position of the black woman should be prone." Thus, there appears to be a distinctly conservative and backward-looking view in much of what black males write today about black women, and many black women have been led to believe that the restoration of the black male to his lost manhood must take precedence over the claims of black women to equalitarian status. Consequently, there has been a tendency to acquiesce without vigorous protest to policies which emphasize the "underemployment" of the black male in relation to the black female and which encourage the upgrading and education of black male youth while all but ignoring the educational and training needs of black female youth, although the highest rates of unemployment today are among black female teenagers. A parallel tendency to concentrate on career and training opportunities primarily for black males is evident in government and industry.

As this article goes to press, further confirmation of a patriarchal view on the part of organizations dominated by black males is found in "Black Declaration of Independence" published as a full-page advertisement in *The New York Times* on July 3, 1970. Signed by members of the National Committee of Black Churchmen and presuming to speak "By Order and on Behalf of Black People," this document ignores both the personhood and the contributions of black women to the cause of human rights. The drafters show a shocking insensitivity to the revitalized women's rights/women's liberation movement which is beginning to capture the front pages of national newspapers and the mass media. It evidences a parochialism which has hardly moved beyond the eighteenth century in its thinking about women. Not only does it paraphrase the 1776 Declaration about the equality of "all Men," with a noticeable lack of imagination, but it also declares itself "in the Name of our good People and our own Black Heroes." Then follows a list of black males prominent in the historic struggle for liberation. The names of Harriet Tubman, Sojourner Truth, Mary McLeod Bethune, or Daisy Bates, or any other black women are conspicuous by their absence. If black male leaders of the Christian faith—who concededly have suffered much through denigration of their personhood and who are committed to the equality of all in the eyes of God—are callous to the indivisibility of human rights, who is to remember?

In the larger society, of course, black and white women share the common burden of discrimination based upon sex. The parallels between racism and sexism have been distinctive features of American society, and the movements to eliminate these two evils have often been allied and sometimes had interchangeable leadership. The beginnings of a women's rights movement in this country is linked with the Abolitionist movement. In 1840, William Lloyd Garrison and Charles Remond, the latter a Negro, refused to be seated as delegates to the World Anti-Slavery Convention in London when they learned that women members of the American delegation had been excluded because of their sex and could sit only in the balcony and observe the proceedings. The seed of the Seneca Falls Convention of 1848, which marked the formal beginning of the women's rights struggle in the United States, was planted at that London conference. Frederick Douglass attended the Seneca Falls Convention and rigorously supported Elizabeth Cady Stanton's daring resolution on woman's suffrage. Except for a temporary defection during the controversy over adding "sex" to the Fifteenth Amendment, Douglass remained a staunch advocate of women's rights until his death in 1895. Sojourner Truth and other black women were also active in the movement for women's rights, as indicated earlier.

Despite the common interests of black and white women, however, the dichotomy of a racially segregated society which has become increasingly polarized has prevented them from cementing a natural alliance. Communication and cooperation have been hesitant, limited, and formal. In the past Negro women have tended to identify discrimination against them as primarily racial and have accorded high priority to the struggle for Negro rights. They have had little time or energy for consideration of women's rights. And, until recent years, their egalitarian position in the struggle seemed to justify such preoccupation.

As the drive for black empowerment continues, however, black women are becoming increasingly aware of a new development which creates for them a dilemma of competing identities and priorities. On the one hand, as Dr. Jeanne Noble has observed, "establishing 'black manhood' became a prime goal of black revolution," and black women began to realize "that black men wanted to determine the policy and progress of black people without female participation in decision-making and leadership positions." On the other hand, a rising movement for women's liberation is challenging the concept of male dominance which the black revolution appears to have embraced. Confronted with the multiple barriers of poverty, race, and sex, the quandary of black women is how best to distribute their energies among these issues and what strategies to pursue which will minimize conflicting interests and objectives.

Cognizant of the similarities between paternalism and racial arrogance, black women are nevertheless handicapped by the continuing stereotype of the black "matriarchy" and the demand that black women now step back and push black men into positions of leadership. They are made to feel disloyal to racial interests if they insist upon women's rights. Moreover, to the extent that racial polarization often accompanies the thrust for Black Power, black women find it increasingly difficult to make common cause with white women. These developments raise several questions. Are black women gaining or losing in the drive toward human rights? As the movement for women's liberation becomes increasingly a force to be reckoned with, are black women to take a backward step and sacrifice their egalitarian tradition? What are the alternatives to matriarchal dominance on the one hand or male supremacy on the other?

Much has been written in the past about the matriarchal character of Negro family life, the relatively favored position of Negro women, and the tensions and difficulties growing out of the assumptions that they are better educated and more able to obtain employment than Negro males. These assumptions require closer examination. It is true that according to reports of the Bureau of the Census, in March 1968 an estimated 278,000 nonwhite women had completed four or more years of college—86,000 more than male college graduates in the nonwhite population (Negro women constitute 93 percent of all nonwhite women), and that in March 1966 the median years of school completed by Negro females (10.1) was slightly higher than that for Negro males (9.4). It should be borne in mind that this is not unique to the black community. In the white population as well, females exceed males in median years of school completed (12.2 to 12.0) and do not begin to lag behind males until the college years. The significant fact is that the percentage of both sexes in the Negro population eighteen years of age and over in 1966 who had completed four years of college was roughly equivalent (males: 2.2 percent; females: 2.3 percent). When graduate training is taken into account, the proportion of Negro males with five or more years of college training (3.3 percent) moved ahead of the Negro females (3.2 percent). Moreover, 1966 figures show that a larger proportion of Negro males (63 percent) than Negro females (57 percent) was enrolled in school and that this superiority continued into college enrollments (males: 5 percent; females: 4 percent). These 1966 figures reflect a concerted effort to broaden educational opportunities for Negro males, manifested in recruitment policies and scholarship programs made available primarily to Negro male students. Though later statistics are not now available, this trend appears to have accelerated each year.

The assumption that Negro women have more education than Negro men also overlooks the possibility that the greater number of college-trained Negro women may correspond to the larger number of Negro women in the population. Of enormous importance to a consideration of Negro family life and the relation between the sexes is the startling fact of the excess of females over males. The Bureau of the Census estimated that in July 1968 there were 688,000 more Negro females than Negro males. Although census officials attribute this disparity to errors in counting a "floating" Negro male population, this excess has appeared in steadily increasing numbers in every census since 1860, but has received little analysis beyond periodic comment. Over the past century the reported ratio of black males to black females has decreased. In 1966, there were less than 94 black males to every 100 females.

The numerical imbalance between the sexes in the black population is more dramatic than in any other group in the United States. Within the white population the excess of women shows up in the middle or later years. In the black population, however, the sex imbalance is present in every age group over fourteen and is greatest during the age when most marriages occur. In the twenty-five to forty-four age group, the percentage of males within the black population drops to 86.9 as compared to 96.9 for white males.

It is now generally known that females tend to be constitutionally stronger than males, that male babies are more fragile than female babies, that boys are harder to rear than girls, that the male death rate is slightly higher and life expectancy for males is shorter than that of females. Add to these general factors the special hardships to which the Negro minority is exposed—poverty, crowded living conditions, poor health, marginal jobs, and minimum protection against hazards of accident and illness—and it becomes apparent that there is much in the American environment that is particularly hostile to the survival of the black male. But even if we discount these factors and accept the theory that the sex ratio is the result of errors in census counting, it is difficult to avoid the conclusion that a large number of black males have so few stable ties that they are not included as functioning units of the society. In either case formidable pressures are created for black women.

The explosive social implications of an excess of more than half a million black girls and women over fourteen years of age are obvious in a society in which the mass media intensify notions of glamour and expectations of romantic love and marriage, while at the same time there are many barriers against interracial marriages. When such marriages do take place they are more likely to involve black males and white females, which tends to aggravate the issue. (No value judgment about interracial marriages is implied here. I am merely trying to describe a social dilemma.) The problem of an excess female population is a familiar one in countries which have experienced heavy male casualties during wars, but an excess female ethnic minority as an enclave within a larger population raises important social issues. To what extent are the tensions and conflicts traditionally associated with the matriarchal framework of Negro family life in reality due to this imbalance and the pressures it generates? Does this excess explain the active competition between Negro professional men and women seeking employment in markets which have limited or excluded Negroes? And does this competition intensify the stereotype of the matriarchal society and female dominance? What relationship is there between the high rate of illegitimate births among black women and the population figures we have described?

These figures suggest that the Negro woman's fate in the United States, while inextricably bound with that of the Negro male in one sense, transcends the issue of Negro rights. Equal opportunity for her must mean equal opportunity to compete for jobs and to find a mate in the total society. For as long as she is confined to an area in which she must compete fiercely for a mate, she will remain the object of sexual exploitation and the victim of all the social evils which such exploitation involves.

When we compare the position of the black woman to that of the white woman, we find that she remains single more often, bears more children, is in the labor market longer and in greater proportion, has less education, earns less, is widowed earlier, and carries a relatively heavier economic responsibility as family head than her white counterpart.

In 1966 black women represented one of every seven women workers, although Negroes generally constitute only 11 percent of the total population in the United States. Of the 3,105,000 black women eighteen years of age and over who were in the labor force, however, nearly half (48.2 percent) were either single, widowed, divorced, separated from their husbands, or their husbands were absent for other reasons, as compared with 31.8 percent of white women in similar circumstances. Moreover, six of every ten black women were in household employment or other service jobs. Conversely, while 58.8 percent of all women workers held white-collar positions, only 23.2 percent of black women held such jobs.

As working wives, black women contribute a higher proportion to family income than do white women. Among nonwhite wives in 1965, 58 percent contributed 20 percent or more of the total family income, 43 percent contributed 30 percent or more, and 27 percent contributed 40 percent or more. The comparable percentages for white wives were 56 percent, 40 percent, and 24 percent respectively.

Black working mothers are more heavily represented in the labor force than white mothers. In March 1966, nonwhite working mothers with children under eighteen years of age represented 48 percent of all nonwhite mothers with children this age as compared with 35 percent of white working mothers. Nonwhite working mothers also represented four of every ten of all nonwhite mothers of children under six years of age. Of the 12,300,000 children under fourteen years of age in February 1965 whose mothers worked, only 2 percent were provided group care in day-care centers. Adequate child care is an urgent need for working mothers generally, but it has particular significance for the high proportion of black working mothers of young children.

Black women also carry heavy responsibilities as family heads. In 1966 one-fourth of all black families were headed by a woman as compared with less than one-tenth of all white families. The economic disabilities of women generally are aggravated in the case of black women. Moreover, while all families headed by women are more vulnerable to poverty than husband-wife families, the black woman family head is doubly victimized. For example, the median wage or salary income of all women workers who were employed full-time, year-round in 1967 was only 58 percent of that of all male workers, and the median earnings of white females were less than those of black males. The median wage of nonwhite women workers, however, was $3,268, or only 71 percent of the median income of white women workers. In 1965 one-third of all families headed by women lived in poverty, but 62 percent of the 1,132,000 nonwhite families with a female head were poor.

A significant factor in the low economic and social status of black women is their concentration at the bottom rung of the employment ladder. More than one-third of all nonwhite working women are employed as private household workers. The median wages of women private household workers who were employed full-time, year-round in 1968 was only $1,701. Furthermore, these workers are not covered by the federal minimum wage and hours law and are generally excluded from state wage and hours laws, unemployment compensation, and workmen's compensation.

The black woman is triply handicapped. She is heavily represented in non-union employment and thus has few of the benefits to be derived from labor organization or social legislation. She is further victimized by discrimination because of race and sex. Although she has made great strides in recent decades in closing the educational gap, she still suffers from inadequate education and training. In 1966 only 71.1 percent of all Negro women had completed eight grades of elementary school, compared to 88 percent of all white women. Only one-third (33.2 percent) of all Negro women had completed high school, as compared with more than one-half of all white women (56.3 percent). More than twice as many white women, proportionally, have completed college (7.2 percent) as black women (3.2 percent).

The notion of the favored economic position of the black female in relation to the black male is a myth. The 1966 median earnings of full-time, year-round nonwhite female workers was only 65 percent of that of nonwhite males. The unemployment rate for adult nonwhite women (6.6) was higher than for their male counterparts (4.9). Among nonwhite teenagers, the unemployment rate for girls was 31.1, as compared with 21.2 for boys.

In the face of their multiple disadvantages, it seems clear that black women can neither postpone nor subordinate the fight against sex discrimination to the black revolution. Many of them must expect to be self-supporting and perhaps to support others for a considerable period or for life. In these circumstances, while efforts to raise educational and employment levels for black males will ease some of the economic and social burdens now carried by many black women, for a large and apparently growing minority these burdens will continue. As a matter of sheer survival black women have no alternative but to insist upon equal opportunities

> **As a matter of sheer survival black women have no alternative but to insist upon equal opportunities without regard to sex in training, education, and employment.**

without regard to sex in training, education, and employment. Given their heavy family responsibilities, the outlook for their children will be bleak indeed unless they are encouraged in every way to develop their potential skills and earning power.

Because black women have an equal stake in women's liberation and black liberation, they are key figures at the juncture of these two movements. White women feminists are their natural allies in both causes. Their own liberation is linked with the issues which are stirring women today: adequate income maintenance and the elimination of poverty, repeal or reform of abortion laws, a national system of child-care centers, extension of labor standards to workers now excluded, cash maternity benefits as part of a system of social insurance, and the removal of all sex barriers to educational and employment opportunities at all levels. Black women have a special stake in the revolt against the treatment of women primarily as sex objects, for their own history has left them with the scars of the most brutal and degrading aspects of sexual exploitation.

The middle-class Negro woman is strategically placed by virtue of her tradition of independence and her long experience in civil rights, and can play a creative role in strengthening the alliance between the black revolution and women's liberation. Her advantages of training and her values make it possible for her to communicate with her white counterparts, interpret the deepest feelings within the black community, and cooperate with white women on the basis of mutual concerns as women. The possibility of productive interchange between black and white women is greatly facilitated by the absence of the power relationships which separate black and white males as antagonists. By asserting a leadership role in the growing feminist movement, the black woman can help to keep it allied to the objectives of black liberation while simultaneously advancing the interests of all women.*

The lesson of history that all human rights are indivisible and that the failure to adhere to this principle jeopardizes the rights of all is particularly applicable here. A built-in hazard of an aggressive ethnocentric movement which disregards the

---

*[Editor's note: A step in this direction was taken in the Fall of 1973 with the formation of the National Black Feminist Organization (285 Madison Avenue, New York 10017). On the West Coast there is Black Women Organized for Action, P. O. Box 15072, San Francisco 94115.]

interests of other disadvantaged groups is that it will become parochial and ultimately self-defeating in the face of hostile reactions, dwindling allies, and mounting frustrations. As Dr. Caroline F. Ware has pointed out, perhaps the most essential instrument for combating the divisive effects of a black-only movement is the voice of black women insisting upon the unity of civil rights of women and Negroes as well as other minorities and excluded groups. Only a broad movement for human rights can prevent the black revolution from becoming isolated and can ensure its ultimate success.

Beyond all the present conflict lies the important task of reconciliation of the races in America on the basis of genuine equality and human dignity. A powerful force in bringing about this result can be generated through the process of black and white women working together to achieve their common humanity.

Women in American Politics: An Overview

Naomi Lynn

The political activities of American women comprise a mixed record that ranges from minimal tokenism to limited achievement. Politics has great strategic importance for women because the ultimate success of the women's movement will rest heavily on effective use of the political process. Women are relatively inactive in politics in part because they are denied opportunities to develop the self-confidence that political scientists have found to characterize the active citizen in a democratic system.

From infancy girls are trained to be passive and dependent, and by the time they reach elementary school the pattern is well established. A 1959 study of elementary school children showed that girls were more likely to solve problems by imitating adults, while boys sought solutions on their own; girls were also more likely to seek adult advice and approval as part of the problem-solving process.[1] As a girl grows up she finds that our culture continues to emphasize the view that women are more dependent and politically less competent than men. All this gives the typical woman a poor opinion of her own political efficacy.

Studies indicate that a woman feels less able

than a man to cope with the complexities of the political process; she feels that her participation would carry little weight anyway. Political competence, in short, is not part of the woman's role as it is taught throughout the process of socialization. More effective political action by women will require, then, not merely knowledge and objective competence but an entirely new self-concept on their part.

WOMEN AS VOTERS

The Women's Suffrage Movement

A major turning point for women came in the 1830's, when the early efforts of Northern women to secure the abolition of slavery demonstrated the effectiveness of agitation for human rights.[2] Soon after slavery was abolished, the issue of women's suffrage came to the fore. The first victories came in areas where women represented a minority of the population, such as the American West and New Zealand. In 1869 the territory of Wyoming gave women the right to vote. Three years later Susan B. Anthony voted illegally in the presidential election, and she was later convicted in court. She drafted the Woman Suffrage Amendment, which was finally ratified in 1920.

After 1920 the women's suffrage movement was faced with a decision. Should it exert its considerable influence in active politics, or should it shift to nonpartisan efforts? The National American Woman's Suffrage Association decided on the second route, and such groups as the League of Women Voters became a main focus of women's political attention for decades.[3] The move was justified by a desire to keep women united and to hold all office holders accountable to all women, but it did dilute the force of women's political power. As one observer has said, "Looking back across the years since the 19th Amendment we can see where women erred. Winning the vote was accepted as an end in itself, which it was not. Having won political power, women have never used it. Therein lies our failure."[4]

Women's Voting Patterns

In the early years of women's suffrage many women not involved in the suffrage movement were uncomfortable about exercising their new voting rights. A 1924 study of Chicago women revealed that 11.4 percent of them still did not believe women should vote.[5] The percentage of women voters increased over the next three decades, but it remained lower than the percentage of men. By the 1950's the difference nationwide was about 10 percent, though in some areas, such as Waukegan, Illinois, there was no difference at all. The gradual increase in women voters can be accounted for in part by the fact that the older generations, who had been brought up with the idea that voting was a man's work, were gradually replaced by later generations who grew up after woman's suffrage had become a fact of life. Table 1 shows the percentages of men and women born in 1898 and 1927 who

TABLE 1   Percentages of Men and Women Born in 1898 and 1927 Voting in the Elections of 1952 and 1964

Year of birth and sex	Percentage Voting	
	1952	1964
1898		
Men	80	76
Women	67	69
1927		
Men	60	75
Women	56	76

Source: Center for Political Studies, Inst. for Political Research, Univ. of Michigan.

voted in the elections of 1952 and 1964. The considerable gap in the percentages of men and women voters in the older group in 1952 was much narrower in 1964. The small gap in the younger group in 1952 was completely wiped out by 1964. In 1972 more women under 30 voted than men in the same age group.[6]

Table 2 shows the overall record of voting by men and women from 1948 to 1972. A small gap has persisted in the past decade, with men's voting percentages remaining 3 or 4 points above women's. But even the small gap in overall voting is unlikely to remain as the voters born in the 1898 period decline in numbers. By 1972 the electorate included people born in 1954—sons and daughters of the voters born in 1927. Moreover, despite the fact that a slightly smaller percentage of women vote than men, in 1972 more votes were cast by women than by men.[7] This

TABLE 2   Percentages of Men and Women Voting in Elections, 1948–1972

	1948	1952	1956	1960	1964	1968	1972
Men	69	72	80	80	73	69	64
Women	59	62	69	69	70	66	62

Source: Center for Political Studies, Inter-University Consortium, Univ. of Michigan. 1972 data were obtained from U.S. Dept. of Commerce, Bureau of the Census, Current Population Reports, Population Characteristics, "Voting Participation in November 1972," Series P-20, no. 244, Dec. 1972.

larger number of votes by women, even with a lower total voting percentage, is due to the fact that there are more women than men in the population.

Even though the Nineteenth Amendment was ratified over half a century ago, women have continued to face barriers to voting. Perhaps the most important is their traditional training and upbringing, which serves to teach girls that political matters are not an area of competence for them. The expected appropriate behavior traditionally required of a woman placed her at home and taught her it was unbecoming and inappropriate to enter the male political world. As sex-typed behavior changes, it is expected that female political behavior will also change. This is best illustrated by looking at the South, where the traditional female role has been the most firmly entrenched and slow to change. Women in the South have a lower voting turnout than women of the same age and with similar education in other regions.[8] Differences in turnout are least among the more highly educated women.

The American Voter, a classic University of Michigan study, made the following observation, based on 1956 survey data about women:

> It is the sense of political efficacy that, with factors like education, age and region controlled, differs most sharply and consistently between men and women. . . . Moralistic values about citizen participation in democratic government have been bred in women as in men; what has been less adequately transmitted to the woman is a sense of political competence vis-a-vis the political world.[9]

In the face of this handicap the voting performance of women since the mid-1960's represents both progress and strength. Women now have the numerical voting strength to be a decisive force and to break down barriers in any other political area they choose. What is needed, of course, is the will.

Before 1948 women apparently did not identify with a particular party as strongly as men, though survey data are not available to prove this point. Since 1948 the party identification of men and women has become generally similar. As Table 3 shows, in 1956, 1960, and 1964 the party identification of women in the high educational category was actually stronger than that of men in the same category. The question that emerges next is how do the party preferences of men differ from those of women? As Table 4 reflects, the answer to this question is mixed. Women voted more heavily for Eisenhower than men did in both 1952 and 1956. More women also voted for Nixon than Kennedy in 1960, despite the myth that women voters are swayed more than men by a candidate's physical appearance. But since 1960 women have supported Democratic candidates at a slightly higher percentage than men. In a Gallup Poll of August 1970, 28 percent of the men interviewed considered themselves Republicans; 42 percent, Democrats; and 30 percent, independents. Of the women interviewed, 30 percent considered themselves Republicans; 45 percent, Democrats; and 25 percent, independents.[10] That is, 5 percent fewer women considered themselves independents, and of these 5 percentage points, three went to the Democrats and two to the Republicans.

TABLE 3 Percentages of Men and Women Who Considered Themselves "Strong" Democrats or Republicans, 1952-1964

Year and educational level	"Strong" Democrats		"Strong" Republicans	
	Men	Women	Men	Women
1952				
High	18%	19%	19%	18%
Medium	22	20	12	14
Low	28	22	11	10
1956				
High	16	17	15	23
Medium	24	22	8	13
Low	26	19	15	16
1960				
High	13	17	16	26
Medium	20	19	10	11
Low	27	24	15	14
1964				
High	19	20	16	18
Medium	27	25	12	7
Low	39	36	4	9

Source: Marjorie Lansing, "Sex Differences in Political Participation." (unpub. Ph.D. diss. Univ. of Michigan, 1970.)

In 1968, 82.2 percent of college-educated women and 84 percent of college-educated men voted. Among people with only a grade school education or less, 59.3 percent of men and only 50 percent of women voted.[11] As more women move into the high education category, more should be voting. A pioneer suffragette once said that if men wanted to keep women down, they made their first mistake when they taught them their ABC's.[12] Women may just be beginning to cash in their educational chips.

The authors of *The American Voter* found that mothers of young children were less likely to vote than fathers of young children, regardless of educational level. The researchers suggested that the demands of child care could keep the women from voting, but their political involvement could still be higher than the

TABLE 4 The Vote by Sex in Presidential Elections,
1952–1972

Year and Candidate	Men	Women
1952		
Eisenhower	53%	58%
Stevenson	47	42
1956		
Eisenhower	55	61
Stevenson	45	39
1960		
Kennedy	52	49
Nixon	48	51
1964		
Johnson	60	62
Goldwater	40	38
1968		
Nixon	43	43
Humphrey	41	45
Wallace	16	13
1972		
McGovern	37	38
Nixon	63	62

Source: Gallup Opinion Index, Dec. 1972, report no. 90.

voting turnout alone would indicate.[13] However, sociologists have noted the primacy of the role of mother in the identification of the adult female, and this author's own research suggests that among women with education above the high school level, motherhood tends to lower their sense of political efficacy and hence their political participation.[14] Further research is needed to examine the full impact that motherhood in our child-centered society has on the development of women's political sense of self.

Women and the Issues

Early voting data on women's stands on issues have been scanty and have emphasized women's moralistic orientation as revealed in their strong stand on prohibition. Women are also described as generally more conservative than men. However, as has been mentioned, women have voted more heavily for Democratic presidential candidates in the last two elections than men have. Recent and more thorough studies have shown that women do differ from men in their stand on some issues. Gallup data and the 1972 Virginia Slims Poll, conducted by Louis Harris, show that women are less likely to seek military solutions to international problems. On the issue of Vietnam more women classified themselves as doves. The greater value women apparently place on human life goes beyond war to the issues of capital punishment and social welfare.[15] Only on issues where their own children were involved, such as busing, were women more conservative than men, once again indicating the predominance of the motherhood role in women.

Whether or not a women's bloc vote will materialize remains to be seen. In close elections, such as the 1968 presidential race, a difference of a few percentage points in the voting choices of men and women could make the critical difference. A real voting bloc has yet to be seen even on issues dealing with women's rights, since no candidate has sought election on a primarily feminist platform. It must always be remembered that women differ in personality, education, income, and social class, and that these variables will continue to affect their political choices.

THE PARTY WOMEN

Modern government is party government. Political power must rest on party power. As women's political activities increase they must necessarily play a greater role in party affairs, and this partisanship presents an important expansion area for women. The parties have admitted women as workers on various levels, but they have not yet admitted them on a level approaching equality.

Level of Party Work

Partisanship among women is as high as it is among men, especially in the more educated groups. This partisanship may develop into an interest in party activity. In 1964, 9.3 percent of college-educated women responded as party "activists," while only 6.9 percent of similarly educated men regarded themselves in this way.[16]

Partisanship and party activity, however, lead to little power for women. Women find ready employment as envelope stuffers and doorbell ringers. They are far less likely to find themselves in a position of responsibility or decision making. A New York study revealed that there was only one woman county party chairman in the 62 counties of the state.[17] Even when a woman does reach high party office, she is likely to find herself treated like a precocious child when she sits in the party councils—an object of benevolent amusement or perhaps pride, but hardly a source of wisdom or power.

Women's powerlessness may stem in part from their general lack of administrative experience and public visibility. In the most active age brackets women have often found it difficult or impossible to get away from home in order to pursue party work enough to build real power. While men who get into party activities are praised for assuming their proper civic responsibilities, the active woman may be chastised for leaving her home. Even such a scholarly observer as Robert E. Lane revealed this bias when he wrote,

> It is too seldom remembered in the American society that working girls and career women, and women who insistently serve the community in volunteer capacities, and women with extra-curricular interests of an absorbing kind are often borrowing their time and attention and capacity for relaxed play and love from their children to whom it rightfully belongs. As Kardiner points out, the rise of juvenile delinquency (and, he says, homosexuality) is partly to be attributed to the feminist movement and what it did to the American mother.[18]

The Woman Convention Delegate

At the county level, the "ceremonial" woman is a common fixture. She brightens the local meeting as she mounts the platform smiling with a red, white, and blue streamer across her chest. If she also works hard, she may be given one of the nominal state offices reserved for women, or she may ultimately have the honor of attending a national convention.

In 1964, 15 percent (416) of the 2,934 delegates to the Democratic National Convention were women. By 1968 the figure had dropped to 13 percent (405 out of 3,045).[19] In 1968, 17 percent of the delegates to the Republican National Convention were women.[20] In 1972, as a result of the efforts of the McGovern-Frasier Commission of the Democratic Party, and women's movement organizations such as the National Women's Political Caucus, the figures increased to 40 percent for the Democrats and 30 percent for the Republicans.

THE FEMALE CANDIDATE

Candidacy for public office is an important threshold for the woman with a strong interest in politics. The few women who cross it must face barriers much higher than those that face women who content themselves with low-level party work.

Prejudice

Shirley Chisholm, member of the United States House of Representatives from New

> By and large, party leaders are even more pre-
> judiced than voters and rival candidates. They
> often permit women to run only in situations
> where they are certain to lose.

York, has summed up the prejudice a woman faces when she seeks public office:

> When I decided to run for Congress I knew I would encounter both antiblack
> and antifeminist sentiments. What surprised me was the much greater viru-
> lence of the sex discrimination. I was constantly bombarded by both men and
> women exclaiming that I should return to teaching, a woman's vocation, and
> leave politics to the men.[21]

A 1969 Gallup Poll showed that 67 percent of the electorate would vote for a black
man for President of the United States. Only 54 percent said they would vote for a
woman, regardless of her race.[22]

Women face this prejudice from members of both sexes. A 1970 Gallup Poll
found that 13 percent of men and 13 percent of women would not vote for a
woman for Congress, even if she was qualified. This is much lower than the percentage who would bar a woman from the presidency, but it represents a hard core of
opposition. Significantly, among college graduates only 8 percent would not vote
for a woman for Congress.[23]

In her unsuccessful bid to win a United States Senate seat in Michigan,
Lenore Romney found that male reporters were biased against her. She explained
this discrimination by the fact that those journalists had no experience dealing with
women who knew and cared about public affairs. She was simply not accepted.[24]

In view of this attitude it is not surprising that in the early 1970's the women
running for office were often those who were equipped by experience and expectation to deal with sex discrimination. In a special survey Georgi Jones of the Urban
Research Corporation found that of fifteen female candidates for various offices,
five were black and six were running on "woman power" platforms. Of the five
women who won, three were black.[25]

Additional Barriers

The woman who wants to run for office might emulate the model of Patsy Mink,
Congresswoman from Hawaii. Mrs. Mink worked behind the scenes in Democratic
politics, doing the dull work of running party headquarters and ringing doorbells.
Ultimately she chose to run for territorial office, and though her name was not well
known, by her own hard work and that of her supporters she won and went on to

higher office later.[26] This sort of story would be easy to duplicate among male members of the House of Representatives, but Mrs. Mink is one of the few women who have been able to follow it to a successful conclusion.

By and large, party leaders are even more prejudiced than voters and rival candidates. They often permit women to run only in situations where they are certain to lose.[27] Then when the inevitable happens, all that may be remembered is that a woman lost.

There are other myths and preconceptions that plague women candidates. It is said that women cannot take the time away from their children that candidacy and public office require. A seat in the state legislature, to cite a common first-rung office, may require two to three months away from home every winter. But this argument does not explain the lack of women candidates from areas near the state capital. Political leaders also argue that it is a waste of time, effort, and money to promote a young woman for office when she is liable to become pregnant at any time. The fact that modern birth control techniques render the pregnancy of a serious candidate highly unlikely may serve to dispel this myth in time. In any event the election in 1972 to the House of Representatives of a young mother (Patricia Schroeder, D. Colorado) and the birth of a daughter to another Congress-woman (Yvonne Braithwaite Burke, D. Calif.) may defuse this argument.

If the barriers of family responsibilities, myths, party organization, and preju-diced voters are not enough, the female candidate often finds that her means of making a living is a barrier too. More women than men proportionately are in civil service jobs or teaching jobs that are not conducive to office seeking. The woman who must go off the payroll to have the privilege of spending large sums of money campaigning is at a disadvantage compared to a business or professional man whose income continues. The legal profession contributes more office holders than any other, and in 1970–71 only 7.8 percent of the students entering law school were women.[28]*

Another barrier faced by many women is their relationship with their hus-band. In 1968 three female lawyers, Martha W. Griffiths (D. Mich.), Patsy Mink (D. Hawaii), and Margaret M. Heckler (R. Mass.) had reached the House of Representa-tives. In her study of these three, Lamson found that each had an unusual degree of solidarity in her relationship with her husband, and each husband had played a vital role in prompting and even managing his wife's campaign. In the present cultural context few husbands are prepared or equipped to do this.[29]

---

*[Editor's note: Over 60 percent of all male congressional representatives are lawyers; however, in 1973–74 15.6 percent of entering law students were women—a significant increase in the pool of potential female politicians.]

Still another barrier the female candidate faces is that male politicians are used to dealing with other men. Congresswoman Margaret Heckler has stated that party leaders do not enjoy drinking with women and sharing with them the sort of camaraderie they have in a stag group.[30] This socializing (it might be termed cronyism) often serves as the foundation for relationships that lead to the selection of candidates.

A special frustration for women candidates is the fact that they tend to fare better in primaries than they do in the general election. One study has hypothesized that among the more informed groups of fellow partisans, sex discrimination is not the strong negative factor that it is among the whole electorate.[31]

Even more serious is the fund-raising problem. Congresswoman Heckler points out that the big givers, who like to back a winner, consider a female candidate a poor investment. Former senator Maureen Neuberger of Oregon has also emphasized that raising money poses an especially difficult challenge for the female candidate.[32] Women tend not to be highly confident fund raisers, since they lack the business experience of most men. All these elements combine to thin the ranks of female candidates considerably.

WOMEN IN PUBLIC OFFICE

The few women who get elected or even appointed to public office are likely to be concentrated in a few posts, such as treasurer, auditor, or (state) secretary of state. Fields dealing with libraries and children are also considered appropriate for women.[33] When women go beyond these fields, they have very high visibility. They are constantly identified as women, and men may act self-conscious or patronizing in their presence. When a woman office holder makes mistakes, they are usually attributed to her sex. Instead of saying "Nobody's perfect," people are likely to say, "Just like a woman."[34]

State and Local Offices

Although women's progress in gaining office at the state and local level is modest, it is at this level that the greatest advances have been made. Women's greatest strength is in the state legislatures. In 1920 there were 29 women in state legislatures; by 1963 the figure had reached 351 (141 Democrats, 206 Republicans, 4 independents), from which it dropped back to 318 in 1967.[35] In 1972 there were 344 women in state legislatures. As a result of the November 1972 election, the figure went up to 424, representing an increase of 18.8 percent.[36]

Women's progress in state legislatures is concentrated in the smaller states of the Northeast and the West, and in the lower houses of the legislature. In 1963–64 the highest percentages of women were in Vermont (17.8 percent), New Hampshire (14.6 percent), Connecticut (14.6 percent), Oregon (10.0 percent), Arizona (8.3 percent), and Colorado (7.0 percent).[37] All of these states rank in the lower half of the states in population; Vermont is forty-seventh. Half the women in state legislatures in 1963–64 were in Vermont, New Hampshire, and Connecticut, which had combined populations of 3.5 million. California, at present the largest state in population, with 18 million, had only one woman legislator.[38] Emmy E. Werner attributes the success of women candidates in the smaller, nonurbanized states to the easy accessibility campaigners have to voters, the low cost of campaigning in these areas, and the small districts that result from the large New England legislatures.[39]

Only three women have been elected state governors, and all of them came to office largely or entirely in their capacity as wives. Miriam A. ("Ma") Ferguson of Texas was elected in 1924 and 1932; her husband was the former governor and had been impeached. Nellie Taylor Ross was elected in 1925 to serve her dead husband's unexpired term in Wyoming. Lurleen Wallace was elected in Alabama in 1966, when her husband, George, was prohibited by the state constitution from succeeding himself in office. One explanation for the lack of women in governorships is that they are especially resented in the authoritative administrative role. A woman is much more readily accepted as a representative in the legislative branch than as a leader in the executive.*

Women have made the greatest gains in local government, but primarily in positions traditionally reserved for women, such as on library boards or in part-time, poorly paid elective offices. The first woman elected mayor of a major city was Patience Latting, who was elected mayor of Oklahoma City (population 366,000) on April 13, 1971. Ms. Latting got into politics after being active in the Parent-Teachers Association and the League of Women Voters, and after serving a four-year term on the city council. There are now fifteen women heading city governments in cities of more than 30,000 population.[40]

Congress

The first woman to be elected to the United States House of Representatives was Jeanette Rankin of Montana in 1916.** Throughout a long life she kept up her

---

*[Editor's note: Frances "Sissy" Farenthold ran on the Democratic ticket for the office of Governor of Texas in 1972, winning 45% of her party's vote. She is expected to run again.]

**[Editor's note: Jeanette Rankin was the only representative to vote against U.S. entry into both World Wars I and II.]

interest in public affairs. Although her last term in the House was over thirty years ago, she led an antiwar march in Washington in 1968 at the age of 87. The first woman who actually served in the Senate was Hattie W. Caraway of Arkansas, who was appointed in 1932 to fill her dead husband's unexpired term. Later she won election to a six-year term, the first of only three women ever to do this.

Mrs. Caraway's record is part of a pattern that characterized women in Congress before 1949: they entered via "widow's succession." Since then this pattern has broken down. Margaret Mead has pointed out that widows are the only women society allows to be both dominant and respectable at the same time. If power is thrust upon a woman by her husband's death, she may accept it without blame.[41]

In the Senate a woman is more likely to enter by appointment than by election, even when the vacancy is caused by something other than her husband's death. Of the ten women who served in the Senate between 1917 and 1973, six were appointed to fill a vacancy. Of these vacancies, four were caused by the death or resignation of a nonrelative.[42]

Table 5 shows the number of women members of the House and Senate from 1947 to 1973. There is certainly no very clear growth pattern. Despite the fact that the total rose from 8 in the 80th Congress to 19 in the 87th, it was only 16 in the 93rd.

TABLE 5 Number of Women Members of Congress, 1947-1973

Congress	Year	Senate	House
80th	1947–48	0	8
81st	1949–50	1	9
82nd	1951–52	1	10
83rd	1953–54	2	11
84th	1955–56	1	16
85th	1957–58	1	15
86th	1959–60	1	16
87th	1961–62	2	17
88th	1963–64	2	11
89th	1965–66	2	10
90th	1967–68	1	11
91st	1969–70	1	10
92nd	1971–72	1	12[a]
93rd	1973–74	0	16[b]

[a]Charlotte Reid left Congress to accept a Presidential appointment.

[b]Two widows, Lindy Boggs and Cardiff Collins, were elected in special elections in 1973 to succeed their late husbands.

During the entire 1917–73 period, 38 of the 50 states sent women to Congress. Table 6 shows the record of all the states. Despite New York's leading position with 10, the Western states have sent more women relative to their populations. It is interesting to note that Vermont and New Hampshire, the states with the largest number of women in state legislatures, had no women in Congress in the entire 56-year period.

TABLE 6   States Represented by Women in Congress, 1917–1973

State	No. of Congresswomen	State	No. of Congresswomen
North Atlantic		**North Central**	
Maine	1	Ohio	1
New Hampshire	0	Indiana	2
Vermont	0	Illinois	8
Massachusetts	3	Michigan	2
Rhode Island	0	Wisconsin	0
Connecticutt	3	Minnesota	1
New York	10	Iowa	0
New Jersey	2	Missouri	1
Pennsylvania	3	North Dakota	0
	22	South Dakota	2
		Nebraska	2
South Atlantic		Kansas	1
Delaware	0		20
Maryland	2		
Virginia	0	**Western**	
West Virginia	1	Montana	1
North Carolina	1	Wyoming	0
South Carolina	3	Colorado	1
Georgia	4	New Mexico	1
Florida	1	Arizona	1
	12	Utah	1
		Nevada	0
South Central		Idaho	1
Kentucky	1	Washington	2
Tennessee	2	Oregon	3
Alabama	2	California	4
Mississippi	0	Hawaii	1
Louisiana	2	Alaska	0
Texas	1		16
Oklahoma	4		
Arkansas	4		
	16		

As might be expected, the women in Congress fall into the older age brackets. Only three women under 35 were ever elected to the House, and only 11 under the age of 40 were elected in the 1917-73 period. The modal age at which Congresswomen began their service was 52. A study of Congresswomen during the 1917-64 period found that over half of them were college graduates. Some 90 percent were wives or widows, and half of their husbands had also served in Congress. Twenty percent of the women in Congress had been teachers, 10 percent had been lawyers, and 10 percent farmers. No other occupation was shared by as many as 10 percent.[43] The prior political activity listed most often was service in a state House of Representatives.[44] It is interesting to note that all five of the Congresswomen newly elected in 1972 were lawyers. All five also ran as professional politicians and not on the basis of familial connections.

It is well known that the secret of success in Congress is to acquire seniority. The freshman legislator is expected to serve inconspicuously, his only hope of wielding influence being to keep winning reelection until he inevitably becomes a committee chairman. Unfortunately, few of the women who have served in Congress have been reelected enough times to reach this level. From 1918 to 1973 only 17 Congresswomen served five or more terms, the minimum length of time generally required to gain power in the House. The only woman Senator to gain extensive seniority is Margaret Chase Smith of Maine. Senator Smith was elected to the House in 1940 when her Congressman husband was seriously ill from a heart attack, from which he later died.[45] She was elected to the Senate for the first time in 1948 and served until she was defeated in 1972. She was renowned for her service to her constituents, her independence of thought, and her record of never missing a roll call.

Among women who have gained substantial seniority in the House are Frances Bolton (R. Ohio), Mary T. Norton (D. New Jersey), Martha Griffiths (D. Michigan), and Edith Green (D. Oregon).* On one occasion it is reported that a new Congresswoman (who was not reelected later) came into the House chamber chewing gum and with her hair in curlers. Mrs. Bolton turned pale at this sight, and Mrs. Norton, since the newcomer was a Democrat, advised her on proper decorum.[46] This incident reflects the hypersensitivity of senior women with respect to the image of women members of the House.

In Congress, women are not accepted in the "club," an informal organization that can have considerable influence. Another traditional gathering in the House is known as the "Board of Education"; in the "Board" the Speaker and a chosen few compare notes and have a few drinks. It is used informally to plan strategy and

---

*[Editor's note: Griffiths and Green retired in 1974.]

occasionally to educate new members in the ways of the House. One Congresswoman with twenty years' seniority had never heard of it when asked by a researcher.[47] The male administrative aide to a Congresswoman summed up the problem this way: "No woman can quite make it. The power structure doesn't operate that way. So much of the power structure is built around the golf course, the bar, over cards, in the gym shower room, etc. I doubt that the best or most able women can ever get to the inner circle where there is complete acceptance."[48]

No woman has ever been elected to any of the party leadership roles, which are sources of considerable power. These would include Speaker of the House, Majority Leader, and party whips. Women who have shown competence and who have received recognition, such as choice committee posts, have tended to adopt role behavior more like that ascribed to the male stereotype than like that ascribed to the female stereotype.[49] Despite such successes, a woman is never accepted as fully as a man might be. We must conclude, then, that the overall record is one of stagnation. A token degree of representation has occurred, but there has not been continuing progress.

The Record in Other Nations

The problems faced by American women as they run for office are not unique. Lena Jager, a British Member of Parliament, cites the familiar story of women having to raise their families first and then having to deal with "patronizing young men on selection committees" who think they are too old to run for office.[50] It is true, however, that among not only the Western democracies but also other nations, the United States has one of the worst records for having women in national public office. A 1970 survey showed that the percentage of women office holders in Norway had increased from 4 percent to 9.3 percent. In Rumania 14 percent (67 out of 465) of the Grand National Assembly members were women. Among the few nations to match the low United States percentage of 2.4 percent in 1970 were Guatemala, with 2 percent, and Thailand, with 2.2 percent.[51] The American record is not one to be proud of.

THE FEMALE ADMINISTRATOR

Women's progress in attaining high appointive posts and administrative jobs in government has been spotty. The record reveals areas of no progress at all, areas where there has been retrogression, and areas where advances have taken place in spite of prejudice.

High Appointive Posts

Certain appointive posts have never been held by women. The most conspicuous example is that no woman has ever been appointed to the United States Supreme Court. The Circuit Court of Appeals has only one woman. Four of the 307 United States district judges in 1973 were women. Two Cabinet members have also been women: Frances Perkins, Secretary of Labor from 1933 to 1945; and Olveta Culp Hobby, Secretary of Health, Education, and Welfare from 1953 to 1955. The Treasurer of the United States is traditionally a woman, but since the duties of this post consist largely of the honorary function of signing currency, the tradition hardly stands as a tribute to women's ability.

From 1920 to 1970 only ten ambassadors and ministers have been women, and only three chiefs of missions abroad are currently women out of a total of 103.[52] Of the 1,700 posts classified by the Women's Division of the National Republican Party as high-level, policy-making positions, President Nixon appointed women to 39.[53] One of Nixon's top female appointees was Jayne Baker Spain, a Cincinnati businesswoman who got a $38,000 post as a member of the Civil Service Commission. Nixon was the first to appoint a woman to be head of a Veterans Administration facility.[54]

Discrimination and Stereotyping

Representative Shirley Chisholm (D. New York) has stated that women hold only 2 percent of all managerial jobs, public and private, in the United States. This happens to be about the proportion of women in Congress. It might be thought that because of civil service regulations, the percentage of women holding federal administrative jobs would be higher, but such is not the case.

Of some ten thousand federal jobs that pay over $26,000 per year, only 1.5 percent are held by women. These, of course, are the upper administrative posts. Even in the middle salary range (G.S. 7 to 12) only 19.7 percent of the jobs are held by women. It is at the lower levels that women are in the majority. In the Department of Health, Education, and Welfare, for example, 57.8 percent of the 113,811 employees are women, but at the highest level, G.S. 18 and over, there is only one woman out of 40 employees.[55] In 1971 it was reported that Tally Palmer, a 39-year-old career Foreign Service officer, had to go to both the National Association of Government Employers and the Civil Service Commission to get a promotion to Foreign Service Officer III, with a raise from $19,537 to $22,135. The State Department finally admitted that she had earned the promotion but had been denied it through the usual processes because of her sex.[56]

When a woman gets an administrative post, she must contend with the problem posed by the many men who find it hard to work under a woman. These feelings were well expressed by Herbert A. Miller, who testified for the National Woman's Party on behalf of the Equal Rights Amendment in 1970:

> The difficulties I had working under a woman largely stemmed from my own feelings concerning her status in a bureaucratic hierarchy. Many men for whom I have worked, frankly, have been more difficult to please than the woman for whom I worked, but I accepted the difficulties of working for a man as part of the working world in which I lived. . . .
>
> The cause of my difficulty was not so much the woman under whom I worked, but my own feelings of resentment and unwillingness to accept a woman as a professional equal or superior.[57]

Meeting this problem remains a major challenge.

THE OUTLOOK

The growth of the women's movement may signal the end of complacency on the part of an increasing group of women, but there are still many obstacles to overcome. Many girls still equate intellectual achievement with a lack of femininity. The idea of woman as a "sex object" has been deeply socialized. The National Organization of Women points to self-hatred as a trait possessed by many women.[58] When it comes to political activity, women are apt to use their family responsibilities as an excuse for inaction.

In the present cultural climate, a woman's success in politics may expose her to criticism that she is a poor wife and a worse mother, especially if she has young children. Even when a woman has confidence in her ability to handle the dual functions of politician and mother, she may hesitate to seek political office and busy herself instead with the equally time-consuming voluntary associations that society has defined as suitable for young matrons. A study of women delegates to the 1972 Democratic and Republican conventions from Kansas, Nebraska, South Dakota, and North Dakota found that half the mothers sampled reported they had misgivings about their political activity because of their children. No woman interviewed belonged to fewer than two nonpolitical organizations, and one woman listed 13. Children were found to have no statistical effect on women's nonpolitical organizational activity. In the sample, women with children—even those with eight children—were as likely to participate in as many organizations as those with no children or very few children.[59] Women are not as criticized for leaving their children to cook and serve for political functions—it is only when they attempt to figure in the decision making that leaving their children becomes relevant. If women are to become active in politics at all levels, clearly the motherhood role must be redefined and basic attitudes on the part of both men and women must be restructured.

There are signs that these traditional attitudes and barriers to women's involvement in politics can be broken down. A 1970 Harris Poll revealed a coalition of 40 to 45 percent of American women favoring major changes in women's power status. This coalition was made up of women at the upper end of the educational spectrum and at the lowest end of the economic spectrum. Younger women college graduates, black women, single women, and divorced women were among the major components of the group. A majority of women still favored no change in women's power status. This group is largely made up of white married women who have not attended college.[60] Congresswoman Catherine May (R. Wash.) expresses the belief that women now in college will not be as inhibited about participating in politics as the older generation has been.[61]

In 1972 many women were elected to public office, especially at the local level. A 1971 Gallup Poll showed that 66 percent of voters would vote for a woman for President of the United States. This is a dramatic jump upward from the 54-percent figure in the 1969 poll cited earlier.[62] The earlier poll reflects traditional attitudes that have been entrenched over a long term; the newer one shows that even these attitudes can be changed.

There are several other signs that the forces pushing women into fuller political participation are strong and irreversible. Women's labor force participation rates have been increasing and are forecasted to continue to increase.[63] Education is probably the most important force propelling women into various aspects of political activity, and the number and percentage of women completing college will undoubtedly continue to rise for many years to come. Younger women are more active politically than older women, and the greater percentage of people in the younger age brackets will have significant political impact in the 1970's. Finally, urban women are more politically active than nonurban women, and despite the problems of the cities, there seems to be no end in sight to the trend toward urbanization.[64] Acting as a catalyst to these basic forces will be such organizational elements as the National Women's Political Caucus. In 1972 the NWPC sponsored conferences and encouraged women to play an active political role in all aspects of the campaign. Such efforts may represent a small start, but given the basic demographic trends cited above, all the elements of the women's movement are likely to play an important role in making women a decisive political force before the decade is over. A very popular button passed out at various women's meetings in 1972 may turn out to be prophetic. It says, "Make policy not coffee."

Notes

1. This study and other related studies reaching the same conclusion are cited in Sandra L. Bem and Daryl J. Bem, "Case Study of a Nonconscious Ideology: Training the Woman to Know Her Place," in D. J. Bem, *Beliefs, Attitudes and Human Affairs* (Belmont, Calif.: Brooks-Cole, 1970).
2. Andrew Sinclair, *The Emancipation of the American Woman* (New York: Harper and Row, 1965), p. 39.
3. *Ibid.*, pp. 326-27.
4. Mrs. Gladys O'Donnell, President, National Federation of Republican Women, in a statement before the Constitutional Amendments Subcommittee of the Judiciary Committee, U.S. Congress, Senate, Committee on the Judiciary, *The "Equal Rights" Amendment,* Hearings before the Subcommittee on Constitutional Amendments, Senate, on S.J. Res. 61, 91st Cong., 5th sess., May 1970, p. 664.
5. Charles E. Merriam and Harold F. Gosnell, *Non-Voting* (Chicago: Univ. of Chicago Press, 1924), p. 47.
6. U.S. Dept. of Commerce, Bureau of the Census, *Current Population Reports, Population Characteristics,* "Voting Participation in Nov. 1972," series P-20, no. 192, series P-20, no. 244, Dec. 1972.
7. *Ibid.*
8. Angus Campbell, Philip E. Converse, Warren E. Miller, and Donald E. Stokes, *The American Voter* (New York: Wiley and Sons, 1964), pp. 485-87.
9. *Ibid.*, p. 490.
10. Gallup Opinion Index, Sept. 1970, report no. 63.
11. U.S. Census Bureau, "Voting and Registration in the Election of 1968."
12. Sinclair, p. 92.
13. Campbell et al., pp. 487-88.
14. Naomi B. Lynn and Cornelia B. Flora, "Child-Rearing and Political Participation: The Changing Sense of Self," *Journal of Military and Political Sociology* (Spring 1973).
15. The 1972 Virginia Slims American Women's Opinion Poll, conducted by Louis Harris and Associates; Gallup Opinion Index, Sept. 1970, report no. 63; Gallup Opinion Index, April 1972, report no. 82.
16. Center for Political Studies, Inst. for Social Research, Univ. of Michigan.
17. U.S. Congress, House of Representatives, Committee on Education and Labor, *Discrimination Against Women,* Hearings before the Special Subcommittee on Education on Section 805 of H.R. 16098, 91st Cong., 2d sess., June 1970, pt. 1, p. 179.
18. Robert E. Lane, *Political Life* (New York: Free Press, 1959), p. 355.
19. Democratic National Committee, *National Democrat* (Washington D.C.: National Democratic Committee, Spring 1971), p. 12.
20. *New York Times,* July 22, 1972, p. 22.
21. U.S. Congress, House of Representatives, Committee on Education and Labor, *Discrimination Against Women,* Hearings before the Special Subcommittee on Education on Section 805 of H.R. 16098, 91st Cong., 2d sess. July 1970, pt. 2, p. 913.
22. Gallup Opinion Index, April 1968, report no. 46.
23. Gallup Opinion Index, Sept. 1970, report no. 63.
24. Quoted in *Women Today,* vol. 1, no. 5 (April 2, 1971).
25. *The Spokeswoman,* vol. 1, no. 14 (June 1, 1971), p. 12. *The Spokeswoman* is a new bulle-

tin published at the Urban Research Corporation, 5464 South Short Drive, Chicago, Ill. 60615. Subscriptions are $9 per year.

26. Peggy Lamson, *Few Are Chosen: American Women in Political Life Today* (Boston: Houghton Mifflin, 1968), pp. 98-109.
27. *Ibid.*, p. xxiii. Lamson quotes both the chairman and the second vice-chairman of the Democratic National Committee on this point.
28. "Appendix: The Status of Women in American Law Schools," *Rutgers Law Review*, 25 (Fall 1970), 77.
29. Lamson, pp. 87-123.
30. "How Women Are Doing in Politics," *U.S. News and World Reports*, Aug. 31, 1970, p. 26.
31. M. Kent Jennings and Norman Thomas, "Men and Women in Party Elites: Social Roles and Political Resources," *Midwest Journal of Political Science*, 12 (Nov. 1968), 482.
32. "Increase in Female House Members in 1971 Expected," *Congressional Quarterly Weekly Report*, 28 (July 10, 1970), 1746.
33. Margaret Mead and Frances Begley Kaplan, eds., *American Women: The Report of the President's Commission on the Status of Women and Other Publications of the Commission* (New York: Scribner's, 1965), p. 73.
34. U.S. Congress, Senate, Committee on the Judiciary, *Equal Rights, 1970*, Hearings on S.J. Res. 61 and S.J. Res. 231, 91st Cong., 2d sess., Sept. 1970, p. 243.
35. Emmy E. Werner, "Women in Congress, 1917–1964," *Western Political Quarterly*, 19 (March 1966), 28; Emmy E. Werner, "Women in the State Legislatures," *Western Political Quarterly*, 21 (March 1968), 42-46; *Discrimination Against Women*, Hearings, pt. 2, pp. 912-13.
36. *The Spokeswoman*, vol. 3, no. 6 (Dec. 1, 1972), p. 4.
37. Werner, "Women in the State Legislatures," p. 43.
38. *Ibid.*, p. 44.
39. *Ibid.*, pp. 43-45.
40. *The Spokeswoman*, vol. 1, no. 12 (May 1, 1971), p. 4.
41. *Discrimination Against Women*, Hearings, pt. 2.
42. Werner, "Women in Congress," p. 26.
43. *Ibid.*, p. 23.
44. *Ibid.*, p. 25.
45. Lamson, p. 10.
46. *Ibid.*, p. 44.
47. Frieda L. Gehlen, "Women in Congress," *Trans-action*, 6 (Oct. 1969), 38.
48. *Ibid.*, p. 39.
49. *Ibid.*
50. Lena Jager, M.P., "Has It Made Any Difference," *New Statesman*, 75 (Feb. 16, 1968), 199.
51. United Nations, General Assembly, Report of the Secretary General, *Political Rights of Women*, Addendum, A/18132/Add. 1 (Dec. 1970), p. 11.
52. U.S. Civil Service Commission, Statistics Section, *Study of Employment of Women in Federal Government, 1967* (Washington, D.C.: Government Printing Office, June 1968).
53. Robenia Smith, ed., *Women in Public Service* (Washington, D.C.: Republican National Committee, 1970).
54. *Women Today*, vol. 1, no. 8 (May 17, 1971), p. 2.
55. *Discrimination Against Women*, Hearings, pt. 2, p. 652.

56. *Time,* Sept. 6, 1971, p. 20.
57. *Equal Rights, 1970,* Hearings, p. 266.
58. *Discrimination Against Women,* Hearings, pt. 1, p. 144.
59. Naomi B. Lynn and Cornelia B. Flora, "Women Delegates to the National Conventions: A Regional Perspective" (paper delivered at the 31st annual meeting of the Midwest Political Science Association, Chicago, 1973).
60. *Women Today,* vol. 1, no. 15 (Aug. 23, 1971), p. 1.
61. "Increase in Female House Members in 1971 Expected," p. 1748.
62. *Women Today,* vol. 1, no. 15 (Aug. 23, 1971), p. 1.
63. Valerie Kincade Oppenheimer, *The Female Labor Force in the United States: Demographic and Economic Factors Governing Its Growth and Changing Composition,* Population Monograph Series, no. 5 (Univ. of California, Berkeley: Institute of International Studies, 1970), esp. chap. 1.
64. Abbott L. Ferriss, *Indicators of Trends in the Status of American Women* (New York: Russell Sage Foundation, 1971), pp. 179-82.

Marriage and Psychotherapy

Phyllis Chesler

Many American women enter individual psychoanalysis or psychotherapy just as they enter marriage: with a sense of urgency and desperation, and without questioning their own motives. This is not surprising. Both psychotherapy and marriage are the two major socially approved institutions for women, especially for middle-class women. There is some evidence that single and divorced women seek psychiatric help more often than people in other groups—as if not being married is experienced as an "illness" which psychotherapy can cure (Gurin, 1965; Bart, 1968; Chesler, 1970). Both psychotherapy and marriage isolate women from each other; both institutions emphasize individual rather than or before collective solutions to a woman's problems. Both institutions may be viewed as redramatizations of a little girl's relation to her father in a male-dominated society. Both institutions are based on a woman's helplessness and dependence on a "stronger" male or female authority figure— as husband or psychotherapist. Most women, as well as most men, seem to prefer men as "doctors," just as they prefer male children rather than or before female children. For example, in analyzing the records

Reprinted with permission from *Radical Therapist*, 1, 3 (August-September 1970): 16.

of a middle-class clinic population, I have found that preference for a male rather than a female therapist is voluntarily stated twice as often by both male and female patients.

Both psychotherapy and marriage may be viewed as a way of socially controlling and oppressing women. At the same time, both institutions may be viewed as the two safest havens for women in a society that offers them no others. Psychotherapy and marriage are ways in which a woman can safely express (and politically defuse) her anger and unhappiness—by experiencing them as a form of emotional "illness." Many women experience headaches, terrible fatigue, chronic depression, frigidity, and an overwhelming sense of inferiority. (In Freud's Vienna this was all called "hysteria").[1] Each woman patient thinks these symptoms are unique and are her own fault. She is "neurotic"—rather than economically and psychologically oppressed. She wants from a psychotherapist what she wants—and often can't get—from a husband: attention, understanding, merciful relief, a *personal solution* —in the arms of the "right" husband, on the couch of the "right" therapist. In a complicated way, the institutions of marriage and psychotherapy not only mirror each other: therapy is a way of shoring up the marriage institution by substituting for it, by supplementing it, by encouraging an intrapsychic rather than a political vision. Specifically, the institution of psychotherapy may be used by many women as a way of keeping a bad marriage together, or as a way of terminating it in order to form a "good" marriage. Some women may use psychotherapy as a way to learn how to "catch" a husband—by practicing with a male therapist. Seventy-one out of 105 women patients at a middle-class clinic were single; 48 preferred male therapists. (It is interesting that 43 out of 71 male patients were also single; however, only eight of them volunteered a preference for a female therapist.) It seems likely that women probably spend more time during a therapy session talking about their husbands or boyfriends—or lack of them—than they do talking about their lack of an independent identity or their superficial relations to other women.

Both the institution of psychotherapy and of marriage encourage women to talk—often endlessly—rather than to act (except in their socially prearranged roles as passive "women" or "patients"). In marriage the talking is usually of an indirect nature. Open expressions of rage are too dangerous and ineffective for isolated and economically dependent women. (Often, such "kitchen" declarations end in tears, self-blame, and in the husband graciously agreeing with his wife that she was "not herself.") Even control of a simple—but serious—conversation is usually impossible for most wives when several men, including their husbands, are present. The "wife"-women talk to each other, or they listen silently while the men talk. Very rarely, if ever, do men listen silently to a group of women talking. Even if there are a number of women talking, and only one man is present, he will question the women, per-

Both husbands (beginning with Adam) and psychotherapists (beginning with Freud and including most *female* psychotherapists) tend to view women as children.

haps patiently, perhaps not, but always in order to ultimately control the conversation, and always from a "superior" position.

In psychotherapy the "patient"-woman is encouraged, in fact *directed* to talk—and by a therapist who is at least expected to be, or is perceived as, "superior" or objective. The traditional therapist may be viewed as ultimately controlling what the patient says—through a subtle system of rewards (attention, "interpretations," etc.). In a sense, the treatment monologue or dialogue is taking place in a "laboratory." At its best, such conversation cannot be successfully transferred by the woman—acting by herself alone—to those people in her office, on the streets, or in her bedroom who directly profit from her oppression. (She would be laughed at, viewed as "silly" or "crazy," and if she persisted, would be out of a job—as secretary or wife.) Psychotherapeutic "talking" is indirect in the sense that it does not involve the woman in a verbal confrontation with the significant people in her life. It is indirect also in that words—*any* words—are permitted, so long as certain actions of consequence are avoided. (Such as not paying one's bill, or having—or refusing to have—sexual relations with one's therapist.)

The traditional psychoanalytic theories about women are at best confused and incomplete, and at worst false. However, what takes place in therapy may be more determined by the therapist's personality and ideas, and by the patient's expectations, than by any psychoanalytic "theory." Both husbands (beginning with Adam) and psychotherapists (beginning with Freud and including most *female* psychotherapists) tend to view women as children. For example, in a recent study by Broverman et al. on clinicians' judgments of what is "normal, adult behavior," what is male behavior, and what is female behavior, both male and female clinicians correlated masculine rather than feminine behavior with what they considered to be "normal," and "adult." Specifically, women were viewed as more emotional, more concerned about their appearance, less objective, less independent, less adventurous, more easily influenced, less aggressive, less competitive, more excitable in minor crises than were men. And these traits were not considered "normal" or "adult." Obviously, the ethic of mental health is a masculine one in our society. Two sociologists, writing in 1968 (Phillips and Segal), suggested that women seek psychiatric help (as well as medical help) more often than men because the social role of "woman" allows her to display emotional and physical distress more easily than men. "Sensitive or emotional behavior is more tolerated in women, to the point of aberration, while self-assertive, aggressive, vigorous physical demonstrations are more tolerated among men. . . . Our argument is simply that it is more culturally appropriate and acceptable for women to be expressive about their difficulties." And women can "express" themselves away—in both marriage and in psychotherapy.

Many psychoanalytic concepts and values were and are revolutionary and liberating ones. What I've been objecting to throughout this paper is the way in which these concepts have been institutionalized. For most women the psychotherapeutic encounter is just one more instance of an unequal relationship, just one more instance of a power relationship in which she is submissive and the authority figure is dominant. I wonder how well such a structure can encourage independence—or healthy dependence—in a woman? I wonder what a woman can learn from a male therapist (however well-intentioned) whose own values are sexist, who has been conditioned to view women as inferior, as threatening, as childish, as castrating, as *alien* to himself? How free from the dictates of a sexist society can a female as *patient* be with a *male* therapist? And if therapy could, theoretically, be used to overcome such oppressive sex-role stereotyping, why should the female patient pay money for it—rather than her male therapist, who presumably would be learning to relate to women in a non-sexist way? (And who may, in fact, be enjoying a psychological "service" from his female patient, namely being able to feel superior to, or in control of, his own forbidden longings for dependence, emotionality, etc.—longings he has been trained to project onto women as a *caste;* projections which he can experience most safely with a woman who is a patient, rather than with a wife or a girlfriend or a mother.) How much can a male therapist empathize with a female patient? In Masters and Johnson's recently published *Human Sexual Inadequacy* they state that their research supported unequivocally the "premise that no man will ever fully understand a woman's sexual function or dysfunction . . . (and the same is true for women). . . It helps immeasurably for a distressed, relatively inarticulate or emotionally unstable wife to have available a female cotherapist to interpret what she is saying and even what she is attempting unsuccessfully to express to the uncomprehending husband and often to the male cotherapist as well." I would go one step further here and ask: and what if the female cotherapist is male-oriented, is elitist, is as much a sexist as a male therapist? What if the female therapist has never realized that she is oppressed—*as a woman?* What if the female therapist views marriage and children as "fulfillment" for all women—other than herself?

What practical suggestions can be made following such an analysis of what the institution of psychotherapy has in common with the institution of marriage?

1. Women therapists must begin talking about feminism and about women's liberation with other women—and with other women therapists. A new—rather a *first*—psychology of women must be struggled for—and its outlines communicated to male therapists.[2] Perhaps, for a period of time, male therapists should not attempt to treat female patients. Perhaps all women must join a feminist conscious-ness-raising group—as well as remain in therapeutic treatment.

Notes

1. Many researchers (Szasz, 1961; Hollingshead and Redlich, 1958; Gurin, et al., 1960) have traced the missing Viennese hysteric for us: "she" has turned up in the American lower classes; "she" is either male or female and is not psychologically sophisticated enough to ex-perience physical illnesses as having a psychic origin or meaning. The doctors they consult, often in clinics, are not *ethically* sophisticated enough to do anything other than administer the "pills and needles" expected by their lower-class patients.

2. Male therapists might want to work in new ways with their *male* patients.

Bibliography

1. Bart, Pauline B., "Social Structure and Vocabularies of Discomfort: What Happened to Female Hysteria?" *J. Health and Social Behavior*, vol. 9, no. 3, 1968.
2. Broverman, I. K., Broverman, D. M., Clarkson, R., Rosenkrantz, P., and Vogel, S., "Sex Role Stereotypes and Clinical Judgments of Mental Health," *J. Consulting Psychology*, 1969.
3. Chesler, P., "Psychotherapy and Marriage: Parallel Dependency Structures," *J. of Social Issues* (in press).
4. Gurin, G., et al., *Americans View Their Mental Health* (New York: Basic Books, 1960).
5. Hollingshead, A. B., and Redlich, F. C., *Social Class and Mental Illness* (New York: Wiley, 1958).
6. Masters, W. H., and Johnson, V. E., *Human Sexual Inadequacy* (Boston: Little, Brown, 1970).
7. Phillips, P. L., and Segal, B. E., "Sexual Status and Psychiatric Symptoms," *American Sociological Review*, Feb. 1969.
8. Szasz, T., *The Myth of Mental Illness* (Hoeber-Harper, 1961).

The Sexual Politics
of Interpersonal Behavior

Nancy Henley and Jo Freeman

Social interaction is the battlefield where the
daily war between the sexes is fought. It is
here that women are constantly reminded where
their "place" is and here that they are put back in
their place, should they venture out. Thus, social
interaction serves as the most common means of
social control employed against women. By being
continually reminded of their inferior status in
their interactions with others, and continually compelled to acknowledge that status in their own
patterns of behavior, women learn to internalize
society's definition of them as inferior so thoroughly that they are often unaware of what their status
is. Inferiority becomes habitual, and the inferior
place assumes the familiarity—and even desirability—
of home.

Different sorts of cues in social interaction aid
this enforcement of one's social definition, particularly the verbal message, the nonverbal message
transmitted within a social relationship, and the
nonverbal message transmitted by the environment.
Our educational system emphasizes the verbal message and teaches us next to nothing about how we
interpret and react to the nonverbal ones. Just how

391

. . . environmental cues set the stage on which the power relationships of the sexes are acted out, and the assigned status of each sex is reinforced.

important nonverbal messages are, however, is shown by the finding of Argyle et al. (1970) that nonverbal cues have over four times the impact of verbal ones when both verbal and nonverbal cues are used. Even more important for women, Argyle found that female subjects were more responsive to nonverbal cues (compared with verbal ones) than male subjects. If women are to understand how the subtle forces of social control work in their lives, they must learn as much as possible about how nonverbal cues affect people, and particularly about how they perpetuate the power and superior status enjoyed by men.

Even if a woman encounters no one else directly in her day, visual status reminders are a ubiquitous part of her environment. As she moves through the day, she absorbs many variations of the same status theme, whether or not she is aware of it: male bosses dictate while female secretaries bend over their steno pads; male doctors operate while female nurses assist; restaurants are populated with waitresses serving men; magazine and billboard ads remind the woman that home maintenance and child care are her foremost responsibilities and that being a sex object for male voyeurs is her greatest asset. If she is married, her mail reminds her that she is a mere "Mrs." appended to her husband's name. When she is introduced to others or fills out a form, the first thing she must do is divulge her marital status, acknowledging the social rule that the most important information anyone can know about her is her legal relationship to a man.

These environmental cues set the stage on which the power relationships of the sexes are acted out, and the assigned status of each sex is reinforced. Though studies have been made of the several means by which status inequalities are communicated in interpersonal behavior, they do not usually deal with power relationships between men and women. Goffman (1956, pp. 64, 78–79) has pointed to many characteristics associated with status:

> Between status equals we may expect to find interaction guided by symmetrical familiarity. Between superordinate and subordinate we may expect to find assymetrical relations, the superordinate having the right to exercise certain familiarities which the subordinate is not allowed to reciprocate. Thus, in the research hospital, doctors tended to call nurses by their first names, while nurses responded with "polite" or "formal" address. Similarly, in American business organizations the boss may thoughtfully ask the elevator man how his children are, but this entrance into another's life may be

blocked to the elevator man, who can appreciate the concern but not return it. Perhaps the clearest form of this is found in the psychiatrist-patient relation, where the psychiatrist has a right to touch on aspects of the patient's life that the patient might not even allow himself to touch upon, while of course this privilege is not reciprocated.

Rules of demeanor, like rules of deference, can be symmetrical or asymmetrical. Between social equals, symmetrical rules of demeanor seem often to be prescribed. Between unequals many variations can be found. For example, at staff meetings on the psychiatric units of the hospital, medical doctors had the privilege of swearing, changing the topic of conversation, and sitting in undignified positions; attendants, on the other hand, had the right to attend staff meetings and to ask questions during them . . . but were implicitly expected to conduct themselves with greater circumspection than was required of doctors. . . . Similarly, doctors had the right to saunter into the nurses' station, lounge on the station's dispensing counter, and engage in joking with the nurses; other ranks participated in this informal interaction with doctors, but only after doctors had initiated it.

A status variable widely studied by Brown and others (1960, 1961, 1965) is the use of terms of address. In languages that have both familiar and polite forms of the second person singular ("you"), asymmetrical use of the two forms invariably indicates a status difference, and it always follows the same pattern. The person using the familiar form is always the superior to the person using the polite form. In English, the only major European language not to have dual forms of address, status differences are similarly indicated by the right of first-naming; the status superior can first-name the inferior in situations where the inferior must use the superior's title and last name. An inferior who breaks this rule by inappropriately using a superior's first name is considered insolent (see Brown, 1965, pp. 92–97).

According to Brown, the pattern evident in the use of forms of address applies to a very wide range of interpersonal behavior and invariably has two other components: (1) whatever form is used by a superior in situations of status inequality can be used reciprocally by intimates, and whatever form is used by an inferior is the socially prescribed usage for nonintimates; (2) initiation or increase of intimacy is the right of the superior. To use the example of naming again, friends use first names with each other, while strangers use titles and last names, though "instant" intimacy is considered proper in some cultures, such as our own, among status equals in informal settings. Status superiors, such as professors, specifically tell status inferiors, such as students when they can use the first name, and often rebuff them if they assume such a right unilaterally.

Although Brown did not apply these patterns to status differences between the sexes, their relevance is readily seen. The social rules say that it is boys who are supposed to call girls for dates, men who are supposed to propose marriage to

> Females who make "advances" are considered
> improper, forward, aggressive, brassy, or
> otherwise "unladylike." By initiating intimacy
> they have . . . usurped a [male] prerogative.

women, and males who are supposed to initiate sexual activity with females. Females who make "advances" are considered improper, forward, aggressive, brassy, or otherwise "unladylike." By initiating intimacy they have stepped out of their place and usurped a status prerogative. The value of such a prerogative is that it is a form of power. Between the sexes, as in other human interaction, the one who has the right to initiate greater intimacy has more control over the relationship. Superior status brings with it not only greater prestige and greater privileges, but greater power.

These advantages are exemplified in many of the various means of communicating status. Like the doctors in Goffman's research hospital, men are allowed such privileges as swearing and sitting in undignified positions, but women are denied them. Though the male privilege of swearing is curtailed in mixed company, the body movement permitted to women is circumscribed even in all-woman groups. It is considered unladylike for a woman to use her body too forcefully, to sprawl, to stand with her legs widely spread, to sit with her feet up, or to cross the ankle of one leg over the knee of the other. The more "feminine" a woman's clothes are, the more circumscribed the use of her body. Depending on her clothes, she may be expected to sit with her knees together, not to sit cross-legged, or not even to bend over.

Prior to the 1920's women's clothes were designed to be confining and cumbersome. The dress reform movement, which disposed of corsets and long skirts, was considered by many to have more significance for female emancipation than women's suffrage (O'Neill, 1969, p. 270). Today women's clothes are designed to be revealing, but women are expected to restrict their body movements to avoid revealing too much. Furthermore, because women's clothes are contrived to reveal women's physical features, rather than being loose like men's, women must resort to purses to carry their belongings instead of pockets. These "conveniences" have become, in a time of blurred sex distinctions, one of the surest signs of sex, and thus have developed the character of stigma, a sign of woman's shame, as when they are used to ridicule both women and transvestites.

Women in our society are expected to reveal not only more of their bodies than men but also more of themselves. Female socialization encourages greater expression of emotion than that of the male. Whereas men are expected to be stolid and impassive, and not to disclose their feelings beyond certain limits, women are expected to express their *selves*. Such self-expression can disclose a lot of oneself, and, as Jourard and Lasakow (1958) found, females are more self-disclosing to others than males are. This puts them at an immediate disadvantage.

The inverse relationship between disclosure and power has been reported by other studies in addition to Goffman's earlier cited investigation into a research hospital. Slobin, Miller, and Porter (1968) stated that individuals in a business organization are "more self-disclosing to their immediate superior than to their immediate subordinates." Self-disclosure is a means of enhancing another's power. When one has greater access to information about another person, one has a resource the other person does not have. Thus not only does power give status, but status gives power. And those possessing neither must contribute to the power and status of others continuously.

Another factor adding to women's vulnerability is that they are socialized to *care* more than men—especially about personal relationships. This puts them at a disadvantage, as Ross articulated in 1921 in what he called the "Law of Personal Exploitation": "In any sentimental relation the one who cares less can exploit the one who cares more," (p. 136). The same idea was put more broadly by Waller and Hill (1951) as the "Principle of Least Interest": "That person is able to dictate the conditions of association whose interest in the continuation of the affair is least." (p. 191). In other words, women's caring, like their openness, gives them less power in a relationship.

One way of indicating acceptance of one's place and deference to those of superior status is by following the rules of "personal space." Sommer (1969, Chap. 2) has observed that dominant animals and human beings have a larger envelope of inviolability surrounding them—i.e., are approached less closely—than those of a lower status. Willis (1966) made a study of the initial speaking distance set by an approaching person as a function of the speakers' relationship. His finding that women were approached more closely than men—i.e., their personal space was smaller or more likely to be breached—is consistent with their lower status.

Touching is one of the closer invasions of one's personal space, and in our low-contact culture it implies privileged access to another person. People who accidentally touch other people generally take great pains to apologize; people forced into close proximity, as in a crowded elevator, often go to extreme lengths to avoid touching. Even the figurative meanings of the word convey a notion of access to privileged areas—e.g., to one's emotions (one is "touched" by a sad story), or to one's purse (one is "touched" for ten dollars). In addition, the act of touching can be a subtle physical threat.

Remembering the patterns that Brown found in terms of address, consider the interactions between pairs of persons of different status, and picture who would be more likely to touch the other (put an arm around the shoulder or a hand on the back, tap the chest, hold the arm, or the like): teacher and student; master and servant; policeman and accused; doctor and patient; minister and parishioner; adviser and advisee; foreman and worker; businessman and secretary. As with first-naming, it is considered presumptuous for a person of low status to initiate touch with a person of higher status.

There has been little investigation of touching by social scientists, but the few studies made so far indicate that females are touched more than males are. Goldberg and Lewis (1969) and Lewis (1972) report that from six months on, girl babies are touched more than boy babies. The data reported in Jourard (1966) and Jourard and Rubin (1968) show that sons and fathers tend to refrain from touching each other and that "when it comes to physical contact within the family, it is the daughters who are the favored ones" (Jourard, 1966, p. 224). An examination of the number of different regions in which subjects were touched showed that mothers and fathers touch their daughters in more regions than they do their sons; that daughters touch their fathers in more regions than sons do; and that males touch their opposite-sex best friends in more regions than females do. Overall, women's mean total "being-touched" score was higher than men's.

Jourard and Rubin take the view that "touching is equated with sexual intent, either consciously, or at a less-conscious level" (p. 47), but it would seem that there is a sex difference in the interpretation of touch. Lewis reflects this when he writes, "In general, for men in our culture, proximity (touching) is restricted to the opposite sex and its function is primarily sexual in nature" (p. 237). Waitresses, secretaries, and women students are quite used to being touched by their male superordinates, but they are expected not to "misinterpret" such gestures. However, women who touch men are often interpreted as conveying sexual intent, as they have often found out when their intentions were quite otherwise. Such different interpretations are consistent with the status patterns found earlier. If touching indicates either power or intimacy, and women are deemed by men to be status inferiors, touching by women will be perceived as a gesture of intimacy, since it would be inconceivable for them to be exercising power.

A study by Henley (1970) puts forward this hypothesis. Observations of incidents of touch in public urban places by a white male research assistant, naive to the uses of his data, in which age, sex, and approximate socioeconomic status were recorded, indicated that higher-status persons do touch lower-status persons significantly more. In particular, men touched women more, even when all other variables were held constant. When the settings of the observations were differentially examined, the pattern showed up primarily in the outdoor setting, with indoor interaction being more evenly spread over sex combinations. This finding cannot be unequivocally interpreted, but it may be that outdoor interaction, being more public, necessitates stricter attention to the symbols of power, while indoor interaction, especially in the relatively impersonal yet public settings visited, is more informal and encourages relaxation of the power relationship. Alternatively, one could say that indoors, power may be more easily communicated by cues other than touching.

The other nonverbal cues by which status is indicated have likewise not been adequately researched—for humans. But O'Connor (1970) argues that many of the gestures of dominance and submission that have been noted in the primates are equally present in humans. They are used to maintain and reinforce the status hierarchy by reassuring those of higher status that those of lower status accept their place in the human pecking order.

The most studied nonverbal communication among humans is probably eye contact, and here too one finds a sex difference. It has repeatedly been found that women look more at another in a dyad than men do (Exline, 1963; Exline, Gray, & Schuette, 1965; Rubin, 1970). Exline, Gray, and Schuette suggest that "willingness to engage in mutual visual interaction is more characteristic of those who are oriented towards inclusive and affectionate interpersonal relations" (p. 207), but Rubin concludes that while "gazing may serve as a vehicle of emotional expression for women, [it] in addition may allow women to obtain cues from their male partners concerning the appropriateness of their behavior" (p. 272). This interpretation is supported by Efran and Broughton's (1966) data showing that even male subjects "maintain more eye contact with individuals toward whom they have developed higher expectancies for social approval" (p. 103).

Another possible reason why women gaze more at men is that men talk more (Argyle, Lalljee, & Cook, 1968), and there is a tendency for the listener to look more at the speaker than vice versa (Exline et al., 1965).

It is especially illuminating to look at the power relationships established and maintained by the manipulation of eye contact. The mutual glance can be seen as a sign of union, but when intensified into a stare it may become a way of doing battle (Exline, 1963). Research reported by Ellsworth, Carlsmith, and Henson (1972) supports the notion that the stare can be interpreted as an aggressive gesture. These authors write, "Staring at humans can elicit the same sort of responses that are common in primates; that is, staring can act like a primate threat display" (p. 310).

Though women engage in mutual visual interaction in its intimate form to a high degree, they probably back down when looking becomes a gesture of dominance. O'Connor points out, "The direct stare or glare is a common human gesture

> . . . contrary to popular myth, men do talk
> more than women, both in single-sex and in
> mixed-sex groups.

of dominance. Women use the gesture as well as men, but often in modified form. While looking directly at a man, a woman usually has her head slightly tilted, implying the beginning of a presenting gesture or enough submission to render the stare ambivalent if not actually submissive."

The idea that the averted glance is a gesture of submission is supported by the research of Hutt and Ounsted (1966) into the characteristic gaze aversion of autistic children. They remark that "these children were never attacked [by peers] despite the fact that to a naive observer they appeared to be easy targets; this indicated that their gaze aversion had some signalling function similar to 'facing away' in the kittiwake or 'head-flagging' in the herring gull—behavior patterns which Tinbergen (1959) has termed 'appeasement postures.' In other words, gaze aversion inhibited any aggressive or threat behavior on the part of other conspecifics" (p. 354).

Gestures of dominance and submission can be verbal as well as nonverbal. In fact, the sheer use of verbalization is a form of dominance because it can quite literally render someone speechless by preventing one from "getting a word in edgewise." As noted earlier, contrary to popular myth, men do talk more than women, both in single-sex and in mixed-sex groups. Within a group a major means of asserting dominance is to interrupt. Those who want to dominate others interrupt more; those speaking will not permit themselves to be interrupted by their inferiors, but they will give way to those they consider their superiors.

Other characteristics of persons in inferior status positions are the tendencies to hesitate and apologize, often offered as submissive gestures in the face of threats or potential threats. If staring directly, pointing, and touching can be subtle nonverbal threats, the corresponding gestures of submission seem to be lowering the eyes from another's gaze, falling silent (or not speaking at all) when interrupted or pointed at, and cuddling to the touch. Many of these nonverbal gestures of submission are very familiar. They are the traits our society assigns as desirable secondary characteristics of the female role. Girls who have properly learned to be "feminine" have learned to lower their eyes, remain silent, back down, and cuddle at the appropriate times. There is even a word for this syndrome that is applied only to females: coy.

In verbal communication one finds a similar pattern of differences between the sexes. As mentioned earlier, men have the privilege of swearing, and hence access to a vocabulary not customarily available to women. On the surface this seems like an innocuous limitation, until one realizes the psychological function of swearing: it is one of the most harmless and effective ways of expressing anger. The alternatives are to express one's feelings with physical violence or to suppress them and by so doing turn one's anger in on oneself. The former is prohibited to both sexes (to different degrees) but the latter is decisively encouraged in women. The result is that women are "intropunitive"; they punish themselves for their own anger rather than somehow dissipate it. Since anger turned inward is commonly viewed as the basis for depression, we should not be surprised that depression is considerably more common in women that in men, and in fact is the most prevalent form of "mental illness" among women.

Swearing is only the most obvious sex difference in language. Key (1972) has noted that sex differences are to be found in phonological, semantic, and grammatical aspects of language as well as in word use (see also Lakoff, 1973). Austin (1965) has commented that "in our culture little boys tend to be nasal . . . and little girls, oral" (p. 34), but that in the "final stages" of courtship the voices of both men and women are low and nasal (p. 37). The pattern cited by Brown (1965), in which the form appropriately used by status superiors is used between status equals in intimate situations, is again visible: in the intimate situation the female adopts the vocal style of the male.

In situations where intimacy is not a possible interpretation, it is not power but abnormality that is the usual interpretation. Female voices are expected to be soft and quiet—even when men are using loud voices. Yet it is only the "lady" whose speech is refined. Women who do not fit this stereotype are often called loud —a word commonly applied derogatorily to other minority groups or out groups (Austin, 1963, p. 38). One of the most popular derogatory terms for women is "shrill," which, after all, simply means loud (out of place) and high-pitched (female).

In language, as in touch and in most other aspects of interpersonal behavior, status differences between the sexes mean that the same traits are differently interpreted when displayed by each sex. A man's behavior toward a woman might be interpreted as an expression of either power or intimacy, depending on the situation. When the same behavior is engaged in by a woman and directed toward a man, it is interpreted only as a gesture of intimacy—and intimacy between the sexes is always seen as sexual in nature. Because our values say that women should not have power over men, women's nonverbal communication is rarely interpreted as an expression of power. If the situation precludes a sexual interpretation, women's assumption of the male prerogative is dismissed as deviant (castrating, domineering, unfeminine, or the like).

Of course, if women do not wish to be classified either as deviant or as perpetually sexy, then they must persist in playing the proper role by following the interpersonal behavior pattern prescribed for them. Followed repeatedly, these patterns function as a means of control. What is merely habitual is often seen as desirable. The more men and women interact in the way they have been trained to from birth without considering the meaning of what they do, the more they become dulled to the significance of their actions. Just as outsiders observing a new society are more aware of the status differences of that society than its members are, so those who play the sexual politics of interpersonal behavior are usually not conscious of what they do. Instead they continue to wonder that feminists make such a mountain out of such a "trivial" molehill.

References

Argyle, M., Lalljee, M., & Cook, M. The effects of visibility on interaction in a dyad. *Human Relations,* 1968, 21:3–17.

Argyle, M., Salter, V., Nicholson, H., Williams, M., & Burgess, P. The communication of inferior and superior attitudes by verbal and non-verbal signals. *British Journal of Social and Clinical Psychology,* 1970, 9:222–31.

Austin, W. M. Some social aspects of paralanguage. *Canadian Journal of Linguistics,* 1965, 11:31–39.

Brown, R. *Social psychology.* Glencoe, Ill.: Free Press, 1965.

Brown, R., & Ford, M. Address in American English. *Journal of Abnormal and Social Psychology,* 1961, 62:375–85.

Brown, R., & Gilman, A. The pronouns of power and solidarity. In T. A. Sebeak, ed., *Style in language.* Cambridge, Mass.: M.I.T. Press, 1960.

Efran, J. S., & Broughton, A. Effect of expectancies for social approval on visual behavior. *Journal of Personality and Social Psychology,* 1966, 4:103–7.

Ellsworth, P. C., Carlsmith, J. M., & Henson, A. The stare as a stimulus to flight in human subjects: A series of field experiments. *Journal of Personality and Social Psychology,* 1972, 21:302–11.

Exline, R. Explorations in the process of person perception: Visual interaction in relation to competition, sex, and need for affiliation. *Journal of Personality,* 1963, 31:1–20.

Exline, R., Gray, D., & Schuette, D. Visual behavior in a dyad as affected by interview content and sex of respondent. *Journal of Personality and Social Psychology,* 1965, 1:201–9.

Goffman, E. The nature of deference and demeanor. *American Anthropologist,* 1956, 58:473–502. Reprinted in E. Goffman, *Interaction ritual.* New York: Anchor, 1967, pp. 47–95.

Goldberg, S., & Lewis, M. Play behavior in the year-old infant: Early sex differences. *Child Development,* 1969, 40:21–31.

Henley, N. The politics of touch. American Psychological Association, 1970. In P. Brown, ed., *Radical psychology.* New York: Harper & Row, 1973.

Hutt, C., & Ounsted, C. The biological significance of gaze aversion with particular reference to the syndrome of infantile autism. *Behavioral Science*, 1966, 11:346–56.

Jourard, S. M. An exploratory study of body accessibility. *British Journal of Social and Clinical Psychology*, 1966, 5:221–31.

Jourard, S. M., & Lasakow, P. Some factors in self-disclosure. *Journal of Abnormal and Social Psychology*, 1958, 56:91–98.

Jourard, S. M., & Rubin, J. E. Self-disclosure and touching: A study of two modes of interpersonal encounter and their interrelation. *Journal of Humanistic Psychology*, 1968, 8:39–48.

Key, M. R. Linguistic behavior of male and female. *Linguistics*, 1972, 88:15–31.

Lakoff, R. Language and woman's place. *Language in Society*, 1973, 2, 1:45–79.

Lewis, M. Parents and children: Sex-Role development. *School Review*, 1972, 80:229–40.

O'Connor, L. Male dominance: The nitty gritty of oppression. *It Ain't Me Babe*, 1970, 1:9.

O'Neill, W. L. *Everyone was brave: The rise and fall of feminism*. Chicago: Quadrangle, 1969.

Ross, E. A. *Principles of sociology*. New York: Century, 1921.

Rubin, Z. Measurement of romantic love. *Journal of Personality and Social Psychology*, 1970, 16:265–73.

Slobin, D. I., Miller, S. H., & Porter, L. W. Forms of address and social relations in a business organization. *Journal of Personality and Social Psychology*, 1968, 8:289–93.

Sommer, R. *Personal space*. Englewood Cliffs, N.J.: Prentice-Hall, 1969.

Tinbergen, N. Comparative study of the behavior of gulls: A progress report. *Behavior*, 1959, 15:1–70

Waller, W. W., & Hill, R. *The family: A dynamic interpretation*. New York: Dryden, 1951.

Willis, F. N., Jr. Initial speaking distance as a function of the speakers' relationship. *Psychonomic Science*, 1966, 5:221–22.

Women As a Minority Group

Helen Mayer Hacker

Although sociological literature reveals scattered references to women as a minority group, comparable in certain respects to racial, ethnic, and national minorities, no systematic investigation has been undertaken as to what extent the term "minority group" is applicable to women. . . .

Yet it may well be that regarding women as a minority group may be productive of fresh insights and suggest leads for further research. The purpose of this paper is to apply to women some portion of that body of sociological theory and methodology customarily used for investigating such minority groups as Negroes, Jews, immigrants, etc. It may be anticipated that not only will principles already established in the field of intergroup relations contribute to our understanding of women, but in the process of modifying traditional concepts and theories to fit the special case of women, new viewpoints for the fruitful re-examination of other minority groups will emerge.

In defining the term "minority group," the presence of discrimination is the identifying factor. As Louis Wirth has pointed out, "minority group" is not a statistical concept, nor need it denote an alien group, Indeed for the present discussion I have

Reprinted from *Social Forces*, 30 (October 1951): 60-69, by permission of the University of North Carolina Press.

adopted his definition: "A minority group is any group of people who because of their physical or cultural characteristics, are singled out from the others in the society in which they live for differential and unequal treatment, and who therefore regard themselves as objects of collective discrimination." It is apparent that this definition includes both objective and subjective characteristics of a minority group: the fact of discrimination and the awareness of discrimination, with attendant reactions to that awareness. A person who on the basis of his group affiliation is denied full participation in those opportunities which the value system of his culture extends to all members of the society satisfies the objective criterion, but there are various circumstances which may prevent him from fulfilling the subjective criterion.

In the first place, a person may be unaware of the extent to which his group membership influences the way others treat him. He may have formally dissolved all ties with the group in question and fondly imagine his identity is different from what others hold it to be. Consequently, he interprets their behavior toward him solely in terms of his individual characteristics. Or, less likely, he may be conscious of his membership in a certain group but not be aware of the general disesteem with which the group is regarded. A final possibility is that he may belong in a category which he does not realize has group significance. An example here might be a speech peculiarity which has come to have unpleasant connotations in the minds of others. Or a lower-class child with no conception of "class as culture" may not understand how his manners act as cues in eliciting the dislike of his middle-class teacher. The foregoing cases all assume that the person believes in equal opportunities for all in the sense that one's group affiliation should not affect his role in the larger society. We turn now to a consideration of situations in which this assumption is not made.

It is frequently the case that a person knows that because of his group affiliation he receives differential treatment, but feels that this treatment is warranted by the distinctive characteristics of his group. A Negro may believe that there are significant differences between whites and Negroes which justify a different role in life for the Negro. A child may accept the fact that physical differences between him and an adult require his going to bed earlier than they do. A Sudra knows that his lot in life has been cast by divine fiat, and he does not expect the perquisites of a Brahmin. A woman does not wish for the rights and duties of men. In all these situations, clearly, the person does not regard himself as an "object of collective discrimination."

For the two types presented above: (1) those who do not know that they are being discriminated against on a group basis; and (2) those who acknowledge the propriety of differential treatment on a group basis, the subjective attributes of a

Like those minority groups whose self-castigation outdoes dominant-group derision of them, women frequently exceed men in the violence of their vituperations of their sex.

minority-group member are lacking. They feel no minority-group consciousness, harbor no resentment, and, hence, cannot properly be said to belong in a minority group. Although the term "minority group" is inapplicable to both types, the term "minority-group status" may be substituted. This term is used to categorize persons who are denied rights to which they are entitled according to the value system of the observer. An observer, who is a firm adherent of the democratic ideology, will often consider persons to occupy a minority-group status who are well accommodated to their subordinate roles.

No empirical study of the frequency of minority-group feelings among women has yet been made, but common observation would suggest that, consciously at least, few women believe themselves to be members of a minority group in the way in which some Negroes, Jews, Italians, etc., may so conceive themselves. There are, of course, many sex-conscious women, known to a past generation as feminists, who are filled with resentment at the discriminations they fancy are directed against their sex. . . . Yet the number of women who participate in "women's affairs" even in the United States, the classic land of associations, is so small that one cannot easily say the the majority of women display minority group consciousness. . . .

Still, women often manifest many of the psychological characteristics which have been imputed to self-conscious minority groups. Kurt Lewin[1] has pointed to group self-hatred as a frequent reaction of the minority-group member to his group affiliation. This feeling is exhibited in the person's tendency to denigrate other members of the group, to accept the dominant group's stereotyped conception of them, and to indulge in "mea culpa" breast-beating. He may seek to exclude himself from the average of his group, or he may point the finger of scorn at himself. Since a person's conception of himself is based on the defining gestures of others, it is unlikely that members of a minority group can wholly escape personality distortion. Constant reiteration of one's inferiority must often lead to its acceptance as a fact.

Certainly women have not been immune to the formulations of the "female character" throughout the ages. From those (to us) deluded creatures who confessed to witchcraft to the modern sophisticates who speak disparagingly of the cattiness and disloyalty of women, women reveal their introjection of prevailing attitudes toward them. Like those minority groups whose self-castigation outdoes dominant-group derision of them, women frequently exceed men in the violence of their vituperations of their sex. They are more severe in moral judgments, especially in sexual matters. A line of self-criticism may be traced from Hannah More, a blue-stocking herself, to Dr. Marynia Farnham, who lays most of the world's ills at women's door. Women express themselves as disliking other women, as preferring to work under men, and as finding exclusively female gatherings repugnant. The *Fortune* polls conducted in 1946 show that women, more than men, have misgivings concerning women's participation in industry, the professions, and civic life. And more than one-fourth of women wish they had been born in the opposite sex.[2]

Militating against a feeling of group identification on the part of women is a differential factor in their socialization. Members of a minority group are frequently socialized within their own group. Personality development is more largely a resultant of intra- than inter-group interaction. The conception of his role formed by a Negro or a Jew or a second-generation immigrant is greatly dependent upon the definitions offered by members of his own group, on their attitudes and behavior toward him. Ignoring for the moment class differences within the group, the minority-group person does not suffer discrimination from members of his own group. But only rarely does a woman experience this type of group belongingness. Her interactions with members of the opposite sex may be as frequent as her relationships with members of her own sex. Women's conceptions of themselves, therefore, spring as much from their intimate relationships with men as with women. . . .

Even though the sense of group identification is not so conspicuous in women as in racial and ethnic minorities, they, like these others, tend to develop a separate subculture. Women have their own language, comparable to the argot of the underworld and professional groups. It may not extend to a completely separate dialect [such] as has been discovered in some preliterate groups, but there are words and idioms employed chiefly by women. Only the acculturated male can enter into the conversation of the beauty parlor, the exclusive shop, the bridge table, or the kitchen. In contrast to men's interest in physical health, safety, money, and sex, women attach greater importance to attractiveness, personality, home, family, and other people. . . .

We must return now to the original question of the aptness of the designation of minority group for women. . . . Formal discriminations against women are too well-known for any but the most summary description. In general they take the form of being barred from certain activities or, if admitted, being treated unequally. Discriminations against women may be viewed as arising from the generally ascribed status "female" and from the specially ascribed statuses of "wife," "mother," and "sister." . . .

As females, in the economic sphere, women are largely confined to sedentary, monotonous work under the supervision of men, and are treated unequally with regard to pay, promotion, and responsibility. With the exceptions of teaching, nursing, social service, and library work, in which they do not hold a proportionate number of supervisory positions and are often occupationally segregated from men, they make a poor showing in the professions. Although they own 80 percent of the nation's wealth,* they do not sit on the boards of directors of great corporations. Educational opportunities are likewise unequal. Professional schools, such as [those of] architecture and medicine, apply quotas. Women's colleges are frequently inferior to men's. In co-educational schools women's participation in campus activities is limited. As citizens, women are often barred from jury service and public office. Even when they are admitted to the apparatus of political parties, they are subordinated to men. Socially, women have less freedom of movement, and are permitted fewer deviations in the proprieties of dress, speech, manners. In social intercourse they are confined to a narrower range of personality expression.

In the specially ascribed status of wife, a woman—in several States—has no exclusive right to her earnings, is discriminated against in employment, must take the domicile of her husband, and in general must meet the social expectation of subordination to her husband's interests. As a mother, she may not have the guardianship of her children, bears the chief stigma in the case of an illegitimate child, is rarely given leave of absence for pregnancy. As a sister, she suffers unequal distribution of domestic duties between herself and her brother, must yield preference to him in obtaining an education, and in such other psychic and material gratifications as cars, trips, and living away from home.

If it is conceded that women have a minority-group status, what may be learned from applying to women various theoretical constructs in the field of intergroup relations?

One instrument of diagnostic value is the measurement of social distance between dominant and minority groups. But we have seen that one important difference between women and other minorities is that women's attitudes and self-conceptions are conditioned more largely by interaction with both minority- and dominant group members. Before measuring social distance, therefore, a continuum might be constructed of the frequency and extent of women's interaction with men, with the poles conceptualized as ideal types. One extreme would represent a complete "ghetto" status, the woman whose contacts with men were of the most secondary kind. At the other extreme shall we put the woman who has prolonged and repeated associations with men, but only in those situations in which

---

* [Editor's note: See, however, the Bernard article in this volume.]

sex-awareness plays a prominent role, or the woman who enters into a variety of relationships with men in which her sex identity is to a large extent irrelevant? . . .

Social distance tests as applied to relationships between other dominant and minority groups have for the most part adopted prestige criteria as their basis. The assumption is that the type of situation into which one is willing to enter with average members of another group reflects one's estimate of the status of the group relative to one's own. When the tested group is a sex-group rather than a racial, national, religious, or economic one, several important differences in the use and interpretation of the scale must be noted.

1. Only two groups are involved: men and women. Thus, the test indicates the amount of homogeneity or we-feeling only according to the attribute of sex. If men are a primary group, there are not many groups to be ranked secondary, tertiary, etc., with respect to them, but only one group, women whose social distance cannot be calculated relative to other groups.

2. Lundberg[3] suggests the possibility of a group of Catholics registering a smaller social distance to Moslems than to Catholics. In such an event the group of Catholics, from any sociological viewpoint, would be classified as Moslems. If women expressed less social distance to men than to women, should they then be classified sociologically as men? Perhaps no more so than the legendary Negro who, when requested to move to the colored section of the train, replied, "Boss, I'se done resigned from the colored race," should be classified as white. It is likely, however, that the group identification of many women in our society is with men. The feminists were charged with wanting to be men, since they associated male physical characteristics with masculine social privileges. A similar statement can be made about men who show greater social distance to other men than to women.

Social distance may be measured from the standpoint of the minority group or the dominant group with different results. In point of fact, tension often arises when one group feels less social distance than the other. A type case here is the persistent suitor who underestimates his desired sweetheart's feeling of social distance toward him.

3. In social distance tests the assumption is made of an orderly progression—although not necessarily by equal intervals—in the scale. That is, it is not likely that a person would express willingness to have members of a given group as his neighbors, while simultaneously voicing the desire to have them excluded from his country. On all scales marriage represents the minimum social distance, and implies willingness for associations on all levels of lesser intimacy. May the customary scale be applied to men and women? If we take the expressed attitude of many men and women not to marry, we may say that they have feelings of social distance toward the opposite sex, and in this situation the usual order of the scale may be preserved.

Men will accept women at the supposed level of greatest intimacy while rejecting them at lower levels.

In our culture, however, men who wish to marry must perforce marry women, and even if they accept this relationship, they may still wish to limit their association with women in other situations. The male physician may not care for the addition of female physicians to his hospital staff. The male poker player may be thrown off his game if women participate. A damper may be put upon the hunting expedition if women come along. The average man may not wish to consult a woman lawyer. And so on. In these cases it seems apparent that the steps in the social-distance scale must be reversed. Men will accept women at the supposed level of greatest intimacy while rejecting them at lower levels.

But before concluding that a different scale must be constructed when the dominant-group attitude . . . being tested is that of men toward women, the question may be raised as to whether marriage in fact represents the point of minimum social distance. It may not imply anything but physical intimacy and work accommodation, as was frequently true in nonindividuated societies, such as preliterate groups and the household economy of the Middle Ages, or marriages of convenience in the European upper class. Even in our own democratic society where marriage is supposedly based on romantic love there may be little communication between the partners in marriage. The Lynds[4] report the absence of real companionship between husband and wife in Middletown. Women have been known to say that although they have been married for twenty years, their husband is still a stranger to them. . . . Part of the explanation may be found in the subordination of wives to husbands in our culture which is expressed in the separate spheres of activity for men and women. A recent advertisement in a magazine of national circulation depicts a pensive husband seated by his knitting wife with the caption, "Sometimes a man has moods his wife cannot understand." In this case the husband is worried about a pension plan for his employees. The assumption is that the wife, knowing nothing of the business world, cannot take the role of her husband in this matter.

The presence of love does not in itself argue for either equality of status nor fullness of communication. We may love those who are either inferior or superior to us, and we may love persons whom we do not understand. The supreme literary examples of passion without communication are found in Proust's portrayal of Swann's obsession with Odette, the narrator's infatuation with the elusive Albertine, and, of course, Dante's longing for Beatrice.

In the light of these considerations concerning the relationships between men and women, some doubt may be cast on the propriety of placing marriage on the positive extreme of the social distance scale with respect to ethnic and religious minority groups. Since inequalities of status are preserved in marriage, a dominant-group member may be willing to marry a member of a group which, in general, he would not wish admitted to his club. The social-distance scale which uses marriage as a sign of an extreme degree of acceptance is inadequate for appreciating the position of women, and perhaps for other minority groups as well. The relationships among similarity of status, communication as a measure of intimacy, and love must be clarified before social distance tests can be applied usefully to attitudes between men and women.

Is the separation between males and females in our society a caste line? Folsom[5] suggests that it is, and Myrdal[6] in his well-known Appendix 5 considers the parallel between the position of and feelings toward women and Negroes in our society. The relation between women and Negroes is historical, as well as analogical. In the seventeenth century the legal status of Negro servants was borrowed from that of women and children, who were under the *patria potestas,* and until the Civil War there was considerable cooperation between the Abolitionist and woman suffrage movements. According to Myrdal, the problems of both groups are resultants of the transition from a pre-industrial, paternalistic scheme of life to individualistic, industrial capitalism. Obvious similarities in the status of women and Negroes are indicated in Chart 1.

While these similarities in the situation of women and Negroes may lead to increased understanding of their social roles, account must also be taken of differences which impose qualifications on the comparison of the two groups. Most importantly, the influence of marriage as a social elevator for women, but not for Negroes, must be considered. Obvious, too, is the greater importance of women to the dominant group, despite the economic, sexual, and prestige gains which Negroes afford the white South. Ambivalence is probably more marked in the attitude of white males toward women than toward Negroes. The "war of the sexes" is only an expression of men's and women's vital need of each other. Again, there is greater polarization in the relationship between men and women. Negroes, although they have borne the brunt of anti-minority-group feeling in this country, do not constitute the only racial or ethnic minority, but there are only two sexes. And, although we have seen that social distance exists between men and women, it is not to be compared with the social segregation of Negroes.

At the present time, of course, Negroes suffer far greater discrimination than women, but since the latter's problems are rooted in a biological reality less susceptible to cultural manipulation, they prove more lasting. Women's privileges exceed those of Negroes. Protective attitudes toward Negroes have faded into abeyance, even in the South, but most boys are still taught to take care of girls, and many evidences of male chivalry remain. The factor of class introduces variations here. The middle-class Negro endures frustrations largely without the rewards of his white class-peer, but the lower-class Negro is still absolved from many responsibilities. The reverse holds true for women. Notwithstanding these and other differences between the position of women and Negroes, the similarities are sufficient to render research on either group applicable in some fashion to the other.

Exemplary of the possible usefulness of applying the caste principle to women is viewing some of the confusion surrounding women's roles as reflecting a conflict between class and caste status. Such a conflict is present in the thinking and feeling of both dominant and minority groups toward upper-class Negroes and educated women. Should a woman judge be treated with the respect due a judge or the gallantry accorded a woman? The extent to which the rights and duties of one role permeate other roles so as to cause a role conflict has been treated elsewhere

CHART 1 Castelike Status of Women and Negroes

NEGROES	WOMEN
1. High Social Visibility	
a. Skin color, other "racial" characteristics	a. Secondary sex characteristics
b. (Sometimes) distinctive dress—bandana, flashy clothes	b. Distinctive dress, skirts, etc.
2. Ascribed Attributes	
a. Inferior intelligence, smaller brain, less convoluted, scarcity of geniuses	a. ditto
b. More free in instinctual gratifications. More emotional, "primitive" and childlike. Imagined sexual prowess envied.	b. Irresponsible, inconsistent, emotionally unstable. Lack strong super-ego. Women as "temptresses."
c. Common stereotype, "inferior"	c. "Weaker"
3. Rationalizations of Status	
a. Thought all right in his place	a. Woman's place is in the home
b. Myth of contented Negro	b. Myth of contented women—"feminine" woman is happy in subordinate role

CHART 1 Continued

NEGROES	WOMEN

4. Accommodation Attitudes

NEGROES	WOMEN
a. Supplicatory whining intonation of voice	a. Rising inflection, smiles, laughs, downward glances
b. Deferential manner	b. Flattering manner
c. Concealment of real feelings	c. "Feminine wiles"
d. Outwit "white folks"	d. Outwit "men-folk"
e. Careful study of points at which dominant group is susceptible to influence	e. ditto
f. Fake appeals for directives; show of ignorance	f. Appearance of helplessness

5. Discriminations

NEGROES	WOMEN
a. Limitations on education— should fit "place" in society	a. ditto
b. Confined to traditional jobs— barred from supervisory positions. Their competition feared. No family precedents for new aspirations.	b. ditto
c. Deprived of political importance	c. ditto
d. Social and professional segregation	d. ditto
e. More vulnerable to criticism	e. e.g., conduct in bars [women drivers]

6. Similar Problems

a. Roles not clearly defined, but in flux as result of social change. Conflict between achieved status and ascribed status.

by the writer. Lower-class Negroes who have acquired dominant-group attitudes toward the Negro resent upper-class Negro pretensions to superiority. Similarly, domestic women may feel the career woman is neglecting the duties of her proper station.

Parallels in adjustment of women and Negroes to the class-caste conflict may also be noted. Point 4 "Accommodation Attitudes" of the foregoing chart indicates the kinds of behavior displayed by members of both groups who accept their caste status. Many "sophisticated" women are retreating from emancipation with the support of psycho-analytic derivations.[7] David Riesman has recently provided an interesting discussion of changes "in the denigration by American women of their own sex" in which he explains their new submissiveness as in part a reaction to the weakness of men in the contemporary world.[8] "Parallelism" and "Negroidism" which accept a racially restricted economy reflect allied tendencies in the Negro group.

Role segmentation as a mode of adjustment is illustrated by Negroes who indulge in occasional passing and women who vary their behavior according to their definition of the situation. An example of the latter is the case of the woman lawyer who, after losing a case before a judge who was also her husband, said she would appeal the case, and added, "The judge can lay down the law at home, but I'll argue with him in court."

A third type of reaction is to fight for recognition of class status. Negro race leaders seek greater prerogatives for Negroes. Feminist women, acting either through organizations or as individuals, push for public disavowal of any differential treatment of men and women.

The "race relations cycle," as defined by Robert E. Park,[9] describes the social processes of reduction in tension and increase of communication in the relations between two or more groups who are living in a common territory under a single political or economic system. The sequence of competition, conflict, accommodation, and assimilation may also occur when social change introduces dissociative forces into an assimilated group or causes accommodated groups to seek new definitions of the situation. The ethnic or nationality characteristics of the groups involved are not essential to the cycle. In a complex industrialized society, groups are constantly forming and reforming on the basis of new interests and new identities. Women, of course, have always possessed a sex-identification though perhaps not a group awareness. Today they represent a previously accommodated group which is endeavoring to modify the relationships between the sexes in the home, in work, and in the community.

The sex-relations cycle bears important similarities to the race-relation cycle. In the wake of the Industrial Revolution, as women acquired industrial, business, and professional skills, they increasingly sought employment in competition with men. Men were quick to perceive them as a rival group and made use of economic, legal, and ideological weapons to eliminate or reduce their competition. They excluded women from the trade unions, made contracts with employers to prevent their hiring women, passed laws restricting the employment of married women, caricatured the working woman, and carried on ceaseless propaganda to return women to the home or keep them there. Since the days of the suffragettes there has been no overt conflict between men and women on a group basis. Rather than conflict, the dissociative process between the sexes is that of contravention, a type

Arising out of the present contravention of the sexes is the marginal woman, torn between rejection and acceptance of traditional roles and attributes.

of opposition intermediate between competition and conflict. . . . It includes rebuffing, repulsing, working against, hindering, protesting, obstructing, restraining, and upsetting another's plans.

The present contravention of the sexes, arising from women's competition with men, is manifested in the discriminations against women, as well as in the doubts and uncertainties expressed concerning women's character, abilities, motives. The processes of competition and contravention are continually giving way to accommodation in the relationships between men and women. Like other minority groups, women have sought a protected position, a niche in the economy which they could occupy, and, like other minority groups, they have found these positions in new occupations in which dominant-group members had not yet established themselves and in old occupations which they no longer wanted. When women entered fields which represented an extension of services in the home (except medicine!), they encountered least opposition. Evidence is accumulating, however, that women are becoming dissatisfied with the employment conditions of the great women-employing occupations and present accommodations are threatened.

What would assimilation of men and women mean? Park and Burgess in their classic text define assimilation as "a process of interpenetration and fusion in which persons and groups acquire the memories, sentiments, and attitudes of other persons or groups, and, by sharing their experiences and history, are incorporated with them in a cultural life." If accommodation is characterized by secondary contacts, assimilation holds the promise of primary contacts. If men and women were truly assimilated, we would find no cleavages of interest along sex lines. The special provinces of men and women would be abolished. Women's pages would disappear from the newspaper and women's organizations would pass into limbo. The sports page and racing news would be read indifferently by men and women. Interest in cookery and interior decoration would follow individual rather than sex lines. Women's talk would be no different from men's talk, and frank and full communication would obtain between the sexes.

Group relationships are reflected in personal adjustments. Arising out of the present contravention of the sexes is the marginal woman, torn between rejection and acceptance of traditional roles and attributes. Uncertain of the ground on which she stands, subjected to conflicting cultural expectations, the marginal woman suffers the psychological ravages of instability, conflict, self-hate, anxiety, and resentment.

In applying the concept of marginality to women, the term "role" must be substituted for that of "group." Many of the traditional devices for creating role differentiation among boys and girls, such as dress, manners, activities, have been de-emphasized in modern urban middle-class homes. The small girl who wears a playsuit, plays games with boys and girls together, attends a co-educational school, may have little awareness of sexual differentiation until the approach of adolescence. Parental expectations in the matters of scholarship, conduct toward others, duties in the home may have differed little for herself and her brother. But in high school or perhaps not until college, she finds herself called upon to play a new role. Benedict[10] has called attention to discontinuities in the life cycle, and the fact that these continuities in cultural conditioning take a greater toll of girls than of boys is revealed in test scores showing neuroticism and introversion. In adolescence girls find frank, spontaneous behavior toward the neighboring sex no longer rewarding. High grades are more likely to elicit anxiety than praise from parents, especially mothers, who seem more pleased if male callers are frequent. There are subtle indications that to remain home with a good book on a Saturday night is a fate worse than death. But even if the die is successfully cast for popularity, not all problems are solved. Girls are encouraged to heighten their sexual attractiveness, but to abjure sexual expression.

Assuming new roles in adolescence does not mean the complete relinquishing of old ones. Scholarship, while not so vital as for the boy, is still important, but must be maintained discreetly and without obvious effort. Komarovsky[11] has supplied statements by Barnard College girls of the conflicting expectations of their elders. Even more than to the boy is the "allround" ideal held up to girls, and it is not always possible to integrate the roles of good date, good daughter, good sorority sister, good student, good friend, and good citizen. The superior achievements of college men over college women bear witness to the crippling division of energies among women. Part of the explanation may lie in women having interiorized cultural notions of feminine inferiority in certain fields, and even the most self-confident or most defensive woman may be filled with doubt as to whether she can do productive work.

It may be expected that as differences in privileges between men and women decrease, the frequency of marginal women will increase. Widening opportunities for women will call forth a growing number of women capable of performing roles formerly reserved for men, but whose acceptance in these new roles may well remain uncertain and problematic. This hypothesis is in accord with Arnold Green's[12] recent critical re-examination of the marginal-man concept in which he points out that it is those Negroes and second-generation immigrants whose values and behavior most approximate those of the dominant majority who experience the most severe personal crises. He believes that the classicial marginal-man symptoms appear only when a person striving to leave the racial or ethnic group into which he was born is deeply identified with the family of orientation and is met with grudging, uncertain, and unpredictable acceptance, rather than with absolute rejection by the group he is attempting to join. [He must also be] committed to success-careerism. Analogically, one would expect to find that women who display marginal symptoms are psychologically bound to the family of orientation in which they experience the imperatives of both the traditional and new feminine roles, and are seeking to expand the occupational (or other) areas open to women rather than . . . content themselves with established fields. Concretely, one might suppose women engineers to have greater personality problems than women librarians.

Other avenues of investigation suggested by the minority-group approach can only be mentioned. What social types arise as personal adjustments to sex status? What can be done in the way of experimental modification of the attitudes of men and women toward each other and themselves? What hypotheses of inter-group relations may be tested in regard to men and women? For example, is it true that as women approach the cultural standards of men, they are perceived as a threat and tensions increase? Of what significance are regional and community variations in the treatment of and degree of participation permitted women, mindful here that women share responsibility with men for the perpetuation of attitudes toward women? This paper is exploratory in suggesting the enhanced possibilities of fruitful analysis if women are included in the minority-group corpus, particularly with reference to such concepts and techniques as group belongingness, socialization of the minority-group child, cultural differences, social-distance tests, conflict between class and caste status, race-relations cycle, and marginality. I believe that the concept of the marginal woman should be especially productive [as a subject for scholarly investigation].

Notes

1. Kurt Lewin, "Self-Hatred Among Jews," *Contemporary Jewish Record,* 4 (1941): 219–32.
2. *Fortune,* Sept. 1946, p. 5.
3. George A Lundberg, *Foundations of Sociology* (New York: McKay, 1939), p. 319.

4. Robert S. and Helen Merrell Lynd, *Middletown* (Cambridge, Mass.: Harvard University Press, 1929), p. 120; and *Middletown in Transition* (Cambridge, Mass.: Harvard University Press, 1937), p. 176.

5. Joseph Kirk Folsom, *The Family and Democratic Society* (London: Routledge, 1948), pp. 623–24.

6. Gunnar Myrdal, *An American Dilemma* (New York: Harper, 1944), pp. 1073–78.

7. As furnished by such books as Helene Deutsch, *The Psychology of Women* (New York: Grune & Stratton, 1944–45); and Ferdinand Lundberg and Marynia F. Farnham, *Modern Woman: The Lost Sex* (New York: Harper, 1947).

8. David Riesman, "The Saving Remnant: An Examination of Character Structure," in John W. Chase, ed., *Years of the Modern: An American Appraisal* (New York: Longmans, Green, 1949), pp. 139–40.

9. Robert E. Park, "Our Racial Frontier on the Pacific," *The Survey Graphic,* 56 (May 1, 1926): 192–96.

10. Ruth Benedict, "Continuities and Discontinuities in Cultural Conditioning," *Psychiatry,* 1 (1938): 161–67.

11. Mirra Komarovsky, "Cultural Contradictions and Sex Roles," *The American Journal of Sociology,* 52 (Nov. 1946): 184–89.

12. Arnold Green, "A Re-Examination of the Marginal Man Concept," *Social Forces,* 26 (Dec. 1947): 167–71.

Jesus was a Feminist

EQUAL RIGHTS FOR WOMEN

WOMAN POWER it's much too good to waste!

WOMAN'S PLACE IS IN THE WORLD

I AM A CASTRATING BITCH

Trust in GOD She will provide-

SEXISM IS A SOCIAL DISEASE

BAN DISCRIMINATION BASED ON RACE-CREED-COLOR OR SEX

FEMINISTS DEMAND IMMEDIATE WITHDRAWAL

DON'T LET MEN FLY YOURSELF

SISTER

I AM FURIOUS FEMALE

MAKE WOMEN'S AMERICAN REVOLUTION NOT LOVE

I AM MY SISTERS KEEPER!

SECRETARIES ARE MORE THAN TYPEWRITERS

BLACK SISTERS UNITE

SISTERHOOD IS POWERFUL

publish women or perish

LIBERALIZE DIVORCE LAWS

Margaret Chase Smith

EQUAL FRANCHISE

Girls Need a Future too

THE WOMEN'S VOTE IS THE PEACE VOTE

WOMEN'S LIBERATION

CHISHOLM for PRESIDENT '72

The Historical Background

Viola Klein

O ur historical memory is so short, and our imagination so limited, that we fail to be sufficiently
aware of the striking contrast between our present
attitudes and those of, say, a hundred years ago.
[Since we are unaware that women who were not
slaves could be sold in the open market, it is with]
amazement [that] we read the following note in *The
Times* of July 22, 1797: "The increasing value of the
fair sex is regarded by many writers as the certain
index of a growing civilization.[1] Smithfield[2] may for
this reason claim to be a contributor to particular
progress in finesse, for in the market the price was
again raised from one half a guinea to three-and-one
half." This trend in the "progress of finesse" (to
adopt for a moment the standard of *The Times* of
1797) does not seem to have persisted, as the following story indicates:[3]

> In 1814 Henry Cook of Effingham, Surrey, was
> forced under the bastardy laws to marry a
> woman of Slinfold, Sussex, and six months
> after the marriage she and her child were re-
> moved to the Effingham workhouse. The gover-
> nor there, having contracted to maintain all the
> poor for the specific sum of £210, complained
> of the new arrivals, whereupon *the parish*

Reprinted with permission of
the publisher from Viola
Klein, *Feminine Character:
History of an Ideology* (Ur-
bana: University of Illinois
Press, 1973), chapter 2.

officer to Effingham prevailed on Cook to sell his wife. The master of the workhouse, Chippen, was directed to take the woman to Croydon market and there, on June 17, 1815, *she was sold to John Earl for the sum of one shilling* which had been given to Earl for the purchase. To bind the bargain the following receipt was made out:

5/— stamp   June 17, 1815

Received of John Earl the sum of one shilling, in full, for my lawful wife, by me,

HENRY COOK.

Daniel Cook   }
John Chippen   } Witnesses.

In their satisfaction of having got rid of the chargeability of the woman the parish officers of Effingham paid the expenses of the journey to Croydon, including refreshments there, and also allowed a leg of mutton for the wedding dinner which took place in Earl's parish of Dorking . . .''

Miss Pinchbeck rightly remarks: "That the expenses incurred by such trans-action could be entered up in the parish accounts and regularly passed by a parish vestry, is sufficient evidence, not only of the futility of parish administration under the old Poor Laws, but also of the straits to which women were reduced by the weakness of their economic and social position."

These instances do not seem to be isolated cases. More examples are recorded in the "Sale of Wives in England in 1823," by H. W. V. Temperley (in *History Teachers' Miscellany* for May 1925), and as late as 1856 such a benevolent critic of this country as R. W. Emerson has to report, in his *English Traits*: "The right of the husband to sell his wife has been retained down to our times." All this in England, a country which was proverbially called a "Wives' Paradise," and of which Defoe had said in 1725 that, if there were only a bridge between the Continent and England, all Continental women would like to come across the Straits.

Judging this situation from our distant point of observation we must not, however, adopt an attitude of righteous indignation and fail to see the facts in their correct perspective. We must not overlook the fact that we are dealing with a pre-individualistic period: and although women's lot no doubt was, in every respect, harder than men's, woman was no more than one stage behind man in the social evolution. We should misrepresent the situation if we conceived of the "Subjection of Women" as the submission of the weaker sex to the superior physical and eco-nomic power of free and independent males. It would seem more exact to say that women remained serfs after men had already outgrown the state of serfdom. If we adopt Muller-Lyer's[4] classification of the historic development into three main

Before the agricultural and industrial revolution there was hardly any job which was not also performed by women.

phases—the Clan Epoch, the Family Epoch, and the Individual Epoch—according to the social unit which ideologically forms the basic element of the social organization, and which is felt to be the ultimate "end in itself" at a given period, we should say that the capitalist period marks the transition from the family phase to the individual phase generally, but that this transition was delayed in the case of women. Keeping in mind the power of persistence of all those attitudes, customs, and traditions which are linked with the family and handed down by the very personal, very emotional contact within the primary group, we cannot be surprised at the retarded social development in the case of women.

Another error . . . is the idea that women were, of old, excluded from the economic life of society, and are only now reluctantly and gradually being admitted into the masculine sphere of work. This is a misrepresentation of facts. Before the agricultural and industrial revolution there was hardly any job which was not also performed by women. No work was too hard, no labour too strenuous, to exclude them. In fields and mines, manufactories and shops, on markets and roads as well as in workshops and in their homes, women were busy, assisting their men or replacing them in their absence or after their death, or contributing by their own labour to the family income. Before technical inventions revolutionized the methods of production the family was, first of all, an economic unit in which all members, men, women and children, played their part. The advice given in *A Present for a Servant Maid* in 1743: "You cannot expect to marry in such a manner as neither of you shall have occasion to work, and none but a fool will take a wife whose bread must be earned solely by his labour and who will contribute nothing towards it herself,"[5] expresses a general attitude. Society as a whole was not rich enough, and the methods of work not sufficiently productive individually to admit of dispensing with anyone on the score of age or sex. Marriage, at that time, was not looked on, as it was later, as a liability for the man and as a sort of favour conferred upon woman, involving for her a life insurance for a minimum premium, but was regarded as a necessity for all, both for their personal fulfilment and their economic benefit. Only when growing industrialization transferred more and more productive activities from the home to the factory, when machines relieved woman of a great part of her household duties, and schools took over the education of her children, woman's economic value as a contributor to the family income declined, particularly in the middle classes. Where before women and children had assisted in providing for the needs of the family, this responsibility now devolved upon one man. Women and children became an economic liability rather than an asset, and marriage was increasingly felt to be a burden for the man. The emotional satisfaction which it may have offered to both, man and woman, was not enough to make good the loss of self-respect incurred by women by the knowledge of their economic uselessness. The endeavour to reinstate women in the economic process, on the one hand, and to restrict the size of families, on the other, has continued from then on up to the present day.

At all times, however, the common characteristic of women's work, as contrasted with men's was, first of all, that it was subsidiary, i.e. that it involved assisting the men of the family—fathers, husbands, brothers—rather than independent; secondly, and closely connected with this fact, that it was paid at a lower rate, if it received any payment at all and was not included in the family wage; and, thirdly, that it was mostly unskilled. Although they were accepted as members by some guilds and apprenticed in their crafts, women generally played the part of odd hands, doing useful work of many kinds, but acquiring their skill in a casual way rather than by systematic training. Here we find one of the reasons for the emphasis on education which was so prominent in the feminist movement ever since Mary Wollstonecraft first raised her voice in support of the emancipation of women. It seems significant that prior to her famous *Vindication of the Rights of Women* (1792) she should have published her *Thoughts on the Education of Daughters* (1786). The lack of sufficient training was felt to be one of the major disabilities in women's struggle for independence.

For her personal happiness, her social status, and her economic prosperity, marriage was for woman an indispensable condition. But it was left to a later period, when all the economic and social advantages of marriage seemed to have weighed in her favor alone, that she had to develop the "clinging vine" type as a feminine ideal in order to "appease" men. Only by flattering his vanity could she make up for the loss of the practical contribution she had to offer in the matrimonial relation.

> A good woman has no desire to rule [says Mrs. Graves] where she feels it to be her duty, as it is her highest pleasure "to love, honour and obey"; and she submits with cheerful acquiescence to that order in the conjugal relation which God and nature have established. Woman feels she is not made for command, and finds her truest happiness in submitting to those who wield a rightful sceptre in justice, mercy and love.[6]

'Nothing is so likely to conciliate the affection of the other sex," advises Mrs.

Sandford, "as the feeling that women look to them for guidance and support."[7] In other words, nothing befits the slave so well as servility.

To win a husband—woman's only aim and preoccupation—must, in fact, have been a formidable job at that time, if we keep in mind what enormous obstacles Victorian morality put in the way of the only end they thought worth achieving. "Acquaintances with the other sex should be formed with excessive caution"[8] was the general opinion held at the time, and everything was done to prevent free association of the sexes. "It would be improper, nay, indecorous, to correspond with the gentleman unknown to your father," an anxious questioner is warned. Young ladies were, however, protected not only from contact with "gentlemen unknown to their father," but from their brothers' friends and all other men who were not selected as prospective husbands by their parents.

> J. should not walk with a gentleman much her superior in life, unless she is well assured that he seeks her society with a view to marriage, and she has her parents' approbation of her conduct. All young girls should study so to conduct themselves that not even the whisper of envy or scandal should be heard in connection with their names.

Moreover, apart from seclusion, her job of finding a husband was rendered more difficult by the "maidenly reserve" enjoined on her which forbade her to seek a man's attention or to show him signs of sympathy.

> All the poets and prose-writers who have written upon love are agreed upon one point [is one advice given in the correspondence column of the *London Journal*], and that is that delicate reserve, a rosy diffidence, and sweetly chastened deportment are precisely the qualities in a woman that mostly win upon the attention of men, whether young or old. The moment she begins to seek attention, she sinks in the esteem of any man with an opinion worth having.

A few more quotations from the same source will make it clear with what immense difficulties, imposed by etiquette, the Victorian girl had to struggle in her main pursuit of captivating a husband.

> We cannot lend any countenance to such glaring impropriety as trying to "catch the gentleman's attention!" It is his duty to try to catch yours; so preserve your dignity and the decorum due to your sex, position and usages of society.
> Violet must wait. Is she not aware of the motto *Il faut me chercher* (I must be sought after)? The gentleman will propose when he finds Violet is really a timid, bashful girl.
> Mary F. is deeply in love with a young gentleman and wishes to know the best way to make him propose; she thinks he is fond of her, but is rather bashful. The best way is to wait. He will propose quite time enough. If Fanny

Frailness and disease were . . . the only means by which a woman could "catch" attention without offending contemporary morality.

were to give him a hint, he might run away. Some men are very fastidious on the subject of feminine propriety.

Lavina wants to be married—but cannot obtain even a sweetheart. She is afraid her commanding appearance intimidates the young gentlemen of her acquaintance. Nothing of the kind. It is her anxiety, her feverish stepping out of her maidenly reserve, which has shocked their preconceived notions of feminine propriety—and so frightened them into dumb significance. Lavina must be more retiring, think less of herself, and learn to spell better.

The number of quotations, all in the same vein, could be increased indefinitely. They go to show that almost insuperable obstacles were laid on the Victorian girl's only road to happiness, and it seems as if the peculiar feminine affliction called "decline," which consisted in "a form of suicide by acute auto-suggestion,"[9] was by no means only a matter of fashion and a "desire for ethereality." "It might be said of a large number of Victorian ladies that there was, literally, 'no health in them.' The ideal of a fair young maiden wasting away for no apparent reason or from love unrequited was universally upheld in polite literature," cays C. J. Furness in his interesting book. But, considering the inner conflicts and the shattering frustration which must have resulted from the circumstances just described, it is questionable whether the melancholy and "decline" of so many Victorian girls were entirely due to fashion and literary model (the two classic examples quoted by Furness are Dickens's "little Nell" and "little Eva" in *Uncle Tom's Cabin*). It is probable that they were at least partly the outcome of a situation which made marriage for woman the only career and purpose in life, while at the same time depriving her both of the sense of social usefulness and of the means of successfully pursuing her interests or of expressing her emotions. Frailness and disease were, moreover, the only means by which a woman could "catch" attention without offending contemporary morality.

The number of characters in Victorian fiction—sometimes meant to be touching, sometimes not (but always tiresome viewed from the standpoint of today)—who could not put a foot on the ground for weakness and yet had no actual disease is amazing. To most Victorian women, this type of invalidism appeared not merely interesting but attractive: it was almost the only way in which they could attract attention to themselves, while remaining models of propriety, in a world indifferent to their potential intellectual or athletic endowments; and the fancies of young girls who would nowadays see themselves pleading at the bar or playing championship tennis at Wimbledon, dwelt then on pictures of themselves as pathetically helpless creatures in the grip of lingering (but not painful) illness and the objects of the constant concern of their doting families.[10]

A radical change in the life of Western society had been brought about in the second half of the eighteenth and in the beginning of the nineteenth century by new technical inventions which caused an entire reorganization of the productive process. The economic and social effects of the Industrial Revolution are familiar enough to everyone for a brief summary to suffice. Not at once but gradually

> the industrial revolution cast out of our rural and urban life the yeoman cultivator and the copyholder, the domestic manufacturer and the independent handicraftsman, all of whom owned the instruments by which they earned their livelihood; and gradually substituted for them a relatively small body of capitalist entrepreneurs employing at wages an always multiplying mass of propertyless men, women and children, struggling like rats in a bag, for the right to live. This bold venture in economic reconstruction had now been proved to have been, so it seemed to me, at one and the same time, a stupendous success and a tragic failure. The accepted purpose of the pioneers of the new power-driven machine industry was the making of pecuniary profit; a purpose which had been fulfilled, as Dr. Johnson observed about his friend Thrale's brewery, "beyond the dreams of avarice." Commodities of all sorts and kinds rolled out from the new factories at an always accelerating speed with an always falling cost of production, thereby promoting what Adam Smith had idealized as "The Wealth of Nations." . . . On the other hand, that same revolution had deprived the manual workers—that is, four-fifths of the people of England—of their opportunity for spontaneity and freedom of initiative in production. It had transformed such of them as had been independent producers into hirelings and servants of another social class; and, as the East End of London in my time only too vividly demonstrated, it had thrust hundreds of thousands of families into the physical horrors and moral debasement of chronic destitution in crowded tenements in the midst of mean streets.[11]

The decline of domestic industries deeply affected the life of women. While the increasing specialization of labor created a multitude of new jobs in factories and homes with very low wages for the women of the new proletariat, it narrowed the lives of the middle-class women and robbed them of their economic usefulness. Not only industrial activities, but more and more of the specifically feminine types of work formerly connected with household duties, were carried out on an increasing scale by the factories, e.g. bread-baking, beer-brewing, soap-making, tailoring, etc. Moreover, the enormous prosperity created by the new industrial organization produced a growing veneration of wealth (now no longer expressed in terms of landed property but of the more flexible commodities of money, shares, factories and interest-bearing securities). It produced, in the new upper and middle classes, an ambition to compete with each other in the outward signs of prosperity; in consumption, in finery, in the idleness of women. A man's prestige required that his wife and daughters did not do any profitable work. The education of girls was aimed at producing accomplished ladies, not educated women. Frances Power Cobbe recalls in her memoirs:[1][2]

> Nobody dreamed that any of us could, in later life, be more or less than an ornament to society. That a pupil in that school should become an artist or authoress would have been regarded as a deplorable dereliction. Not that which was good and useful to the community, or even that which would be delightful to ourselves, but that which would make us admired in society was the *raison d'etre* of such a requirement. The education of women was probably at its lowest ebb about half a century ago. It was at that period more pretentious than it had even been before, and infinitely more costly, and it was likewise more shallow and senseless than can easily be believed.

If by ill chance the daughter of a middle-class family had to earn her living, there were only two possible careers open to her: that of the much-despised governess, or that of needlewoman. Both involved a loss of caste, and, besides, were not sufficiently remunerative to make her self-supporting.

Under these circumstances it was not surprising that, among the women of the middle classes, more and more voices were clamoring for equal opportunities and higher education.

It is worth recalling that these were aspirations of the upper and middle classes. They were not identical with the interests of the working women. Whereas the women of the upper and middle classes claimed political freedom, the right to work, and improved educational facilities, working women wanted protection; while middle-class women were fighting for equality, working-class women demanded differential treatment. This claim for differential treatment of women in industry has been recognized by everyone except the doctrinaire feminists and the rigid free-trade economists, and, in fact, the first historic examples of State interference in private enterprise are those laws protecting women and children: the Factory Acts applying to the cotton industry, from 1802 onwards; the Mines Act in 1842 which made illegal the employment underground of women and children under the age of seven; and the Ten Hours Act (1847), which limited the working hours of women and children in industry. The flogging of women had been prohibited in the eighteen-twenties.

The appalling conditions of the industrial proletariat on one side, the increase of wealth on the other, gave rise to a growing concern about social problems. The poverty of the masses gradually penetrated public consciousness and created among the ruling classes of Victorian England what Beatrice Webb characterizes as a collective "sense of sin." No longer was poverty accepted as a necessary evil with devout resignation. It was realized more and more that the misery of the poor was not unavoidable and, therefore, that it should be remedied. Charles Booth's extensive investigation into the *Life and Labour of the People* and Karl Marx's *Kapital* are two outstanding examples of this development.

The decline of Christianity, brought about by the unprecedented progress of physical science during the nineteenth century, no longer admitted of the passive acquiescence in the state of affairs as being ordained by God. No longer was one satisfied that human suffering would be rewarded by heavenly bliss beyond the grave, but one asked for remedy here and now. The poverty of the poor—and, to some extent also the "Subjection of Women"—were no longer considered as irremediable natural states, but as the result of social institutions for which Man and not God was responsible. The following quotation from John Stuart Mill's *Utilitarianism*[13] gives a very good illustration of this new attitude towards human misery and the prevailing optimism with regard to the power of science and education:

> No one whose opinion deserves a moment's consideration can doubt that most of the great positive evils of the world are in themselves removable, and will, if human affairs continue to improve, be in the end reduced within narrow limits. Poverty in any sense implying suffering, may be completely extinguished by the wisdom of society, combined with the good sense and providence of individuals. Even that most intractable of enemies, disease, may be infinitely reduced in dimensions by good physical and moral education and proper control of noxious influences; while the progress of science holds out a promise for the future of still more direct conquests over this detestable foe.

The characteristic state of mind of that period cannot be better summed up than in Beatrice Webb's words:

> It seems to me that two outstanding tenets, some would say, two idols of the mind, were united in this mid-Victorian trend of thought and feeling. There was the current belief in the scientific method, in that intellectual synthesis of observation and experiment, hypothesis and verification, by means of which alone all mundane problems were to be solved. And added to this belief in science was the consciousness of a new motive; the transference of the emotions of self-sacrificing service from God to man.[14]

Philanthropic activities expanded on an increasing scale, and, in keeping with the scientific spirit of the time, systematic investigations were made into the conditions of the poor, investigations which mark the beginning of social science. Underlying, and partly motivating, these activities were the prevailing optimism of the period, created by the success of expanding capitalism, and the almost naive belief in the power and possibilities of science.

> It was a forward looking age, simple and serious, believing in the worthwhile-ness of things. The reigning theory still regarded the removal of restrictions as the one thing needful; it trusted human character and intellect to dominate their environment and achieve continued progress. It was an age content with its ideals, if not with its achievements, confident that it was moving on, under the guidance of Providence, to the mastery of the material world and the creation of certain nobler races, now very dimly imagined.[15]

There is a peculiar affinity between the fate of women and the origin of social science, and it is no mere coincidence that the emancipation of women should have started at the same time as the birth of sociology. Both are the result of a break in the established social order and of radical changes in the structure of society; and, in fact, the general interest in social problems to which these changes gave rise did much to assist the cause of women. Both, too, were made possible by the relaxation of the hold which the Christian Churches had for centuries exercised over people's minds. But the relation of woman's emancipation to social science does not only spring from a common origin; it is more direct: the humanitarian interests which formed the starting-point of social research, and practical social work itself, actually provided the back door through which women slipped into public life.

Owing, presumably, to the emotional character of philanthropic work and to the absence of pecuniary profit attaching to it, it did not seem "improper" for women of standing to engage in charitable activities, and soon we find ladies of rank and consequence running charity organizations, working for prison reform, collecting rent in the slums of the East End of London, embarking on propaganda for the abolition of slavery, against cruelty to children, against alcoholism and prostitution, and for the emancipation of women. The social history of the nineteenth century is full of women pioneers in all fields of social reform. [The American] *Frances Wright*, a disciple of Robert Owen, who worked for the practical solution of the slavery problem; *Harriet Martineau*, the political economist, translator of Auguste Comte, who became one of the most distinguished publicists and political leader-writers of her day and who worked for the Reform Bill; *Octavia Hill*, one of the founders and leading spirits of the Charity Organization Society, who became famous by her work for the improvement of working-class houses; *Elizabeth Fry*, the Quaker, who worked for prison reform, founded committees of visiting ladies to care for the prisoners, and who made missionary journeys for her cause all over Europe; *Florence Nightingale*, who during the Crimean War reorganized the military health services after their complete breakdown under the military authorities and who created a new career for women as hospital nurses and probationers; *Louisa Twining*, one of the most active pioneers in Poor Law Reform and in improving the lot of the inmates of workhouses; *Frances Power Cobbe* and *Mary Carpenter*, who tried in Ragged Schools and Reformatories to promote the welfare of neglected children; *Beatrice* and *Katherine Potter*, who were rent collectors in the east End of London and social investigators into the living and working conditions of the poor (Beatrice, later married to Sidney Webb, becoming one of the outstanding social investigators of our time); the Baroness *Angela Burdett-Coutts*, who, with money and influence, actively supported most of the charitable organizations; *Josephine Butler*, reputed for her agitation for the repeal of the Contagious Diseases Acts, but equally active in promoting better education for women—these are only a few selected names, and do not include those who worked more directly as the propagandists of the women's cause: for their parliamentary suffrage, their university education and occupational equality, and against discrimination in moral questions.

All this work helped, first, to demonstrate women's ability to organize, to investigate, to do administrative and all kinds of intellectual work; and, second, to create a new feminine type, distinct from the prevailing Victorian ideal of the submissive and "respectable" wife whose sphere of activities and interests was circumscribed by the triad Church, Child, Kitchen.

Speaking of Miss Cons, another social worker in the East End slums, Beatrice Webb notes in her diary (1885): "To her people she spoke with that peculiar *combination of sympathy and authority which characterized the modern type of governing women*," and she prophetically adds: "These governing and guiding women may become important factors if they increase as they have done lately." As distinctive characteristics of this new type of women she stresses their "eyes clear of self-consciousness" and their "dignity of habitual authority."

Not a few of these women were aware of the fact that, while they were fighting poverty, slavery, and disease, they were, at the same time, fighting in the cause of women. And many of them had consciously accepted this as a secondary aim. They felt that, by creating new openings for women and by furnishing evidence of their ability to work, they contributed to the future improvement of women's position, and they preferred their method of missionary work to the political and journalistic activities of their feminist sisters. As Harriet Martineau put it in a refutation of feminist polemics: "The best advocates are yet to come—in the persons of women who are obtaining access to real social business—the female physicians and other professors in America, the women of business and the female artists in France; and the hospital administrators, the nurses, the educators and substantially successful authoresses of our own country."[16] This prognosis seems to be essentially correct.

The fact that women entered "social business" by way of public relief work, as journalists, and as "substantially successful authoresses of novels," illustrates an interesting sociological phenomenon: the fact, namely, that new crafts, new industries, or new arts afford the opportunities for hitherto excluded social groups to take part in the life of the community and to rise in the social scale. It is not by admittance to the traditionally established professions that newcomers are accepted. The old taboos excluding specific groups from certain spheres of work live on in the form of prejudices and are an effective barrier to their admission. It is the development of new branches of trade, of art, or industry, which enables outsiders to force their way, or to slip, into the established system. Once they are settled there they may have a chance of making an entry into the formerly reserved occupations if they have succeeded by their skill, their acknowledged character, or the power that they have meanwhile accumulated, in conquering old prejudices. The same process may be observed in the case of women, of Jews, of foreign immigrants. In the case of women it was the spheres of social investigation, of charity organization, of the expanding educational system, and of social health services which were the places of least resistance through which the bastion of masculine business was penetrated. The expansion of industry further increased the scope of possible work and created new types of occupation. In the same way, for instance, shorthand typing has today replaced the needlework of times past as a characteristic feminine occupation.

In the arts it was the novel, developing during the nineteenth century as a new literary form, which attracted women and in which some of them won fame as writers of the first rank. One has only to mention the names of Jane Austen, the three Bronte sisters, George Eliot, and Olive Schreiner, to illustrate this point. Among the lower ranks of fiction the number of successful women authors was legion.

Women thus began, by their achievements, to make themselves conspicuous. The fact could no longer be overlooked that there were a number of women—a small minority still, but an impressive *elite* which could be increased—who did not conform to the traditional definition of the type. There was in consequence a feeling among some contemporaries that the definition needed readjustment. In this way women became a problem for philosophers, psychologists and sociologists.

Women themselves became restless. Some of them felt frustrated by the lack of useful work and did not think, with Dr. Gregory, that passing their time with "needlework, knitting and such like" was a sufficiently agreeable way of "filling up their many solitary hours."[17] Even more of them felt humiliated by the fact that their sex was their only means of getting a livelihood and thought it a degradation of marriage that it should, first of all, have to be considered a business arrangement securing their income and social status. Love and marriage being the main concern of women, it was only natural that their revolt should not have sprung from thirst for knowledge or a desire for freedom or adventures, but that, first of all, it should have been expressed as a protest against the humiliation of having to barter their love for support. As Olive Schreiner said in *The Story of an African Farm*:[18]

> It is for love's sake yet more than for any other that we look for that new time. . . . When love is no more bought or sold, when it is not a means of making bread, when each woman's life is filled with earnest, independent labour, then love will come to her, a strange sudden sweetness breaking in upon her earnest work; not sought for, but found.

Moreover, the chances of marriage were more uncertain than they had ever been before, owing, partly, to the increased economic difficulties arising from a social ideal which required the dependence of a whole family on the remunerative work of one member only, partly to the greater liabilities involved in rising social standards, and partly to a growing individualism. The number of people remaining single became large enough to permit their being termed, as a group, "protestants of marriage" and for these to become a social problem. Contrary to the general assumption, however, the surplus of women which would at any rate have deprived a number of them of the chances of getting married, and which as a serious problem was very much on women's minds at the time, was not a new phenomenon. Although the data available are incomplete it appears, according to Karl Bucher,[19] that during the Middle Ages the numerical superiority of women was even greater, varying from 10 percent to 25 percent (the present rate is on an average 7.5 percent in most European countries). But owing to the fact that most industrial activities were carried out in the house the chances of female employment then were bigger. Women were admitted to a number of trades, such as woolen and linen weaving, braiding, tailoring, fur-dressing and tanning, baking, leather-cutting and armorial embroidery, goldsmith's work and gold-spinning. In addition they worked in trades not submitted to regulations, in marketing, huckstering, copying, as musicians in taverns, as nurses, doctors, midwives, as sutler-women accompanying armies and crusades, as porters, gaolers, in the excise, in money-changing, in herding, and in many other professions. Living in homes of relatives they were no useless addition to the household. Moreover, various institutions were provided—apart from nunneries—where single women or widows found board and accommodation. It was industrialization with its separation of home and work, and with its improvement of the social standards of the middle and upper classes, which made the fate of the unmarriageable woman so acute a problem from the nineteenth century onward.

In this way it happened that

> middle class women, by force of circumstances, were being more and more
> compelled to seek a greater development of their powers in order to become
> better able to maintain themselves in an honourable independence in case of
> need. . . . Great numbers of women have, of course, aimed at higher educa-
> tion who are in no possible need of it for the purposes of gaining a livelihood
> thereby; but the incentive spoken of has been one of the strongest factors in
> the situation. As large numbers of women became more and more dependent
> on their own exertions for self-maintenance they found that school French,
> and school music, dancing, flower-painting, needlework, and a diligent use of
> the back-board, did not necessarily qualify them to undertake remunerative
> employment, and play their part in the struggle for existence; while as for the
> old tradition that anything more than elementary education might unfit a
> woman for becoming a wife and mother, that was set aside by the stern logic
> of statistics, which proved that there were many thousands of women who
> could not hope to enter the matrimonial state at all or who became widows
> and self-dependent after doing so.[20]

The need for making some provision in the event of their having to depend on
their own resources was felt by women to be imperative. The following quotation
from a report on the "Emigration of Educated Women" read by Miss Rye at a
meeting of the Social Science Congress in Dublin in 1861 will shed some light on
the urgency of the problem:

> My office is besieged every day by applicants for work, and there is scarcely a
> county or city in the United Kingdom that has not sent some anxious en-
> quiries to me. Unfortunately my experience on this point is not singular: Miss
> Faithfull at the Printing Press, Miss Crowe at the Register Office, Mrs. Craig at
> the Telegraph Station, have all a surplus list of applicants. A short time since
> 810 women applied for one situation of £15 per annum; still later (only ten
> days ago) 250 women applied for another vacancy worth only £12 a year (the
> daughters of many professional men being among the numbers); and, on the
> authority of Mrs. Denison, lady superior of the Welbeck Street Home,
> London, I may state that at an office similar to those already alluded to 120
> women applied in *one day* to find that there was literally *not one situation
> for any one of them.*[21]

The demand not only for a better general education, but for such special
training as would enable women to take up independent careers, had its root in the
practical necessity of not having to rely on one's feminine charm only in providing
for one's future.

In addition, ideological factors played an important part in creating a
"Women's Cause." The contrast between their position as the dependents of men

and the prevalent individualist philosophy was one of the things which gave women most cause and most incitement to protest. The spreading democratic ideology taught that all human beings had equal rights by nature; that man must never be used as a means to anything else but is to be considered an "end in himself"; and that everyone should have an equal chance of free development as an individual.

Although the ideal of the Rights of Man did not explicitly include the rights of women (and these were certainly not endorsed by all who stood up for the democratic ideal), they may be assumed to be implicit. The demands for women's emancipation, i.e. for their equal citizenship and rights to education, were engendered by the democratic propaganda for equality and liberty and were its logical consequence. Women's struggle for enfranchisement, for equal opportunities, and for full legal rights was incidental to the struggle of the rising bourgeoisie for political power and social ascendancy.

Whether they fought for a reform of the marriage laws on the ground that no one should have property rights over other persons, whether they fought for equal educational facilities, or whether they emphasized the importance of the suffrage as a means and the expression of their equality, the trend of thought behind all shades of feminist opinion was the democratic ideology. (The same is true with regard to the illusion, held by a section of feminists, that the vote was the key to the earthly paradise.)

The opposition to feminist claims was strong and bitter not only among those who had vested interests in the legal, political and personal submission of women. It was at least equally strong among the majority of women themselves. While the claim to equality challenged the masculine feeling of power and superiority, it attacked, in women, those symbols which they had developed as substitute gratifications for their lack of real power, and which were no less close to their hearts than the feeling of superiority was to man's. Queen Victoria's appeal to all women of good will "to join in checking this mad, wicked folly of Women's Rights with all its attendant horrors, on which my poor feeble sex is bent, forgetting every sense of womanly feeling and propriety"[22]—certainly found a readier emotional response among the majority than the unorthodox claim of the feminists. Queen Victoria was not the only eminent woman who, though by her own character and achievement defying the familiar notion of the weak and mentally inferior female, objected to the equalitarian claims of Feminism. Hannah More, the moral writer, for instance, held that "that providential economy which has clearly determined that women were born to share with men the duties of private life, has clearly demonstrated that they were not born to divide with them its public administration,"[23] and although "pestered to read the *Rights of Women*," Mary Wollstonecraft's famous book, she was "invincibly resolved not to do it."

Caroline Norton, known for her struggle to secure for mothers some rights over their children, wrote in 1838: "The wild and stupid theories advanced by a few women of 'equal rights' and 'equal intelligence' are not the opinion of their sex. I, for one (I, with millions more), believe in the natural superiority of man, as I do in the existence of God. The natural position of woman is inferiority to man." And Beatrice Webb (who, however, later regretted this action) signed a manifesto in 1889, drafted by Mrs. Humphry Ward and some other distinguished ladies, against the enfranchisement of women, and in indignant protest against the suffragettes she allowed herself to be carried away at a public luncheon to make the statement: "I have never met a man, however inferior, whom I do not consider to be my superior."[24]

Nowhere were feminists more than a small, much-despised, and even more ridiculed minority. Their unpopularity resulted in part from their militant methods of agitation; in part from their over-emphasis on enfranchisement, which was a repetition of the struggle for the Reform Bill, with similar methods and bound to have the similar result described (with regard to the workers) by Esme Wingfield-Stratford in these words: "They had roared for the Bill, the whole Bill and nothing but the Bill, and it took them a little time to discover that what they had got was—nothing but the Bill."[25] But the main shortcoming of Feminism was that, a child of the Victorian era, it presented woman as a sort of sexless creature, as a mere abstraction without flesh and blood. The suffragettes' exaltation of woman into a rational super-person "beyond the coarseness of animal instincts," their hatred of Man as their Enemy Number One, their contempt of his unsatiable sensuality, were the weakest points in their theory. It laid feminists open to ridicule and attack, and deprived them of the sympathy of the younger generation of women who, in the dilemma between "Rights" and emotions, would always be prepared to sacrifice abstract principles to emotional satisfaction. In spite of all its revolutionary *elan* the feminist movement had but little appeal to youth, and the report published in the *Vossische Zeitung* in 1932 is probably characteristic not only for Germany but to some extent of other countries as well: "Almost all meetings of women's organizations . . . show the same picture. At least three-fourths of the women present are over forty. The generation between twenty and thirty is almost completely lacking; that between thirty and forty is sparsely represented."[26]

It is the more remarkable that in spite of all their failings feminists saw almost all their demands gradually realized—in several instances by frankly anti-feminist statesmen (such as Asquith in this country or President Wilson in the United States, who, himself an anti-suffragist, enfranchised the women of his country in 1917)—simply by force of practical necessity, and because their claims were in accordance with the general trend of social development.

Notes

1. Quoted from S. D. Schmalhausen and V. Calverton, eds., *Woman's Coming of Age: A Symposium* (New York: Liveright, 1931).
2. A market particularly reputed for its sales of women.
3. Recorded by Ivy Pinchbeck in *Women Workers and the Industrial Revolution* (London: George Routledge & Sons, 1930), p. 83.
4. E. Muller-Lyer, *The Evolution of Modern Marriage* (London: Allen & Unwin, 1930), from *Phasen der Liebe,* first pub. in Munich, 1913.
5. Quoted in Dorothy George, *London Life in the 18th Century* (London: Kegan Paul, 1925).
6. A. J. Graves, *Women in America* (New York: Harper Bros., 1858), quoted from Schmalhausen and Calverton, eds.
7. Quoted from *Ibid.*
8. This and the following quotations are taken from *Advice to Young Ladies,* a collection of answers to correspondents published in the *London Journal* between 1855 and 1862 (London: Methuen, 1933).
9. Clifton J. Furness, ed., *The Genteel Female: An Anthology* (New York: Knopf, 1931).
10. Irene Clephane, *Towards Sex Freedom* (London: John Lane, 1935).
11. Beatrice Webb, *My Apprenticeship* (London: Longmans, 1926).
12. *The Life of Frances Power Cobbe as Told by Herself* (London: Swan Sonnenschein & Co., 1904).
13. Chapter 2.
14. Webb, *op. cit.*
15. R. M. Butler, *A History of England, 1815–1918* (London: Home University Library, 1928).
16. Quoted from Janet E. Courtney, *The Adventurous Thirties: A Chapter in the Women's Movement* (Oxford: Oxford University Press, 1933).
17. The pertinent paragraph in Dr. John Gregory's *A Father's Legacy to His Daughters* runs: "The intention of your being taught needlework, knitting and such like is not on account of the intrinsic value of all you can do with your hands, which is trifling, but . . . to enable you to fill up, in a tolerably agreeable way, some of the many solitary hours you must necessarily pass at home." (Quoted from John Langdon-Davies, *A Short History of Women* (London: Cape, 1928.)
18. First published in London, 1833.
19. Karl Bucher, *Die Frauenfrage im Mittelalter* (Tubingen, 1882).
20. Edwin A. Pratt, *Pioneer Women in Victoria's Reign* (London: Newnes, 1897).
21. *Ibid.*
22. Quoted from Courtney, ed.
23. Quoted from Clephane.
24. Webb, *op. cit.*
25. Esme Wingfield-Stratford, *The Victorian Tragedy* (London: Routledge, 1930).
26. Hiltgunde Graef, "Die vergreiste Frauenbewegung" (The senile feminist movement), *Vossische Zeitung,* Nov. 20, 1932.

The First Feminists

Judith Hole and Ellen Levine

The contemporary women's movement is not the first such movement in American history to offer a wide-ranging feminist critique of society. In fact, much of what seems "radical" in contemporary feminist analysis parallels the critique made by the feminists of the nineteenth century. Both the early and the contemporary feminists have engaged in a fundamental reexamination of the role of women in all spheres of life, and of the relationships of men and women in all social, political, economic and cultural institutions. Both have defined women as an oppressed group and have traced the origin of women's subjugation to male-defined and male-dominated social institutions and value systems.

When the early feminist movement emerged in the nineteenth century, the "woman issue" was extensively debated in the national press, in political gatherings, and from church pulpits. The women's groups, their platforms, and their leaders, although not always well received or understood, were extremely well known. Until recently, however, that early feminist movement has been only cursorily discussed in American history textbooks, and then only in terms of the drive for suffrage. Even a brief

Reprinted from Judith Hole and Ellen Levine, *Rebirth of Feminism* (New York: Quadrangle, 1973), pp. 1–14 with permission of the publisher.

reading of early feminist writings and of the few histories that have dealt specifically with the woman's movement (as it was called then) reveals that the drive for
suffrage became the single focus of the movement only after several decades of a
more multi-issued campaign for women's equality.

The woman's movement emerged during the 1800's. It was a time of geographic expansion, industrial development, growth of social reform movements, and
a general intellectual ferment with a philosophical emphasis on individual freedom,
the "rights of man," and universal education. In fact, some of the earliest efforts to
extend opportunities to women were made in the field of education. In 1833,
Oberlin became the first college to open its doors to both men and women. Although female education at Oberlin was regarded as necessary to ensure the development of good and proper wives and mothers, the open admission policy paved
the way for the founding of other schools, some devoted entirely to women's education.[1] Much of the ground-breaking work in education was done by Emma
Willard, who had campaigned vigorously for educational facilities for women beginning in the early 1820's. Frances Wright, one of the first women orators, was also a
strong advocate of education for women. She viewed women as an oppressed group
and argued that, "Until women assume the place in society which good sense and
good feeling alike assign to them, human improvement must advance but feebly."[2]
Central to her discussion of the inequalities between the sexes was a particular
concern with the need for equal educational training for women.

It was in the abolition movement of the 1830's, however, that the woman's
rights movement as such had its political origins. When women began working in
earnest for the abolition of slavery, they quickly learned that they could not function as political equals with their male abolitionist friends. Not only were they
barred from membership in some organizations, but they had to wage an uphill
battle for the right simply to speak in public. Sarah and Angeline Grimke, daughters
of a South Carolina slaveholding family, were among the first to fight this battle.
Early in their lives the sisters left South Carolina, moved north, and began to speak
out publicly on the abolition issue. Within a short time they drew the wrath of
different sectors of society. A Pastoral letter from the Council of the Congregation-
alist Ministers of Massachusetts typified the attack:

> The appropriate duties and influence of woman are clearly stated in the New
> Testament. . . . The power of woman is her dependence, flowing from the
> consciousness of that weakness which God has given her for her protec-
> tion. . . . When she assumes the place and tone of man as a public re-
> former . . . she yields the power which God has given her . . . and her charac-
> ter becomes unnatural.[3]

The brutal and unceasing attacks (sometimes physical) on the women convinced the

Grimkes that the issues of freedom for slaves and freedom for women were inextricably linked. The women began to speak about both issues, but because of the objections from male abolitionists who were afraid that discussions of woman's rights would "muddy the waters," they often spoke about the "woman question" as a separate issue. (In fact, Lucy Stone, an early feminist and abolitionist, lectured on abolition on Saturdays and Sundays and on women's rights during the week.)

In an 1837 letter to the President of the Boston Female Anti-Slavery Society —by that time many female anti-slavery societies had been established in response to the exclusionary policy of the male abolitionist groups—Sarah Grimke addressed herself directly to the question of woman's status:

> All history attests that man has subjugated woman to his will, used her as a means to promote his selfish gratification, to minister to his sensual pleasure, to be instrumental in promoting his comfort; but never has he desired to elevate her to that rank she was created to fill. He has done all he could to debase and enslave her mind; and now he looks triumphantly on the ruin he has wrought, and says, the being he has thus deeply injured is his inferior. . . . But I ask no favors for my sex. . . . All I ask of our brethren is, that they will take their feet from off our necks and permit us to stand upright on that ground which God designed us to occupy.[4]

The Grimkes challenged both the assumption of the "natural superiority of man" and the social institutions predicated on that assumption. For example, in her *Letters on the Equality of the Sexes* . . . Sarah Grimke argued against both religious dogma and the institution of marriage. Two brief examples are indicative:

> . . . Adams's ready acquiescence with his wife's proposal, does not savor much of that superiority *in strength of mind*, which is arrogated by man.[5]
> . . . man has exercised the most unlimited and brutal power over woman, in the peculiar character of husband—a word in most countries synonymous with tyrant. . . . Woman, instead of being elevated by her union with man, which might be expected from an alliance with a superior being, is in reality lowered. She generally loses her individuality, her independent character, her moral being. She becomes absorbed into him, and henceforth is looked at, and acts through the medium of her husband.[6]

They attacked as well the manifestations of "male superiority" in the employment market. In a letter "On the Condition of Women in the United States" Sarah Grimke wrote of:

> . . . the disproportionate value set on the time and labor of men and of women. A man who is engaged in teaching, can always, I believe, command a higher price for tuition than a woman—even when he teaches the same branches, and is not in any respect superior to the woman. . . . [Or] for example, in tailoring, a man has twice, or three times as much for making a

waistcoat or pantaloons as a woman, although the work done by each may be equally good.[7]

The abolition movement continued to expand, and in 1840 a World Anti-Slavery Convention was held in London. The American delegation included a group of women, among them Lucretia Mott and Elizabeth Cady Stanton. In Volume I of the *History of Woman Suffrage,* written and edited by Stanton, Susan B. Anthony, and Matilda Joslyn Gage, the authors note that the mere presence of women delegates produced an "excitement and vehemence of protest and denunciation [that] could not have been greater, if the news had come that the French were about to invade England."[8] The women were relegated to the galleries and prohibited from participating in any of the proceedings. That society at large frowned upon women participating in political activities was one thing; that the leading male radicals, those most concerned with social inequalities, should also discriminate against women was quite another. The events at the world conference reinforced the women's growing awareness that the battle for the abolition of Negro slavery could never be won without a battle for the abolition of woman's slavery:

> As Lucretia Mott and Elizabeth Cady Stanton wended their way arm in arm down Great Queen Street that night, reviewing the exciting scenes of the day, they agreed to hold a woman's rights convention on their return to America, as the men to whom they had just listened had manifested their great need of some education on that question.[9]

Mott and Stanton returned to America and continued their abolitionist work as well as pressing for state legislative reforms on woman's property and family rights. Although the women had discussed the idea of calling a public meeting on woman's rights, the possibility did not materialize until eight years after the London Convention. On July 14, 1848, they placed a small notice in the *Seneca* (New York) *County Courier* announcing a "Woman's Rights Convention." Five days later, on July 19 and 20, some three hundred interested women and men, coming from as far as fifty miles, crowded into the small Wesleyan Chapel (now a gas station) and approved a Declaration of Sentiments (modeled on the Declaration of Independence) and twelve Resolutions. The delineation of issues in the Declaration bears a startling resemblance to contemporary feminist writings. Some excerpts are illustrative:[10]

> We hold these truths to be self-evident: that all men and women are created equal; that they are endowed by their Creator with certain inalienable rights; that among these are life, liberty, and the pursuit of happiness. . . .
>   The history of mankind is a history of repeated injuries and usurpations on the part of man toward woman, having in direct object the establishment

of an absolute tyranny over her. To prove this, let facts be submitted to a candid world. . . .

He has compelled her to submit to laws, in the formation of which she has no voice. . . .

He has made her, if married, in the eye of the law, civilly dead. . . .

He has monopolized nearly all the profitable employments, and from those she is permitted to follow, she receives but a scanty remuneration. He closes against her all the avenues to wealth and distinction which he considers most honorable to himself. As a teacher of theology, medicine, or law, she is now known.

He allows her in church, as well as State, but a subordinate position, claiming Apostolic authority for her exclusion from the ministry, and, with some exceptions, from any public participation in the affairs of the Church.

He has created a false public sentiment by giving to the world a different code of morals for men and women, by which moral delinquencies which exclude women from society, are not only tolerated, but deemed of little account in man.

He has usurped the prerogative of Jehovah himself, claiming it as his right to assign for her a sphere of action, when that belongs to her conscience and to her God.

He has endeavored, in every way that he could, to destroy her confidence in her own powers, to lessen her self-respect, and to make her willing to lead a dependent and abject life.

Included in the list of twelve resolutions was one which read: "*Resolved,* That it is the duty of the women of this country to secure to themselves their sacred right to the elective franchise."

Although the Seneca Falls Convention is considered the official beginning of the woman's suffrage movement, it is important to reiterate that the goal of the early woman's rights movement was not limited to the demand for suffrage. In fact, the suffrage resolution was included only after lengthy debate, and was the only resolution not accepted unanimously. Those participants at the Convention who actively opposed the inclusion of the suffrage resolution:

> . . . feared a demand for the right to vote would defeat others they deemed more rational, and make the whole movement ridiculous. But Mrs. Stanton and Frederick Douglass seeing that the power to choose rulers and make laws, was the right by which all others could be secured, persistently advocated the resolution. . . .[11]

Far more important to most of the women at the Convention was their desire to gain control of their property and earnings, guardianship of their children, rights to divorce, etc. Notwithstanding the disagreements at the Convention, the Seneca Falls meeting was of great historical significance. As Flexner has noted:

[The women] themselves were fully aware of the nature of the step they were taking; today's debt to them has been inadequately acknowledged. . . . Beginning in 1848 it was possible for women who rebelled against the circumstances of their lives, to know that they were not alone—although often the news reached them only through a vitriolic sermon or an abusive newspaper editorial. But a movement had been launched which they could either join, or ignore, that would leave its imprint on the lives of their daughters and of women throughout the world.[12]

From 1848 until the beginning of the Civil War, Woman's Rights Conventions were held nearly every year in different cities in the East and Midwest. The 1850 Convention in Salem, Ohio:

. . . had one peculiar characteristic. It was officered entirely by women; not a man was allowed to sit on the platform, to speak, or vote. *Never did men so suffer.* They implored just to say a word; but no; the President was inflexible —no man should be heard. If one meekly arose to make a suggestion he was at once ruled out of order. For the first time in the world's history, men learned how it felt to sit in silence when questions in which they were interested were under discussion.[13]

As the woman's movement gained in strength, attacks upon it became more vitriolic. In newspaper editorials and church sermons anti-feminists argued vociferously that the public arena was not the proper place for women. In response to such criticism, Stanton wrote in an article in the Rochester, New York, *National Reformer:*

If God has assigned a sphere to man and one to woman, we claim the right to judge ourselves of His design in reference to *us,* and we accord to man the same privilege. . . . We have all seen a man making a jackass of himself in the pulpit, at the bar, or in our legislative halls. . . . Now, is it to be wondered at that woman has some doubts about the present position assigned her being the true one, when her every-day experience shows her that man makes such fatal mistakes in regard to himself?[14]

It was abundantly clear to the women that they could not rely on the pulpit or the "establishment" press for either factual or sympathetic reportage; nor could they use the press as a means to disseminate their ideas. As a result they depended on the abolitionist papers of the day, and in addition founded a number of independent women's journals including *The Lily, The Una, Woman's Advocate, Pittsburgh Visiter* [sic], etc.

One of the many issues with which the women activists were concerned was dress reform. Some began to wear the "bloomer" costume (a misnomer since Amelia Bloomer, although an advocate of the loose-fitting dress, was neither its

Although Anthony and Stanton continued arguing that any battle for freedom must include woman's freedom, the woman's movement activities essentially stopped for the duration of the [Civil] war.

originator nor the first to wear it) in protest against the tight-fitting and singularly uncomfortable cinched-waisted stays and layers of petticoats. However, as Flexner has noted, "The attempt at dress reform, although badly needed, was not only unsuccessful but boomeranged and had to be abandoned."[15] Women's rights advocates became known as "bloomers" and the movement for equal rights as well as the individual women were subjected to increasing ridicule. Elizabeth Cady Stanton, one of the earliest to wear the more comfortable outfit, was one of the first to suggest its rejection. In a letter to Susan B. Anthony she wrote:

> We put the dress on for greater freedom, but what is physical freedom compared with mental bondage? . . . It is not wise, Susan, to use up so much energy and feeling that way. You can put them to better use. I speak from experience.[16]

When the Civil War began in 1861, woman's rights advocates were urged to abandon their cause and support the war effort. Although Anthony and Stanton continued arguing that any battle for freedom must include woman's freedom, the woman's movement activities essentially stopped for the duration of the war. After the war and the ratification of the Thirteenth Amendment abolishing slavery (for which the woman activists had campaigned vigorously), the abolitionists began to press for passage of a Fourteenth Amendment to secure the rights, privileges, and immunities of citizens (the new freedmen) under the law. In the second section of the proposed Amendment, however, the word "male" appeared, introducing a sex distinction into the Constitution for the first time. Shocked and enraged by the introduction of the word "male," the women activists mounted an extensive campaign to eliminate it. They were dismayed to find that no one, neither the Republican administration nor their old abolitionist allies, had any intention of "complicating" the campaign for Negroes' rights by advocating women's rights as well. Over and over again the women were told, "This is the Negroes' hour." The authors of *History of Woman Suffrage* analyzed the women's situation:

> During the six years they held their own claims in abeyance to the slaves of the South, and labored to inspire the people with enthusiasm for the great measures of the Republican party, they were highly honored as "wise, loyal, and clear-sighted." But again when the slaves were emancipated and they asked that women should be recognized in the reconstruction as citizens of

the Republic, equal before the law, all these transcendent virtues vanished like dew before the morning sun. And thus it ever is so long as woman labors to second man's endeavors and exalt *his* sex above her own, her virtues pass unquestioned; but when she dares to demand rights and privileges for herself, her motives, manners, dress, personal appearance, character, are subjects for ridicule and detraction.[17]

The women met with the same response when they campaigned to get the word "sex" added to the proposed Fifteenth Amendment which would prohibit the denial of suffrage on account of race.[18]

As a result of these setbacks, the woman's movement assumed as its first priority the drive for woman's suffrage. It must be noted, however, that while nearly all the women activists agreed on the need for suffrage, in 1869 the movement split over ideological and tactical questions into major factions. In May of that year, Susan B. Anthony and Elizabeth Cady Stanton organized the National Woman Suffrage Association. Six months later, Lucy Stone and others organized the American Woman Suffrage Association. The American, in an attempt to make the idea of woman's suffrage "respectable," limited its activities to that issue, and refused to address itself to any of the more "controversial" subjects such as marriage or the church. The National, on the other hand, embraced the broad cause of woman's rights of which the vote was seen primarily as a *means* of achieving those rights. During this time Anthony and Stanton founded *The Revolution,* which became one of the best known of the independent women's newspapers. The weekly journal began in January, 1868, and took as its motto, "Men, their rights and nothing more; women, their rights and nothing less." In addition to discussion of suffrage, *The Revolution* examined the institutions of marriage, the law, organized religion, etc. Moreover, the newspaper touched on "such incendiary topics as the double standard and prostitution."[19] Flexner describes the paper:

> [It] made a contribution to the women's cause out of all proportion to either its size, brief lifespan, or modest circulation. . . . Here was news not to be found elsewhere—of the organization of women typesetters, tailoresses, and laundry workers, of the first women's clubs, of pioneers in the professions, of women abroad. But *The Revolution* did more than just carry news, or set a new standard of professionalism for papers edited by and for women. It gave their movement a forum, focus, and direction. It pointed, it led, and it fought, with vigor and vehemence.[20]

The two suffrage organizations coexisted for over twenty years and used some of the same tactics in their campaigns for suffrage: lecture tours, lobbying activities, petition campaigns, etc. The American, however, focused exclusively on state-by-state action, while the National in addition pushed for a woman suffrage

Amendment to the Constitution. Susan B. Anthony and others also attempted to gain the vote through court decisions. The Supreme Court, however, held in 1875[21] that suffrage was not necessarily one of the privileges and immunities of citizens protected by the Fourteenth Amendment. Thus, although women were *citizens* it was nonetheless permissible, according to the Court, to constitutionally limit the right to vote to males.

During this same period, a strong temperance movement had also emerged. Large numbers of women, including some suffragists, became actively involved in the temperance cause. It is important to note that one of the main reasons women became involved in pressing for laws restricting the sale and consumption of alcohol was that their legal status as married women offered them no protection against either physical abuse or abandonment by a drunken husband. It might be added that the reason separate women's temperance organizations were formed was that women were not permitted to participate in the men's groups. In spite of the fact that temperance was in "woman's interests," the growth of the women's temperance movement solidified the liquor and brewing industries' opposition to woman suffrage. As a result, suffrage leaders became convinced of the necessity of keeping the two issues separate.

As the campaign for woman suffrage grew, more and more sympathizers were attracted to the conservative and "respectable" American Association which, as noted above, deliberately limited its work to the single issue of suffrage. After two decades "respectability" won out, and the broad-ranging issues of the earlier movement had been largely subsumed by suffrage. (Even the Stanton-Anthony forces had somewhat redefined their goals and were focusing primarily on suffrage.) By 1890, when the American and the National merged to become the National American Woman Suffrage Association, the woman's movement had, in fact, been transformed into the single-issue suffrage movement. Moreover, although Elizabeth Cady Stanton, NAWSA's first president, was succeeded two years later by Susan B. Anthony, the first women activists, with their catholic range of concerns, were slowly being replaced by a second group far more limited in their political analysis. It should be noted that Stanton herself, after her two-year term as president of the new organization, withdrew from active work in the suffrage campaign. Although [she had been] one of the earliest feminist leaders to understand the need for woman suffrage, by this time Stanton believed that the main obstacle to woman's equality was the church and organized religion.

During the entire development of the woman's movement, perhaps the argument most often used by anti-feminists was that the subjugation of women was divinely ordained as written in the Bible. Stanton attacked the argument head-on. She and a group of twenty-three women, including three ordained ministers, produced *The Woman's Bible*[22] which presented a systematic feminist critique of woman's role and image in the Bible. Some Biblical chapters were presented as proof that the Scripture itself was the source of woman's subjugation; others to show that, if reinterpreted, men and women were indeed equals in the Bible, not superior and inferior beings. "We have made a fetich [*sic*] of the Bible long enough. The time has come to read it as we do all other books, accepting the good and rejecting the evil it teaches."[23] Dismissing the "rib story" as a "petty surgical operation," Stanton argued further that the entire structure of the Bible was predicated on the notion of Eve's (woman's) corruption:

> Take the snake, the fruit-tree and the woman from the tableau, and we have no fall, nor frowning Judge, no Inferno, no everlasting punishment;—hence no need of a Savior. Thus the bottom falls out of the whole Christian theology. Here is the reason why in all the Biblical researches and higher criticisms, the scholars never touch the position of women.[24]

Not surprisingly, *The Woman's Bible* was considered scandalous and sacrilegious by most. The Suffrage Association members themselves, with the exception of Anthony and a few others, publicly disavowed Stanton and her work. They feared that the image of the already controversial suffrage movement would be irreparably damaged if the public were to associate it with Stanton's radical tract.

Shortly after the turn of the century, the second generation of woman suffragists came of age and new leaders replaced the old. Carrie Chapman Catt is perhaps the best known; she succeeded Anthony as president of the National American Woman Suffrage Association, which by then had become a large and somewhat unwieldy organization. Although limited gains were achieved (a number of western states had enfranchised women), no major progress was made in the campaign for suffrage until Alice Paul, a young and extremely militant suffragist, became active in the movement. In April, 1913, she formed a small radical group known as the Congressional Union (later reorganized as the Woman's Party) to work exclusively on a campaign for a *federal* woman's suffrage Amendment using any tactics necessary, no matter how unorthodox. Her group organized parades, mass demonstrations, hunger strikes, and its members were on several occasions arrested and jailed.[25] Although many suffragists rejected both the militant style and tactics of the Congressional Union, they nonetheless did consider Paul and her followers in large part responsible for "shocking" the languishing movement into actively pressuring for the federal Amendment. The woman suffrage Amendment (known as the "Anthony Amendment"), introduced into every session of Congress from 1878 on, was finally ratified on August 26, 1920.

Nearly three-quarters of a century had passed since the demand for woman suffrage had first been made at the Seneca Falls Convention. By 1920, so much energy had been expended in achieving the right to vote that the woman's movement virtually collapsed from exhaustion. To achieve the vote alone, as Carrie Chapman Catt had computed, took:

> . . . fifty-two years of pauseless campaign . . . fifty-six campaigns of referenda to male voters; 480 campaigns to get Legislatures to submit suffrage amendments to votes; 47 campaigns to get State constitutional conventions to write woman suffrage into state constitutions; 277 campaigns to get State party conventions to include woman suffrage planks; 30 campaigns to get presidential party conventions to adopt woman suffrage planks in party platforms, and 19 campaigns with 19 successive Congresses.[26]

With the passage of the Nineteenth Amendment the majority of women activists as well as the public at large assumed that having gained the vote woman's complete equality had been virtually obtained.

It must be remembered, however, that for most of the period that the woman's movement existed, suffrage had not been seen as an all-inclusive goal, but as a means of achieving equality—suffrage was only one element in the wide-ranging feminist critique questioning the fundamental organization of society. Historians, however, have for the most part ignored this radical critique and focused exclusively on the suffrage campaign. By virtue of this omission they have, to all intents and purposes, denied the political significance of the early feminist analysis. Moreover, the summary treatment by historians of the nineteenth and twentieth-century drive for woman's suffrage has made that campaign almost a footnote to the abolitionist movement and the campaign for Negro suffrage. In addition, the traditional textbook image of the early feminists—if not wild-eyed women waving placards for the vote, then wild-eyed women swinging axes at saloon doors—has further demeaned the importance of their philosophical analysis.

The woman's movement virtually died in 1920 and, with the exception of a few organizations, feminism was to lie dormant for forty years.

Notes

1. Mount Holyoke opened in 1837; Vassar, 1865; Smith and Wellesley, 1875; Radcliffe, 1879; Bryn Mawr, 1885.
2. Quoted in Eleanor Flexner, *Century of Struggle: The Woman's Rights Movement in the United States* (Cambridge, Mass.: The Belknap Press of Harvard University Press, 1959), p. 27.
3. *History of Woman Suffrage* (republished by Arno Press and *The New York Times*, New York, 1969), Vol. I, p. 81. Hereafter cited as *HWS*. Volumes I–III were edited by Elizabeth Cady Stanton, Susan B. Anthony, and Matilda Joslyn Gage. The first two volumes were

published in 1881, the third in 1886. Volume IV was edited by Susan B. Anthony and Ida Husted Harper and was published in 1902. Volumes V and VI were edited by Ida Husted Harper and published in 1922.

4. Sarah M. Grimke, *Letters on the Equality of the Sexes and the Condition of Woman* (Boston: Isaac Knapp, 1838, reprinted by Source Book Press, New York, 1970), p. 10ff.

5. *Ibid.*, pp. 9-10.

6. *Ibid.*, pp. 85-86.

7. *Ibid.*, p. 51.

8. *HWS,* p. 54.

9. *Ibid.*, p. 61.

10. *Ibid.*, pp. 70-73.

11. *HWS,* p. 73.

12. Flexner, p. 77.

13. *HWS,* p. 110.

14. *Ibid.*, p. 806.

15. Flexner, p. 83.

16. *Ibid.*, p. 84.

17. *HWS,* Vol. II, p. 51.

18. The Thirteenth Amendment was ratified in 1865; the Fourteenth in 1868; the Fifteenth in 1870.

19. Flexner, p. 151.

20. *Loc. cit.*

21. *Minor v. Happersett,* 21 Wall. 162, 22 L. Ed. 627 (1875).

22. (New York: European Publishing Company, 1895 and 1898. Two Parts.)

23. *Ibid.*, Part II, pp. 7-8.

24. Stanton, letter to the editor of *The Critic* (New York), March 28, 1896, quoted in Aileen S. Kraditor, *The Ideas of the Woman Suffrage Movement, 1890–1920* (New York: Columbia University Press, 1965), n. 11, p. 86.

25. A total of 218 women from 26 states were arrested during the first session of the Sixty-fifth Congress (1917). Ninety-seven went to prison.

26. Carrie Chapman Catt and Nettie Rogers Shuler, *Woman Suffrage and Politics* (New York, 1923), p. 107. Quoted in Flexner, p. 173.

Women's Liberation ement: Its Origins, Structures, Impact, and Ideas

Jo Freeman

ometime during the 1920's, feminism died in
the United States. It was a premature death—
feminists had just obtained that long-sought tool, the
vote, with which they had hoped to make an equal
place for women in this society—but it seemed an
irreversible one. By the time the suffragists' grand-
daughters were old enough to vote, social mythology
had firmly ensconced women in the home, and the
very term "feminist" had become an insult.

Social mythology, however, did not always
coincide with social fact. Even during the era of the
"feminine mystique," the 1940's and 1950's, when
the relative numbers of academic degrees given to
women were dropping, the absolute numbers of such
degrees were rising astronomically. Women's participation in the labor force was also rising, even while
women's position within it was declining. Opportunities to work, the trend toward smaller families, plus a
change in preferred status symbols from a leisured
wife at home to a second car and a color television
set, helped transform the female labor force from one
of primarily single women under 25, as it was in
1940, to one of married women and mothers over 40,
as it was by 1950. Simultaneously, the job market

became even more rigidly segragated, with the exception of traditional female jobs such as teaching and social work which were flooded by men. Thus women's share of professional and technical jobs declined by a third, with a commensurate decline in women's relative income. The result of all this was the creation of a class of highly educated, underemployed, and underpaid women.

In the early 1960's, feminism was still an unmentionable, but it was slowly awakening from the dead. The first sign of new life was President Kennedy's establishment of a national Commission on the Status of Women in 1961. Created at the urging of Esther Petersen of the Women's Bureau, the shortlived Commission thoroughly documented women's second-class status. It was followed by the formation of a citizens' advisory council and fifty state commissions. Many of the people involved in these commissions, dissatisfied with the lack of progress made on their recommendations, joined with Betty Friedan in 1966 to found the National Organization for Women (NOW).

NOW was the first new feminist organization in almost fifty years, but it was not the sole beginning of the organized expression of the movement. The movement actually has two origins, from two different strata of society, with two different styles, orientations, values, and forms of organization. In many ways there have been two separate movements that have not entirely merged. Although the composition of both branches tends to be predominantly white, middle-class, and college-educated, initially the median age of the activists in what I call the older branch of the movement was higher. Too, it began first. In addition to NOW, this branch contains such organizations as the Women's Equity Action League, Federally Employed Women (FEW), and some 50 different organizations and caucuses of professional women. Their style of organization has tended to be traditionally formal, with numerous elected officers, boards of directors, bylaws, and the other trappings of democratic procedure. All started as top-down organizations lacking a mass base. Some have subsequently developed a mass base, some have not yet done so, and others don't want to.

In 1967 and 1968, unaware of and unknown to NOW or to the state commissions, the other branch of the movement was taking shape. Contrary to popular myth, it did not begin on the campuses; nor was it started by Students for a Democratic Society. However, its activators were on the younger side of the generation gap. Although few were students, all were under 30 and had received their political education as participants in or concerned observers of the social-action projects of the preceding decade. Many came direct from New Left and civil rights organizations where they had been shunted into traditional roles and faced with the contradiction of working in a freedom movement but not being very free. Others had attended various courses on women in the multitude of free universities springing up around the country during those years.

During 1967 and 1968 at least five groups formed spontaneously and independently of each other in five different cities—Chicago, Toronto, Detroit, Seattle, and Gainesville, Florida. They arose at a very auspicious moment. The blacks had just kicked the whites out of the civil rights movement, student power had been discredited by SDS, and the organized New Left was on the wane. Only draft-resistance activities were on the rise, and for women whose consciousness was sufficiently advanced, this movement more than any other movement of its time exemplified the social inequities of the sexes. Men could resist the draft. Women could only counsel resistance.

There had been individual temporary caucuses and conferences of women as early as 1964 when Stokeley Carmichael of the Student Nonviolent Coordinating Committee made his infamous remark that "the only position for women in SNCC is prone." But it was not until 1967 that the groups developed a determined, if cautious, continuity and began to expand. In 1968 they held their first, and so far only, national conference, attended by over 200 women from around this country and Canada on less than a month's notice. For the next three years they expanded exponentially.

This expansion was more amoebic than organized, because the younger branch of the movement prides itself on its lack of organization. Eschewing structure and damning leadership, it has carried the concept of "everyone doing her own thing" almost to its logical extreme. The thousands of sister chapters around the country are virtually independent of each other, linked only by journals, newsletters, and cross-country travelers. Some cities have a coordinating committee that tries to maintain communication among local groups and to channel newcomers into appropriate ones, but none of these committees has any power over the activities, let alone the ideas, of any of the groups it serves. One result of this style is a very broadly based, creative movement, to which individuals can relate as they desire, with no concern for orthodoxy or doctrine.

Another result is political impotence. It would be virtually impossible for this branch of the movement to join together in a nation-wide action, even assuming there could be an agreement on issues. Fortunately, the older branch of the movement does have the structure necessary to coordinate such actions, and is usually the one to initiate them, as NOW did for the August 26 national strike in 1970.

It is a common mistake to try to place the various feminist organizations on the traditional left/right spectrum. The terms "reformist" and "radical" are convenient and fit into our preconceived notions about the nature of political organization, but they tell us nothing relevant. As with most other kinds of categories, feminism cuts across the normal political categories and demands new perspectives in order to be understood. Some groups often called reformist have a platform that would so completely change our society it would be unrecognizable. Other groups called radical concentrate on the traditional female concerns of love, sex, children, and interpersonal relationships (although with nontraditional views). The activities of the organizations are similarly incongruous. The most typical division of labor, ironically, is that those groups labeled radical engage primarily in educational work whereas the so-called reformist ones are the activists. It is structure and style of action rather than ideology that more accurately differentiates the various groups, and even here there has been much borrowing on both sides. In general, the older branch has used the traditional forms, often with great skill, while the younger branch has been experimental.

The most prevalent innovation developed by the younger branch has been the "rap group." Essentially an educational technique, it has spread far beyond its origins and become a major organizational unit of the whole movement, most frequently used by suburban housewives. From a sociological perspective the rap group is probably the most valuable contribution by the women's liberation movement to the tools for social change. As such it deserves some extended attention here.

The rap group serves two main functions. One is simply bringing women together in a situation of structured interaction. It has long been known that people can be kept down as long as they are kept divided from each other, relating more to their social superiors than to their social equals. It is when social development creates natural structures in which people can interact with one another and compare their common concerns that social movements take place. This is the function that the factory served for the workers, the church for the Southern civil rights movement, the campus for students and the ghetto for urban blacks.

Women have generally been deprived of structured interaction and been kept isolated in their individual homes, relating more to men than to each other. Natural structures for the purpose are still largely lacking, although they have begun to develop. But the rap group has provided an artificial structure that does much the same thing. The second function of the rap groups is to serve as mechanisms for social change in and of themselves. They are structures created specifically for the purpose of altering the participants' perceptions and conceptions of themselves and of society at large.

The process is known as "consciousness-raising" and is very simple. Women come together in groups of five to fifteen and talk to one another about their personal problems, personal experiences, personal feelings and personal concerns. From this public sharing of experiences comes the realization that what was thought to be individual is in fact common; that what was considered a personal

> **It is this process of deeply personal attitude change that makes the rap group such a powerful tool. . . . Once women have gone through such a resocialization, their views of themselves and the world are never the same again. . . .**

problem has a social cause and probably a political solution. Women see how social structures and attitudes have limited their opportunities and molded them from birth. They ascertain the extent to which women have been denigrated in this society and how they have developed prejudices against themselves and other women.

It is this process of deeply personal attitude change that makes the rap group such a powerful tool. The need for any movement to develop "correct consciousness" has long been known. But usually this consciousness is not developed by means intrinsic to the structure of the movement and does not require such a profound resocialization of one's self-concept. This experience is both irreversible and contagious. Once women have gone through such a resocialization, their views of themselves and the world are never the same again even if they stop participating actively in the movement. Those who do drop out rarely do so without spreading feminist ideas among their own friends and colleagues. All who undergo consciousness-raising feel compelled themselves to seek out other women with whom to share the experience.

There are several personal results from this process. The initial one is a decrease in self- and group-depreciation. Women come to see themselves and other women as essentially worthwhile and interesting. With this realization, the myth of the individual solution explodes. Women come to believe that if they are the way they are because of society, they can change their lives significantly only by changing society. These feelings in turn create a consciousness of oneself as a member of a group and the feeling of solidarity so necessary to any social movement. From this awareness comes the concept of "sisterhood."

The need for group solidarity explains why men have been largely excluded from women's rap groups. Sisterhood was not the initial goal of these groups, but it has been one of the more beneficial by-products. Originally, the idea of exclusion was borrowed from the Black Power movement, which was much in the public consciousness when the women's liberation movement began. It was reinforced by the unremitting hostility of most of the New Left men at the prospect of an independent women's movement not tied to radical ideology. Even when this hostility was not evident, women in virtually every group in the United States, Canada, and Europe soon discovered that when men were present, the traditional sex roles reasserted themselves regardless of the good intentions of the participants. Men inevitably dominated the discussions, and usually would talk only about how women's liberation related to men, or how men were oppressed by the sex roles. In all-female groups women found the discussions to be more open, honest, and extensive. They could learn how to relate to other women, not just to men.

Although the two branches of the movement do not have significantly differing ideologies, their different structure and style has resulted in significantly different activities. The women and men who formed NOW, and its subsequent sister organizations, created a national structure prepared to use the legal, political, and media institutions of our country. This it has done. The Equal Employment Opportunity Commission has changed many of its prejudicial attitudes toward women in its rulings of the last few years. Numerous lawsuits have been filed under the sex provision of Title VII of the 1964 Civil Rights Act. The Equal Rights Amendment has passed Congress. The Supreme Court has legalized some abortions. Complaints have been filed against more than 400 colleges and universities, as well as many businesses, charging sex discrimination. Articles on feminism have appeared in virtually every news medium, and a whole host of new laws have been passed prohibiting sex discrimination in a variety of areas.

These groups have functioned and continue to function primarily as pressure groups within the limits of traditional political activity. Consequently, their actual membership remains small. Diversification in the older branch of the movement has been largely along occupational lines and primarily within the professions. This branch has stressed using the tools for change provided by the system, however limited these may be. It emphasizes short-range goals and does not attempt to place them within a broader ideological framework.

Initially, this structure hampered the development of older branch organizations. NOW suffered three splits between 1967 and 1968. As the only action organization concerned with women's rights, it had attracted many different kinds of people with many different views on what to do and how to do it. With only a national structure and, at that point, no local base, individuals found it difficult to pursue their particular concerns on a local level; they had to persuade the whole organization to support them. This top-down structure, combined with limited resources, placed severe restrictions on diversity and, in turn, severe strains on the organization. Local chapters were also hampered by a lack of organizers to develop new chapters and the lack of a program into which they could fit.

Eventually these initial difficulties were overcome. NOW and the other older branch organizations are thriving at this point because they can effectively use the institutional tools our society provides for social and political change. Yet, these groups are also limited by these tools to the rather narrow arenas within which they are designed to operate. The nature of these arenas and the particular skills they require for participation already limit both the kind of women who can effectively work in older-branch groups and the activities they can undertake. When their scope is exhausted, it remains to be seen whether organizations such as NOW will wither, institutionalize themselves as traditional pressure groups, or show the imagination to develop new lines for action.

The younger branch has had an entirely different history and faces different prospects. It was able to expand rapidly in the beginning because it could capitalize on the New Left's infrastructure of organizations and media and because its initiators were skilled in local community organizing. Since the primary unit was the small group and no need for national cooperation was perceived, multitudinous splits increased its strength rather than drained its resources. Such fission was often "friendly" in nature, and even when not, served to bring ever-increasing numbers of women under the movement's umbrella.

Unfortunately, these newly recruited masses lacked the organizing skills of the initiators, and, because the very ideas of "leadership" and "organization" were in disrepute, they made no attempt to acquire them. They did not want to deal with traditional political institutions and abjured all traditional political skills. Consequently, the growth of the movement institutions did not go beyond the local level, and they were often inadequate to handle the accelerating influx of new people into the movement. Although these small groups were diverse in kind and responsible to no one for their focus, their nature determined both the structure and the strategy of the movement. To date, the major, though hardly exclusive, activities of the younger branch have been organizing rap groups, putting on conferences, putting out educational literature, and running service projects such as bookstores and health centers. This branch's contribution has lain more in the impact of its new ideas than in its activities. It has developed several ideological perspectives, much of the terminology of the movement, an amazing number of publications and "counter-institutions," numerous new issues, and even new techniques for social change.

Nonetheless, this loose structure is flexible only within certain limits, and the movement has not yet shown a propensity to transcend them. The rap groups have afforded excellent techniques for changing individual attitudes, but they have not been very successful in dealing with social institutions. Their loose, informal structure encourages participation in discussion, and their supportive atmosphere elicits personal insight; but neither is very efficient in handling specific tasks. Thus, although they have been of fundamental value to the development of the movement it is the more structured groups that are the more politically effective.

Individual rap groups tend to flounder when their members have exhausted

The feminist perspective starts from the premise that women and men are constitutionally equal and share the same human capabilities; observed differences therefore demand a critical analysis of the social institutions that cause them.

the virtues of consciousness-raising and decide they want to do something more concrete. The problem is that most groups are unwilling to change their structure when they change their tasks. They have accepted the ideology of "structure-lessness" without recognizing the limitations of its uses.

This shortcoming is currently causing an organizational crisis within the movement, because the formation of rap groups as a major movement function has become obsolete. In the last few years women's liberation has become a household word. Its issues are discussed and informal rap groups formed by people who have no explicit connection with any movement groups. Ironically, this subtle, silent, and subversive spread of feminist consciousness is causing a situation of political unemployment. With educational work no longer such an overwhelming need, women's liberation groups have to develop new forms of organization to deal with new tasks in a new stage of development. The resurgence of feminism tapped a major source of female energy, but the younger branch has not yet been able to channel it. New groups form and dissolve at an accelerating rate, creating a good deal of consciousness and very little action. Most of the women who go through these groups do not stay within the younger branch. They are either recruited into NOW and the other national organizations or drop out. The result is that most of the movement is proliferating underground. It often seems mired in introspection, but it is in fact creating a vast reservoir of conscious feminist sentiment that only awaits an appropriate opportunity for action.

The widely differing backgrounds and perspectives of the women in the movement have resulted in many different interpretations of women's status. Some are more sophisticated than others, and some are better publicized, yet there is no single comprehensive interpretation that can accurately be labeled the women's-liberationist, feminist, neofeminist, or radical feminist analysis. At best one can say there is general agreement on two theoretical concerns. The first is the feminist critique of society, and the second is the idea of oppression.

The traditional view of society assumes that men and women are essentially different and should serve different social functions; their diverse roles and statuses simply reflect these essential differences. The feminist perspective starts from the premise that women and men are constitutionally equal and share the same human capabilities; observed differences therefore demand a critical analysis of the social institutions that cause them. Since these two views start from different premises, neither can refute the other in logical terms.

The term "oppression" was long avoided by feminists out of a feeling that it was too rhetorical. But there was no convenient euphemism, and "discrimination" was inadequate to describe what happens to women and what they have in common with other disadvantaged groups. As long as the word remained illegitimate, so did the idea, and that was too valuable not to use. Oppression is still largely an undeveloped concept in which the details have not been sketched, but it appears to have two aspects related much as the two sides of a coin—distinct, yet inseparable. The sociostructural manifestations are easily visible as they are reflected in the legal, economic, social, and political institutions. The sociopsychological ones are often intangible; hard to grasp and hard to alter. Group self-hate and distortion of perceptions to justify a preconceived interpretation of reality are just some of the factors being teased out.

Sexism is the word used to describe the particular kind of oppression that women experience. Starting from the traditional belief of the difference between the sexes, sexism embodies two core concepts. The first is that men are more important than women. Not necessarily superior—we are far too sophisticated these days to use that tainted term—but more important, more significant, more valuable, more worthwhile. This presumption justifies the idea that it is more important for a man, the "breadwinner," to have a job or a promotion, to be paid well, to have an education, and in general to have preference over a woman. It is the basis of men's feeling that if women enter a particular occupation they will degrade it and that men must then leave it or be themselves degraded; it is also at the root of women's feeling that they can raise the prestige of their professions by recruiting men, which they can do only by giving men the better jobs. From this value comes the attitude that a husband must earn more than his wife or suffer a loss of personal status and a wife must subsume her interests to his or be socially castigated. The first core concept of sexist thought, then, is that men do the important work in the world, and the work done by men is what is important.

The second core concept is that women are here for the pleasure and assistance of men. This is what is implied when women are told that their role is complementary to that of men; that they should fulfill their natural "feminine" functions; that they are "different" from men and should not compete with them. From this concept comes the attitude that women are and should be dependent on men for everything, especially their identities, the social definition of who they are. It defines the few roles for which women are socially rewarded—wife, mother, mistress; all pleasing or beneficial to men—and leads directly to the Pedestal theory that extols women who stay in their place as good helpmeets to men.

It is this attitude that stigmatizes those women who do not marry or who do not devote their primary energies to the care of men and their children. Association with a man is the basic criterion for a woman's participation in this society, and one who does not seek her identity through a man is a threat to the social values. It is similarly this attitude that causes women's-liberation activists to be labeled as man-haters for exposing the nature of sexism. People feel that a woman not devoted to looking after a man must hate men or be unable to "catch" one. The effect of this second core concept of sexist thought, then, is that women's identities are defined by their relationship to men, and their social value is determined by that of the men they are related to.

The sexism of our society is so pervasive that we are not even aware of all its manifestations. Unless one has developed a sensitivity to its workings, by adopting a self-consciously contrary view, its activities are accepted with little question as "normal" and justified. People are said to "choose" what in fact they never thought about. A good example of sexism is what happened during and after World War II. The sudden onslaught of the war radically changed the whole structure of American social relationships as well as the American economy. Men were drafted into the army and women into the labor force. Now desperately needed, women had their wants provided for as were those of the boys at the front. Federal financing of day-care centers in the form of the Lanham Act passed Congress in a record two weeks. Special crash training programs were provided for the new women workers to give them skills they were not previously thought capable of exercising. Women instantly assumed positions of authority and responsibility unavailable to them only the year before.

But what happened when the war ended? Both men and women had heeded their country's call to duty to bring the struggle to a successful conclusion. Yet men were rewarded for their efforts and women punished for theirs. The returning soldiers were given the G.I. Bill and other veterans' benefits. They got their old jobs back and a disproportionate share of the new ones created by the war economy. Women, on the other hand, saw their child-care centers dismantled and their training programs cease. They were fired or demoted in droves and often found it difficult to enter colleges flooded with ex-GIs matriculating on government money. Is it any wonder they heard the message that their place was in the home? Where else could they go?

The eradication of sexism, and of sexist practices like those described above, is obviously one of the major goals of the women's-liberation movement. But it is not enough to destroy a set of values and leave a normative vacuum. The old values have to be replaced with something. A movement can begin by declaring its opposition to the status quo, but eventually, if it is to succeed, it has to propose an alternative.

**The social institutions that oppress women
as women also oppress people as people and
can be altered to make a more humane
existence for all.**

I cannot pretend to be definitive about the possible alternatives contemplated by the numerous participants in the women's liberation movement. Yet from the plethora of ideas and visions feminists have thought, discussed, and written about, I think that two predominant ideas have emerged. I call these the Egalitarian Ethic and the Liberation Ethic. They are closely related and merge into what can only be described as a feminist humanism.

The Egalitarian Ethic means exactly what it says. The sexes are equal; therefore sex roles must go. Our history has proven that institutionalized difference inevitably means inequity, and sex-role stereotypes have long since become anachronistic. Strongly differentiated sex roles were rooted in the ancient division of labor; their basis has been torn apart by modern technology. Their justification was rooted in the subjection of women to the reproductive cycle. That has already been destroyed by modern pharmacology. The cramped little boxes of personality and social function to which we assign people from birth must be broken open so that all people can develop independently, as individuals. This means that there will be an integration of social functions and life-styles of men and women as groups until, ideally, one cannot tell anything relevant about a person's social role by knowing that person's sex. But this greater similarity of the two groups also means more options for individuals and more diversity in the human race. No longer will there be men's work and women's work. No longer will humanity suffer a schizophrenic personality desperately trying to reconcile its "masculine" and "feminine" parts. No longer will marriage be an institution in which two half-people come together in hopes of making a whole.

The Liberation Ethic says this is not enough. Not only the limits of the roles must be changed, but their content as well. The Liberation Ethic looks at the kinds of lives currently being led by men as well as women and concludes that both are deplorable and neither is necessary. The social institutions that oppress women as women also oppress people as people and can be altered to make a more humane existence for all. So much of our society is hung upon the framework of sex-role stereotypes and their reciprocal functions that the dismantling of this structure will provide the opportunity for making a more viable life for everyone.

It is important to stress that these two ethics must work in tandem. If the first is emphasized over the second, then we have a women's rights movement, not one of women's liberation. To seek for equality alone, given the current male bias of the social values, is to assume that women want to be like men or that men are worth emulating. It is to demand that women be allowed to participate in society as we know it, to get their piece of the pie, without questioning whether that society is worth participating in. Most feminists today find this view inadequate. Those women who are personally more comfortable in what is considered the male role must realize that that role is made possible only by the existence of the female sex role; in other words, only by the subjection of women. Therefore women cannot become equal to men without the destruction of those two interdependent, mutually parasitic roles. To fail to recognize that the integration of the sex roles and the equality of the sexes will inevitably lead to basic structural change is to fail to seize the opportunity to decide the direction of those changes.

It is just as dangerous to fall into the trap of seeking liberation without due concern for equality. This is the mistake made by many left radicals. They find the general human condition to be so wretched that they feel everyone should devote her/his energies to the millennial Revolution in the belief that the liberation of women will follow naturally the liberation of people.

However, women have yet to be defined as people, even among the radicals, and it is erroneous to assume their interests are identical to those of men. For women to subsume their concerns once again is to ensure that the promise of liberation will be a spurious one. There has yet to be created or conceived by any political or social theorist a revolutionary society in which women were equal to men and their needs duly considered. The sex-role structure has never been comprehensively challenged by male philosophers, and the systems they have proposed have all presumed the existence of a sex-role structure.

Such undue emphasis on the Liberation Ethic can also lead to a sort of Radical Paradox. This is a situation in which the New Left women frequently found themselves during the early days of the movement. They found repugnant the possibility of pursuing "reformist" issues that might be achieved without altering the basic nature of the system, and thus would, they felt, only strengthen the system. However, their search for a sufficiently radical action or issue came to naught and they found themselves unable to do anything out of fear that it might be counter-revolutionary. Inactive revolutionaries are much more innocuous than active reformists.

But even among those who are not rendered impotent, the unilateral pursuit of Liberation can take its toll. Some radical women have been so appalled at the condition of most men, and the possibility of becoming even partially what they are, that they have clung to the security of a role they know while waiting for the Revolution to liberate everyone. Some men, fearing that role-reversal is a goal of the women's liberation movement, have taken a similar position. Both have failed to realize that the abolition of sex roles must be a part of any radical restructuring of society and thus have failed to explore the possible consequences of such role integration. The goal they advocate may be one of liberation, but it does not involve women's liberation.

Separated from each other, the Egalitarian Ethic and the Liberation Ethic can be crippling, but together they can be a very powerful force. Separately they speak to limited interests; together they speak to all humanity. Separately, they afford but superficial solutions; together they recognize that sexism not only oppresses women but limits the potentiality of men. Separately, neither will be achieved because both are too narrow in scope; together, they provide a vision worthy of our devotion. Separately, these two ethics liberate neither women nor men; together, they can liberate both.

Index

Bosch, Hieronymus, 310n
Boston Female Anti-Slavery Society, 438
Botticelli, Sandro, 310n, 312, 313
Boucher, Francois, 314, 315, 319
Bouguereau, Adolphe William 317
Bowlby, John, cited, 96
Boys, sex-role stereotypes of, 111. *See also under* Children; Socialization
Breen, Ann, cited, 37
Brim, Orville G., cited, 120
Bronfenbrenner, Urie, cited, 94-95, 118
Brontë, Charlotte, 430
Brontë, Emily, 430
Bronzino, 11, 313
Brotherhood of Locomotive Firemen and Enginemen, 264
Brotherhood of Railway and Steamship Clerks, 266
Brotherhood of Sleeping Car Porters, 251-52
Brown, Charles Brockden, innovative treatment of fictional heroines by, 281
Brown, Daniel G., cited, 112-13
Brown, Nacio, 299
Brown, William Hill, 280
Bucher, Karl, cited, 431
Burdett-Coutts, Baroness Angela, 429
Burgess, E. W., quoted, 413
Burke, Yvonne Braithwaite, 373
"Burning judges," 342, 343
Butler, Josephine, 429

Cabanel, Alexandre, 318
California, 375; Fair Employment Practices Commission of, 271
Calvin, John: on witchcraft, 341
"Can't Help Lovin' Dat Man of Mine," 303
Capitalism, 421, 428. *See also* Industrialization; Industry
Cap Makers, 256
Caraway, Hattie W., 376
Career: attitudes toward, 132-33, 201-2; commitment of university women to, 119; new career concept, 232-33; orientation of college women toward, 131-32; patterns, 228-29; return to,

after motherhood, 11, 12. *See also* Professional women; Working women
Carmichael, Stokely, quoted, 450
Carlsmith, J. M., quoted, 397
Carpenter, Mary, cited, 429
Caste and Class in a Southern Town, cited 154
Castration complex of American male: revealed in popular songs, 305-6; suggested in fiction, 285-89
Catharism, 338
Cathars, 337
Cather, Willa, 291
Catt, Carrie Chapman, cited and quoted, 445, 446
Census, U. S. Bureau of, statistics on blacks, 358
Cezanne, Paul, 318n
Charity Organization Society, cited, 428
Charity organizations, rise of, during Victorian era, 428-29
Charlotte Temple, 280
Chastity, 30; and double standard, 33
Chesterfield, Lord, condescending view of women, quoted, 298, 300
Chicago, 365
Childbearing, 8, 157
Child, Irwin, cited, 121
Child care: black women's need for, 360; as brake on women's political involvement, 368-69, 373, 381-82; evolution of, 51; planning for, 88; statistics on, for children of working mothers, 93; as women's work in marriage, 84-85
Childlessness, social acceptability of, 9
Children: born out of wedlock, 12; early alienation of, 17; economic responsibility of, 10; effect of, on marital power distribution, 83-84; forms of punishment of, 118; importance of, to middle-aged women, 163, 164; as industrial workers during 18th-19th centuries, 212, 213, 215; rearing of, 12, 89, 157; sex-role and, 110-13, 116-17, 125; social pressure to bear, 9; status of, in post-industrial society, 422, 428; in

Crane, Stephen, 286
Crisis, psychological, 22
Cronan, Sheila, cited, 71
Crown Zellerbach Corp., 275n, 51
Cultural alienation, 23
Cuneo Eastern Press, 260, 267
Customs, instinctual basis of, 48

Dante, cited, 409
David, Hal, 301
Day, Doris, 285
Day Care: attitudes toward, 94-96; cost of,
96-97; in Depression, 90-91; under
Economic Opportunity Act, 92-93;
effects of, on children, 95-96; financing
of, 98; history of, 89-92; need for,
93-94, 360; in New York City, 92;
organization of, 97, 98; planning of, 98;
policy, 88; in Soviet Union, 94-95;
teachers in, 90; union negotiations for,
258, 260; universal, 98, 99; at univer-
sities, 183; during World War II, 90-92,
457; as work incentive for mothers,
98-99
Day nurseries, 89, 90, 91. See also Day Care
Death rate, 4
Decision-making: areas of, in marriage, 66-
67; as measure of power in marriage,
66; power of, within family, 74
Declaration of Sentiments, quoted, 439-40
Defense, as factor in male dominance of
primates, 49
Defoe, Daniel, cited, 420
Degas, H. G. E., 309, 319
Degrees. See Educational degrees
"Dejeuner sur L'Herbe" (painting), 318
De Kooning, Willem, 320
Delacroix, F. V. E., 310n, 317
Democratic Party: McGovern-Frasier
Commission, 371; women delegates to
National Convention of, 371, 381;
women's support for, 367, 368, 369, 372
Demonic possession, 338-42 passim, 347
Demonologie, 341
Demorphism, sexual: of chimpanzees, 49;
of humans, 49

Dependency: of Americans on world resources, 5; as female sex-role
characteristic, 117, 118, 364; of married
women, 74; of middle-aged women, 167;
of suburban wives, 80; of women with
children, 84
Depression: ethnic background and, 165;
in menopausal women, 157; of middle-
aged professional women, 166; of
middle-aged women, 164, 165, 166;
theories of, 167. See also Alienation;
Psychiatric disorders
Desertion: as grounds for divorce, 73; in
marriage, 72-73
Deutsch, Helene, cited, 166, 167
Devil, in witchcraft mythology, 335-40
passim
Dewey, Lucretia M., cited, 251
Dialectic of Sex, The, quoted, 21
Dickens, Charles, 281; cited, 424
Dickinson, Emily, 291
Didion, Joan, 291
Dinerman, Beatrice, cited, 173
Discrimination. See Racial discrimination;
Sex discrimination
Division of labor, 56; in hunting societies,
53; in primate societies, 45, 47; as result
of language, 51; sexual, history of, 50-
51, 52, 61
Divorce: desertion as grounds for, 73; in
hunting societies, 57; statistics on, 10,
74; violence as reason for, 78
Divorced women, 146-47; in psycho-
therapy, 386
Dixon, Marlene, cited, 195
Doll, woman as: cuddly-toy image in
Western art, 314-15, 329; paper-doll
image in popular songs, 293-94
Dollard, John, cited, 154
Doll-play, and female conformity, 118
Domestics. See Household employees
Domestic services of wife. See Homemaking
Dominance: gestures of, 397-98; sexual, 20,
22, 28-29; of wife, 76. See also Power
——male: in hunting societies, 58-59, 60; in
marriage, 66, 68-69, 78-82 passim; in

Equal Rights Amendment of 1972 (ERA), 262, 381, 453; effect on sex discrimination, 328-29

Eroticism: male, physical violence as, 27-28; and sado-masochism, 19, 21, 22, 28; in Western art, 313-20 passim. *See also* Sexuality

Esterson, A., cited, 18n

Eve: as major theme in Western art, 309-12 passim; representation of woman as oppressor, 37

Evolution: of family life, 44, 50, 51, 52, 55, 61, 62; of hominids, 51-52; human, history of, 49-52; of human body, 51; of language, 50, 52

Executive Orders 11246, 11375, and 11478, sex discrimination barred by, 180, 189, 262, 267, 330

Exline, R., quoted, 397

Exogamy: band, in hunting societies, 60

Extended families, 44, 54, 89, 158

Eye contact, as nonverbal communication, 397-98

Factory Acts, 426

Faculty, 194-95; attitude toward women, 202-3; interaction with students, 198-99, 201-2; wives, status of, 181-82; women on, 179-80, 182

Faithfulness, in marriage, 30, 148

Fallen woman, 30-31

Families of Schizophrenics, cited 18n

Family: American, history of, 64-65; attitudes of, toward children's education, 201; black (*see* Blacks, families); decline of, 54-55; definition of, 44-56; effect of industrialization on, 7; extended, 44, 54, 89, 158; future of, 55, 63; in hunting societies, 44, 53-54, 55; as ideal, 44; male authority in, 45, 68-69, 73; as motivation to achieve, 135; origin and evolution of, 43, 44, 51, 52, 55, 61, 62; planning, by the poor, 6n; poor, 6; power differentials in, 66-67, 74, 81, 82-84; in pre-industrial society, 421; sexual taboos of, 44-45; size of, 6, 8; as source

of sex-role behavior learning, 119, 120; structures of, 44, 343, 421-22; structure of, in primates, 46, 47; traditional, 38-39. *See also* Matriarchal family; Nuclear family; Parents

Family Assistance Plan (FAP), 97

Family Epoch, 421

Famine, in medieval Europe, 345

Faerie Queene, The, 283

Fair Employment Practices Act, 250

Fair Employment Practices Commission, California, 271

Fair Labor Standards Act, 243, 247

Fantasy: female sexual, 19-22 passim; male sexual, 22, 27. *See also* Art (Western), image of women in; Popular songs, image of women in

Farenthold, Frances "Sissy," 375n

Farmer, James, 352

Farm workers, women: excluded from NLRA coverage, 263; low earnings of, 242, 244; unionization of, 251, 257

Farnham, Marynia, cited, 405

Fathers, 45; effect of, on sex-typing in children, 110; sex-role expectations of, for daughters, 124, 136

Faulkner, William, 288, 291; quoted, 279

Fear: of aging in women, 145; of castration, 288-89, 305-6; female, of self, 36; of rape, 24, 25, 33; of rejection in girl children, 118

Federal Commission on Crimes of Violence, 27

Federal Emergency Relief Administration (FERA), 90

Federally Employed Women (FEW), 449

Federal minimum wage, 247; extension of, 250; workers not covered by, 243, 244, 245, 361

"Fellow Needs a Girl, A," 300

"Female character," formulation of, 404-5

Femaleness, as culturally determined, 106-7

Female sexual value, cultural definition of, 146

Feminine Character: History of an Ideology, cited, 419n

Feminine inferiority, cultural concepts of, 414

Feminine mystique, era of, 448

"Feminine nature," 184, 193 n. 40

"Feminine roles," socialization to, 185

"Feminine" traits, 398

Femininity: in code of chivalry, 36; definition of, 118; relation of, to menopause, 166-67

Feminism: in early 20th century, 448; and law (*see* Law, feminism and); in media, 453; as "race suicide," 7; in Victorian era, 434. *See also* Feminist organizations; Feminists; Women's Liberation Movement; Women's movement

Feminist movement. *See* Women's movement

Feminist organizations: ideologies of, 450-51; structure and style of, 451

Feminists: attitudes of society toward, 407, 433-34, 436, 457; attitudes of, toward motherhood, 9. *See also* Women's movement; Women's Liberation Movement

Ferdinand (king of Spain), 340

Ferguson, Charles W., cited and quoted, 295, 296, 305

Ferguson, Miriam A. ("Ma"), 375

"Fete Champetre" (painting), 318

Fiction (American), women in, 150, 279-92; American Bitch stereotype, 288, 289; Charles Brockden Brown's innovative treatment of, 281; degradation of, by Mailer and others, 288n, 289; Dew Drop heroine, 285-86, 287, 289; in domestic novels of early women novelists, 284-85; evolution from flower to Venus's flytrap, 279-80; Fair Maiden and Dark Woman symbolized by, 282-84; Kate Chopin and fate of her career and novel, 290-91; male critics' distorted view and "biological put-down" of women authors and, 291; mother-savior image, 288, 289; Nancy Drew stories and, 287; New Woman as heroine, 281, 286-87; role and goals of women authors in rebalancing image of, 290-92; Romantic movement, Puritanical tradition, and desexed quality of, 281-82; sentimental and historical heroines of earliest novels, 280; sex-connected image of, 283n, 289

Fiedler, Leslie, cited and quoted, 281-82

Fifteenth Amendment, 357, 443

Fifth Amendment, sex discrimination and, 327

Financial aid, for higher education, 174

Firestone, Shulamith, quoted, 21

Fitzgerald, F. Scott, 288

Fitzpatrick, Robert, cited, 205

Flaubert, Gustave, 291

Flexner, Eleanor, quoted, 440-41, 442

Flogging of women, laws against, 426

Florida, sex-discriminatory law in, 327

Ford Motor Co., 259, 265

Fortune polls (1946), results of, cited, 405

For Whom the Bell Tolls, 288

Foster, Hannah, 280

Fourteenth Amendment, 442; abortion and, 331; duty of fair representation and, 267; sex discrimination and, 326-27; and suffrage, 444

Fragonard, Jean Honore, 314, 315, 319, 320

Franchised day care centers. *See* Day Care

Frazier, F. Franklin, quoted, 352, 353

Frederick II (king of Prussia), 342

Freed, Arthur, 299

Freeman, Jo, cited, 126, 134, 180

Freud, Sigmund, 282n; quoted, 300; theory of sex-role identification, 109-10, 135

Fried, Ellen, cited, 196n

Friedan, Betty, 449; cited, 137; quoted, 177

Friedman, Bruce J., 163

Friendship patterns, among suburban men and women, 79

Froebel, Friedrich, 89

Fry, Elizabeth, 428

Furness, Clifton J., cited, 424

Gage, Matilda Joslyn, quoted, 439

Gantry, Chris, 299

Garbo, Greta, cited, 33

"Garden of Earthly Delights, A" (painting), 310n

Heckler, Margaret M., 373; cited, 374
Heer, David M., cited, 84
"He Hasn't a Thing Except Me," 303
Heilbrun, Alfred B., Jr., cited, 136, 137
"Helene Fourment in a Fur Coat" (painting), 312
Hemingway, Ernest, 288
Henson, A., quoted, 397
Heretics, 337
Hermaphrodites, sex determination of, 107
Hewitt, S. C., cited, 255n
Higher education. *See* Education
Hill, Octavia, 428
Hill, R., quoted, 395
History of Woman Suffrage, quoted, 439, 442-43
Hobby, Oveta Culp, 380
Hofstadter, Beatrice K., quoted, 286
Hokada, Elizabeth, quoted, 110-11
Holliday, Billie, account of rape quoted, 36
Holmes, Oliver Wendell, 283
Home life, evolution of, 51, 52
Homemaking: image of, in popular songs, 296-97, 300-302; role of homemaker, 164, 166; as a service, 71-72, 84-85; as sex-role socialization, 115
Homogamous marriage, 69
Homo-sapiens, 50, 52
Horner, Matina, cited, 138, 185, 198, 205
Horticultural societies, 60
Hospitalization, of middle-aged women, 165
Hospital workers, women as, 221, 264
Hotel and Restaurant Employees and Bartenders International Unions, 266n
Household employees, female: blacks as bulk of, 82, 219, 243-44, 360, 361; degradation and exploitation of, 242, 243-44; denied federal minimum wage and fringe benefits, 243, 361; excluded from NLRA coverage, 263; extreme poverty of, 242, 243, 361; unionization of, 251-52, 257
Household industries: economic importance during Colonial period, 212-13; of urban women during 19th century, 216
Housewife, popular-song image of, 300. *See*

also Homemaking
Howells, William Dean, 284
How to Be a Jewish Mother, 163
Huckleberry Finn, 281
Hughes, Everett, cited, 230
Hull House, 90
Human body, evolution of, 51
Human Sexual Inadequacy, quoted, 389
Hundred Years' War, 346
Hunting, in human evolution, 50
Hunting societies: family structure in, 53-54, 55-56; infanticide, 59; male power in, 58-59; modern, 52; position of women in, 57-58; sexual customs in, 56-57
Husband: attitude toward politically involved wife, 373; legal responsibilities of, 72, 73; legal rights of, 64-65, 71, 73; power of, 69-70, 74-75, 79, 80-81; role of, in post-industrial society, 422, 431

Idaho, sex-discriminatory statute in, 327
"I Enjoy Being a Girl," 299
"If You Love Her Tell Her So," 302
"I Like What You're Doing," 303
Illinois, 326
Immigrant women in labor force, 218; in 19th century, 215
"In Bondage" (painting), 317
Incest, 25, 44; prohibitions, 44-45, 47-48, 51, 52
Income, as measure of marital power, 75, 80n, 85, 449. *See also* Income of women
Income of women: difference in earnings between union and nonunion members; Equal Pay Act and, 260, 262, 267, 273 329; matriarchal family and lack of, 224, 239-40, 246, 248, 360-61; as measure of marital power, 85, 449; in political posts, 380; sex discrimination and, 222-24, 239-49 passim, 253 n. 14, 258, 260, 262, 268, 273, 360-61; statistics on, 85, 238, 245-46, 360-61
——low earnings and financial needs: 222-24, 238-52 passim, 360-61; of black women, 81-82, 222, 224, 242, 243,

Matza, David, cited, 118
May, Catherine, cited, 382
Mead, Margaret, cited and quoted, 26, 106, 156, 301-2, 376
Melville, Herman, 282, 283; quoted, 279
Menopause, 156-57, 166-67
Middle-age, definition of, 157n. *See also* Middle-aged men; Middle-aged women
Middle-aged men, 148, 150
Middle-aged women: cultural attitude toward, 148, 150; dependency of, 167; discrimination against, 151-53, 154, 169; importance of children to, 163-65; psychiatric disorders of, 151, 157, 164-67 passim; rejection of, 159; role loss of, 168; roles of, 156-57, 158, 169; social conditioning of, 150-51
Middle Ages, rise of witchcraft in, 336
Midwives, 347
Mill, John Stuart, quoted, 427
Miller, Arthur, 293
Miller, Herbert A., quoted, 381
Millett, Kate, cited, 22, 289; quoted, 35, 39
Mines Act (1842), 426
Mink, Patsy, 372-73; quoted, 193n.40
Minnesota Multiphasic Personality Inventory (MMPI), 167
Minority group, women as: definition of, 402-3; psychology of, 404-5
Miranda Fuel Co., 265, 267
Missionary work, of women in Victorian era, 429
Moby Dick, 281
Money, John, cited, 107
Monogamy; in chivalry code, 30; in hunting societies, 56
More, Hannah, 405; quoted, 433
Morgan, Lewis H., cited and quoted, 46n, 49, 54, 55, 61
Morris (Philip), Inc., 269
Moss, Howard A., cited, 108, 205
Mother-child relationship, 159
Mother-in-law role, 158
Mothers: American industry's attitude toward, 8; feminists' attitudes toward motherhood, 9-10; influence of, on sex-

role perceptions, 120, 126, 135; as martyrs, 159-63; mother-child relationships, 136, 159, 168; motherhood as identity, 11-12; motherhood as primary role, 3-4, 149, 163, 164, 166, 369, 370, 371; motherhood as role factor in alienation, 18; political involvement of, 368-73 passim, 381-82; social expectations re, 248; status of women as, 406; unintentional, 13; on welfare, 95; Victorian ideal of, 284, 296-97. *See also* black women; Middle-aged women; Working women, mothers
A Mother's Kisses, 163
Mother-son relationship: effect of, on male achievement, 136
Motivation, 135, 136; and professional woman, 228-29
Mott, Lucretia, 439
Muller-Lyer, E., cited, 420-21
Munch, Edvard, 312
Murdock, G. P., cited, 53, 56
Mythology: and image of women in Western art, 315-19 passim; of witchcraft, 346-47. *See also* Social myths about women

NAACP Legal Defense Fund, 271
Naegele, Kasper, quoted, 124
Name change of woman, in marriage, 73
Narcissism, 21
National American Woman Suffrage Association (NAWSA), 365, 443, 444, 445
National Association of Government Employers, 380
National Black Feminist Organization, 362n
National Committee of Black Churchmen, 256
National Committee on Household Employment (NCHE), 250; cited, 243, 252
National Conference of Social Work, 90
National Farm Workers Organization, 251
National Federation of Day Nurseries, 90
National Labor Relations Act of 1935 (NLRA): coverage, 263-67; effectiveness in re sex discrimination, 265-67, 270, 272; exclusions detrimental to women

workers, 263-64; and violation of duty of fair representation, 264-67, 272

National Labor Relations Board (NLRB), 259; role in regulating discrimination in trade unions, 263, 265, 272

National Organization for Women (NOW), 381; founding of, 449; future of, 454; national strike initiation of (1970), 450; lawsuit of, against colleges and universities, 180, 183; legal defense through, 180, 183, 271; structure of, 453

National Woman's Party, 381

National Woman Suffrage Association, 443

National Women's Political Caucus (NWPC), 382

Natural Science Education Resources, 234

"Natural superiority of man," 19th century assumption of, 438

NCHE, See National Committee on Household Employment

Neanderthal man, 52

"Need to fail," women's, 186

"Negro Washerwoman, The: A Vanishing Figure," 354

Neuberger, Maureen, cited, 374

Neugarten, Bernice, quoted, 149, 150

Neurosis, 387. See also Depression; "Jewish mother"; Psychiatric disorders

New England textile mills, women workers in: during 19th century, 213, 215, 255; and strike of 1828 in Dover, N.H., 255

New Hampshire, 375, 377

New Left, 449, 450, 452, 454, 459

"New Model, The" (painting), 315

"New Olympia, The" (painting), 318n

New York, 377

New York Times, The, 356

Nightingale, Florence, 428

Nineteenth Amendment, 365, 367, 445, 446

Nixon, Richard M., 9, 367, 380; quoted, 252

NLRA. See National Labor Relations Act

NLRB. See National Labor Relations Board

Noble, Jeanne, quoted, 357

Nonverbal communication, 392; eye contact, 395-98, touching, 393-94

Normand, Ernest, 317

Norm of universal marriage, 8

Norris, Frank, quoted, 286

Norton, Caroline, cited, 434

Norton, Mary T., 378

Norway, 379

Novelists, women, 430; domestic novels of 19th century by, 284-85; Kate Chopin and fate of her career and novel, 290-91; male criticism and "biological put-down" of, 291; role and goals of, 290-92

Novels, women in. See Fiction (American), women in

NOW. See National Organization for Women

Nuclear family, 44; condition of, 99, 154; in hunting societies, 53-54; as related to child care, 88-89

Null Environment Hypothesis, 197-200

Nurseries, day, 89, 90, 91. See also Day care

Nursery schools: private, establishment of, 90

Nurturance, 3, 95. See also Mothers

Oberlin College, 437

Ochs, Phil, 305-6

O'Connor, L., quoted, 78, 397-98

O'Donnell, Gladys, quoted, 365

Oestrus, of monkeys and apes, 47

Office of Economic Opportunity (OEO), 92

"Oh, You Beautiful Doll," 294

Oklahoma City, 375

Old age, cultural attitude toward, 145

Oltman, Ruth, cited, 172

"Olympia" (painting), 318

One Flew Over the Cuckoo's Nest, 289

"One Hundred Easy Ways (to Lose a Man)," 304

"On the Condition of Women in the United States," quoted, 438-39

Oppenheimer, Valerie, cited, 219

Oppression: as defined by women's movement, 455-56; of women in psychotherapy, 387

"Oreades, Les" (painting), 317-18

Oregon, 375; litigation re discriminatory state law in, 326

Organizational participation, as power in marriage, 76, 84

record in other nations, 379; Congress, 375-79; state and local offices, 375
——as voters: stands on issues, 369-70; suffrage campaigns, 356-57, 364-67 passim, 412, 434, 443-46 passim; voting patterns, 365-69
Pollaiuolo, Antonio, 426
Polyandrous societies, fatherhood in, 45
Polygyny, in hunting societies, 53-57 passim
Poor Law Reform, 429
Poor Laws, 420
Popular songs, images of American woman in, 293-308; angel as major theme, 296, 299; castration complex and, 305-6; and dominance of male values and prejudices, 295; and domineering female and male hostility, 304-6; double standard reinforced by, 297-98; effect on adolescent girls, 306-7; "female female" theme, 299; "everyday housewife" theme, 299-300; formula ingredients and, 294-95; glorification of home, motherhood, domestic life, 296-98; independence, discouragement of, 303-4; love as major topic, 296, 302; marriage and, 300-302; masochism cliche and, 302-3; Pandora creature as major theme, 296; paper-doll image, persistence of, 293-94, 304; paternalism and, 298-99; service as major topic, 296, 300-301; sex as major or underlying theme, 296, 299, 306; and songs as culture symbols, 293-94; stereotypes and prejudices perpetuated by, 306-7
Population: in Depression, 7; in medieval Europe, 344; post-war, 7-8; problem, 4-5, 13; relation of, to women's liberation movement, 3
Population Education Act, 9
Population Stabilization Resolution, 9
Possession, by the devil in witchcraft, 339
Portnoy's Complaint, 163
Potter, Beatrice, 429
Potter, Elmer, cited, 121
Potter, Katherine, 429
Poverty, 5, 6n, 88; in medieval Europe, 344-45; in Victorian era, 427; and women,

238-53. See also Income of women
Power, 19, 20, 28, 39, 186; of black male, 80-83; expressed through body language, 397-98 passim; of female, as depicted in fiction and popular songs, 288-89, 304-6; of husband, 69-70, 74-75, 79, 80-81; of male, as presented in Western art, 315-17; of male, in hunting societies, 58-59, 60; political, of women, 370-71, 372, 379, 382. See also Black Power; Dominance
——in marriage: distribution of, 65-70 passim, 83-84; male, 66, 69-70, 75, 79, 80-83; measurement of, 66-67; sources of, 66, 74-75, 77-78, 85-86
Powerlessness, female, 17, 18, 22; as depicted in Western art, 315-17; in politics, 364, 370-71, 379. See also Dependency; Passivity
Power of Sympathy, The, 280
Prehistoric humans, tools and home sites of, 44
Prejudice: against women, 195; against women entering professions, 430; of women against other women, 184, 185, 405, 412, 452. See also Racial discrimination; Sex discrimination
Premarital sex: in hunting societies, 56, 57; in U.S., 12
A Present for a Servant Maid, cited, 421
President's Commission on Population and the American Future, 9
President's Commission on the Status of Women, 183, 188
Press, Jean M., cited, 138
Prestige, as function of age, 150
"Pretty Smart on My Part," 305
Primates, non-human: family structure, 44, 46; incest prohibitions, 47-48; male dominance among, 49; mating practices, 48; sexual bons, 47
"Primavera" (painting), 310n
Primitive societies: family as framework in, 61; sexual equality in, 61-62
"Principle of Least Interest," defined, 395
Professional Household Workers Union, 251

Professional men, as husbands, 75
Professional women, 134-35; acceptance, recognition, and interaction, problems of, 138-39, 231-32, 233, 236, 381, 430; attitude of other women toward, 205; black career women, 82, 355; career patterns and motivations of, 228-29; caucuses of, 449; depression of, in middle age, 166; identity and self-esteem problems, 227-28, 231, 232, 233; in law, 329, 373, 378; new career concept, 232-33; number of, 220; part-time opportunities for, 234, 236; in political posts, 379-81; as politicians, 373, 378; preponderance of teachers and nurses, 220, 264; professional socialization, 229-30; psychological and social barriers to, 227-37; retraining programs and reentry techniques, 234-35, 236; sense of competence, 227, 229; suggested remedies for barriers faced by, 233-36; special and lower status of Ph.D.'s, 231; sponsorship, importance of, 230-31, 233; in Victorian era, 426, 430. *See also* Career
Project Headstart, 92-93
Promiscuity, 20; "original" state of, 49
Pronatalism, as government policy, 9
Property: jurisdictions of, in marriage, 72-73
Property tax, 9
Prostitution, 345, 428, 443
"Protestants of Marriage," 431
Protestant witch hunts, 340
Proto-humans, tools and home sites of, 44
Proust, Marcel, cited, 408
Psychiatric disorders, of middle-aged women, 151. *See also* Alienation; Depression; Neurosis
Psychoanalysis, 386
Psychoanalytic theories about women, 388
Psychological Perspectives on Population, cited, 6n
Psychology of women, creation of, 390
Psychotherapy, 386-88
Public Welfare Amendments to Social Security Act (1962), 92

Punaluan, 55
Punishment; forms of, for girls and boys, 118
Puritan ethic, 9
"Queen of the House," 302
Quinney, Richard, cited, 186
Quotas, in educational admissions policies, 175

Rabban, Meyer L., cited, 109, 112, 119
Race-relation cycle, compared with sex-relations cycle, 412-13
"Race suicide," as outcome of feminism, 7
Racial discrimination: in American South, 37-38; parallels between sexism and, 351; Title VII of Civil Rights Act, and affirmative action against, 270-71; in trade unions, 259, 264-65, 267, 269-71. *See also* Blacks; Black women
Racism. *See* Racial discrimination
Radcliffe Institute, fellowship program at, 227-28, 236-37 n. 1
Ragged Schools, 429
Railway Labor Act of 1926 (RLA; as amended in 1936), 263; coverage and exclusion of women workers, 264; and duty of fair representation, 264, 267, 272
Rainwater, Lee, cited, 8
Rankin, Jeanette, 375-76
Rape: cultural attitudes toward, 16, 25-26, 39; fear of, 24-25, 33; statistics on, 25, 26, 27, 33, 38; male mythology of, 27-28, 29, 30; legalities of, 27, 28, 34-35; in American South, 37-38, 353; black male attitude toward, 38; as theme in Western art, 314-18 passim
— —rape victim: attitude toward, 30-35 passim; third world women as, 35-36, 37
— —rapist: black, 38; psychology of, 26, 29; trial of Jerry Plotkin, 31
"Rape of Dejanira, The" (painting), 316
"Rape of Lucretia, The" (painting), 316
Rap groups, 451-55 passim
Red Badge of Courage, The, 281
Reformation, 340, 342, 343
Reformatories, 429

Self concepts, of women, 405, 406-7
Self-disclosure, of women, 395
Self-hatred, of minority groups, 404-5
Self-realization, in modern marriage, 70
Self-reliance: in male children, 118; tradition of, among black women, 352, 353, 360, 362
Seneca Falls Convention (1848), 356, 439, 440; suffrage resolution of, 356-57, 440, 445-46
Seniority system: in Congress, 378; sex discrimination institutionalized by, 268-70
Serfdom, 420
Service Workers International Union, 251
Service workers, women: black women as, 82; high percentage of, 219-21, 244; low earnings of, 221, 244; unionization of 251, 257
Sewell, William H., cited, 124
Sex, 17-21 passim; attitude of organized religion toward, 7; in black marriage, 83; as main or underlying theme in popular songs, 296, 299, 306; in marriage contract, 71; pre-marital, 12, 56, 57. *See also* Sex object, woman as
Sex and Temperament, quoted, 26
Sex discrimination, 189, 456, 457; age distinctions and, 151-54, 169, 329; against black women, 81, 82, 351-63 passim; against childless women, 9; in education, 172-82 passim, 194-95, 406; in job opportunities and earnings, 83, 85, 151-54 passim, 169, 219-25 passim, 239-49 passim, 253 n. 14, 262-73 passim, 361, 406, 412-13, 438-39; in language of job ads, 153; lawsuits against, 453; legal protection against (*see* Law, feminism and); as measure of minority status, 403-4; parallels between sexism and racism, 351, 356-57; against single women, 9; in trade unions (*see* Trade unions, sex discrimination in); toward women in politics, 372-74, 378-79; in traditional roles, 405. *See also* Art (Western), sexism in

Sexism: parallels between racism and, 351, 356-57; in Western art, 309-21. *See also* Sex discrimination
Sex object, woman as, 152, 184-85, 381; black woman and, 355, 362; in Western art, 313-20 passim
Sex ratio, among blacks, 358-59; social implication of imbalance in, 359-60
Sex-relations cycle, compared with race-relations cycle, 412-13
Sex role, 3, 169, 459; abolishment of, 458, 460; assignments of, 106-7; definition of, 114; differentiation, comparison of lower and middle class families, 119; expectation, 124-25, 126, 131; learning, 108-9, 110, 117, 120; norms, sanctioned by U.S. government, 8; preferences, of children, 112-13, 116-17; as result of socialization, 20, 105; socialization (*see* Socialization); standards, 117, 118-19; studies on cross-cultural variation in, 106
—behavior: of black women, 119, 125; changes in, with age, 120 deviation from, 114; effect of family constellation on, 120; effect of school on, 121; in interaction with opposite sex, 135-36; in males, 114, 118; parental reinforcement of, 109
—stereotyping, 458; of adults, as perceived by children, 112; in psychotherapy, 389; school reinforcement of, 121; tracking system for, 121-22
Sex segregation. *See* Sex discrimination
Sexual activity, male initiation of, 394
Sexual adjustment, psychology of, 20
Sexual alienation, 17, 21, 22, 23
Sexual attraction, effect of aging on, 145
Sexual behavior, psychological study of, 20
Sexual culture, male, 16-22 passim
Sexual customs, in hunting societies, 56-57
Sexual dimorphism, in humans and chimpanzees, 49
Sexual freedom, 12, 13, 16, 23
Sexual equality, in primitive societies, 61-62
Sexuality: of apes and monkeys, 47-48; female, 12, 20, 21-22; male, 26-27; in

socialization of women in, 423-25;
working women in, 426-27
Vidal, Gore, 289
Vietnam issue, women's stand on, 370
View from the Bridge, A, 293
Vindication of the Rights of Women,
cited, 422
Violence. *See* Physical violence
Virginity, 30
Virgin Mary: cult of, 344; as depicted in
Western art, 310-11, 316, 318
Voice, as measure of feminity, 399
Volunteer work, as female achievement, 138
Voters, women as. *See under* Politics,
women in

Wages. *See* Income; Income of women
Waldensianism, 338
Wallace, George, 375
Wallace, Lurleen, 375
Waller, W. W., quoted, 395
Walpurgis night, 336n
War between the sexes, 391
Ward, Mrs. Humphrey, cited, 434
Ware, Caroline F., cited, 363
Wartime nurseries, 90-92
Wasserstrom, William, cited, 288-89
Waukegan, Ill., 365-66
"Wealth of Nations, The," 425
Wealth of women, cliches discredited re,
238, 240-41
Weaving, as female trade, 212-13, 345
Webb, Beatrice, quoted, 427, 429, 434
"Wedding Cake Blues," 302
Weisstein, Naomi, quoted, 70-71
Weitzman, Lenore J., cited and quoted,
110-11, 121, 188
Welfare: children on, 89, 95; disproportion-
ate number of women on, 240; eligi-
bility requirements, 248-49; exploitation
of recipients, 249; mothers on, 95
Wellesley College, 235
Wells-Barnett, Ida B., 353
"We Never Speak As We Pass By," lyrics
quoted, 297-98
Werner, Emmy E., cited, 375

Wesselman, Tom, 320
West, Mae, quoted, 30
Wharton, Edith, 284, 291
"What's the Use of Wonderin'," 303
Wheaton Glass Co., 260
White-collar husbands, 74, 77
White male ethos, 36
White womanhood, myth of, 38
Whitman, Walt, 282
Whitney, Fraine E., cited, 138
Widows, 146-47; succession to political
office, 376
Wieland, 281
"Wild One," lyrics quoted, 305
Willard, Emma, 437
Wilson, Augusta Jane Evans, 284
Wilson, Woodrow, 434
Wingfield-Stratford, Esme, quoted, 434
Wirth, Louis, cited, 402-3
Witchcraft, 404; crusade against, 337; in
ecclesiastical period, 336-40; mythology
of, 346-47; during Reformation and
Counter Reformation, 340-42; during
Thirty Years' War, 342
Witches' Hammer, The, 338-39, 343, 347
Wives: faculty, 181-82; image of, in popular
songs, 296-302 passim; legal responsibilities of, 71-72; in politics, 373, 375; as
portrayed in media, 37; role of, 74;
status of, 406, 408; subordination of,
408; suburban, 80; as supporters of
student-husbands, 175
——in labor force: 68, 76, 218, 227-37 passim, 249; changing attitudes toward,
219; and financial needs, 223-24;
increased participation, 217-24 passim;
during 19th century, 215-16; trade-
union discrimination, 266
——in professions: 227-37 passim; identity
and self-esteem problems, 227-28; new
career concept, 232-33; reentry, 228,
234-35. *See also* Science, women in
"Wives and Lovers," 301
Wolfe, Donald M., cited and quoted, 65-68
passim, 75, 76, 80-81
Wolfson, Teresa, cited, 257